# The Fantasy Benefit
# 2020 Fantasy Baseball Draft Guide

Brought to you by FriendswithFantasyBenefits.com

D1303021

**Table of Contents**

## About FWFB

Friends with Fantasy Benefits launched in 2014 as an uncensored, unabashed fantasy baseball podcast. Since that time, we have added over 60 staff members who write and podcast on all fantasy sports. Members of FWFB have gone on to work at some of the best fantasy sports sites and businesses in the industry including Fangraphs, Baseball HQ, Baseball Prospectus, and many more. We are FSWA nominated and have been invited to represent FWFB at events like Tout Wars and LABR. In our third annual draft guide, you will find all the information you need to win your leagues no matter the depth, format, or style. The eBook and PDF versions of the guide will be updated through March and if you buy a paperback, you can receive updates via email if you contact us at friendswithfantasybenefits@gmail.com. You can find more information about FWFB at friendswithfantasybenefits.com, follow us on Twitter @fantasybenefits, like us on Facebook or join our Facebook discussion group.

# Starting Your Own League
## By Jim Bay

In one study, it was reported that over 25% of adult males in America have participated in fantasy leagues at some point in their lives. Fantasy sports leagues have become a fun way to stay competitive for those of us who never had or no longer have the ability to play. As baseball season approaches, you can join this cultural phenomenon and be one of the many that enjoy participating in a fantasy baseball league.

The first decision to be made is where you want your league to be hosted. There are several websites out there that offer league services. ESPN, CBS Sports, Yahoo, and Fantrax are sites that host fantasy baseball leagues, with all of them being more than capable of successfully hosting your league. Most will offer mock drafting to help you prepare for your upcoming draft. It would be wise to check out all of these sites to see which one meets your needs.

If you are the person to start a league, you will probably be the person with the less than glamorous job of being the league commissioner. If that is the case, there are few things that you need to know to run a league smoothly and fairly. The first thing to consider is that is a tricky proposition to have more authority and power than friends, family, colleagues or even acquaintances who are in your league. You need to make sure your league is made up of people who you can trust, who are reliable, and who have good reputations. To help with this, it would be wise to consider appointing a co-commissioner in order to maintain a balance of power and to help in possible disputes that involve the team you are managing. This person can also help you to pick and choose what they want to include in their league's rules, but there are some conventions which should apply to all leagues that seek to maintain order and integrity. This includes clearly explaining any rules on teams making dump trades once they are eliminated from playoff contention. All of the sites mentioned earlier have settings that allow the commissioner or the league itself to decide whether trades should be allowed. Many have debated the merits of both methods but many use the league voting method as the commissioner being the person who breaks ties. One of the best ways to avoid this or any other conflict is to make sure that there is a good avenue of communication in your league.. It is recommended that you use email or other electronic communications so that you can write to all league members and be able to confirm delivery and give you the assurance that your message has been sent and received by everyone in the league.

The next decision you have to make is whether it will be a keeper/dynasty or redraft league. A redraft league means that you would draft an entirely new team each year that you decided to play. This is usually the choice for casual players who are running their league on a year to year basis. Keeper/dynasty leagues allow a person to retain a certain number of players from year to year which incentivizes long-term thinking when it comes to drafting, roster management and trade strategy. If you are starting a new keeper/dynasty league, then the rules regarding keepers, contracts, and trading draft picks must be clearly defined well before the draft takes place. This is an option if you want to keep your same league going year after year and would like to dig deeper into the intricacies that make up fantasy baseball.

Next, you will have to decide whether your league will be a rotisserie or points-based league. Rotisserie leagues are played using a certain number of categories in which statistics are accumulated collectively and the standings are determined based on where each team in the league ranks in each category. This is the classic version of fantasy baseball that developed independently and popularized in the 1980s by a group of journalists and formalized under the title Rotisserie League Baseball in 1980, named after the New York City restaurant La

Rotisserie Française, where its founders met for lunch and first played the game. Head-to-head points-based leagues have specific point values associated with each statistic where league members face a different opponent each week and the winner is determined by which team has the most amount of total points at the end of a scoring period. Many leagues with family and/or co-workers like head-to-head because it allows them the one on one battle that can talk about around the water cooler at work or during family gatherings. Finally, when creating your league you will need to decide if your league will include all of MLB or be a specialized NL-only or AL-only league. The league-specific format is much more difficult simply because the pool of available players is smaller than using all of the MLB teams.

You now have been given the information to start and participate in your own fantasy baseball league and join the estimated 60 million people plus in the country who have participated in fantasy sports. Also, feel free to check the Friends with Fantasy Benefits website for information to help you draft and run your own successful team.

# Hindsight Injury Breakdown for the 2020 Fantasy Baseball Season
By: Reuven Guy, RPA-C, Orthopedics and Physical Medicine

Last year, in this same publication, I discussed how injuries affected MLB teams and their push to the playoffs. The injury bug hit major league baseball year almost as hard in 2019 but it did not seem to affect the teams in their push for the playoffs as teams like the New York Yankees, the team with the most IL trips in all of baseball (30), ended the regular season with 103 wins- the 3rd most in all of baseball. The Los Angeles Dodgers had the 5th most players on the IL and they finished with the best record in baseball. The Tampa Rays had the 4th most and made the playoffs as a wild card team. This year, I am going to look at the injuries in baseball from a different perspective.

With the 2020 baseball season comes a few changes in the rules in baseball. They are as follows-

1- There will be a 26 man roster, up from the original 25 man roster.

2- There will be a 28 man roster in September instead of the usual 40 man roster.

3- There will again be a 10 day IL stint for hitters but now a mandatory 15 day IL stint for all pitchers.

4- Pitchers must pitch to at least 3 batters or finish an inning when they are inserted into the game.

These changes in the game will have a profound effect on how players are used. The increase from 25 to 26 man roster will mean, almost assuredly, that there will be another relief pitcher on each roster. Pitchers having to pitch to at least 3 batters will eliminate, for the most part, the use of "specialists" late in games.

I would like to concentrate on the rules regarding the 28 man September roster and the change in IL stay for pitchers. The roster being limited to 28 players in September will force MLB teams to utilize the IL in September, something teams have not done in the past. Players, even when injured, were not put on the IL with the hope that they could be utilized on a day they are feeling good or just for a pinch hit at bat here or there. There will be more clarity regarding injured players and if they are actually able to play. This means less lineup issues- not knowing whether a player should be put in a locked lineup for an entire week without the knowledge that they may not even be available to play even though they were not on the IL. This is a positive when it comes to the end of the season and possible playoffs for fantasy teams. There is also the possibility of teams not bringing up a player only to pinch run or only to pitch vs lefties. There may be less stolen bases available on the waiver wire and clearer bullpen roles come September.

I want to concentrate on the rule of the 10 day hitter IL and 15 day pitcher IL. This rule was put in place for a few reasons. First and foremost, it was done to protect the health of the pitchers. In baseball last year, there were 321 pitchers put on the IL at some point last year for a total of 23,612 days on the IL. There were 251 position players to hit the IL totaling 14,285 days on the IL. There were 26 pitchers who were on the IL the whole season compared to 8 position players who missed the entire season. The average of non- full season injured pitchers comes out to 63.6 days on the IL. There were 45 pitchers who spent 15 days or less on the IL last year. These numbers include pitchers who spent the minimum of 10 days on the IL because they were "injured" but were really put there to miss a start or two for rest only. What do we do with these numbers?

First, let's take a look at the IL trend over the past few years-

| Year | Total Pitchers | |
|------|------|------|
| 2015 | 597 | |
| 2016 | 592 | |
| 2017 | 607 | |
| 2018 | 616 | |
| 2019 | 645 | |
| | 10 inn min. | |

This is a list of the amount of pitchers in baseball who threw at least 10 innings. I use the 10 inning mark as this eliminates the "non-pitcher" players who pitched.

| Year | Total Hitters | |
|------|------|------|
| 2015 | 472 | |
| 2016 | 462 | |
| 2017 | 463 | |
| 2018 | 475 | |
| 2019 | 482 | |
| | 70 abs | |

This is a list of the total amount of position players who had at least 70 at bats during the course of the season. I use the mark of 70 at bats as this eliminates at bats from pitchers.

| Year | Total IL players |
|------|------|
| 2015 | 408 |
| 2016 | 473 |
| 2017 | 528 |
| 2018 | 585 |

| | 2019 | 574 |
|---|---|---|

This is a chart of the total amount of players on the IL over the past 5 seasons. Last year was the first down year, or leveling off, of the IL trend.

| Year | Pitchers on IL | % Injured |
|---|---|---|
| 2015 | 240 | 40.2 |
| 2016 | 272 | 45.9 |
| 2017 | 292 | 48.1 |
| 2018 | 344 | 55.8 |
| 2019 | 321 | 49.7 |

| Year | Position Players on IL | % |
|---|---|---|
| 2015 | 168 | 35.6 |
| 2016 | 200 | 43.3 |
| 2017 | 234 | 50.5 |
| 2018 | 241 | 50.7 |
| 2019 | 253 | 52.4 |

These two charts show the overall percentage of players hitting the IL.

| Year | avg IL time | |
|---|---|---|
| 2015 | 61.8 | |
| 2016 | 59.1 | |
| 2017 | 54.89 | |
| 2018 | 48.7 | |
| 2019 | 65.1 | |

This chart shows the overall average IL time in baseball, pitchers and position players. As you can see, the trend of the percentage of pitchers and hitters on the IL may be beginning to level off but the amount of time spent on the IL continues to increase. With the change in the rule that pitchers now must spend at least 15 days on the IL per stint, I only expect this average to go up next year- even if the amount of pitchers on the IL declines again.

What to Do?

The question then arises- how can we combat this and field a competitive fantasy team all year long. There are top players that, if injured, could sink your team. Losing 2 or 3 of your top picks in a draft or auction usually spells doom for your team. That is just a luck aspect. However, if we can take a guess as to how long these players may be out due to their injuries, we may be able to keep our teams afloat. In that way, we will know how much money to spend on FAAB or how many players should be picked up on FAAB or via trade to help fill the holes left by these injuries.

## Pitchers

As shown above, the amount of pitchers on go on the IL declined slightly in 2019 when compared to 2018. In 2019, 22 pitchers were lost to Tommy John Surgery. Here is a listing of the top 15 reasons pitchers were placed on the IL in 2019 along with the amount of time they spent on the IL. Some injuries not listed here include illness (6 players for 245 day) and IL stint listed as Other (4 for 146 days).

| Body Part | # of Players | Days on IL |
| --- | --- | --- |
| Shoulder | 76 | 3,905 |
| Elbow | 64 | 5,861 |
| Arm | 45 | 3,192 |
| Neck/Back | 26 | 959 |
| Knee | 19 | 1009 |
| Oblique | 14 | 488 |
| Hamstring | 13 | 359 |
| Finger | 11 | 275 |
| Biceps | 10 | 749 |
| Hip | 9 | 505 |
| Groin | 6 | 142 |
| Wrist | 5 | 491 |
| Pectoral | 4 | 182 |
| Foot/Toe | 7 | 284 |
| Calf | 4 | 111 |

For obvious reasons, pitchers tend to have more shoulder/elbow/arm injuries than position players. Shoulder injuries dominate this injury category, averaging 51.3 days on the IL per player. Elbow injuries sideline pitchers, on average 91.5 days per IL stint. A lot of these pitchers experience elbow "discomfort" or pain and are shut down due to the concern that

Tommy John surgery is in their future and one of the mainstays to treat elbow pain in a pitcher is rest. General arm injuries keep pitchers out of average 70.9 days.Finger injuries last about 68 days. Oblique and knee issues can cause an IL stay of around 1 month. Wrist injuries keep pitchers even longer than elbow issues, an average of 98.2.

With these numbers in hand, once a pitcher develops an injury, one could know, on average, how long the player will be out for. This will help your in- season strategy when replacing your injured pitchers. However, this is only how long they are out of action for- this does not account for effectiveness following the injury. That needs a study in its own right.

## Hitters

Over the past 3 years, in Major League Baseball, an average of 243 position players landed on the IL. There has been a slow but steady increase in these numbers over the past 5 years, however, the increase from year to year has gone down over the past 3 years. This may mean another slight increase in IL stints this coming year. The position player IL stay remains at 10 days for the 2020 season.

Some of the injuries, like pitchers, have a full year lost to injury- such as ACL tears (surgery required) or the need for Tommy John surgery. Six position players had those types of injuries last year. Here is a listing of the top 15 injuries accrued to position players last year and how many days they were out-

| Body Part | # Injured Players | Days on IL |
|---|---|---|
| Hamstring | 33 | 954 |
| Hand/Finger | 27 | 1241 |
| Neck/Back | 25 | 1248 |
| Oblique | 23 | 811 |
| Knee | 21 | 1,769 |
| Shoulder | 21 | 1,294 |
| Concussion | 19 | 567 |
| Groin/Hip | 18 | 1024 |
| Wrist | 17 | 601 |
| Calf | 14 | 692 |
| Ankle | 13 | 371 |
| Quad | 12 | 440 |
| Foot/Toe | 12 | 814 |

| Elbow | 10 | 449 |
|---|---|---|
| Biceps/Arm | 9 | 460 |

The average time on the IL for some of these injuries makes complete orthopedic sense. Non-ACL knee injuries cost a position player 84.2 days. Typically, a player tries rehab, injections and rest for about 4-5 weeks and then possible arthroscopic surgery, which has a recovery time of about 4-6 weeks. Hand and finger injuries (fractures or torn tendons/ligaments which may or may not require surgery) usually have an average recovery time of 5-8 weeks (depending on severity). The average time a player spends on the IL for this type of injury was about 46 days. Wrist injuries/fractures take 4-6 weeks to heal, hence an average of 35 days on the IL . Ankle injuries/sprains take 3-4 weeks to heal and there was an average of 4 weeks on the IL.

Then there are the wild card injuries- sprains/strains of the neck, low back, oblique and hamstring and injuries related to concussions. Neck, back, groin and oblique injuries should be considered muscle sprains/strains unless testing shows otherwise. Neck and back injuries take the longest to recover from (average of 49 days) with oblique injuries taking around 35 days and hamstring injuries taking about 39 days.Concussion protocol and IL maintains at least an 8-10 day stay on the IL with an average stay of 1 month. Groin and hip injuries average a 56 day stay on the IL.

Again- the point of this exercise is not to teach you orthopedics but to give you an idea of how long a certain player will be sidelined. With this knowledge, one can manage a team better with trades and the waiver wire- knowing how long the replacement will be in there.

## Conclusion

Injuries are unpredictable. Managing your fantasy team with injuries should not be. Equipped with the knowledge of injury types and average length of stay away from the baseball diamond is huge. Some injuries to top players could cripple your team but with an average in baseball of 1 out of every 2 players (pitcher or hitter) ending up on the IL at some point in the season, everyone will have to deal with injury replacements at some point during the season. Being able to navigate these injuries will make the chances of finishing near the top of your standings feasible. To help keep up with all current players injuries, follow me on Twitter @mlbinjuryguru and PM or tweet to me any questions you may have regarding any player or injury. Also, your injury questions could also be answered weekly throughout the year on the TGFBI podcast Beat the Shift edition.

Happy 2020 Fantasy Baseball Season!

## Player Injuries and Timetables
By Reuven Guy

### Injured/Recovering Player List

This a list of fantasy relevant players (by team) who missed significant time at the end of 2019 and how they are faring in their rehab process. Also included in this listing is the updated status of other injured players. Injured free agents (at the time of this printing) are listed at the end. Ages are in parentheses. All of my injury reports come from a composite of various sources. The medical opinion and length of time for recovery is my own opinion based on my medical background as an orthopedic PA with 15+ years experience.

By: Reuven Guy, RPA-C, Orthopedics and Physical Medicine

Follow me on Twitter- @mlbinjuryguru

Updated January 14 2020

### Arizona Diamondbacks

Luke Weaver (26)- Elbow- Was sidelined mid May with mild flexor pronator strain and a minor UCL sprain. No surgery was performed. Came back to pitch but was then shut down again, but a healthy shut down. Should be fine for Spring Training.

David Peralta (32)- Shoulder- Had shoulder surgery August 2019 to clean out loose bodies from his right shoulder. Should be good to go for Spring Training.

Corbin Martin (24)- Elbow- Had Tommy John surgery July 2019 and is expected to miss almost the entire 2020 season.

### Atlanta Braves

Ender Inciarte (29)- Hamstring- Was shut down at the end of last year with a grade 2 right hamstring strain. He should be good to go for Spring Training.

AJ Minter (26)- Shoulder- Minter was shut down in September 2019 with left shoulder inflammation. He also dealt with the same issue earlier in the year. No report of MRI findings. Should be fine for Spring Training

Joahn Camargo (26)- Shin- Camargo fractured his right shin in September 2019. This should be fully healed by Spring Training.

### Baltimore Orioles

Alex Cobb (32)- Hip- Cobb had 3 trips to the IL last year, culminating with hip surgery June 2019. He is expected to be close to full strength by Spring Training.

### Boston Red Sox

Chris Sale (30)- Elbow- Sale was shut down at the end of last year due to elbow issues. Met with Dr. James Andrews in November and was cleared to begin his off-season throwing program. No surgery was performed but he did receive a PRP injection for his elbow last August. Should not have any restrictions at Spring Training.

Michael Chavis (24)- Oblique- Chavis was shut down last August due to an oblique strain. He also skipped winter ball due to the injury but no setbacks were noted. He is expected to be ready for Spring Training.

David Price (34)- Wrist- Price underwent surgery to remove a cyst from his left wrist September 2019. Assistant general manager Brian O'Halloran said the surgery "went well" and added that the team expects him fully ready to go for spring training.

Dustin Pedroia (36)- Knee- Pedroia had left knee surgery in August 2019, followed by a 12 week strengthening program. No word at this time about his status for Spring Training.

Nathan Eovaldi (29)- Elbow- Had elbow surgery to remove loose bodies April 2019. He came back to pitch later in the season. Healthy.

## Chicago Cubs

Brandon Morrow (35)- Elbow- Had arthroscopic surgery performed on his right elbow in November 2018 and had a few setbacks last year. His status for Spring Training is unknown.

Jharel Cotton (27)- Elbow- Had Tommy John surgery mid March 2018. He pitched in rehab games last year and should be healthy to start Spring Training.

## Chicago White Sox

Michael Koepech (23)- Elbow-Had Tommy John surgery performed in September 2018. Koepech is fully healthy entering the offseason and is good to go for Spring Training.

Carlos Rodon (27)- Elbow- Rodon had Tommy John surgery May 2019 and is expected to be back sometime midseason 2020, around June.

Lucas Giolito (25)- Lat- Giolito was shut down September 2019 with a lat injury. The White Sox have no long-term concerns about Giolito's health and he is expected to be good to go for the start of Spring Training.

Nicky Delmonico (27)- Shoulder- Delmonico underwent season-ending surgery to repair the labrum in his left shoulder June 2019. He should be healthy coming into Spring Training.

## Cincinnati Reds

Jesse Winker (26)- Neck- Winker was out since the end of August with a cervical strain. He did not respond well to treatment at the end of the year and did not return. No word on any setbacks this offseason and he should be fine for Spring Training.

Nick Senzel (24)- Shoulder- Senzel has surgery for his right shoulder in September 2019to repair his labrum. Senzel is on track to begin hitting and throwing during the second week of January.

Derek Dietrich (30)- Shoulder- According to his manager David Bell, Dietrich has "been dealing with a shoulder [injury] off and on all year….It's just kind of some wear and tear in the shoulder." He should be ready for Spring Training barring any off-season setbacks.

Jose DeLeon (27)- Elbow- Had Tommy John surgery March 2018. Healthy.

### Cleveland Indians
Tyler Naquin (28)- Knee- Naquin had right knee surgery in September 2019 for a torn ACL. He is expected to return about 8 months after the surgery. He should be back at the end of May beginning of June 2020.

Carlos Carrasco (32)- Healthy

### Colorado Rockies

Brendan Rodgers (23)- Shoulder- Rodgers said in November that he is progressing well from June surgery to repair the labrum in his right shoulder. "A couple of months ago, I couldn't even feel my arm and now I'm back to pretty much full activity, other than throwing and hitting a baseball," Rodgers said. He should be healthy by Spring Training.

David Dahl (25)- Ankle- Dahl suffered an ankle sprain in August which ended his season 2 months early. He is expected to be fully healthy come Spring training.

Scott Oberg (29)- Arm- Oberg was dealing with blood clots and that shut him down at the end of August 2019. The Rockies must feel he is healthy again as they signed him to a contract extension this off-season.

Kyle Freeland (26)- Groin- Freeland missed 1 month- from the end of August to end of September- with a groin strain. He came back at the end of the year for a few outings. He should be good for Spring Training.

Jon Gray (28)- Foot- Gray had surgery for a fractured left foot at the end of August 2019. Gray made it clear that he thinks the surgery will not affect his availability for the 2020 season.

German Marquez (24)- Arm- Marquez was shut down at the end of August due to right arm inflammation, and Manager Bud Black later clarified that he was dealing with a "tired arm." Marquez pitched 174 innings last year, down from the previous year, 2018, when he pitched 196 innings. He should be good to go for Spring Training.

Julian Fernandez (24)- Elbow- Fernandez had Tommy John surgery April 2018 and was never activated last year. His status is unknown.

## Detroit Tigers

Michael Fulmer (26)- Elbow- had Tommy John surgery March 2019 and it was reported that he is playing catch. He is expected back around June/July 2020.

Jacoby Jones (27)- Wrist- Had a fractured left wrist in August 2019 that did not require surgery. Should be fully healed by Spring Training

Niko Goodrum (27)- Groin- Missed the last month of the season with a left groin strain. Expected to be healthy to start Spring Training.

## Houston Astros

Lance McCullers (26)- Elbow- Had Tommy John surgery performed November 2018. Proclaimed healthy and finished rehab and is good to start Spring Training

Carlos Correa (25)- Healthy

Brad Peacock (31)- Healthy

Francis Martes (24)- Elbow- Had elbow surgery to repair his UCL August 2018 and comes into 2020 healthy.

Colin McHugh (32)- Elbow- Was shut down the last month of the season due to pain in his elbow. McHugh comes into SpringTraining with his injury status in question.

## Kansas City Royals

Jesse Hahn (30)- Elbow- Had surgery to repair his UCL in August 2018. Healthy.

Salvador Perez (29)- Elbow- Perez had Tommy John surgery March 2019 and is expected to be healthy and see more playing time at first base in 2020.

## Los Angeles Angels

Keynan Middleton (26)- Had Tommy John surgery performed mid May 2018. Healthy .

Tommy LaStella (30)- Leg- Fractured his right leg July 2019. Healthy.

Felix Pena (29)- Knee- Had ACL surgery August 2019. May not be ready to start Spring Training.

Griffin Canning (23)- Elbow- Canning was shut down at the end of August 2019 with right elbow inflammation. Began throwing again November 2019. Trending toward health for Spring Training.

Cam Bedrosian (28)- Forearm- Bedrosian was shut down the entire September 2019 due to a right forearm strain. Questionable to start Spring Training.

Shohei Ohtan (25)i- Elbow- Had Tommy John surgery October 2018. Completed Tommy John rehab December 2019. Fully healthy.

Justin Upton- Knee- Missed the last 2.5 weeks of the season with right knee patellar tendonitis. Had a PRP injection to the knee in September 2019 and is expected to be ready for Spring Training.


## Los Angeles Dodgers

Alex Verdugo (23)- Oblique- Verdugo missed the last 2 months of the season with an oblique strain and was yet to resume baseball activities as of mid- December. His status for Spring Training is not yet known.

Tyler White (29)- Trap- White missed the last 2 months of the season due to a right trapezius strain. Not word on his status for Spring training yet.

Ross Stripling (30)- Biceps- healthy after dealing with right biceps tightness during the month of August.

Jimmy Nelson (30)- Healthy.

## Miami Marlins

Brian Anderson (26)-  Finger- Anderson missed the last 6 weeks of the season with a broken finger on his left hand. No surgery was required and should be healthy for Spring Training.

Chad Wallach (28)- Concussion- Wallach continued to suffer from the side effects of a concussion that he suffered in May through the end of the season. Spring Training status is unknown.

Drew Steckenrider (28)- Elbow- Steckenrider had elbow surgery August 2019 and his status for Spring Training is unclear at this point.

Jordan Yamamoto (23)- Forearm- Yamamoto was sidelined in September with a right forearm strain but did return before the season ended. Healthy.

Garret Cooper (29)- Healthy.

Corey Dickerson (30)- Foot- Dickerson missed the last few weeks of the season due to a fractured left foot. Expected to be healthy to start the season.

## Milwaukee Brewers

Corey Knebel (28)- Elbow- Knebel had Tommy John surgery at the end of March 2019. He is expected to start throwing off flat ground January 2020. He is expected back mid 2020 season.

Brent Suter (30)- Elbow- Had Tommy John surgery done August 1, 2018. Healthy.

Ryon Healy (27)- Hip- Healy had season ending hip surgery August 2019. He is expected to be ready for Spring Training.

Christian Yelich- Knee- Suffered a fractured kneecap in September 2019. Began a running program mid November and was expected to have fully healthy winter workouts.

Logan Morrison (32)- Healthy

## Minnesota Twins

Blaine Hardy (32)- Elbow- Had a forearm strain in August 2019 and had a PRP injection performed mid August. Health status to start the season is not yet known.

Byron Buxton (26)- Shoulder- Buxton required season-ending surgery to repair the labrum in his left shoulder in September 2019. Recovery time is usually about 6 months which puts his availability for Spring Training in question

Rich Hill (39)- Elbow- Hill had elbow surgery in late October 2019 and will not be ready for Opening Day, looking at June/July activation.

## New York Mets

Yoenis Cespedes (34)- Heels/Ankle- Cespedes underwent bilateral heel surgery in 2018 and had a fractured ankle during his time away in 2019. Cespedes is expected to be ready for Spring training.

Jeff McNeil (27)- Wrist- McNeil had surgery October 2, 2019 to repair a fractured right wrist. He is expected to be fully recovered by Spring training.

Jed Lowrie (35)- Knee- Lowrie missed the majority of the 2019 season with left knee/calf  issues and was activated at the end of last year. Lowrie is expected to be healthy to start Spring Training.

Robert Gsellman (26)- Triceps- Gsellman missed the last 6 weeks of the season with a partially torn right triceps. He is expected to be healthy to start Spring Training.

Robinson Cano (37)- Multiple- Cano dealt with multiple injuries throughout the 2019 season but ended the season healthy.

Dominic Smith (24)- Foot- Smith missed about 3 months last year due to a stress fracture in his left foot. He returned for the last game of the season and is healthy to start Spring Training.

Brandon Nimmo (26)- Neck- Nimmo missed 3 months last year with a bulging disc in his neck. He returned in September and is healthy.

Delin Betances (31)- Achilles- Betances suffered a partial torn Achilles in his only appearance in 2019 after missing the first part of the season with shoulder/lat injury. He is expected to be healthy to start Spring Training.


**New York Yankees**

Jordan Montgomery (27)- Elbow- Had Tommy John surgery June 2018. Healthy

Mike Tauchman (29)- Calf- Tauchman missed the last month of the season with a calf strain. He is expected to be ready for Spring Training.

Aaron Hicks (30)- Elbow- Hicks had Tommy John surgery performed October 2019. He is expected back around August 2020.

Giancarlo Stanton (30)- Knee/Biceps- Stanton missed most of the 2019 season with knee and biceps injuries but returned healthy for the playoffs.

Miguel Andujar (24)- Shoulder- Andujar had shoulder surgery ending his season May 2019. He is expected to be close to 100% by Spring Training.

Luis Severino (25)- Lat- Severino missed all but 3 starts last year due to a grade 2 lat strain. Pitched in the playoffs and is healthy.

Luke Voit (28)- Abdomen- Voit had off-season surgery to address core muscle injuries and is expected to be ready for Spring Training.

Masahiro Tanaka (31)- Elbow- Tanaka had arthroscopic elbow surgery to remove a bone spur in his pitching elbow but is expected to be ready for spring training.

**Oakland Athletics**

AJ Puk (24)- Elbow- Had Tommy John surgery in April 2018.  Healthy.

Daniel Gossett (27)- Elbow- Had Tommy John surgery August 2018. Expected to be healthy to start Spring Training.

Stephen Piscotty (28)- Ankle- Healthy

James  Kaprielian (25)- Lat- Healthy

Khris Davis (32)- Hand/Hip- Davis dealt with hand and hip injuries throughout the season. Healthy.

## Philadelphia Phillies

Jake Arrieta (33)- Elbow- Arreita had surgery for his elbow to remove a bone spur August 2019. Expected to be ready for Spring Training.

Roman Quinn (26)- Oblique/Groin- Quinn played in only 44 games last year due to oblique and groin strains. Expected to be healthy to start Spring Training.

Adam Morgan (29)- Elbow- Morgan missed the last 2 months of the season with a left flexor strain. No surgery was required. Status for Spring Training is unknown at this time.

Andrew McCutchen (33)- Knee- McCutchen had ACL repair surgery in June 2019. He is expected to be at full strength at Spring Training.

Tommy Hunter (33)- Elbow- Hunter underwent surgery on his right flexor tendon July 2019. His status for Spring Training is not yet known.

Seranthony Dominguez (25)- Elbow- Dominguez missed the last 4 months of the season due to a UCL injury that did not require surgery. He is said to be having a normal off-season and will be ready for Spring training.

David Robertson (34)- Elbow- Robertson had Tommy John surgery August 2019 and is expected to miss the entire 2020 season.

## Pittsburgh Pirates

Chad Kuhl (27)- Elbow- Had Tommy John surgery performed September 2018. Should be healthy and ready for Spring Training.

Nick Burdi (26)- Biceps- Burdi underwent surgery to relieve symptoms of thoracic outlet syndrome June 2019. His availability will be re-evaluated around the time of Spring Training.

Jameson Taillon (28)- Elbow- Taillon had his 2nd Tommy John surgery performed in August 2019 and may miss the entire 2020 season.

Chris Archer (31)- Shoulder- Archer missed the last 6 weeks of the season due to right shoulder inflammation. He was deemed fully healthy in December 2019 and is having a normal offseason.

Chris Stratton (29)- Healthy

Gregory Polanco (28)- Shoulder- Polanco had shoulder surgery in September 2018. Dealt with persistent pain throughout the 2019 season, playing only 42 games. Status for Spring Training remains in question but mid-December was throwing 120 feet with no issues.

## San Diego Padres

Dinelson Lamet (27)- Elbow- Had Tommy John surgery in April 2018. Healthy.

Garrett Richards (31)- Elbow- Had Tommy John surgery in July 2018. He returned to the majors in September 2019. Healthy

Franchy Cordero (25)- Quad/Elbow- Cordero played only 9 games in 2019 due to elbow and quad injuries. Considered healthy and was playing Winter ball.

FernandoTatis Jr (20)- Back- Tatis missed the last 6 weeks of the 2019 season due to a back injury. Expected to be healthy to start Spring Training.

Francisco Mejia (24)- Oblique- Healthy

## San Francisco Giants

Johnny Cueto (35)- Elbow- Had Tommy John surgery performed in August 2018. Healthy.

Andrew Triggs (30)- Shoulder- Had thoracic outlet surgery in September 2018. Dealt with hip issues in 2019 and missed the entire season. He is expected to be ready for Spring Training.

Reyes Moronta (26)- Shoulder- Moronta underwent shoulder surgery to repair a torn labrum in his right shoulder. He is expected back August/September 2020.

Pablo Sandoval (33)- Elbow- Sandoval underwent surgery on his right elbow September 2019 to repair his UCL and have loose bodies removed. Expected to miss the first half of the 2020 season.

Steven Duggar (26)-Shoulder- Had left shoulder surgery in September 2018. Missed the last 2 months of the 2019 season with a left shoulder sprain, no surgery required. Expected to be healthy for Spring training.

Jeff Samardzija (34)- Shoulder- Healthy

Tyler Anderson (30)- Knee- Anderson had left knee surgery June 2019 and is expected to start the 2020 season on the IL.

Tyson Ross (32)- Elbow/Neck- Had an elbow injury that did not require surgery and then had a setback with neck discomfort. Status for next year is not yet known.

## Seattle Mariners
Kendall Gravemen (29)- Elbow- Graveman missed all of 2019 after undergoing Tommy John surgery in July 2018. Healthy going into the 2020 season.

Mitch Haniger (29)- Back- Haniger missed the last 4 months of the season following testicular surgery and a back injury. Haniger stated in September 2019 that he expected to be fully healthy in 1 month and will have no restrictions for Spring Training.

Dee Gordon (31)- Wrist/Quad- Healthy.

## St. Louis Cardinals

Alex Reyes (25)- Pectoral- Reyes is healthy and is having a normal offseason.

Bret Cecil (33)- Wrist- Cecil had carpal tunnel surgery performed April 2019 and missed the entire 2019 season. Status for Spring Training is not yet known.

Jordan Hicks (23)- Elbow- Hicks had Tommy John surgery June 2019 and is expected to miss the majority of the 2020 season.

Tony Cingrani (33)- Shoulder- Cingrani missed the 2019 season after having shoulder surgery (labrum) in June 2019. Status for 2020 Spring Training is not yet known.

Tyler O'Neil (24)- Wrist/Elbow- Healthy


## Tampa Bay Rays

Tyler Glasnow (26)- Forearm- Glasnow missed 4 months with a mild left forearm strain.He came back to pitch in September and the playoffs. Healthy.

Yandy Diaz (28)- Foot- Daiz missed 2 months last season with a left foot contusion but returned for the playoffs.

Brandon Lowe (25)- Quad- Lowe missed 2 and a half months with a quad injury. Healthy.

Blake Snell (27)- Elbow- Snell missed 2 months in 2019 due to arthroscopic surgery to remove a loose body in his left elbow. Came back healthy.

Yonny Chirinos (26)- Finger- Chirinos missed 6 weeks mid season with right middle finger inflammation. Healthy

## Texas Rangers

Corey Kluber (33)- Forearm/Oblique- Kluber was hit by a line drive fracturing his right forearm May 2019 and injured his oblique during a rehab assignment. He is expected to be at full strength for Spring Training.

Joey Gallo (26)- Wrist- Gallo missed the last 2+ months of the 2019 season after undergoing surgery for a right hamate bone fracture in his wrist in July 2019. He is expected to be at full strength for Spring Training.

Jesse Chavez (36)- Elbow- Chavez underwent surgery to remove loose bodies from his right elbow in September 2019. He is expected to be ready by Spring Training.


## Toronto Blue Jays

AJ Cole (27)- Shoulder- Cole was shut down mid August with shoulder impingement. His health coming into the season is questionable.

Ryan Borucki (25)- Elbow- Borucki pitched in only 2 games due to an elbow injury and underwent surgery to remove bone spurs from his left elbow in August 2019. Status for Spring Training is not yet known.

Matt Shoemaker (33)- Knee- Shoemaker made only 5 starts last year until he required knee surgery due to a torn ACL. Began throwing bullpen sessions in October 2019 and is expected to be ready for Spring Training.

Lourdes Gurriel Jr (26)- Quad- Gurriel missed time last year due to a quad injury and his season ended early due to appendicitis. Expected to be ready for Spring Training.

## Washington Nationals

Sean Doolittle (33)- Knee- Healthy

## Free Agents

Steven Souza (30)- Knee- Tore his ACL March 2019 and is fully healed and ready for Spring training.

Taiujan Walker (27)- Elbow- Came back from Tommy John surgery to pitch in the last game of 2019. Fully healthy.

Chad Bettis (30)- Hips- Bettis' season came to an end after he underwent surgery on both hips at the end of August, but he doesn't anticipate missing any time next season. "It's going to be a normal off-season for me," stated Bettis. He is expected to be at full strength for the beginning of Spring Training.

Cody Anderson (29)- Elbow- Anderson threw 8.2 innings last season. He underwent surgery on the flexor tendon in his right elbow in mid-June and did not return to action. His status heading into next year's Spring Training is unclear.

Jon Jay (34)- Hip- Had season ending surgery August/September 2019. His status for 2020 is as of yet unknown.

Nate Karns (31)- Forearm- Had a forearm strain and was recommended not to have surgery. Status for next year is unknown at this time.

Aaron Sanchez (27)- Shoulder- Sanchez had shoulder surgery September 2019 to repair a torn capsule in his shoulder. Sanchez is expected to miss most if not all of the 2020 season.

Cesar Puello (28)- Hip- Puello was sidelined the last 2 months of the season with a left hip flexor strain. Puello should be healthy heading into Spring Training.

Jeremy Jeffress (31)- Hip- Jeffress was shut down for all of September due to a left hip strain. He is expected to be ready by Spring Training.

Marco Estrada (36)- Healthy.

Jerad Eickhoff (29)- Biceps- Eickhoff dealt with a biceps injury and missed the last 3 months of the season. Healthy.

Pat Neshek (39)- Hamstring- Neshek underwent surgery for his left hamstring September 2019. Status for Spring Training is not yet known.

Lonnie Chisenhall (31)- Calf- Chisenhall missed the entire 2019 season due to a fractured finger a calf injury. Status for Spring Training remains unclear.

Domingo Santana (27)- Elbow- Santana missed about 5 weeks with his right elbow. inflammation. Returned in September healthy.
Matt Duffy (28)- Hamstring- Healthy

Nate Jones (33)- Elbow- Jones had season ending surgery May 2019 to repair a tear in his flexor mass. Spring Training status is not yet known.

Hunter Pence (36)- Back/Hamstring- Pence missed the last month of the season due to hamstring and back injuries. He is expected to be ready for Spring Training.

Devon Travis (28)- Knee- Travis had left knee surgery March 2019 but had setbacks and never played last year. Expected to be healthy for Spring training.

Spencer Kieboom (28)- Elbow- Kieboom finished the 2019 season on IL due to elbow inflammation. Spring Training status is not yet known.

Johnny Venters (34)- Shoulder- Venters underwent surgery in mid-August for a torn capsule in his left shoulder. Status for Spring training is uncertain.

Jeremy Helickson (32)- Shoulder- Healthy.

Austin Brice (27)- Forearm- Brice missed the last 2 months of the season with a right forearm strain. No word on his status for Spring training.

Zack Cozart (34)- Shoulder- Began hitting November 2019 and looks to be on track for Spring Training.

Dylan Covey (28)- Shoulder- Covey was shut down mid September 2019 with a shoulder issue. No recent word of any issues this off-season and he should be good for Spring Training.

# Catcher Outlook
By Ray Kuhn


When it comes to fantasy baseball, catchers are generally met with a great deal of frustration. However, that doesn't mean we get to ignore the position, as there is still value to be found.

Whether or not your league utilizes one or two starting catchers greatly impacts your strategy, but at the end of the day, we have to remember that it is stats we are compiling, and it doesn't necessarily matter what position they are coming from.

**Tier One:**
J.T. Realmuto

Having questions about catchers is normal, but when it comes to Realmuto, he has the least. After getting off to a slow start in Philadelphia last season, we really saw him pick things up in the second half, and Realmuto ultimately finished with career best totals of 25 home runs and 83 RBI while also contributing nine stolen bases (six in the second half), after just three in 2018. What really solidifies Realmuto's place in a tier all his own, is the fact that we saw legitimate skill surges in the second half, both with hard contact and power, that give you comfort in his ability to repeat those 15 home runs, 46 RBI and .286 batting average.

**Tier Two:**
Gary Sanchez
Mitch Garver
Willson Contreras
Yasmani Grandal

This is an interesting tier as about 35 picks separate Sanchez from Contreras, and at first glance, that is telling you to wait. Despite the fact that Sanchez very easily could have found himself in Realmuto's tier had he lived up to the 2019 expectations some had for him, the next three catchers are a lot more attractive. Sanchez is the better player, but you can do a lot with those two or three other draft picks if you pass on him. In fact, bypassing this tier all together might be the best thing for building your team.

We know that Sanchez is going to bat in the middle of a very strong Yankees' lineup, but as with most catchers, health is something that we do need to be mindful of. The power is real, but the home run upside has been, and will continue to be until proven otherwise, limited by Sanchez's ability to stay on the field. It is also no secret that Sanchez struggles to make contact, and while he isn't going to hit .232 again (or .184 like he did in 2018), we aren't looking at an asset in the batting average department either. As far as those home runs go, Sanchez did get his fly ball rate up to 48% last season. At the right price, Sanchez works, but there is just too much risk here as his ADP leaves out much of the room for profit.

The first thing we have to do is resist the urge to project Garver's 31 home runs in 359 at bats from last season out to 500-550 at bats. But at this price, why wouldn't we take a repeat of what we saw from the Twins' catcher last season even though we should be able to expect some more playing time. After all, Garver certainly earned it as he consistently hit the ball hard and increased his fly ball rate from 38% to 47%. Garver has also shown the ability to draw a walk, and with a batting average in the .260 range, he isn't a liability either. While Minnesota did acquire Alex Avila to ease the burden on Garver behind the plate, he will likely see some time at first base as well to keep his bat in the lineup.

Contreras rebounded from a lackluster 2018 season, and the big thing for him was watching his fly ball rate rise as he went deep 24 times. I wouldn't expect much more than that and a batting average .270, but Contreras can also be a sneaky source of RBI depending on his spot in the batting order. As we saw his power metrics rebound last season, there is the hope that Contreras continues to improve, but you don't want to pay for it just yet as 25 home runs, 70 RBI, and a .270 batting average is very possible.

Let's not judge Grandal solely on the basis of his rough second half season as he hit .225 with just 10 home runs. Over the last three seasons, Grandal has averaged about 25 home runs while showing the ability to be a solid run producer, and now he slides into the middle of the White Sox's batting order. Just don't expect much from the batting average.

**Tier Three:**
Will Smith
Sal Perez
Wilson Ramos
Christian Vasquez

And this is where I start to gain some comfort with diving into the position. As with the previous tier though, we are talking about a wide range; this time about 50 picks. And we also aren't without questions either, as we begin to lack in the way of upside.

I, and likely many others, would like to see Smith take the next step in 2020, but I'm not sure how plausible it is. Upon his promotion last season, the hard contact and power metrics were there, but how much of that power do we believe, and Will Smith's contract issues hinder his progress? My guess is that there will be some ups and downs in his performance, but the power numbers will be there despite some streakiness and batting average struggles.

While Perez is a year older, he doesn't have the load of catching last season on him, and the Kansas City backstop is also a known quantity. Yes, there is no upside with Perez, but his skills are stable and we know we can expect roughly 25 home runs and 70 RBI with a decent batting average.

Ramos was never a home run hitter, but his power certainly took a step back last season. With a 62% ground ball rate, Ramos' upside is limited despite the fact that he was in the middle of the Mets' lineup for the majority of last season. The batting average is there, especially for a catcher, which makes Ramos a solid option as even with all of the ground balls, he is a solid source of run production.

Not to be negative, but the only place for Christian Vasquez's performance to go as compared to last season is down. After hitting .207 with three home runs and 16 RBI in 2018, Vasquez made a 180-degree flip as he finished with .276 with 23 home runs and 72 RBI. With a league average barrel rate and just a slightly above average launch rate, we likely saw the best of what Vasquez has to offer last season. But with that being said, he should be drafted as a starting catcher.

**Tier Four:**
Omar Navarez
Jorge Alfaro
Carson Kelly

And we now get to the point in the rankings, and it didn't take long, where a lot of this is a matter of personal preference.

Prior to last season, the knock on Navarez was always his lack of power. The line drive rate was there, along with contact rate and therefore a solid batting average (around .275), but things went in the right direction in 2019. While his home run to fly ball rate remained relatively unchanged, Navarez's home runs went from nine to 22 thanks to a drastically improved fly ball rate (29% to 41%) and increased power metrics. The fact that this didn't negatively impact his batting average is also a positive development. Even despite the improvement, Navarez's hard hit rates and exit velocity were still below average as compared to the league. While we can expect a regression from the 22 home runs, his improved launch angle should allow for him to keep some of those improvements.

Overall, it was a solid campaign for Alfaro as he hit .262 for the second straight season while bringing his home run total up from 10 to 18. Alfaro's 64% contact rate will hold him back from likely making any further progress, but we know the playing time will be there, and you can do a lot worse than the Miami backstop.

In just 365 at bats last season, Kelly took a nice step forward in his first crack at extended playing time. If we are looking at a catcher who could move up the board by the end of the season, Kelly is it as we saw his power metrics surge in 2019. With a 13.2% walk rate, Kelly has shown the ability to get on base, and with a 40.4% hard hit rate, along with other favorable power metrics, there is room for even more improvement. To be the complete package, we just need Kelly to improve on his 75% contact rate to bring up his .245 batting average.

**Tier Five:**
Yadier Molina
Travis d'Arnaud
Robinson Chirinos
Roberto Perez

Last year was the first time in the last five years that Molina finished with less than 500 at bats, and it was just a thumb injury as he is showing no signs of slowing down. The one thing is that we are starting to see a decrease in his home runs as we can longer expect him to reach 20, but a .270 batting average along with 60-70 RBI are still a quite reasonable expectation. Just no, that perhaps this could be the year he really slows down, and that there is no upside.

Just stay healthy. That would make life so much easier for d'Arnaud. It will be interesting to see how things work with d'Arnaud in the National League without the benefit of the DH spot. But even if he is healthy, can we expect him to hit more than .250? Over the past two seasons, d'Arnaud has shown an impressive hard-hit rate, but should we be banking on 500 at bats? And I'm not sure we should expect more than 20 home runs either? I'm not against Atlanta's new catcher, I'm just not looking to make a sizable investment.

With his .238 batting average last season, Chirinos, surprisingly in fact, right in line with the average production from the position. He likely will find his way into another 400 at bat season, which will amount to decent home run production, some RBI, and just a solid season. Chirinos begins the replacement level portion, at best, of our programming.

Perez is essentially a younger version of Chirinos, but can we expect him to hit 24 home runs again? While he does have above average power metrics, I'm not sure we can bank on a repeat performance due to his 28% home run to fly ball rate and 32% fly ball rate. A 4.3% launch rate also doesn't leave me with a great deal of confidence.

**Tier Six:**
Francisco Mejia
Sean Murphy

Ranking these two young catchers here, likely means they won't end up on any of my teams in 2020. The potential is there for them to surge into the third or fourth tiers, but there are also some questions to be answered, and we might be a year too early.

The fly balls were there for Mejia last season, but with just eight home runs in 265 at bats, the results didn't follow. To this point, he hasn't shown that the batting average potential and production he displayed in the minor leagues can translate to the big-league level. While success is possible, don't invest too heavily.

Without more fly balls, I'm not sure how many home runs we can expect from Murphy moving forward, and while the batting average upside is limited, there could be some value here. And at least with Murphy, there is some growth potential.

**Tier Seven:**
Tom Murphy
Danny Jansen
Buster Posey
James McCann
Wellington Castillo

With the trade of Navarez to Milwaukee, we will see a lot more of Murphy behind the plate for Seattle. Despite leaving Coors Field, we finally got to see what he is capable of in the home run department (18 in 281 at bats). Splits are an issue, Murphy is a lot better against southpaws, and thanks to a 67% contact rate, the batting average is questionable. But with a 47% fly ball rate and improved power metrics, 15-20 home runs should be there from Murphy with the potential for more based on playing time.

After a disappointing rookie season, I might be a little low on Jansen, but this could also represent a buying opportunity if others share a similar sentiment. From a hit rate standpoint, Jansen was unlucky, but close to a league average contact rate should mean good things for his batting average; at least better than what we saw last season. In reality, things can't really be any worse than they were in 2019 as his power metrics did improve in the second half of last season, although his upside is limited.

How far has Posey fallen? At this point the former All-Star is a shell of himself, and his skills are just not what they once were. We can't expect him to make it through the season healthy, the power and run production is a fraction of what it once was, and now we can't count on an elite batting average any longer.

Despite the White Sox acquiring Grandal, McCann should still receive a regular amount of playing time with first base and the DH spot being utilized. Regardless of the Grandal signing, McCann wasn't going to repeat his All-Star campaign from a year ago. In 476 at bats, McCann had 18 home runs and 60 RBI, and that will likely go down as a career year for him as despite a seven percent decrease in fly balls, his home run to fly ball rate spiked and he struggled to make contact in the second half of the season (65%).

Castillo is a proven commodity that will offer some home runs and RBI commensurate with his playing time. While he hit .209 last season, the career .254 hitter should bounce back, but the new Texas catcher should essentially be free on draft day.

**Tier Eight:**
Tucker Barnhart
Kurt Suzuki
Mike Zunino
Tyler Flowers
Pedro Severino
Jacob Stallings
Yan Gomes

And this is where we get to the desperation portion of events. All of these options will receive enough at bats to at least be fantasy relevant and add some home runs and RBI, but we also have to be aware of what they could potentially do to your batting average.

Barnhart doesn't do anything that jumps off the page, but with a .250 batting average, he won't hurt you much, and the at bats will be there.

I wouldn't hold it against Suzuki that he is in a timeshare with Gomes, as he provides a solid batting average along with being legitimate source of run production. In 309 at bats last season, Suzuki hit 17 home runs (that number will likely decrease by a few in 2020) while driving in 63 runs. Even in weekly leagues, you could make that work from the catcher position, but in leagues that allow daily roster moves, Suzuki could prove to be a valuable, and cost-effective option.

Zunino has power, but that batting average is just bad. At this point, I'm not sure if it shows any signs of getting better, so the question is, can you tolerate it and are the home runs worth it? And how much playing time will Tampa Bay give him?

We can figure that the Braves will tread carefully with d'Arnaud and his playing time, which means Flowers will receive his share of playing time. And while we won't do much out of the ordinary, Flowers does offer replacement level value as he did hit 11 home runs in 310 at bats last season. But the .238 career hitter won't be an asset in the batting department.

While he did make some improvements last season, Severino is still just a league average option at best. Looking elsewhere is the way to go, but the Baltimore backstop will likely end up on his share of rosters simply based on supply and demand.

There were a few flashes of success from Stallings last season, but nothing that was really worthy of your attention. With a league average contact rate, batting average won't be a liability, but the problem is that we aren't dealing with much power here.

Gomes' best days are behind him, but we know he is going to have a role next season. There is some power production, but nothing really of note.

**First Base Outlook**
By Ray Kuhn

This is your friendly reminder that each year is different. We go through trends, and there is always the need for change and adaptation. Specifically, this comes into play when talking about first base, because it is not the position it once was. Far from it in fact.

Things thin out quite quickly these days at first base, and it is no longer a position you can simply afford to wait on. Of course, that brings us to another set of problems, because depending on how early you look to select your first baseman, it could leave you lacking in speed or starting pitching. This is why tiering is so critical, as you can't be left without a top 15 option. Additionally, the by-product of this, is how it impacts the corner infield position as well.

Now that we have sounded the alarm, let's jump into how our options rank:

**Tier One:**
Cody Bellinger
Freddie Freeman

After a down 2018 campaign, Bellinger bounced back in a big way last season, and it makes for an interesting evaluation for 2020. Right now, it looks like we can write off that down campaign of 25 home runs and 76 RBI, but at the same time, I'm not sure we can expect him to go deep 47 times once again. However, the power is real, and perhaps more importantly, Bellinger's contact rate rose from 73% to 81% last season. Factor in 15 stolen bases, and we are talking about a top option, but the concern for Bellinger, is that his .259 batting average in the second half is going to stick around. Even if that's the case, no one would complain based on his elite launch angle.

With 38 home runs and 121 RBI, Freeman also took part in the power revolution, and it shouldn't come as a surprise. It feels like Freeman has been around forever, but at age 30, there is still plenty of time left for him to continue his success. At this point, nothing should come as a surprise with Freeman, as his skill set and production is as solid and predictable as it gets.

**Tier Two:**
Pete Alonso
Matt Olson
Paul Goldschmidt
Jose Abreu
Anthony Rizzo
Josh Bell

This is likely where I would look to secure my first baseman, but despite what the early ADP suggests, there isn't that much of a difference between Alonso and the rest of the tier. Yes, we know everything that Alonso did in his rookie season, and his power tool and skill set is as real as it gets, but expecting 53 home runs once again might not be prudent. With a 69% contact rate last season, the concern for Alonso is that he is closer to his .241 second half batting average, and that isn't exactly what you want out of your second or third round pick. But 45 home runs and 100 RBI are a very reasonable expectation.

I came close to others in this tier ahead of Alonso, but that is leaving a lot of home runs on the table. Granted based on the market place, I have a much better shot at leaving a draft with Olson than Alonso, but I still can't do it. Early season surgery on his hamate bone didn't seem to impact the Oakland first baseman, as his power and hard-hit rate didn't come close to missing a beat. There is more of a concern with the batting average here, but after hitting .262 last season, Olson shouldn't be a liability. In fact, it wouldn't surprise me to see Olson and Alonso finish 2020 with identical stat lines.

It wasn't exactly a smooth campaign for Goldschmidt in his new home, but at the end of the day, he got pretty close to his previous performance. Well, with what major exception; stolen bases. Goldschmidt simply doesn't run anymore, and he is more of a .280 hitter than anything else. The good news though, is that Goldschmidt picked things back up, especially in the power department, over the second half of the season, and that is something we should see continue.

If it is predictability you after, then Abreu is your man. The improvements Chicago is making to their lineup should serve to benefit the veteran, as there is no reason why he can't continue to produce at his expected levels. There have been some slight dips to Abreu's metrics, but based on his 33 home runs and 123 RBI last season, you wouldn't know it. Even with slight regression, you should be perfectly fine here once again.

Expecting 100 RBI along with a .280 batting average has become common place for Rizzo, but after 25 and 27 home runs the last two seasons, after averaging 32 in the three prior years, along with a dip in fly ball percentage in the second half of last season, there have to be some doubts in place. And then there is the nagging back injury from the second half of last season as well.

Everyone waiting for Bell to emerge certainly got their wish last season, but the first half was better than the second. The plate skills were always there for Bell, but his swing changes from last off-season unlocked something as he jumped from 12 home runs all the way to 37; although he did hit 26 in 2017. Everything did take a step back in the second half of last season, but even that pace was better than what we had become accustomed to. There is still some upside there, but don't pay for it, and instead pay for 25-30 home runs, 100 RBI, and a .265 average.

**Tier Three:**
D.J. LeMahieu
Max Muncy
Trey Mancini
Danny Santana

The opinion entering last season, was that leaving Coors Field would adversely impact LeMahieu, but that certainly wasn't the close. Throughout the season, LeMahieu was one of the true constants in the Yankees' lineup as he hit .327 with 25 home runs and 102 RBI. With below average power, LeMahieu's home run outburst wasn't exactly expected, but his home run to fly ball rate rose from 11% to 19%. The run production, at least most of it, and the .300 batting average are believable, but regardless of what the metrics say, I have a hard time banking on

25 home runs once again. Regardless, we know that he can hit, and LeMahieu will be a key part of one of the best lineups in baseball while also offering positional flexibility.

We just have two years of track record with Muncy, but they have been pretty close to identical, and his profile backs that up. There is the elite power and walk rate, but that comes along with a sub-standard contact rate and a .250 batting. The good thing though, is that you know what you are getting with Muncy, and his dual eligibility at second and third base also helps. It is pretty crazy though, to think that he might be more valuable at first base.

I guess the Orioles have to have one legitimate, middle of the order threat, and that is Mancini. Of course, part of the problem, is that he doesn't exactly have protection around him, and you have to be at least slightly concerned as to who will even be on base for him to drive in. Always a solid hitter, we saw a nice across the board increase to Mancini's metrics, but most importantly his fly ball rate rose from 26% to 32%. An above average power rate means that Mancini should come close to another 35-home run season, but even with a little regression, you likely won't notice much of a difference in his performance. Sometimes, there isn't anything wrong with a situation lacking upside, if you get production you can bank on.

Talk about coming out of nowhere. As a perfect example of why you should never ignore the waiver wire early in the season, Santana did 28 home runs while adding 21 stolen bases for essentially no cost. The problem now, is expecting to see a repeat of that performance in 2020. Of everything, the stolen bases are the most likely thing we can expect to see again thanks to his elite speed, and considering he once was a five-tool prospect (although like five years ago), his success didn't really come out of nowhere; even if it did. Santana's 69% contact rate will be a problem, and it remains to be seen how sustainable his 24% home run to fly ball rate will be. Even with that being said, there is still value in a 20/20 player who hits .250-.260.

**Tier Four:**
Yuli Gurriel
Rhys Hoskins
Carlos Santana

Gurriel often flies under the radar with the Astros in their prolific lineup, but he is a proven run producer. The concern here is that fantasy owners are going to pay for the 31 home runs he hit last season, but the launch angle and batted ball metrics don't really support much more than 20. Even with that being said though, his 88% contact rate and above average hard contact rates, support a .290 batting average and 90 RBI.

With the explosion of power that we have seen recently, 30 home runs don't mean the same as it used to. And when you factor in Rhys Hoskins' .226 batting average last season, we are dealing with a liability, and that's not even taking into account his ADP from last season. The last month and half was especially bad for Hoskins after a hand injury, but there is no denying power as an elite skill set that he owns. What does hold him back though, is his home run to fly ball rates of 16% and 14% the last two seasons. If the price is right, there is some value, but don't expect much more than a .250 batting average at best.

Santana is an all-around solid hitter, and while last season was likely his peak, the regression that comes shouldn't be all that large based on his solid skill set the plate. Being back in

Cleveland seemed to truly help his cause, but don't expect a 34-home run season once again. Santana makes a solid case for spending early round picks elsewhere as he can be a nice complementary piece to your lineup.

**Tier Five:**
Eric Hosmer
Edwin Encarnacion
Christian Walker
Joc Pederson
Luke Voit
Nate Lowe

Yes, we know, Hosmer hits too many ground balls and he isn't worth the contract San Diego gave him, but we also shouldn't hold that against him. At a 56% ground ball rate, we know that Hosmer certainly doesn't elevate the ball nearly as much as he should, and his contact rate is now below average (67% in the second half of last season is something to keep an eye on). However, a .260 batting average with 20 home runs and 90 RBI is right in his wheelhouse as we know that Hosmer is still going to be a solid run producer in the middle of the Padres' batting order with bankable playing time.

At this point, maybe we shouldn't write off Encarnacion, but his power and home run production are no longer truly elite. However, that doesn't mean we still can't bank on 30 home runs once again. He isn't going to hit much better than .250, and there were some health issues last season, but he is as predictable as they come at hitting the ball over the wall. And while he will likely finish short, 40 home runs and 100 RBI are both possible, with the benefit being that you aren't paying for it.

Walker was an early season stat-cast darling, and 2019 was the first time he was able to put that together as that resulted in 29 home runs and 73 RBI, along with a .259 batting average. Yes, the exit velocity and hard-hit rate was elite, but with just a 38% fly ball rate we are left banking on his 20% home run to fly ball rate. Thanks to a 71% contact rate, which was an improvement on years past, he is really just power dependent, and leaves him without much upside.

We know that Pederson has elite level power, but he is truly a platoon player. Based on his struggles against southpaws, that might be better for him and his .250 batting average, but he likely won't get much more than 500 at bats. What holds me back from going crazier though, is his 26% home run to fly ball rate and the doubts on him repeating his 36 home runs from last season.

The playing time is there for the taking, but Voit needs to stay healthy. Voit does have above average power, but he doesn't do anything that truly stands out from a fantasy perspective. We have also never seen what Voit can do with a full season's worth of playing time, and there just isn't much upside. In reality, there is nothing stopping Voit from being 10 spots lower on this list depending on how things go, and I would treat him as such with his propensity for strikeouts being a concern.

We know how things go with Tampa Bay and their plethora of options, but let's just go based on the skill level Lowe possesses and bank on 500 at bats. For that to happen though, Lowe needs to be a lot more disciplined at the plate. He did it in Triple-A, and 169 plate appearances is a small sample size and he was also up and down, so the tools are there. Lowe's power isn't much more than league average, so we won't see him hit 30 home runs, but with playing time and experience, we are looking at a solid contributor.

**Tier Six:**
Yandy Diaz
C.J. Cron
Daniel Murphy
Joey Votto
Michael Chavis
Renato Nunez
Evan White
Jesus Aguilar
Rowdy Tellez

With 14 home runs in 347 plate appearances, Diaz finally figured out how to get the ball in the air with a 32% fly ball rate. He makes hard contact at an elite level, the power metrics are there and seemingly improving based on the second half of the season, and Diaz also has a league average contact rate. Let's now see what the 28-year-old can do with a full season's worth of playing time.

Detroit decided to bolster the right side of their infield with some veteran reinforcements, and that includes Cron. At this point, Cron owns his power production, and we can bank on 30 home runs with a batting average that won't be a liability. There are some situations where not having any upside is perfectly acceptable, because there is value in predictability and playing time.

We can likely count on at least one stint on the Injured List from Murphy, and likely more. While Murphy does have above average contact skills (83%), it is no longer elite (88%), and his power is also on the decline. Murphy is no longer what he once was, but with a 24%-line drive rate, he is still a solid option at the plate.

If you want to talk about a player on the decline, Votto certainly stands out. After 36 home runs and 100 RBI campaign in 2017, the last two seasons have been ugly for the Reds' first baseman, and at age 36, I'm not sure we should be expecting a rebound. After carrying a 20% home run to fly ball rate, it has dropped to 10% in each of the last two seasons, as he is simply not barreling the ball to nearly the same level as he once did. Votto is still a solid option, but without the .300 batting average, he just blends into the background.

Chavis has power, but maybe not as much as he showed upon his initial promotion, but there are also some holes in his swing that do present a cause for concern. In the second half of the season, Chavis' was also dealing with a shoulder injury, so I'm not sure we should be sounding any alarms just yet. But we should proceed with caution here until we at least see how strong his power really is.

If Baltimore was any other team, Nunez likely wouldn't have gotten 599 plate appearances last season or batted in the middle of the lineup. That translated to 31 home runs and 90 RBI, but Nunez also hit .244. The batting average is real, but expecting a repeat of his power production and his 46% fly ball rate, might not be prudent as his power metrics aren't all that much more than league average (although his first half production was a lot better than his second half, and maybe health was the cause). Through Nunez on your bench or the back end of your roster, but be prepared to move on quickly.

Prior to the season, the Mariners gave White a nice contract extension (six years and $24 million), so you have to think they are committed to giving him a chance to show what he can do at the start of the season. White finally found some power last season, 18 home runs and 55 RBI, to go along with his .293 batting average, and that gives us some insight into what we can expect from him moving forward. The career .296 hitter has solid plate skills, but it remains to be seen how that translates to major league pitching. This is a ranking that reflects caution, as his contract is the only reason why I would expect him to start the season with Seattle.

Talk about a steep fall. After hitting .274 with 35 home runs and 108 RBI in 2018, Aguilar had just a disaster of a season in 2019 as he hit just .236 with 12 home runs and 50 RBI. After being over drafted last season, Aguilar represents a nice value proposition for 2020 as he we can likely expect him to receive 500 at bats with the Marlins. He really just needs his power to rebound, and after being bogged down by a slow start in 2019, it's possible that takes place. And at this price, why not figure it out.

Playing time is still in doubt for Tellez, and his plate skills are also a cause for concern, but the power is real. There is probably a .250 hitter in there, and 30 home runs are possible, as there are some things to work with here, but I'm not paying to find out. But that doesn't mean I'm not keeping Tellez on my radar either.

With an influx of youth and some multi-positional players available for second base (2B), there are a lot of options to consider at the position this year. As with most years, you'll have to pay up for the top players but for those who are patient, there is some middle-infield gold to mine later in the draft.

NOTE: The names in these tiers are listed based on their Fantrax ADPs. However, placement within the respective tiers are based on my own rankings, and in some cases conflict with the Fantrax ADPs and possibly your own rankings. I provide my arguments below. Let's get into it:

**Tier 1**
Altuve (34)

Jose Altuve remains at the top of the 2B rankings again heading into the 2020 season but may be overtaken by some of the youth in the next tier by season's end. The soon-to-be 30-year-old saw a dip in his BA and OBP in 2019 but took advantage of the new baseball by hitting almost as many HRs as the previous 2 seasons combined. His stolen base (SB) numbers stand out as a concern, certainly related to the 5 weeks missed due to a hamstring injury, so keep an eye on this aspect of his game in the early part of the season. All-in-all, Jose remains the most complete 2B player for your team. If he's still available past the middle of Round 3, someone will be getting a bargain.

Unlike last season when Javier Baez qualified at the position after having played over half of his games at 2B in 2018, he was exclusively at shortstop (SS) for the Cubs in 2019 so does not make this list. However, if he still carries the eligibility in your league for some reason, target him over Altuve.

**Tier 2**
Marte (40)
Hiura (54)
Merrifield (55)

Here is a tier I really dislike, not because the players in it, but primarily the cost it'll take to own any of the three.

Not many predicted the magnitude of Ketel Marte's breakout last season. If you were one of those astute owners who drafted him or saw the early-season trends and traded for him by the end of May, he probably carried many of your team toward a league title. By making significant increases in all the power categories and maintaining a low strikeout (K) rate, he turned his third season in Arizona into MVP consideration. He's primed for another productive season but it comes at a high risk. A lot of his power can be linked to the 2019 baseball. Should there be a significant correction there, I suspect you'll see it with Marte as well. His current ADP in the low 40s is just too high for me and I don't expect to own many shares of him on Opening Day. However, I'll have my eye on him if he slides another round or two.

If I were going to reach for one of these Tier 2 players in a redraft, Keston Hiura is the one. By next year, I fully expect my fellow prognosticators will be debating if he has overtaken Altuve as the top 2B in fantasy. I tend to think he will. From his first call-up on May 13, he showed a confidence that indicated he was ready for the full-time gig in Milwaukee. That first visit only lasted 17 games but, in that time, Keston delivered with 5 HRs and a .281/.333/.531 slash. By comparison, Travis Shaw provided 4 HRs and a .163/.266/.281 slash before Huira's call-up. Despite this, the Brewers sent him back down for a few more weeks until the Shaw experiment at 2B was finished. Keston came up for good on June 26 and went on to post a total of 19 HRs and a .303/.368/.570 slash after playing only half the season. With a full-time role in 2020, it's hard not to expect a rise in both his production and his rank amongst MLB second basemen. In a dynasty or keeper league, he's the guy you want to buy and hold.

Whit Merrifield is another player I will likely own a few shares of. He remains a 20/20 threat but there are some warning signs that a regression is coming. The 2019 baseball did not benefit him like we saw with so many other players as his home run (HR) totals ticked up just slightly, from 12 in 2018 and 16 in 2019. Likewise, he was probably drafted in your 2019 league as a premier source of SBs but in 162 games only produced 20, a 56% decrease from 2018. Merrifield also turns 31 before Spring Training so we may see the age bias drive his ADPs down a bit once we get closer to the season. Despite all this, I have him in my Tier 2 rankings because I believe he can still be a huge asset to your fantasy team. However, I caution you to temper expectations a bit when developing your draft queue.

**Tier 3**
Villar (28)
Torres (38)
LeMahieu (75)
Muncy (79)
McNeil (101)
Moustakas (128)

In some lists, Jonathan Villar is still ranked as the top 2B in fantasy. With his placement in my third tier, I tend to disagree. Placed on waivers by the Orioles, Villar moves on to Miami where he'll continue to get every day playing time. In that regard, this was an ideal landing point since most other teams would likely adjust his role to more of a utility player. Every day ABs mean he should remain a significant source of speed for your fantasy baseball teams. Marlins Park has never been mistaken for Camden Yards to a hitter and moving the wall in by 12 feet in some areas may only mask the inevitable decline in Villar's HR totals. I really see Villar becoming another Dee Gordon, which is why I will not likely own any shares of him this season.

The Yankee infielders come up next in the ADPs. I struggled a bit with Glebar Torres' placement in Tier 3 because I really see him on the verge of cracking Tier 2. His power numbers are not in doubt and although primarily a pull hitter from the right side, he did take advantage of the short porch at Yankee Stadium enough to please his fantasy owners. The main concern I still see is his high strikeout rate. If he gets that in check, he'll definitely move up. Conversely, one of his teammate's strengths is his low strikeout rate, leading DJ LeMahieu to a very high AVE and strong offensive numbers across the board, with 25+ HRs and 100+ runs (R) and runs batted in (RBI) in 2019. DJ doesn't run much, so you'll have to look for SB somewhere else as everyone else in your league is doing at this point in the draft. Overall, I see upside in both players at their current ADPs.

Max Muncy is somewhat an enigma. Will he play 2B? Will he move to 1B for Lux? Does Turner move to 1B and Muncy shift to the hot corner? Maybe Bellinger moved to 1B and Muncy becomes a platoon player? There's no doubt he provides the power numbers you crave in a middle infield (MI)-qualified player but the current uncertainty in the Dodgers' lineup makes me a little hesitant (but just a little). Will he get enough ABs this season to justify his high ADP? Over the past 2 years, he's averaging 139 games so I'm fairly confident the Dodgers will work it out. For us early drafters, I wish there was a little more playing time clarity, as well as a reduction in his strikeout rate, but I'm certainly not going to pass on him in the early 6th round of my next 15-team draft. I suspect he won't be available there though.

I really like these next two players at their current ADP. On paper, Jeff McNeil looks a lot like DJ LeMathieu, high AVE, low K-rate, moderate power, and minimal speed. He is another player that benefited from the 2019 baseball, and is coming off wrist surgery this off-season, so temper your HR estimations a bit. He may play more 3B than 2B, but if you can pair him with a power-hitting corner infielder on your fantasy squad, the two can provide a significant boost to your team. Another multi-positional player that fits this same recommendation is Mike Moustakas. Moose will never win a batting title but is an all-around solid player with a career .252/.310/.441 slash and averaging 33 HRs over the past 3 seasons. Playing half his games in Cincinnati should see him comfortably exceed these power numbers and thus his current ADP. In fact, I wouldn't be surprised to see his ADP cut in half by Spring Training so take advantage where you can and buy at a significant discount.

**Tier 4**
Albies (50)
Escobar (80)
D Santana (117)
Biggio (154)
Edman (170)

The current ADPs of my Tier 4 players are all over the map. Albies remains an extremely popular selection in fantasy circles but I apparently continue to miss the boat on this one. He'll play this year at age 23 so there's certainly time to grow but as of now, we seem to be looking at a 25 HR/15 SB player with good average and counting stats. If you start the draft focused on starting pitching, I can see Albies being an attractive pick near the 3/4 turn. For the more traditional drafter, he just doesn't translate to a top 50 overall pick for me. I'd prefer to wait 2 rounds and select a player like Eduardo Escobar, who gains 2B eligibility for the first time. Escobar appears to be getting better with age. Playing in 150+ games in each of his age 29 and age 30 seasons have been his best yet, averaging 29 HRs, 84 R, 101 RBI, and .270 AVE. As with many others, he will not help in the SB category, attempting an average of only 6 per season, so look elsewhere after drafting this roster anchor.

We all have players that burned us in the past, maybe multiple times, and we promised ourselves on draft day to avoid at all costs. How many of you have included Danny Santana on that list over the years? Yes, I have my hand up too. I was very high on Santana after his 2014 season where he slashed .319/.353/.472 and gave us 20 SBs. Much to my dismay, 2015 ...and

2016…..and 2017 …and 2018 (I'm stubborn that way) made me seriously question my player evaluation skills. I'm not sure who showed up in Texas last spring wearing his uniform but he quickly played his way onto my fantasy rosters (again). Danny put together a fantasy all-star season with 28 HRs and 21 SBs, slashing .283/.324/.534, gaining multi-positional eligibility. Will he break my heart again in 2020? Maybe, but for an 8th round pick, I'm willing to roll the dice (again).

Cavin Biggio is part of an exciting group of young Blue Jays that are going to be fun to watch for years to come. However, Biggio's moderate power/speed combo, along with a low AVE, suggests a maximum 20/20 player in the making. He also reminds me of the lesson I should have learned after Danny Santana's rookie year (see above). Biggio turns 25 in April and will undoubtedly grow into a more complete player but I'll likely let someone else live through the growing pains in my redraft leagues.

If I'm skeptical of Biggio, why am I very high on Tommy Edman this season? The quick answer is his advanced hit tools, specifically his high hard-hit rate and low K-rate. Edman approached 15/15 with a .300+ average over just 92 games, also gaining multi-position eligibility along the way. What can we expect with a full season of production? I'm betting on a 20/20 floor and will be drafting him as much as possible, at or before his Rd 11 ADP.


**Tier 5**
Lux (128)
Kingery (184)
McMahon (197)
Newman (216)
Chavis (245)

As we move into this tier, we find a number of players with lots of potential, but obvious concerns as well. Gavin Lux is going to be a very popular player in 2020 drafts, especially in dynasty formats, but the short-term warning signs (playing time, high K-rate, low power indicators, lack of speed, etc.) make his 9th round ADP hard to consider in your redraft leagues. Scott Kingery is another player with multi-position eligibility and a potential for 20/20 production. His high K-rate will be a batting average drain but the price is probably about right at his current ADP. When I see Ryan McMahon and Michael Chavis, I see two young Mike Moustakas clones (good power, moderate AVE, multiple positions, etc.). Who wouldn't take a shot with Moose at Coors Field in the 13th round or Fenway Park in the 16th round, respectively? Count me in! Kevin Newman got called up in May 2019 and quickly displayed the ability to get on base with high average and low K-rate. Although he won't ever be invited to the HR Derby, his 12 HRs over 130 MLB games eclipsed 4 years of combined AA and AAA production, rewarding his fantasy owners with a boost of power along with 16 SBs. At an ADP of 216, he'll be a low risk/moderate reward player on draft day.

**Tier 6**
Hampson (163)
B Lowe (174)
Wong (214)
Odor (219)

Hernandez (284)
Fletcher (292)
Madrigal (333)

By this point, you should have someone on your roster to fill the 2B position and looking for MI or roster depth. You're not likely to find someone to fill the stat sheet here but there are a number of players who can fill a needed category gap. Garrett Hampson was drafted last year to provide elite speed and contact skills. He "rewarded" his owners by converting 15 of 18 SB attempts and a .247/.302/.385 slash – yet is being drafted a full 100 spots ahead of last year's early ADP lists. Unless you're desperate for speed, you may want to consider passing on him. If he can stay healthy, Brandon Lowe makes for an intriguing pickup. Lowe had a stellar first-half slashing .276/.339/.523 with 16 HR and 5 SB before the All-Star Break. He spent the summer on the injured list, only playing a handful of games in September. He should have a lock on the position for the Rays and worth a speculative add in the 11th or 12th round. Kolten Wong makes for a good MI candidate as well, with above average speed and decent batting average potential. His exit velocity and hard-hit rate are below average though meaning you shouldn't expect more than a dozen home runs. Overall, he's a solid player in the mid rounds. If you're desperate for counting stats and looking for a 30/15 player with low batting average, Rougned Odor is probably your guy. There are a number of outfielders with this same profile so plan to balance your draft accordingly, unless you plan to just punt AVE. Cesar Hernandez lands with the Indians and likely has a marginal fantasy relevant role in 2020. He cut is K-rate in 2019, leading to a nice boost in AVE but we're seeing declining speed here and little/no power. David Fletcher profiles very similar to Hernandez, a little better AVG but even less power/speed potential. Despite this, Fletcher remains an attractive pick due to his positional versatility. If I'm picking between Hernandez and Fletcher, I'm going Fletcher most of the time. I expect someone in your league will overdraft Nick Madrigal and the inevitable "I told you so" if he becomes the next rookie sensation. Nobody debates the elite bat-to-ball skills and plus speed potential but there is absolutely no power to speak of and plenty of uncertainty on his playing status. He's a dynasty gem in the making but for those in redraft leagues, it's best to stay away on draft day.

**Tier 7**
D Murphy (260)
Arraez (265)
Dee Gordon (285)
Castro (281)
Profar (323)
Urias (327)
Hoerner (333)
Galvis (356)
Dubon (383)
C Taylor (386)
Schoop (413)

As we move into the later tiers, you should only be looking at these players for roster depth or adding help for one or two specific categories. While none of these players will likely provide instant pop to your fantasy team, there are some intriguing players to consider late. Daniel Murphy may no longer qualify at 2B after playing only 3 games at the keystone in 2019. Those considering him at this ADP are likely drafting a familiar name and Coors Field. He may continue to be useful starter once in a while for your fantasy teams, but note his plate skills are clearly trending down and draft accordingly. Luis Arraez is an interesting player to keep an eye on. He doesn't hit for power or have much speed to offer but has shown he can consistently get on base with an excellent walk rate and very low K-rate. Draft him for a BA boost. Dee Gordon's best asset, his SB potential, is still there but clearly much lower than we are accustomed to. I also expect his playing time will suffer as he yields to younger talent. He remains an option later in drafts but do so with extreme caution. After playing all 162 games for the Marlins last year, Starlin Castro continues to look for a new job. He makes decent contact and should have some appeal off the bench for a MLB team in a Howie Kendrick-type role in 2020. Jurickson Profar gets to start fresh in San Diego after a miserable season in Oakland. He's currently the favorite for the Padres 2B job so there's some late-draft appeal here. His power reward comes with a significant BA risk so use caution when plugging him into your roster. The former San Diego 2B, Luis Urias, was shipped to Milwaukee and a likely UTIL role for the Brewers. The move provides a much-needed fresh start in an attempt to transition from a top prospect to MLB talent. He remains a good roster stash in dynasty leagues but I don't see much immediate appeal here in redraft leagues. Nico Hoerner is a player to track during Spring Training. The young infielder was called up by the Cubs a bit earlier than expected but held his own at the MLB level. His good BA and low K-rate suggests he was not intimidated by MLB pitching but doesn't bring a lot of power or speed. He has a real opportunity to break camp with the Cubs at 2B but it wouldn't be a complete surprise if he spends April in Iowa first. Either way, Hoerner should have an everyday role, perhaps hitting at the top of the lineup, by mid-season. Freddie Galvis was traded to the Reds last year in a UTIL role and now likely finds himself the starting SS this season. As a fantasy player, he doesn't generate a lot of excitement on draft day or in free agency but usually finds his way onto our rosters as a source of moderate power without killing your AVE. This season in Cincy looks promising though and he may be a sneaky good "Mr. Irrelevant" pickup in your draft. It's hard to tell yet if Mauricio Dubon is a quad-A player or legitimate MLB talent. Regardless, the ceiling for the Giants 2B looks to be 15/15, which is ok to take a flyer on, but try not to be influenced by unrealistic projections. Chris Taylor is a player I seem to always own on my fantasy teams. I draft him for positional versatility knowing he will eventually have a stretch as an everyday starter and provide a short-term boost for my team. He plays his best with consistent ABs but projects to start the season again in a super-utility role once again for the Dodgers. As long as you know what you're getting with Taylor, he can be an asset to your teams too. Jonathan Schoop's signing with the Tigers gives him a chance at everyday ABs and makes him an attractive depth candidate for our fantasy teams, especially at this ADP. His 2017 numbers may be a thing of the past but he should continue to provide his fantasy owners with a source of late power without destroying the BA category.

**Tier 8**
Asd Cabrera (360)
Cano (346)
Goodrum (343)
Kendrick (336)
Dozier (476)

I wrap up my 2B outlook with a handful of old guys, plus Nico Goodrum (sorry Nico). Many of these guys are decent depth options very late in drafts. Those with positional flexibility, like

Cabrera and Goodrum, provide extra insurance for your lineups and saves a roster spot for an extra SP or RP to roster. Draft these guys for the value you can readily extract, rather than any potential fantasy upside they may have. These will also be the first to get cut from your roster if space is needed for an early-season prospect call up. Unless you're in a super-deep league, players like this are always available on the waiver wire so don't let any sentimental value cloud your fantasy judgement (generally good advice for any player).

There you have it, my outlook for 43 second base-eligible players heading into your fantasy baseball drafts. You'll note my outlooks differed from current Fantrax ADPs, significantly in some cases, but that's one of the things that makes fantasy baseball so much fun. We will always agree or disagree on projections so read and research as much as you can before you make your draft plan. Most importantly, just enjoy the process.

## Shortstop Outlook
By Corey Steiner

Shortstop is rightly being cast by many as a position of unprecedented depth entering into the 2020 season. Many owners will have to make a difficult decision between focusing on scarcer positions (3B, 1B) in the early rounds of drafts, knowing that SS and MI can be filled later on, or simply drafting the best player available and figuring out the remaining slots later. Both routes should prove viable as long as the drafter approaches team construction with a concrete plan.

Despite the positional depth, it's not wise to wait *too* long to fill the SS and MI positions. After around pick 200, the options begin to thin out. If you can maintain awareness of this drop-off during the draft, you should be able to navigate the early rounds by filling positional needs without having to worry about filling these slots later on.

The list below is numbered and divided into tiers. The early Fantrax ADP of the player is provided in parentheses in order to highlight the difference between my picks and consensus opinion. The rankings are based on traditional 5x5 Roto categories with standard eligibility.

### First Tier
Francisco Lindor, CLE (8)
Trevor Story, COL (12)
Alex Bregman, HOU (8)
Trea Turner, WAS (9)

What separates this group from the players that follow is the reliability and consistency of their output when healthy. If you are picking in the mid-to-late first round and decide to forgo a starting pitcher, you may have to make a difficult choice between these players. Lindor's ability to contribute significantly in every category helps him to stand out from the pack. His 40 HR upside should not be ignored. He has the best chance at providing value compared to the high cost you are paying in drafting him. Bregman's lack of SB contribution hurts, especially since you are not getting a traditional power profile with him, either. Consider holding off on drafting him unless he falls several spots below ADP. Drafting Turner establishes a particular strategy that you must take for the rest of the draft, as you are essentially exclaiming that you intend to be near the top of the league in SB by season's end. This means that you can't let up on drafting speed later on, as a Turner injury would devastate your chances in that category. The inflexibility that comes with drafting Turner has me looking elsewhere at this point in the draft.

Story offers the highest upside in the group, particularly due to his home venue. Ideally, Story's output would look similar to Lindor's by the end of the year, with the exception of perhaps 10 to 15 fewer points in batting average. Because you can get him near the end of the first round, this means that he is a good value pick at this stage in the draft. However, his consistently high strikeout rate suggests that his floor is lower than those of the other three players. The worst-case-scenario for Story was realized in 2017 (.239 average, 24 home runs, 7 stolen bases). Those who choose to draft Story would be wise to pair him with someone who is less liable to fluctuation in output, such as Soto or Rendon.

### Second Tier
Fernando Tatis, SD (17)

While Tatis is close in ADP to the first tier, I separate him because, at his age, we have not had the chance to observe him put together a complete season in the majors; the key question is whether or not he can maintain the level of production we saw in stretches of 2019 over the course of a full season. His upside might look similar to a strong season from Lindor or Story. On the downside, his (at times overly) aggressive plate approach indicates that a middling batting average is a realistic possibility. With that could come a drop in the batting order, leading to fewer stolen bases and run-scoring opportunities. At 21 years old, Tatis certainly looks like a future MVP-caliber player; however, his progression towards that status may not be completely linear.

**Third Tier**
Javier Baez, CHC (39)
Adalberto Mondesi, KC (40)
Gleyber Torres, NYY (27)
Xander Bogaerts, BOS (36)
Jonathan Villar, MIA (32)

This tightly-bunched group isn't likely to put up the stellar seasons that you will see from the first group, but they offer their own forms of consistency that can be key in putting a team together. The one exception to this description is Mondesi, whose age and SB potential (note that he had 43 in only 443 plate appearances last year) offer a promising amount of upside considering the price (close to where he was drafted entering 2019, after putting together a successful 2019 campaign). For those that prefer the piecemeal approach to the SB category, Baez offers stability along with the ability to hit for power: his 34 HR in 2018 is certainly repeatable.

Torres is capable of hitting 40 home runs this year, but there are players at positions with more scarcity who offer similar profiles available later on in the draft (for example, Matt Olson). Bogaerts seems capable of putting together a season similar to Bregman's, indicating that he can be a valuable choice here. However, as with Bregman, a regression in the HR total is likely. Since Bogaerts will not contribute much in terms of speed, his production is replaceable through more affordable options. Villar's move to Miami hurts his value, particularly in terms of counting categories, and it is hard to imagine him reproducing his 2019 season in Baltimore, which would need to happen in order for him to return value at his current ADP.

**Fourth Tier**
Bo Bichette, TOR (76)
Marcus Semien, OAK (80)
Manny Machado, SD (60)
Tim Anderson, CHW (97)
Carlos Correa, HOU (91)

Bichette's aptitude for baserunning and ability to hit for average, combined with decent power, makes him the player with the most upside outside of this group and a great value in the fifth round. Those that have taken gambles or focused on pitching early may prefer to target Semien, who provides consistency paired with power upside and thus is a great value at this stage in the draft. Machado profiles similarly to Semien, with perhaps a few less stolen bases. Because his ADP is 20 picks earlier than Semien's, I recommend passing on Machado unless he falls well below ADP. Anderson's poor plate discipline makes him a risky play. With that said, the fact that you can draft him in the seventh round reflects this fact. If he were to continue to progress in the direction he demonstrated in 2019, he is capable of outperforming Villar, Tatis and even Story this year. This makes him a worthy gamble if you can surround this pick with players whose profiles suggest more consistency from year to year (e.g. Eddie Rosario, Benintendi, etc.). Correa has been unable to demonstrate the ability to put together a healthy season of late and name recognition seems to be keeping his price higher than it should be.

**Fifth Tier**
Elvis Andrus, TEX (126)
Amed Rosario, NYM (131)
Corey Seager, LAD (153)
Jorge Polanco, MIN (151)

Andrus' consistent ability, when healthy, to steal 25-30 bases without hurting you in any of the other categories helps to separate him from the rest of the players in this tier, and his current ADP is a little late considering the skill set that he offers. Rosario is a riskier play, as he has demonstrated an upward trajectory over the last several years, but has yet to put it all together and is likely to contribute fewer stolen bases than Andrus. Polanco's profile is less appealing than both because of the limited upside in both speed and power. However, if you are looking for average at this point in the draft, Polanco can contribute on that front. Still, I prefer Seager to Polanco because Seager is capable of providing a similar average while, if healthy, hitting 5-10 more home runs. It's unusual to see Seager (who is still only 25 years old) getting drafted this late, and a bounceback season could easily re-establish him in the elite tier of players, making this a potential buy-low opportunity.

**Sixth Tier**
Didi Gregorius, PHI (215)
Kevin Newman, PIT (199)
Paul DeJong, STL (191)
Jean Segura, PHI (186)

At this point in the draft, your choices will heavily depend on team needs, and each of these players offers a different skill set that is capable of complementing the team that you have constructed to this point. Still, the degree of risk inherent in each profile becomes more obvious at this stage of the draft. If you haven't yet filled your SS position, it would be wise to grab two players in this range in order to balance out that risk. Gregorius, in particular, offers value at his current ADP due to the fact that he can hit 25 home runs with a decent average in the Phillies' park while also significantly contributing in both runs scored and RBIs. At his best, he is capable of matching or surpassing Bogaerts in four out of five categories (Bogaerts will likely have a higher batting average by 20 to 25 points). Newman's combination of speed and hit tool makes him a valuable pick at his current ADP. Consider passing on Amed Rosario in favor of Newman, as their ultimate production shouldn't differ too greatly. Segura's recent drop in SB (10 in 2019) limits his upside. DeJong offers the most power in this group (30 HR in 2019), but he will also hurt you the most in terms of batting average.

**Seventh Tier**
Dansby Swanson, ATL (258)
Willy Adames, TB (277)

These two make appealing MI options. Both showed promising growth in 2019 and are capable of hitting 20 HR, stealing 10 bases, and contributing in runs and RBIs without hurting you in average. Adames has demonstrated less stability in his short MLB career and thus is the riskier play between the two.

**Eighth Tier**
Andrelton Simmons, LAA (347)
Jon Berti, MIA (216)
Luis Urias, MIL (310)
Niko Goodrum, DET (295)
David Fletcher, LAA (308)

This group offers more risk and less upside than the rest of the pool, and ideally you will already have filled your MI spot *before* reaching this tier. Simmons offers some stability in contributing minimally in all categories. Berti's profile is extremely risky and he may be squeezed for playing time as a result of the Marlins' recent off-season acquisitions (Dickerson, Villar, etc.). Urias' move to Milwaukee helps his power upside, but he has not shown enough ability to make contact in the majors to warrant jumping ADP to select him here. Goodrum offers more stability than both and can be a valuable pick if you have already established a strong batting average base. Fletcher's strong command of the zone suggests that there is more power upside than he has demonstrated so far, but with many talented players available at pick 300 at other positions, selecting him – or anyone else in this group – seems like an overly speculative move, considering the talent available at SS earlier in the draft.

# Third Base Outlook
## By Ray Kuhn

As far as positional eligibility goes, third base is a very versatile position. A lot of options here can also be used at other positions, and that does skew the ADP slightly. With that being said, things do go deep here, and with first base not being as deep as it once was, your corner infield spot will likely be filled from this list. So, let's jump right into how those options rank.

**Tier One:**

Nolan Arenado
Alex Bregman

As of this writing, late December, Arenado is still a member of the Rockies, and the trade speculation seems to be just that. Of course, Coors Field agrees with the third baseman, but his skill level and production plays anywhere. On the surface, a .315 batting average with 41 home runs and 118 RBI couldn't get much better, but his power metrics have taken a slight dip. Yes, Coors Field does help to mitigate some of that, but it might be something to keep in the back of your mind. At the same time though, we really are just trying to poke holes in one of the best, and most consistent, players in the game.

Bregman's eligibility at shortstop does help to push his ADP over Arenado's. While we saw his power and hard-hit metrics improve to career high levels, does that explain his rise from 31 to 41 home runs? Even if he loses those gains, his barrel rate of 5.4% is below average, but his launch angle (19.6 degrees) is well above the league average, 30 home runs is very viable. This is also true considering the fact that he hit 31 home runs in 2018 while eclipsing the 100 RBI mark for the first of two consecutive seasons. There is also no reason why Bregman shouldn't come close to hitting .300 after hitting .296 last season.

**Tier Two:**
Jose Ramirez
Anthony Rendon
Rafael Devers

Can we just forget about the first half of Ramirez's season when he hit .214 with just five home runs? The fact that he stole 18 bases in that stretch did help preserve some value, but things returned to normal in the second half of the season when he hit .321 with 18 home runs and 53 RBI. Despite hitting 38 home runs in 2018, and the aforementioned surge to close out last season, Ramirez's power metrics are merely above average, not elite. Instead, it is his 46% fly ball rate that helps to get the job done, but that in conjunction with an elite contact rate and 30 stolen base potential, is what makes him an elite option. There is no reason why Ramirez can't be a 30/30 option, and taking him in the second round of your draft could be a nice start to your roster. The batting average, probably around .275, does keep him from being a true five category stud, but it's not enough to keep me away.

At this point, we know what we are going to get from Rendon, as his slight and steady improvements over the past few seasons, have helped to establish quite the portfolio at the plate. The main adjustment for Rendon, has been his improvements against right-handed pitching, but there is no doubting his ability and the potential for another .300/30/100 campaign thanks to his elite power and hard contact ability.

It's difficult to forget sometimes that Devers is still just 23 years old, and that is especially the case after what he did last season. He has managed to get his line drive rate up to 21%, from 15% in the last two years, and getting his contact rate up to 82% really paid dividends. With a launch angle slightly below average, I still have minimal doubts about Devers' ability to repeat his 32 home runs from a year ago, but I might just be overly cautious here. After all, Devers had a 9%-barrel rate along with a 92.1 mile per hour exit velocity last season, and we know that the talent is there.

**Tier Three:**
Eugenio Suarez
Kris Bryant
Manny Machado
Vlad Guerrero, Jr

Suarez's 73% contact rate was never elite, but it also didn't previously hold him back. Last season, it did take another step back, 67%, but he does walk at an 11% clip and Suarez's .271 batting average last year was still pretty solid. But let's be honest, it's all about the elite power and 49 home runs from last year. I'm not sure we can expect Suarez to reach a 30% home run to fly ball rate again in 2020, but a drop to 40 home runs along with a 100 RBI will be just fine.

At this point, Bryant has established what he is, but we have to question whether he will reach the 100 RBI mark once again after missing for three straight years. Even with that being said, a .280 batting average and 30 home runs seems to be a foregone conclusion from Bryant, but there are some concerns about his power and hard-hit metrics after the decreases they have taken in the last three seasons.

It's not like Machado had a terrible debut season in San Diego, but it wasn't up to elite levels either. Machado squeaked past the 30-home run mark once again, but there isn't much here that really jumps off the page anymore, and his contact rate also dropped to 78% last season. There is still a lot to work with here, but it also seems like, even though he is still just 27, the upside has seemed to subside.

And now we get to one of the most buzz worthy players in the league. There haven't been many debuts that grabbed more attention than Guerrero, but his rookie season was kind of ordinary. But with a fourth or fifth round ADP, he isn't exactly cheap, but then we have to ask if he is worth it? Of course, I'm sure everyone has seen the pictures and heard the stories about the transformation that Guerrero has made to his body so far this winter, and we know all about his hitting ability. The upside is there, and the power is real, but we only saw it in spurts last season. Overall, Guerrero hit .272 with 15 home runs and 69 RBI in 514 plate appearances, and we know that is not top-60 ADP, but it is all about what he can do. In re-draft leagues, I'm not willing to pay that price to find out. But if he figures out that launch angle, 6.7 degrees last season, look out.

**Tier Four:**

Yoan Moncada
D.J. LeMahieu
Jeff McNeil
Josh Donaldson
Matt Chapman
Max Muncy

Finally, it's long enough. After hitting .235 in 2018, saying Moncada took a huge step forward last year would be an understatement. The 25-year old hit .317, but based on his 41% hit rate, he might have a hard time repeating it. As it is, Moncada brought his contact rate up from 62% to 70%, so while it's quite possible those gains stick, we are dealing with more a .260 hitter here. But with his 25-30 home run and 10-15 stolen base potential, quite realistic in fact considering he hit 25 last year, there is a lot to like. In fact, it's hard to argue with much of anything in his batted ball profile from last season (12.2% barrel rate, 92.8 mile per hour exit velocity, and 47.9% hard hit rate), and as long as you aren't looking for a .300 hitter, there is a lot to like here.

The opinion entering last season, was that leaving Coors Field would adversely impact LeMahieu, but that certainly wasn't the close. Throughout the season, LeMahieu was one of the true constants in the Yankees' lineup as he hit .327 with 25 home runs and 102 RBI. With below average power, LeMahieu's home run outburst wasn't exactly expected, but his home run to fly ball rate rose from 11% to 19%. The run production, or at least most of it, and the .300 batting average are believable, but regardless of what the metrics say, I have a hard time banking on 25 home runs once again. Regardless, we know that he can hit, and LeMahieu will be a key part of one of the best lineups in baseball while also offering positional flexibility.

McNeil's plate skills aren't a surprise, but his second half power surge was to some degree. After posting an 86% contact rate in 2018, he followed that up with an 85% rate last season while also hitting .318 and showing that power we mentioned. After hitting just six home runs in the first half of the season, McNeil followed that up with 23 in the second half as he started attacking first pitches while driving in 75 runs overall. As a whole, McNeil's power metrics are really just slightly above average, but everything here says a repeat is quite possible.

When it comes to Donaldson, the main thing here is for the veteran to stay healthy. Last year that was the case, and the results (37 home runs and 94 RBI) matched. The power and hard contact is still there, but the contact rate and batting average won't get over .260, and we just have to hope for health. Donaldson's ability though, is still there.

Exit velocity, barrel rate, and hard-hit rate. All three of those batted ball metrics paint a very favorable picture of the A's third baseman and Chapman's 36 home runs last season should not be taken as a fluke. Instead, his power ability is quite real, as is the 100 RBI potential, but we are going to have to live with a batting average in the .250 range. That is the only thing that suppresses his value, but over the past two years, Chapman has brought his contact rate from 65% to 75% as he continues to improve and solidify his skill set.

We just have two years of track record with Muncy, but they have been pretty close to identical, and his profile backs that up. There is the elite power and walk rate, but that comes along with a sub-standard contact rate and a .250 batting. The good thing though, is that you know what you are getting with Muncy, and his dual eligibility at second and third base also helps. It is pretty crazy though, to think that he might be more valuable at first base.

**Tier Five:**
Eduardo Escobar
Mike Moustakas
Justin Turner
Yuli Gurriel

Escobar saw a nice spike in his power metrics, and therefore home runs (23 to 35), last season, but other than that, nothing much changed with the infielder. There is no reason not to expect Escobar to continue his solid production. Over the past three seasons, Escobar has established a base level of performance and consistency, but going forward, I would expect more 2018 than 2019 as it is going to be hard for him to reach 118 RBI once again. At the same time though, we know that he can do it, and there wasn't really anything too fluky in his performance, but 2019 was his best-case scenario.

Moustakas is now in Cincinnati and manning second base, but that shouldn't impact his production at the plate. Let's take him for what he is, and that's a .250 hitter with 30 home runs and 90 RBI. Based on what we have seen from him over the past three seasons, Moustakas' plate skills and power metrics have been consistent, and that should result in more of the same from him.

When it comes to Turner, we just can't factor in health throughout the entire season. But when Turner is in the lineup, the production is there. Health and age are both issues, but it's hard to argue with his hard contact and power metrics. Perhaps age will catch up to Turner at some point from a skills perspective, but that just hasn't happened yet. If you aren't expecting elite production, and look at Turner as a corner infielder while factoring in replacement value, then you shouldn't be disappointed.

Gurriel often flies under the radar with the Astros in their prolific lineup, but he is a proven run producer. The concern here is that fantasy owners are going to pay for the 31 home runs he hit last season, but the launch angle and batted ball metrics don't really support much more than 20. Even with that being said though, his 88% contact rate and above average hard contact rates, support a .290 batting average and 90 RBI.

**Tier Six:**
Hunter Dozier
Tommy Edman
Miguel Sano
Yandy Diaz
J.D. Davis
Scott Kingery
Ryan McMahon
Jon Berti
Gio Urshela
Brian Anderson

Dozier was on the cusp of being more of a Quad-A type player, but he seemingly flipped a switch last season and became a middle of the order threat and capable regular with the Royals. He brought some solid power to the table while increasing both his fly ball (44%) and contact rates (72%), although there is still some room for improvement with the latter. I'm not sure he hits .279 again, but Dozier could be a solid, late round, source of production as his 26 home runs and 84 RBI are repeatable.

Out of nowhere, Edman emerged last season and hit .304 with 11 home runs in 342 plate appearances. While there is clear value in that, we likely wouldn't be discussing Edman at this point in the rankings if it weren't for his 15 stolen bases. Granted, the batting average was nice too, but then the bigger question, can it be repeated? The contact rate is average, and there is some power, but it's the elite speed and quest for 20 stolen bases that will keep him on your radar. If we plan for a little less, and maybe a .280 batting average, then things should be just fine with Edman.

We know all about Sano's power skills, but his propensity for striking out is just as large. That means, you have to deal with the lackluster batting average in the .240's as the price for his 35 to 40 home runs. Again, that power tool is elite, but consistency and health have also been two tools that Sano has struggled with. Keep in mind though, if he does stay healthy and refine a few things, Sano could potentially make a fantasy owner very happy.

With 14 home runs in 347 plate appearances, Diaz finally figured out how to get the ball in the air with a 32% fly ball rate. He makes hard contact at an elite level, the power metrics are there and seemingly improving based on the second half of the season, and Diaz also has a league average contact rate. Let's now see what the 28-year-old can do with a full season's worth of playing time.

Finding consistent playing time was key for Davis last season, but the fact that he delivered when in the lineup did lead to more at bats. Where he plays this season, most likely between left field and third base, will somewhat impact his value, but if you draft based on skills, there is a solid base to work with at the plate. While he likely won't hit .307 again, Davis' contact and line drive rates do support a solid batting average with power metrics that led to 14 home runs in 240 second half plate appearances being repeatable. More playing time could lead to 30 home runs, but pay for 20.

When the Phillies gave Kingery a contract extension prior to last season, they envisioned him grabbing a regular role in their lineup, and that will come in 2020, but just at multiple positions. The batting average won't be great, but Kingery owns nice power and speed tools. What will really dictate his value though, is what happens to his 15 stolen bases from last year. Maybe we have a 20/20 player here, and his 26%-line drive rate should help there, and that along with his multiple position eligibility could push his value up based on the scarcity of stolen bases.

Last season, when it comes to McMahon, we saw both the blessing and the curse associated with Coors Field based on his splits. It's unclear as to where his regular playing time will come from, but he did get 539 plate appearances last season, but I would stay away on the road.

There is some power to work with, but a 51% ground ball rate and 67% contact rate will limit his upside.

Berti is going to be one of the more divisive players this winter. Last season he stole 17 bases in 287 plate appearances, but opportunity was key here. The Marlins are clearly rebuilding so that led to both playing time and the chance to run at the top of the order for Berti. With Jonathan Villar now at the top of Miami's lineup, it remains to be seen how that will impact Berti, but with no real power to speak of and just a marginal batting average, you need those stolen bases for him to return any potential value. And that you have to weigh at what opportunity cost are those 20 to 25 stolen bases worth?

Entering the season, or at least Spring Training, Gio Urshela appears to hold the Yankees' third base job, but that is really a case of finder's keepers after Miguel Andujar missed last season due to injury. Urshela certainly earned the playing time last year though as he hit .314 with 21 home runs and 74 RBI. With 15 second half home runs, the power really took off, and the metrics back it up. This was the first period of success we saw from Urshela, but expected a repeat of at least 80-90% is quite reasonable.

Anderson is both as boring and as steady as they come. But for 172 plate appearances in the second half of the season, prior to his season ending pinky injury, Anderson hit nine home runs while driving in 28 and experiencing a nice boost to his power metrics, fly ball rate, and launch angle. The floor isn't terrible for the back end of your roster, and it might be worth seeing if he can continue those power improvements considering the price shouldn't be too steep.

# Outfield Outlook
By Joe Drake

When it comes to fantasy, the outfield is the cream of the crop. It boasts the unanimous top 3 players in the entire sport: Mike Trout, Ronald Acuna Jr., and Christian Yelich right off the top and follows up with bangers like MVP winners Mookie Betts, Cody Bellinger, Bryce Harper, Kris Bryant, and Giancarlo Stanton. You've got the old guard still hanging around in J.D. Martinez and the booming babes like Juan Soto. There's power, speed, and everything in between. The fantasy world is at your fingertips in the outfield.

It's so difficult to rank outfielders, and players in general, without knowing the league setup. An owner will draft very differently in a 15 team roto league where you have 5 OF slots, as opposed to a 12 team points league with just 3. This is where a tier-based system comes in handy. Rather than one glob of ranked players, you'll have pools of players to pick from. You'll know when you can wait longer on a certain caliber of outfielder and when it's now or never. It's not perfect, but having tiers will give you a better feel for the caliber of players on the board during the draft -- it allows you to focus on a level of production rather than specific names.

## Strategies
So, let's talk about strategy. Of course, you can find specialists who may be able to help in a specific category late in the draft, but most multi-category contributors are going to go early. It's important to note where the drop-offs occur at the position in terms of power, speed, average, etc. As you know, home runs exploded across the league in 2019 due to the juiced ball. That doesn't mean that you can take a back seat on drafting sluggers -- if anything, it means you may need to be more vigilant because everyone and their slap-hitting brother were knocking them over the fence. You need to make sure you're keeping up.

That said, don't bank on the same ball for 2020. MLB has shown that they're going to do anything they want with the baseball and we'll only find out after the fact. It could be more "dead" like we saw in the postseason, it could be the same ball, maybe they'll use a random one every pitch, or maybe they'll scrap it all and put seams on a dang Super Ball. We won't know until April.

Draft smart and don't forget to prepare for a variety of circumstances. When it comes down to it, your final categorical stats put up against your opponents' stats matter more than if you drafted the most highly ranked player when given the opportunity. You may find yourself deep into your draft and looking to grab your last OF or perhaps a UTIL or bench bat. Rather than just taking the top player left on your rankings, make sure you take into account your categorical needs and select a player that will give you an edge in a category or fill a need in another. Don't be a slave to your ranks!

One last note, the ranks below are based on standard 5x5 roto leagues and eligibility. These rankings will cover my top 100 for 2020 as we enter the draft season, but there are most certainly guys being left off the list who may have value into the season due to trades, free agent signings, injuries, breakouts, or call ups to the majors.

**Tier 1 (1-3)**
Mike Trout
Ronald Acuna Jr.
Christian Yelich

For the first time in what feels like a decade, Mike Trout has legitimate competition as the top pick in drafts and go figure, that competition comes from two other outfielders. Trout is still my number one, but you can't go wrong with any of these three. Trout offers the highest floor, Acuna the highest ceiling and most steals, and Yelich feels like a slight mix of both. If you really can't choose, close your eyes and throw a dart and you'll be okay.

**Tier 2 (4-7)**
Mookie Betts
Cody Bellinger
Juan Soto
JD Martinez

The second tier at outfield is still incredibly strong and you don't have to squint to see how each of these guys could finish as the #1 overall player in 2020. Betts had a down year in 2019 by his standards but remains a true five-category stud. Bellinger bounced back from a sophomore slump with a huge third-year campaign that netted him the NL MVP. Juan Soto's debut was so nice he decided to do it twice -- and he's still just 20, in case you hadn't heard. J.D. Martinez is the elder statesman here and perhaps the most underrated of this bunch given his age in relation to the others and the lack of "upside". He's the most likely to slip a little further down the board than he should, but remember, he's averaged .313/41/98/113/4 over the last 3 seasons. Not too shabby.

**Tier 3 (8-12)**
Aaron Judge
Bryce Harper
Giancarlo Stanton
George Springer
Starling Marte

Things don't cool down much in Tier 3. We've got 4 sluggers here with AVG questions and 1 do-it-all guy in Marte. Since his sensational rookie season, Judge has fallen short of 500 PAs the last two years but has still been exceptional when on the field. Bryce Harper is starting to feel underrated somehow. The AVG probably isn't coming back, but there are very few guys who hit the ball harder than Bryce does and Statcast agrees. Stanton is a projection darling: Steamer has him leading the majors in HR with 52. Springer is coming off a career year where his power numbers took another step forward. Starling Marte doesn't have the same pop as his tier-mates, but he's a true 5-category contributor to build around.

**Tier 4 (13-20)**
Ketel Marte
Marcell Ozuna
Charlie Blackmon

Austin Meadows
Kris Bryant
Joey Gallo
Eddie Rosario
Eloy Jimenez

Now we're starting to get into talented players with a few more question marks than the top tiers. Ketel Marte broke out in a huge way and before you ask, yes, the power is legit: he had the 12th highest Max Exit Velocity in all of baseball. Marcell Ozuna rebounded from his lackluster 2018 and the Statcast profile suggests he could be even better in 2020. Blackmon continues to mash in his early 30s, but the SBs are gone. Austin Meadows might have the most upside of the whole group if he gets a little better at swiping bags. Kris Bryant looks healthy again and should be primed for another big year. Joey Gallo was great in his half-season, but xBA doesn't support the AVG growth - pay for his career number, not 2019. Rosario continues to be a sneaky 4 category contributor in a stacked lineup. Eloy caught fire to end 2019 and may be primed for a big year at age 23 with a much-improved lineup around him.

**Tier 5 (21-30)**
Yasiel Puig
Tommy Pham
Ramon Laureano
Victor Robles
Byron Buxton
Jorge Soler
Andrew Benintendi
Kyle Schwarber
Trey Mancini
Whit Merrifield

We're outside of the top 20 now and starting to get into some category specialists and all-around guys with lower ceilings. The biggest question about Puig is where he'll land. If he ends up on a team that doesn't let him run, his value will take a big hit and drop at least a tier. Pham moves to San Diego and you can't help but wonder if he'll still be able to top the 20-HR mark. Sign me up for 25 and 15 from Ramon Laureano and toss in a solid .275 AVG -- he's more than just a human highlight reel in centerfield. Victor Robles didn't deliver on the hype in his first full season, but there's still plenty of time to grow into the power/speed threat he was billed as. Speaking of power/speed potential... Hey, there, Byron Buxton. If you know, you know. Jorge Soler barreled up more balls in 2019 than literally everyone in 2019 and the AVG should have been even better if you believe xBA. Benintendi is a curious case as he took a step back in just about every hitting category, but I would trust the skills and buy the dip. Don't look now but the K% went down and the AVG went up for Schwarber. Trey Mancini solidified his status as too good for the Orioles, so expect a trade to a better lineup for the 4-category masher. Merrifield's SB success rate fell off a cliff last year and he attempted just 10 SBs in the second half. Still a great source of SB and AVG who won't kill your power categories.

**Tier 6 (31-38)**
Michael Conforto
Jeff McNeil

Kyle Tucker
Franmil Reyes
Max Kepler
Michael Brantley
Nicholas Castellanos
Luis Robert

Conforto has established himself as a reliable power source who will chip in a few steals and won't hurt your AVG. Jeff McNeil broke out at 27 and can carry your average to the promised land with a little pop mixed in. Tucker went 38 & 35 between AAA and MLB last year. I'm betting he can get to 25 & 20 with a decent AVG this year. The Franimal is in his natural habitat now: the American League. The sky's the limit for his power potential with every day PAs. Kepler had a major power breakout that was fueled by a swing change that has lifted Avg LA +5.5 degrees since 2017. Michael Brantley remains as solid as ever and can anchor your AVG category without hurting you elsewhere. Castellanos is still without a team, but he came alive after he was traded to the contending Cubs. Any contending lineup will be a major improvement for him over Detroit. Luis Robert is well-hyped and super intriguing. Possible 30-30 guy in the future, but don't expect a good AVG in 2020.

**Tier 7 (39-46)**
Lourdes Gurriel Jr
Oscar Mercado
Lorenzo Cain
Bryan Reynolds
Aristides Aquino
Adam Eaton
Willie Calhoun
JD Davis

Lourdes Gurriel Jr. looks like he's going to be a 3 or 4-category guy in a lineup with some of baseball's best young players. Mercado went 19-29 if you include AAA and he's got an outside shot to do it again with a full season in the big leagues. Cain is losing the race against time and it's showing in his stats. Hope for a 10/15 season and be thankful for anything more. Reynolds had a very nice debut in Pittsburgh and will be an AVG asset for your team who chips in with some power and steals. Aristides Aquino is one of the toughest to project for 2020 as he managed to be both incredible and awful in the span of 2 months. Clearly, he has tremendous power if he can continue to find the ball with his bat and don't overlook his sneaky good SBs. Adam Eaton reached 600 PAs for the first time since 2015 and rewarded us with a 15-15 year with 100 runs and .279 AVG. The only question is whether he can stay healthy again. Willie Calhoun can't run but the kid can mash. He has 35 HR, .275 upside for 2020 if the hit tool takes a step forward. J.D. Davis is a Statcast stud who needs playing time to capitalize on all his hard contact, but there could be 30-.300 upside here if he gets 600 PAs -- his xBA and Exit Velocity agree. Remember, we're talking ceiling and not the most likely outcome.

**Tier 8 (47-59)**
Jo Adell
Danny Santana
Ryan Braun

Andrew McCutchen
Justin Upton
Joc Pederson
Mitch Haniger
David Dahl
Shin-Soo Choo
Mark Canha
Scott Kingery
Brian Anderson
Garrett Hampson

Jo Adell is most likely starting the year in AAA, but he has the tools to make an impact in 2020 for both the Angels and your fantasy team. Danny Santana came out of nowhere to drop a 28-21 season with a .283 AVG and the Statcast data suggests it's real -- even still, I'm drafting with caution. Ryan Braun is aging gracefully with good production in reduced PAs and reps at 1B will keep him in the lineup. McCutchen might score 150 runs if he got 650 PAs at the top of that lineup (he'll probably miss time to start the season). The power was still there when Justin Upton returned from injury, but the AVG cratered. Pederson is going to continue to crank homers with an okay AVG in 450-500 PAs.

Haniger suffered a brutal injury to the crown jewels in 2019 that cut his season in half. He's healthy coming into 2020 and is expected to start, look for 2018 numbers but note that the AVG died last season. Dahl is super talented and could be a 4-cat stalwart if he ever got to 500+ PAs - just don't bet on it. Shin-Soo Choo doesn't believe in age. Pencil him in for 20-10-260 - he was in the 95th percentile for Hard Hit rate in 2019. Canha isn't sexy, but he plays all 3 OF spots and 1B, guaranteeing playing time - bank on .250 AVG though, not .275. Speaking of playing everywhere, Kingery was much better in 2019 despite striking out even more. Pay for 15-15-245, but 600 PA upside is 20-20 with a good AVG if the plate skills take a step forward. Brian Anderson is currently slated to hit 3rd for a surprisingly decent Marlins lineup with Villar ahead of him and Aguilar and Dickerson behind him. Call me crazy but I like his upside here for 25 and 260 with useful counting stats and a handful of steals. Garrett Hampson floundered most of 2019 before a torrid September. Everyday playing time brings upside for a 15/30 season and positive AVG.

These last few tiers are a bit larger because we have a bunch of players who all offer similar values but in different shapes. These are the guys who will round out your 5th OF slots and reserve slots. This is where the shape of the production becomes much more important. There's no need to grab a 7th slugger because he's at the top of your cheat sheet if what you actually need is the speed guy 10 spots down. Go get your guys here.

**Tier 9 (60-73)**
Shogo Akiyama
David Peralta
Jackie Bradley Jr
Luis Arraez
Nick Markakis
Anthony Santander
Hunter Dozier

AJ Pollock
Nick Senzel
Jason Heyward
Kevin Kiermaier
Nomar Mazara
Corey Dickerson
Mallex Smith
Alex Verdugo

Shogo Akiyama is coming over to the Reds from the NPB and projected to leadoff against RHPs by Roster Resource. A good 2020 from him might be 15/10/.275 -- expect more contact than power and a handful of SBs. David Peralta should rebound from the shoulder injury, AVG is his best asset. JBJ consistently bounces between legendarily hot and cold streaks - best as a bench bat you can plug in during hot streaks. Luis Arraez had a great debut, but is a one-trick pony for fantasy right now - could win the batting title. Markakis is still penciled in to start for ATL and he just keeps hitting (but not for power). Santander is back in the mix after a couple of lost years. Should get full-time PAs and has a shot at 30 HRs without tanking your AVG. Dozier had a big 1st half, but you'd do better paying for the career AVG and not 2019's -- power upside is real though. Pollock's body still hates him, but he produces whenever he's on the field - pay for 400 PAs and pray for more. While we're on the topic of finding ways to get hurt, Nick Senzel feels like Pollock but with more upside - 15-20-260?

If Heyward didn't hit for big power in 2019, then it's never coming. Take your 10-15 HR and moderate counting stats and move along. Kiermaier hasn't had 500 PAs since 2015 - bet on 10 and 15, not 15 and 20. Mazara has amassed 2000+ PAs despite not turning 25 until this April. Yes, there may still be untapped upside, but it's becoming less and less likely - expect 20 & 260. Corey Dickerson will get you 20+ HR and .280 in a full season, but who knows if he'll stay on the field. At least he's got a starting spot in Miami. Mallex Smith might lead the majors in SBs… but also might be out of a job by May if he hits .227 again. Verdugo is a talented player at the mercy of the LAD lineup roulette game. There's 20 HR-.280 upside here if he ever gets 600 PAs.

**Tier 10 (74-88)**
Steven Souza Jr
Gregory Polanco
Hunter Renfroe
Niko Goodrum
Kevin Pillar
Marwin Gonzalez
Avisail Garcia
David Fletcher
Kole Calhoun
Austin Riley
Ian Happ
Victor Reyes
Ender Inciarte
Dexter Fowler
Austin Hays

Souza's last full season, 2017, was 30/78/78/16/.239 in 600 PAs and he is supposedly fully healthy again. If he can catch on and get regular PAs, there's nice power/speed upside here. Polanco's 2019 was lost to injury, but he still has 20/10/.250 upside. Hunter Renfroe is difficult. The Rays traded for him, but they're also platoon happy. Best not to assume more than 400 PAs for the slugger. Goodrum is a 10/10/.240 hitter eligible at 2B/SS/OF - flexible roster filler. Pillar hit more home runs but had a worse exit velocity… not buying the power surge. Marwin is triple-eligible (1B/3B/OF) but only offers 15-.260. Avisail Garcia moves to Milwaukee, but don't put him down for a career year just yet. He's been anything but consistent year to year - but I won't blame you if you like the upside. David Fletcher is a super-utility (2B/3B/SS/OF) guy with a great average and a handful of steals. Love him as a bench guy in daily leagues to cover off days.

Kole Calhoun projects to be a middle of the order guy in AZ but unlikely to repeat HR total. Austin Riley was way up and way down in 2019. He's slated to start for now and the power is so good he could still hit 30+ HR even if the Ks don't come down. The biggest question regarding Ian Happ is whether he's going to play or not. Roster Resource likes him as the CF right now, but the Cubs are proving pretty unpredictable this offseason. Victor Reyes should start in DET and be a solid source of SB and AVG (bet .275, not .300) - it's not like they have anyone better who could take his place. Inciarte could be the odd man out in the ATL outfield if Riley is pushed out there. He's a 10/20 candidate with full-time PAs. Dexter Fowler bounced-back to league average in 2019, but with so many outfield mouths to feed in STL, it's hard to see him getting 600 PAs again. Austin Hays is a former top prospect with exciting tools and a great September call-up, but best to temper expectations a tad in his first full season (25-10-.250).

**Tier 11 (89-101)**
Brett Gardner
Jesse Winker
Mike Yastrzemski
Trent Grisham
Sam Hilliard
Kyle Lewis
Tyer O'Neill
Teoscar Hernandez
Domingo Santana
Mike Tauchman
Christin Stewart
Harrison Bader

Brett Gardner was back from the dead in 2019 but there's not much reason to believe he can repeat the HRs, 15-20 is a much better bet. The Reds seemingly have 7-8 OFs for just 3 spots and I'm not sure that Jesse Winker's average bat and weak defense are going to keep him in the lineup the whole year -- the AVG should bounce back though. Mike Yastrzemski should play all year in that weak SFG lineup, but it's hard to see him exceeding last year's production as a 28-year old rookie. Trent Grisham moves from one of the most friendly hitters' parks to one of the least friendly which means some of those HRs will turn into 2Bs and 3Bs now. Has the speed to swipe bags if he starts running again (37 steals in 2017 at AA but only 32 attempts since then). Sam Hilliard is an intriguing power/speed option who had a terrific 2019 campaign at AAA. The biggest obstacle for him is finding playing time on a team that always seems to play crusty, old, underperforming vets.

Mariners former 1st rounder Kyle Lewis will get his first full season after an impressive 75 PA cameo in 2019. He's never hit for much AVG and combined with rough K%, it's hard to see him tapping into that exciting power too much this year. Did someone say power? Tyler O'Neill's profile reads a lot like Lewis' but maybe even more extreme. Huge power with little contact, but isn't coming into the season with a starting role like Lewis is. A trade might do him good. Teoscar Hernandez is coming off his best year as a pro in which he repeated his 2018 production but in fewer at-bats. Probably won't get to 600 PAs in TOR's crowded OF. Domingo Santana took a step back in 2019 and is currently without a job. Bump him up a tier or two if he lands a full-time role, but it's becoming less likely that he does. Mike Tauchman is slated to start the year in the Yankee OF but the leash is going to be short with a roster that stacked. He needs to hit early if he wants to keep his role, but even if he doesn't, his plus defense may buy him some extra time. Christin Stewart is a power bat in a bad lineup. You're looking at 20-30 HRs depending on how much contact he can make. Harrison Bader could have a 15/30 season with the Cardinals running wild if he can quell his breaking ball woes. If he can't, Randy Arozarena or Lane Thomas might be taking his place in May. Okay, I went to 101, please don't sue me. Bader's ceiling was too good to leave off this list.

Honorable Mentions: Jon Berti, Wil Myers, Dylan Carlson, Josh Rojas

Are you still with me? Props to you if you made it through all 101 players. I tried to provide a brief but insightful look at what they may provide in 2020. Remember, OF offers you players with every shape of production that you can imagine. Use that to your advantage and take the players who will round out your squad the best, not just the best guy available. If you've already stacked your team with enough speed to finish at the top of your league, but aren't looking so hot in the HR category, a power hitter is going to be a lot more valuable to your team than another 20-steal guy. And remember, you need to do as well as you can in each category if you're in league with an overall competition like the NFBC Main Event or TGFBI. Good luck in 2020 and let's play ball!

# Starting Pitcher Outlook
## By Michael Simione

2019 was not the year of the pitcher by any means. The league average ERA was an astounding 4.50. To put it into perspective the league average ERA in 2018 was 4.15 and it hasn't been this high since 2005. This can easily be blamed on the "juiced" ball that was used all season long. Which begs the question, will it be juiced in 2020? If only anyone knew. While some suspect they used different balls in the playoffs, no one is too sure. Not only do we have the ball in question but we also have to account for how hitters have changed their approach. Hitters are sacrificing average for power thus resulting in more strikeouts. So where does this leave us? Personally, I am aiming for pitchers who keep the ball in the park while providing high strikeout numbers.

Last year this section was written by Bruce Cagle Jr and his approach is one that I did last year and will proceed to do this year. The approach is to discount innings pitched and go with quality over quantity. For instance, don't downplay what Chris Sale did in 2019. Sure he only pitched 147.1 innings but he produced a 13.32 K/9 with a 3.39 FIP and 2.93 xFIP. Those are "Ace" numbers and when he pitches he will produce. While Sale is somewhat of an extreme example you get the point. Take quality over quantity and just stream pitchers with good matchups if a pitcher hits the IL. Always draft someone you know will provide value when they are on the mound.

Below are my top 100 starting pitcher rankings. Some might move a little as time goes on but that is why I put them into tiers. Tiers are great because they help you target players better. Basically everyone in the same tier I value the same.

## Tier 1 - The Elite

1. Gerrit Cole
2. Jacob deGrom
3. Justin Verlander
4. Max Scherzer

These four are without a doubt no brainers. While age and injuries might worry some you can't doubt their skills and what they bring to the table. Gerrit Cole lead the league in SwStr%, Zone Swing & Miss%, Out of Zone Swing & Miss%, and Whiff%. If only he was staying in Houston. Jacob deGrom has the best ERA in baseball in the last two years combined.

## Tier 2 - The Possible Elites

5. Walker Buehler
6. Mike Clevinger
7. Blake Snell
8. Luis Castillo
9. Shane Beiber
10. Chris Sale
11. Stephen Strasburg

I can see all of these pitchers taking the next step and joining the core four. Mike Clevinger finished the year top 5 in FIP, xFIP, K-BB, and K%. Blake Snell suffered an injury and might have been the unluckiest pitcher in baseball. He still produced an insane 17.8 SwStr% which is highest in the league (min 20 starts). Luis Castillo dominated all year with his lethal changeup. Shane Beiber burst onto the scene pitching 214 innings with a 25.5 K-BB%.

## Tier 3 - The Safe and Sound

12. Patrick Corbin
13. Clayton Kershaw
14. Jack Flaherty
15. Luis Severino
16. Aaron Nola
17. Charlie Morton
18. Lucas Giolito
19. Corey Kluber
20. Carlos Carrasco

Right off the bat, some of you might be saying how are Kluber and Carrasco in a safe and sound tier?! Well, this is more in terms of skill. Anyone can get hurt at any time. But with Kluber and Carrasco I have no doubts in their arsenal. Kluber's ERA in 2018 was 2.89 and Carrasco's was 3.38. A lot of people will rank Jack Flaherty higher and while he had a ridiculous second half, it was just one half. Also, we can't be too sure if his fastball is really *that* good. Lucas Giolito had a nice breakout season with an 11.62 K/9 and 15.0 SwStr%. This was largely due to his velocity which went up 1.5 ticks.

## Tier 4 - The Glob

21. Yu Darvish
22. James Paxton
23. Tyler Glasnow
24. Noah Syndergaard
25. Chris Paddack
26. Sonny Gray
27. Zac Gallen
28. Frankie Montas
29. Brandon Woodruff
30. Zack Greinke
31. Lance Lynn
32. Jose Berrios
33. Hyu-Jin Ryu
34. Trevor Bauer
35. Robbie Ray
36. Dinelson Lamet
37. Max Fried
38. Madison Bumgarner
39. Mike Soroka

40. David Price

This tier is called the glob because it consists of 20 pitchers who are all capable of providing draft day value. Yu Darvish changed his release point in the second half and produced a 2.76 ERA and 13.00 K/9. The main question is if he will keep his control and those walks down. Zac Gallen pitched from June 20th - September 15th. In that period he had an ERA of 2.81 (13th) which was better than Soroka, Greinke, Hendricks, Strasburg, Kershaw, and Buehler. Gallen might become the most inflated pitcher in terms of ADP in 2020. Speaking of inflated ADP's everyone knows of Dinelson Lamet. In the second half of the season here are the K/9 leaders with at least 12 starts: Cole, Verlander, Darvish, and...Lamet. He also posted a 3.97 ERA, 3.85 FIP, and 3.36 xFIP. He seems like a Robbie Ray to me. One of my favorite sleepers for 2020 is Max Fried. His last two months of baseball: 10.32 K/9 (17th) 0.95 HR/9 (17th) 22.4 K-BB% (10th) 3.65 ERA (26th) 3.09 FIP (9th) 2.91 xFIP (5th) 3.39 SIERA (7th). I would love to grab two pitchers in this tier.

**Tier 5 - The What Ifs**

41. Shohei Ohtani
42. Mike Minor
43. Kyle Hendricks
44. Zack Wheeler
45. Domingo German
46. Lance McCullers
47. Jesus Luzardo
48. Andrew Heaney
49. Caleb Smith
50. Matt Boyd

A lot of questions in this tier. Whether it is experience, injuries, or extreme first and second half splits; these guys all have potential. Hendricks has never had an ERA over four. His limited strikeout potential hurts his value but he would be great to pair with a risky pitcher. If Zack Wheeler lands in a good situation he can be a sneaky draft pick. He has three solid pitches and maybe a fresh start is what he needs. Lance McCullers comes off of Tommy John but we can't forget his numbers back in 2018. In 2018 he had a 3.86 ERA, 3.50 FIP, 3.43 xFIP to go with a very good 13.5 SwStr%.

**Tier 6 - The Sleepers**

51. Griffin Canning
52. Eduardo Rodriguez
53. Sean Manaea
54. Jake Odorizzi
55. Luke Weaver
56. Mike Foltynewicz
57. Ryan Yarbrough
58. Mitch Keller
59. Kenta Maeda
60. Yonny Chirinos

61. Sandy Alcantara
62. Brendan McKay
63. Julio Urias
64. Carlos Martinez
65. Joe Musgrove
66. Nathan Eovaldi
67. Garrett Richards
68. Masahiro Tanaka

In this tier, most of these pitchers can be classified as sleepers or value picks. I truly believe a lot of these pitchers will provide draft day value. Luke Weaver's breakout was taken away due to injury. Through 12 starts he had a 2.94 ERA, 3.07 FIP, 3.87 xFIP and 21.2 K-BB%. Luke Weaver's best pitch is his changeup. It had a pVAL of 6.3, which was 5th best in the league. Mitch Keller had a 24.1 K-BB% in his first major league stint. That ranked 14th among starters in the last 3 months. Sandy Alcantara increased his sinker usage in August and September. In those months he had a 2.78 ERA with a 3.74 FIP. He also hit the edge of the zone 43.5% of the time while the league average is 39%. Dodgers president of baseball operations has announced Julio Urias will be in the season in the rotation. The problem is you have to figure he will get limited innings, but those should be very solid productive innings.

### Tier 7 - The Old/Decent/Deep Sleeper pitching tier

69. German Marquez
70. Jon Gray
71. Dallas Keuchel
72. Wade Miley
73. Chris Archer
74. Michael Kopech
75. Dylan Cease
76. Johnny Cueto
77. Joey Lucchesi
78. Merrill Kelly
79. Julio Teheran
80. Miles Mikolas
81. Steven Matz
82. Marcus Stroman
83. Adrian Houser

A lot of random pitchers are in this tier. Some are deep sleepers, some are pitchers getting up there in age, and some are high floor low ceiling options. Dylan Cease is a deep sleeper of mine that I find very intriguing. His upside will rely on his control issues, but maybe Grandal can help with that. Merill Kelly's stats when his fastball velocity is 93mph or higher (5 starts): 1.74 ERA, 3.35 FIP, 16.0 K-BB%, and an 11.1 SwStr%. Keep an eye on that velocity come spring training. Miles Mikolas had a down year in 2019. He threw his slider a lot less. He really needs to go back to rocking that slider often. He is a safe bet for a low 4 ERA with maybe some room for improvement. Adrian Houser is an intriguing option as long as he makes the rotation. He relies on two fastballs and in the second half both his four-seam and two-seam were top 10 in xwOBA and K%.

## Tier 8 - A Shot in The Dark

84. Jose Urquidy
85. Anthony DeSclafani
86. Justus Sheffield
87. Pablo Lopez
88. Reynaldo Lopez
89. Dakota Hudson
90. John Means
91. Jeff Samardzija
92. Rich Hill
93. Mike Fiers
94. Cole Hamels
95. Jose Quintana
96. Jon Lester
97. Josh James
98. Dylan Bundy
99. Dustin May
100. Aaron Civale

This is the last of the bunch! I wanted to put Anthony DeSclafani higher but his pitches were kind of meh in 2019. Maybe the Reds pitching coach can get him to reach his potential. Pablo Lopez quietly had a good season and will be a dark horse sleeper for me. Reynaldo Lopez needs that velocity to be up, at times he was hitting high 90's. Josh James, Dustin May, Aaron Civale, and Jose Urquidy all depend on if they make the rotation. If so I would definitely bump any of these guys up a tier. Dylan Bundy's stock will start to go up since he is out of Baltimore. The Angels are an organization who loves to use the slider which benefits Bundy greatly.

# Middle Relievers Outlook
## By Michael Alexander

Pitching in fantasy baseball is a constantly changing landscape. Juiced baseballs, increased usage of the opener, and changing IL rules make it a challenge to keep up. One way to bridge a gap or smooth your roster's back end is a cheap middle reliever.

Here are some of my favorite RPs by category.

Enhanced Ks: Padding your strikeouts is one of the best ways to utilize a cheap middle reliever.
- Nick Anderson
- Andres Munoz
- Adam Ottavino
- Matt Barnes
- Giovany Gallegos

Ratio Coverage: Anchor those ratios by deploying an RP who keeps clean sheets.
- Ryan Pressly
- Zach Britton
- Aaron Bummer
- Blake Treinen
- Kevin Ginkel

Sneaky Saves: It's the most frustrating category in rotisserie baseball. Stash an arm or two before they become the week's top FAAB target.
- Will Harris
- Jalin Garcia
- Chris Martin
- Jose Alvarado
- Tony Watson

Longmen: Effective longmen give you a little bit of everything, typically at higher innings than the average reliever.
- Most of the Tampa Bay pitchers.
- Robert Gsellman
- John Gant
- Chad Green
- Juan Nicasio
- Freddy Peralta

The one thing you don't want to do is overpay for a middle reliever. They bear too much risk to spend significant draft capital on. They're also one of the least mined resources in fantasy. A new crop is always ripening. Don't go nuts for Nick Anderson's Ks when you can find the next Anderson in April for free. Anderson himself was on no one's draft radar just a year ago. The free profit is the biggest part of the deal with middle relievers. Stay in your lane, churn them in season, and enjoy the category boost.

# Closer Outlook
By Paul Mammino

Closers are one of the most interesting commodities in all of fantasy baseball. They are solely responsible for a singular category and due to the nature of the position are an extremely scarce resource. Multiple are required to compete in the category and there are only a finite number of available ones. Many people refuse to pay the high prices associated with the "elite" closers and as a result, prefer to speculate and take their chances on the waiver wire. This can be a valuable strategy but can also be a costly one in terms of FAAB.

Overall, it is hard to rank closers as it is entirely team and opportunity dependent and values can change so much due to a manager's preference. I have below the top projected saves getter for each team based on Steamer Projections broken up into ADP tiers based on early NFBC drafts. Easily one of the most volatile year to year positions it is very unlikely the final rankings look anything like this after the season ends.

## Tier 1
Josh Hader (68.8 ADP)
The top tier is inhabited solely by the Brewers' stud left-hander Josh Hader. His insane strikeout numbers and incredible ratio stabilization make him a valuable asset and worth the high pick it takes to get him. The biggest threat to his value is the return of Corey Knebel which, could push Hader back into a relief ace role. However, even in a relief ace role he provides an insane amount of value and can be paired with a low-K ratio stabilizing starter.

## Tier 2
Kirby Yates (83.7)
Aroldis Chapman (88.3)
Roberto Osuna (94.4)
2019 was a terrible year for the top tiers of closers as both Edwin Diaz and Blake Treinen failed spectacularly. However, this season the second tier contains two of the most reliable closers in recent memory. Chapman has exceeded 35 saves six times in the last eight seasons while posting elite strikeout rates. He is no longer a unicorn in terms of velocity but he is the closer on arguably the best team in all of baseball. He should return value easily as long as he stays healthy. Osuna is one of the best closers in the game on one of the best teams, he does not have the elite strikeout rates but his low walk rates and HR prevention have made him a reliable option. Yates is the newcomer to the group. He has shown an elite skill set over the last two seasons in San Diego and should have plenty of opportunities for saves as the Padres are one of the most improved teams in baseball.

## Tier 3
Liam Hendriks (121.1)
Brad Hand (121.3)
Taylor Rodgers (132.9)
Kenley Jansen (134.9)
Edwin Diaz (136.3)
Ken Giles (139.5)
Craig Kimbrel (143.2)
Once we hit this tier the reliable options begin to dissipate. I preferably want to have at least closer from this list by this point in a draft. Hendriks was the prize for the fade closer crowd and

he became one of the best relievers in all of baseball. The Athletics have proven to be willing to make a change if someone struggles so be careful investing heavily in the Athletics closer. The Indians have two closers in waiting in James Karinchak and Emmanuel Clase so Hand and his salary could be traded this off-season. His potential landing spot will have a lot of impact on his value. Rodgers was another FAAB All-Star but his skill set is solid and he closes for a talented Twins team. I am buying into him this season. Jansen was once a member of the elite but the skill set has regressed. The Dodgers brought in Treinen and he could be a replacement in Jansen struggles again in 2020. I will be avoiding him if I can this season. Diaz was a massive flop last season but he is one of a handful of relievers with number one ranking upside. The skillset is an extremely volatile one but the upside is insane. Ken Giles has long been one of my favorite closer buys and he is perennially underrated. He pairs double-digit K/9 rates with better than average walk numbers. The Blue Jays are on the upswing. It's a great price for a talented arm. Kimbrel was not good in his short stint with the Cubs but he could benefit from a normal off-season. I won't be investing in him in 2020.

**Tier 4**
Hector Neris (154.7)
Raisel Iglesias (159.0)
Alex Colome (169.3)
Emilio Pagan (171.2)
Jose LeClerc (172.0)
Hansel Robles (174.6)
Archie Bradley (186.1)
Brandon Workman (189.8)
Carlos Martinez (190.5)
This tier is where the question marks start to get significant. For many of these guys, the main question is if their team will replace them with a better option if their skill sets can hold up over the length of the season. However, for some, it is solely just because they are closing for a bad team. Neris has had a rocky few seasons but could provide a massive payday if he holds the job all season. Iglesias showed some signs of regression last season and the Reds have a quietly solid bullpen behind him. He could be included in an off-season trade to improve the team elsewhere. Colome has been able to hold down several jobs in recent seasons but the skills leave a lot to be desired. If the White Sox want to compete in 2020 they could look for a replacement. The Rays have several potential closers and could easily replace Pagan at the first sign of struggle. LeClerc should be given another chance to close for an improving Ranger roster. If he holds the job he has Tier 2 upside. Robles was great in 2019 but has a poor track record and there are a few players on that roster who could step in. I have never been an Archie Bradley fan and they have seemed reluctant to use him as a true closer in the past. I would avoid him. Workman stepped up and took over the Boston pen and should get the first crack at it again. I like the price and will most likely be buying in. Martinez may be the closer he may return to the rotation or he may be replaced by Giovanny Gallegos who looked like a future stud. I will be avoiding and prefer Gallegos in that pen.

**Tier 5**
Ian Kennedy (206.3)
Sean Doolittle (210.9)
Joe Jimenez (222.7)
Mark Melancon (232.2)

Keone Kela (242.1)

Scott Oberg (271.9)

There is a good chance most of these guys do not lead their respective teams in saves by the end of the season but hitting on one of these options can win you a league. There is a reason to like almost all of the options here. The Royals seemed to give Kennedy full trust and he was solid in 2019. It is unlikely a team wants to trade for him but he should post solid rations while approaching 20 saves. Doolittle was one of the best closers in baseball but fell on hard times in 2019. He was replaced and the Nationals won a World Series as a result. I think he gets another chance but will be on a short leash. Jimenez closes for a bad team and while Shane Greene was excellent for the same team last season I cannot see Jimenez repeating that success. Melancon was a great addition for the Braves but they already added will Smith who I think ends up with the lion's share of saves there. Kela has the talent but the Pirates could give a different option a chance as they have seemed reluctant to trust Kela fully in the past and he did struggle in 2019. Oberg is extremely talented but any pitcher in Coors is a tough one to bet on. Plus they have historically sided with those they are paying big money to so I would not be surprised if this job goes to Wade Davis.

**Tier 6**

Mychal Givens (353.7)/Hunter Harvey (505.7)

Shaun Anderson (420.5)

Jose Urena (523.3)

Sam Tuivailala (524.3)

These are the projected closers for four of the worst teams in baseball and there is little else to be excited about. Anderson did show some intriguing skills coming out of the pen and is a guy I am willing to bet on without much in the way of expectations. Harvey could be a stud reliever but the team is terrible and they do not project for many save opportunities. Givens has shown flashes but the situation is poor. Urena was better than he was as a starter but that was not a very high bar to clear. Let someone else deal with it. Same with whatever mess is going on in Seattle, Tuivailia is unlikely to keep this job all season.

# Looking at Multi-Positional Players
## By Mike Alexander

What's the worth of a player with multiple position eligibility? That depends on the positions they add and the format you're playing. In a standard roto league, they typically mean bench depth. That's led to the frequent answer being to bump their dollar value a buck or two. In a best ball or draft and hold universe that allows multiple eligibility, they're practically worth their weight in gold. The main reason being that it allows you to carry an extra pitcher on a fixed roster. As for leagues that do allow roster management, I think the buck or two approach is still light. In any non-shallow league being able to mix and match your pitchers to address current stat needs has value. The ability to roster an extra pitcher helps greatly there.

Here are some of my favorite utility men by category.

The Studs: There's nothing like having a premium player that can fill multiple openings.
- Alex Bregman
- Cody Bellinger
- DJ LeMahieu
- Max Muncy

The Whole Shebang: Our current fantasy baseball landscape is rife with landmines. You need easy fixes wherever you can find them. These are some of the best bandaids.
- Jeff McNeil
- Tommy Edman
- Chris Taylor
- Niko Goodrum
- David Fletcher

MI/CI Combo: Slightly less valuable than the above group, but they'll still provide immense depth for your roster.
- Mike Moustakas
- Eduardo Escobar
- Ryan McMahon
- Michael Chavis

OF Add On: Depending on how many OFs your league uses these double dips may be fairly appealing.
- Ketel Marte
- Whit Merrifield
- Kris Bryant
- Hunter Dozier
- Joc Pederson
- Trey Mancini

MI/CI only: Up the middle dual-eligible doesn't carry the weight it once did. It's still nice to be able to kick someone to the other side of the diamond when searching for a free agent add, though.
- Gleyber Torres

- Jonathan Villar
- Luis Urias
- Kevin Newman

Catcher: I'm much more interested in a position player that's managed to snag catcher eligibility than vice versa.
- John Hicks
- Victor Caratini
- Isaiah Kiner-Falefa
- Kyle Farmer (possibly earns in-season)

I'd still add $2-4 of value for the better utility men in standard leagues. Depending on what positions you need help with that could be even higher. When the bullets start flying and the waiver grind gets into full swing, you'll be glad you made the investment in versatile fantasy assets like these.

# Building Your Own Baseball Data Warehouse
## By Andrew Dewhirst

Have you ever wanted to be able to know every player who hit more than 30 home runs while making contact over 70% of the time? Or do you want to know which pitchers have a k/9 over 11 and an xfip under 4? Building your own data warehouse of baseball information is a great way for you to go and look at groups of players based on the stats you value, is devalue the most. What I am going to do here is walk you through where to find a free SQL database software that works on both PC and Mac, how to build your tables, and where to get your data, and clean it up so you can start bringing it in.

Step 1 Getting Your Database

There are lots of different options on the market. If you are using a PC, you can look at MSSQL lite, or MySQL. macOS has fewer options, and because of that, we are going to deal with PostgresSQL. They all use slightly different SQL commands, but whichever you choose for yourself, you can find plenty of command guides on the web.

You can download Postgres using this link, https://www.postgresql.org/. It is typically recommended that you grab the latest version, which is version 12 right now. Additionally, if you prefer to have an interface to work from, I recommend this if you are new to databases, or Postgres, I recommend adding a client like Postico(https://eggerapps.at/postico/) on the Mac, or dBeaver(https://dbeaver.io/) on PC. Go ahead and install your applications. And create your new database. Depending on your client you should be able to create a new database from here, or if you choose not to use a client you can create a new database using the command "CREATE DATABASE {DatabaseName}.

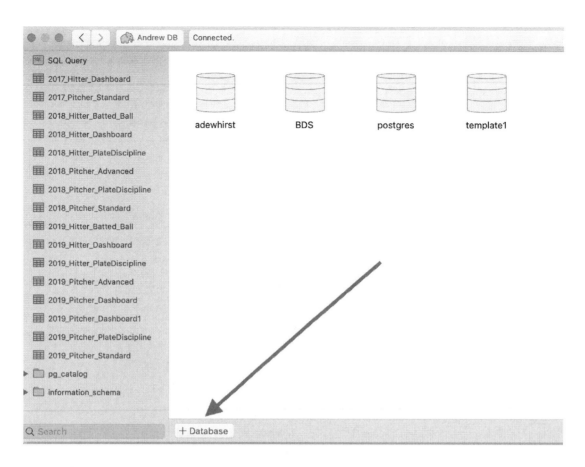

Step 2 Gathering Your Data

After you have installed your database and your database client, it is time to start thinking about building your tables. Before we can do that though we need a source for our data. We want to understand the data we are going to bring in before we start to build a table in our database as they will need to align directly. In this case, I cannot recommend FanGraphs enough. You can get your data from their site by doing the following;

1) Go to Fangraphs.com
2) Navigate to Leaders, and choose either Batting or Pitching and the year you want to bring in.

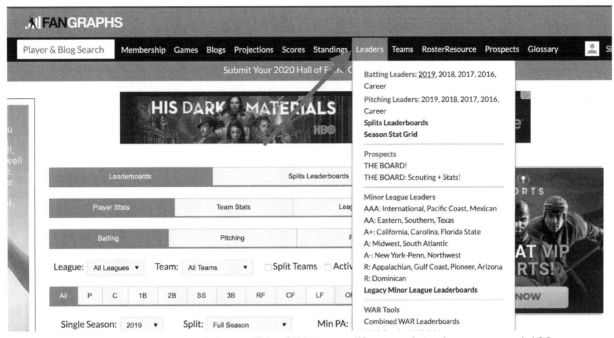

3) You will then want to set your minimum PA of IN, to qualify your data. I recommend 100 PA for hitters and 40 innings for pitchers. We want to make sure we are bringing in all of the relevant players. You can set the bar even lower if you wish, it just means your database will be a little bit bigger. I am going to use Hitters with 100 PA.

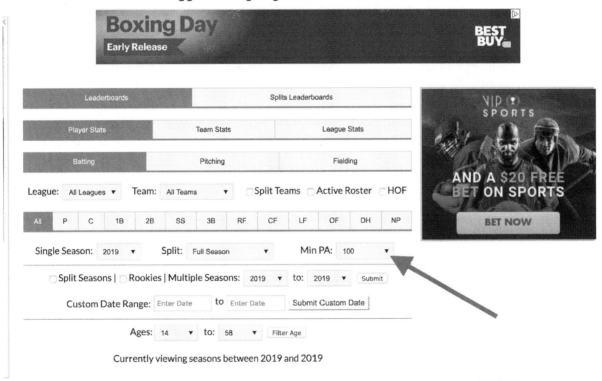

4) Next, you will want to choose the dataset you are looking at on the Fangraphs site. To get started we will use Standard. This gives us all of the base stats. Then you can click export data. This will give you all of the standard data for all hitters with 100 plate appearances or more

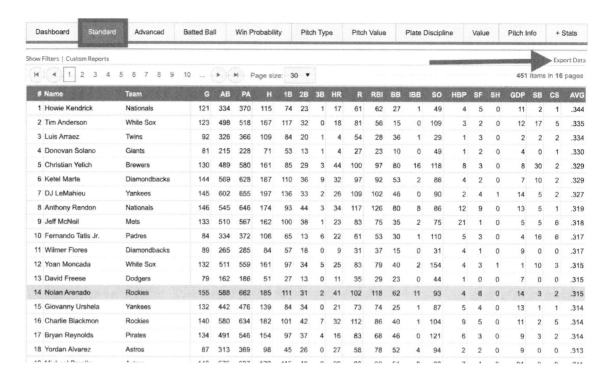

| # | Name | Team | G | AB | PA | H | 1B | 2B | 3B | HR | R | RBI | BB | IBB | SO | HBP | SF | SH | GDP | SB | CS | AVG |
|---|------|------|---|----|----|----|----|----|----|----|---|-----|----|-----|----|-----|----|----|-----|----|----|----|
| 1 | Howie Kendrick | Nationals | 121 | 334 | 370 | 115 | 74 | 23 | 1 | 17 | 61 | 62 | 27 | 1 | 49 | 4 | 5 | 0 | 11 | 2 | 1 | .344 |
| 2 | Tim Anderson | White Sox | 123 | 498 | 518 | 167 | 117 | 32 | 0 | 18 | 81 | 56 | 15 | 0 | 109 | 3 | 2 | 0 | 12 | 17 | 5 | .335 |
| 3 | Luis Arraez | Twins | 92 | 326 | 366 | 109 | 84 | 20 | 1 | 4 | 54 | 28 | 36 | 1 | 29 | 1 | 3 | 0 | 2 | 2 | 2 | .334 |
| 4 | Donovan Solano | Giants | 81 | 215 | 228 | 71 | 53 | 13 | 1 | 4 | 27 | 23 | 10 | 0 | 49 | 1 | 2 | 0 | 4 | 0 | 1 | .330 |
| 5 | Christian Yelich | Brewers | 130 | 489 | 580 | 161 | 85 | 29 | 3 | 44 | 100 | 97 | 80 | 16 | 118 | 8 | 3 | 0 | 8 | 30 | 2 | .329 |
| 6 | Ketel Marte | Diamondbacks | 144 | 569 | 628 | 187 | 110 | 36 | 9 | 32 | 97 | 92 | 53 | 2 | 86 | 4 | 2 | 0 | 7 | 10 | 2 | .329 |
| 7 | DJ LeMahieu | Yankees | 145 | 602 | 655 | 197 | 136 | 33 | 2 | 26 | 109 | 102 | 46 | 0 | 90 | 2 | 4 | 1 | 14 | 5 | 2 | .327 |
| 8 | Anthony Rendon | Nationals | 146 | 545 | 646 | 174 | 93 | 44 | 3 | 34 | 117 | 126 | 80 | 8 | 86 | 12 | 9 | 0 | 13 | 5 | 1 | .319 |
| 9 | Jeff McNeil | Mets | 133 | 510 | 567 | 162 | 100 | 38 | 1 | 23 | 83 | 75 | 35 | 2 | 75 | 21 | 1 | 0 | 5 | 5 | 6 | .318 |
| 10 | Fernando Tatis Jr. | Padres | 84 | 334 | 372 | 106 | 65 | 13 | 6 | 22 | 61 | 53 | 30 | 1 | 110 | 5 | 3 | 0 | 4 | 16 | 6 | .317 |
| 11 | Wilmer Flores | Diamondbacks | 89 | 265 | 285 | 84 | 57 | 18 | 0 | 9 | 31 | 37 | 15 | 0 | 31 | 4 | 1 | 0 | 9 | 0 | 0 | .317 |
| 12 | Yoan Moncada | White Sox | 132 | 511 | 559 | 161 | 97 | 34 | 5 | 25 | 83 | 79 | 40 | 2 | 154 | 4 | 3 | 1 | 1 | 10 | 3 | .315 |
| 13 | David Freese | Dodgers | 79 | 162 | 186 | 51 | 27 | 13 | 0 | 11 | 35 | 29 | 23 | 0 | 44 | 1 | 0 | 0 | 7 | 0 | 0 | .315 |
| 14 | Nolan Arenado | Rockies | 155 | 588 | 662 | 185 | 111 | 31 | 2 | 41 | 102 | 118 | 62 | 11 | 93 | 4 | 8 | 0 | 14 | 3 | 2 | .315 |
| 15 | Giovanny Urshela | Yankees | 132 | 442 | 476 | 139 | 84 | 34 | 0 | 21 | 73 | 74 | 25 | 1 | 87 | 5 | 4 | 0 | 13 | 1 | 1 | .314 |
| 16 | Charlie Blackmon | Rockies | 140 | 580 | 634 | 182 | 101 | 42 | 7 | 32 | 112 | 86 | 40 | 1 | 104 | 9 | 5 | 0 | 11 | 2 | 5 | .314 |
| 17 | Bryan Reynolds | Pirates | 134 | 491 | 546 | 154 | 97 | 37 | 4 | 16 | 83 | 68 | 46 | 0 | 121 | 6 | 3 | 0 | 9 | 3 | 2 | .314 |
| 18 | Yordan Alvarez | Astros | 87 | 313 | 369 | 98 | 45 | 26 | 0 | 27 | 58 | 78 | 52 | 4 | 94 | 2 | 2 | 0 | 9 | 0 | 0 | .313 |

## Step 3: Building Your Database Tables

Now we know the data we are going to bring in, it's time to build our database tables. What you are going to do here is you're going to name the rows based on how they look in the file you go from Fangraphs, we are going to assign it a data type(text, integer, or numeric). Then you will assign a primary key or a secondary key. Given this is a pretty simple database, we won't be assigning any foreign keys. The primary key in each database will be the unique identifier for each row. With FanGraphs data, this will always be the playerid. Using Hitters as an example there are their expected data types. Keep in mind, text should be used for anything that is going to include a non-numeric value, integer should be used for anything that is a whole number, and numeric will be used for anything that will have a decimal point.

| Column Name | Data Type | Primary Key |
|-------------|-----------|-------------|
| Name | text | No |
| Team | text | No |
| G | integer | No |
| AB | integer | No |
| PA | integer | No |
| H | integer | No |

| | | |
|---|---|---|
| 1B | integer | No |
| 2B | integer | No |
| 3B | integer | No |
| HR | integer | No |
| R | integer | No |
| RBI | integer | No |
| BB | integer | No |
| IBB | integer | No |
| SO | integer | No |
| SF | integer | No |
| GDP | integer | No |
| SB | integer | No |
| CS | integer | No |
| AVG | numeric | No |
| playerid | integer | Yes |

Step 4: Cleaning Your Data and Bringing It In

This is likely the most boring step, you're not building anything, you're not going to see anything cool, but if you don't clean your data you will never be able to bring it into your database. Clearing data, is the process of removing anything about your data that the database won't like. These things are often extra characters that get added. In terms of this data you will commonly want to look for quotation marks, and percentage signs. There are 2 main ways that you can clean your data, you can either A) build a script if you have that kind of know how, or you can do it manually. I typically do it manually, because it's easier than it might sound. To do this, you will want to make sure you have a program like NotePad++ on a PC, or Word Wrangler on Mac. What you do is open the file(s) you downloaded from Fangraphs in Step 2. Now you can hit control+F or command+F, which allows you to do a find and replace. So you will find the " and replace it with nothing. You just leave that field blank, and it will remove the character for you. You then do it again for you the % and then save your files. They should now be ready to be imported.

To perform the import  you will need to use the following command,

COPY "{TableName}" FROM '{location the file you cleaned up is saved}' DELIMITER ',' CSV HEADER;

What this command is doing is saying copy the data to this table from this file, its delimited by csv, and it has a header. Here is an example

COPY "2019_Pitcher_Standard" FROM '/users/adewhirst/downloads/Fangraphs LeaderBoard.csv' DELIMITER ',' CSV HEADER;

When you import data a second time into the same table, you will want to make sure you use this command

TRUNCATE "{tableName}";

Part 5: The Pay Off.

This will clear out all of the data, so that you can quickly move in your new data. The only cases you wouldn't want to do this is if you are storing information based on date, so your new data wouldn't be the same as the previous.

It's time to have fun now. You now know how to bring in all of your data, so you just need to start thinking about the things you want to know about. Here are some sample queries to get you started. If you are new to SQL queries, you will want to learn how to perform joins so you can get information from more than one table at once. This information can be found with ease by doing a search on a search engine. There are also some examples below.

This query provides you with every player who is above average in all of the 5 standard fantasy categories.

```
SELECT d."Name", d."Team","HR", "R", "RBI", "SB", "AVG"
FROM "2019_Hitter_Dashboard" as d
INNER JOIN "2019_Hitter_Batted_Ball" as bb
on d.playerid = bb.playerid
INNER JOIN "2019_Hitter_PlateDiscipline" as pd
on d.playerid = pd.playerid
WHERE "SB" > (SELECT AVG("SB")FROM "2019_Hitter_Dashboard")
and "HR" > (SELECT AVG("HR")FROM "2019_Hitter_Dashboard")
and "RBI" > (SELECT AVG("RBI")FROM "2019_Hitter_Dashboard")
and "R" > (SELECT AVG("R")FROM "2019_Hitter_Dashboard")
and "AVG" > (SELECT AVG("AVG")FROM "2019_Hitter_Dashboard")
Order BY "Name"
```

This query will give you a grouping of stats for 6 players, and put them in order from highest to lowest Hard contact rate.

```
SELECT d."Name", "HR", "R", "RBI", "SB", "BB", "K", "ISO", d."BABIP", "AVG", "OBP",
"SLG","wOBA", "LD", "GB", "FB", "Soft", "Med", "Hard", "Swing", "Contact"
FROM "2018_Hitter_Dashboard" as d
```

```
INNER JOIN "2018_Hitter_Batted_Ball" as bb
on d.playerid = bb.playerid
INNER JOIN "2018_Hitter_PlateDiscipline" as pd
on d.playerid = pd.playerid
WHERE d."Name" = 'JustinUpton'
OR d."Name" = 'StarlingMarte'
OR d."Name" = 'TommyPham'
or d."Name" = 'ByronBuxton'
or d."Name" = 'KhrisDavis'
or d."Name" = 'MarcellOzuna'
ORDER BY "Hard" DESC;
```

# Building Draft Values
By Ray Kuhn

Projections are wrong. Well at least most of the time that is. But that doesn't stop us from undertaking the exercise each winter as we get ready for the next baseball season.

So, if they are wrong, why do we keep on doing it? And should we?

Yes, this is an article about building draft values, after all it is one of the fundamentals of fantasy baseball, but without projections we don't have values to draft off of. And by values, we can translate that into both auction values and projected ADP. This means, we have to start with said projections.

With that being said, let's start with the idea of projections, and why/how they are fundamentally wrong. As much as we, and our computer programs and models know what we are doing (or at least think we do), it's impossible to get everything right. There are just too many variables to deal with, and trying to get as granular as saying Mike Trout will have 41 home runs compared to 39, is just not worth it.

First, let's address our initial statement. If we project Trout to have 41 home runs and he hits 39, that would be considered as "wrong". But, is it really? And does either result really impact our thoughts on Trout and how we are going to value him for the upcoming season? Of course, the answer is a resounding, no.

But again, this isn't an article about projections and a reasonable margin of error, so let's move forward while embracing the potential inefficiencies in them. We also need to realize that there are essentially three types of incorrect projections that come with their own characteristics:

·       We have the Trout scenario that was mapped out earlier. This can go in either direction, and it doesn't really bring much risk with it.

·       You can project a hitter for 40 home runs, and they hit 15. That could potentially be a huge problem, but their "draft value" (alright, now we are getting somewhere) will dictate the level of disaster it can be.

·       Then you have the hitter that is projected for 15 home runs and hits 40. A few of these can make your season.

Those were very simplistic examples, and they can be applied to each statistical category.

Now that we have that out of the way, there are a great deal of projections available, and they generally operate under most of the same assumptions, so either pick one or do your own, and go from there. While it's not exactly efficient to grind it down and sweat each home run, you can adjust the projections for each player as you see fit. Before you set out to build your draft values, you should feel comfortable with said projections, because that is the starting point of those values.

Any good draft plan requires awareness of your targets, and that means looking at your league standings from last year. That will tell you what stats you need to hit in 2020 as you look to translate those projections into actionable values.

Next, move on to your league settings:

·       How many teams are there?

·       What do the starting lineups look like?

·       How many players are in the player pool?

·       What is the salary cap?

·       What split will you use between hitting and pitching? For a rough estimate, I would go with 67% on hitting and 33% on pitching, but you could tweak that by a few percentage points in either direction based on preference. Something else that would be helpful with this, is to look back at how previous auctions have gone.

·       If we are building draft values for ADP and not auction prices, then you should have a rough plan based on your ranking, tiering, and previous league behavior of how to proceed.

·       Are there keepers? Those prices, and their respective values need to be factored in as inflation will then come into play. What if Trout is being kept for $6? If he is a $40 player, then we have to add $34 to the dollar pool.

Now, we have projections, know the player pool, and league settings, so then what?

For example, if you are in a 15-team league that starts five outfielders, take your top 60 outfielders. What is the average stat line for that population? To what level the player is above or below that average will start to dictate their dollar value, but make sure your total player pool comes out to 15 teams' times $260.

Once those values are completed, look at them. Don't just take the paper of the printer and sit down to draft. Do the values illustrate your research has told you and what you expected to see? If not, perhaps your values need to be adjusted, or maybe you should do some more research or there is something you missed.

We should also note that Steamer and other projection models do provide auction values and NFBC ADP data is readily available. But those auction values are likely in a vacuum and they will need to be adjusted to account for, perhaps OBP instead of AVG, or to ensure that every dollar in the pool is accounted for.

Now, what happens, if there is a player that model is saying should be $10, but you think it should be $20? Don't pay $20, but maybe pay $11 to make sure you get them. Similar logic applies to the end game in both drafts and auctions. There is nothing wrong with making a mistake at that point in the draft, as you can throw as many darts as you want in the 40th round or in dollar derby. But don't take that player in the 15th round or pay $10 for them.

Again, this is very simplistic, but we have to be nimble here too. The main thing is to understand the player pool, and this was just a very high-level overview. Projections and values are very important, and critical, but understanding the player pool is most important. Well that, developing a plan, and staying nimble.

No two drafts are the same, and none are going to go according to plan. As soon as the first player is drafted, or bought at the auction, those values are out of the window. With each player taken, a new level of inflation comes into play. The most important thing you can do, and must do in fact, is to adjust. And remember that everything requires context.

# Variance And Fantasy Baseball
## By Andrew Dewhirst

While I have only been writing about Fantasy Baseball and sports in general for a little over a year; I have spent many years as a player. At a young age, I developed a love of numbers and sports and fantasy was an easy way for me to combine those passions. In college, I studied statistics eventually earning a master's degree in analytics. This background has helped me become a much better fantasy player.

The biggest thing that this knowledge and experience has taught me is that as an industry, we do not spend nearly enough time discussing variance or range of outcomes. We often hear it discussed when talking about prospects, or sometimes on draft day disguised in the terms ceiling and floor. However, I think there are several different places where this discussion is lacking significantly.

## Pre-Season Projections

Below is a chart showing the 5x5 projected numbers (via Streamer) for five players I selected with between 15-20 HRs/SBs projected and their early-season ADP via NFBC.

| HR | R | RBI | SB | AVG | ADP |
|----|----|-----|----|-------|--------|
| 20 | 75 | 75 | 20 | 0.274 | 81.56 |
| 16 | 86 | 68 | 19 | 0.277 | 182.31 |
| 15 | 71 | 68 | 20 | 0.275 | 135.50 |
| 18 | 75 | 67 | 20 | 0.239 | 300.25 |
| 17 | 64 | 66 | 15 | 0.259 | 176.19 |
| 19 | 65 | 66 | 18 | 0.248 | 120.38 |

As you can see most of these players fall into the 120-180 ADP range but there are two massive outliers. For the most part, these players are very similar overall in nature with regards to their projections but there are some glaring differences. The player with an ADP of 300; has the lowest projected AVG by far which helps to explain his giant disparity in the draft cost. However, looking at the player being drafted around pick 80; there is nothing major that seems to stand out as different when looking at the projections.

However, what his draft day cost appears to be baking in here, is the variance associated with him. The player in question is Blue Jay's SS Bo Bichette. In his 212 PA sample, Bichette hit eleven HRs and swiped four bags; numbers that suggest he could easily outpace his projection. Owners tend to do a good job in understanding this potential and reflect it with draft cost. Projections for young players with little MLB track record tend to be extremely conservative and possess the largest error bars. No matter the prospect history; the systems will never truly know what to do with these players until we have a reasonable MLB sample. The rest of the list contains several veterans. In order we have: Lorenzo Cain, Amed Rosario, Kevin Kiermaier, Nick Senzel, and Danny Santana.

For players such as the first three names, the projection system has a decent amount of history to work off of. As a result, the error bars are fairly small, and we can usually take these projections at face value. Senzel is in a similar boat to Bichette but we do have more MLB data to work with him. He should still have a larger error bar and as a result, his ADP should rise over time. Santana is an interesting case as a late-career breakout. Projection systems also have a hard time with players like him as they may be slow to realize if there was a true change.

Overall, ADP tends to follow the conventional wisdom on players on which players the projections could be most wrong on. However, I think if the industry was more cognizant of displaying variance a better way of looking at things would be to present a 95% confidence interval. That way instead of projecting a mean total, we could show a range of projected outcomes it is most likely to fall in. This would likely show a larger range for a player such as Bichette versus a player like Cain.

**Stat Pages**

The second place I feel a general understanding of variance would help fantasy players become even better is looking at individual stat pages. Over the past few seasons, we as an industry have fallen in love with Statcast metrics, citing exit velocity, launch angle, and spin rates in our everyday conversations. These new metrics have allowed us to understand and quantify things we have long tried to but could never successfully do. This also spurred a launch angle revolution of sorts and seems to have completely changed the game as we know it.

During this season I started to take a better look at these numbers to see if there was something that these average totals were not showing. For example, let's take two players, both of whom have an average exit velocity of 95 MPH on 100 balls in play. I wanted to see if there was a significant difference between the guy who hits 50 balls at 90 MPH and 50 at 100 MPH versus the guys who hits 50 at 85 and 50 and 105. Overall these guys would have the same average number but would have gotten there in vastly different ways. This is variance or standard deviation in action. Is there a benefit to the more consistent hitter or the one who can reach higher totals? Overall, I determined that average matters more in this example, but it is also important to know that higher top exit velocities are even more important for determining power.

However, this led me on a similar path concerning launch angle. Much has been made about the guys who raise their launch angles and join the fly-ball revolution. Hundreds of articles have been written trying to find the next Josh Donaldson, Justin Turner, or JD Martinez using average launch angle. However, I determined that the standard deviation of launch angle was even more important. These findings were replicated and built upon by Alex Chamberlain of Fangraphs. The standard deviation of launch angle tracks better with wOBA than the average launch angle does. This is also an extremely useful tool for determining breakouts. A hitter's average LA may not change at all but if he is making more consistent contact, he may be in line for a breakout. Since changes like this can appear quickly in a season, we may have a new tool for finding breakout hitters quicker. A prime example of this phenomenon in action is Ketel Marte. Below is his 30-day rolling charts comparing his contact consistency to his wOBA on contact.

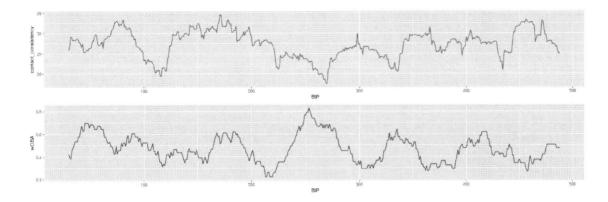

This is not the only example of a statistic where the standard deviation proves to hold more value than the average itself. Baseball is made up of hundreds and thousands of little plays throughout the season and it is important to understand the interaction of each of these. I believe another place to look into is individual pitch metrics such as spin rates and movement numbers.

## League Context

One of the most important applications of variance in fantasy baseball is in one's league context. Without getting too technical, there are three major formats for fantasy ball. Head to Head, Roto, and Best Ball. I know that more exist outside of this list but these are the most common of formats. In the case of Roto, weekly variance does not matter nearly as much as it does in the other leagues. If I have Mike Trout on my roster I do not care how he gets to his end of season stats, all I care about is those end of season results. However, in H2H and Best Ball, the week to week consistency of a player is massive. For example, in a best ball style, the platform automatically selects your lineup for a given week based on what players scored the most points in that week. Fairly simple concept and requires no in-season management. However, when drafting for these leagues we need to consider the weekly variance of a given player. After running the scoring settings through a projection system we may end up with a list of players with extremely similar projected point totals. This means that these guys should all go in the same range, obviously considering for position. However, in reality, we need to find out how we best anticipate these players to reach those totals.

For example, a player who sees much of his end of season value driven by HR or SB totals will likely be a much more volatile asset. A player who sees a large boost from solid on-base skills will likely be safer. In the context of a Best Ball format, the build of your roster will likely determine which is better for you. If you have already taken a significant number of risks, you may want to take the floor option. You know if the remainder of your roster has a down week you can expect that solid floor player to perform and keep the roster in a reasonable position. However, if you have the safety, then you need to take the volatility. One strong week of power or stolen base output could be huge for your team and due to the overall floor of the rest of the roster, that no homer no steal week that will inevitably come will not hurt as much.

This same concept comes through in an H2H Categories league. It is a little harder here because you need to make the choices but comparing your roster to your opponents you can see what player type will fit best. Say your opponent has a balanced roster and typically puts up league average results across all the categories. Then for that given week, the balanced player type who provides a solid floor should be one who can help you win. While such a player does not exist, if you knew a player would hit two homers every week and another player had a 50% chance of four and 50% chance of 0. All else is equal. The expectation for both players averages to two homers per week. On average your opponent hits three more homers than you. If you are aiming to win that category it makes more sense to chase the upside. Now, these perfect scenarios do not exist in baseball but I plan to do some more off-season research delving into weekly trends for players to see if there exist groups of players who have consistent or inconsistent value week to week.

My initial research into this topic showed that based solely on 2019 data, players who see a large portion of their value tied to their ability to hit home runs are more volatile week to week than those tied to stolen bases. This could because home runs impact not only the single category but it also impacts Runs and RBIs. This is a topic I plan to investigate further and will be dedicating an entire article to it in the coming weeks.

## Conclusion

These are just three examples of specific aspects of fantasy baseball that I think can be improved with a deeper understanding of standard deviation and variance. At its core, fantasy baseball is a game of statistics and being able to apply and interpret a simple statistical concept can only make you a better player. This is an aspect of the game that has been instrumental for those who play DFS and is one of the key tenets of a successful DFS player. I believe that these same concepts can make us better full-season players. It can also help to build enhance our ability to make FAAB bids and to make savvy pickups in the context of our teams. I know I have often been guilty of always chasing upside with my pickups even when a solid contributor fits the general build and goal of my roster better. Variance underlies every part of fantasy baseball, understanding that and leveraging it better than your opponent could be the difference in a championship and another year outside the money.

# Head-to-Head Leagues
By Jim Bay

Ali vs. Frazier, David vs. Goliath, Skywalker vs. Vader, Achilles vs Hector, Shamrock vs. Ortiz. There is something about epic head to head battles that get our juices flowing. That is part of the appeal of Head to Head fantasy leagues. There is something about looking at your current weekly match up and seeing that your opponent is your archrival/co-worker/ family member, knowing that you really want to defeat this person.

Yes, we know that there are many out there who believe that the best and the only way to play fantasy baseball is to use the Rotisserie method, in which your drafted team is getting points based on how your entire team does in a specific category. After all, this is how the original version of the game has been traced back to when in 1979 a group of friends got together at a New York City restaurant, La Rôtisserie Française (where the name "Rotisserie" comes from) to have a little fun with stats. Regardless, there are many that would prefer to play in a Head to Head league. H2H leagues can be run with two different scoring systems, involving categories or points that we will discuss here.

CATEGORIES

Category leagues are generally the more popular league, as they require less focus than points leagues and you only have to care about accumulating numbers in however many categories are being scored within the league. Category leagues are similar to rotisserie, but you play against a single opponent each week. Whichever one of you "wins" a particular category, gets a win. So, each week, every team racks up some combination of 10 wins, losses, and ties, one for each of the 10 rotisserie categories. For example, if you beat your opponent in six of the 10 categories that week, your record would be 6-4.

In a category league, having a balanced roster usually leads to a better team. As with roto leagues, you need to be thinking about all 10 categories during your draft. You certainly can ignore a category or two in categories leagues if you must, but for the most part, you're pretty much looking to put together a well-rounded team that will be competitive in every category each week. Depth is also important when playing in a category league. The reason for this is to have the ability to mix and match depending on your opponent's lineup is critical for this type of league. That means drafting a deep roster with a bench that can easily plug holes in pretty much any category, and be able to tailor your lineup to exploit the weaknesses in your opponent's lineup. All-in-all category leagues are great for active managers who don't want to memorize an entire list of points, or who want to focus on only the glamor categories.

POINTS

Points leagues are a great way to account for every aspect of the game and are more player-oriented and straight forward. Whoever gets the most points each week gets the win. In a head-to-head points league, however, you're basically playing against another opponent each week. Each statistical category is assigned a point value much like you would find on DFS sites like DraftKings, where a single is worth one point, a home run is worth four points, etc. Then, each scoring period's winner is determined by which team accumulates the most fantasy points versus your opponent, just like in fantasy football. So if you won that week, your record would be 1-0.

One of the highlights for points league is when you are selecting a player you need to consider a player's real-world skills a bit more. How many innings pitched and strikeouts will that starting pitcher provide for you? What is that hitter's OPS? That is because, in points leagues, the volume is very important. You get at least a fraction of a point for every inning your pitchers throw, and wins are worth quite a bit. Therefore, pitchers who throw a lot of innings are far more important in the points format.  Points leagues are a lot of fun, however, make sure you know your league scoring inside and out - there are a lot more ways to score or lose points in fantasy baseball than fantasy football.

With adding the thrill of facing an opponent one-on-one, H2H does truly offer a different and enjoyable way to play fantasy baseball. This is especially true since the level of understanding needed to play in a head-to-head league doesn't necessarily mean you have to be a "baseball Einstein" in order to enjoy a league. In these leagues, you really need to know the big hitters and stud pitchers, which will give a decent chance to field a good team.  In reality, H2H is more like playing real baseball.  After all, baseball is a matchup of two teams, the way the real game is played, and that's the way many feel fantasy should be played as well. If you're thinking about creating or joining a fantasy baseball league, feel free to go with head-to-head. You won't be disappointed.

# Points Leagues
By Jorge Montanez

Points leagues are a good transition for new players entering the fantasy baseball arena. It's the format that most resembles fantasy football. You draft a team, set your lineup, and watch your players accumulate points throughout the week. Points leagues often get a bad rap in the industry. Truth be told, I think they're pretty fun.

My longest-running league with friends is a points league. It was my introduction to fantasy baseball. One year in and I was hooked. A couple seasons ago, I made it to the championship. There I was down by 0.33 points going into the final game of the fantasy season between the Astros and Angels. My opponent had Justin Upton and I had Alex Bregman. Bottom of the third inning, Alex Bregman goes deep to put me up by 5.66. Then at the top of the eighth inning, Justin Upton hits a solo shot to give my opponent the lead again. Bregman got one more at-bat in the bottom of the ninth, and he hit a pop-up to third. My championship dreams came crashing down into the fielder's glove. While I lost, it's those kinds of exciting weeks that make points leagues fun, even if it doesn't necessarily reward the best fantasy team that season. That's just the nature of head-to-head formats of any fantasy sport. Anything can happen in a given week.

## Strategy

The most important thing to know when entering a points league is your league settings. In category leagues, you have your set categories that will count towards your scoring. In points leagues, just about any activity on the field can be scored. If you catch on to a point system that favors a particular stat, you can find a way to exploit it in the draft. Find a league or create one with the settings that you like best. Sometimes you hear that steals are devalued in points leagues, well just make them worth more points! It's that simple. Just don't make any particular stat overpowering. We tend to complicate things trying to come up with the perfect, most balanced system. Too much tinkering could ruin a league.

That said, points leagues generally tend to favor high-volume strikeout pitchers and home run hitters. Not much different than in category leagues, but in points leagues, not having a base stealer or someone to stabilize your ratios won't necessarily hurt you. Let's take a look at pitching in points leagues.

## Pitching in Points Leagues

Strikeouts and volume are king, plain and simple. The more volume a pitcher has, the more strikeouts he'll accumulate. Rack up the strikeouts and the points come with it. Pitchers who eat up innings tend to record more wins and quality starts as well. If your league scores for that, it's easy to see why pitchers tend to stand atop the leaderboards in points leagues.

While it's important to have pitchers with a good overall skill set, you aren't necessarily worried about ratios like WHIP and ERA. A baseline quality start would get you a 4.50 ERA. That wouldn't exactly help you in a roto league. If it gets you those points for a quality start, then the 4.50 ERA really doesn't matter. That leads to my next point about pitching in points leagues, streaming.

Streaming pitchers is absolutely vital to winning in a points league. Pitchers with two starts in a week can give you a massive advantage over your opponent. This is why I like to keep my bench full of pitchers throughout the season. The more pitchers you are rostering, the more two-start options you'll have. Even if a pitcher has a bad matchup for one of those starts, you're likely to start him that week because VOLUME IS KING. There's less risk in starting a mediocre two-start pitcher in a points league than there is in a roto league. That's because one bad start of the two won't hurt you as much as if it killed your ERA or WHIP category for the week. I've seen it time and again, there's always someone in a points league that has a bench full of hitters. Hitters can't score you points from the bench. Don't be that person.

### Hitting in Points Leagues

Now on to hitting. Similar to pitching, you aren't limited to how a player can score by which categories your league counts. Players who hit for a high average or get on base at a high clip change in value based on your roto categories. But in points leagues, they can both be valuable. It doesn't matter how a player scores points, as long as they score more than your opponent. That said, there are a few things to keep in mind when looking at hitters in points leagues.

Hitters with a high BB/K ratio generally perform better in points leagues. Walks are usually counted the same as a single. So if a hitter has a high on-base percentage, he's scoring you points while also increasing his likelihood of scoring a run. This is important for sluggers who strikeout at a high rate. If a hitter strikes out too much but doesn't walk enough, he's going to kill you some weeks. Plate discipline is crucial. Guys like Billy Hamilton are always the perfect example of players that have drastically different values in points leagues and roto. Sure he might steal a bunch of bases, but that's it. They aren't getting on base enough to accumulate points. This is why Carlos Santana is the reverse extreme. His value is drastically higher in points leagues because of his ability to get on base. The same goes for players like Michael Conforto and Anthony Rendon. Think of OBP as a point-scoring percentage. If a player has an OBP upwards of .400, they're scoring you at least one point 40% of the time!

Another area to look at is slugging percentage. In a standard roto league, a hitter isn't rewarded for extra-base hits. Whereas in points leagues, a double is worth twice as many points as a single. And of course, home runs are the big point scorers. If you want to put the two stats together and look for players with a high OPS, that would be a good way to go when evaluating hitters in points leagues.

### Extra Points

Draft players with multi-positional eligibility. The fewer hitters you need to carry on your bench, the better. As I alluded to before, those reserve spots are better used for pitchers to give you more two-start options week by week. Drafting hitters eligible at multiple spots allows you to do that.

Starting pitchers eligible as relief pitchers gain value in points leagues. Relief pitchers are volatile. You have no idea when they'll be used or if a save opportunity will come up. So being able to start a pitcher in a relief spot could give you a nice point floor in that position. It also gives you an extra opportunity to have the all-important two-start pitcher.

Be careful when looking at rankings. Most rankings you'll see online will be made for roto leagues unless otherwise specified.

That just about covers points leagues for you. So, don't hesitate to give it a chance. You just might have more fun than you think.

# Best Ball Leagues
By Zachary Meyer

Fantasy Baseball has many different formats, whether it be head to head, rotisserie or points leagues. There are also so many different customized formats that are exploding onto the scene. One format that really has taken off the past couple of years is called Bestball Leagues. Best Ball leagues are unique leagues that have set rosters for the whole year and use points league scoring systems. What I mean by set rosters is that there is no trading or adding people during the complete baseball year allowed. The players you draft are the players you have. It makes the draft the most important and only part of the league since there is no other movement allowed. The set rosters in this league make this type of league hard since you have to plan ahead for injuries of players since you cannot just simply add another player from waivers. However, one nice thing is you never have to set your roster. In Best Ball leagues the computer automatically puts in your best roster at the end of the week based on what players scored the most points during that week. No more wishing you would have benched the pitcher that got crushed in a game, or missing out on a hot streak from one of your hitters.

## Rules

A couple things to keep in mind with Best Ball leagues. Always know your rules!!! You want to take a look at the scoring systems that your league uses. Some leagues use different scoring models, Fantrax have different scoring than NFBC. Make sure to look at these before you start drafting.

Another thing to keep in mind is how many players will you be drafting and how many players in each position count for a given week. The common settings are that you will start your top 9 pitchers each week, no differentiation between starters and relief pitchers. Hitting differs in both leagues and you will want to make sure you are drafting accordingly. NFBC has 2 catchers and a 2b/ss and 1b/3b slot and utility slot while Fantrax has only 1 catcher and 3 utility spots instead of the 2b/ss and 1b/3b slots. They both do require starting 5 outfielders each week.

## Other Important Reminders with Best Ball

1. No trading during the season. What you draft is what you get, one positive is you do not have to worry about bad trades ruining your season.
2. No Waivers or FAAB runs: means you do not have to worry about anything during the in season process that you usually would with other fantasy leagues.

## Strategies

I have only drafted Fantrax leagues so far this year so I will mainly focus on Fantrax in this section and how I have seen things play out.

The one thing I have been trying to do in each draft is to make sure that I have 3 hitters in position except for outfield where I have been focusing on getting 8-9. You want to make sure you have depth in each position just to make sure injuries do not crush you during the season. Taking 0's each week at a position is a sure-fire way to lose your league.

Position scarcity exists more on Fantrax since players do not qualify for multiple positions. The players positions are set at the beginning of the year and will remain that way. A few positions to keep an eye on are outfielders since you have to start 5 of them every week and also 2nd base in this format is very thin this year. A couple of other positions that are fairly top heavy are

1st base and also Catcher.  After the big 4 at catcher Realmuto, Grandal, Sanchez and Contreras it is a fairly steep drop off.  This does not mean you have to overreach at this position, but if I have not been getting a top 4 catcher, I am happy with waiting for the later round guys and building up the rest of my roster.  The deepest position is Shortstop.  That doesn't mean you do not want to draft one early, but you can definitely wait for a viable one in the draft.

Watch for drop offs and tiers at each position.  You never know when a run will happen at a certain position, but you want to make sure you are not at the end of it and end up forcing yourself to take a player you did not want.  I like to look at the positions separately instead of as overall rankings.  You can start to see the dips in each position and can tell what position is weak.  Also make sure to look at other teams and what they haven't drafted.  By looking at other teams it helps you visualize what position they might take.

Since Innings pitched gives you points and Quality Starts, starters are more valuable than relievers.  The top 2 relievers for pitchers only were ranked 16th and 24th and that was Josh Hader and Kirby Yates.  I tend to only draft Starters, but if an elite closer falls down in the draft it doesn't hurt to take one.  I avoid closers at the end of drafts just because Saves and job security are much harder to come by than innings pitched.

I also try to avoid prospects in this format.  They can turn out great if they hit, but a player like Walker Beuhler actually scored less points than Kyle Schwarber and Shin-Soo Choo.  Vlad Jr. scored less than Todd Frazier and Evan Longoria.  Playing time is a big thing to focus on, try not to be an ageist in these drafts.  The hardest thing to do is to predict when a prospect will be called up.  Players like Forrest Whitley and Kyle Tucker gave players no points last year.

## Early Draft ADP

**Top 10 early ADP for Fantrax** :  1. Acuna 2. Mike Trout 3. Christian Yelich 4. Cody Bellinger 5. Mookie Betts 6. Gerrit Cole 7. Francisco Lindor 8. Alex Bregman 9. Juan Soto 10. Justin Verlander

**Top 10 Pitchers with ADP listed:**  6. Cole 10. Verlander 13.DeGrom 15. Scherzer 19. Beuhler 23. Beiber 27. Strasburg 28. Clevinger 30. Flaherty 40. Snell


**Good luck this year and happy drafting!!!**

# Daily Fantasy Sports (DFS) Strategy
## By Ray Kuhn

At this point, DFS (Daily Fantasy Sports) have been shoved down our throats, risen from obscurity to the mainstream, and have now settled somewhere in between. This is not to disparage, put down, or take a cranky, "get off my lawn" stance, but we are just stating facts.

And by no means am I against DFS.

In fact, just the opposite, as it is just one more way to enjoy each and every game on the slate. Aside from the excitement and competitive benefit to it, DFS also grants you the benefit of drafting each and every day. Or, multiple times each day. And isn't drafting the best part of fantasy baseball?

Here, you can draft a fresh squad for each slate of games you wish to play, with the elimination of a great deal of risk. Yes, your player can still leave the game in the first inning with an injury, but that only hinders you for that day as opposed to staring at Jose Altuve on your bench for a month.

Fantasy baseball is often referred to as a "grind", and sometimes, unfortunately, life gets in the way and doing your research and/or setting a lineup is just not a plausible situation. The benefit of DFS, yes there are many, is that when that is the case, you simply don't play that slate of games.

But to me, the biggest positive to playing DFS, besides the adrenaline and profit potential, is the positive impact it has on your season long game. Not like you aren't dialed into baseball on a daily basis, but playing DFS, if you are doing it the right way, forces you to really be logged in to everything. Often times, the research you are doing to set a DFS lineup, or something uncovered while monitoring a specific slate of games, will make a difference and translate to season long success.

At this point, there is a great deal of attention paid to specific DFS strategies, theories, and ways to attack the game. Not to overly simplify things, and you can never do enough refreshing your memory and do enough homework, you don't want to over complicate things either.
With that being said, let's take a look at some general points or bullets to keep in mind, dig further into, and be aware of being throwing your hat into the DFS ring:

**Bankroll Management** – Let's not lose sight of the fact that, while there are a wide variety of free and extremely cheap (ie. $0.25) tournaments available, this is for money. Real life cash. And while each team plays 162 games a season, there are a lot more days to the baseball season. Also, within that, while there is a "main" slate each day that holds the majority of the games, there are multiple slates available for your pleasure on a daily basis. All that enjoyment could be extremely profitable, but it could also get to be very expensive. That is especially true if you hit a rough patch. Prior to the season, or each month or week, establish what you can stand to lose. Based on that amount, apply a percentage, maybe 5% to 10%, to each day's action.

**Contest Selection** – This works hand in hand with bankroll management. Try to spread the wealth around to a few contests each day. Also, don't put all your eggs in the tournament basket. While it may be more exciting, and it has the potential for a larger profit, there is also the greatest amount of risk and volatility here. Mix in one tournament with some cash games, 50/50s (half of the field evenly splits the prize pool) or head-to-head contests. The idea is to grind along with a small profit each day for a nice prize at the end of each season, and also so you can sustain your tournament entries for a chance at a larger payout. In cash situations, you want to play for a little less upside and more certainty than in tournaments where some risks must be taken for the possibility at a higher reward.

**Scoring System/Salary Cap** – Each site has a slightly different set-up and point structure, and it is to your advantage to be aware of it. Not every lineup is created equal, and there are some details that can be exploited. By the same token, salaries, in some cases, are different between sites, so that is another factor to consider. While the research and knowledge base may be the same, it would be irresponsible to set identical lineups across websites.

Now that we got some administrative things out of the way, let's jump into some items to consider in your research before setting that "perfect lineup":

**Check out the Starting Lineups/Batting Order** – While it's common sense to confirm that all of the players you use on a given day are in fact playing, there is more to it than that. By looking at where a given player is batting in the lineup, a potential advantage, or disadvantage, could present itself. It may sound like common sense, but higher in the order a player is, the more valuable they are, as that will lead to more at bats; and therefore, more fantasy production. Also, when a player moves up in the lineup, either due to an injury situation or platoon split, it often presents some value when it comes to their salary. Players that don't play every day, or are returning from injury, could also have a cheaper cost. But don't use them just for the sake of using them either.

**Target Bad Pitching** - Yes, some of these are self-explanatory, but it needs to be said. While the best players in baseball are the best players in baseball for a reason, their pricing often reflects that. And let's keep in mind, that no one hits a home run or picks up an RBI every day, and the best hitters fail 70% of the time. I know I just threw some clichés at you, they are facts you must keep in mind when setting your lineup. But when it comes to targeting bad pitching, don't just look at the starting pitcher. For the most part, we don't see starting pitchers last much more than five or six innings, so the bullpen is just as important. Not only should we go after the bad bullpens, but take a look at the last few games a team had. If a bullpen is tired, beat up, or their best option will be getting a rest day, it is a situation to be exploited.

**Be Aware of Travel Schedules & Late Games** – This works both ways. Starting pitchers often travel ahead of their teams on the road, but he is the only one. Everyone else, the offense, defense, and bullpen, did not get to travel ahead, they are likely running on fumes. Yes, we are dealing with highly compensated professionals here and there is no excuse, but it is also the truth. And they are humans who are at the mercy of their bodies. With the entire league at your disposal, you should look for every possible advantage while also avoiding any potential source of struggle.

**Recent Statistics** – Right here, this is the big one. We can go all day here and probably spend half the book going over various stats, their meanings, and why they are useful. But at this point, you likely have at least some measure of understanding of various statistics and data points that are available to us. And if not, head over to the trusty internet, and let your favorite search engine guide you to their meanings. With that being said, while baseball is played on the field, a lot can also be found from a spreadsheet. You must be careful, and this is huge, to put whatever data you can find into context with the actual results and what you are seeing on the field. Don't just look at the surface stats, but also the underlying trends and metrics. This is really the same thing you do each off-season for your season long leagues, so the only difference is that it is now occurring on a daily basis. But this is also what I was getting at when talking about how playing DFS can help you with your seasonal leagues.

**Batter vs. Pitcher** – This (BVP) might be one of the more widely thrown out terms or acronyms when it comes to DVS. presume is actually quite simple; how good does a batter do against a specific pitcher, with the same being true for the other side of the match-up. While this data is important to consider, also look at how batters or pitchers did against comparable counterparts, there is also the tendency for it to be overused. Consider the data, put it into context, and use it as one of your tools. The important thing to consider, is when the data is from and how relevant and recent it is.

**Platoon Splits** -There is a lot of overlap here, as this often influences starting lineups each day. Some teams are better at exploiting this than others, and platoon advantages could open up value opportunities for position players allowing you to also fit in more big-name studs. Those studs are also more often considered to be "platoon indifferent", but it is something that must be carefully considered. By the same token, and I'm not sure this is discussed as often, but if a left-handed pitcher is facing a line-up of all or mostly right-handed hitters, the opposite is also true, then perhaps that is a pitcher to be avoided as well.

**Know the Ballpark** – There are plenty of stats on each ballpark performs with respect to both pitchers and hitters and whether they are left-handed or right-handed. This sometimes could be the deciding factor between two otherwise equal players. And it goes without saying that Coors Field is its own animal.

**Weather** – Just like it seems pretty obvious that you should check the line-up each day, the weather should get the same attention. Be aware of the forecast and whether or not the game will be played; either to completion or if it all. And if there is the possibility of a rain delay, stay away from that particular starting pitcher as their workload and chance for a win will be either greatly reduced or eliminated.
.

**News** – This likely isn't something that needs to be clearly mentioned, but follow along with the news. Is a player dealing with, or was dealing with a nagging injury? Are there any explanations for recent performance, either for the better or for the worst? There is overlap between this bullet, starting lineups, and recent statistics, but they are all intertwined.

Now that we have considered all of those factors, nothing should be a surprise here, we get to the most important part. And that is the eye test. For as much as following along with the news and statistics is a very necessary part of the game, nothing beats actually watching the game. Baseball is played out on the field each and every day, and watching the games will prove to be the most reliable form of research.

And most of all, have fun.

# Drafting a New Dynasty League
## By Walter McMichael

So, you joined a dynasty league, it's a daunting task to determine exactly how to handle all of the intricacies that come with building a dynasty. I generally do not like step by step instructions but there are a few things you MUST do before even looking at players or how to value them. They must be followed 100% or you will fail.

1. Does your league have a constitution?
   a. No, then find a new league.
   b. Yes, then read it. Read it again. Then, try to understand it. If there is anything you do not understand, ask the commissioner. We want to know every rule so nothing surprises us during the draft/season. The rules of your league determine players you want. Ohtani's value in a daily moves league is so much higher than in weekly. Does your league require an active MLB roster? When does the FAAB run? How often does the FAAB run? All of these questions need to be answered before who you are drafting can be.
2. Determine what type of player you are
   a. Do you want to win now?
   b. Do you want to build from youth but not necessarily care about year one?
3. Ensure no half measures based on the type of player you are

Okay, so we have determined the league rules, confirmed the type of player you are, and determined to ensure no half measures are taken when drafting. Now...who do you draft and how do you determine it?

Let's say you have determined you want to win now, you should take every redraft value who falls your way. Yes, I know you really like random 18-year-old prospect for the value but, this is where the no half measures kicks in, he does not help you THIS season. We want to win now so we are taking the veteran who still has a few valuable seasons left. For this method, I recommend creating dollar values out of projections (you can use your own or any publically available source). Draft it like redraft and research as many upside prospects as you can to fill out your minor league roster.

Here is where it gets tricky, let's say we have decided to build from youth and no not care about this year. This method is much harder in my opinion since you have to consider every single player in the player pool no matter their age or how much they will contribute in the upcoming season. One mistake I see people make when they "tank" is they disregard veterans in their late 20s and early 30s but when I am drafting in this manner, I want to draft as many undervalued assets as possible.

My biggest consideration when drafting for to win in future seasons is trade value. Not just my own trade value but how I perceive the market will treat them when I try to trade them. What is the point of drafting a veteran no other team will want when I am looking to trade them to contending teams? In this scenario, I continuously draft who I believe has the most trade value in every round.

All of these strategies "work" but the most important takeaway from this argument is to do the steps before ever thinking about which players you plan on drafting. Know your league, know yourself, and no half measures.

# Auction Strategies
By Justin Mason

## LIMA (Low Investment Mound Aces):

The LIMA plan, invented by Ron Shandler, is a bargain pitching strategy. In an auction league you would spend a total of $60 on pitching. Spend $20-30 on an elite closer and the rest of it on high strikeout starters or relievers. In a snake draft you would take a closer in the top 80 picks, one starter somewhere in the 100 and then not take another pitcher until late in the draft. The plan relies on your ability to identify undervalued guys or ones primed for a breakout. However, if you are good at identifying breakout pitchers, it is a great strategy.

## ZIMA (An Unfortunate Alcoholic Drink from the 90's):

Aside from the alcoholic beverage, this was a twist on Shandler's LIMA plan developed by Matthew Berry. In this adaptation, you still spend $200 on hitting, but instead of spending the $30 on a closer, you spend it on a high strikeout pitcher and you punt saves. In a draft you take a starter in the first two rounds or two in the first five rounds then ignore pitching. I actually prefer this one to the LIMA strategy. I think it is easier to pull off and comes with less risk.

## MRI Theory:

This strategy was developed by Pierre Becquey. In the strategy you draft or buy two elite high strikeout pitchers and then abandon starting pitchers for relievers. This allows you to cushion your ERA and WHIP while stacking up your offense. Then about halfway through your season you acquire starters through free agency or via trade to catch up in Wins and Strikeouts. While I have never attempted this strategy, it seems like it would be best served for deeper auction leagues.

## Labadini Plan:

This is a personal favorite of all the strategies. Named after Larry Labadini, who tried it in LABR in 1996, it calls for you to spend $251 on your offense and $1 each on all your pitchers or in a draft you draft only offense until you have filled up every offensive slot. I love this strategy because it is so unique. You will crush everyone in offense and hopefully get lucky with a $1 reliever that turns into a closer, then you can trade some offense for a starter or two to help catch up in some of the pitching stats because you should have a pretty great lead in offense by the halfway point. With the glut of starting pitchers these days, this is a fun out of the box idea.

## The Modified Labadini:

In this strategy you take the top pitcher in the pool, so Clayton Kershaw or in an AL only Chris Sale. Then you don't take another pitcher until you have filled all your offensive slots in a draft or spend only $1 on the rest in an auction. This gives you the best pitcher in the pool to anchor your staff while still giving you an amazing offense.

## The Volume Play:

This plan is sometimes called by a few different names like the Bernhard Plan (because it is so ugly, but it works), the Randy Bush (a former MLB role player), or the $20 Plan. The idea behind it is that in an AL or NL only auction instead of buying studs, don't spend more than $20 on any player but concentrate on getting the most at bats from your offensive players. That will allow you to spend more on pitching but still get enough offense to be near the top of each category. You have to play this one carefully and make sure you are buying a balanced team. This is the anti-"stars and scrubs" plan, but if you can fill up your offense with all the guys that are getting you at least 450 at bats the sheer volume should have you near the top of each counting category.

**Drowning the Pool:**

Now this is a strategy I don't really like, but it has been employed multiple times last season in two major expert mixed drafts LABR and Tout Wars, so I felt compelled to mention them.

**Positional:**

This strategy was employed in 2015 by Anthony Perri in the Mixed Tout Wars draft and by Mike Gianella and Brett Sayre in the Mixed LABR drafts. In both drafts the teams took the top two shortstops off the board with the 15th and 16th picks. The idea was to cause chaos with the rest of the field by taking the two best options of the most shallow position, therefore cornering the market. My main issue with this strategy is by attempting to corner the market both gave up value on their teams and that value was extracted by the other participants in the league. To employ a strategy that plays on positional scarcity seems short sighted and not to mention is way too focused on other's teams instead of their own. Gianella and Sayre won LABR, but it was not because of this strategy, it was because they nailed the middle rounds and had very good in season management.

**Categorical:**

This is where you drown a scarce category, like stolen bases. The issue with this is that the chances that they will be able to get full value for one of these players are minimal. The other is when you drown the pool of a category in a roto league it doesn't cause the panic one would think. Who cares if you get the most points in one category? Even if you are 50 steals ahead of second place, it is still just one more point in the standings.

# Snake Draft Strategies
By Ray Kuhn

Alright, we are here. It is draft day. So, now what?

First of all, and something tells me this isn't the case since you have already purchased our wonderful draft guide that is teeming with information, but your preparation should not be starting today. In fact, the preparation should be completed by this point as it should have begun weeks, or even months ago.

This isn't the time or place to discuss said preparation, but at a very high level, your research should have been done at this point. That means the following:

·     Either find a trusted source or projections or create your own. At any rate, this isn't just a mathematical exercise or a one-way street. Sure, that is the start of it, but it has to be interactive, and some tweaks are likely required.

·     But before you get to that point, do your research, and pore through each player and all of the available data.

·     Next, turn your projections into rankings, and then those rankings into positional tiers.

·     If there are keepers, we have to account for that, but this is the time to brush up on your league rules. Everything prior to the tiers is your general research, and should be done before even thinking about a real draft.

Now, we get into best practices for your specific snake draft. Aside from having your positional tiers of available players and knowing the settings, statistical targets are also pretty important. You know the parameters of the league and what you must consider, so how do you put it into practice?

Once your draft starts, the plan is gone. Any plan you could possibly have is pointless, and really should go right in the trash. But that doesn't mean you don't need a plan entering the draft. In fact, the complete opposite is true.

A plan is needed. But it can't be a single layered plan. Perhaps a seven-layer dip? You have to plan for the plan not to work, and to be blown pretty quickly. The nimbler you can be, the better.

We know that statistical targets that need to be hit, and there are multiple ways to get there. This is where tiering and knowing the player pool comes into play. For all the preparation and planning you can do, no two drafts are never going to be the same, and ADP isn't always going to be followed.

Essentially, each draft pick builds off the last, and it is a cumulative effect until your roster is built. How you reach your statistical targets doesn't really matter as long as each starting spot is filled. To do this, being proactive is required. You can't let the other owners dictate your draft or how you build your team, because that will never work out in the end. Now, that doesn't mean you should avoid a position run, but at the same time, don't reach and take a catcher or a closer two to three rounds earlier than you have them ranked just to follow the pack. If other owners are reaching, that means they are leaving value for you on the draft board.

Trying to spit out general strategy tips isn't practical, because it is all dependent. If I tell you to take a pitcher in the first round, and one of the top three outfielders (Mike Trout, Ronald Acuna, Christian Yelich) falls, you can't ignore them. We can go on and on with situations like this, but at the end of the day, be aware of your statistical targets, and follow the tiers.

That is the most critical part of draft strategy, as you have to know when the drop offs at each position are going to come, and where you are going to get your stolen bases, home runs, and other fantasy production from. But to do this, you really need to know the player pool.

Of all the players that will be drafted, let's be honest, there are some you just aren't interested in for one reason or another. Have different targets at each position and part of the draft, as that will help streamline your decision-making process.

And when it comes to actually sitting down at the draft table, computer, less is more. The time between picks is minimal, so be organized in order not to get bogged down.

We need to also keep in mind that the draft isn't just about the starting lineup. Proper bench construction is key and shouldn't be forgotten. Yes, all of the players you draft at this point will likely remain on your team all season, but that doesn't mean they can't. You want some upside, but not too many dart throws, versatility is key, as is depth, but the main thing is to maximize those bench spots.

If this article was vague, I apologize, but it was intentionally so. Preparation and being reactive are probably the most important things you can do. Have your cheat sheet ready to go with tiers and targets, and trust yourself. You have done your research, so have faith in it.

# Punting Categories
By Justin Mason

In fantasy football, punters are usually irrelevant. However, in fantasy baseball, punting can be a strategy that, if employed properly, can win leagues or at least throw off your opponents and their draft/auction values.

In a traditional rotisserie or head-to-head categories league, most people look to build a balanced roster. You tend to spread auction money and draft picks on different types of players to make sure you acquire enough of each of the category's statistics to be competitive in every category. For instance, let's say in your average 12-team 5x5 league the winner (on average) usually accumulates 100 total roto points. This would mean that in order to win, you would be targeting third place in each of the ten categories, if you employed a balanced approach.

However, when you punt a category, you flip the script. The premise is simple: if you ignore one category during your draft and auction you can load up on the others. So, instead of attempting to finish third in ten categories, you are looking to get a second in nine and the one point for last in the punted category. The strategy allows you to load up in the other categories without chasing another statistic. Obviously, this is a strategy that has a bit more risk as you really need to nail the other categories, but if implemented properly, punting can be a winning strategy that allows you to simplify your draft targets by eliminating one (or more) of the categories from your equations.

## Punting Saves

We all know the variance in saves from year to year. Closers are the most volatile position in fantasy baseball. It is estimated that in any given year about 40% of opening day closers lose their jobs. Punting saves in a draft allows you to put money in other places in your pitching staff and in your offense. You also should still draft relievers because they can fall into closing roles and help keep your ERA and WHIP down. Saves usually become available in every league. Whether it is because of people losing jobs or because there is always that one guy in every league that drafts too many closers, saves are usually easy to acquire after the draft.

## Punting Stolen Bases

2018 saw the fewest stolen bases in Major League Baseball since 1994. Combine that with the fact it coincided with the fourth largest home run totals in during that span and now we have a huge discrepancy in how stolen bases are valued in fantasy baseball. With prices rising, it may be more cost effective to punt saves than chase them. Punting stolen bases allows you to put those big dollars you would have used into players that can help you dominate other categories. If needed, the lack of stolen bases into today's game can allow you a chance to catch up by acquiring extreme speedsters via trade later on.

## Punting Average

Just like saves, average has a ton of variance from year to year. Guys who routinely have a certain average vary from year to year. For instance, Mike Moustakas' averages the last five years have been: .212, .284, .240, .272, .251. Good luck trying to project his average for this year correctly. This strategy takes that variance out of the equation. In this process you devalue batting average. The plan is not to finish last however, but stack up on the other categories while hopefully allowing the variance in average to place you somewhere in the middle third of that category. However, punting on base percentage, while it can be done, is a riskier proposition. It can be harder to compete in runs and sometimes stolen bases when you punt OBP. Typically when you punt average, you look for those low average, but high OBP guys (i.e. Chris Davis, Steven Souza) to make sure you are getting guys who can get on base so that way they have the ability to score some runs in spite of the lower averages.

## Punting Wins

Wins is my least favorite category to punt that I will actually do. While wins are fluky, they can be a hard category to make up for without hurting your ratio categories. For the most part I don't really project out wins to begin with and devalue them in my rankings and dollar values. It can be done, but I believe it to be the riskiest of the four most commonly punted categories to pull off.

Now for the truly risk and a bit insane, here are a couple of versions that can be fun to employ, involve a ton of skill, but can be difficult to pull off:

## The Double Punt

The idea is simple. Punt two categories that have no correlation (i.e. Batting Average and Saves.) This allows you to really stock up in the other categories and either giving you the opportunity later trade for them or allow the variance of ratios to work themselves out hopefully in a favorable way. While I have used this strategy with success in a few different formats, it is hard to employ. I reserve it most for H2H leagues or in mono keeper leagues where the majority of established closers will be kept by others.

## The Sweeney Plan

This plan is a variation of The Double Punt, but it calls to punt two linked categories traditionally home runs and RBIs, ERA and WHIP, or even stolen bases and Average. In all of these approaches you would really have to nail the other eight categories and even if you do, it may not be enough to outright win your league. Any missteps or major injuries would destroy your season, thus this strategy is too risky for me.

Now these strategies all add a degree of difficulty to your draft or auction, but don't forget they can throw off your opponents. A good fantasy player tracks what their opposition still needs and how much they are likely to spend on any given category of position. So, by punting something, you throw off their values. For example, if an owner in a 12-team league thinks on average each opponent is going to spend around $78 (30% of a $260 budget) on pitching and $25 on closers for a total of $300 of $936 for the entire pitching part of the auction, if you can move that $25 somewhere else in reduces what the value for each closer should have been and increases the value of where that money ends up without the other owners knowing that it is happening, which gives you a strategic advantage.

# Stats for Dummies
## By Matthew Simmons

No sport is as attached to measuring itself as baseball is. There are statistics for everything you can think of. Major league teams have entire departments devoted to not only dissecting the stats we have now, but creating new ones that measure aspects of a players game that were not even thought of 30 years ago.

If you have played fantasy baseball before and want to get into deeper stats, or if you dominated your football league last winter and got pulled into baseball for the first time, this is your place to learn more about the numbers we tend to look at throughout the course of the season. If you are still figuring out the difference between plate appearances and at-bats, or if you want to know what those Statcast and Fangraphs columns mean, read on and hopefully you will see your ability to analyze players grow.

We will first hit some of the absolute basics, skipping categories like HR, but quickly explaining the difference between things like R and RBI or AVG and OBP. Then we will take a look at some of the MLB Statcast metrics found on the baseball savant page. Then we will dive into the deep end and break down some stats you can find on the Fangraphs website (side note: if you are not using Fangraphs for your player analysis, you are leaving wins/points on the table).

## Baseball Basics

So this is your first foray into fantasy baseball. You are a casual fan and know that a .300 average is really good, but don't necessarily know why a .295 OBP is not. This is the place for you. In this section we will be breaking down a few of the statistical categories you will come across in many if not most fantasy leagues, skipping some counting stats like HR and SB. Those basic statistical categories are usually defined on the web platform you are using.

Which leads me to my first quick definitions. Statistical categories are often referred to as either counting stats (HR, SB, R, RBI, W, QS, Sv, H, K's) or rate stats (AVG, OBP, ERA, WHIP, K%, K/9). The difference being that the counting stats simply count how many times an event happens, i.e. Babe Ruth hit a home run 714 times. Rate stats are ones in which something is calculated, i.e. Babe Ruth had a career batting average of .342.

The second quick definition we need to know before going on deals with the difference between an at-bat (AB) and a plate appearance (PA). An at bat happens when a player comes to the plate and gets a hit or an out, so long as that is not a sacrifice. Sacrifice hits, walks, hit by a pitch, and interferences do not count as an at-bat. A plate appearance counts every time the player comes to the plate.

The most basic reading of baseball stats that has been around for decades is the triple slash, or slash line. It is made up of a player's batting average, on-base percentage and slugging percentage. When written down it looks something like this .315/.364/.463

The first stat we will cover is basic for most, and is the first number in the slash line. **Batting average** (Avg) is how many hits a player gets per at-bat. This is the standard stat that has been mainstream for over 100 years.

**On-base percentage** (OBP) is different in that it counts all plate appearances, including walks. If you are playing in an OBP league you need to remember that a player that has a .300 OBP is actually below average because you are counting hits and walks. The MLB average has hovered around .320 for the last decade.

**Slugging Percentage** (SLG) or sometimes called a players slug is his total bases divided by at bats. Similar to batting average, except all hits in batting average count as 1 towards the total divided by at bats, where as slug counts every base touched by the batter in the hit. Slugging is sometimes confused for a power stat since it requires the ball to get deep in the outfield to garner more bases. However, power is not as important as speed for triples and stretching the occasional single to a double. Meaning it is more of a jumping off point to look at a players overall skill set.

**ISO** is isolated power, or the average of extra base hits. Usually measured as SLG-AVG.

**Runs Batted In** (RBI) vs. **Runs** (R) can be a little confusing for someone new to baseball. Runs are the number of times a player crosses the plate to score a run. RBI is the runs scored as a result of a player's at bat. For example, if player A is on second and player B hits one to far right field the man on second may score, resulting in an RBI for player B and a run for player A. Now if player C comes up and hits one to left as well then player B can get a run.

An important thing to remember when building your team is that a leadoff hitter may score a lot of runs, but will likely be somewhat limited in RBI since he will either be the first batter of the inning, or come up following the bottom of the order. Either way it is less likely he will have men on base to drive in than others in the batting order.

On the pitching side we have a few stats that the baseball newbie might get a little confused with.

**Wins** (W) Traditionally, to qualify for a win a starting pitcher must go 5 innings, leave with the lead and not have the lead lost by the bullpen. With the use of the opener by teams like Tampa Bay this has changed a little, but still mostly holds true.

**Quality Start** (QS) To qualify for a quality start a starting pitcher must go at least 6 innings and give up no more than 3 runs.

The difference between the two stats is that QS is not reliant on the team scoring runs, which has made it a popular choice to use as a category in fantasy leagues over the last decade. Of course, with so many starters getting less work in the modern game it can sometimes be frustrating when your guy goes 5 ⅔ innings of scoreless work and gets pulled.

**Saves** (SV) have been the measure of a reliever for decades and are awarded if a pitcher finishes a game in relief, entering with a lead of no more than 3 and not relinquishing said lead.

**Holds** (HLD) are a newer stat we use in fantasy to give middle relievers some more value. The definition of a hold is the same as a save except the pitcher does not finish the game. Most leagues that use holds will just combine them with saves, though more and more we are seeing the category weighted to value saves more, i.e. HLD + SV2 or SV + HLD/2.

**Be a Statcast Savant**

The modern statistical revolution has gifted us a treasure trove of info we never had before. MLB has a place for some of those new measurements found at baseballsavant.mlb.com, commonly referred to as Statcast, the Statcast page as well as Baseball Savant. The following are some useful stats to look at when breaking down a player, or looking to see who is performing well at the moment. One thing to remember is when you are looking at a graph or chart on Statcast you will notice a color code. Blue means bad and red means good and unhighlighted means average. The darker the color the more extreme.

Many of the Baseball Savant stats are relatively easy to figure out while looking at the charts. A players Hard Hit Rate is a measure of how many hits left the bat at or above 95 mph, which is of course good for hitters and bad for pitchers. Others are not quite as straightforward, or at least could use some clarification as to how they can fit into fantasy analysis.

**Exit Velocity** is one that is pretty straightforward in definition, it is the speed in which the ball leaves the bat. How it affects outcomes is a little different though. Common sense says a hitter wants more exit velocity and a pitcher wants less. However, this doesn't mean a lighter hitter will have to hit less home runs. In 2019 Victor Robles was dead last among qualified hitters with an average exit velo of 81 mph. Only 14 spots better was Jose Altuve with a light breeze of an 86.1 mph exit velo... and 31 home runs. In the same way more exit velocity does not equal homeruns. Nick Markakis did not get enough at bats to be a qualified hitter, but if he had his 91.2 mph average would have made him top 25 and all it got him was 9 home runs in over 400 at bats. The difference comes in part from the next stat.

**Launch Angle** is at what angle the ball leaves the bat. While the Baseball Savant page gives amazing definitions on what launch angles are and which ones are the best, the dumbed down version is that there is a goldilocks zone that keeps the ball high enough not to ground out, but low enough not to pop up.

**Barrels** is the name of that goldilocks zone. It starts with a ball hit at least 98 mph with a launch angle between 26-30 degrees. As the velocity increases so does the range for acceptable degrees. Barrels have a minimum batting average of .500 and a slugging of 1.500. Why am I telling you this basic definition that the folks over at Baseball Savant have defined themselves? Because it is that important. Barrels are an amazing tool for a quick rundown of players who are getting great contact. If you are short on time and want to see who is making quality contact this is the place to go. If you want to do some deep research on players, but don't want to waste time on every Joe out there, this is where you can start.

**Sprint Speed** can be a tricky stat. It is the average feet per second in the players fast one second of a play. When looking at the chart it is obviously a rank of who has the best wheels. Remember, this does not equate directly to stolen bases. There will always be players who are absolute jack rabbits in the field who are average to mediocre base stealers just as every once in a while there is a guy with no range in the field who can lead his team in steals. Sprint speed also obviously does not take into account a team's philosophy on base stealing. If the coach doesn't send a guy he can't swipe a bag. It can be used as a clue as to why a player may not be stealing as much in a season as it can show if he has lost a step due to age or injury. It also is just fun to look over now and again.

**Expected Stats** or *\*Xstats** are a useful tool to gauge if a player is over or underperforming in a certain category and are usually designated by placing an x in front of a stat. (i.e. xSLG, xERA, xBA) They work by taking in all the measurements like pitch velocity, exit velo and the like to determine what was likely to happen when compared to historical instances that fit the same criteria. I know, it sounds like voodoo math, but the xstats usually hold pretty close to the real life averages. For example, in 2019 the MLB batting average was .252 and the expected average was .250. The miniscule .002 difference in batting average and expected average shows that overall we can predict with some accuracy what the end result should be for a player.

Sometimes though, a player's numbers will begin to deviate. If that is the case it is a sign to look deeper. Is a player's expected average significantly higher than his real average? Maybe he is coming back from a long injury, or happened to face a couple of ace pitchers with solid defenses behind them recently. Such a player might be a buy low candidate. How about when a player's numbers are reversed? When his real average is dominating his expected numbers it could be a sign that some regression is coming and you may want to trade him while the value is high.

None of the Baseball Savant Statcast numbers should be taken as the only piece of info needed on a player. However, when looked at as a whole they give a massive picture on why a player is doing what he is doing.

*Xstats, for some, has become a shorthand for expected stats and should not be confused with the old site xstats.org, which was run by Andrew Perpetua, before he was stolen away from us in the public realm by the Mets front office.

### Find it on Fangraphs

First off, I know, a lot of this is not Fangraphs exclusive, but it is a great source to find them all in one place. Second, like on baseball savant, none of these are the stats you will use as categories in your league unless you have accidently stumbled into some oddball specialty league. They are however invaluable tools to help sift through players who are underperforming, overperforming, about to break out, or close to cratering.

A couple of these first few stats you may know, but we will go over as they will be needed for the rest of the stats.

**BABIP** stands for Batting Average of Balls In Play, or the batting average of only the balls hit into the field of play. This means everything from strikeouts to home runs are not counted. Only batted balls which have to be fielded. To over simplify things, this number can be used as a measure of luck. When you see a player with an outlier number, up or down, it is likely they will show some regression back towards the mean. There are some exceptions that make BABIP not the end all of luck. For instance, an incredibly speedy player can have a higher BABIP since his wheels allow him to outrun an infield hit. While babip can show if a player has been lucky, it is not a strictly luck stat

*For pitchers*, BABIP can show when a pitcher has had some bad luck in the field, inflating his ERA and giving hope of some positive regression. On the other hand, it may mean he is pitching in front of a horrendous defense and has less room for improvement.

**BACON** stands for Batting Average on Contact. So, it's BABIP, but with home runs added. I like to say BACON makes everything better, and for the hitter it does. A player like Judge or Stanton will hit enough home runs over the course of a healthy season to significantly outpace their BABIP. The same goes for some pitchers who likes to give up the long ball. Both units have their place in research though.

**wOBA** is the Weighted On Base Average. It combines the aspects of a plate appearance in a weighted format. To over simplify, it takes the components of the triple slash and combines them according to impact on run values (another can of statistical worms we will not cover in this chapter). Basically, imagine a somewhat better barometer of a hitter than just batting average or OBP alone, making it a good tab to sort by when starting your research.

**wRC+** stands for Weighted Runs Created Plus. The simplest way to understand it is take wOBA and add in park factors making an even more precise number. wRC+ works on a scale with 100 being league average.

**GB%, FB%, LD%** refers to the percentage of Ground Balls, Fly Balls, and Line Drives a player hits. Generally speaking, a player doesn't want too many ground balls unless he is a speedster that can beat the throw to first. In the same way, a player doesn't want too many fly balls unless he is a masher that can get it out of the park. Line drives are the sweet spot that usually produce the best batting averages for all types of hitters. *For pitchers*, These rates basically work in reverse. You do not want to see your pitcher having a high line drive rate as that will raise his WHIP and most likely his ERA. The best thing for a pitcher is to have a high GB% as that will also suppress the ISO he gives up as well. Some pitchers can live with a high FB% if they are also good at suppressing their HR/FB rate.

**GB/FB** is the rate of Ground Balls hit to Fly Balls. This useful tool gives you a look into players who can get the ball in the air, meaning more chances for home runs. The caveat to this is some players who normally have warning track power have been trying to lift the ball more since the ball has changed, resulting in some crazy power spikes. GB/FB rates over the course of the last several seasons may help you to know why a player has spiked, and possibly identify players who could spike if they just adjust their rate.
*For pitchers* you really want to see a higher rate of ground balls as it will limit extra base hits, including home runs.

**HR/FB** is the rate at which a player's Fly Balls turn into Home Runs. The top power hitters in the game usually have rates around 25% and up. Sometimes, there is a worry that players with high percentages are due for regression. This is especially true when it is a player we are not used to hitting the long ball. That is a possibility, however, you also have to take into account possible changes in the ball and a change of scenery. Christian Yelich had a spike when he moved from Miami to Milwaukee. This makes total sense though as Miami is a noted pitchers park that suppresses home runs. Jose Altuve had a massive spike this year, going from a career average of 9.5% to 23.3%. He is an example of a player you would want to look deeper as to why this spike happened. Of course Altuve is on a Hall of Fame trajectory, so I say all of this as an example, I'm not worried about his hitting profile going forward.

*For pitchers* this is an important number. Some pitchers have a skill at suppressing home runs, allowing them to give up more fly balls, but turning them into pop ups. Although, it should not be assumed that a pitcher with a high HR/FB is a bad pitcher. A quick look at the 2019 standings shows names like Garrett Cole, Clayton Kershaw, Stephen Strasburg, Justin Verlander, Shane Bieber and Luis Castillo all in the top 20 highest rates. Thats 20% of the top 20 that either already have a Cy Young award or will likely come close to one in the next 5 years. So what does the ratio tell us? It can be a reason as to why a pitcher's ERA is oddly high or low, hopefully helping you decide if a change is going to stick.

**IFFB** is the Infield Fly Ball rate. You do not want your players high on this list. It is the measure of how often a player pops up to the infield. This is the list where you see guys who need to lower their launch angle because an infield fly is almost as bad as a strikeout. Also, remember when we talked about players who may have a low babip regressing back up to their peers? A player with a high IFFB rate is not as likely to have that positive regression as they are giving up to many easy outs.

*For pitchers* it's simple. You want in field fly balls as they are simple pop ups that are almost a guaranteed out.

**Pull%, Cent%, Opp%** are references to a batters directional tendencies when he makes contact. Normally, it is easier to hit a homerun to the pull side, but guys that hit that way too much are often times candidates for defensive shifts.

*For pitchers* this can help show if a particular pitcher has an exaggerated lefty/righty split. This could be useful if your pitcher has an upcoming game against a team that he might not be able to handle as well, giving you the opportunity to bench him for a better option. It could also hint at a pitcher's defense letting him down and the need for the manager to tinker with the shift for him.

**Soft%, Med%, Hard%** refers to the quality of contact for a hitter as measured by hangtime, trajectory, and landing spot. These Fangraphs metrics do not take into account exit velocity. However, they are still a great tool for finding a good hitter. Especially one who's babip may actually be just bad luck. As a general rule, you want more Hard% and less Soft%.

*For pitchers* it is kind of obvious. The softer the better. A pitcher who allows more hard contact will usually have a higher HR/FB rate and BABIP, and will not necessarily regress back down.

**O-Swing% & Z-Swing%** refer to percentages of swings at pitches outside of the zone (O) and inside the zone (Z). Obviously, it is better to lay off pitches outside of the zone and to swing at pitches inside the zone. These numbers do seem to be better at looking back than they do looking ahead, but if you have a guy going through a slump you can look back and see if there has been any changes. Conversely, if a mediocre guy is on a hot streak, you can see if this is something sustainable or if it is likely just a flash in the pan.

*For pitchers* a swing out of the zone is usually good. It means the pitcher is getting batters to chase pitches that aren't usually hitable. Generating swings in the zone could go either way. A pitcher could be fooling guys with deceptive movement, or he could just be tossing in cantaloupes.

**O-Contact% & Z-Contact%** is the percent of times contact is made one the swings mentioned above. Very similar in usefulness to the swing numbers, it can also highlight a batter who has that odd knack for hitting the outside pitch. Which doesn't make him more valuable, but makes a high O-Swing% less detrimental.

*For pitchers* contact out of the zone is usually good as pitches out of the zone are often times harder to make good contact with, generating fouls, ground balls and pop ups. So a high O-contact can sometimes be a good thing. Contact in the zone usually means you are giving up hits of some kind. Yes, a good pitcher can still induce weak contact in the zone, so be sure to look at that. However, as you will see in a simple search, there are not many good pitchers with a high rate. In 2019, of the top 20 highest O-contact rates only 4 pitchers were below a 3.50 ERA, while another 3 had ERA's over 5.00

**FIP** is Fielding Independent Pitching, which is an attempt to measure ERA based solely on things the pitcher does. So it takes into account hit by pitch, walks, strikeouts and home runs and ignores all other outs and hits, giving a snapshot of what happened when the pitcher was responsible for the outcome. This number can help with identifying what a pitcher's true talent should be when compared to his ERA. For example, Jose Quintana had a 4.68 ERA in 2019 versus a 3.80 FIP. You may want to look deeper at his games and the defense around him to see if there might be some positive regression ahead. On the other side of the coin, Mike Soroka posted a 2.68 ERA and a 3.45 FIP. You would want to look deeper into his numbers to see if he was the beneficiary of good defense or good luck or something else that may leave him regressing to a higher ERA in the coming season.

**SIERA** stands for Skill Interactive ERA and is similar to FIP in that it tries to find a pitchers true talent ERA, but different in that it also tries to limit park factors and allows for some batted ball data. In SIERA, pitchers who have higher GB% and FB% will get a bump as these skills can usually lead to quicker outs.

**K/9, BB/9, H/9, HR/9** are all pretty obvious. They are the rate of Strikeouts, Walks, Hits, and Home Runs per 9 innings accumulated by the pitcher. You want K to be as high as possible and the rest to be as low as possible. Remember, a pitcher with a high K rate will not only be affecting your strikeouts category, but it will also suppress your ERA and WHIP. On the same token, high numbers in the other three stats will inflate ERA and WHIP.

**K% & BB%** are the percentage of Strikeouts and Walks a pitcher earns. Very similar to the above in its use for fantasy, expressed as a percentage of the whole instead of a per 9 inning rate.

**K/BB** is the ratio of strikeouts to walks for the pitcher. This direct comparison of non-batted ball outcomes is a good indicator of control for a pitcher.

**WAR** is an all encompassing number that stands for Wins Above Replacement. It is a backwards looking attempt to quantify every aspect of a players game. It can be really fun to sort by and look over, but at best it has near zero value in evaluating a player in fantasy baseball. It would be much easier to look at any number of top 500 fantasy player lists that will have at least as much value as WAR if not much more. If you are paying enough attention to buy this book, then you are paying enough attention for WAR to be useless to you.

There are very few stats that can be taken 100% on their own to determine if you should roster a certain player or not. However, I hope that this has helped you to understand some of the mountains of information available to you and also to understand what someone is saying when you read an article or listen to a podcast about fantasy baseball this season. If you come across a stat that is not listed above and get confused, don't be afraid to ask. Reach out to any of us at Friends With Fantasy Benefits and we would love to help.

## Using Expected Stats
### By Dylan White

With the advent of publicly available StatCast data, fantasy baseball analysis has been afforded brand new tools. Rather than diving deep into sprint speed or xwOBA, in this article I will explore the underlying metrics for a pitcher's K%-BB%.

Pitcher K%-BB%

Whether we are fantasy baseball novices or experts, K%-BB% is a key metric that most of us look at, whether we know it or not. Not only are strikeouts a category in most leagues, but most predictive ERA indicators (such as SIERA or FIP) are derived directly from K% and BB%. (And for dynasty leagues, Bill James as early as the late 1980s showed that one of the best predictors of whether a pitcher would have longevity was correlated to their strikeout to walk rate ratio.) In other words, this is one of the key metrics that we should be looking at for pitchers.

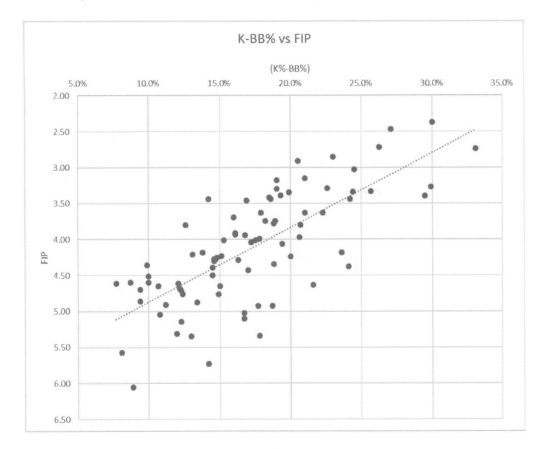

Running a quick correlation, we see that there is a 0.65 correlation between K%-BB% and a combination of z-Con%, SwStrk%, and O-Sw% (for pitchers with more than 70 innings pitched in 2019). I will call this "*expected K%-BB%*". For those of you mathematically inclined, the formula for "expected K%-BB%" is 0.26 − 0.44*z-Con% + 1.01*SwStrk% + 0.49*O-Sw%

Comparing the actual K%-BB% for 2019 and the expected K%-BB%, we can potentially find some pitchers who underperformed their K%-BB% (and who, perhaps, the projections are therefore under-projecting).

I took the top 45 starting pitchers in 2019 (by K%-BB%) and the top 45 starting pitchers (by expected K%-BB%) and looked at the difference between the two statistics.

Pitchers who will perhaps are being undervalued

There were ten (10) pitchers who threw a minimum of 70 innings and were not in the top 45 of K%-BB% but *were* in the top 45 of expected K%-BB%. Some of these pitchers had their role change in 2019 between the rotation and the bullpen, and hence their underlying metrics are potentially misleading (or exaggerated because they can 'air out' when in the bullpen). Therefore, I removed Kevin Gausman, Kenta Maeda, Trevor Richards, and Elieser Hernandez from the analysis and examined the following pitchers:

**Caleb Smith** (16.7 K%-BB%, 20.1% expected K%-BB% [14th]).

The Marlin 'ace' started off extremely strong in 2019 with a 3.50 ERA in the first half. Unfortunately, the second half wasn't kind to Smith as he tossed a 5.42 ERA, leading to an overall season ERA of 4.52 (which was around 50th best, had he thrown enough innings to qualify). According to his full year's underlying peripherals, however, he was "expected to have" the 14th best K%-BB% among starting pitchers. That intrigues me. Don't be surprised if he out-earns his projections of, per Steamer, a 4.57 ERA in 2020).

**Chris Archer** (16.7 K%-BB%, 18.8% expected K%-BB% [22nd])

The pitcher who will likely be plagued for the rest of his career as being associated with one of the worst real life baseball trades of all time (having been traded for Tyler Glasnow, Austin Meadows and Shane Baz) actually was unlucky last year before being shut down with a shoulder issue. In 2016, Archer had a K%-BB% close to last year's expected K%-BB% and ended 2016 with a 4.02 ERA. This would have been a much more palatable outcome than the 5.19 mark he actually put up last year. The Pirates must agree (or don't understand sunk costs) as they picked up his 2020 option.

**Dylan Bundy** (14.9 K%-BB%, 18.3% expected K%-BB% [26th])

The former Oriole is getting some helium after he was moved to the Los Angeles Angels. Rather than just chalking any potential 2020 improvement to the change of scenery, his 2019 expected K%-BB% was higher than any K%-BB% he has ever had in his career. In other words, it could be argued that Bundy "should" have had his best year in 2019. Looking over his career, that would mean that he easily could have bested his career best 4.02 ERA as opposed to the 4.79 he did hurl. Color me intrigued.

**Kyle Gibson** (14.6 K%-BB%, 17.9% expected K%-BB% [30th])

Another pitcher who changed scenery, the former Twin also should have outperformed his 2019. Just like Bundy, had his 2019 K%-BB% actually met his expected K%-BB%, it would have been the highest mark he has ever thrown in his career. Again, that implies he theoretically 'should have' bested his career best 3.62 ERA from 2018. Judging from Lance Lynn and Mike Minor's 2019 performances, the Texas Rangers' major league pitching coaching seems to be able to extract high performance from their crew. Could Gibson be the next one to follow suit?

Others: **Eduard Rodriguez** (17.7% expK%-BB%) and **Joe Musgrove** (17.3% expK%-BB%)

Pitchers who are potentially being overvalued

There were seven (7) starting pitchers whose K%-BB% was in the top 45 but fell out of the top 45 when ranked by expected K%-BB%. Perhaps, they are not as good as we superficially think?

**David Price** (21.0 K%-BB% [18th], 15.8% expected K%-BB%)

Just by looking at Price's 21.0% K%-BB% – his highest since 2014 and good enough for 18th of all 2019 SPs who threw a minimum of 70 IP – many pundits are calling for a partial return to form for the once dominant Ray ace. As part of the argument, they argue that his FIP and xFIP were 3.62 and 3.73 respectively. I urge caution, however, as his expected K%-BB% was actually outside of the top 45 (and the lowest he would have put up since 2010). Drafters seem to agree, as his ADP puts him as a SP4, despite projections having him as an SP3.

**German Marquez** (19.4 K%-BB% [24th], 17.0% expected K%-BB%)

Last year's popular sleeper frustrated many owners as he finished with a 4.76 ERA. Those expecting a bounceback in 2020 may be disappointed as positive regression isn't baked in, judging from his underlying metrics.

**Sonny Gray** (19.3 K%-BB% [25th], 13.6% expected K%-BB%)

Sonny Gray helped many owners in 2019 by putting up a 2.87 ERA, good enough for 7th in the league. A lot of that could likely be attributed to his K%-BB% rate. Note though that his expected K%-BB% rate for 2019 was 13.6%, which incidentally closely matches his 13.8% career rate. In other words, don't be surprised if his 2020 ERA is closer to his career ERA of 3.53 than the scintillating numbers he put up last year in Cincinnati. Steamer has him going into his age 30 season underperforming his career numbers and hurling a 3.90 ERA but recent December ADP has him as the 31st starting pitcher off the board. That's a bit too rich for me.

Others: **Zack Greinke** (15.7% expK%-BB%), **Trevor Bauer** (16.3% expK%-BB%), **Madison Bumgarner** (16.8% expK%-BB%), and **Max Fried** (15.3% exp K%-BB%).

Hitters (OPS and deserved OPS)
The single best statistic to capture a hitter's production is OPS. It is more closely correlated to fantasy production than even wOBA or wRC. Therefore, if we could find hitters who had either "deserved" OPS that were higher than their actual, we could potentially find sleepers for next

year or potential breakouts. Conversely, those who overperformed their deserved OPS, would suggest that they may not meet their 2020 projections.

To investigate further, using Excel, I took 2019 hitters (with a minimum of 200 PAs) and found that the best descriptive correlation to OPS (with an $R^2$ of 0.72) could be found with a combination of HR/FB, BB%, K%, GB%, and Hard%. Intuitively this makes sense as BB% contributes to OBP, HR/FB is an indicator of home run rate (which obviously provides the best 'bang for buck' for slugging percentage). We also know that how hard a batter hits the ball is correlated to slugging percentage and that hitting fly balls (ie the launch angle revolution – which is highly correlated to groundball rate) is desired.

The descriptive formula for 'deserved' OPS was:
**deservedOPS = 1.01 x HR/FB – 0.23 x GB% + 0.31 x Hard% + 0.52 x BB% - 0.86 x K% + 0.730**

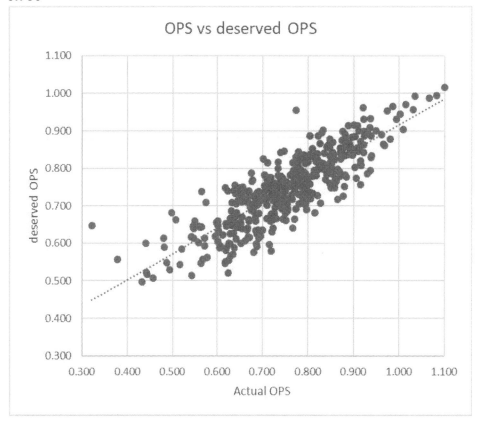

One way to think of it is that you start with an OPS of 0.730 and move the needle upward based on your BB%, Hard%, and HR/FB (with walk rate being slightly more 'important' than Hard hit rate, and HR/FB being twice as important as walk rate) and downward based on groundball rate and strikeout rate (with strikeout rate being three times more important than groundball rate).

The first thing that jumps out is that the most significant component of OPS is *home run per flyball* rate. Although this makes complete sense – the batters that hit the most home runs per flyball would obviously have a high slugging percentage – it is also unsatisfying. For one, we know that this regresses toward the batter's career mean every year and is often thought of as a "luck" stat. Saying "the guy who hit a lot of home runs had good offensive numbers is clearly not #Analysis. However, what if we went one layer further and derived a *deserved* HR/FB?

Essentially performing the same steps as for OPS, we find that HR/FB is again highly correlated ($R^2$ of 0.72) to Launch Angle, Pull%, Velocity (on fly balls and line drives), and Barrels/PA. Again, this makes complete sense that a combination of launch angle, velocity on balls in the air and the rate at which the batter is barreling the ball would all contribute to a hitter's HR/FB rate.

The deserved HR/FB formula is described by:
**deservedHR/FB = 0.019 x Brl/PA + 0.0054 x V(fb+LD) + 0.149 x Pull% - 0.003 x LA – 0.47.**

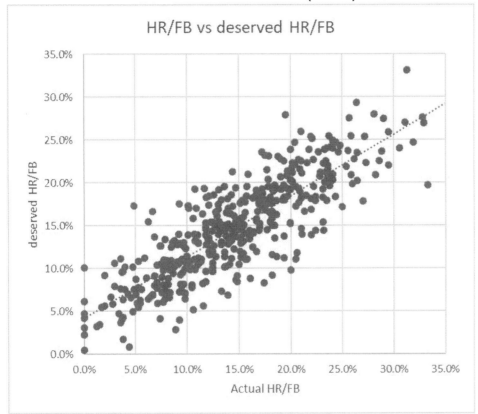

Now that I have a variable whose luck component has been normalized out, I can then plug this variable into "HR/FB" within the deserved OPS formula above in order to compare a hitter's actual 2019 OPS with what the underlying metrics (of Exit Velocity$_{FLYBALLS+LINEDRIVES}$, Barrels-per-PA, Pull%, GB%, Launch Angle, etc.) suggest his "deserved" OPS could/should have been.

For ease of understanding of the analysis, instead of just comparing OPS to deserved OPS (e.g. 0.780 vs 0.813), I sorted OPS and deserved OPS into *percentiles*. This (to me) seems like a better way to see where a hitter's OPS and underlying OPS fell within the context of the pool of players. If a player's OPS suggests he is in the 90th percentile and his deserved OPS is in the 95th percentile, it is not that large of a jump (even if the absolute value of the OPS change is large). But if he was in the 50th percentile (league average) and his deserved OPS was in the 90th percentile, this gets my attention.

Without further ado, here are some hand-plucked players whose actual OPS underperformed their deserved OPS. I consider these hitters as potential sleepers for 2020 who have a high likelihood of exceeding their projections.

Hitting Sleepers (based on deserved OPS)

**Marcell Ozuna**: actual OPS of 0.804 (65th percentile), dsvOPS of 0.917 (98th percentile)
**C.J. Cron**: actual OPS of 0.780 (55th percentile), dsvOPS of 0.887 (93rd percentile)
**Yandy Diaz**: actual OPS of 0.816 (68th percentile), dsvOPS of 0.879 (93rd percentile)
**Eddie Rosario**: actual OPS of 0.800 (64th percentile), dsvOPS of 0.854 (88th percentile)

This is a cluster of hitters whose 2019 OPS production was in the middle 'glob' (within one standard deviation of 'average'). However, their underlying peripherals suggest that they are actually elite hitters.

**Jason Castro**: actual OPS of 0.767 (49th percentile), dsvOPS of 0.850 (87th percentile)
**Albert Pujols**: actual OPS of 0.734 (34th percentile), dsvOPS of 0.844 (84th percentile)
**Jake Lamb**: actual OPS of 0.676 (16th percentile), dsvOPS of 0.823 (77th percentile)
**Danny Jansen**: actual OPS of 0.640 (9th percentile), dsvOPS of 0.783 (61st percentile)
**Jurickson Profar**: actual OPS of 0.711 (27th percentile), dsvOPS of 0.824 (78th percentile)

The hitters in this group all had below average (sometimes **well** below average) OPS's but whose batted ball profiles all suggest they should have had above average offensive projection. I think we all expect a bounce back from Profar and Jansen but this provides some of the justification behind it. Don't count them out just yet. And perhaps the Diamondbacks shouldn't write off Lamb either.

Hitters to Potentially Avoid (based on OPS vs deserved OPS):

Now for the depressing flipside of players who overperformed their OPS, based on their underlying peripherals.

**Tim Anderson**: actual OPS of 0.865 (82nd percentile), dsvOPS of 0.671 (15th percentile)
**Danny Santana**: actual OPS of 0.857 (80th percentile), dsvOPS of 0.732 (35th percentile)

Yikes. I think we all expected last year's American League batting champ to regress (mostly citing his unsustainable 0.399 BABIP) but this suggests an even more significant regression is in the cards. His deserved OPS for 2019 was actually in the bottom 15% of the league! I know that I will be avoiding him – despite the ~20 SBs that helps cushion the blow.

Danny Santana is another one who broadly outperformed expectations. If the question is whether I think he has taken a step forward to another talent level and can therefore sustain this level of performance into 2020, my answer is sadly that he likely will not.

**Bo Bichette**: actual OPS of 0.930 (94th percentile), dsvOPS of 0.741 (40th percentile)
**Keston Hiura**: actual OPS of 0.938 (95th percentile), dsvOPS of 0.757 (49th percentile)

**Fernando Tatis Jr.**: actual OPS of 0.969 (97$^{th}$ percentile), dsvOPS of 0.788 (63$^{rd}$ percentile)

I don't mean to be a party pooper and take some of the luster off of these new favorite things, but these rookies – who were all in the elite percentile of production – "actually" should have been somewhere in the middle of the pack (to varying degrees). Don't get me wrong: these hitters are above average and will no doubt have long productive careers. However, don't be surprised if their 2020 doesn't live up to your sky high expectations.

**Kevin Newman**: actual OPS of 0.800 (64$^{th}$ percentile), dsvOPS of 0.695 (21$^{st}$ percentile)
**Bryan Reynolds**: actual OPS of 0.880 (85$^{th}$ percentile), dsvOPS of 0.757 (50$^{th}$ percentile)

These two Pittsburgh Pirates are trendy names for 2020 as they broke out last year and are expected to continue to be full time regulars under the new Pirate regime. Unfortunately, they appear to actually be below-average to average hitters. Newman especially, seems poised to disappoint.

Takeaways
The beauty of this analysis is not just that you have some names to have before your draft. For those of us with the time and energy, within the season we can calculate some 'deserved' OPS's of hitters to see who is under or over performing. This should help you with potential trades or waiver wire add/drops.

# Trading
By Justin Mason

We all remember our best and worst trades. Trading is a huge part of fantasy sports and often a badge of honor we tote around our leagues. However, every league has THAT GUY. You know him, the one that no one wants to trade with for a variety of reasons. I want to help you not be "that guy." So, here are my 10 Rules for Trading.

## 1) Trading is a Relationship

When trading with a partner, it is important to remember that you are attempting to seduce the other person. Be gentle at first and turn it up a notch when need be. Make your partner feel like you are looking out for their needs as well as your own. Don't be greedy. Taking advantage of them only works out once. Don't publicly brag with your buddies that won a trade. It could embarrass the other party. If you get a bad reputation as a selfish trader, you may find yourself without a partner later on. Always cuddle after.

## 2) Win Your League, Not the Trade

In a poker tournament , when someone else is all-in, the proper strategy is to stop betting unless you hit an unbeatable hand. The rationale being that the end goal is to be the last man standing in the tournament, not win every hand. You have a better chance to do that with less people in the tournament. The same can be applied for fantasy. I know everyone wants to win every single trade, but sometimes you don't need to win. The objective is to win the championship. Your league mates may think it is dumb to trade Giancarlo Stanton for Dee Gordon, but if you have a surplus of power and speed puts you over the top, then it's a move you have to make. Don't be afraid to give too much, if you think it guarantees you a championship.

## 3) Know Your Opponents

Some people like to haggle. Some people don't have the time. Some people always want the best player in a deal. Some love prospects. Knowing what each person in your league values gives you a leg up in negotiations. Something I started doing this year is keeping a folder in my email of all trade offers I have made and received. It allows me to go back and see what players my league mates have been interested in the past and gives me the ability to better figure out who I am dealing with on the opposite side of the table. In an era of fantasy sports when you can often be playing with people you have never met in real life, it is good to get to know your competition to the best of your ability. I always friend my league mates on facebook and follow them on twitter. They won't come to me most of the time for help in our league, but I'll be able to see when they tweet at other industry professionals.

## 4) Flag Fly Forever

If you are in a keeper or dynasty league, everyone loves prospects and young MLB stars. People tend to overvalue these players to their own detriment. If you are in the hunt for a championship, it is often the right move to sacrifice your future to win now. There are a couple of reasons for this. First, no one remembers who second place was, but everyone remembers champions. Second, tomorrow may never come. I was in a long time AL Only keeper league until a year ago. The league had been in existence for over 30 years and I had been in it for the last 15. I went all out in my last season, trading away all my keepers for this season to win my second championship in three seasons. However, I was not invited back to the league the following season. Am I bitter? Sure, but I won the money. Tomorrow isn't guaranteed. Don't forget, for every top prospect that turns into Mike Trout, Ronald Acuna, and Alex Bregman, there are plenty of the Dominic Smith's, Brandon Wood's, and Jesus Montero's that never amounted to much and even more that never amounted to anything. Play to win now.

## 5) Make The First Offer

This is not a popular piece of advice. Many people don't like to make the first offer because they worry that if they offer too much, they may have left some meat on the bone. While that can be true, in the larger majority of circumstances, often the framework of a deal is set up by the original offer. Rarely do people counter a trade offer with something completely different than was first offered by the other person. This gives you a distinct advantage in getting what you want from a deal.

## 6) Check In

There is nothing more frustrating than seeing a deal go down in your league and feeling like you would have given a better offer for a particular player. To avoid this from happening too often, check in with your league mates on a regular basis to see what the availability of their players are. However, don't be annoying about it. You don't want your league mates to dread when they see a message from you in their inbox.

## 7) Don't Make Bad Offers

Nothing ruins a reputation quicker than being the guy that always sends awful trade offers. No, I do not want to give you Cody Bellinger for Sean Doolittle. I am usually pretty cordial about it, but that will end the conversation for me. There is nothing wrong with starting with a low-ball offer, but don't start a negotiation by insulting your trade partner's intelligence.

## 8) Don't Be a Jerk

Few things are more annoying than someone honestly telling you "that player sucks, you should trade him to me for cheap." If he sucks so much, then why do you want him? Talking players down doesn't lower their value as a player, it lowers your value as a trade partner. Sure, sometimes it is beneficial to keep your motives hidden, but don't think you can fleece someone by putting them down. On a similar note, don't insult the owner you are trying to trade with or may want/need to trade with later on. Remember, relationships are key and people don't forget when you insult them.

## 9) More is Often Less

Ever get this offer? "I will give you Dansby Swanson, Josh Reddick, and Jake Arrieta for Mike Clevinger." Of course you have. There is always one guy in your league that will consistently offer quantity for quality. The only time that ever works is in the deepest of leagues. This insults the intelligence of the person you are playing. Very rarely do these trades ever make sense, so while sometimes you can package depth for higher end talent, if you are trying to sell trash for treasure, you are approaching it wrong.

## 10) The Best Move Sometimes is the One You Don't Make

I like to trade more than most, but sometimes the best decisions I ever made were trades I chose not to make. Sometimes you can feel obligated to make a move once you have gone far enough down a negotiation. Always be sure that the deal as constructed works for you and walk away if you need to. You never HAVE to make a trade. If you are desperate, others will smell blood in the water.

## Post Hype Sleepers
By Walter McMichael

A quick recap of the the 2019 list:

Gary Sanchez - was not the number one catcher and underperformed again

Joc Pederson - set a career high with 36 HRs and was a great source of power late in drafts with a decent batting average

Maikel Franco - started out extremely hot but flopped soon after.

Jorge Soler - one of the best values of 2019 as he crushed the second half of the season on his way to an AL leading 48 HRs

Domingo German - off-field issues aside, German provided a strong 150 innings with an okay ERA, strong WHIP, and an extremely useful 18 wins.

Matt Shoemaker - he was one of the darlings of the first month of the season but like Shoemaker often does, he was injured and out for the season

Caleb Smith - he had a strong first half of the season but fell apart in the second half. He was still a useful addition to a fantasy staff at the cost

Luiz Gohara - he did not pitch in 2019

Now, to the 2020 list:

### Luis Urías

Urías was traded to the Brewers in the trade that brought Trent Grisham to the Padres. Urías seemed to have worn out his welcome in the Padres system with his displeasure being left in AAA. The one constant with Urías is he has hit while being young for the level at every stop. He has struggled in his short samples in the majors but he appears to be the Brewers everyday SS and will have enough playing time to prove he can hit. The profile does not have a ton of upside due to the lack of steals, however, the Brewers have an opening at the top of their lineup and Urías' contact and OBP would fit perfectly. If he were to take the leadoff role, a plus AVG, plus runs scored profile could be very valuable at his current price.

### Jose Peraza

Peraza is not a new name to fantasy owners, he has previously been drafted in the top 100. His profile (AVG and speed who is not burner with little power) is not the type I like to invest in when the price is pushed into the top 100 but now his cost is outside of the top 300. He actually showed decent power in 2018 where he is not a negative in the HR and RBI categories. He was a low-key signing by the Red Sox where it seems his playing time should be relatively safe at 2B and in a good lineup. One issue is his runs and RBI will be low due to his slot in the lineup but he is a great pick for AVG and SB (the two hardest categories to find late) at a weak position late in drafts.

### Ian Happ

It seems like so long ago when everyone's favorite breakout lead off the season with a HR. Ever since that moment in 2018, MLB pitching has been a struggle for Happ. He showed improvement last year on his previously extreme strikeout to a more manageable 25% due to becoming more aggressive and making more contact in the zone. These improvements should be able to keep his batting average at a reasonable number (.240-.260). He comes into 2020 as the Cubs' starting CF and his profile is very fantasy friendly due to his combination of solid

20-25 HR power with the ability to chip in 8-10 SBs. He should be a target for fantasy owners needing a potential well-rounded fantasy producer while being a non-zero in SBs.

## Gregory Polanco
"THIS is the year of the Gregory Polanco breakout", said in 2016, 2017, 2018….okay, it has not fully happened. I do not think the actual upside many believe existed when he was called up from the minor leagues is there but at his 2020 price, it does not need to. 2019 was a lost season due to his recovery from a major shoulder injury in 2018. In 2018, he provided 23 HRs, 75 runs, 81 RBIs, 12 SBs, and .254 AVG in only 535 PAs which is a really good player. If he can replicate his 2018 season, he's a major bargain outside of the top 300.

## Cal Quantrill
Quantrill's three start stretch from 8/27 to 9/9 : 12.1 IP, 24 ER, 28 H, 6 BB, and 10 K. His other 15 starts: 79.1 IP, 35 ER, 72 H, 18 BB, and 68 K. These three starts completely tanked his final numbers but it appears Quantrill wore down as the season went on. His numbers outside of those three starts are good for a 3.97 ERA and 1.13 WHIP which are great ratios for a back-end starter. I do not see a ton of strikeout upside but he can be a valuable ratio play late in drafts.

## Garrett Richards
It has literally been years since he was able to pitch a full season. He missed the majority of 2019 healing from TJ in the middle of the 2018 season. He came back and pitched extremely poorly but it was encouraging to see his fastball velocity at a pre-surgery level. I would not expect many innings from Richards but when he pitches (outside of the small 2019 sample), he has been effective and will likely be one of most fantasy team's top nine pitchers.

## Tyler Anderson
Tyler Anderson's name brother (Tyler Chatwood) has struggled since he has left the beast that is Coors field but his skills were never as good as Anderson's. Anderson signed a one year deal to stay in the NL West but the park he pitches in could not have changed more moving from Colorado to San Francisco. He has always shown a solid strikeout rate with an ability to limit walks and now moves to the best park for his home run issues. I think he could be a great addition to teams in the last round of drafts.

## Ross Stripling
The Dodgers always seem to have five must-start pitchers in their rotation no matter who they plug into their rotation. Stripling lost his rotation spot in 2019 when their rotation was fully healthy but with the departures of Rich Hill and Hyun Jin-Ryu, he should have the opportunity to compete for one of their rotation spots. It seems people have forgotten about Stripling with the inclusion of the Dodgers young starting pitchers but I believe he gets the first shot at the job and can contribute awesome ratios, wins, and strikeouts in comparison to other pitchers going outside of the top 300.

# Baltimore Orioles Team Preview
By Daniel Rotter

**Projected Order:**
1- Hanser Alberto, 2B
2- Austin Hays, CF
3- Trey Mancini, 1B
4- Anthony Santander, LF
5- Renato Nunez, DH
6- Rio Ruiz, 3B
7- Dwight Smith Jr., RF
8- Jose Iglesias, SS
9- Chance Sisco, C

**Projected Bench:**
Pedro Severino, C
Chris Davis, 1B
Richard Urena, INF
Stevie Wilkerson, INF/OF

**Projected Rotation:**
John Means, LHP
Alex Cobb, RHP
Asher Wojciechowski, RHP
Kohl Stewart, RHP
Brandon Bailey, RHP

**Bullpen:**
Mychal Givens, RHP
Richard Bleier, LHP
Hunter Harvey, RHP
Miguel Castro, RHP
Paul Fry, LHP
Shawn Armstrong, RHP
Tanner Scott, LHP
Michael Rucker, RHP

**Catchers:**
Chance Sisco, age 25, eligible at C
2019 Stats: 198 PA, 8 HR, 29 Runs, 20 RBI, 0 SB, .210/.333/.395
Thought to be the future at the catching position in Baltimore prior to the arrival of #1 draftee Adley Rutschman, Sisco comes into 2020 with plenty to prove after what has been an abysmal showing in the majors thus far. Sisco, a career .203 hitter in the bigs in 132 games, is penciled in to be the starter behind the dish due to his platoon advantage over the righty Severino and his strong showing in the upper minor leagues in 2016. Sisco should only be on your preseason fantasy radar in deep two-catcher leagues, but with good play could gain value seeing as though the Orioles have plenty of holes to fill in their lineup.

Pedro Severino, age 26, eligible at C
2019 Stats: 341 PA, 13 HR, 37 Runs, 44 RBI, 3 SB, .249/.321/.420
After coming over from the Nationals where he would get occasional starts as a backup, Severino was a pleasant surprise for the rebuilding O's in 2019. Including a three-homer game in Arlington against the Rangers, Severino clubbed 13 home runs and showed the most offensive prowess of any of the Orioles' catching options. Defendingly, he also recorded the fastest pop time of all major league catchers last year, which should help his argument to manager Brandon Hyde for making the team out of camp. Severino figures to get semi-regular at-bats while splitting the catching duties with Sisco.

**Infielders**:
Trey Mancini, age 28, eligible at 1B, OF
2019 Stats: 679 PA, 35 HR, 106 Runs, 97 RBI, 1 SB, .291/.364/.535
Perhaps one of the biggest All-Star snubs of the 2019 season, Mancini cemented his spot in the center of the O's lineup early in the year and enters 2020 as the best bat the squad boasts at the major league level. There was a lot of uncertainty around Mancini entering 2019 after hitting .242 with 24 homers, but he made his plans very certain from the get-go from Opening Day, to be the clubhouse leader of the young, Adam Jones and Manny Machado-less Orioles. Now entering his age-28 season, the Orioles are certain to humor offers for Mancini for a quality return considering he is under team control through the 2023 season, but will be looking for a very talent-laden package to part ways with their best bat after refusing to pay Jonathan Villar and shipping him off to Miami. No matter where he ends up finishing the season in 2020, Mancini is the only Oriole that will be selected in all of your drafts, no matter the league size.

Hanser Alberto, age 27, eligible at 2B, 3B
2019 Stats: 550 PA, 12 HR, 62 Runs, 51 RBI, 4 SB, .305/.329/.422
Hanser Alberto had a heck of an offseason leading up to his surprising 2019 campaign, as he was claimed off of waivers by the Yankees from the Rangers, then claimed by the Orioles, then claimed by the Giants from the Orioles, THEN the Orioles claimed him back off of waivers from San Francisco on March 1, where he would remain for the rest of the year. After Alberto hit .305 in 139 games and providing versatility in the infield, he appears to have as secure a spot as any Oriole in the lineup entering 2020. A free swinger, Alberto struck out only 50 times but also walked just 16 times, and you know what they say, good things happen when you put the ball in play. Alberto possessed a BABIP of .318 last season, so while some regression should be expected he could have fantasy relevance if he can stay above the .300 threshold for a second-straight season. Alberto does not exactly possess the most gaudy tools compared to the athletic phenoms in the infield nowadays, but will hold an everyday spot in the Orioles lineup so he should accumulate some numbers in volume-based stats.

Renato Nunez, age 25, eligible at 1B
2019 Stats: 599 PA, 31 HR, 72 Runs, 90 RBI, 1 SB, .244/.311/.460
Probably the least known 30 home run hitter of the 2019 season, Renato Nunez was a consistent source of power in a lineup that needed to put runs on the board at any opportunity with the horrid situation that is their pitching staff. Nunez's ISO went way up in 2019 from .161 to .216 and his BABIP went way down from .316 to .272, so hopefully he can see improvement in his batting average and slugging % as more of those balls fall in the gap in 2020. Nunez's wRC+ of 99 shows that he is actually just about a league average hitter, and given that he was only playing in his first whole major league season last year at the age of 25, he could actually

be a nice value in larger league sizes given his everyday role in the O's lineup and the power he has displayed thus far. Nunez also has received time at 3B in his Orioles tenure as well, so if Rio Ruiz were to struggle or succumb to injury, Nunez could have dual position eligibility.

Rio Ruiz, age 25, eligible at 3B
2019 Stats: 413 PA, 12 HR, 35 Runs, 46 RBI, 0 SB, .232/.306/.376
Ruiz is a player that Orioles GM Mike Elias coveted for years, as Elias was a part of the Astros draft room that selected Ruiz in the 4th round of the 2012 draft. After taking the reins of the Orioles last off-season, one of Elias' first transactions was snagging the left-handed Ruiz off of waivers from Atlanta and giving him a chance at consistent at-bats. Though he didn't exactly wow anyone with his numbers, he is a young strong side platoon option at the hot corner, and had maybe the most clutch at-bat of the Orioles season in 2019, blasting a walk-off home run onto the flag court at Camden Yards off of Roberto Osuna as the O's beat Justin Verlander and the Astros 8-7 a day after getting obliterated 23-2 at home. Ruiz shouldn't be on any preseason draft radars.

Jose Iglesias, age 30, eligible at SS
2019 Stats (with CIN):  530 PA, 11 HR, 62 Runs, 59 RBI, 4 SB, .288/.318/.407
Brought on to replace the major league void filled by flipping Villar, Jose Iglesias signed for just $3 million and will bring great defense in addition to coming off of a career best season with the bat as well. Iglesias will be in line for everyday at-bats with no competition from the upper levels of the Orioles minor league system up the middle, and will anchor the O's infield in 2020.

Chris Davis, age 34, eligible at 1B
2019 Stats: 352 PA, 12 HR, 26 Runs, 36 RBI, 0 SB, .179/.276/.326
Here we go again. The Angelos family refuses to eat the remainder of Davis' 7 year, $161 million contract (three years remaining, $93 million remain in total with deferred money through 2037), so the O's front office has to bite the bullet and continue to run out #19 in the lineup this year. If you had to rank every team's 26 man rosters for fantasy purposes for 2020, Davis would probably be the last ranked hitter on your draft board. Not only does he strike out a tremendous amount and hit for a horrible average, but he just looks completely lost every time he sets foot in the batter's box. Do not draft.

Richard Urena, age 23, eligible at SS
2019 Stats (with TOR):  80 PA, 0 HR, 4 Runs, 4 RBI, 0 SB, .243/.273/.324
Even though there's probably a good chance that Urena doesn't make the major league roster with plenty more time for moves to flurry in, he is a switch-hitting utility infielder and could provide relief for Alberto and Iglesias up the middle after being claimed off  waivers from Toronto. Not worthy of preseason draft consideration.


**Outfielders**:
Austin Hays, age 24, eligible at OF
2019 Stats: 75 PA, 4 HR, 12 Runs, 13 RBI, 2 SB, .309/.373/.574
Hays is one of the first glimmers of hope of a potentially impactful player to a good Orioles team hitting the major leagues, and he should get a shot full-time in 2020. After going bananas in his first full minor league season in 2017 and gracing the cover of Baseball America entering 2018, Hays looked the part of a major league outfielder when he came up for a cup of joe in the bigs in

2019. In addition to his solid batting line, Hays played spectacular defense and had more highlight reel plays than some center fielders who got 600 at-bats. I think Hays is a good bet to bat leadoff in 2020, and could be a nice sleeper in the late rounds of your draft.

Anthony Santander, age 25, eligible at OF
2019 Stats: 405 PA, 20 HR, 46 Runs, 59 RBI, 1 SB, .261/.297/.476
Santander proved to be a steady source of offense towards the top of the Orioles lineup in 2019, and he appears to be an early lock for a starting gig in 2020. After hitting 20 home runs in 405 plate appearances, Santander could easily be looking at a season where he hits 25-30 home runs with a good enough average for him to be a top 75 outfielder in roto leagues where batting average is a stat, and maybe a little lower in OBP leagues. Santander doesn't walk a whole lot and isn't very aggressive on the basepaths, but his ability to hit and hit for power makes him worth a look in larger leagues.

Dwight Smith Jr., age 27, eligible at OF
2019 Stats: 392 PA, 13 HR, 46 Runs, 53 RBI, 5 SB, .241/.297/.412
At the start of 2019, it had appeared that Smith thrust himself into a starting gig after showing some nice pop and usable speed in his first 200 plate appearances (.270 AVG, 9 HR, 4 SB, .799 OPS). Things went downhill from there for Smith, and he struggled to see consistent at-bats in the second half. There's a good chance he makes the team as a 4th outfielder, but he doesn't have much more upside than that.

Stevie Wilkerson, age 28, eligible at OF
2019 Stats: 361 PA, 10 HR, 41 Runs, 35 RBI, 3 SB, .225/.286/.383
Wilkerson may have set a record for the most eventful season that ended up with the least eventful fantasy statline I have ever seen. Wilkerson became the first position player ever to record a save when he did so against the Angels in Anaheim on July 26, and on the final game of the season made maybe the catch of the year with a home run robbery near the bullpen in right field at Fenway. Wilkerson will probably make the team because he can be used basically anywhere, but his tools are not particularly exciting on the hitting end of things.

DJ Stewart, age 26, eligible at OF
2019 Stats: 142 PA, 4 HR, 15 Runs, 14 RBI, 1 SB, .238/.317/.381
The 2015 first round pick has yet to live up to his draft position, and there is a good chance that he starts 2020 in the minors after having right ankle surgery in October. He'll be in Baltimore soon after, but he is not likely to be near fantasy relevance.

**Starters:**
John Means, age 26, LHP
2019 Stats: 155 IP, 121 K, 12 W, 3.60 ERA, 1.14 WHIP
Throughout his minor league career, John Means had never had a K/9 of over 7.4 or a WHIP of under 1.26, and because of this he never even sniffed any top prospect lists, for the MLB as a whole or even just his club! Means didn't even make the Orioles' rotation out of camp, and logged four bullpen appearances before Hyde deemed him worthy of a go in the rotation. He didn't disappoint. Means and his nasty changeup took off as he gained confidence, en route to being selected an All-Star and American League Rookie of the Year runner-up in an amazing and unexpected first campaign in the bigs. Means is a hard guy to peg as far as his preseason value because he still didn't miss a lot of bats last year and is certainly not in line for a lot of

wins playing for this team, either. I still think he's worth a look around the 250-300 range, because he's taken over as the ace of the staff and will look to get back into the All-Star game and prove his 2019 wasn't a fluke.

Alex Cobb, age 32, RHP
2019 Stats: 12.1 IP, 8 K, 0 W, 10.95 ERA, 1.87 WHIP
Orioles fans had finally been freed of the crippling Ubaldo Jimenez deal after four long and painful years after the 2017 season, but then-GM Dan Duquette decided that the Orioles needed to issue another risky four year deal to a pitcher who has dealt with injuries and that man was Alex Cobb. Cobb's Orioles tenure has been just about as close to a nightmare as they come, in 31 starts he is 5-17 with a 5.36 ERA and a 6.0 K/9 only to undergo season-ending hip surgery in April in 2019 at age 31. The Orioles need more from Cobb than he is probably going to give, as his combination of age, injury, and performance does not bode well for his prospects in 2020.

Asher Wojciechowski, age 31, RHP
2019 Stats: 82.1 IP, 80 K, 4 W, 4.92 ERA, 1.31 WHIP
Brought over from the Indians in July, Wojciechowski was nothing too special but did give the Orioles innings that they desperately needed. Though his numbers left something to be desired, Wojciechowski owned the Red Sox last year: in three starts he went 17.2 innings and allowed only two runs to go with 20 strikeouts. That alone should give him a spot in the 2020 rotation.

Kohl Stewart, age 25, RHP
2019 Stats (with MIN): 25.1 IP, 10 K, 2 W, 6.39 ERA, 1.46 WHIP
Signed over from the Twins to give the club major league innings, it remains to be seen if Stewart can stay in the big leagues after not posting particularly encouraging numbers in his two stints with Minnesota, or even in Triple-A for that matter. Obviously Elias sees something in him, but Kohl Stewart should not be selected in any drafts.

Brandon Bailey, age 25, RHP
2019 Stats (with HOU AA): 92.2 IP, 103 K, 4 W, 3.30 ERA, 1.22 WHIP
Another one of Elias' acquisitions from his former club, Bailey was selected with the second overall pick in the Rule 5 draft and thus will get an extended look to see how he can perform in the majors. His numbers in Double-A were respectable, and if he can't stick in the rotation he will get an opportunity in long relief to show he belongs. The club held onto the #1 pick in the 2019 Rule 5 draft, Richie Martin, for the entire season last year despite his .208 batting average, so Bailey will have to perform really poorly to be shipped back to Houston in all likelihood.

Keegan Akin, age 24, LHP
2019 Stats (AAA): 112.1 IP, 131 K, 6 W, 4.73 ERA, 1.51 WHIP
Akin may not make the team out of camp, but Elias and Hyde have made it known that 2016 second rounder Akin will get some turns in the starting rotation in 2020. His ERA wasn't admirable last year which is why he will probably pitch the first few weeks in Norfolk, but he has posted solid strikeout numbers across all levels of the minors and is someone to watch to get innings for the club.

**Relievers:**

Mychal Givens, age 29, RHP
2019 Stats: 63 IP, 86 K, 2 W, 11 SV, 4.57 ERA, 1.19 WHIP
2019 may have looked like a lost season for Givens, and that's not to say he had a great year by any stretch, but he posted the best strikeout numbers of his career last year and his FIP shows that he was a bit unlucky. He should see his ERA dip a bit this coming season, but despite his lackluster ERA he is the leading candidate for saves in 2020. Givens is their most reliable reliever and should take the few save chances that come his way in a bullpen that was an absolute embarrassment last year and gave games away on a regular basis. Givens is also a strong candidate to be traded at the deadline, he is only under team control through 2022 and there are always clubs searching for relief help. Givens will be one of the lowest ranked closers in fantasy baseball in 2020 purely because of a lack of volume.

Richard Bleier, age 32, LHP
2019 Stats: 55.1 IP, 30 K, 3 W, 4 SV, 5.37 ERA, 1.32 WHIP
The most likely candidate to get saves against lefty-heavy teams, Bleier also saw his ERA balloon after a horrible follow-up to his outstanding 2017 and 2018 campaigns. Never much of a strikeout guy, Bleier relies on finesse and weak contact to get outs but he wasn't getting a whole lot of weak contact in 2019. I expect Bleier to be surpassed as the best lefty in the bullpen because his stuff is just not super impressive and he got a late start to his major league career, so there's not really any room for growth.

Hunter Harvey, age 25, RHP
2019 Stats: 6.1 IP, 11 K, 1 W, 1.42 ERA, 1.11 WHIP
Picked in the first round of the 2013 draft out of high school, Harvey dealt with a great deal of injuries to his arm and eventually gave up on starting after a lack of success at any minor league level. Once Harvey committed to being a reliever, his electric fastball rose him all the way to the major leagues in 2019, where he looked to be arguably the most effective pitcher in the O's bullpen in September. If Givens underperforms or is traded, Harvey would be his most likely replacement and I believe he could anchor this bullpen for years to come, because he has an electric arm.

Miguel Castro, age 25, RHP
2019 Stats: 73.1 IP, 71 K, 1 W, 2 SV, 4.66 ERA, 1.42 WHIP
A hard throwing sinkerballer, Castro has the makeup of an effective reliever with a 98 mph fastball and a wipeout slider, but Castro's control has always been a major issue and when he's not missing out of the zone, he's missing right over the plate. His stuff alone will keep him in the Orioles bullpen, but his control issues will keep him from getting many innings in meaningful scenarios.

Paul Fry, age 27, LHP
2019 Stats: 57.1 IP, 55 K, 1 W, 3 SV, 5.34 ERA, 1.45 WHIP
A steady left-handed arm in the bullpen, Fry is likely to make the team out of camp and get some hold chances early in the year against lefty-heavy lineups.

Shawn Armstrong, age 29, RHP
2019 Stats (with SEA/BAL): 58 IP, 63 K, 1 W, 4 SV, 5.74 ERA, 1.64 WHIP
Armstrong saw a lot of opportunities because he is a hard thrower, but he rarely made it through innings cleanly last year and is just a bullpen depth piece entering 2020.

Tanner Scott, age 25, LHP
2019 Stats: 26.1 IP, 37 K, 1 W, 4.78 ERA, 1.79 WHIP
Scott is almost like the left-handed Harvey in the Orioles bullpen, he has a great arm and pumps in fastball at 97-98 with a great slider. He has yet to make the jump in brief stints in 2017-18, but in my opinion is best situated to be the best southpaw in this bullpen this year.

Michael Rucker, age 25, RHP
2019 Stats (with CHC AA/AAA): 79.2 IP, 93 K, 0 W, 4.18 ERA, 1.32 WHIP
Selected from the Cubs in the second round of the Rule 5 draft, Rucker will likely have to earn his way on the roster with a good spring. For reference, last year Elias sent back his 2019 Rule 5 second rounder Drew Jackson after only a couple weeks with the club. He is most likely going to earn opportunities in long relief.

# Baltimore Orioles Prospects
By Matt Thompson

### 1. Adley Rutschman- C
The switch-hitting catcher was the most hyped draft prospect since Bryce Harper. He projects as an all-around superstar, and a franchise cornerstone. He has an easy, uppercut swing that generates loft and is ideal for his plus raw pop. He has elite plate skills and walk rates, and uses all fields. This is Paul Goldschmidt with catchers gear. The defensive skills are polished, and the arm will shut down the running game. Four-category fantasy contributor and one of the few catchers that you can own with confidence. **ETA: 2022.**

### 2. Grayson Rodriguez- RHP
The big Texan stands six-foot-five and is a well filled out 220 pounds. His fastball/curveball combo is lethal and he largely dominated in his full season debut because of this. His sinking mid-90s heater has natural run in on right-handed hitters, and his big 12-6 curve is a putaway pitch. He will get hitters to chase his slider and his changeup has a chance to be an above-average pitch. Rodriguez has number two starter upside, and his stock is on the rise. Likely starts in High-A in 2020. **ETA: 2022.**

### 3. DL Hall- LHP
The lefty combines three potential plus pitches with athleticism, and projects as a future number three starter, and two for tantasy due to the strikeout potential. Hall can bump up to 97 but sits in the mid-90s with late movement. The harder he throws, the straighter the fastball. His curveball and changeup can both be big league out pitches, and it provides more safety in case one isn't working on a given day. Hall needs to become more efficient, high pitch counts have chased him starts early. He's been working on a cutter as well and can jump up to a number two with more refinement. This is an exciting arm. **ETA: 2022.**

### 4. Austin Hays- OF
Back on the radar after a strong 2019 washed out bad 2018 after taste. Hays came up in September and flashed his skills. I was shocked at how good he looked in center and he quieted some of his aggressiveness in the box. He wasn't selling out for power as much, and just letting his natural skills take over. He's got plus raw power, could hit 25 this year with 30-homer pop likely soon after. He should steal 10-12 bases and while he may only hit .250 there are enough secondary skills to carry the average. Draft Hays with confidence this spring. **ETA: Arrived.**

### 5. Ryan Mountcastle- 1B/3B/OF
Mountcastle is an unconventional profile, but one that's nearly big league ready. He can hit and has plus bat speed and strong wrists and will hit some majestic homers in Camden Yard. He's an easy 30-homer bat. His offensive game is brought down a bit by an over-aggressive mindset in the box. He will swing early and often at a pitch he likes, often posting walk rates around 4-5%. Defensively he's limited to first or left, and won't be an asset at either position. He's already on the 40-man, so we should see Mountcastle in Baltimore this summer. **ETA: 2020.**

### 6. Yusniel Diaz- OF
The crown jewel of the Manny Machado trade, Diaz isn't as advanced of a prospect as initially hoped. Despite the strong, sturdy frame, his power hasn't translated in games yet. He has

above-average bat speed and will sting the ball but doesn't generate enough loft to get to the levels needed for a corner outfielder. He does have a strong arm and is a prototypical right fielder, but he needs to tap into that power. He will take a walk, but isn't a threat to run. Some danger that becomes a tweener; not enough speed and glove for center, not enough power for a corner. **ETA: 2021.**

## 7. Michael Baumann- RHP
Perhaps the most underrated arm in the minors. Baumann has a big,upper 90s heater that headlines his four pitch mix. His cutter and curveball are above-average secondaries now, the cutter gets weak contact while the hook misses bats. He tunnels his change exceptionally with his fastball which adds deception. The ideal frame at 6'4" and a lean 200, Baumann is athletic and will succeed in whatever role Baltimore puts him in. A plus bat misser with overall above-average command, Baumann's stuff could pop with Major League instruction.**ETA: 2021.**

## 8. Dean Kremer- RHP
Another piece from the Machado deal, Kremer has five potential above-average pitches but lacks one that projects as plus. His fastball moves, and will sit in the low-90s. It plays up due to above-average extension. His 12-6 hook is his primary swing and miss pitch, and his slider and change are average with a chance for a half grade more. He also mizes in a cutter which he uses against lefties. Pitched well in the AFL during my looks. Could hit Baltimore in the second half. **ETA: 2020.**

## 9. Gunnar Henderson- SS
Henderson was the Orioles second rounder in 2019 out of the Alabama prep ranks. Posted strong numbers in his pro debut despite the aggressive assignment to short-season ball. It's a powerful, but linear swing. He's a bigger bodied kid but will have to make adjustments to tap into the raw power in the frame. May have to move to third, but is agile enough to play a below-average shortstop, which may be good enough due to shifting. Natural feel for hitting carries the profile though, don't expect any stolen base bonuses here either. **ETA: 2024**

## 10. Adam Hall- SS
Canadian middle infield prospect with an above-average hit tool, above-average wheels but below-average pop. Higher floor than most kids making their full-season debut. Average defender that will work counts, Hall is a tough out. Modest (10-15) homer and stolen base upside, but that should come with a strong average and OBP. **ETA: 2022.**

**Next Five:**
Rylan Bannon- 2B/3B
Ryan McKenna- OF
Keegan Akin- LHP
Zac Lowther- LHP
Elio Prado- OF

**Top Five in FYPDs:**
Adley Rutschman- C
Gunnar Henderson- SS
Kyle Stowers- OF
Zach Watson- OF

Toby Welk- 3B

By Paul Martin

## Projected Order:
1- Alex Verdugo (L)
2- Rafael Devers (L)
3- Xander Bogaerts (R)
4- J.D. Martinez (R)
5- Andrew Benintendi (L)
6- Michael Chavis (R)
7- Jackie Bradley Jr. (L)
8- Christian Vázquez (R)
9- José Peraza (R)

## Projected Bench:
Kevin Plawecki (R), Catcher
Jonathan Arauz (S), Infield/Shortstop
Marco Hernández (L), Infield/Second Base
Tzu-Wei Lin (L), Infield/Utility

## Projected Rotation:
Chris Sale, LHP
Eduardo Rodriguez, LHP
Nathan Eovaldi, RHP
Martin Pérez, LHP
Matt Hall LHP

## Bullpen:
Brandon Workman, RHP
Matt Barnes, RHP
Josh Taylor, LHP
Ryan Brasier, RHP
Darwinzon Hernandez, LHP
Colton Brewer, RHP
Heath Hembree, RHP
Marcus Walden, RHP

## Catchers:
Christian Vázquez, age 29.4, eligible at C
2019 Stats: 521 PA, 23 HR, 66 Runs, 72 RBI, 4 SB, .276/.320/.477
The longest tenured member of the Red Sox (sorry Pedroia) was a revelation at the dish last season. Vázquez provided owners one of the most potent bats at the catcher position in the first half of 2019, slashing .299/.332/.520 with 14 HR, 38 runs, and 41 RBI. Heading into 2020 drafts, the question remains: was Vázquez' power legit? Well, even if he sold out for more home runs in 2019, the Statcast numbers do not paint a Picasso. In fact, Vázquez looks about as average as it gets, which luckily for him is only exciting for fantasy at the position he plays. While you could choose much worse at catcher in this year's drafts, I suggest holding off on Vázquez

where he currently sits. There are plenty of viable options later on that can provide the same power upside.

Kevin Plawecki, age 28.9, eligible at C
2019 Stats: 174 PA, 3 HR, 13 Runs, 17 RBI, 0 SB, .222/.287/.342
There isn't much to say about this profile. Your standard, garden-variety back-up catcher and pitch-framing extraordinaire. There isn't even anything to get excited about if Christian Vázquez was to get injured. You can pretty much disregard this name in 2020, unless there is some massive overhaul to his entire offensive skill-set.

**Infielders**:
Michael Chavis, age 24.4, eligible at 1B/2B
2019 Stats: 382 PA, 18 HR, 46 Runs, 58 RBI, 2 SB, .254/.322/.444
After garnering some hype as a Top-100 MLB prospect, Chavis made his debut in 2019. What began as a torrid display of titanic power, ended as a prime example of a rookie in over his head. There are plenty of holes in his swing, including the low-inside breaking ball which Chavis cannot seem to lay off. However, there is significant power upside for someone eligible at 1B and 2B, with value where he is currently drafted. He should get every opportunity to prosper, or fail, at the big league level next year and is worth the risk at a middle or corner infield position in fantasy leagues.

José Peraza, age 25.7, eligible at 2B/SS/OF
2019 Stats: 403 PA, 6 HR, 37 Runs, 33 RBI, 7 SB, .239/.285/.346
After a full season breakout in 2018, Peraza took a major step-back last year. Starting off poorly was compounded by the rise of Derek Dietrich and his extravagant home run pimp jobs. Unfortunately for Peraza, moving to the Red Sox does not guarantee a return to everyday playing time. Brock Holt never surpassed 509 PA in his six full seasons as the Sox utility specialist, and averaged only 358.5 PA over that span. With Peraza inheriting the "Holt" role, it won't be enough opportunity to project a return to 20+ stolen bases. However, an injury could add intrigue as Alex Cora is not averse to letting his players run. There are better late speed options, but monitor the situation for an opening as Peraza can fill multiple positions on the diamond.

Rafael Devers, age 23.2, eligible at 3B
2019 Stats: 702 PA, 32 HR, 129 Runs, 115 RBI, 8 SB, .311/.361/.555
Devers took one of the biggest steps forward of any player in 2019. After being a top Red Sox prospect for a few years, his debut in 2017, and injury shortened stint in 2018, there were still questions as to whether he would be able to make enough contact to be an everyday player. Last year erased all doubt, as he was able to simply become a better hitter. As hard as it is to explain, there were very little changes in his plate discipline profile, and he even started swinging at more pitches outside the zone. However, he somehow managed to swing more than ever and make more contact than ever in what seems to be an improvement in overall bat-to-ball skills. Devers proved his natural hitting abilities and showcased the power with an exit velocity in the Top 6% of the league. The draft price leaves little value to be had, but he is still extremely young and it wouldn't shock me to see another power uptick while he continues to refine his plate approach. Devers should continue to post near-.300/30 lines for years to come.

Xander Bogaerts, age 27.3, eligible at SS

2019 Stats: 698 PA, 33 HR, 110 Runs, 117 RBI, 4 SB, .309/.384/.555

Xander is about as consistent as it gets at the shortstop position. He's been a cornerstone for the Red Sox since 2015 when he broke out as a 22-year old, slashing .320/.355/421 in 156 games. Going into his age 27 season, he is trying to build on a career high power output in 2019. Boges doesn't steal nearly as many bases as he used to, so the draft price scares me at the moment. He is a very selective hitter, according to the Statcast Swing Take Profile, and last season proves he's growing into his power. The lack of stolen bases means his value will be carried by the batting average, power, and counting stats. I have no problem buying into Xander excelling in those categories, but I may still pass on him come draft day if there are 5-category players on the board.

Bobby Dalbec, age 24.5, eligible at 3B
2019 Stats (AA/AAA): 562 PA, 27 HR, 69 Runs, 73 RBI, 6 SB, .239/.356/.460

Dalbec is the only prospect listed, but has a high potential of seeing time in the majors this season. His statline clearly shows a power upside with low batting average and high OBP, a true three outcome talent. He is very similar in ways to Michael Chavis, but without the 2B eligibility. Dalbec can provide a spark to this team at some point in 2020 and may be one of those promotions to catch fire immediately. There are HR, runs and RBI to be had as long as the batting average stays palatable.

**Outfielders**:


J.D. Martinez, age 32.4, eligible at OF
2019 Stats: 657 PA, 36 HR, 98 Runs, 105 RBI, 2 SB, .304/.383/.557

J.D. also looks just as good as the stats do on his Fangraphs page. The consistency has been unbelievable, hitting at least 36 HR and surpassing 100 RBI in 4 of the last 5 seasons. Another underrated piece to his fantasy profile is the batting average that has been above-.300 the past 4 years, and 5 times in the last 6 seasons. I have zero issue with him going in the 2nd round at what I perceive to be an excellent value.

Andrew Benintendi, age 25.5, eligible at OF
2019 Stats: 615 PA, 13 HR, 72 Runs, 68 RBI, 10 SB, .266/.343/.431

I never seem to draft Andrew Benintendi. No matter where he's being taken, he's never enticed me to the point where I think I should press the button. However, digging into him a little deeper for this write-up, I can't seem to deny a value at his price this season. People are finally starting to fade him a bit and there's no reason to believe he still can't grow into slightly more over-the-fence power in his age-26 season. He's had a 20/20 season in the past, he's shown an ability to hit for high average and, despite the lack of blazing speed, he can steal a base without getting caught at an alarming rate. There's still a chance for it all to come together in one magical season, and this could be a prime time to buy-in.

Alex Verdugo, age 24, eligible at OF
2019 stats: 377 PA, 12 HR, 43 Runs, 44 RBI, 4 SB, .294/.342/.475

In 377 plate appearances last season, we finally got a nice peak at Verdugo's potential becoming a reality. He improved against southpaws, boosted his fly ball rate (22% to 29%), doubled his home run to fly ball rate (up to 14%), and saw his elite level hard hit rate get even better. Verdugo's power metrics are never going to be great, but thanks to his overall plate skills and 86% contact rate, we have a .300 hitter here. Don't go crazy, as 20 home runs are likely it, but Verdugo is a solid option.

Jackie Bradley Jr., age 29.7, eligible at OF
2019 Stats: 567 PA, 21 HR, 69 Runs, 62 RBI, 8 SB, .225/.317/.421
This may be the only season JBJ doesn't have some variation of sleeper hype. He is going extremely late in drafts after posting his lowest batting average in 4 years. The power and speed potential is still there, but there is no sign of improvement in the contact profile. His Statcast Swing Take graphics are very depressing, as Bradley really struggles with pitches over the heart of the plate. Barring another jump in stolen bases, a la 2018 which looks to be an outlier, there isn't enough in the profile to get excited about in fantasy.

**Starters:**
Chris Sale, age 30.8, LHP
2019 Stats: 147.1 IP, 218 K, 6 W, 4.40 ERA, 1.09 WHIP
This season, Chris Sale has the opportunity to make 2019 look like an outlier within a career of greatness. He struggled with velocity to start the year, and never fully recovered from a few IL stints. Despite the velocity dip, he was able to strike out 218 batters in only 147.1 thanks to increased slider usage and a deadly changeup. Outside of high ERA, and notable lack of wins, his strikeouts and WHIP allowed him to provide value to fantasy teams even in a down year. This offseason looks to be a perfect time to buy back in to a pitcher who projects, in nearly every major system, as a top tier arm that you can draft outside of the first two rounds.

Eduardo Rodriguez, age 26.7, LHP
2019 Stats: 203.1 IP, 213 K, 19 W, 3.81 ERA, 1.33 WHIP
E-Rod finally provided fantasy owners a healthy season in 2019, his first since debuting in 2015. He accumulated 200+ strikeouts and 200+ innings, and he was fine. There's nothing gaudy in the profile, he may even be a slight WHIP liability, but players can make unpredicted skill jumps at his age. His biggest skill was limiting hard contact, which he had actually shown before in 2016. Rodriguez can be considered a solid pitcher when healthy but the problem is he's only done that in 2019, as stated earlier. Pitchers are risky enough as it is and there are plenty of other names that can provide higher strikeout potential than E-Rod.

Nathan Eovaldi, age 29.9, RHP
2019 Stats: 67.2 IP, 70 K, 2 W, 5.99 ERA, 1.58 WHIP
Despite having a fastball velocity in the 89th percentile, Eovaldi posted an exit velocity in the bottom 3rd percentile and one of the worst Hard Hit% in limited innings last season. He never seems to strike out as many people as you expect, and there is extreme liability in WHIP and ERA. He's going late in drafts and there are things to like, but I think it's time to lower the overall expectations that have previously been as high as the MPH on his fastball.

Martin Pérez, age 28.8, LHP
2019 Stats: 165.1 IP, 135 K, 10 W, 5.12 ERA, 1.52 WHIP
Pérez has been pitching in the majors since age 21, and sadly has never been a great addition to a fantasy roster. The occasional streamer that has never galloped the glorious meadows of "must-own". This season is no different. I see no reason to be giddy over Martin Pérez being on your team and outside of a miraculous skills jump, or the home Orioles start, I would stay away completely.

**Relievers:**

Brandon Workman, age 31.4, RHP

2019 Stats: 71.2 IP, 104 K, 10 W, 16 SV, 1.88 ERA, 1.03 WHIP

Since recovering from Tommy John surgery in 2016, Workman has made a comfortable living in the bullpen. He wasn't overused in his first two seasons back, but impressed with a sub-3.25 ERA and 1.21 WHIP. However, 2019 was a completely different animal. The curve usage skyrocketed, the four-seamer gained velocity, and the strikeouts began to flow like a duck boat in the Charles River. While there were a handful of names to garner save opportunities for the Red Sox last season, Workman was by far the best. I could never project a sub-2.00 ERA, but I do think he is a reliever that can hold down a job for the entirety of the season while providing high strikeouts and decent peripherals.

Matt Barnes, age 29.5, RHP

2019 Stats: 64.1 IP, 110 K, 5 W, 4 SV, 3.78 ERA, 1.38 WHIP

Barnes may not have posted the brilliant final stat-line of Workman, but he was still a beast. His superb strikeout numbers have me thinking he is the fallback going into this season; he also was able to mop up a handful of saves last year. Workman and Barnes both have some issues with walking batters, but they are very underrated for the numbers they posted in 2019. Barnes may not be worth taking on draft day, but someone to spend a hefty amount of FAAB on if Workman goes down with an injury.

Josh Taylor, age 26.8, LHP

2019 Stats: 47.1 IP, 62 K, 2 W, 0 SV, 3.04 ERA, 1.18 WHIP

Taylor will go into the year as the main lefty specialist without much fantasy upside at all. He actually posted a decent K% last season and is talented for the role he is asked to fill. The Red Sox are known for having a lack of bullpen depth, but these three names are reasonable talents. Taylor doesn't have the opportunity for saves like Workman and Barnes, but he won't kill their chances by blowing the game before they enter.

Ryan Brasier, age 32.4, RHP

2019 Stats: 55.2 IP, 61 K, 2 W, 7 SV, 4.85 ERA, 1.29 WHIP

Ah, the times of Ryan Brasier "Red Sox closer" are now long in the past. That was fun while it lasted though, right? Actually, it really wasn't if you spent a high draft pick on him being the opening day closer. Now let's pray this doesn't happen to Brandon Workman in 2020, but Brasier never showed the skill set that Workman was able to display last season. We can safely ignore Brasier in drafts this year, as hard as that is for some of you to hear.

Darwinzon Hernandez, age 23.0, LHP

2019 Stats: 30.1 IP, 57 K, 0 W, 0 SV, 4.45 ERA, 1.75 WHIP

Hernandez adds some extra left-handed depth to the bullpen. On top of that, he actually has a proper two-pitch repertoire with a 95+ MPH fastball and a highly graded breaker. The problem is that the command has never been able to click. He should miss bats, but will be prone to blow-ups and will not have a chance at many save opportunities at all.

Colton Brewer, age 27.2, RHP

2019 Stats: 54.2 IP, 52 K, 1 W, 0 SV, 4.12 ERA, 1.70 WHIP

Another non-viable for fantasy bullpen option. This one isn't too exciting in real life either, so he may be replaced by an intriguing minor league arm at some point.

Heath Hembree, age 31.0, RHP
2019 Stats: 39.2 IP, 46 K, 1 W, 2 SV, 3.86 ERA, 1.31 WHIP
Hembree was somehow able to gather up 2 SV last season, but that won't be the case this year. Outside of an anecdotal opportunity or two, Hembree shouldn't be considered for saves, or fantasy for that matter. Another arm that may be rotated in and out if there are pitchers at AAA that deserve a look.

Marcus Walden, age 31.3, RHP
2019 Stats: 78.0 IP, 76 K, 9 W, 2 SV, 3.81 ERA, 1.19 WHIP
Walden has a modest skill-set and should prove to be an adequate major leaguer. For fantasy purposes, we don't have to worry about studying the profile. Save chances will be minimal, and amassing 9 wins will be hard to replicate in a bullpen role. Stick to Brandon Workman and Matt Barnes as the two main guys. Then Walden and Hernandez have the most talent after that, with Walden being the first of the two I would project for saves.

**Boston Red Sox Prospects**
By Matt Thompson

### 1. Triston Casas- 1B
The Red Sox stopped Casas' draft day slide by taking the Florida prep at pick 26. His large frame and 70-grade raw power are what you are looking for from a first base prospect, and his high walk rates sweeten the profile. The hit tool is above-average right now, but if you factor in the strong plate skills I'm comfortable putting a plus tag on him. He's a back half of the top 100 type prospect due to his upside, and this is the ideal hitter to pepper the Monster with doubles to left-center. Casas was limited to two games in 2019 due to a thumb injury, but came back healthy for 2019. He will start 2020 in the tough Florida State League. **ETA: 2023.**

### 2. Brusdar Graterol- RHP
I'm a little bummed that the Twins are moving forward with Graterol as a reliever. He gets his hype from his big triple digit fastball, but his slider is actually his best pitch. His slider is a wipeout swing and miss offering with a tight, two-plane break. His fastball lacks movement, but his two-seamer does have some run. His changeup is essentially just a slower version of his fastball. It doesn't have much in the way of fade or movement. This is a future closer if he sticks in the bullpen long term. Depending on your league format a closer can have more value than a mid-rotation starter, so don't write him off just yet. The trade to the Red Sox as part of the Mookie Betts return doesn't change much as I don't view Graterol as a starter, but as a lockdown reliever. **ETA: Arrived.**

### 3. Bobby Dalbec- 3B
The powerful former Arizona Wildcat went off the board in the fourth round in the 2016 draft. Two things stick out right away from Dalbec, and that's his 70-raw power and the strikeout concerns that come with it. His K rates have been over 30% every year until 2019, and we was able to cut it down to 25% in 2019. Still too high, but I'm encouraged that he's headed in the right direction. Dalbec is athletic for a big man, and has an absolute cannon of an arm from third base. With the way the Red Sox depth chart at first and second base looks there's a chance Dalbec is the starting first baseman by the end of April, with Chavis sticking at second. His power and high walk rates make him interesting, but the strikeouts pour some cold water on him. **ETA: 2020.**

### 4. Jay Groome- LHP
If it wasn't for bad luck Groome would have no luck at all. It's been a rocky start to Groome's professional debut, and he's only started 20 games due to a back injury and then Tommy John. We got some strong reports from the fall on Groome and he reportedly looked sharp in his return to the mound. They have to push him aggressively due to him being Rule 5 eligible next winter, but this was a former Vanderbilt commit that had three above-average offerings and and a mid-90s fastball before the injuries, so if he's that guy again he will shoot up these lists with no problem. Groome should join Casas in High-A to begin 2020. **ETA: 2022.**

### 5. Jarren Duran- OF

Duran received a lot of top 100-prospect buzz after he lit the Carolina League on fire hitting .387/.456/.543 in 50 games. He predictably came down to earth as he faced more age appropriate competition at Double-A Portland. Duran is a plus runner with a plus plus hit tool, but his lack of power might cut the hit tool out at the knees. Reports on his defense were mixed, and some of the talk in Arizona during the AFL was how bad he looked in centerfield. The defense will decide whether his line drive approach unseats Jackie Bradley Jr as the everyday centerfielder. That can happen as soon as 2021. **ETA: 2021.**

### 6. Gilberto Jimenez- OF

The switch-hitting Jimenez broke out in the lower minors by hitting .359 with strong plate skills in 2019. Strong bat to ball skills with true 80-grade speed, Jimenez projects as a future top of the order bat. He's a slap hitter with very little power projection, but do think he can hit 10-12 homers at peak. He should be a strong batting average and stolen base asset, but patience is required here. He should join Casas and Groome in the Florida State League to start 2020. **ETA: 2023.**

### 7. Thad Ward- RHP

A reliever while at UCF, the Red Sox drafted Ward in the fifth round in 2018 and have transitioned him to a starter. His first full season was a strong one, and he led all Red Sox farmhands in strikeouts. He can manipulate his low-to-mid 90s heater, he can cut it or sink it and get grounders and weak contact in addition to the strikeouts. He added a cutter to the mix, and he will attack lefties with it. He's pitched better than his stuff thus far, but Ward projects as a number four starter or late inning reliever for me. **ETA: 2023.**

### 8. Bryan Mata- RHP

Mata climbed all the way to Double-A as a 20-year-old and found some success as he missed bats at a higher rate than he ever had before. Mata has multiple versions of his fastball, and depending on how you classify the fastball types, can throw as many as five different pitches. He recently added a cutter to his four-seam and two-seam, and also throws a curveball and a changeup. He threw more strikes, but needs to improve his overall command, but his new uptick in stuff doesn't require him to be as precise. Mata thrives on getting grounders and misses enough bats, and I get a strong Marcus Stroman vibe here. **ETA: 2021.**

### 9. Matthew Lugo- SS

Lugo was drafted in the second round by the Red Sox this summer, and became the highest upside position player I can remember the Sox drafting in years. The Puerto Rican kid is tooled up with a plus arm, plus bat speed, good hands and feet at short and projectable raw power. He had a strong summer in the GCL before an end of season promotion. There's a wide range of outcomes here, but Lugo is a very interesting stash. **ETA: 2024.**

### 10. Noah Song- RHP

Before I tell you about Song it's important to understand the questions about his future and the military requirement he may or may not have to serve. Song is an officer in the Navy, and his appeals to start his professional baseball career are waiting for a resolution. Look into that before drafting. Song throws four pitches; a mid 90's fastball with two breaking balls and a changeup. He's a future mid-rotation arm that misses bats, but if he's forced to take some time off he may fit better in the bullpen upon return. **ETA: 2021?**

**Next Five:**
C.J. Chatham- SS
Nick Decker- OF
Chih-Jung Liu- RHP
Tanner Houck- RHP
Cameron Cannon- 2B/3B


**Top Five in FYPDs:**
Matthew Lugo- SS
Noah Song- RHP
Chih-Jung Liu- RHP
Cameron Cannon- 2B/3B
Juan Chacon- OF

**The New York Yankees Team Preview**
By Jim Bay

**Projected Order:**
1- DJ LeMahieu, 2B
2- Aaron Judge, RF
3- Gleyber Torres, SS
4- Giancarlo Stanton, DH
5- Gary Sanchez, C
6- Brett Gardner, CF
7- Gio Urshela, 3B
8- Mike Tauchman, LF
9- Luke Voit, 1B

**Projected Bench:**
Miguel Andujar, 3B
Tyler Wade INF/OF
Clint Frazier, OF
Kyle Higashioka, C
Aaron Hicks (out till at least mid-season 2020 after Tommy John surgery)

**Projected Rotation:**
Gerrit Cole, RHP
James Paxton, LHP
Masahiro Tanaka, RHP
Luis Severino, RHP
JA Happ, LHP

**Bullpen:**
Aroldis Chapman, LHP
Zack Britton, LHP
Adam Ottovino, RHP
Tommy Kahnle, LHP
Chad Green, RHP
Ben Heller, RHP
Stephen Tarpley, LHP
Luis Cessa, RHP

**Catchers:**
Gary Sanchez, age 27, eligible at C
2019 Stats: 446 PAs, 34 HR, 62 Runs, 77 RBI, 0 SB, .232/.316/.525
Injuries have hampered Sanchez's production in the last couple of years. After a miserable injury-plagued 2018 campaign, Sanchez bounced back in a big way, but still only played in 106 games. The second half of the 2019 season was a struggle for him in large part because of the injuries. After the All-Star break, he hit .207 with 10 HR, 20 RBI, and a .785 OPS after posting a clip of .871 during his first 261 at-bats. A healthy Sanchez is a top 5 fantasy catcher and should be drafted as such.

Kyle Higashioka, age 29, eligible at C
2019 Stats: 57 PA, 3 HR, 8 Runs, 11 RBI, 0 SB, .214/.211/.464
Will be the backup to Gary Sanchez. Given the injury history of Sanchez, fantasy owners should at least keep Higashioka on their radar.

**Infielders:**
DJ LeMahieu, age 31, eligible at 2B/1B/3B
2019 Stats: 655 PAs, 26 HR, 109 Runs, 102 RBI, 5 SB, .327/.375/.518
When he signed with the Yankees in 2019, the thought was that LeMahieu would be a nice super-utility player. There were concerns that LeMahieu's stats had been inflated by the thin air in Coors Field, where he spent seven of his first eight years in the big leagues. However, LeMahieu not only exceeded expectations, but he was also the most productive player the Yankees had in 2019. Even with a slight drop off from last year, his multi-position eligibility will make him a valuable fantasy asset.

Gleyber Torres, age 23, eligible at 2B/SS
2019 Stats: 604 PAs, 38 HR, 96 Runs, 90 RBI, 5 SB, .278/.337/.535
Torres should be the everyday shortstop, now that Didi Gregorious signed a free-agent deal with the Phillies. After a rookie year that had him finish as the third finalist for the Rookie of the Year, he followed up with a break-out power season in 2019, adding 55 points to his slugging percentage. There is no reason to think that he won't post similar, if not better numbers in 2020.

Gio Urshela, age 28, eligible at 3B
2019 Stats: 476 PAs, 21 HR, 73 Runs, 74 RBI, 1 SB, .314/.355/.534
Over the course of Urshela's career prior to 2019, he had never played more than 81 games in a single season. Last year, not only did Urshela set a career-high in games played but every major offensive category. He was also able to find his power stroke in pinstripes. In 167 games leading up to 2019, he had just eight career home runs -- in 132 games with the Yanks, Urshela hit 21 homers. A definite starter in all fantasy formats in 2020.

Luke Voit, age 29, eligible at 1B
2019 Stats: 510 PAs, 21 HR, 72 Runs, 62 RBI, 0 SB, .263/.378/.464
In 2019, Voit had a sports hernia that derailed a potential All-Star campaign and full-season breakout. Voit hit an outstanding .280/.393/.509 in the first half of 2019 but limped to a dismal .228/.348/.368 after, mainly due to the injury. After having successful surgery for the problem, Voit remains a nice sleeper pick for 2020.

Miguel Andujar, age 25, eligible at DH/3B
2019 Stats: 49 PAs, 0 HR, 1 Run, 1 RBI, 0 SB, .128/.143/.128
Andujar missed most of the 2019 season when it was revealed in May that he was going to undergo surgery on his shoulder to repair a partial glenoid labrum tear. Potential fantasy owners will want to see if he can put up numbers similar to 2018 when he hit 27 home runs with 92 RBIs and a slash line of .297/.328/.527 through 149 games.
Potential owners will also want to check their league settings to see if he qualifies for 3B.


**Outfield**
Aaron Judge, age 27, eligible at OF

2019 Stats: 447 PAs, 27 HR, 75 Runs, 55 RBI, 3 SB, .272/.381/.540
When healthy, Judge is one of the best hitters in the game. Injuries have limited Judge over the past two seasons, playing in just 112 games in 2018 and 102 games last year while hitting just 27 homers each of those years. If he stays healthy, Judge could produce 200 runs-plus-RBI and is one of the few players with 50 homer potential. His early draft projection in the late twenties is reasonable and could be a comparative bargain.

Giancarlo Stanton, age 30, eligible at OF/DH
2019 Stats: 72 PAs, 3 HR, 8 Runs, 13 RBI, 0 SB, .288/.403/..492
Stanton was injured most of last season, so take a look at the 2018 numbers to gauge what a healthy Stanton could do. That year he had a more Stanton-like season of 38 home runs with 100 RBI. Last year's numbers could see him slide in drafts, making him a bargain for a prudent fantasy owner.

Brett Garner, age 36, eligible at OF
2019 Stats: 550 PAs, 28 HR, 86 Runs, 74 RBI, 10 SB, .251/.325/.503
Gardner is the model of consistency for fantasy owners, In 2020, he should provide the same as he should see a good amount of playing time, especially with Aaron Hicks' injury status uncertain heading into next season.It may be a stretch to see him post a career-best .828 OPS, 28 home runs and 74 RBI, but something close to that will be just fine for fantasy owners.

Clint Frazier, age 25. Eligible at OF
2019 Stats: 246 PAs, 12 HR, 31 Runs, 38 RBI, 1 SB, .267/.317/.489
Frazier deserves a look on draft day. Playing on a deep team that seems to struggle with injuries could make him a nice addition to a fantasy roster, especially in deep leagues.

Mike Tauchman, age 29, eligible at OF
2019 Stats: 296 PAs, 13 HR, 46 Runs, 47 RBI, 6 SB, .277/.361/.504
After slashing .228/.318/.404 with four home runs in 42 games before the All-Star break, Tauchman turned it on after the break.. In his final 45 games, Tauchman hit nine home runs, 20 extra-base hits, 30 RBI and slashed .315/.395/.582. He will make a nice depth addition to fantasy rosters.

Tyler Wade, age 25, eligible at 2B (18) 3B (5) SS (4) LF (14) CF (2) RF (2)
2019 Stats: 108 PA, 2 HR, 16 Runs, 11 RBI, 7 SB, .245/.330/.362
Wade versatility at many positions, on a talented team, could make him worthy of a roster spot, especially in deeper leagues.

**PITCHERS**

**Starting Pitchers**
Gerrit Cole, age 29, RHP
2019 Stats: 212.1 IP, 326 Ks, 20 Wins, 2.50 ERA, 0.89 WHIP
One of the biggest free-agent signings in the off-season, Cole will now spend half his season pitching at Yankee Stadium. Things shouldn't change dramatically for Cole in New York. There is no reason to expect his numbers will change dramatically and he could easily be a top-three pitcher for the 2020 fantasy season.

James Paxton, age 31, LHP
2019 Stats: 150.2 IP, 186 Ks, 15 Wins, 3.82 ERA, 1.28 WHIP
Like many Yankees in 2018, Paxton had a few health issues that sidelined him for some time.
Regardless, he put up solid numbers and putting health concerns aside, he is a fantastic
strikeout arm to target in your draft.

Masahiro Tanaka, age 31, RHP
2019 Stats: 182 IP, 149 Ks, 11 Wins, 4.45 ERA, 1.24 WHIP
After the 2019 season, Tanaka had arthroscopic surgery to remove a bone spur in his pitching
elbow but is expected to be ready for spring training. He still won't be able to lead your fantasy
rotation to a championship, but he's a reliable third or fourth starter on all fantasy rosters.

Luis Severino, age 25, RHP
2019 Stats: 12 IP, 17 Ks, 1 Win, 1.50 ERA, 1.00 WHIP
Severino started 2019 on the IL and did not return until September. If healthy, Severino can put
up the kind of season that involves 200 innings pitched, 220-plus strikeouts, and many wins.
The promising news is that at the end of last season, Severino pitched 20.1 innings and gave up
only four runs. He essentially looked healthy and pitched like his normal self.

J.A. Happ, age 37, LHP
2019 Stats: 161.1 IP, 140 Ks, 12 Wins, 4.91 ERA, 1.30 WHIP
After struggling for most of 2019, Happ was decent in September. In five games, including a
relief appearance, Happ allowed just five runs in 27 1/3 innings for a 1.65 ERA. He still has
enough in the tank to be on most fantasy rosters as a mid to late-round pickup.

**BULLPEN**
Aroldis Chapman, age 31, LHP
2019 Stats: 57 IP, 85 Ks, 3 Wins, 37 Saves, 2.21 ERA, 1.11 WHIP
The veteran left-hander was again one of the top closers in baseball in 2019, and will still be a
reliable choice for saves in 2020. He should be one of the first relievers to go off the board in
most fantasy drafts.

Zack Britton, age 31, LHP
2019 Stats: 61.1 IP, 53 Ks, 3 Wins, 3 Saves, 1.91 ERA, 1.14 WHIP
Britton has value as a Chapman backup for saves. Also valuable in a league that awards points
for holds. Like all relievers, it will be curious to see how the new 3 batter rule affects Britton.

Adam Ottavino, age 34, RHP
2019 Stats: 66.1 IP, 88 Ks, 6 Wins, 2 Saves, 1.90 ERA, 1.31 WHIP
Like Britton, Ottavino could be source of late-round saves. The Yankees are a team that loves to
use their bullpen so opportunities will be plenty.

Luis Cessa, age 27, RHP
2019 Stats: 81 IP, 75 Ks, 2 Wins, 1 save, 4.11 ERA, 1.31 WHIP
Cessa is slated to be the long reliever but should be kept on a fantasy owner's radar for spot
starts or if anyone in the rotation goes down with an injury.

Tommy Kahnle, age 30, RHP

2019 Stats: 61.1 IP, 88 Ks, 3 Wins, 0 Saves, 3.67 ERA, 1.06 WHIP
As the Yankees like to use the bullpen, he has some value in very deep leagues.

Chad Green, age 28, RHP
2019 Stats: 69 IP, 98 Ks, 4 Wins, 2 Saves, 4.17 ERA, 1.23 WHIP
Like Kahnle, Green has value in very deep leagues.

Stephen Tarpley, age 26, LHP
2019 Stats: 24.2 IP, 34 K's, 1 Win, 2 Saves, 6.93 ERA, 1.99 WHIP
No real fantasy value

Ben Heller, age RHP
2019 Stats: 7.1 IP, 9 Ks, 0 Wins, 0 Saves, 1.23 ERA, 1.23 WHIP
No real fantasy value

## New York Yankees Prospects
### By Matt Thompson

**1. Jasson Dominguez- OF**
The man. The myth. The legend. The hype machine is rolling along in an almost unprecedented manner with "The Martian". I don't have much to add here as I haven't seen anything other than the same twitter clips or youtube videos with Dominguez that you have. If you want him though it's going to cost you. He's a candidate for the number one pick in your FYPD, and is going off the board in the top 15 amongst prospects in most dynasty drafts I've seen. The success of the last two big J-2 guys, Wander Franco and Marco Luciano, is partially to blame here. Potential plus runner with a plus or double-plus power tool. Dominguez is potentially a five-category star. Or not? Does anyone really know? **ETA: 2024.**

**2. Deivi Garcia- RHP**
Tiny right-hander that pitches bigger than his stuff, Garcia is knocking on the door of the big leagues. Despite his small, 5'9' 165 pound frame, he gets his fastball up to 97 in short bursts but sits 92-93 as a starter. His high spin curveball is the star of the show, and is a plus big league pitch now. The movement and tempo in his delivery showcase his athleticism, but the main knock is a lack of durability. His build doesn't help, but Garcia has only eclipsed the 100 inning mark once in his pro career. Needs to get up to 150 in 2020, and some of those may come in the Bronx in the second half. **ETA: 2020.**

**3. Clarke Schmidt- RHP**
The Yankees picked Schmidt in the first round in 2017 despite knowing that he was going to require Tommy John surgery. 2019 was his statement season thus far. The stocky righty showed he was healthy and welcomed the return of his plus fastball and his split-change, which is also a plus pitch. Schmidt sits 92-95 and touches 97 with life. His split-change is his fastball, except there's a trap door in front of home plate. The pitch just disappears. He also throws a slider that grades out to above-average. He can get crafty as well and mess with timing and arm angles and give hitters a different sight line. He needs to build innings. Should start in Double-A, and if he has enough of his likely 120-130 innings left he could end the season in New York. **ETA: 2021.**

**4. Luis Medina- RHP**
Medina has been blessed by the gods with an absolute cannon for an arm. Dude was hitting triple digits as a teenager before signing. It's an absolute 80-grade heater with life. Unfortunately the command and control is non-existent. Scattershot is a better word for it. He averaged 98 with the pitch last year, and was clocked as high as 101. The pitch had a 32% SwStr%!!! His slider is a two-plane pitch that piles up the swing and miss as well. Also has a near 90 mph changeup that has shown the ability to be a plus pitch. A strong finish to 2019 makes Medina very interesting, and if he can get is command up to a playable level, this is the best pitcher in the game upside. Slim chance he hits that, sure, but it exists. **ETA: 2023.**

**5. Luis Gil- RHP**
Yet another teenage firebreather. The Yankees acquired Gil from the Twins and the early returns look strong. Armed with a double-plus high 90s heater that's touched 101, he has the ability to miss bats in bunches. His two secondaries should be average, which is more than enough when

blessed with an arm like this. Missed some time in 2019 with a biceps injury, but did return to the mound and throw in side sessions. Gil is a future SP 2 or 3, or late inning reliever. **ETA: 2022.**

### 6. Alexander Vargas- SS

Probably the high man on Vargas, but it's sort of a pick 'em from here on out with Yankees prospects all being in the lower minors. Vargas was signed for $2.5 million out of Cuba in 2018. Vargas has plus speed and strong defensive instincts at short, and has strong bat-to-ball skills and advanced feel for the zone for such a young age. Was a perfect 13-for-13 on the base paths, and I think he can be a future stolen base weapon. **ETA: 2024.**

### 7. Canaan Smith- OF

An offense only prospect, Smith's value is entirely tied to his production in that left-handed batters box. Armed with future plus power and hit tools, and an advanced feel for the zone, Smith was amongst the league leaders in doubles and OBP/walks. He's going to turn those doubles into potential 30-homer thump in the future. I like Smith, but this profile sounds a lot like Clint Frazier, and that's not good enough to play everyday in the Bronx. **ETA: 2023.**

### 8. Kevin Alcantara- OF

Alcantara is a tooled up J2 signing from the 2018 class. He's a plus runner that was getting big exit velocity numbers on the showcase circuit, and should add bulk to his lean and potentially powerful frame. He gets positive marks for his defense and overall feel for the game, and Alcantara is a similar power/speed asset to the guy below him on this list, just hope he stays healthy and makes more consistent contact. **ETA: 2023.**

### 9. Estevan Florial- OF

A myriad of injuries and a stagnant hit tool has taken the bloom off the rose here. Florial has missed a lot of development due to freak injuries, and was added to the 40-man this off-season despite never taking an at-bat above High-A. IF everything clicks we have a potential five category producer, but judging by his ranking you can tell I've soured a bit. The quality of his at-bats haven't improved and the same bad habits that plagued him years ago are still very prevalent. **ETA: 2021**

### 10. Anthony Volpe- SS

Their 2019 first rounder out of the New Jersey prep ranks, Volpe has a well rounded skill set that all plays up due to his high baseball acumen. A future plus defender at the six, Volpe profiles similarly to Dansby Swanson to me. He does a bit of everything, nothing elite (except his defense) and gets the most out of his skill set. He had a rough introduction to pro ball but was also recovering from a bout with mono, so I'll toss it. I wouldn't be shocked if the Yankees push him aggressively here, knowing that he has the skills and mindset to handle it. **ETA: 2023.**

**Next Five:**
Antonio Cabello- OF
Oswald Peraza- SS
Roansy Contreras- RHP
Alexander Vizcaino- RHP
Ezequiel Duran- 2B

**Top Five in FYPDs:**
Jasson Dominguez- OF
Anthony Volpe- SS
Josh Smith- SS
T.J. Sikkema- LHP
Enger Castellano- 3B

**Projected Order:**
1- Brandon Lowe, 2B
2- Austin Meadows, LF
3- Yandy Díaz, 3B
4- Ji-Man Choi, 1B
5- Hunter Renfroe, RF
6- Yoshi Tsutsugo, DH
7- Willy Adames, SS
8- Kevin Kiermaier, CF
9- Mike Zunino, C

**Projected Bench:**
Michael Perez, C
Jose Martinez, INF/OF
Daniel Robertson, INF/OF
Joey Wendle INF/OF

**Projected Rotation:**
Charlie Morton, RHP
Blake Snell, LHP
Tyler Glasnow, RHP
Yonny Chirinos, RHP
Ryan Yarbrough, LHP

**Bullpen**:
Emilio Pagán, RHP
Nick Anderson, RHP
Diego Castillo, RHP
Colin Poche, LHP
Chaz Roe, RHP
José Alvarado, LHP
Oliver Drake, RHP
Austin Pruitt, RHP

**Catchers:**
Mike Zunino, age 29, eligible at C
2019 Stats: 289 PA, 9 HR, 30 Runs, 32 RBI, 0 SB, .165/.232/.312
Zunino has shown flashes of fantasy relevance in the past due to his power potential but the batting average has gotten to the point that he is not worth rostering hoping for one of his hot streaks.

Michael Perez, age 27, eligible at C
2019 Stats: 55 PA, 0 HR, 6 Runs, 2 RBI, 0 SB, .217/.345/.326
Perez is only a backup catcher and would not carry any fantasy value even if Zunino were to be injured.

**Infielders**:

Ji-Man Choi, age 28, eligible at 1B
2019 Stats: 487 PA, 19 HR, 54 Runs, 63 RBI, 2 SB, .261/.363/.459
Choi fits in nicely for what the Rays like to do, platoon above average hitters at multiple positions. Choi has more value in OBP and/or daily roster move leagues as his batting average is not strong enough to carry his average power and his playing time decreases due to the platooning. He is a great streamer when the Rays face a right handed heavy schedule.

Brandon Lowe, age 25, eligible at 2B
2019 Stats: 327 PA, 17 HR, 42 Runs, 51 RBI, 5 SB, .270/.336/.514
Lowe had an extremely promising rookie year and on the surface should be a great buy as the Rays' potential leadoff hitter. His problem is he had a 34.6% strikeout rate which spikes to 52.9% versus left-handed pitchers. Due to his struggles against left-handed pitching and the Rays love of platooning, I do not see him getting full-time plate appearances. His playing time risk along with the batting average downside, I see him as a very risky investment.

Yandy Díaz, age 28, eligible at 1B/3B
2019 Stats: 347 PA, 14 HR, 53 Runs, 38 RBI, 2 SB, .267/.340/.476
Díaz started extremely hot and it appeared he was finally producing the power and batting average profile fantasy owners have always wished out of the muscle flexing pictures. He cooled down but still seems to have improved his power swing and should be able to produce mid-20s home run power with a solid batting average and counting stats hitting in the middle of the Rays order

Willy Adames, age 24, eligible at SS
2019 Stats: 584 PA, 20 HR, 69 Runs, 52 RBI, 4 SB, .254/.317/.418
Adames was finally given a full season of playing time and produced a strong all-around season for the Rays. His fantasy output was nothing special and he does not project above average in any category but he should be a nice late-round MI for people who waited on the position.

Daniel Robertson, age 26, eligible at 2B/3B
2019 Stats: 237 PA, 2 HR, 23 Runs, 19 RBI, 2 SB, .213/.312/.295
Robertson has always shown some intriguing OBP value due to strong walk rates but he is strictly a short-side platoon middle infielder.

Joey Wendle, age 29, eligible at 2B/3B
2019 Stats: 263 PA, 3 HR, 32 Runs, 19 RBI, 8 SB, .231/.293/.340
2019 was a lost season for Wendle after his surprisingly strong 28-year-old rookie season in 2018. He does not have much power but at his best, Wendle will combine a plus batting average with mid-teens stolen bases at a weak 2B position. If he starts the season hot, be prepared to add him for the potential steals.

**Outfielders**:

Austin Meadows, age 24, eligible at OF
2019 Stats: 591 PA, 33 HR, 83 Runs, 89 RBI, 12 SB, .291/.364/.558
The former top 10 prospect and top 10 overall pick is making the Chris Archer trade look better and better. Meadows completely crushed during the 2019 and every underlying metric proves

he is a potential fantasy superstar. He provides batting average, power, speed, and counting stats in a good Rays lineup. He is a five category producer with top 20 overall potential.

Kevin Kiermaier, age 29, eligible at OF
2019 Stats: 480 PA, 12 HR, 60 Runs, 55 RBI, 19 SB, .228/.278/.398
In the year of stolen base contributors being pushed up draft boards, Kiermaier is still relatively affordable. He does come with the batting average downside we saw in 2019 but with a little BABIP luck, he could contribute mid-teens home runs with 20+ stolen bases and a .250 average. While he has sustained injuries over the years, his glove keeps him in the lineup every day when healthy.

Hunter Renfroe, age 28, eligible at OF
2019 Stats: 494 PA, 33 HR, 64 Runs, 64 RBI, 5 SB, .216/.289/.489
Renfroe comes over to the Rays from the Padres and seems to have a more likely path to every day playing time than he did in San Diego. He is a power-only, low-OBP, corner outfielder which is not highly valued in modern baseball but the Rays traded for him so I would assume they want to play him. I worry he could fall into a short-side platoon role as they have plenty of lefties who can play the OF since he finished 2019 with a .208/.274/.459 slash line against right handed pitching with a 34% strikeout rate.

Yoshi Tsutsugo, age 28, eligible at OF (check your league's website)
2019 Stats: No stats
Tsutsugo signed with the Rays this offseason for two years and $12 million. He has played 1B, 3B, and OF in his career and should split time at DH and 1B with Choi, Renfroe, and who the Rays decide is the other right handed platoon partner. Tsutsugo is the prototypical left-handed power hitting corner bat. During his years in Japan, he displayed great power numbers and good patience while limiting his strikeouts. He should be a good addition to fantasy teams looking for power.

Jose Martinez, age 31, eligible at OF
2019 Stats: 373 PA, 10 HR, 45 Runs, 42 RBI, 3 SB, .269/.340/.410
Jose Martinez has been a fantasy darling for a few years but his lack of defensive value, congested Cardinals roster, and no DH has left him with little fantasy value due to playing time. The one thing Martinez has shown is the ability to hit for a strong batting average with modest power. Unfortunately, even though he made his way to the AL, the platoon happy Rays is not a great landing spot for his playing time. He should at a minimum be a short-side platoon player for the Rays with the upside to be their every day DH/1B. Invest assuming limited PAs.

**Starters:**
Charlie Morton, age 36, RHP
2019 Stats: 194.2 IP, 240 K, 16 W, 3.05 ERA, 1.08 WHIP
Ground Chuck gets no respect after his dominant 2019 season because, well, he's old. There honestly is no other reason for him to be going outside of the top 10 starting pitchers. He checks all the boxes: elite strikeout rate, good walk rate, good ground ball rate, innings volume, great team, and great pitchers park. I think he is a steal at his current ADP considering he is going at a discount due to age unlike Justin Verlander and Max Scherzer.

Blake Snell, age 27, LHP

2019 Stats: 107 IP, 147 K, 6 W, 4.29 ERA, 1.27 WHIP

Snell's 2019 after his Cy Young winning 2018 was nothing short of a disaster. He started the season great and was pitching like an ace but then dropped a decorative bathroom foot and broke his toe. He returned soon after and was lit up in 23.1 June innings to the tune of a 9.64 ERA. Snell's price has not been discounted too much from last year's cost but he is still an ace in my opinion and should be off the board in the third round.

Tyler Glasnow, age 26, RHP

2019 Stats: 60.2 IP, 76 K, 6 W, 1.78 ERA, 0.89 WHIP

Glasnow finally put it all together last year but it was cut short by an elbow injury that cost him three months. He always had the "stuff" to be an ace with an upper 90s fastball and wipeout curve but the control was never there. My concerns with his 2020 outlook are can he hold up over a full season and if he can, are there diminishing returns as the innings pile up? I have always been very high on Glasnow but these concerns have me out on his at his current price.

Yonny Chirinos, age 26, RHP

2019 Stats: 133.1 IP, 114 K, 9 W, 3.85 ERA, 1.05 WHIP

Chirinos was one of the original "followers" or bulk-inning pitchers after the opener and was great in the role. Last year, he started more than he had an opener start the game which is actually a slight downgrade for fantasy since it lowers his win potential. He is a great ratio boost to fantasy rosters but his lack of strike out upside and low innings total makes him hard to use in weekly leagues where he only has one start.

Ryan Yarbrough, age 28, LHP

2019 Stats: 141.2 IP, 117 K, 11 W, 4.13 ERA, 1.00 WHIP

Yarbrough was used more as the bulk reliever than Chirinos was in 2019. Again, his statistical profile is pretty similar to Chirinos in that they are both good ratio boosts with limited strikeout upside and hard to use in one-start weeks due to the low innings total.

**Relievers:**

Emilio Pagán age 28, RHP

2019 Stats: 70 IP, 96 K, 4 W, 2.31 ERA, 0.83 WHIP

Pagán looks to be the most recent dominant Rays relief pitcher to come out of relative obscurity. His surface numbers look awesome with a 31.1% K-BB% backed by 17.6% swinging strike rate. One concern is the Rays like to mix and match at the back end of the bullpen. The last concern is he may not be the best pitcher in his own bullpen because...

Nick Anderson, age 29, RHP

2019 Stats: 65 IP, 110 K, 5 W, 3.32 ERA, 1.08 WHIP

Nick Anderson from the day he was acquired by the Rays: 21.1 IP, 41 K, 2.11 ERA, and 0.66 WHIP with a 50%(!!!) K-BB%. Many relievers dominate over a small sample size of 20 innings but the degree to which Anderson did was special. He is pretty pricey as a ratio and strikeout boosting reliever but if he were to take the closer role, he could be the best closer in fantasy.

Diego Castillo, age 25, RHP

2019 Stats: 68.2 IP, 81 K, 5 W, 3.41 ERA, 1.24 WHIP

Castillo had a chance at the closer role in 2019 but he was clearly a worse choice than Pagán as the season went on. He was the opener for a few games last year which shows me he is down on the Rays' list of potential closers. I can see him eventually popping up as a waiver wire addition for ratios and strikeouts.

Colin Poche, age 25, LHP
2019 Stats: 51.2 IP, 72 K, 5 W, 4.70 ERA, 1.01 WHIP
Poche had a really tough MLB debut if you strictly look at his ERA but the underlying skills have the look of another dominant Rays bullpen arm. He should be their top lefty in the bullpen but since he primarily throws his fastball, I do not think he has the arsenal to be their closer.

Chaz Roe, age 33, RHP
2019 Stats: 51 IP, 65 K, 1 W, 4.06 ERA, 1.57 WHIP
Roe is a decent middle reliever but the walk rate keeps him off the fantasy radar since he has the risk of hurting your ratios. He does not have the stuff to jump all the more talented arms in the pen.

José Alvarado, age 24, LHP
2019 Stats: 30 IP, 39 K, 1 W, 4.80 ERA, 1.87 WHIP
The Rays' closer to start the 2019 and one of the most GIFable pitchers, Alvarado was one of the bigger flops among 2019 relief pitchers. His control completely fell apart and was unable to keep his job. He has the talent where everyone should be keeping him on their watch list in case he returns to his 2018 form.

Oliver Drake, age 33, RHP
2019 Stats: 56 IP, 70 K, 5 W, 3.21 ERA, 0.98 WHIP
Drake is a very interesting real-life bullpen arm and on another team, he would have some fantasy intrigue. Unfortunately, him and his 16.8% swinging strike rate is second class in this ridiculously deep bullpen. He, like the rest of the middle relievers on this team, will likely have weeks of intrigue for ratios and strikeouts.

Austin Pruitt, age 30, RHP
2019 Stats: 47 IP, 39 K, 3 W, 4.40 ERA, 1.26 WHIP
Pruitt was used often as the bulk reliever but his profile is less interesting than Chirinos or Yarbrough because he does not have the miniscule walk rate. He should be left on waiver wires no matter which role he is in.

**Tampa Bay Rays Prospects**
By Matt Thompson

### 1. Wander Franco- SS

The only knock against Franco as a prospect is he hasn't hit Double-A yet. That will change in 2020 after a 2019 season that saw the top prospect in the game destroy two levels in his first season of full-season ball. He torched the Midwest League by hitting .318/.390/.506 and following that with a .339/.408/.464 line in the Florida State League. For his professional career he's walked 83 times while only striking out 54 times. Unbelievable plate skills and the quickest hands in the minor league game. It's an 80-hit tool and I predict something like .330 with 30+ homers and 10-15 steals at peak. **ETA: 2021.**

### 2. Vidal Brujan- 2B/SS

The switch-hitting Brujan stole 48 bases last season between High-A and Double-A, and his speed is of the game changing variety. He also has plus plate skills, and projects as the Rays leadoff hitter of the future. There isn't much power in his game. He has good hands and actions at second base, but I was talking to an evaluator who suggested centerfield as his future long-term home. Brujan is knocking on the door and was added to the 40-man this winter. **ETA: 2021.**

### 3. Brendan McKay- LHP

I'm not even factoring in McKay's two-way abilities here, as the Rays depth chart is already incredibly crowded at DH and first base. McKay's best trait on the mound is his plus command, and while none of his four-pitch mix strays too far from above-average, they all play up and he can throw any pitch in any count. His fastball sits around 93, and he has a cutter, curveball and a change. He's a big league ready mid-rotation arm. He was one inning shy of graduating from prospect lists, and pitched a combined 120 innings or so across three levels last season. Look for him to throw 150 innings or so, bouncing between Durham and Tampa. **ETA: Arrived.**

### 4. Greg Jones- SS

Another switch-hitting middle infield prospect with 70-speed and questions about power. Jones was the 19th pick in the 2019 draft, and isn't as polished as most collegiate bats tend to be. He will take a walk, and posted strong OBP numbers since entering pro ball, but there's a significant amount of swing and miss present here. Jones is going off the board between pick 8-12 in FYPDs. Significant upside but it comes with risk. **ETA: 2022.**

### 5. Xavier Edwards- 2B

The fourth switch-hitting middle infielder on the list, Edwards was the prospect return in the Tommy Pham deal with the Padres this winter. Edwards was the 38th pick in the 2018 draft due to his 80-grade speed and ability to make contact. Both of those skills have translated to pro ball, and an optimistic comp is Dee Gordon with the ability to take a walk. The lack of power is alarming, but he knows that's not his game. Patience is required, but Edwards should have significant fantasy value due to the stolen bases. **ETA: 2022.**

### 6. Shane Baz- RHP

Baz can bring the heat. The six-foot-two righty can dial it up to triple digits with movement. He pairs it with a 70-slider to form one of the most lethal one-two punches of all minor league baseball. He also has a curveball and a change. His changeup has the potential to be a plus pitch, but he has trouble with feel and comes and goes on a per inning basis. Baz has the stuff to be a number one, but command and control get in the way. There is some reliever risk here due to how well the fastball and slider play together, but you let this arm start as long as you can. **ETA: 2022.**

### 7. Josh Lowe- OF
A productive 2019 mitigated some of the strikeout concerns that have followed him since he was picked in the first round in 2016. Lowe is tooled up and his power and speed skills finally busted through, and he posted an 18 homer, 30 steal campaign in Double-A. He's always been a guy that's posted double-digit walk rates in his career, and he's also a strong defender in centerfield. He handles lefties well which should lead to full time at-bats with time. He seems like a future trade piece for the Rays, and could be ready this summer if he produces in Triple-A. Lowe is an exciting future asset, but there is some risk with the strikeouts. **ETA: 2021.**

### 8. Kevin Padlo- 3B
The 23-year old former Rockies prospect has hit his way back onto prospect lists. It's not too often that an offensive prospect gains value after leaving the Rockies organization, but here we are. In 110 games between Double-A and Triple-A, Padlo mashed. He hit .265/.389/.538 with a near 16% walk rate and 21/12 homers/steals. Sure the strikeouts are an issue, at nearly 27%, but his batted ball data is a thing of beauty. His line drive rate is high, and he hits the ball in the air, to his pull side. He was added to the 40-man roster this winter. The range of outcomes is wide, but Padlo is worth a mid-round flier in a prospect draft. **ETA: 2021.**

### 9. Shane McClanahan- LHP
The now 22 year-old lefty was the Rays first round pick in 2018. He can touch triple digits with the fastball, and the curveball is a plus pitch. His slider and changeup lag behind, and the overall arsenal lacks consistent command and control. There's some reliever risk here, and most of that is due to the organization. If his slider or change don't catch up to the other pitches he could find himself in a multi-inning relief role, and avoiding facing hitters multiple times. His range of outcomes is anywhere from a high strikeout number two fantasy arm, to a multi-inning reliever. **ETA: 2022.**

### 10. JJ Goss- RHP
This pairing has me very excited for the future. Goss is the perfect arm for an organization like the Rays, who selected him with the 36th pick in 2019. Goss gets elite extension on his mid-to-high 90s heater, and will give hitters an uncomfortable look due to the perceived velocity and funky arm slot. Goss' upside is similar to McClanahan and Baz above him. Significant risk but potentially a monsterous reward. **ETA: 2023.**

**Next Five:**
Brent Honeywell Jr.- RHP
Joe Ryan- RHP
Ronaldo Hernandez- C
Randy Arozarena- OF
Seth Johnson- RHP

**Top Five in FYPDs:**
Greg Jones- SS

JJ Goss- RHP
Seth Johnson- RHP
Jhon Diaz- OF
Graeme Stinson- LHP

## Toronto Blue Jays Team Preview
By Andrew Dewhirst

**Projected Order:**
1- Bo Bichette, SS
2- Cavan Biggio, 2B
3- Lourdes Gurriel Jr., LF
4- Vladamir Guerrero Jr., 3B
5- Travis Shaw, 1B
6- Randal Grichuk, LF
7. Dany Jansen, C
8- Teoscar Hernandez, DH
9- Derek Fisher, CF

**Projected Bench:**
Reese McGuire - C
Brandon Drury - 3B/OF
Breyvic Valera - INF
Anthony Alford - OF

**Projected Rotation:**
Hyun-Jin Ryu, LHP
Chase Anderson, RHP
Tanner Roark, RHP
Matt Shoemaker, RHP
Ryan Borucki, LHP

**Bullpen**:
Ken Giles, RHP
Anthony Bass, RHP
Shun Yamaguchi, RHP
Jordan Romano, RHP
Thomas Pannone, LHP
Sam Gavigleo, RHP
Trent Thornton, RHP
Wilmer Font, RHP

**Catchers:**
Dany Jansen, age 24, eligible at C
2019 Stats: 384 PAs, 13 HRs, 41 Runs, 43 RBIs, 0 SBs, .207/.279/.360
Jansen didn't have the rookie season that many envisioned on draft day. That being said, he is in prime post-hype sleeper territory. He will turn 25 just after the season starts and now has a full season under his belt. Catchers notoriously have slow starts to their careers, and Jansen may just do the same. He should be owned in all 2 catcher leagues, and 15 teams or larger.

Reese McGuire, age 24, eligible at C

2019 Stats: 105 PAs, 5 HRs, 14 Runs, 11 RBIs, 0 SBs, .299/.346/.526

I don't expect much from McGuire in 2020. At best he is likely hollow average and not much else. At worst he spends most of the year in AAA. He shouldn't be drafted in any league size.

**Infielders**:
Travis Shaw, age 29, eligible at 1B
2019 Stats: 270 PAs, 7 HRs, 22 Runs, 16 RBIs, 0 SBs, .157/.281/.270

Shaw will get the opportunity to bounce back in Toronto, where there will be much less pressure. If he can get anywhere close to his 2017 or 2018 where he hit over 30 HR, he will be a great value. He is worth a late-round flyer, in 12 and 15 team leagues.

Cavan Biggio, age 24,  eligible at 2B, SS
2019 Stats: 430 PAs, 16 HR, 66 Runs, 48 RBIs, 14 SB, .234/.364/.429

Biggio could easily go 25/20 this year. The question is will he sink you in leagues that use average. Odds are that he will. He is a pull heavy hitter, who will see the shift a lot. So keep that in mind on draft day. If you're willing to live with his poor batting average, you could get a steal, just try to make sure you have a couple of good pillows.

Vladimir Gurerero Jr, age 21, eligible at 3B
2019 Stats: 514 PAs, 15 HR, 52 Runs, 69 RBIs, 0 SB, .272/.339/.433

There was some disappointment in Vlad's rookie season. Many expected 25 Hr, and an average over 300. There isn't a lot of reason to not believe that he could deliver that this year and more, as the Blue Jays lineup is considerably better now than it was this time last year. However, you are still going to be asked to pay up to find out in many situations, if you're willing to pay up there is upside there, but you might prefer to play it safer at his draft cost.

Bo Bichette, age 21, eligible at SS
2017 Stats: 220 PAs, 11 HR, 32 Runs, 21 RBI's, 4 SB, .311/.358/.571

What a debut Bichette had last year. He could easily give you 0.275 with 20 HR and 20 steals. The thing to keep in mind with Bichette is that because of his small sample, the league hasn't adjusted to him as of yet, so there could be some rough stretches. This won't hurt his value much in Roto leagues, but it will create some warts in points leagues.

Brandon Drury, age 27, eligible at 3B/OF
2019 Stats:: 447 PA, 15 HR, 43 Runs, 41 RBI, 0 SB, .218/.262/.380

Drury likely doesn't make a big impact in 2020. With no clear path to playing time, as the Blue Jays need to let much of their infield grow in their positions. His best path is going to either be an injury or Shaw's continued struggles. He isn't worth drafting in any format this year.

Breyvic Valera, age 27, eligible at 2B
2019 Stats: 52 PAs, 1 HR, 7 Runs, 6 RBI's, 0 SB, .234/.308/.383

Valera shouldn't be on your draft radar in 2020.

**Outfielders:**

Randal Grichuk age 28, eligible at OF
2019 Stats: 628 PAs, 31 HRs, 75 Runs, 80 RBIs, 2 SBs, .232/.280/.457

If you can take on his poor average, Grichuk can be a useful outfielder. It's reasonable to believe that there isn't anyone who is going to be taking playing time from him, so he should be in line for another 30 HR season, and you could see an uptick in his runs and RBIs as the team improves.

Lourdes Gurriel Jr. age 26, eligible at OF
2019 Stats: 343 PAs, 20 HRs, 52 Runs, 50 RBIs, 6 SBs, .277/.327/.541

Health is a big concern with Gurriel. He had a fantastic 2019 but appeared in less than 100 games. I think he is a risk that is worth taking though in your OF. He has 30 HR and 15 steals upside while hitting for a nice average.

Teoscar Hernandez, age 27, eligible at OF
2019 Stats: 464 PAs, 26 HRs, 58 Runs, 65 RBIs, 6 SBs, .230/.306/.472

Another interesting power-speed combination for the Blue Jays. Like so many of their players 30 HR and 10 steals are in play for Teoscar if he can steal healthy, however, like many of his teammates the batting average is a concern. I expect you will get Teoscar relatively cheap, so he could be worth the investment.

Derek Fisher age 26, eligible at OF
2019 Stats: 167 PAs, 7 HRs, 23 Runs, 17 RBIs, 5 SBs, .185/.287/.370

In his time in the majors Fisher has struggled to hit for any sort of average, which has led to him never really getting much more than a cup of coffee. The Blue Jays appear to be ready to give him a shot as a regular player so if he can bring his average closer to his AAA level, then he could be a very useful fantasy player.

Anthony Alford age 25, eligible at OF
2019 Stats: 30 PAs, 1 HRs, 3 Runs, 1 RBIs, 2 SBs, .179/.233/.286

Alford is likely the 5th outfielder, so he will not have any relevance on draft day.


**Starters:**
Hyun-Jin Ryu, age 33, LHP
2019 Stats: 182.2 IP, 163 Ks, 14 Wins, 3.32 ERA, 1.01 WHIP

As the newly anointed ace of the staff, there will be some pressure on Ryu to perform. This likely wasn't the best landing spot for Ryu, moving not only from the NL to the AL, but to the AL East. He won't produce big strikeout totals for you, but he should stabilize your WHIP.

Additionally, if he can keep his fly ball rate close to the 25% it was last year, he should provide a solid return in the ERA department as well.

Chase Anderson age 32, RHP
2019 Stats: 139 IP, 124 Ks, 8 Wins, 4.21 ERA, 1.27 WHIP

It's hard to envision Anderson having a positive impact on your 2020 fantasy team. He is draftable in 20 team leagues or larger, but he likely won't help you in any particular category, you're just hoping for volume.

Tanner Roark, age 33, RHP
2019 Stats: 165.1 IP, 158 Ks, 10 Wins, 4.35 ERA, 1.40 WHIP

Any value that Roark has in 2020 will be tied to leagues where innings pitched matters. His ratios won't be good, he won't strike a lot of people out, and well, he might not even win that many games.

Matt Shoemaker, age 33, RHP
2019 Stats: 28.2 IP, 24 Ks, 1 Win, 4.25 ERA, 1.72 WHIP

2019 was a lost year for Shoemaker. He only made 5 starts but was effective in those prior to injuring his knee(torn ACL). The only good news in this is that he will be ready to go for spring training. If healthy, he can have value in 15 team leagues, and AL-only.

Ryan Borucki, age 25, LHP
2019 Stats: 6.2 IP, 6 Ks, 0 Wins, 10.80 ERA, 3.15 WHIP

Borucki will likely never be exciting but in leagues larger than 15 teams and AL-only he can have value as a pitcher who will get you some strikeouts and is capable of a sub 4 ERA.


**Relievers:**
Ken Giles, age 29, RHP
53 IP, 83 K's, 23 Saves, 1.87 ERA, 1.00 WHIP

Giles has a solid 2019, even though he missed time with injuries. His 39% strikeout rate is promising, and if healthy could provide 30 saves this year for the Blue Jays. He should be owned in all formats this year.

Anthony Bass, RHP, age 32, RHP
48 IP, 43 K's, 5 Saves, 3.56 ERA, 0.98 WHIP

If Bass maintains his gains in WHIP from 2019, he could provide value in deep leagues. That said, you really have no need to think about him much on draft day.

Shun Yamaguchi, age 32, RHP
181 IP, 194 K's, 0 Saves, 2.78 ERA, 1.17 WHIP

While listed as a reliever, it is very possible that Yamaguchi starts this year. He was quite effective in his time last year in Japan. He isn't getting a lot of hype, but if he gets a starting role he can be relevant in 15 team leagues or bigger.

Jordan Romano, age 26, RHP
15.1 IP, 21 Ks, 0 Wins, 7.63 ERA, 1.70 WHIP

Romano had great strikeout numbers in his big league time last season. If those numbers are maintained, he will have value in 15 team leagues and h2h points and categories leagues that have designated reliever spots.

Thomas Pannone, age 25, LHP
73 IP, 69 SO, 0 Saves, 6.16 ERA, 1.42 WHIP

Pannone has no fantasy relevance this year.

Sam Gaviglio, age 29, RHP
95.2 IP, 88 K's, 0 Saves, 4.61 ERA, 1.12 WHIP

Gaviglio has no fantasy value this year.

Trent Thornton, age 26, RHP
154.0 IP, 149 K's, 0 Saves, 4.84 ERA, 1.41 WHIP

As a reliever, I think Thornton could be interesting. He has an awkward delivery and was able to show as a starter the ability to strike people out. You can look at him in AL-only, and in all other formats, I would want to wait and see what his role is.

Wilmer Font age 29, RHP
84.1 IP, 95 K's, 0 Saves, 4.48 ERA, 1.27 WHIP

Font has no fantasy value this year.

## Toronto Blue Jays Prospects
By Matt Thompson

### 1. Nate Pearson- RHP
Big Nate with the big fastball, Pearson stole all the headlines in the AFL in 2018 with his 103 MPH heater. Pearson sits 95-99 with the fastball and pairs it with a 89-91 MPH slider. It's a powerful arsenal. He also throws a curveball and a changeup. Despite the big stuff Pearson doesn't pile up the strikeouts like he should. Instead he generates weak contact. His command and control have a long way to go. He alternated short and longer starts for most of 2019 in an effort to keep him on the mound. He's had limited exposure to turning a lineup over three times, and for someone that lacks a viable third pitch to pair with the fastball/slider, that is something I'm watching for 2020. Pearson likely hits the big leagues early in 2021, but there's a chance he could be the team's best potential reliever not named Ken Giles, and there's a slim chance he will debut in the second half as a reliever. **ETA: 2021.**

### 2. Jordan Groshans- 3B/SS
It looked like we were witnessing a breakout as Groshans hit .337/.427/.482 as one of the league's youngest players, but the 2018 first rounders season was cut short due to a foot injury. He has been deemed healthy for 2020, and I expect Groshans to start back in the Midwest League, but the presence of Orelvis Martinez may push him to Dunedin. At present it's a hit over power profile for Groshans, but the expectation is the power catches up as he bulks up and slides over to third base. It's a small sample, full of questions, but I love what we've seen thus far. **ETA: 2023.**

### 3. Orelvis Martinez- SS/3B
Martinez received the largest signing bonus of the 2018 international class and was immediately brought stateside and thrown into the Gulf Coast League despite being only 17 years-old. He proved he could handle the aggressive assignment with strong plate skills and an impressive 150 wRC+ as one of the league's youngest players. He's going to fill out and should start 2020 in Low-A with Lansing. It will be interesting to see what the infield looks like with Groshans and Orelvis in the future. Both teenagers are expected to outgrow shortstop and slide over to the hot corner. **ETA: 2023.**

### 4. Simeon Woods-Richardson- RHP
The Jays acquired SWR in the Marcus Stroman trade with the Mets. The young righty just turned 19, and he's been outstanding since entering pro ball. His ability to throw strikes is strong for his age, and his three pitch arsenal plays up due to his ability to pound the zone. It's an over the top arm slot for SWR and he works up in the zone with the heater to set up the big, power breaking ball. One downside to being in the strike zone so much is the stuff becomes too hittable, and that is the main issue here. SWR should start 2020 in the Florida State League with a bump up to New Hampshire in the summer. **ETA: 2022.**

### 5. Alek Manoah- RHP
Manoah was the Blue Jays first round pick this past June. I ultimately slotted him behind SWR due to SWR's command and untapped potential. Manoah is a more polished arm that lacks the front of the rotation upside that SWR has, but brings a much higher floor. On a real baseball list you'll likely see these two profiles flipped, but this makes sense to me for fantasy. Manoah sits 94-97 with the fastball and put hitters away with a late biting slider. He reminds me of Lance

Lynn physically, and will miss bats in the future. The focus for 2020 will be developing that changeup, and if the Jays can accomplish that he should move quickly. Manoah should start with SWR in the Florida State League to begin 2020. **ETA: 2022.**

### 6. Miguel Hiraldo- 2B/SS

One of the crown jewels of the Jays 2017 international class, Hiraldo had a strong 56 game stint in the Appalachian League, as he slashed .300/.348/.481 despite only being 18 years old. Hiraldo made contact at an impressive 85% rate. He split time between short and second base, but his best long term home is second, although he doesn't profile as much beyond average defensively there. He's an aggressive, pull-heavy kid so just a warning, the numbers may not look great during his introduction to pro ball. Pitchers that can command a breaking ball or have the ability to sequence will give him fits. I'm interested in seeing how he adjusts. The foundation here is solid, think .270-.280, 15-20 homers, 10-12 steals, but it's not one with significant upside. Hiraldo should start in the Midwest League in 2020. **ETA: 2022.**

### 7. Adam Kloffenstein- RHP

Kloffenstein is a massive human. The 2018 third rounder stands six-foot-five, and weighs over 240 pounds. The Jays liked him enough to give him a big $2.45 million bonus to get him in the organization. Despite the large frame, Kloffenstein doesn't light up radar guns, and will sit in the low-90s with his sinking fastball. He also throws a slider, a curveball and a changeup, and all four pitches project as above-average or better offerings. His curveball is the more likely of his secondaries to take a step up. His heavy groundball profile should play, especially in the Midwest League, and Kloffenstein can become a stingy number two starter if the curveball makes that jump, or just settle in as a number three or four with a solid arsenal if it doesn't. **ETA: 2023.**

### 8. Anthony Kay- LHP

Anthony Kay won't soon forget the whirlwind that was his 2019 season. The former Boston College arm began the season in Double-A for the Mets and pitched his way to Triple-A. He was then shipped from the Mets to the Blue Jays in the Marcus Stroman deal. Kay would later make his big league debut with the Blue Jays. Kay has an average fastball around 92-93 with some wiggle to it. He compliments it with an above-average curveball and changeup. His fastball has enough movement to stay off barrels and he didn't give up much in the way of hard contact in his big league debut. The Blue Jays added Ryu, Anderson, and Yamaguchi to the fold, so Kay is likely to return to Triple-A Buffalo to begin 2020. He's likely a number four starter long term, and Kay should spend the majority of the season in Toronto. **ETA: Arrived.**

### 9. Eric Pardinho- RHP

The Jays have moved the now 19 year-old Pardinho along slowly, since he signed for $1.4 million in 2017. The start of his 2019 was delayed due to elbow soreness, but he was deemed healthy enough to throw 37 innings at the end of the season. The small-framed righty throws in the low-90s with a future plus curveball and an average change. His command makes the stuff play up. He's likely going to have strict innings and pitch count restrictions again in 2020, and should begin the season in Low-A. Pardinho has number two starter profile, and the hope is the frame catches up with the stuff. **ETA: 2022.**

### 10. Gabriel Moreno- C

Moreno is an athletic catcher who had a very successful full season debut. Moreno made contact at a strong 88% clip, and the foundation of his offensive game is his ability to hit for average. Moreno hit 12 homers in the Midwest League in 2019, and has the bat speed and bat-to-ball skills to post a similar .280 12-15 homer statline at his peak. Moreno needs to fine tune the defensive side of his game, but does have the arm to stick. **ETA: 2023.**

**Next Five:**
Kendall Williams- RHP
Alejandro Kirk- C
Kevin Smith- SS
Otto Lopez- 2B
Dasan Brown- OF

**Top Five in FYPDs:**
Alek Manoah- RHP
Kendall Williams- RHP
Dasan Brown- OF
Will Robertson- OF
Estiven Machado- SS

**Chicago White Sox**
By Gabe Zammit

**Projected Order:**
1- Yoán Moncada, 3B
2- Tim Anderson, SS
3- Jose Abreu, 1B
4- Yasmani Grandal, C
5- Edwin Encarnación, DH
6- Eloy Jiménez, LF
7- Nomar Mazara, RF
8- Luis Robert, CF
9- Leury García, 2B

**Projected Bench:**
James McCann, C
Zack Collins, C/1B
Danny Mendick, INF
Adam Engel, OF

**Projected Rotation:**
Lucas Giolito, RHP
Dallas Keuchel, LHP
Reynaldo López, RHP
Gio Gonzalez, LHP
Dylan Cease, RHP

**Bullpen**:
Alex Colomé, RHP
Aaron Bummer, LHP
Evan Marshall, RHP
Kelvin Herrera, RHP
Jace Fry, LHP
Jimmy Cordero, RHP
Tayron Guerrero, RHP
Carson Fulmer, RHP

**Catchers:**
Yasmani Grandal, age 31, eligible at C
2019 Stats: 632 PA, 28 HR, 79 Runs, 77 RBI, 5 SB, .246/.380/.468
The catcher position is still not looking great, and here you have a top 3 option at the position. Grandal's projected to bat cleanup and should knock in a load of runs in what has suddenly become a particularly interesting lineup. Expect his average to hover right around .250 again

while knocking in 25-30 HR. Be prepared to push Grandal up your draft boards in OBP leagues (17% walk rate last year).

James McCann, age 29, eligible at C
2019 Stats: 476 PA, 18 HR, 62 Runs, 60 RBI, 4 SB, .273/.328/.460
McCann was a decent find at the catcher position last year and looked to be a bargain again in drafts this year. He's made strides across the board, but then the White Sox went and signed a slew of bats and Yasmani Grandal, effectively blocking his chance for at bats. Barring injuries or trade, McCann is not worth more than a speculative stash in 2 catcher leagues.

Zack Collins, age 25, eligible at C
2019 Stats: 102 PA, 3 HR, 10 Runs, 12 RBI, 0 SB, .186/.307/.349
Similar to McCann, it is hard to envision much of a role for Collins given the off-season additions. He flashed intriguing power hitting 19 HR in 2019 in triple-A, but he's not worth a spot even in the deepest of leagues.

**Infielders**:
Jose Abreu, age 33, eligible at 1B/DH
2019 Stats: 693 PA, 33 HR, 85 Runs, 123 RBI, 2 SB, .284/.330/.503
Well, last year was quite the resurgence for Jose Abreu. He improved his barrel and hard hit percentage and it's not hard to envision a repeat performance this year. Abreu seems to be a relative bargain right now in drafts as he isn't quite as flashy as the top options at the position. If you wait at first base, he is a great high floor guy to fall back on.

Edwin Encarnación, age 37, eligible at 1B/DH
2019 Stats: 486 PA, 34 HR, 81 Runs, 86 RBI, 0 SB, .244/.344/.531
E5 is not quite what he was in terms of his average, but he still seems to have plenty of thump in his bat. He found the perfect landing spot on the South Side and should see 500+ at bats as the resident DH provided that BA doesn't continue to slide. He gets an obvious boost in OBP but keeps an eye on those plate skills.

Danny Mendick, age 26, eligible at SS
2019 Stats: 40 PA, 2 HR, 6 Runs, 4 RBI, 0 SB, .308/.325/.462
It's easy to look at Mendick's numbers in the minors (17 HR & 19 steals) and his successful cup of coffee and think the Sox have found their second baseman of the future. Mendick's pedigree and BABIP last year point to a better fit as a utility infielder than a full-time starter. Add to that hot prospect Nick Madrigal waiting for the call from the minors, and it's hard to invest in Mendick.

Tim Anderson, age 26, eligible at SS
2019 Stats: 518 PA, 18 HR, 81 Runs, 56 RBI, 17 SB, .335/.357/.508
Some might say Anderson's BA last year was an outlier, but his xBA still points to him hitting right around the .300 mark. Combine that with his 20 + homer and 20+ steal potential, and you have an incredible bargain where Anderson is going in drafts. I get the feeling I will own him on plenty of teams.

Yoán Moncada, age 24, eligible at 3B
2019 Stats: 559 PA, 25 HR, 83 Runs, 79 RBI, 10 SB, .315/.367/.548

I was all out on Moncada last year, but oh baby I'm all in on him this year. Moncada's k% since coming into the league was alarming, and gave him the look of a bust. However, last year he showed strides cutting his k% down from 33.4% to 27.5%. While that's still high, his hard hit%, exit velocity, and xBA are all tops across the league. To me, that signals growth from Moncada rather than an outlier year. I'm buying it.

**Outfielders:**
Eloy Jiménez, age 23, eligible at OF
2019 Stats: 504 PA, 31 HR, 69 Runs, 79 RBI, 0 SB, .267/.315/.513
Eloy's much anticipated debut in Chicago did not disappoint. A rookie who can hit 30 dongs, even in the year of the juiced ball, is very tantalizing. I'm not crazy about him striking out at 26.6% clip, but his FB% and hard hit% would indicate that the power is very real. Another 30 HR year is more than reasonable with the potential for better counting stats given the improved lineup.

Luis Robert, age 22, eligible at OF
2019 Stats: Did Not Play in the Majors
White Sox fans probably thought they were getting pranked when they read that Robert has signed a long-term deal with the Sox, effectively signaling his role as the opening day CF. Robert is an exciting top prospect who could stun the fantasy community by hitting 20 homers and stealing 30 bags. There is risk here though. Robert really doesn't walk and he struck out at a near 25% clip in the minors. It wouldn't be a surprise if there were some bumps along the way this year.

Leury García, age 29, eligible at OF
2019 Stats: 618 PA, 8 HR, 93 Runs, 40 RBI, 15 SB, .279/.310/.378
While Luery Garcia's year wasn't bad, it really wasn't anything to write home about either. Top prospect Luis Robert signing in the off-season pushed Garcia off CF. Take that into account when considering Garcia. He might be relegated to a 4th OF or maybe see some time at 2B.

Nomar Mazara, age 24, eligible at OF
2019 Stats: 469 PA, 19 HR, 69 Runs, 66 RBI, 4 SB, .268/.318/.469
A December trade brought the underwhelming Mazara from the Rangers over to the Sox. He has never quite lived up to the hype having yet to exceed 20 HR in a season. Maybe the White Sox can unlock that power potential and he can finally become the power hitter he was pegged to be. His advanced stats all point to the contrary, and are why I am hesitant about buying in this year.

Adam Engel, age 28, eligible at OF
2019 Stats: 248 PA, 6 HR, 26 Runs, 26 RBI, 3 SB, .242/.304/.383
If you are on the lookout for run of the mill, then look no further. Without some injuries, he won't see enough playing time to warrant more than a passing glance.

**Starters:**
Lucas Giolito, age 25, RHP
2019 Stats: 176.2 IP, 228 K, 14 W, 3.41 ERA, 1.06 WHIP
Oh Hallelujah! White Sox fans rejoiced at the arrival of the ace they didn't even know they had. Giolito broke out in a big way last year and lived up to his pedigree. His swinging strike rate

jumped close to 7 points to 15.5% and his FB velocity also ticked up almost 2 mph. It's hard not to get excited about Giolito not only repeating, but maybe even taking another step forward this year. The only knock on him could be the home ballpark, but Giolito is making that easy to overlook.

Dallas Keuchel, age 32, LHP
2019 Stats: 112.2 IP, 91 K, 8 W, 3.75 ERA, 1.37 WHIP
Keuchel's incredible 2015 seems like a distant memory. His K/9 sat at 7.27 last year and his BB/9 bloated to 3.12. I wouldn't want Keuchel for anything other than to eat innings or hopefully to get some wins. He just doesn't have the type of skill set that offers much upside anymore for fantasy.

Reynaldo López, age 26, RHP
2019 Stats: 184 IP, 169 K, 10 W, 5.38 ERA, 1.46 WHIP
Yeesh… An initial glance at López 2019 induces some serious cringing. However, a closer look would indicate a lot of an equal amount of solid performances mixed in with the crappy ones. His biggest problem was keeping the ball in the yard, his HR/9 rocketed up to 1.71 from 1.19. Call me a sucker, but I'm cautiously optimistic that he can make the necessary changes to return SP3 value. At his current cost, he's worth the dart throw.

Gio Gonzalez, age 34, LHP
2019 Stats: 87.1 IP, 78 K, 3 W, 3.50 ERA, 1.29 WHIP
Here we have an aging pitcher with a skill set that offers little upside. You could do worse, but you could also do much better. I'd rather put a pitcher on my bench with more upside and cut him if it didn't pan out than waste space on a guy I'd never feel inclined to start.

Dylan Cease, age 24, RHP
2019 Stats: 73 IP, 81 K, 4 W, 5.79 ERA, 1.55 WHIP
Now here's an example of a pitcher I'd rather stash than the aforementioned Gio Gonzalez. Cease did not have a good debut last year, but as a speculative add I will roll the dice. He has the potential to well exceed a strikeout per inning, he just needs to work on his control as his BB/9 was a sickly 4.32. His fastball/curveball combo could end up being a nightmare for opposing batters.

**Relievers:**
Alex Colomé, age 31, RHP
2019 Stats: 61 IP, 55 K, 30 SV, 2.80 ERA, 1.07 WHIP
The return on saves here was pretty good last year, but I would not be surprised if he cedes the role this year. Colomé's FIP was over a run higher than his ERA at 4.08, which signals a bit of luck behind his numbers last year. Granted, the best reliever in the bullpen isn't always the closer, so maybe he could hold the job all year even if his numbers decline.

Aaron Bummer, age 26, LHP
2019 Stats: 67.2 IP, 60 K, 2.13 ERA, 0.99 WHIP

While Bummer is a good reliever, it's hard to see him getting more than the occasional save here and there. He doesn't quite have the ability to punch guys out the way you'd want a closer to. However, for those of you in leagues that count Holds, Bummer is a guy to target.

Evan Marshall, age 29, RHP
2019 Stats: 50.2 IP, 41 K, 2.49 ERA, 1.30 WHIP
Another bullpen arm with decent enough stuff, but who just doesn't strike out enough batters to make him worth rostering. Marshall is somewhat interesting in Holds leagues though as he racked up 19 last year.

Kelvin Herrera, age 30, RHP
2019 Stats: 51.1 IP, 53 K, 6.14 ERA, 1.62 WHIP
Last year Herrera was drafted by those who thought they might be getting the team leader in saves if Colomé were to falter. What they got instead was a relief pitcher who gave up more free passes than he ever has in addition to an unsightly 1.4 HR/9. The innings and strikeouts are encouraging signs, but unless Herrera gets his control back, you can find better relief options elsewhere.

Jace Fry, age 26, LHP
2019 Stats: 55 IP, 68 K, 4.75 ERA, 1.58 WHIP
I went out on a limb last year and said Fry was the dark horse for saves on this roster. His 2018 K/9 (12.27) and his BB/9 (3.51) matched with a FIP of 2.67 gave every indication that there was a closer in the making here. Things didn't go as planned last year for Fry though. His BB/9 doubled to 7.04 and his FIP jumped up to 4.90.

Jimmy Cordero, age 28, RHP
2019 Stats: 37.1 IP, 31 K, 2.89 ERA, 0.99 WHIP
Out of all the guys currently in the bullpen, I'd put my money on Cordero to grab saves if Colomé gets hurt or is traded. Cordero can pump it up to 97mph and has made some strides with his control. He doesn't quite have the gaudy strikeout numbers you want in a potential closer, but he has the raw stuff to maybe improve in that area. Definitely a guy to keep an eye on and maybe someone I'd toss a buck at if the closer job was up for grabs.

Tayron Guerrero, age 29, RHP
2019 Stats: 46 IP, 43 K, 6.26 ERA, 1.70 WHIP
Dialing it up to 99 MPH is great and all, unless you can't keep it over the plate. The White Sox claimed him off waivers from the Marlins and it wouldn't be a shock to see him on a different roster at some point this year too if he can't figure things out.

Carson Fulmer, age 26, RHP
2019 Stats: 27.1 IP, 25 K, 6.26 ERA, 1.68 WHIP
Fulmer couldn't quite hack it as a starter so here's hoping he can join the list of failed starters who become effective relievers. He has a huge problem with free passes and needs to get that sorted out or he could end up on the chopping block.

# Chicago White Sox Prospects
By Matt Thompson

### 1. Luis Robert- OF
The high priced Cuban import has passed every challenge thrown at him thus far. Robert is a physical specimen, with a tool belt full of potentially above-average or better tools across the board. He has the ideal frame, and looks like he could excel at any sport if given the opportunity. Robert's speed and power tools are his most appealing from a fantasy standpoint, but he also projects as a stud defender that will occupy centerfield for the better part of the next decade. There are some concerns with the hit tool that takes a little luster away from the profile. He has trouble recognizing spin, and just questionable reaction skills altogether. I don't doubt that he figures it out, but just be patient here. He will likely break camp with the team now that he's signed the extension. **ETA: 2020.**

### 2. Andrew Vaughn- 1B
The White Sox selected Vaughn with the third overall pick in the most recent draft. Vaughn was an incredibly productive collegiate player at Cal, hitting .376/.497/.691 with 50 homers over his 160 game career. As a right-handed hitting and throwing first baseman there's a bit of a stigma there, especially one that is under six foot tall. I think Vaughn's bat is too good to worry about those, but his small samples in full season ball were more good than great. It was also a long season for him, so fatigue could be a factor there. Vaughn has top five first baseman upside, and is my top pick in FYPDs. The addition of Edwin Encarnacion likely pushes Vaughns debut back to 2021, but he's advanced and is going to hit. **ETA: 2021.**

### 3. Michael Kopech- RHP
Kopech has ace level stuff with his big fastball and slider combo. The fastball may be 80-grade with high-90s velocity and movement, and his slider is double-plus with tight, two-plane break. His fastball was a high-spin pitch, and when he works up in the zone with that pitch he's extremely tough on the opposition. His change is also above-average, and it flashed plus during his big league debut. Kopech is likely to spend the beginning of 2020 in Charlotte, but will be up in Chicago in about a month or so. **ETA: Arrived.**

### 4. Nick Madrigal- 2B
Madrigal is a unique player, and you either love him or just like him. There's no doubt that he will be a useful big leaguer, but just how useful? Well there's no denying his elite bat-to-ball skills. His lowest contact rate at any stop in his professional career is 96%. He's an athletic middle infielder who has a chance to be an elite defender at second base, and he's a plus runner that is an efficient baserunner. He doesn't pull the ball enough to tap into his fringe power, and his natural inside-out swing naturally takes the ball to the right side, and mostly on the ground. Madrigal will start in Charlotte in 2020, and should be in Chicago by the summer. **ETA: 2020.**

### 5. Jonathan Stiever- RHP
Stiever is a midwestern kid that popped and had a career year in 2019. The former Indiana Hoosier began missing more bats while also cutting his walk rate. He's got two plus pitches in his fastball and slider. His fastball jumped from 92-94 to 94-96 while maintaining the late movement that makes it difficult to square up. His changeup and curveball are average pitches at present, and if one of those improves he could be a number two. Right now Stiever is a bat

missing number three, and is an arm to track going forward. He will start 2020 in Double-A. **ETA: 2021.**

### 6. Dane Dunning- RHP
Dunning was on the verge of the big leaguers before blowing out in Spring Training. He should be through with his rehab around June or July of this year, and there's a chance he could make his debut later this season. Dunning gets a lot of grounders with his heater but uses his slider to miss bats. He throws strikes while also limiting walks and profiles as a number three with a solid ratio. He pitched for a stacked University of Florida squad and showed well out of the bullpen, which is something to watch. **ETA: 2021.**

### 7. Benyamin Bailey- OF
You can't put much stock into DSL statistics, but Bailey performed well in the one aspect that has shown the ability to translate to stateside ball. Bailey led the DSL in OBP with a .477 mark. He drew 52 walks to just 40 strikeouts in 243 plate appearances. Not bad for a $35,000 signing. Bailey actually signed in April and is part of the 2018 international class, so he may actually still be eligible for your FYPDs. He's six-foot-five and his plus raw pop, and is an average runner. It all depends on how often he strikes out. **ETA: 2024.**

### 8. Micker Adolfo- OF
The Dominican slugger has an injury history as long as those majestic homers he's capable of. He was only limited to 128 at-bats due to Tommy John surgery, but did come back to play in the Arizona Fall League. He's missed so much playing time that the White Sox were granted an extra option, but this is also the last time he can get sent down without being exposed on waivers. He's only had 95 plate appearances at Double-A. There are some serious defensive concerns here, but he had a strong arm before surgery. He will always strikeout, so he really has to get into that power. **ETA: 2021.**

### 9. Zack Collins- C
When talking about Collins and his fantasy potential, I challenge you to explain it to someone without saying "if this" or "if that". It's almost impossible. There are so many variables when describing Collins. First thing, he's not a catcher. He's a DH, but one that posts elite walk rates. His batted ball profile wasn't encouraging, but it wasn't enough of a sample to write him off completely. He's going to have to be more direct to the ball to reach the power ceiling, but OBP makes him interesting. **ETA: Arrived.**

### 10. Luis Alexander Basabe- OF
Basabe is a plus runner with above-average raw pop that's dealt with his share of injuries in the past. The missed time is troublesome for someone that struggles to make consistent contact. His 67% contact rate in Double-A last season is problematic, and he hasn't been able to tap into his pop consistently. He struggles with pitch recognition skills, and will strike out, but the hope is he can get to enough of his secondary skills. He may be a fourth outfielder, but his fantasy skills are worth the investment. **ETA: 2020.**

**Next Five:**
Matthew Thompson- RHP
Blake Rutherford- OF
Andrew Dalquist- RHP

Luis Gonzalez- OF
Jimmy Lambert- RHP

**Top Five in FYPDs:**
Andrew Vaughn- 1B
Matthew Thompson- RHP
Andrew Dalquist- RHP
Yolbert Sanchez- SS
James Beard- OF

# Cleveland Indians Team Preview
By Jim Bay

## Projected Lineup

1- Francisco Lindor - SS
2- Oscar Mercado - CF
3- Carlos Santana - 1B
4- Jose Ramirez - 3B
5- Franmil Reyes - DH
6- Cesar Hernandez - 2B
7- Jake Bauers - LF
8- Roberto Perez - C
9- Greg Allen - RF

## Projected Bench
Bradley Zimmer - OF
Sandy Leon - C
Christian Arroyo - INF
Delino DeShields - OF
Jordan Luplow - OF

## Projected Rotation

Mike Clevinger - RHP
Shane Bieber - RHP
Carlos Carrasco - RHP
Aaron Civale - RHP
Zach Plesac - RHP

## Projected Bullpen
Brad Hand - LHP
Nick Wittgren - RHP
Emmanuel Clase - RHP
Oliver Perez - LHP
Adam Cimber - RHP
Hunter Wood - RHP
James Karinchak - RHP
Adam Plutko - RHP
## CATCHERS

Roberto Perez, age 31, eligible at Catcher
2019 Stats: 449 PAs, 24 HRs, 26 Runs, 63 RBI, 0 SB, .239/.321/.452
What potential fantasy owners are hoping is that Perez continues improving on his 2019 numbers. It would be based on the fact that Perez demonstrated an increased ability to drive pitches and make his contact count last season, particularly up the middle or to the opposite field. He hit 16 of his 24 homers to the non-pull side, and Perez also increased his average fly

ball distance from 314 feet in 2018 to 343 feet in 2019, per Statcast. Generally considered at the end of the top 20, but with some potential upside.

Sandy Leon, age 30, eligible at C
2019 Stats: 191 PAs, 5 HR, 14 Runs, 19 RBI, 0 SB, .191/.252/.297
Leon has little fantasy value

## INFIELDERS

Francisco Lindor, age 26, eligible at SS
2019 Stats: 654 PAs, 32 HRs, 101 Runs, 74 RBI, 22 SB, .284/.335/.518
Lindor should be considered one of the top shortstops and would generally be taken in the first round in most fantasy drafts. Expect the counting stats to increase in 2020 as he should enter the season completely healthy after missing 19 games last season.

Carlos Santana, age 33, eligible at 1B
2019 Stats: 686 PAs, 34 HRs, 110 Runs, 93 RBI, 4 SB, .281/.397/.515
Santana put up some career type numbers last year but did see a bit of a drop-off in the second half. At age 33, some wonder when age will catch up with him but until that does, he should be considered a top 10 first baseman in fantasy.

Jose Ramirez, age 27, eligible at 3B
2019 Stats: 542 PAs, 23 HRs, 68 Runs, 83 RBI, 24 SB, .255/.327/.479
Ramirez was a bit up and down in 2019, especially in batting average. Ramirez has incredible contact skills and will still put up outstanding numbers. He probably will not be a first-rounder like in 2019, but he should easily be one of the top five third basemen in fantasy this year.

Cesar Hernandez, age 29, eligible at 2B
2019 Stats: (PHI) 667 PAs, 14 HRs, 77 Runs, 71 RBI, 9 SB, .279/.333/.408
Hernandez will get fantasy owners stats across the board, just not exceptionally well. Projecting to start at second base for Cleveland will keep him fantasy relevant and is generally ranked in the bottom half of the second basemen.

Christian Arroyo, age 24, eligible at 3B
2019 Stats: 57 PAs, 2 HR, 8 Runs, 7 RBI, 0 SB, .220/.304.380
Unlikely to see enough playing time to be fantasy relevant

## OUTFIELDERS

Oscar Mercado, age 25, eligible at OF
2019 Stats: 482 PAs, 15 HR, 70 Runs, 54 RBI, 15 SB, .269/.318/.443
Mercado was given the chance to start at Center Field in mid-May and did not give the job up. If he continues to bat second in the Indian's order, he should produce enough to become a starter in most fantasy leagues.

Franmil Reyes, age 24, eligible at OF
2019 Stats: 354 PAs, 37 HRs, 69 Runs, 81 RBI, 0 SB, .249/.310/.512

Reyes should be drafted for his power potential, as he has the skills to hit 40 home runs. Last year he posted a 14.8% Barrel rate and exceptional 51% Hard Hit rate. Reyes hit 37 home runs between Cleveland and San Diego last year, and with a clear path ahead of him with the Indians, most of his stats should improve. The exception would be the batting average.

Jake Bauers, age 24, eligible at OF/1B
2019 Stats: 423 PAs, 12 HRs, 46 Runs, 43 RBI, 3 SB, .226/.312/.371
Bauers may end up in a platoon, getting the start against right-handers. This makes him fantasy relevant in only deep leagues.

Greg Allen, age 25, eligible at OF
2019 Stats: 256 PAs, 4 HRs, 30 Runs, 27 RBI, 8 SB, .229/.290/.346
Allen will have to compete for outfield time and even if he does win, it may only be in a platoon. A deep fantasy sleeper at best.

Jordan Luplow, age 26, eligible at OF
2019 Stats: PAs 261, 15 HRs, 42 Runs, 38 RBI, 3 SB, .276/.332/.551
Luplow will likely be a part of the Cleveland outfield platoon system and have value only in deep leagues.

Bradley Zimmer, age 27, eligible at OF
2019 Stats: 14 PAs, 0 HRs, 1 Run, 0 RBI, 0 SB, .000/.071/.000
Zimmer could start in an outfield platoon. He could also start the year in Triple A. He had shoulder surgery in 2018, which made last year more of his recovery time. If interested in some roster depth, a potential owner will have to monitor him during spring training.

Delino DeShields, age 27, eligible at OF
2019 Stats (Tex): 408 PAs, 4 HRs, 42 Runs, 32 RBI, 24 SB, .249/.325/.347
Acquired from Texas in the Corey Kluber trade, DeShields may end up in the Indians outfield platoon. However, he could provide a cheap source of steals.

## PITCHERS

### Projected Rotation

Mike Clevinger, age 29, RHP
2019 Stats: 126 IP, 169 K's, 13 Wins, 2.71 ERA, 1.06 WHIP
Clevinger has quietly emerged as one of the top starters in the American League over the last three years. He has compiled a 3.20 ERA and 1.19 WHIP in 97 appearances across four seasons with the Indians. He is a top 10 starting pitcher in fantasy.

Shane Bieber, age 24, RHP
2019 Stats: 214.1 IP, 259 K's, 15 Wins, 3.28 ERA, 1.05 WHIP
Last year, Bieber was drafted late in many drafts and posted top-five stats in most fantasy formats. These stats, such as a very strong K/BB ratio among others, will make up an early draft pick this year as he is easily a top 10 pitcher and will be drafted as such.

Carlos Carrasco, age 33, RHP

2019 Stats: 80 IP, 96 K's, 6 Wins, 5.29 ERA, 1.35 WHIP
In 2019, Carrasco was diagnosed with went through treatment and came back to pitch in the same season. He seemed to return to his old form in September when he posted a 3:2 K: BB while allowing just one hit across five innings of relief. Monitor his health over spring training but he is generally considered in the top 125 for 2020 fantasy rankings. Fully healthy, that would be a bargain.

Aaron Civale, age 24, RHP
2019 Stats: 57.2 IP, 46 K's, 3 Wins, 2.34 ERA, 1.04 WHIP
Before being called up in June of 2019, Civale made seven starts between Double-A Akron and Triple-A Columbus going 5–0 with a 2.85 ERA. His nice start at the Majors would make him a nice roster addition in the later rounds.

Zach Plesac, age 25, RHP
2019 Stats: 115.2 IP, 88 K's, 8 Wins, 3.81 ERA, 1.23 WHIP
The nephew of former major leaguer Dan Plesac made his major league debut in May of 2019. If he comes out of spring in the starting rotation, he could have value as a late draft pick in deep leagues.

**BULLPEN**

Brad Hand, age 30, LHP
2019 Stats: 57.1 IP, 84 K's, 6 Wins, 34 Saves, 3.30 ERA, 1.24 WHIP
A solid closer who has no competition behind him. Should be selected among the top 10 closers in drafts, and deservedly so.

Emmanuel Clase, age 22, RHP
2019 Stats:(TEX) 23.1 IP, 21 K's, 2 Wins, 1 Save, 2.31 ERA, 1.11 WHIP
The hard-throwing right-handers came to Cleveland from Texas in the Corey Kluber trade. He is projected to be the set-up man but would be expected to get first shot at closing duties if something were to happen to Brad Hand. His age and flamethrowing abilities make his worth a look in dynasty and keeper leagues as well.

Nick Wittgren, age 28, RHP
2019 Stats: 57.2 IP, 60 K's, 5 Wins, 4 Saves, 2.81 ERA, 1.08 WHIP
Another set-up man for Hand, his fantasy value will come mostly from holds. Could get a chance at closing if something happens to Hand.

Adam Plutko, age 28, RHP
2019 Stats: 109.1 IP, 78 K's, 7 Wins, 0 Saves, 4.86 ERA, 1.29 WHIP
Plutko is targeted to be the long reliever but will be given the opportunity to win the final spot in the rotation. If he does claim the spot, he would have some value in deep leagues only.

James Karinchak, age 24, RHP

2019 Stats: 5.1 IP, 8 K's, 0 Wins, 0 Saves, 1.69 ERA, 0.75 WHIP
No fantasy value

Oliver Perez, age 38, LHP
2019 Stats: 40.2 IP, 48 K's, 2 Wins, 1 Save, 3.98 ERA, 1.23 WHIP
As a lefty, his fantasy value only comes from holds and the occasional poaching of a win or save.

Hunter Wood, age 26, RHP
2019 Stats: 45.1 IP, 39 K's, 1 Win, 1 Save, 2.98 ERA, 1.28 WHIP
No fantasy value

Adam Cimber, age 29. RHP
2019 Stats: 56.2 IP, 41 K's, 6 Wins, 1 Save, 4.45 ERA, 1.32 ERA
No fantasy value

# Cleveland Indians Prospects
By Matt Thompson

### 1. Nolan Jones- 3B
The Indians have aggressively pushed Jones through their system, and the powerful 21-year-old has answered the bell every time. Jones has big time power and he's been beginning to get to it with more frequency in game. His ultimate fantasy value will depend on the format of your league though. Jones will post elite on-base percentages while potentially only hitting .250-.260, but we could be looking at OBPs around .370-.380 with that type of average. Jones arm is plus, and I hope he can stick at third, but there's a high likelihood of a move across the infield in the future. He left the AFL early due to a thumb injury that required surgery, but the lefty should be ready for opening day. Jones should start 2020 in Triple-A. He's a future 30-homer bat. **ETA: 2021.**

### 2. George Valera- OF
Short statured with a stance that's a mirror image of his idol Robinson Cano, Valera has some of the quickest hands/wrists in all the minor leagues. It's the primary reason for the hype he's received thus far. He struggles to make consistent contact, but there's significant hand movement prior to his swing, and a more consistent setup prior to starting his swing can vary the length and cause timing issues here. So, despite the subpar contact rates he's shown, he rarely makes weak contact and this is a relatively simple fix. He missed some time in 2018 due to a wrist injury, so it could just be a matter of adding strength and getting his timing back. The upside here is a corner outfielder that can hit .280 with 25-30 homers but no speed. Very solid secondary piece for fantasy. **ETA: 2023.**

### 3. Ethan Hankins- RHP
As an amateur Hankins may have had the best stuff for a kid his age that I've ever seen. The run on his two-seamer was absolutely filthy, and his curveball and slider were impossible to square up. He had some talk of potentially going number one overall until a shoulder injury ended those. Hankins hasn't seen the stuff fully return, but he's missed bats and kept the ball on the ground thus far. His slider is his best breaking ball, and his curveball and change are improving, but everything lacks that bite that it had while pitching for Team USA. The overall command is lacking a bit as well, and while he still throws strikes, it's the quality of those pitches that leaves a bit to be desired. He needs to be sharper, and right now I project him as a number two fantasy arm but a number three for the Indians. **ETA: 2022.**

### 4. Tyler Freeman- SS/2B
Freeman does everything on offense except hit for power. Like at all. I don't think Freeman has enough power in the bat to even reach double digits in homers. He's also super aggressive, and won't walk very much but his high batting averages will carry the offensive profile. His hard contact rates are below average, and the swing is very much geared towards contact. Finding power will result in a complete overhaul of his game. That's unlikely. His hands are good enough to stick in the middle infield. He's a gap-to-gap offensive player that will get extra base hits and can steal 15-20 bases. **ETA: 2021.**

### 5. Daniel Espino- RHP

Espino has the highest upside of any prep arm in the 2019 draft, and falling to the Indians is an arrangement that will benefit both the team and the player. The Indians will find a way to get the most out of his big fastball which can sit in the mid-90s and top out at 99. He pairs it with two plus breaking balls, and a changeup that is coming along. He needs to work on two things. The quality of the strikes he throws, and just building up innings. He's incredibly athletic and has the big frame to pile up innings. It's going to be a slow burn here, but should pay off with a nice SP 2, or high strikeout closer. **ETA: 2023.**

### 6. Aaron Bracho- 2B/SS

The 18-year-old Bracho is the first in the wave of high upside middle infield prospects in the Indians system. (Freeman is more of a floor guy). Bracho is a short, almost bad-bodied likely second baseman with a plus hit tool, potential plus power, and average speed. He's posted elite walk rates and a swing with an uppercut perfect for generating loft. Bracho is looking to sting the ball every time, and he will not get cheated. He's got serious 25-homer pop. That should come with a strong average and a few steals. Bracho should start in the Midwest League in 2020. **ETA: 2024.**

### 7. Brayan Rocchio- SS/2B

A short but powerful middle infielder, Rocchio is switch-hitter with strong feel for the barrel. He's a plus runner with surprising power for his small frame. It's still below-average pop, but Rocchio will spray the ball everywhere, gap-to-gap, from either side of the plate. He was above-average in the NYPL despite being three years younger than the average player for the level. It's a hit over power profile, but he also has 20-homer upside. He will join Bracho in the Midwest League to start 2020. **ETA: 2023.**

### 8. Alexfri Planez- OF

A teenage outfield prospect with double-plus power, Planez is flying up fantasy prospect lists. In addition to the plus-plus raw, he's also an above-average runner with a chiseled frame. His kryptonite is his poor pitch recognition skills. Toolsy players like this are normally scooped up and are already on your radar, but Planez fractured his hamate just six games into his AZL season. My colleague Jason Pennini raved about what he saw, and this is the type of athlete that can shoot up lists like this as more people see the tools. The 18-year-old should see short-season ball to start in 2020 and could see the Midwest League later on. **ETA: 2024.**

### 9. Gabriel Rodriguez- SS/3B

Power is the name of the game for Rodriguez. His plus-plus raw is outstanding, but there are some issues with the swing and approach that need to be addressed. Rodriguez is overly aggressive, and pitchers that can sequence and command a breaking ball will eat him up. He has issues recognizing spin, and needs to keep the lower half more engaged in his swing. He pulls off the ball frequently, and can also be caught off balance with regularity. These are all fairly normal issues with 17-year-old mashers, but it makes this a risky profile. He's also likely going to slide over to third, but I think he hits enough to handle the move. There's no speed and below average athleticism here, but G-Rod is a nice dart throw. **ETA: 2023.**

### 10. Daniel Johnson- OF

Johnson's plus defensive skills in right field combined with his plus raw power and heavy pull profile makes him the Indians likely everyday outfielder in the second half. He's already on the 40-man, and the rest of the alternatives aren't that inspiring. He's also a plus runner and could chip in double digit stolen bases as well. There's some struggles against lefties that could lead to a platoon situation, but at least Johnson would be on the strong side of that. Definitely worth a flier in the later portion of a draft and hold league. **ETA: 2020.**

**Next Five:**
Triston McKenzie- RHP
Emmanuel Clase- RHP
James Karinchak- RHP
Angel Martinez- INF
Will Benson- OF

**Top Five in FYPDs:**
Daniel Espino- RHP
Joe Naranjo- 1B
Yordys Valdes- SS
Christian Cairo- 2B/3B
Xzavion Curry- LHP

# Detroit Tigers Team Preview
By Andrew Dewhirst

**Projected Order:**
1. JaCoby Jones - CF
2. Niko Goodrum - SS
3. Miguel Cabrera - DH
4. C.J. Cron - 1B
5. Christian Stewart - LF
6. Jonathan Schoop - 2B
7. Jeimer Candelario - 3B
8. Austin Romine - C
9. Victor Reyes - RF

**Projected Bench:**
Grayson Greiner - C
Dawel Lugo - INF
Harold Castro - INF/OF
Travis Demeritte - OF

**Projected Rotation:**
Matthew Boyd - LHP
Jordan Zimmerman - RHP
Daniel Norris - LHP
Spencer Turnbull - RHP
Tyler Alexander - LHP

**Bullpen:**
Joe Jimenez - RHP
Buck Farmer - RHP
Jose Cisnero - RHP
David McKay - RHP
Bryan Garcia - RHP
John Schreiber - RHP
Gregory Soto - LHP
Rony Garcia - RHP

**Catchers:**
Austin Romine, age 31, eligible at C
2019 Stats: 240 PAs, 8 HRs, 29 Runs, 35 RBIs, 1 SBs, .281/.310/.439
It's hard to think of Romine as much more than a guy. He is roster able in a 15 team 2 catcher leagues, with the hope that he can be an average asset, and the extra PA's as the everyday catcher get him close to average stats, but the upside is pretty limited.

Grayson Greiner, age 27, eligible at C
2019 Stats: 224 PAs, 5 HRs, 18 Runs, 19 RBIs, 0 SBs, .202/.251/.308

Greiner will continue to be the back up this year in the Motor City. Unless he can start hitting he will likely not be much more than a 2nd catcher in his career. He is also at risk of being demoted for the Tigers to see what they have in Jake Rogers.

**Infielders**:
Miguel Cabrera, age 36, eligible at 1B
2019 Stats: 549 PAs, 12 HRs, 41 Runs, 59 RBIs, 0 SBs, .282/.346/.398
The good news is that Miggy was largely healthy, his exit velocity, hard hit%, his BA, and his xBA were all well above average. The bad news is that none of that really translated into production, in 2019. I wouldn't expect the outcome to change too much in 2020, unless he can raise his launch angle from 12 degrees to something closer to 15. I think he could be worth a flyer in 15 team leagues or larger, in hope of that launch angle change.

Jeimer Candelario, age 26, eligible at 3B
2019 Stats: 386 PAs, 8 HR, 33 Runs, 32 RBIs, 3 SB, .203/.306/.337
Candelario should not be on anyone's draft list this year. He was below average in exit velocity, hard hit%, xwOBA,xBA, and xSLG. The production wasn't there in his MLB career, and it's hard to see it coming at this point.

Harold Castro, age 26, eligible at 2B, OF
2019 Stats: 369 PAs, 5 HRs, 30 Runs, 38 RBIs, 4 SBs, .291/.305/.384
Harold Castro is at best a batting average asset. He hit for a good average in his first real major league stint last year, and you could see him hitting in the range of 0.270 this year. However, he has yet to show any power in his career, and the team context will keep his batting average from turning his counting stats from being of any real value.

Dawel Lugo, age 24, eligible at 3B
2019 Stats: 288 PAs, 6 HRs, 28 Runs, 26 RBIs, 0 SBs, .245/.271/.381
I can't think of a good reason why you should pay any attention to Dawel Lugo during draft season. Cross the name off your list and move on. He doesn't hit particularly well, and he likely wouldn't be on the roster of 28 other MLB teams.

C.J. Cron, age 29, eligible at 1B
2019 Stats: 499 PAs, 25 HRs, 51 Runs, 78 RBIs, 0 SBs, .253/.311/.469
Cron had a good year with the Twins, coming off a good year with the Rays. He should provide you with 25-30 HR, as the full time 1B and see time at DH with the Tigers. He could reach 80+ RBI, but I don't expect his runs to be very high as the back half of the Tigers lineup isn't strong.

Jonathan Schoop, age 28, eligible at 2B
2019 Stats: 464 PAs, 23 HRs, 61 Runs, 59 RBIs, 1 SBs, .256/.304/.473
Schoop could have some sneaky value in 2020, especially with how shallow 2B looks this year. He is nearly a lock for 20 HR, and if he can get to 600 PA's again you could see 30 HR upside, while not crushing your average.

**Outfielders**:
Victor Reyes, age 26, eligible at OF
2019 Stats: 292 PAs, 3 HRs, 29 Runs, 25 RBIs, 9 SBs, .304/.336/.431

Reyes has a little interest in deep leagues. With a full season of PA's 20 steals in the cards. He is likely more of a 0.275 hitter than a 0.300 guy, and his walk rate doesn't offer a lot of safety, but when steals are this rare, he could be a cheap source.

Niko Goodrum, age 25, eligible at 2B, SS, OF
2019 Stats: 472 PAs, 12 HR, 61 Runs, 45 RBIs, 12 SB, .248/.322/.421
Niko's value hasn't changed much from last year. There is still 15/15 upside there which holds weight in 15 teams are larger leagues. His eligibility also adds a lot to his value in daily moves leagues.

JaCoby Jones, age 26, eligible at OF
2019 Stats: 333 PAs, 11 HRs, 39 Runs, 26 RBIs, 7 SBs, .235/.410/.430
Like many of the Tigers players, there is some steal potential here. Projections systems have him around 16 HR, and 12 steals, but means he is a fill in at best in a 15 team league, but fiable in deeper formats. Unfortunately his batting average hurts you too much to use him in shallower formats.

Christin Stewart, age 26, eligible at OF
2019 Stats: 416 PAs, 10 HRs, 32 Runs, 40 RBIs, 0 SBs, .233/.305/.388
Stewart didn't have the year that Tigers fans had hoped. His average was closer to where people thought it would be, but the power didn't show up. The projection systems are bearish on his 2020 outlook, but I am not sure I want to sleep on his power, which makes him a nice late game flyer in 15 team leagues.

Travis Demeritte, age 25, eligible at OF
2019 Stats: 186 PAs, 3 HRs, 24 Runs, 10 RBIs, 3 SBs, .225/.286/.343
This is going to be an upside play. He could be 25 HR, 10 steals, if he gets a full season worth of at bats. However, he could play once every 4th day and you could drop him in the first week. You might want to take a wait and see approach with him as he likely will go undrafted in most leagues.

**Starters:**
Spencer Turnbull, age 27, RHP
148.1 IP, 146 Ks, 3 Wins, 4.61 ERA, 1.44 WHIP
Turnbull will offer some value in formats where innings are valuable. He will get you some strikeouts, but if you play in a points format where losses hurt you, you will need to stay far away from Turnbull.

Daniel Norris, age 26, RHP
144.1 IP, 125 Ks, 3 Wins, 4.49 ERA, 1.33 WHIP
Do you play in a dynasty league where you are trying to tank but still need to hit an innings limit. If that is the case, Norris is the guy for you. He isn't going to strike many people out, he is going to give up runs, and it's likely that the Tigers will run him out as long as he is healthy.

Jordan Zimmerman, age 33, RHP
112 IP, 82 Ks, 1 Wins, 6.91 ERA, 1.52 WHIP

Zimmerman might be the worst starting pitcher in baseball who will see regular starts in 2020. Don't draft him, try to avoid seeing his name if you can, just encase viewing his name somehow affects your life as negatively as he is going to affect the Tigers in 2020.

Matthew Boyd, age 28, LHP
185.1 IP, 238 Ks, 9 Wins, 4.56 ERA, 1.23 WHIP
Boyd surprisingly had value considering in 2019. The ERA wasn't good, but much of that came in the second half of the year. His k's make him draftable, and if he should land on a better team, you could get him as a nice value as the win potential will go up quite a bit.

Tyler Alexander, age 25, LHP
53.2 IP, 47 Ks, 1 Wins, 4.86 ERA, 1.40 WHIP

Don't expect Alexander to have any fantasy value in 2020.

## Relievers:

Joe Jimenez, age 24, RHP
59.2 IP, 82 SO, 7 Saves, 4.37 ERA, 1.32 WHIP
Jimenez didn't have the year that many expected. Shane Greene held the job for much of the year while Jimenez posted an ERA over 4. That being said, the closer job is his, so he is going to have value, and should be worth 20+ saves. He also strikes out nearly 32% of the betters he saw in 2019, which is also really nice.

Buck Farmer, age 28, RHP
67.2 IP, 73 K's, 0 Saves, 3.72 ERA, 1.27 WHIP
Farmer would likely be the next guy up if Jimenez was to get injured. His fantasy value though is capped, as he doesn't strike enough batters out to give you much if he isn't getting saves.

Jose Cisnero, age 30, RHP
35.1 IP, 40 K's, 0 Saves, 4.33 ERA, 1.53 WHIP
Cisnero could be a nice story in 2020, after being completely out of the league in 2017 and 2018, but I wouldn't expect him to have any impact in fantasy terms this season.

David McKay, age 24, RHP
26.1 IP, 34 K's, 0 Saves, 5.47 ERA, 1.41 WHIP
McKay has no fantasy relevance this year.

Bryan Garcia, age 24, RHP
6.2 IP, 7 K's, 0 Saves, 12.15 ERA, 2.10 WHIP
Garcia has no fantasy relevance this year.

John Schreiber, age 25, LHP
13 IP, 19 K's, 0 Saves, 6.23 ERA, 1.54 WHIP
Schreiber has no fantasy relevance this year.

Gregory Soto, age 24, LHP
57.2 IP, 45 K's, 0 Saves, 5.77 ERA, 1.86 WHIP

Soto has no fantasy relevance this year.

Rony Garcia, age 22, RHP
105.1 IP, 104 K's, 0 Saves, 4.44 ERA, 1.25 WHIP
Garcia was a Rule 5 pick for the Tigers. He will get some work, but is likely on the roster for the year and will spend next year in AAA. He has no fantasy relevance this year.

### 1. Matt Manning- RHP

The six-foot-six, athletic right-hander has developed into one of the top pitching prospects in the game. His fastball sits 92-95 with wiggle, but he can reach back and touch 97 when he needs it. The fastball plays up due to the extension he gets. His curveball is a plus pitch, and it's a high-spin offering with sharp downward break. It's his out pitch. Manning's changeup drastically improved and transformed from a fringe offering to now one that projects to be above-average. His control also improved and he dominated Double-A. He is likely to start 2020 in Triple-A, and should make his debut this summer. He pitched 117 innings in 2018, bumped up to 133 in 2019 so he should be allowed to get to around 160 this year. He's not draftable outside of the deepest leagues, but is a must add when he gets the call. Likely settles in as a #2/3 starter. **ETA: 2020.**

### 2. Casey Mize- RHP

The former number one overall pick started out hot in 2019. Over his first four starts in the Florida State League he only allowed one earned run over his first 28 innings while striking out 25 and walking just one. He followed it up by throwing a no-hitter for Erie in his first start in Double-A. Mize has a deep arsenal and advanced command. His fastball and slider are already plus pitches (60-grade) and even more impressive is his splitter, which is plus-plus (70-grade). He's even added another pitch, an above-average (55-grade) cutter that he uses mostly against lefties. The command is above-average, and he's posted tiny walk rates in his pro career. Why is he number two? It's injuries. At Auburn he missed time with a flexor strain in 2017, and in 2018 he looked gassed towards the end of his collegiate season. In 2019 he missed time with a shoulder strain, and returned about a month later. He wasn't the same after he returned, and was shut down soon after. He should begin the season in Triple-A, but likely tops out at around 130-140 innings this year. The last two years he's thrown 114 and 109 innings respectably, so he needs to prove he's healthy entering 2020 and just finish the season strong. **ETA: 2021.**

### 3. Riley Greene- OF

Greene was advertised as the best prep hitter in the 2019 class, and while that may not necessarily be true, he's proven to be the most advanced. His first professional season saw him jump from the GCL to the NY-Penn league and it ended in the Midwest League despite just being 18-years old. He posted a 121 wRC+ for his first season, and should start 2019 back in the tough Midwest League. Greene's built like a Major Leaguer now, but he won't hit the majors this year or next. He uses all fields already and is a line drive gap-to-gap hitter, and will grow into 30-homer pop at peak. He should also hit for a high average and post strong OBPs. His above-average speed will likely disappear, but the production he should post in the box will make up for it. The second half of 2022 is an aggressive ETA for a prep bat, but a summer promotion seems plausible. **ETA: 2022.**

### 4. Tarik Skubal- LHP

Skubal's elbow blew out while he was pitching at Seattle University in 2016. He returned to the mound in 2018 and still was missing bats but struggled to throw strikes consistently. The Tigers used him out of the bullpen after taking him in the 9th round to keep his innings down, but he jumped back into the rotation in 2019 and took off. Of all pitchers that threw more than 70 innings in a full-season league, Skubal had the highest swinging strike rate. His fastball sits in the mid-90s but can touch 97. He throws an average curveball and slider, with his slider potentially becoming a plus pitch. He will also mix in a change. His arsenal plays up with how well he commands his four-pitch mix. Skubal is out-pitching his stuff right now and profiles as a number three starter, with a chance at becoming a number two. He should start the season in Triple-A, but like Mize is unlikely to reach the big leagues due to innings limits. **ETA: 2021.**

### 5. Isaac Paredes- 3B

Paredes was acquired from the Cubs at the 2017 deadline in a deal that sent Justin Wilson and Alex Avila to the Cubs. The Cubs reached into their deep talent rich pipeline in Mexico and signed him for $800,000, and he reached full season ball in his first professional season. He's an advanced prospect for his age due to his advanced bat-to-ball skills, plate approach and ability to hit line drives to all fields. Paredes just doesn't swing and miss. His arm is plus, and his hands are good enough to stick at third, but he may outgrow the position and move over to first base. An 87% contact rate for a 20-year-old in Double-A is unheard of, and Paredes should start 2020 in Triple-A with a small chance he debuts in the big leagues in the late summer. Detroit's competitive window likely keeps Paredes in Triple-A until at least 2021. **ETA: 2021.**

### 6. Daz Cameron- OF

Cameron had a lot of hype as an amateur due to his bloodlines and prep performance, but around draft time the other hitters in his class had caught up to him, and he dropped to the 37th pick in the 2015 draft. Cameron is likely a much better real life player than a fantasy one due to his defensive ability. He's an above-average runner with plus instincts that can cover serious ground in center and he has a strong throwing arm. His best offensive tool is his average raw power that can lead to several 20 homer seasons. The hit tool is below-average, and there is a lot of swing and miss here, and he's likely a .250 hitter unless that changes. He will chip in around 10-12 steals, but he's been inefficient on the base paths. Cameron is a prototypical second division regular. He spent all of 2019 in Triple-A and hit .214/.330/.377 with 13 homers and 17 steals. He will start 2020 back in Toledo but should get to Detroit by the end of the summer. **ETA: 2020.**

### 7. Joey Wentz- LHP

The Braves drafted Wentz out of the Kansas prep ranks with the 40th overall pick in 2016 and traded him to the Tigers as part of the return for Shane Greene in 2019. There have been several inconsistent velocity reports on Wentz in the past, but his fastball sits 91-93 with little to no movement. His changeup is a plus pitch that plays off the fastball with tumble and run. His curveball is above-average with 12-to-6 shape, and plays well off of his fastball. Despite the below-average heater he gets an above-average amount of swing and miss due to his ability to sequence. He's a number four starter for me, and should start 2020 in Triple-A after 25 starts in Double-A last year. He's more likely of any of the arms above him on this list to make his debut in 2020. **ETA: 2020.**

### 8. Jose De La Cruz- OF

De La Cruz was the crown jewel of the Tigers 2018 international class, signing for $1.85 million out of the Dominican Republic. De La Cruz makes frequent hard, loud contact and has a swing that generates easy loft. His swing comes with a large leg kick that can create timing issues and leads to significant swing and miss. He has above-average power potential and that also comes with above-average speed. He's likely a better fit in a corner though because of his body type.

He hit .307/.375/.556 in the DSL with a league leading eleven homers and also 16 steals. **ETA: 2024.**

## 9. Adinso Reyes- 3B
Reyes was signed in 2018 for $1.45 million out of the Dominican Republic. His calling card is his plus raw power that he can already tap into regularly. The power is enough to allow him to survive the move off of shortstop to third base. How good the hit tool is is up for debate. He did put up strong power numbers in the DSL, but those numbers aren't translatable to stateside ball. **ETA: 2024.**

## 10. Willi Castro- SS
Castro was acquired from the Indians at the 2018 deadline for Leonys Martin. The defense first shortstop reached the big leagues at just 22 years-old, and had a strong season for Toledo. He hit .301/.366/.467 with eleven homers and 17 steals. While the upside isn't incredibly high, there's a chance Castro can put up a season similar to what Kevin Newman did in 2019. **ETA: Arrived.**

**Next Five:**
Roberto Campos- OF
Derek Hill- OF
Jake Rogers- C
Alex Faedo- RHP
Wenceel Perez- SS

**Top Five in FYPDs:**
Riley Greene- OF
Roberto Campos- OF
Bryant Packard- OF
Andre Lipcius- 3B
Nick Quintana- 3B

# Kansas City Royals Team Preview
## By Brent Brown

**Projected Order:**
1- Adalberto Mondesi, SS
2- Whit Merrifield, 2B
3- Jorge Soler, RF
4- Hunter Dozier, 3B
5- Maikel Franco, DH
6- Salvador Perez, C
7- Ryan O'Hearn, 1B
8- Brett Phillips, CF
9- Bubba Starling, LF

**Projected Bench:**
Nicky Lopez, 2B
Cam Gallagher, C
Kelvin Gutierrez, 3B
Ryan McBroom, OF

**Projected Rotation:**
Danny Duffy, LHP
Heath Fillmyer, RHP
Jakob Junis, RHP
Brad Keller, RHP
Mike Montgomery, LHP

**Bullpen:**
Ian Kennedy, RHP
Scott Barlow, RHP
Tim Hill, LHP Kevin McCarthy, RHP
Jake Newberry, RHP Josh Staumont, RHP
Randy Rosario, LHP
Kyle Zimmer, RHP

**Catchers:**
Salvador Perez, age 30, eligible at C
2019 Stats: DNP, recovering from TJ Surgery for a catcher.
With surgery being March 11, 2019 he will be past one year post-op when the season begins. The last few seasons the power numbers have stayed consistent, but the AVG and OBP have begun to decline. His days as a locked-in starter are probably behind him.

Cam Gallager, age 27, eligible at C
2019 Stats: 142 PA, 3 HR, 12 Runs, 14 RBI, 0 SB, .238/.312/.677
One of multiple catchers used in 2019 and not much of a fantasy option. He's backing up Perez, but could work his way into more playing time with a hot start to start the season.

**Infielders:**

Hunter Dozier, age 28, eligible at 1B, 3B, OF
2019 Stats: 586 PA, 26 HR, 75 Runs, 84 RBI, 2 SB, .279/.348/.870
Played all both corner spots on the infield and right field in 2019. Still a young player and showed a big improvement in his first full season. Useful to fill up your CI or last OF spot in a deep league.

Adalberto Mondesi, age 24, eligible at SS
2019 Stats: 443 PA, 9 HR, 58 Runs, 62 RBI, 43 SB, .263/.291/.715
Missing about six weeks of the season from a shoulder injury, back until another shoulder injury that resulted in surgery ended his season in late September. He was off to the races, stealing 12 bases in the month. Expect a little power, a ton of steals and a solid amount of runs.

Whit Merrifield, age 31, eligible at 2B, OF
2019 Stats: 735 PA, 16 HR, 105 Runs, 74 RBI, 20 SB, .302/.348/.811
When will he slow down? The steals cut in half from 2018 to 2019, was this age or was it team design to avoid wear and tear? Still likely the best offensive player across the board, keeping the HR total in the upper-teens is important to go with 20+steals.

Ryan O'Hearn, age 26, eligible at 1B
2019 Stats: 370 PA, 14 HR, 32 Runs, 38 RBI, 0 SB, .195/.281/.650
A flash in 2018 led to some promise for 2019, but he didn't deliver. He's going to get another chance, but with the roster flexibility, he could see less playing time than hoped.

Maikel Franco, age 27, eligible at 3B
2019 Stats: 428 PA, 17 HR, 48 Runs, 56 RBI, 0 SB, .234/.297/.705
Falling out of favor in Philly because of his defensive liabilities, so going to an AL team where he can be inserted as the DH could be a blessing in disguise. A useful player in your CI position in deep leagues.

Nicky Lopez, age 25, eligible at 2B, SS 2019 Stats: 402 PA, 2 HR, 44 Runs, 30 RBI, 1 SB, .240/.276/.601 The light-hitting MI made his debut in May, but it wasn't that great. He might get some early action with Mondesi recovering, but it likely won't keep him in the lineup. A backup and bench for fantasy.

Kelvin Gutierrez, age 25, eligible at 3B
2019 Stats: 79 PA, 1 HR, 4 Runs, 11 RBI, 1 SB, .260/.304/.660
Backup player, but showed some life in his small amount of playing time.

**Outfielders**:
Bubba Starling, age 27, eligible at OF
2019 Stats: 197 PA, 4 HR, 26 Runs, 12 RBI, 2 SB, .215/.255/.572
He's going to get his chance to man LF or CF on a full-time basis. The former 1st Round pick made his debut in 2019. I think he's worth a flier, just seeing the potential.

Brett Phillips, age 26, eligible at OF 2019 Stats: 79 PA, 2 HR, 7 Runs, 6 RBI, 3 SB, .138/.247/.508 His defense will keep him on the field, but he's got to produce on offense. Showed a little bit of power and speed in 2019 in a small sample size of playing time.

Jorge Soler, age 28, eligible at OF
2019 Stats: 679 PA, 48 HR, 95 Runs, 117 RBI, 3 SB, .265/.354/.922
Quite possibly was his career year. Spent only 54 games in right-field and the remainder of his time at D.H. Now the Royals single-season HR leader, with a decent average and on-base all the time. Staying healthy could lead to a repeat season or maybe greater.

Ryan McBroom, age 28, eligible at OF
2019 Stats: 83 PA, 0 HR, 8 Runs, 6 RBI, 0. SB, .293/.361/.721
Bench OF in MLB, not really a factor for fantasy.

**Starters:**
Danny Duffy, age 31, LHP
2019 Stats: 130 ⅔ IP, 115 K, 7 W, 4.34 ERA, 1.31 WHIP
Following the disappointment of 2018, 2019 was an improvement. Not great, but an improvement.

Brad Keller, age 24, RHP
2019 Stats: 165 ⅓ IP, 122 K, 7 W, 4.19 ERA, 1.35 WHIP
The most consistent starter for KC the last two seasons during his career. He's not a big K/9 pitcher, maybe that part of his game will come around as he ages and matures.

Jakob Junis, age 27, RHP
2019 Stats: 175 1/3 IP, 164 K, 9 W, 5.24 ERA, 1.43 WHIP
Useful in the deepest of leagues or to eat innings if that is a stat category. There are better options in shallower leagues.

Heath Fillmyer, age 26, RHP
2019 Stats: 22 ⅓ IP, 15 K, 0 W, 8.06 ERA, 1.79 WHIP
After putting up a respectable 4.26 in 2018, I took a big step back in 2019. Much like most of this rotation, stay away unless you are a fan or at minimum desperate.

Mike Montgomery, age 31, LHP
2019 Stats: 91 IP, 69 K, 3 W, 4.95 ERA, 1.62 WHIP
Used out of the pen and as a starter for the Cubs and Royals, he's back to the team that drafted him. Maybe some consistent role will produce better numbers?

**Relievers:**
Ian Kennedy, age 35, RHP
2019 Stats: 63 ⅓ IP, 73 K, 3 W, 30 SV, 3.41 ERA, 1.28 WHIP
The closer on this team, at the back end of a bad bullpen. Not the greatest of ERA and WHIP, but not going to kill you. At some point last season, everyone thought he would be traded. With KC not likely to be contending in 2020, that could again be the case and would most likely take him out of the closer's role on his new team.

Scott Barlow, age 27, RHP
2019 Stats: 70 ⅓ IP, 92 K, 3 W, 4.22 ERA, 1.44 WHIP
Potential Closer? He at least had more K's than Innings pitch, although with a higher than you would like in the bullpen ERA and WHIP. I see a defined role as one of the primary setup guys

leading to some better results.

Tim Hill, age 30, LHP
2019 Stats: 39 2/3 IP, 39 K, 2 W, 3.63 ERA, 1.11 WHIP
A submariner from the left-side, could be a primary weapon late in games and picking up those important holds if you need them. In his two-year MLB career, his numbers have improved.

Kevin McCarthy, age 28, RHP
2019 Stats: 60 ⅓ IP, 38 K, 4 W, 4.48 ERA, 1.48 WHIP
Just not much fantasy value out of the top two guys. He's probably headed towards middle-relief and not an end of the game option.

Jake Newberry, age 25, RHP
2019 Stats: 31 IP, 29 K, 1 W, 3.77 ERA, 1.45 WHIP
A young arm, still trying to establish himself, he's got less than 45 MLB innings under his belt.

Josh Staumont, age 26, RHP
2019 Stats: 19 ⅓ IP, 15 K, 0 W, 3.72 ERA, 1.60 WHIP
Once a starter, he made his debut in 2019 and didn't pitch that much. In a small sample it's hard to tell if the move to the pen was successful. He did make 12 starts at AAA for Omaha in 2019, so a return to a starters role could be an option.

Randy Rosario, age 26, LHP
2019 Stats: 14 ⅓ IP, 13 K, 2 W, 4.40 ERA, 1.40 WHIP
A DFA casualty from the Cubs in September of 2019 and was claimed by KC. He had a very short, but successful six appearances before the season ended. Always had good stuff, good work towards the back of the bullpen if he can find his control.

Kyle Zimmer, age 28, RHP
2019 Stats: 18 ⅓ IP, 18 K, 0 W, 10.80 ERA, 2.56 WHIP
Just don't look at those numbers from 2019. A first round draftee in 2012, the lack of health has delayed his career, but the potential could still be there. Only time will tell if he or his brother Bradley Zimmer will live up to the hype they have been known for.

# Kansas City Royals Prospects
## By Matt Thompson

### 1. Bobby Witt Jr.- SS
Witt has all the tools that you normally associate with a top five pick, and the Texas prep has the makings of a franchise cornerstone and a future fantasy first rounder. Witt is a plus defender at short and also has plus power and speed tools. The question with Witt is the hit tool. The bat speed is plus, but the swing is linear, leading to a lot of weak contact and ground balls. He does struggle a bit with handling breaking balls, but he's only 19. Due to that, I don't expect Witt to move quickly. It was a down year for nearly every offensive player in the Royals organization in 2019, so I expect the Royals to take their time with this potential franchise player. Witt is pretty solidly going off the board with the fourth pick in FYPDs. He's a future 25-30 homer, 20-25 steal shortstop. Wait and see on the type of average we get. **ETA: 2023.**

### 2. Daniel Lynch- LHP
Lynch is one of my favorite arms in the minors. I was a fan of Lynch while he was at the University of Virginia, and became even more of a fan after he altered his pitch mix. Lynch became more fastball heavy with the Royals, and his fastball picked up velocity and movement later on in the season after he returned from a bout of arm soreness. He was sitting around 96, and he even touched 99 during his one inning of work during the Fall Stars Game at the AFL. His slider is a plus pitch as well, and I think the curveball can creep up to above-average with refinement and his changeup can get to average. There's a chance Lynch can become a number one starter, but he more than likely settles in somewhere between a two and a three. He should start 2020 in Double-A, with an eye towards a late season big league call up. **ETA: 2021.**

### 3. Erick Pena- OF
The hype machine has pushed up all top end J2 talent this year, and Pena is one of those guys. I saw Pena while out in Arizona as the 2019 J2 signing made it out to Arizona for the instructional league. He's a quick-twitch athlete with potential plus power and hit tools, and he's also an above-average runner ticketed for rightfield. He squared up two baseballs in my look, and Pena is an exciting prospect to dream on. He's going off the board around pick ten in FYPDs. **ETA: 2024.**

### 4. Jackson Kowar- RHP
A projectable collegiate arm out of the University of Florida, Kowar reminds me a lot of Michael Wacha or Chris Paddack. It's an athletic, lean frame. His fastball sits low-to-mid 90s and can bump up to 97. His best secondary pitch is a changeup that gets double-plus grades due to its excellent fade and drop. He also mixes in a curveball that flashes above-average and can become even better with time. Despite the strong three-pitch mix, Kowar's stuff plays down due to his below-average fastball command. He has a chance to be a strong number two if the command improves, but he's likely to settle in as a three or four that shows flashes. Turning the lineup over three times may be something he struggles with. He should begin the season in Triple-A after pitching 74 innings in High-A and Double-A in 2019. He could be up sometime this summer. **ETA: 2021.**

### 5. Brady Singer- RHP

Singer was teammates with Kowar at the University of Florida, and in fact was even his roommate. The teammates were both first round picks by the Royals in 2018, and have moved through the Royals system together since. Singer has better command of the two, but his stuff lags behind significantly. Singer is primarily a two-pitch guy and his fastball/slider plays up from his ¾ slot. The fastball has plus movement, and the slider has tight, two-plane break. He gets ground balls and missed bats with both offerings, and has the floor of a late-inning pen arm if the changeup doesn't come along. He's a future mid-rotation arm, or closer. He should start in Triple-A. **ETA: 2021.**

### 6. Khalil Lee- OF

The Royals have aggressively promoted Lee through the minors, largely due to his makeup and defensive abilities. Questions with the overall hit tool, and just making contact in general, haven't slowed them down even if it probably should have. He's a patient hitter that has posted double-digit walk rates despite a lackluster hit tool. 53 stolen bases stand out though, and Lee is a plus runner with strong instincts on the bases. His heavy ground ball tilt is troublesome, but not as troublesome as his 67% contact rate in Double-A. He's a strong defender with a plus arm and is a fit in all three outfield spots. He needs to make more contact if he's ever going to post a 30-steal season in the bigs. He will likely get sent to Triple-A to start 2020, even though the contact rate says he probably shouldn't. **ETA: 2021.**

### 7. Kris Bubic- LHP

Yet another arm from the Royals huge 2018 draft. Bubic has proven too advanced for the low minors due to his command/control and plus changeup. He was eating inexperienced hitters alive by simply being able to sequence and put the changeup wherever he wanted. It's only an average fastball, but it plays up due to extension and his ability to hide the ball. His changeup is double-plus due to fade and velocity separation from the fastball. He also has an eye level changing curveball. This is the type of arm that beats projections, and Bubic has been doing that for his entire career thus far. The former Stanford Cardinal projects as a number four starter for me. He should start in Double-A in 2020. **ETA: 2022.**

### 8. Kyle Isbel- OF

Isbel is a short, muscular left-handed hitter with surprising pop despite his sub six foot frame. He's a plus runner with strong defensive skills that can potentially play all over the diamond, which is something I hope happens here. Isbel lacks a standout offensive tool, but he's posted strong walk and contact rates to this point. He battled injuries in 2019 but ended the season on a strong note in the AFL. I think he can hit 12-18 homers with regular playing time, with the ability to also add 10-15 stolen bases. He's played some second base during instructs and hope he gets more time there in the future. Isbel should report to Double-A as he begins his age 23 season in 2020. **ETA: 2021.**

### 9. Brady McConnell- SS

A toolsy collegiate shortstop from the University of Florida, McConnell is the lower ceiling prep version of Bobby Witt. McConnell has plus raw pop, especially to the pull side, and plus speed. He's got above-average bat speed but struggles with spin. McConnell had a sub 60% contact rate in the Pioneer League. That's a disappointing number for a college bat like this. If the hit tool can develop to average McConnell has a chance to hit 25 homers and chip in 12-15 steals. He's likely a second baseman long-term due to his arm, but McConnell could be a power-utility option off the bench as his athleticism makes him a strong candidate to move all over the diamond. First thing's first though, if he doesn't hit enough it's a moot point. **ETA: 2023.**

**10. Brewer Hicklen- OF**
A long-time personal cheese ball of mine, Hicklen showed what he's capable of in the Carolina League posting a 14 homer, 39 steal season in High-A. It did come with a 67% contact rate however. It's worth noting that the former two-sport athlete is raw, and his baseball instincts are lacking on the bases and in the field, but once he's underway his plus speed and athleticism take over. I'm worried about his potential power output, due to his issues with consistent contact and a linear bat path. Hicklen will take his skills to Double-A in 2020, and he's one of the players I'm most interested in tracking as the jump from High-A to Double-A is one of the most challenging in the minors. **ETA: 2022.**

**Next Five:**
Yefri Del Rosario- RHP
MJ Melendez- C
Zach Haake- RHP
Darryl Collins- OF
Jonathan Bowlan- RHP

**Top Five in FYPDs:**
Bobby Witt Jr.- SS
Erick Pena- OF
Brady McConnell- SS
Alec Marsh- RHP
Grant Gambrell- RHP

# Minnesota Twins Team Preview
### By Corey Steiner

**Projected Order:**
1. Max Kepler, RF
2. Jorge Polanco, SS
3. Nelson Cruz, DH
4. Eddie Rosario, LF
5. Josh Donaldson, 3B
6. Mitch Garver, C
7. Luis Arraez, 2B
8. Miguel Sanó, 3B
9. Byron Buxton, CF

**Projected Bench:**
Willians Astudillo, C
Alex Avila, C
Ehire Adrianza, OF
Jake Cave, OF
Marwin Gonzalez, 1B

**Projected Rotation:**
José Berríos, RHP
Jake Odorizzi, RHP
Kenta Maeda RHP
Homer Bailey, RHP
Randy Dobnak, RHP
Devin Smeltzer, LHP
Michael Pineda, RHP
Rich Hill, LHP

**Projected Bullpen:**
Taylor Rogers, LHP
Sergio Romo, RHP
Trevor May, RHP
Tyler Duffey, RHP
Tyler Clippard, RHP
Zack Littell, RHP
Fernando Romero, RHP
Matt Wisler, RHP
Brusdar Graterol, RHP

**Catchers:**
Mitch Garver, age 29, eligible at C
2019 stats: 359 PA, 31 HR, 70 Runs, 67 RBI, 0 SB, .273/.365/.404
As was the case last year, Garver boasts impressive plate skills and power, but enters the season with questions about how much playing time he will receive. With an ADP of 112, he is the fourth catcher being taken off the board. Consider waiting for more affordable options

(Perez, Kelly, even his former teammate Castro) who have the promise of more playing time and thus can match Garver's counting stats despite having less prowess at the plate.

Alex Avila, age 33, eligible at C
2019 stats: 201 PA, 9 HR, 22 Runs, 24 RBI, 1 SB, .207/.353/.421
Avila's ability to draw walks at an elite rate makes him an interesting late-round catcher two in OBP leagues. He doesn't hit for enough average to justify drafting in standard AVG leagues.

Willians Astudillo, age 28, eligible at C
2019 stats: 204 PA, 4 HR, 28 Runs, 21 RBI, 0 SB, .268/.299/.379
Astudillo didn't live up to the hype entering 2019, but this was as much due to limited opportunity as it was to his performance. Unfortunately, he enters a similar situation here, and it would be surprising to see him surpass 250 plate appearances, dramatically limiting his potential upside. As with Garver, consider passing on Astudillo in favor of players with more consistent playing time.

**Infielders:**
Marwin Gonzalez, age 31, eligible at 1B, 3B, OF
2019 stats: 463 PA, 15 HR, 52 Runs, 55 RBI, 1 SB, .264/.323/.414
As is usually the case, the appeal in drafting Gonzalez comes from his positional flexibility, particularly at the CI positions, both of which can be difficult to find depth in during the season. His performance is remarkably consistent from year to year and he has not shown signs of slowing down. He should provide value anywhere past pick 300 in standard leagues.

Luis Arraez, age 22, eligible at 2B, OF
2019 stats: 366 PA, 4 HR, 54 Runs, 28 RBI, 2 SB, .334/.399/.439
The biggest question with Arraez is whether he will be able to turn his amazing contact skills into power production, or whether he will remain a player whose only major contribution is in batting average. Unfortunately, his average exit velocity and hard hit percentage were both near the bottom of the league in 2019. You're probably going to be better off drafting someone who has already demonstrated power upside than selecting Arraez anywhere near his ADP (224). Consider Starlin Castro and Cesar Hernandez for more affordable options at the same position.

Jorge Polanco, age 26, eligible at SS
2019 stats: 704 PA, 22 HR, 107 Runs, 79 RBI, 4 SB, .295/.356/.485
Polanco demonstrated an uptick in his ability to hit for power in 2019, but unfortunately for fantasy purposes, this corresponded with a drop in stolen bases. For this reason, his profile is less unique than it used to be at a deep shortstop position. Consider passing on Polanco in favor of Didi Gregorius or Paul DeJong later in the draft, both of whom can provide similar or better production.

Miguel Sanó, age 26, eligible at 3B
2019 stats: 439 PA, 34 HR, 76 Runs, 79 RBI, 0 SB, .247/.346/.576
Sanó's 34 home runs in 2019 did not receive a lot of attention, making his 134 ADP a place of apparent value entering into this year's drafts. He still strikes out more than almost any full-time player in the majors, so it's certainly possible that we will see a drop in batting average this year. However, this is somewhat counterbalanced by his ability to draw walks, along with the fact that when he does make contact, he hits the ball *hard*. Sanó could very well match or outproduce Matt Chapman and Josh Donaldson this season, both of whom are going much earlier in drafts

than Sanó. Keeping his off-field issues in mind, you can still feel confident making him a target in your drafts.

Nelson Cruz, age 39, eligible at UT
2019 stats: 521 PA, 41 HR, 81 Runs, 108 RBI, 0 SB, .311/.392/.639
Age doesn't seem to apply to the relentless Cruz. He hit the ball harder than he ever has in his career in his age-38 season and hit 41 home runs despite only playing in 120 games as a result of minor injuries. As usual, you can draft Cruz at a discount because he can only be deployed in the DH slot. Feel comfortable targeting him in the pick 90-100 range.

Ehire Adrianza, age 30, eligible at 1B, SS, 3B
2019 stats: 236 PA, 5 HR, 34 Runs, 22 RBI, 0 SB, .272/.349/.416
Adrianza showed improvement in plate discipline in 2019 and offers the ability to hit for some power and steal some bases if given enough playing time. The question is whether he will play enough to be able to contribute in fantasy leagues. Watch out for injuries and poor performances in spring training and early in the season, as both could result in an increased role for Adrianza and thus the opportunity for fantasy value.

**Outfielders:**
Eddie Rosario, age 28, eligible at OF
2019 stats: 59 PA, 32 HR, 91 Runs, 109 RBI, 3 SB, .276/.300/.500
In 2019, we saw the highest power production of Rosario's career, but we also saw a decrease in stolen bases and a drop in walk rate. This could be the result of a change in approach rather than skills, making the 30 HR threshold repeatable in 2020. He is a relatively safe pick at his current ADP (92), but you may be able to find similar or better production a round or two later through players like Ozuna, Benintendi, and Castellanos.

Max Kepler, age 27, eligible at OF
2019 stats: 596 PA, 36 HR, 98 Runs, 90 RBI, 1 SB, .254/.336/.519
The power uptick displayed by Kepler in 2019 is noteworthy and went slightly under the radar, as his current ADP is a modest 142. Kepler again experienced bad luck in batted ball events last year, suggesting that his average could rise another 10 points in 2020. He boasts a strong plate approach and should be a target for anyone who decides to wait on drafting power.

Byron Buxton, age 26, eligible at OF
2019 stats: 295 PA, 10 HR, 48 Runs, 46 RBI, 14 SB, .262/.314/.513
After another injury-shortened campaign in 2019, it is fair to begin to question whether Buxton is capable of putting it all together over the course of a full season. Still, in the time he was on the field, Buxton showed improvements in both plate discipline (his strikeout rate dropped by over 6%) and power (his slugging percentage was the highest of his major league career). Buxton is never likely to hit for a high average, but the ability to hit 20 HR and steal 25 bases makes him a valuable target in the middle rounds (ADP 159) for those that prefer to begin the draft with a high batting average base.

Jake Cave, age 27, eligible at OF
2019 stats: 228 PA, 8 HR, 28 Runs, 25 RBI, 0 SB, .258/.351/.455
An interesting sleeper in deep leagues heading into 2020, Cave is capable of hitting for power, getting on base at a decent rate, and even stealing some bases if he is given the playing time.

The problem is that the outfield in Minnesota is currently crowded and he is not projected to play much, at least at the beginning of the year. A high strikeout rate also increases the possibility that he would not find enough success in a short stint to establish a full-time role.

**Starters:**
José Berríos, age 25, RHP
2019 stats: 200.1 IP, 195 Ks, 14 Wins, 3.68 ERA, 1.22 WHIP
After a very strong 2019 season which flew slightly under the radar, Berríos is going *later* (ADP 94) in drafts than he was a year ago. Berríos boasts elite skills in limiting hard contact and exit velocity, and with strong command and a decent strikeout rate, there is little to suggest that regression is going to significantly affect his results in 2020. Projection systems suggest there is some cause for concern in terms of home runs allowed, but because his profile has remained relatively consistent over the last three years, this may be overstated. Feel safe taking him as your second starter around his current ADP.

Kenta Maeda, age 31, RHP
2019 stats: 153.2 IP, 169 IP, 10 Wins, 4.04 ERA, 1.07 WHIP
It has been a few seasons since Maeda really has been an innings eater, 176 in 2015 and 2016, and we can't expect to see that change. So even if you take his projections with a grain of salt, and factor him in for 140 to 150 innings, there might be some value to be had. Even without elite velocity, Maeda generated a 15.1% swinging strike rate last season. That does translate into strikeouts, and with a relatively stable skill set, what you see from the right-hander is what you get. And there is something to be said for that.

Homer Bailey, age 33, RHP
2019 stats: 163.1 IP, 149 Ks, 13 Wins, 4.57 ERA, 1.32 WHIP
Bailey's minimal ability to garner strikeouts limits his upside, but with a current ADP of 482, there is essentially no risk in taking him at the end of a standard 15-team draft. He is capable of providing consistent innings of moderate ratios and can also be an effective streaming option against weaker divisional opponents.

Jake Odorizzi, age 29, RHP
2019 stats: 159 IP, 178 Ks, 15 Wins, 3.51 ERA, 1.21 WHIP
Due to a breakout 2019 campaign, Odorizzi's stock is on the rise, with a current ADP of 175. He won't necessarily pitch deep into games, but after finding success with his cutter in 2019, Odorizzi's ability to generate more than one strikeout per inning should remain consistent. He also should be able to pick up plenty of wins on a Twins team that is favored to win its division. If you are looking for a stable option at this stage in the draft, Odorizzi can return decent value at his ADP.

Michael Pineda, age 31, RHP
2019 stats: 146 IP, 140 Ks, 11 Wins, 4.01 ERA, 1.16 WHIP
Pineda was showing signs of improvement last year before receiving a suspension due to violating MLB's banned substance policy. Unfortunately, it is difficult to justify drafting him at his ADP (304) knowing that he won't be playing for the first five weeks while he completes his suspension. Consider looking for players that can make an immediate impact and picking him up off the waiver wire a few weeks into the season if he is available in shallower leagues.

Randy Dobnak, age 25, RHP
2019 stats: 28.1 IP, 23 Ks, 2 Wins, 1.59 ERA, 1.13 WHIP
Dobnak's strong rations during his first run in the big leagues can in part be attributed to fortune, as he maintained an unsustainably low home run to fly ball ratio (5.3%) and gave up too much hard contact (42.5%). The lack of strikeout upside really hurts his value and he should only be drafted in deeper leagues and deployed selectively against weaker opponents.

Devin Smeltzer, age 24, LHP
2019 stats: 49 IP, 38 Ks, 2 Wins, 3.86 ERA, 1.27 WHIP
Smeltzer makes for an intriguing streaming option while Pineda serves his suspension for over the first five weeks of the season. Smeltzer's upside is limited because he doesn't generate a lot of swings and misses or strikeouts, but in divisional matchups against teams like the Tigers and Royals, he can be useful in standard leagues.

Rich Hill, age 40, LHP
2019 stats: 58.2 IP, 72 Ks, 4 Wins, 2.45 ERA, 1.13 WHIP
Hill likely won't return to the field until June or July of 2020, making it impossible to justify drafting and holding him in standard leagues or leagues without IL slots. Keep an eye on him on the waiver wires and don't be afraid to pick him up a few weeks early. When healthy, he should be rostered in every league. His production remains solid despite his age with a high strikeout rate and strong command of the zone.

**Projected Bullpen:**
Taylor Rogers, age 29, LHP
2019 stats: 69 IP, 90 Ks, 30 Saves, 2.61 ERA, 1.00 WHIP
After generating the highest strikeout rate of his career in 2019, Rogers projects to be an elite closer in 2020 and is likely to retain the role if his strong performance continues. He was lucky in terms of stranding runners (86.2% LOB) last year, so it wouldn't be surprising to see his ratios take a step back this year, but he presents a higher floor than most relievers drafted in his current ADP range (130-140).

Sergio Romo, age 37, RHP
2019 stats: 60.1 IP, 60 Ks, 20 Saves, 3.43 ERA, 1.11 WHIP
While he should be useful in leagues that credit holds, it seems unlikely that Romo would take over the closer role for the Twins this year. He was fortunate in 2019 in terms of allowing HR, but with an elite ability to limit hard contact through deployment of sliders and changeups, he should continue to post decent ratios this year. Expect to see him used in the opener role and high-leverage situations.

Trevor May, age 30, RHP
2019 stats: 64.1 IP, 79 Ks, 2 Saves, 2.94 ERA, 1.07 WHIP
May posted great results in 2019 despite not getting the opportunity to close on a regular basis. He should remain useful in Holds leagues and has a chance to get some saves if Rogers struggles or misses time due to injury. Note that May was fortunate in 2019 in terms of BABIP (.233) and is projected to experience an increase in HR/9 in 2020, both of which indicate that he won't provide elite ratios, though the strikeouts will likely remain consistent.

Tyler Duffey, age 29, RHP

2019 stats: 57.2 IP, 82 Ks, 5 Wins, 2.50 ERA, 1.01 WHIP

After demonstrating great improvements in 2019 through more successful deployment of his slider, resulting in a now elite strikeout rate, Duffey seems primed to step into a high-leverage role in 2020. Expect him to contribute in Holds leagues, and keep an eye on him in standard leagues, as he could gain opportunities for saves if the players in front of him falter or miss time.

Tyler Clippard, age 35, RHP

2019 stats: 62 IP, 64 Ks, 1 Win, 2.90 ERA, 0.85 WHIP

Projection systems expect Clippard to take a step backwards in production in 2020, but he remains one of the game's best in limiting hard contact. He should provide solid production for the Twins, but he isn't likely to provide fantasy value outside of deeper holds leagues.

Zack Littell, age 24, RHP

2019 stats: 37 IP, 32 Ks, 6 Wins, 2.68 ERA, 1.16 WHIP

Offering a solid four-pitch mix, Littell has the chance to work as a starter at some point in his career. But with the Twins in win-now mode, he isn't likely to receive a significant opportunity this season, making him a player to watch on the waiver-wire rather than drafting this season.

Fernando Romero, age 25, RHP

2019 stats: 14 IP, 18 Ks, 0 saves, 7.07 ERA, 2.14 WHIP

Romero is too low on the depth charts to offer promise for fantasy production this season.

Matt Wisler, age 27, RHP

2019 stats: 51.1 IP, 63 Ks, 3 Wins, 5.61 ERA, 1.40 WHIP

Wisler has some strikeout upside, but like Romero, doesn't project to receive significant opportunities for saves or holds in 2020.

Brusdar Graterol, age 21, RHP

2019 stats: 9.2 IP, 10 K, 1 Win, 4.66 ERA, 1.24 WHIP

An exciting prospect from the Twins' minor league system, Graterol has a chance to start for the Twins eventually, but is more likely to be deployed from the bullpen this year. He is a hard-throwing righty who can generate strikeouts and exhibits strong command of the zone. Keep an eye on his spring training results; if he breaks camp with the big leagues, he is worth a speculative add in the late rounds of standard drafts.

# Minnesota Twins Prospects
## By Matt Thompson

### 1. Royce Lewis- SS
For the first time in his life, Lewis struggled on a baseball field. The number one pick of the 2017 draft, Lewis hit a disappointing .236/.290/.371 between High-A and Double-A. He followed it up by an MVP winning performance at the Arizona Fall League. Lewis suffered an oblique injury in spring training that is likely at least partially to blame for the slow start. Lewis himself said Twins told him to continue to do what he was doing despite the struggles, and that his exit velocities were strong. This is a kid with plus raw power and explosive athleticism. Combine that with true 80-grade makeup and you can see why he was a former number one pick, and still a top prospect despite his struggles. He will likely start 2020 in Double-A, and could see late season work in Minnesota **ETA: 2021.**

### 2. Alex Kirilloff- OF/1B
2019 was essentially a wash for the sweet swingin' lefty, as a wrist injury sapped all power and actually altered his swing mechanically. Don't look into the power outage, he's simply too good of a hitter to only hit nine homers for a season. The lefty has one of the sweetest swings in the minors when he's going right, and the Twins will be able to slot him in at first base without worrying about the bat clearing the new offensive bar. He's a .280 30+ homer bat long term, and he could hit his way to the big leagues in 2020 if injuries hit. He should start in Triple-A, and the more realistic ETA is 2021. There's a small buy low window open here for a guy comfortably within the top 50. **ETA: 2021.**

### 3. Trevor Larnach- OF
There's nothing flashy here with Larnach, but the Oregon State product just absolutely rakes. Larnach gets a boost in OBP formats due to his plus approach, and will use all fields and has the skills to post OBPs above .350 in the big leagues. I have him down for 20-25 homers at present, but he does hit the ball on the ground (47.5%) a bit more than I like. If he can make an adjustment to his batted ball profile there's 30-35 homer upside here. There's not much risk associated with this profile, and while he may not be a star, he's an extremely productive future big league right fielder. He should start 2020 in Triple-A, and is in a similar situation as Kirilloff in that he could come up later in 2020 but the ETA is more likely 2021. **ETA: 2021.**

### 5. Jordan Balazovic- RHP
The six-foot-three, 170 pound righty popped up on prospect lists after striking out over 11 per nine while walking around three per nine in the Midwest League in 2018. He followed it up with a strong 2019 campaign that answered my questions about the legitimacy of this arm. Balazovic is a big arm with a big league ready fastball that he gets in the mid-90s with run and plus extension. His slider is a put away breaking ball, but he still needs his changeup to pop to solidify his future in a big league rotation. My one concern, besides the change, is his long arm action. Look for the future mid-rotation arm to start 2020 in Double-A. **ETA: 2022.**

## 6. Jhoan Duran- RHP

Big, filled out right-hander sits 95-97 with the heater, and backs it up with a curveball that functions as the main put away pitch. He works primarily low in the zone with the fastball, which could be troublesome in today's uppercut heavy offensive game. In addition to the curveball he also throws a split/change, and this pitch is the key to his long term role. With him primarily working low in the zone with the fastball, hopefully he can tunnell the split/change off of that and make it as effective as possible. With the splitter we can have a potential fantasy number three. Without it there's some reliever risk here. Duran should report back to Double-A to start 2020. **ETA: 2021.**

## 7. Keoni Cavaco- SS/3B

Throw out the numbers when rostering Cavaco. He's sushi raw and has a swing on the longer side that is prone to swing and miss. He's toolsy as hell, with plus to double-plus raw thump and plus bat speed. He has an absolute cannon and projects as a third baseman for me due to his frame. He's lean and athletic at present but I anticipate him filling out and moving to his right. I'm really excited for Cavaco and his power over hit profile. He's always going to strikeout, but it's just a matter of keeping them in check. The profile reminds me of a mini-Javier Baez? It's going to be a slow burn throughout the minors but I'm excited for Cavaco's future. **ETA: 2024.**

## 8. Misael Urbina- OF

The 2018 J2 signing had a strong summer in the DSL, flashing strong plate and contact skills and playing a mature centerfield. Urbina is a hit/speed profile, and walked an astounding 23 times with only 14 strikeouts in 217 plate appearances. Urbina should be a strong batting average asset that can chip in 20-25 steals and hit 8-10 homers. A future table setter a top the Twins lineup. He's advanced enough that a full-season assignment right out of the gate wouldn't surprise me. **ETA: 2023.**

## 9. Brent Rooker- OF

Rooker lacks the upside of the names listed above him, but he's a big league ready power bat. Rooker, the 35th pick in the 2017 draft, was limited to just 65 games in 2019 due to a leg/groin injury. When healthy he's a 30-35 homer bat based on raw power alone, but there are some red flags here. His 58% contact rate in Triple-A is really poor, and he will need a strong enough hit tool to fully tap into the power. Rookier can play 1B as well as LF, and would need an injury or two to get big league run in 2020. **ETA: 2020.**

## 10. Travis Blankenhorn- 2B/3B/OF

Blankenhorn had a breakout season in Double-A hitting .278/.312/.474 with 18 homers and 11 stolen bases. He's an underrated prospect because all of his value is tied to what he can do with the bat. He's a below average defender at all three spots, but with this recent power surge I'm ready to invest in dynasty leagues. He made an adjustment to his swing that created more loft without sacrificing any of the components to his hit tool. An offensive minded utility option with above-average pop, an average hit tool and sneaky speed, Blankenhorn is a useful guy in the deepest leagues. **ETA: 2021.**

**10. Matt Wallner- OF**

Wallner was a former two-way player at Southern Miss, and now projects as a future plus right fiedler with a cannon arm. Wallner's best offensive tool is the plus raw power and strong walk rate. The Twins selected him with the 39th overall pick, and he's a nice middle round pick in your FYPD.

**Next Five:**
Devin Smeltzer- LHP
Lewis Thorpe- LHP
Ryan Jeffers- C
Emmanuel Rodriguez- OF
Randy Dobnak- RHP

**Top Five in FYPDs:**
Keoni Cavaco- SS
Matt Wallner- OF
Emmanuel Rodriguez- OF
Spencer Steer- SS
Matt Canterino- RHP

# Houston Astros Team Preview
By Matthew Simmons

## Projected Order
1-George SpringerCF
2-Alex Bregman 3B
3-Jose Altuve 2B
4-Yordan Alvarez DH
5-Michael Brantley LF
6-Carlos Correa SS
7-Yulieski Gurriel 1B
8-Josh Redick RF
9-Martín Maldonado

## Projected Bench
Kyle Tucker OF
Miles Straw SS
Aledmys Diaz SS
Dustin Garneau C
*Garrett Stubbs C

## Projected Rotation
Justin Verlander RHP
Zack Greinke RHP
Lance McCullers Jr RHP
Jose Urquidy
Josh James RHP
Framber Valdez LHP
*Rogelio Armenteros RHP
*Forrest Whitley RHP
*Cristian Javier RHP
*Francis Martez

## Projected Bullpen
Roberto Osuna RHP
Ryan Pressly RHP
Chris Devenski RHP
Brad Peacock RHP
Joe Biagini RHP
Cy Sneed RHP
*Cionel Perez LHP
*Are not likely to be on opening day roster at time of writing, but can force their way in with a good spring.

## Catcher
Martín Maldonado, age 33, eligible at C
2019 stats: 374 PA, 12 HR, 46 R, 27 RBI, 0 SB
At the moment Maldonado is the only catching option with real experience on the roster. His

career .220 average is really all you need to know about his fantasy value. If the Astros were to stand pat, he will only have value in deep two catcher or AL only leagues. That being said, the club has been linked to Wilson Contreras of the Cubs and their own free agent Robinson Chirinos in an attempt to find a backstop with some more bat.

Dustin Garneau, age 32, eligible at C
2019 stats: in minors
With 158 plate appearances in the majors spread over an eleven year career, Garneau is more of a stop gap than anything else. Baring another move he will start the season in the majors over Stubbs not due to an edge in talent, but because he's out of options. Odds are he will be released before the start of the season once the club adds another backstop, or decides that Stubbs is enough. Either way, the fact that he is at best a couple of steps behind Maldonado's weak bat shows his lack of fantasy value.

Garrett Stubbs, age 26, eligible at C 2019 stats: 39 PA, 0 HR, 8R, 2 RBI, 1 SB, .200/.282/.286
The 2015 Johnny Bench award winner finally has a path to playing time with the big club, so long as no one else is added to the roster. He has put up decent numbers in the minors with the most surprising one being double digit steals in each of his first four full professional seasons. However, with the Astros obvious team philosophy of not running I wouldn't expect that to fully translate to the big leagues. The biggest knock on him since his college days is the belief that his smaller frame will not hold up to a season of major league baseball. Odds are that will not matter much this year. If Stubbs gets more than 250 plate appearances this year either the Astros plans behind the plate have gone horribly wrong or Stubbs is having an unexpected breakout.

**Infielders**
Yulieski Gurriel, age 35, eligible at 1st and 3rd
2019 stats: 612 PA, 31 HR, 85 R, 104 RBI, 5 SB, .298/.343/.541 The veteran first baseman is a good option for those who miss out on the top tier guys and are in panic mode right before the floor falls out in the position. Sitting in the middle of the potent Astros lineup he will be a solid run and RBI producer with a batting average that should sit in the mid to high .290's. His power spiked in 2019 after a conversation with retired player Carlos Beltran in which the new skipper for the Mets convinced him to change his batting stance. There
is some question in the fantasy world as to whether or not the power will hold, especially if baseball goes back to the deaderball of 2018.

Jose Altuve, age 30, eligible at 2nd 2019 stats: 548 PA, 31 HR, 89 R, 74 RBI, 6 SB, .298/.353/.550 There are those who think Altuve is past his prime and sliding. I personally do not see that happening for another year or two. However, let's say he is on the downswing, who are you taking over him at 2nd? Marte, Albies, and Moncada may be closing the gap, but they are not above him yet. His steals have been down with the rest of the Astros, but word is he started the season not 100% from his knee surgery. He projects to be on par or better than all the other decent second baseman in the category with the exceptions of outliers Merrifield, Mondesi and Villar. He also projects to be one of the top power producers at 2nd, especially since the Orioles pitching should be just enough improved to possibly cut Glyber Torres output by 8 to 10 home runs.

Carlos Correa, age 25, eligible at SS 2019 stats: 321 PA, 21 HR, 42 R, 59 RBI, 1 SB,

.297/.358/.380 I waited to write the Carlos Correa section up because it is entirely possible he is gone before the season starts. Jeff Luhnow's response to Correa trade rumors was so unconvincing it inspired astros twitter to respond with The Walking Dead memes telling Carlos to just "look at the flowers". No matter who he plays for though the book on him is the same. Talent wise, Correa is a top 3-5 shorstop in all of baseball. If he ever plays 140 games he will be in the MVP race. He has only reached 140 games once, back in 2016. Personally, I was in the camp that it was odd freak injuries and you couldn't call him injury prone. That is until this year when the massage that was meant to keep his back in shape fractured a rib... On NFBC Correa is currently ranked the #14 shortstop going at pick pick 90 on average. If you can get him as the 14th shortstop off the board in the mid 7th round of a 12 team draft I'd say go for it and pair him up with someone else to cover while he is injured. If you do go that route, Amed Rosario the next round or so would be a good pairing if spending that much time on the position doesn't bother you. Or wait a while and take a look at Segura, Newman, DeJong or Kieboom

Aledmys Diaz, age 29, eligible at 1st, 2nd
2019 stats: 247 PA, 9 HR, 36 R, 40 RBI, 2 SB, .271/.356/.467 The backup infielder for the Astros is a position to pay attention to with the health history of Carlos Correa. On his own Diaz is a decent player. In the Astros lineup he would make an OK option at either middle infield or corner. All of this depends on a spot opening up in the starting lineup though so he will probably not be on many draft radars outside of deep leagues or AL only reserve rounds.

Alex Bregman, age 26, eligible at 3rd, SS 2019 stats: 690 PA, 41 HR, 122 R, 112 RBI, 5 SB, .296/.423/.592 The 2019 AL MVP runner up had his best season as a pro and cemented himself as a top 3 third baseman in fantasy. While I am not sure he will reach 41 home runs regularly, I do believe
that is the realistic upper end of his power output with his 31 from 2018 the floor. Bregman should go in the back of the first round to early second in most leagues. His near .400 obp raises his value even more in those leagues.

**Outfielders**
George Springer, age 30, eligible at OF, DH
2019 stats: 556 PA, 39 HR, 96 R, 96 RBI, 6 SB, .292/.383/.591
One of the Astros elder statesmen, Springer looks to lead the team in the outfield and in his normal leadoff role at the plate. The Astros lineup gives him the rare opportunity to be a 100 RBI leadoff man if he can play 150 games. Small nagging injuries have always been a problem for Springer, not eclipsing 140 games played since 2016. He's not a brittle bone guy either. If he can reign in the reckless abandon with which he plays Springer could be a dark horse for MVP this season.

Michael Brantley, age 31
2019 stats: 637 PA, 22 HR, 88 R, 90 RBI, 3 SB, .311/.372/.503
As of this writing, Michael Brantley's average draft position on NFBC (the only platform with adp's this early) was a criminal 128.5 as the 36th OF. He is currently wedged in between Danny Santanna and Max Kepler. Some names just a head of him are: Andrew Benintendi, Nicholas Castellanos, Oscar Mercado, and fellow Astro Kyle Tucker who currently does not have a place to play. He is going 40 spots behind Ramón Laureano who statistically is Brantley plus 10-12 steals and minus 20-30 points in batting average and OBP. The knock on Brantley is that he is injury prone which is not exactly true. Late in 2015 he injured his shoulder diving, requiring

surgery to repair. He managed 11 games back in 2016 before it was confirmed he would need another surgery to fix things. And that is the reason for the missed time in 2017. In reality, Michael Brantley just had some of the worst luck, missing chunks of 3 seasons to repair one injury. I see no reason why you can not take Brantley as early as the 6th round and get a good return on him. Keep an eye on the ADP as the spring rolls on though. If he remains low you should be able to take him in rounds 7-8.

Josh Reddick, age 32
2019 stats: 550 PA, 14 HR, 57 R, 56 RBI, 5 SB, .275/.319/.409
The self proclaimed "Mr. Irrelevant" is still slated to start for the Astros, but everyone including Reddick knows his days are numbered. For several years now Reddick has been a solid contributor for the Houston Astros, but also been known as a placeholder for top prospect Kyle Tucker. He has never had top end value, but a nice bench piece in deeper leagues. This year he is a great late round pick up for who ever takes Kyle Tucker.

Kyle Tucker, age 23
2019 stats: 72 PA, 4 HR, 15 R, 11 RBI, 5 SB, .269/.319/.537 Tucker is the last of the 100 loss Astros hitting prospects to either be promoted or traded. His 2018 much anticipated debut left some fans disappointed with 28 games of a .141 average. In
2019 he saw 22 games of a .269 average and some playoff appearances where he just looked over matched. I honestly thought people would jump off the bandwagon, but in NFBC early drafts he is the 34th OF off the board. While the early results have been somewhat underwhelming for a top prospect they are small samples of a young player just getting to the big leagues. Let me throw some short time up numbers at you,
Player A) year 1: 17 games, .204 Year 2: 48 games, .232 Player B) 40 games, .202 Player C) 5 games, .200 Player D) 127 games, .264 Those players are, in order, Alex Rodrigues, Mike Trout, Babe Ruth, and Ken Griffey Jr. (Side note, I looked up Ted Williams rookie year, 149 games with a slash of .323/.436/.609. Dude was just the greatest) Now, I'm not saying that Tucker will be one of the all time greats. All I'm saying is you can not estimate what he will do this season based on the short samples we have of him in the majors.

**Designated Hitter**
Yordan Alvarez, age 22
2019 stats: 369 PA, 27 HR, 58 R, 78 RBI, 0 SB, .313/.412/.655
For those of you who have not heard of 2019 rookie of the year, Yordan Alvarez, welcome to baseball! First of all, he has said his name is pronounced Jordan, as in Michael, which makes some sense since in Spanish J makes more of a hard H sound. On the baseball field he makes more of a hard crack sound with the bat. In 87 games he hit 27 home runs, including some moonshots. He does have a couple of drawbacks. First, and least important, is that he enters the season as a util/DH only player. Next is his 25.5% K rate. That is a little high, but acceptable for a masher. The one I'm most interested to see if he can fix in the offseason is the way he swung at the high stuff early in an at bat and the low stuff for strike three against the Yankees in the ALCS. Half way through the series my non-baseball fan wife said, "Why does he swing at all on strike 3? At least he could make the pitcher throw another pitch." In the World Series, his numbers did get a bit better. However, the Nationals did not take the same pitching strategy the Yankees did. It appears to be something completely coachable, but it is something to watch in spring training.

**Starters**

Justin Verlander, age 37

2019 stats: 223 IP, 300 Ks, 21 W, 2.58 ERA, 0.80 WHIP

I kind of wanted to leave last year to write up about JV in and see if anyone would notice, because what else can really be said that's new? The future 1st ballot hall of famer (possibly unanimous) just keeps on doing what he does. Strikeouts, innings, and wins with good averages. He is a top tier fantasy ace whose only knock is his age. Yes, it's likely that at some point he will fall off. Of course they've been saying that for 5 years now. In early draft ADP he is the 3rd pitcher off the board. If age is the reason you pass on him I can understand that price being a little rich. However, some of the other pitchers behind him in the top 10 are Scherzer, Strasburg, and Snell. You can't say you think Verlander is going to fall off and not think those guys might as well. If you want to take Cole, deGrom and Buehler ahead of him I understand your fears, I've had them too in the past, but there is no way Verlander does not enter the season as a top 5 pitcher with the same injury worries that every pitcher that steps on the mound has with one exception. He's already proven himself durable.

Zack Greinke, age 36

2019 stats: 208 IP, 187 Ks, 18 W, 2.93 ERA, .98 WHIP

I am writing this section on Greinke before pitchers and catchers report, but let me do a little future reading. OH NO! GREINKE HAS LOST A TICK AND A HALF OFF HIS FAST BALL! Wait, that's what we have said every spring for the last several years. Outside of his disastrous 2016 that saw him miss a month due to injury and have 4 true meltdown games, Greinke has not had a bad season in his career. He's likely to give you decent strike out numbers, better than average percentages and a good number of wins coming from the Astros lineup behind him.

Lance McCullers Jr, age 26

2019 stats: recovered from Tommy John surgery 24 straight curveballs.

Sorry Yankee fans, but you knew it was coming if you are reading anything about Lance McCullers from here to eternity. McCullers missed the 2019 season recovering from Tommy John surgery after the 2018 season. Right now in early draft season he is going around the 60th pitcher off the board. Expect that to rise as the spring unfolds. In the 2017 playoffs he looked to be a pitcher on the brink of breakout. Coming back from a season off I'd expect him to post around 130 innings of mid to upper 3's ERA with an average WHIP and a little more than a K per inning. As the presumed Astros #3 pitcher he should have a decent amount of wins and be a very valuable real life pitcher and a decent middle of the rotation fantasy asset. Do be careful in the spring as his pitches will often times just look amazing, sometimes raising his draft position higher than his fantasy value.

Jose Urquidy, age 24

2019 stats: 41 IP, 40 Ks, 2 W, 3.95 ERA, 1.10 WHIP

Just when things looked the most bleak in the 4 spot during the playoffs, Urquidy comes in and grinds through 5 innings with 0 runs. Right now he has to be considered a front runner for one of the last two rotation spots. Through 41 innings in the majors this season he posted a 24% K rate and a 4% BB rate, add that to a 3.68 FIP and you can see the basis for a quality late round starter. Especially look his way if you decided to skip SP's in the early rounds as he is likely to at least start the season in the rotation and likely has an ERA floor around 5.00, which isn't good, but he should avoid a 9.00+ meltdown season.

Josh James, age 27
2019 stats: 61 IP, 100 Ks, 5 W, 1 SV, 4.7 ERA, 1.32 WHIP
After what appeared to be a breakout season, most people, including yours truly, were on the James bandwagon. I felt he was a lock of the 5th spot. Then came a quad injury in spring and he never seemed to be able to work his way into the rotation. Several minor injuries and inconsistency helped contribute, but it appears the Astros like him in the bullpen. With the apparent loss of Will Harris and Colin McHugh, the Astros will be looking to find new reliable arms in the pen. If he can stay healthy I think that is where they want him. However, the job for the 5th spot is wide open and James could possibly fit well there too. This makes him an interesting late round stash in early drafts and possibly a late round go to as the spring progresses.

Framber Valdez, age 26
2019 stats: 70.2 IP, 68 Ks, 4 W, 5.86 ERA, 1.67 WHIP
Valdez will be hoping to right some of the wrongs from 2019. He saw a marked increase in most of the under the hood stats that you don't want going up, like exit velocity (+2.8mph), hard hit% (+19.7%), and HR/FB (+5.7%). While his GB% dropped 8.2%. The good news is, this is likely due in large part to the rabbit ball. The bad news is we don't know what ball will be used this year and it is evident he was unable to adjust to it. Personally, I'm out on Valdez except in really deep leagues or the very end of an AL only until I see something that convinces me otherwise. If he can make the changes needed though, he can become a usable 5th starter for the Astros, making him usable in fantasy. I expect him to get the opportunity from the club in spring as they seem to want James in the pen and the other options are all inexperienced.

Rogelio Armenteros, age 25
2019 stats: 18 IP, 18 Ks, 1 W, 4.00 ERA, 1.22 WHIP
Armenteros is a three pitch guy with a fastball, changeup, and curve who in the past has been considered a future pen arm. He has been one of the protected prospects in Astros trades in recent years and does have some potential as a starter depending on how things play out in the spring. Personally, I am staying away from him until there is a clearer path to playing time and some indication that the club is ready to lean on him.

Forrest Whitley, age 22
2019 stats: in minors
Whitley feels like Justin Verlander, except not in a good way. Every season we are ready for the breakout to come and see the player that was promised. Every season we see injury or suspension killing his time to develop. Whitley and Tucker are the last two guys drafted off the lean rebuild years. Tucker was discussed earlier and looks ready to go. Whitley has the tools, but has not been able to put it together yet. He does continue to look better in the Arizona Fall League than he does in the regular season. This could be because he is finally getting into the groove after injuries, it could be because he is a bit more fresh than the hitters he's facing, it could just be a small sample size. The fact that the Astros, who seem to know everything about every pitcher in the league still seem to believe in him, so I do as well. He should be a cheap speculative add unless he goes berserker in spring. Then get ready to pay up. Either way the team will probably service clock him and start him at AAA.

Cristian Javier, age 22
2019 stats: in minors

Playing at three levels last year (A+, AA, AAA) Javier appeared to have little problem with any of them. Known as a fastball/slider guy, he has a changeup that could develop into a reliable third pitch. Command has been his Achilles' heel, though when you hear people in the organization talk about it they do not seem that worried long run. He could also make a really solid pen arm if he doesn't stick in the rotation.

Francis Martes, age 24
2019 stat: recovered from Tommy John surgery/ in minors
Martes had a decent surge in the minors leading up to a mixed bag premier in 2017. He is a long shot for the rotation at the moment, but if he can find his groove in the spring he has as good a shot as anyone to be the #5 starter. Unless he absolutely goes off in spring training he will be more of a speculation add in deeper leagues.

## Relievers

Roberto Osuna, age 24
2019 stats: 65 IP, 73 Ks, 4 W, 38 SV, 2.63 ERA, 0.88 WHIP
As the unquestioned starter for the Astros, Osuna will have a lot of save opportunities this season. You will have to pay for him though as he will be in the top 6 relievers off the board this year in all formats. In the top 15 saves getters from last season (excluding Felipe Vasquez) he has the 6th lowest ERA with the 2nd most saves,.... and tied for the 2nd fewest K's. If you for some reason plan on getting all your strikeouts from your relievers, then you should avoid him. If you don't think the 20 odd K's means as much as the saves and ERA, then grab him. It's as simple as that.

Ryan Pressly, age 30
2019 stats: 54 IP, 72 Ks, 2 W, 3 SV, 2.32 ERA, 0.90 WHIP
What a season. Pressly started off the year by setting the MLB record for scoreless appearances at 40, then soon after was injured and looked at it. He didn't seem to be 100% the rest of the year, though he did come up huge in the playoffs on a play in which every Astros fan thought he blew out his knee. With an off-season of rest Pressly will likely resume his role of dominant setup man. If you are looking for a back end fantasy reliever who might get some saves, but will mostly just dominate for you, look no further.

Chris Devenski, age 28
2019 stats: 69 IP, 72 Ks, 2 W, 0 SV, 4.83 ERA, 1.30 WHIP
One of the heroes of the 2017 season and a fan favorite, Devinski has had trouble the last two seasons. His 4.83 ERA is the worst of his career. We are all hoping to see the return of Devo's Dragon Curve, but I'm not buying in until I see it. If someone else in your draft wants to take him, let them.

Brad Peacock, age 32
2019 stats: 91.2 IP, 96 Ks, 7 W, 4.12 ERA, 1.19 WHIP
Don't let the numbers fool you. Peacock was not as bad as his 4.12 ERA last season, he was injured. After a really rocky first few months of the season he was shut down due to shoulder discomfort he said he had been having all season. Once reactivated in August, Peacock pitched 3.2 innings in three games allowing only one run before going on the IL again for the same shoulder problem. He returned at the end of September and pitched 3 more innings of 2 run ball. Really, this was just a lost season. Peacock could become the 5th starter again, but if

healthy it is likely Hinch and company will want him to try to replace the hole left by Will Harris. Peacock is definitely a guy to watch in spring to see how his role develops. He could be a good end of the rotation starter, or he could be a great middle reliever so long as he's healthy.

Cionel Perez, age 23
2019 stats: 9 IP, 7 Ks, 1 W, 0 SV, 10.00 ERA, 1.44 WHIP
The 23 year old rookie has at times shown promise and flashes of brilliance as well as utter collapses. Hopefully this year he can fully get a grasp of the command he needs to make his ability to throw filthy stuff worth while. He could be a dark horse for the rotation, but he is much more likely to be a middle/long reliever without much fantasy upside except in the deepest of leagues.

Joe Smith, age 36
2019 stats: 25 IP, 22 Ks, 1 W, 0 SV, 1.80 ERA, 0.96 WHIP
Smith started the season injured and did not see action until late. And then, when he did see some playing time, he delivered. While 1.80 ERA in 25 innings is a small sample size, the team continued to rely on him in the playoffs and he continued to perform. The fact that the Astros decided to give him two more years seems to indicate that they think his injury is behind him. Smith really looks to be the replacement for Will Harris at the moment as the #3 bullpen arm. Joe Biagini 2019 stats: 64.2 IP, 60 Ks, 2 W, 0 SV, 4.59 ERA, 1.50 WHIP Biagini Came to the Astros along with Aaron Sanchez in the trade for Derek Fisher. He is one of those stereotypical guys with a huge spin rate, but not a lot of results, that the Astros seem to turn into diamonds. His biggest problem is giving up the occasional home run that really blows his numbers up. If the Astros can help him figure that out Biagini has all the makings of a dominant multi-inning reliever/spot starter in the vein of other Astros relievers like, Will Harris, Colin McHugh, Brad Peacock, Josh James and Framber Valdez. Yes, they have a type, and Joe Biagini could easily fit the bill at the top of that list. I am watching him, expecting to take him late in some drafts, though it is likely you can just wait and pick him up after the draft unless he blows up in spring.

# Houston Astros Prospects
## By Matt Thompson

### 1. Forrest Whitley- RHP

A suspension, shoulder fatigue, and a completely reworked delivery have gotten us to this point with former top five prospect Forrest Whitley. The top-end pitching prospect hasn't put a full season together since 2017. He's looking to build off of a strong stint in the AFL and conquer Triple-A before getting a taste of the big leagues this year. Whitley was flat out miserable in Triple-A last season, posting a staggering 12.21 ERA in just under 25 innings of work. He was hit hard by the walks and the homer run ball. Despite the down season Whitley is still a top twenty prospect. While we don't know where the command will settle in with this new delivery, this is a kid armed with three plus or double-plus pitches in his fastball, curveball and changeup. He's got two more above-average to plus offerings in his slider and cutter. It's an incredibly deep arsenal and he very much still has ace upside with five potentially plus pitches. Whitley will play a big role on the 2020 Astros. **ETA: 2020.**

### 2. Jose Urquidy- RHP

A pop-up prospect turned big league rotation piece, Urquidy is the anti-Whitley in a lot of ways. It's a command/control over stuff profile here, with a low-to-mid 90s heater that he can put wherever he wants at the forefront. He also throws a changeup with fade that plays very well off the fastball. He will mix in a curveball that he uses to steal strikes. The stuff is small by today's standards, but he just knows how to attack hitters. Urquidy has already had Tommy John surgery, and he has seen his fastball now sits at 93 and touch 97 since he's returned to the mound. I value Urquidy similarly to how I value Marcus Stroman for 2020. **ETA: Arrived.**

### 3. Abraham Toro- 3B

Toro is essentially the Astros insurance policy protecting them from injuries to any of their non-Altuve infielders. It was a strong 2019 for Toro as he jumped from Double-A to the big leagues for the American League champion Astros. He upped the quality of his at-bats and saw his numbers rise across the board. Hitting his pitch instead of what the pitcher was giving him, Toro led the Texas League in on-base percentage while setting a new career high in homers as well as batting average. The switch-hitter could still use some more time in the minors, and the Astros are in a position to be able to provide that. He's got no real true defensive home, but his best position is third base. Something like .275, with 20-25 homers is a realistic outcome here. He needs a trade to get that opportunity though. **ETA: Arrived.**

### 4. Jeremy Pena- SS/2B

Pena intrigues me. The 2018 third rounder hit .303/.385/.440 with 35 extra base hits (seven homers) and 20 steals. The University of Maine product was advertised as a defense first middle infielder, and that's still the case. He's a sparkling defender up the middle, but I think the words "glove first" often get mistaken for "no bat," and with Pena this isn't the case. He has natural bat-to-ball skills and an advanced feel for the strike zone. Pena fared well across two levels of A-ball and made an appearance in the Arizona Fall League to end his 2019. 2020 will be a big test as Pena will start in Double-A. **ETA: 2021.**

### 5. Bryan Abreu- RHP

Abreu had some eye-popping numbers in Double-A, with a remarkable 126 strikeouts and only 69 hits allowed in 91 innings. There's a little bit of smoke with these numbers though, as the

Astros used a "piggy-back" system in Double-A, which limits appearances to 3-4 innings a game. So he hasn't passed the test of turning lineups over a second or even a third time. It's a big fastball at 95-96 with a slider and a curveball. He's got fringe command of his arsenal, and if he improves the command he can be a future big league number three, or high leverage reliever. Abreu made seven appearances out of the big league bullpen down the stretch for the Astros and performed well. I'd bet on that being his future role. **ETA: Arrived.**

### 6. Christian Javier- RHP

Javier had one of the most dominant seasons we've seen in minor league baseball, striking out 170 hitters in 113 innings of work. Absolutely eye popping numbers but numbers that were aided by that piggy-back arrangement. He's not a flamethrower like the other arms listed. He has a low-90s heater with run and a plus slider. His command lags behind the stuff, but this is yet another potentially high upside arm to take a gamble on. **ETA: 2020.**

### 7. Tyler Ivey- RHP

A tall, lanky six-foot-four righty, Ivey was yet another arm that missed bats at a high clip. He also has the same concerns as the others. Can he start? Can he go deep in games? I think he's less likely to start out of this group due to his high-effort delivery and long arm action. His high-spin curve is his best offering, but he also throws a fastball with good movements and a tight-slider. He throws a changeup but it's not in the same class as his other pitches, and will likely be dropped if he moves to the bullpen. **ETA: 2022.**

### 8. Brandon Bielak- RHP

Yet another arm here, Bielak has a quality four pitch arsenal, but one that lacks a true swing and miss pitch. Bielak will throw any pitch in any count, and can locate them well. He will disrupt the timing of hitters and has a naturally deceptive delivery. His low-90s fastball is backed up by a high spin curveball, an above-average slider and a change. Unlike these other arms above him Bielak has stuff that's unlikely to play up in a bullpen role. He's more likely to remain a backend starter, but lacks the upside of the guys ahead of him. **ETA: 2020.**

### 9. Korey Lee- C

The profile for Lee is a simple, yet potentially productive one. A surprising first round pick out of Cal, Lee brings plus raw power and outstanding plate skills to the table. He has the unteachable ability to read and understand spin, and should post OBPs in the .330-.340 range to go with 20 homer pop. He needs to improve his receiving and blocking skills, but he has a plus arm. This is the type of catcher that gains value with robo-umpires. **ETA: 2022.**

### 10. Freudis Nova- SS/2B

This is an upside play, as the tools play much bigger than the numbers have to this point. There are no plus tools here, except his arm and range defensively. On offense it's a trio of above-average tools, with his power, his legs, and his hit tool. His aggressiveness can make the offensive game play down some, and Nova didn't pop in the tough Midwest League in 2019. **ETA: 2022.**

**Next Five:**
Jordan Brewer- OF
Colin Barber- OF
Dauri Lorenzo- SS

Luis Garcia- RHP
Taylor Jones- 1B

**Top Five in FYPDs:**
Korey Lee- C
Jordan Brewer- OF
Colin Barber- OF
Dauri Lorenzo- SS
Hunter Brown- RHP

**Projected Order:**
1- Tommy La Stella, 1B
2- Mike Trout, CF
3- Anthony Rendon, 3B
4- Shohei Ohtani, DH
5- Justin Upton, LF
6- Brian Goodwin, RF
7- Andrelton Simmons, SS
8- David Fletcher, 2B
9- Jason Castro, C

**Projected Bench:**
Albert Pujols, 1B
Luis Rengifo, INF
Michael Hermosillo, OF
Max Stassi, C

**Projected Rotation:**
Julio Teheran, RHP
Andrew Heaney, LHP
Dylan Bundy, RHP
Griffin Canning, RHP
Patrick Sandoval, LHP
Shohei Ohtani, RHP

**Bullpen:**
Hansel Robles, RHP
Ty Buttrey, RHP
Keynan Middleton, RHP
Cam Bedrosian, RHP
Noe Ramirez, RHP
Mike Mayers, RHP
Adalberto Mejia, LHP
Taylor Cole, RHP

**Catchers:**
Jason Castro, 32, eligible at C
2019 Stats: 275 PR, 13 HR, 39 Runs, 30 RBI, 0 SB, .232/.332/.435
A much needed signing to start the new year and the Angels now have a very good defensive duo of C.  Not known for his bat Castro is interesting for fantasy primarily in 2 C leagues where his starter status in a good lineup automatically makes him relevant.  He did take advantage of the offensive environment last season posting 13HR in 79 games peeking over 100wRC+ at 103 for the first time since 2013.  C is gross and there is a chance you will see him as a plug-in

at the position on a few rosters during the season if he threatens to repeat his offensive performance from last season over a higher number of at bats but not a player I would target at C.

Max Stassi, 28, eligible at C
2019 Stats: 147 PA, 1 HR, 7 Runs, 5 RBI, 0 SB, .136/.211/.167
A defense first C who may not be ready for opening day with a hip injury.  He can be ignored in fantasy drafts

**Infielders**:
Tommy La Stella, age 31, eligible at 2B, 3B (currently projected starting 1B)
2019 Stats: 321 PA, 16 HR, 49 Runs, 44 RBI, _ SB, .295/.346/.486
La Stella has 26 career home runs in 476 games...16 of them came in just under 80 games last year before breaking his leg.  If that power boost is legit La Stella could have a huge season.  Even if the power takes a hit he has a career .345 OBP and is pencilled in batting in front of Rendon/Trout/Ohtani.  Still a significant risk as he has never eclipsed 360 PA in a season and has 10 career HR outside of last season, but a decent later round gamble who comes with some positional flexibility to help his value.

David Fletcher, age 25, eligible at 2B, 3B, SS, OF
2019 Stats: 653 PA, 6 HR, 83 Runs, 49 RBI, 8 SB, .290/.350/.384
Multi-eligibility gives him some nice flexibility for your deeper leagues and as a career .285 hitter in a good lineup could give you a little BA stability and be a decent source of runs.  Not someone I would want to see in my fantasy starting lineup on opening day but could serve as an injury fill in at times during the year.  6 HR in 653 PA with a juiced ball, provides almost no power so if you do end up slotting him in at times make sure you plan accordingly.

Anthony Rendon, age 29, eligible at 3B
2019 Stats: 646 PA, 34 HR, 117 Runs, 126 RBI, 5 SB, .319/.412/.598
Coming off an absolute monster season where he actually out-earned his new teammate Mike Trout according to ESPN Player Rater finishing as the #7 overall hitter.  Early drafts have him coming off the board in the 2nd round in the middle of a group of 3 3rd basemen which feels right.  The depth of 3rd base and a lack of speed are the 2 reasons I am not rallying for Rendon to be pushed into the first round.  I tend to lean to the over on the projections for Tony Two Bags who will have plenty of RBI opportunities batting behind the aforementioned Trout.  He set career highs in every category outside of SB last season so I wouldn't bank on reaching last year's numbers again this year but it certainly raised his ceiling and he has about as safe a floor as you will find.

Andrelton Simmons, age 30, eligible at SS
2019 Stats: 424 PA, 7 HR, 47 Runs, 40 RBI, 10 SB, .264/.309/.364
Injuries limited this defense first SS to only 103 games last year but he did still get to double digit steals.  A healthy season should produce a better BA (.278 was his low mark as an Angel before last season) and some usable numbers from SB/R/RBI.  Probably not a starting SS in a standard mixed as he provides little power but he could be a productive MI who you can pick up pretty late in drafts.

Luis Rengifo, age 23, eligible at 2B
2019 Stats: 406 PA, 7 HR, 44 Runs, 33 RBI, 2 SB, .238/.321/.364
A bench bat with very little power but good on base skills coming of a hamate bone injury. He was only 22 last year so there is still potential for growth but not someone to look for on draft day.

Albert Pujols, age 40, eligible at 1B
2019 Stats: 545 PA, 23 HR, 55 Runs, 93 RBI, 3 SB, .244/.305/.430
Pujols, entering his age 40 season this year, still managed to put up 93 RBI last year but his days of anchoring a lineup, fantasy or real life, are well past. Ohtani getting more run at DH should eat into Pujols playing time. I don't see Pujols as being fantasy relevant except perhaps in our 30 team 40 man roster staff dynasty league.

**Outfielders**:
Mike Trout, age 28, eligible at OF
2019 Stats: 600 PA, 45 HR, 110 Runs, 104 RBI, 11 SB, .291/.438/.645
He real good. Trout is as safe as it comes from a production standpoint and will go in the top 3 in the majority of drafts (as opposed to top 1 as he has the last couple of years). To nitpick some negatives he dropped to 11 steals last year in 134 games and has missed some time in 3 straight seasons after 4 seasons of perfect health. That being said he ended up at 45/110/104 in 134 games, good enough for the 8th overall hitter on the year in 2019. Counting stats and ratios anchor who gives you a strong base and plenty of flexibility as you build your roster. The argument is there for Acuna and Yelich but Trout still goes 1 for me.

Shohei Ohtani, age 25, eligible at UT
2019 Stats: 425 PA, 18 HR, 51 Runs, 62 RBI, 12 SB, .286/.343/.505
Daily or Weekly Lineups? 1 or 2 Ohtani? Those are the most important questions with regards to Ohtani's value. Weekly his value lies mostly in his P numbers, not that his hitting isn't elite when he is getting ABs. If you were starting a dynasty daily league with 1 Ohtani you could make a strong case for Ohtani at 1 overall. An elite pitcher on a per game basis with power and speed from the UT spot when he gets DH starts. This year though, he carries risk coming off of Tommy John surgery and we really don't know how the Angels will deploy him as a pitcher or hitter around his starts. His value falls quite a bit if you are in a weekly league or split Ohtani league; in weekly leagues he could be a frustrating own as we figure out his batting usage and how eager the Angels are to push him deep into games. Expect his start #s to fall well below other top of the rotation SP but expect elite numbers when he toes the rubber and he could make a run at 25-30 HR and double digit steals if he gets enough time at the plate. My guess is in weekly leagues he will go higher than I am willing to spend on him.

Joc Pederson, age 28, eligible at OF and 1B
2019 stats: 514 PA, 36 HR, 83 Runs, 74 RBI, 1 SB, .249/.339/.538
We know that Pederson has elite level power, but he is truly a platoon player. Based on his struggles against southpaws, that might be better for him and his .250 batting average, but he likely won't get much more than 500 at bats. What holds me back from going crazier though, is his 26% home run to fly ball rate and the doubts on him repeating his 36 home runs from last season.

Justin Upton, age 32, eligible at OF

2019 Stats: 256 PA, 12 HR, 34 Runs, 40 RBI, 1 SB, .215/.309/.416

Played only 63 games last year due to lower half injuries. Has 30 HR power if he stays healthy but I'm not sure he will ever get back to his double digitish steals numbers that helped boost his value. Career .266 hitter won't kill your BA but not a huge boost there. A decent back end bat with power potential but one I would be willing to eject from fairly early in the season if injuries pop up or his performance looks more like 2019 and not 2017/8

Brian Goodwin, age 29, eligible at OF
2019 Stats: 458 PA, 17 HR, 65 Runs, 47 RBI, 7 SB, .262/.326/.470

Former 1st round draft pick who hasn't ever met that level of expectations. Goodwin has some deeper league appeal with some pop and a handful of SB with palatable ratio #s as long as he is in the lineup...which is directly tied to how long it takes Jo Adell to break into the big leagues or how long one of the regulars is on the IR.

Michael Hermosillo, age 25, eligible at OF
2019 Stats: 46 PA, 0 HR, 7 Runs, 3 RBI, 2 SB, .139/.304/.222

A September call up as a 24yo last season he is a fringe major leaguer and can be ignored in fantasy drafts

**Starters:**

Julio Teheran, age 29, RHP
2019 Stats: 174.2 IP, 162 K, 10 W, 3.81 ERA, 1.32 WHIP

Teheran has made a habit of outplaying his peripherals as his 3.81 ERA with a 1.32 WHIP from last season indicates. He has had a sub 4 ERA 3 of the last 4 years but a sub 4.66 FIP only 1 of those 4 seasons and has a career 7.82 K/9 Angels have improved their lineup and are definitely looking to compete this year so he could earn some wins but I am not going to end up with shares of Teheran

Andrew Heaney, age 28, LHP
2019 Stats: 95.1 IP, 118 K, 4 W, 4.91 ERA, 1.29 WHIP

There is a definite sleeper appeal with the 28 yo Lefty Heaney who boasts excellent k numbers for an SP with early projections putting him up near 10 per 9. His 1.89 HR/9 from last season will need to drop if he wants to lower that ERA but if he can keep the ball on the ground a bit more and keep up those strikeout numbers he will be an intriguing SP 3 with upside.

Dylan Bundy, age 27, RHP
2019 Stats: 161.2 IP, 162 K, 7 W, 4.79 ERA, 1.35 WHIP

Perhaps a change of scenery can help pull out some of that potential that made Bundy a top prospect in his earlier years. His fantasy value depends on it and it certainly wouldn't be the first time a pitcher showed improvement after escaping Baltimore. He is a fringe fantasy asset with that always elusive upside to develop into more. He might show up on some sleeper lists this year but I am going to have to see it first with Bundy which means if it happens this year it won't help my fantasy squads.

Griffin Canning, age 23, RHP
2019 Stats: 90.1 IP, 96 K, 5 W, 4.58 ERA, 1.22 WHIP

At 23 Canning carries a decent amount of upside coming of his 90 inning debut season in the majors. He doesn't strike me as a future fantasy ace yet and there may be some work load limitations coming off a career high 106.1 innings between AAA and MLB last season but a low to mid 4s ERA with over a K/inning certainly makes him fantasy relevant.

Patrick Sandoval, age 23, LHP
2019 Stats: 39.1 IP, 42 K, 0 W, 5.03 ERA, 1.37 WHIP
The 23 yo prospect made his debut last year and is currently pencilled into the Angels' unconventional 6 man rotation. In addition to keeping Ohtani on schedule the 6 man rotation could have the added benefit of helping manage innings for youngsters Sandoval and Canning. Sandoval holds some deep league value assuming he sticks in the rotation as he is a strikeout pitcher but I wouldn't expect even triple digits in innings pitched.

Shohei Ohtani, age 25, eligible at UT
2019 Stats: Did not Pitch
2018 Stats: 51.2 IP, 63 K, 4 W, 3.31 ERA, 1.16 WHIP
Daily or Weekly Lineups? 1 or 2 Ohtani? Those are the most important questions with regards to Ohtani's value. Weekly his value lies mostly in his P numbers, not that his hitting isn't elite when he is getting ABs. If you were starting a dynasty daily league with 1 Ohtani you could make a strong case for Ohtani at 1 overall. An elite pitcher on a per game basis with power and speed from the UT spot when he gets DH starts. This year though, he carries risk coming off of Tommy John surgery and we really don't know how the Angels will deploy him as a pitcher or hitter around his starts. His value falls quite a bit if you are in a weekly league or split Ohtani league; in weekly leagues he could be a frustrating own as we figure out his batting usage and how eager the Angels are to push him deep into games. Expect his start #s to fall well below other top of the rotation SP but expect elite numbers when he toes the rubber and he could make a run at 25-30 HR and double digit steals if he gets enough time at the plate. My guess is in weekly leagues he will go higher than I am willing to spend on him.


**Relievers:**
Hansel Robles, age 29, RHP
2019 Stats: 72.2 IP, 75 K, 5 W, 23 Sv, 2.48 ERA, 1.02 WHIP
Had a great season last year and if he can carry his skills improvements from last season into the 2020 campaign he could be an excellent pick in the middle of your fantasy draft. He is a #2 closer in most fantasy leagues but at the top end of that list with good ratios and an acceptable K rate.

Ty Buttrey, age 26, RHP
2019 Stats: 72.1 IP, 84 K, 6 W, 2 Sv, 3.98 ERA, 1.27 WHIP
High leverage pitcher with an excellent K rate. Good source of holds and not a bad speculative saves pick if Robles struggles or goes down with an injury. Even if he's not earning saves he will still help you in Ks and can put up good ratios so in leagues where that matters Buttrey is definitely worth a look.

Keynan Middleton, age 26, RHP
2019 Stats: 7.2 IP, 6 K, 0 W, 1.17 ERA, 1.43 WHIP
Only through 7.2 Innings last year as he returned from TJS. Middle reliever still coming back from TJS isn't worth a look in fantasy for this season.

Cam Bedrosian, age 28, RHP
2019 Stats: 61.1 IP, 64 K, 3 W, 1 Sv, 3.23 ERA, 1.14 WHIP
Someone to maybe keep an eye on through the season in case things go awry at the back end of the Angels pen but not someone you should be looking at in your fantasy drafts.

Noe Ramirez, age 30, RHP
2019 Stats: 67.2 IP, 79 K, 5 W, 3.99 ERA, 1.17 WHIP
Middle reliever not worth fantasy consideration.

Mike Mayers, age 28, RHP
2019 Stats: 19 IP, 16 K, 0 W, 6.63 ERA, 1.68 WHIP
Waiver pickup from the Cardinals in the offseason, Mayers is a low inning RP with bad ratios and less than 1K/ip and can be ignored in fantasy drafts

Adalberto Mejia, age 26, LHP
2019 Stats: 31.1 IP, 30 K, 0 W, 6.61 ERA, 1.72 WHIP
No fantasy draft appeal

Taylor Cole, age 30, RHP
2019 Stats: 21.2 IP, 50 K, 3 W, 1.59 ERA, 0.00 WHIP
No fantasy draft appeal

## Los Angeles Angels Prospects
By Matt Thompson

### 1. Jo Adell- OF
Adell missed the first two months of 2019 after a horrific ankle injury sliding into second base in a spring training game. If not for the injury we could've seen Adell in the second half, but he made up for the lost development time with a stint in the Arizona Fall League. After rehab he was sent to Double-A, and performed extremely well. He was promoted to Triple-A Salt Lake, and struggled a bit with a .264/.321/.355 line with an alarming 64% contact rate. He corrected some of the contact concerns while in the AFL, but still struck out 29 times in 24 games. He's not as polished as someone like Vlad was coming up, but the athleticism shines through. He's a 30-35 homer bat at peak due to his plus raw power, and its plus-plus to his pull side. I expect him to chip away at those contact concerns and post a strong .270-.280 average at peak, but don't expect that right away. He can also chip in around 15 steals as well. We will see Adell when he's deemed ready, likely sometime before the middle of May. **ETA: 2020.**

### 2. Brandon Marsh- OF
I came away from the AFL absolutely in love with Brandon Marsh. Marsh did everything on the field. Flashed his improved hit tool, and hit for power. He ran the bases well, flashed his plus defense in center, and even showed off his strong arm. I saw all of that in like a five game sample. He's the epitome of the phrase I always say. Always bet on the athletes. That saying is especially true in the fantasy realm. Marsh likely starts the season in Triple-A, and will position himself for a potential call-up later in the second half. He's good enough to be the fourth outfielder now for the Angels, but Marsh has missed so much development time due to playing football in college and also just injuries that have kept him off the field. I'm investing heavily in Marsh where I can. He's a potential 20/20 kid with plus defense in center. Look for him in 2021. **ETA: 2021.**

### 3. Jordyn Adams- OF
Adams might be one of the best overall athletes to put on a baseball uniform at any level in 2019. A three-sport star, he passed up a football scholarship to sign with the Angels. Adams posted strong double-digit walk rates during his first taste of full-season ball, across two levels of A-ball. He's an 80-grade runner, and that combined with his OBP ability, he is a threat to steal 30 bags at the big league level. The hit tool and power are likely only average, but when you factor in his plate skills and game changing speed he has a chance to be a dynamic offensive player. Adams can also go and get it in center and is yet another all around contributor. Buy! Buy! Buy! Adams has a chance to be a top 25 prospect at this time next year. **ETA: 2023.**

### 4. Jeremiah Jackson- SS/3B/2B
We are now four-for-four on toolsy explosive athletes in this system. Jeremiah Jackson posted power numbers that absolutely jumped off the page as he swatted 23 homers for Orem in the hitter friendly Pioneer League. It's a skinny, lean frame but a powerful one. There's plus raw power in here despite his build. He's currently an average runner, but I expect him to slow down as he fills out, and likely moves to third. His 63% contact rate is alarming, but we will learn a lot about Jackson as he will start 2020 in the Midwest League. There's big power here, and you are gambling on the rest of his offensive skills to come around. **ETA: 2023.**

### 5. Patrick Sandoval- LHP

Sandoval was a personal favorite of mine when he was drafted by the Astros in 2015. His stock may be down a bit after rough stints in Triple-A and with the Angels, but Sandoval is much too young to toss aside. He will be only 23 on Opening Day and he brings an advanced four-pitch mix to the plate. He averaged 93 with the fastball during his big league time, and flashed three average or better secondaries, with hsi plus curveball being the best offering. Sandoval has a strong track record of missing bats, and projects as a solid number four in the big leagues. He will likely be up and down this year between the Angels and Salt Lake, but his price is likely a bit suppressed right now. **ETA: Arrived.**

### 6. Kyren Paris- SS
One of the younger players in the 2019 draft class, the Angels selected Paris in the second round out of the California prep circuit. It's a long slow burn for Paris, but he projects to hit for a strong average with 15-18 homers and steals at peak. Obviously depending on how his body develops that can tip the scale more towards power or speed, but the point here is Paris doesn't have a standout fantasy tool, and will be a well rounded contributor. His defense and advanced feel for the game are his best attributes. **ETA: 2024.**

### 7. Jack Kochanowicz- RHP
The Angels third round pick in this past draft, Kochanowicz is a six-foot-six, long limbed projectable arm with the potential to have three above-average or better offerings. He projects as a bat missing mid-rotation arm with a chance for more while also supplying strong ratios. It's a long term play here, with a likely ETA around 2024. **ETA: 2024.**

### 8. D'Shawn Knowles- OF
A premium athlete, Knowles is a switch-hitting center fielder with a chance to hit at the top of a lineup. He's a plus to double-plus runner that can steal 30 bags if he can get on base at a league average clip. He's struggled to make contact consistently and will likely never post strong batting averages, but .240-.250 with average walk rates and his ability to steal 30 bases and chip in 12-15 homers carries value. Knowles will join Jeremiah Jackson in the Midwest League as he makes his full-season debut in 2020. **ETA: 2023.**

### 9. Arol Vera- SS/3B
Vera was one of the top players in the 2019 J2 class, and the Angels gave the athletic infielder $2 million to sign. The switch-hitter is now six-foot-three, and just under 190 pounds at only 17 years old. Vera projects to have plus raw power that is able to get it to translate in games sooner because he can already command the zone better than most hitters his age. He's a nice power-only high upside play late in your FYPD. **ETA: 2025.**

### 10. Jahmai Jones- 2B/OF
Jones has seen his prospect stock dip over the last two-three seasons due to his lack of production in the minors. The speed is the best tool here, but the overall offensive skill set is propped up due to his above-average walk rates. Jones has constantly tinkered with his hands at setup since entering pro ball, and is trying to find a more consistent power stroke while he makes contact at a higher clip. Jones stock is down and shouldn't cost much, and he should debut in 2021. **ETA: 2021.**

**Next Five:**
Chris Rodriguez- RHP

Hector Yan- LHP
Jose Soriano- RHP
Trent Deveaux- OF
Adrian Placencia- SS

**Top Five in FYPDs:**
Kyren Paris- SS
Jack Kochanowicz- RHP
Arol Vera- SS
Adrian Placencia- SS
Alexander Ramirez- OF

# Oakland Athletics Team Preview
## By Gabe Zammit

**Projected Order:**

1- Marcus Semien, SS
2- Ramón Laureano, OF
3- Matt Chapman, 3B
4- Matt Olson, 1B
5- Mark Canha, OF
6- Khris Davis, DH
7- Stephen Piscotty, OF
8- Sean Murphy, C
9- Franklin Barreto, 2B

**Projected Bench:**

Austin Allen, C
Jorge Mateo, INF
Chad Pinder, INF/OF
Robbie Grossman, OF

**Projected Rotation:**

Mike Fiers, RHP
Sean Manaea, LHP
Frankie Montas, RHP
Jesus Luzardo, LHP
Chris Bassitt, RHP

**Bullpen**:

Liam Hendriks, RHP
Yusmeiro Petit, RHP
Joakim Soria, RHP
Jake Diekman, LHP
Lou Trivino, RHP
J.B. Wendelken, RHP
T.J. McFarland, LHP
Daniel Mengden, RHP

**Catchers:**

Sean Murphy, age 25, eligible at C
2019 Stats: 60 PA, 4 HR, 14 Runs, 8 RBI, 0 SB, .245/.333/.566
Once upon a time Murphy was seen as a defense first catcher with untapped raw power lurking in his bat. He must have figured something out. In 2018 Murphy's HR/FB rate was 13.6% and in 2019 it spiked to 31.3% in triple-A. This power trend continued over to his introduction to the majors last year as he hit 4 homers in 20 games. I would still expect some regression, but 25 HR with a .260 average is definitely a possibility.

Austin Allen, age 26, eligible at C
2019 Stats: 71 PA, 0 HR, 4 Runs, 3 RBI, 0 SB, .215/.282/.277

Allen came over to Oakland in the Profar to San Diego trade. Unfortunately for Allen, Sean Murphy had a mini-breakout last year. The best he can hope for is to catch a couple of games a week. There doesn't seem to be a ton of upside in his bat anyways for now, but he did always hit for a high average in the minors. If Murphy falters, Allen could steal more playing time as the year progresses.

**Infielders**:
Matt Olson, age 25, eligible at 1B
2019 Stats: 547 PA, 36 HR, 73 Runs, 91 RBI, 0 SB, .267/.351/.545
Within the first week of the season, Matt Olson will turn 26 and be right in the prime years of his career. He's about as safe a bet as they come right now at 1B and should be good for another year where he gets between 35-45 HR. The only real knock on Olson is his batting average, but it's not so bad that it will sink you. Just keep in mind he is more likely a .250 hitter, than a .300 hitter.

Khris Davis, age 32, eligible at DH
2019 Stats: 533 PA, 23 HR, 61 Runs, 73 RBI, 0 SB, .220/.293/.387
Here comes Mr. .247 who had his fifth year hitting for… Oh… Khris Davis was bad last year? Yes, he was. Injuries piled up and kept Davis from hitting .247 again, but more importantly completely sapped his power. Don't forget about Davis at the draft table, and don't get scared off by his Util only designation. He could come at a discount and get you 40 HR on the cheap.

Franklin Barreto, age 24, eligible at 2B
2019 Stats: 58 PA, 2 HR, 6 Runs, 5 RBI, 1 SB, .123/.138/.263
The position battle to watch in camp will be for the 2B gig. Barreto, Mateo, and prospect Sheldon Neuse are all being considered. While Barreto is penciled in currently, he is far from a lock if he can't get a hold of his strikeout problem. He has tantalizing speed and power and the upside is a 20/20 season, just not if he can't bat over .200.

Marcus Semien, age 29, eligible at SS
2019 Stats: 747 PA, 33 HR, 123 Runs, 92 RBI, 10 SB, .285/.369/.522
Marcus Semien really doesn't get the love he deserves in fantasy circles, and I can't figure out why. His numbers are slightly inflated due to the insane number of plate appearances he had in 2019, but health is a skill too. Semien has reached at least 600 plate appearances in 4 of the last 5 years. He might not be the flashiest pick, but the floor is set pretty high with Semien.

Matt Chapman, age 26, eligible at 3B
2019 Stats: 670 PA, 36 HR, 102 Runs, 91 RBI, 1 SB, .249/.342/.506
I'm not sure if there are skeptics out there on Matt Chapman, but there really shouldn't be. Sure, Chapman jumped from 24 to 36 HR between 2018 and 2019, but that was fueled by a boost in his barrel percentage and his launch angle. He's really not hitting the ball any harder than 2018, he's just making better contact. This indicates the growth is here to stay and maybe there is the potential for 40+ HR.

Jorge Mateo, age 24, eligible at SS
2019 Stats: Did Not Play in the Majors
This is the guy I'm hoping gets the 2B job and runs with it. Mateo profiles as someone who could push 25 steals, which given the state of speed in the game is obviously pretty exciting.

Last year he hit 19 HR in triple-A, which dwarfed anything he'd done to that point in the minors as far as his power was concerned. If he gets the job, buy him for speed and anything else is just a bonus.

**Outfielders**:
Ramón Laureano, age 25, eligible at OF
2019 Stats: 481 PA, 24 HR, 79 Runs, 67 RBI, 13 SB, .288/.340/.521
There are those who dream of a 30/30 season from Laureano for the 2020 season. That is definitely within the range of outcomes, however, he could just as easily struggle at the plate and be frustrated. Laureano's 25.6% strikeout rate, .342 BABIP, and 5.6% walk rate all point to a guy who could have some peaks and valleys. He's a good play for roto, but could be frustrating in head to head leagues.

Mark Canha, age 31, eligible at OF
2019 Stats: 497 PA, 26 HR, 80 Runs, 58 RBI, 3 SB, .273/.396/.517
For those of you in OBP leagues, take note of Mark Canha and his 13.5% walk rate. Even if his AVG dips to around the .260 range, his on base skills and power stroke will make him an undervalued gem and a great draft day bargain.

Stephen Piscotty, age 29, eligible at OF
2019 Stats: 393 PA, 13 HR, 46 Runs, 44 RBI, 2 SB, .249/.309/.412
Stephen Piscotty had some serious problems with right handed pitching last year batting just .214 against them. This is not in line with his previous seasons, so there is hope he could turn things around. Oakland has depth on their roster though, so a platoon could be coming if Piscotty struggles again this year.

Robbie Grossman, age 30, eligible at OF
2019 Stats: 482 PA, 6 HR, 57 Runs, 38 RBI, 9 SB, .240/.334/.348
Outside of the handful of stolen bases Grossman provides, there is not much else to get excited about. He looks like a 4th OF more than anything else and would need an injury to see full time at bats.

Chad Pinder, age 27, eligible at 2B/OF
2019 Stats: 370 PA, 13 HR, 45 Runs, 47 RBI, 0 SB, .240/.290/.416
Pinder's underlying power metrics from 2018 hinted at the potential for something greater, but he just couldn't seem to level up last year. Because of his defensive versatility, he is likely just a utility player unless his bat breaks out in a big way.

**Starters:**
Mike Fiers, age 34, RHP
2019 Stats: 184.2 IP, 126 K, 15 W, 3.90 ERA, 1.19 WHIP
Here lies the picture of a rotation inning eater. While this role is an important one for a major league club, it holds little value in the fantasy game. A 4.97 FIP indicates an even bleaker picture than you might think. Outside of getting you some cheap wins, it's hard to recommend Mike Fiers.

Sean Manaea, age 28, LHP
2019 Stats: 29.2 IP, 30 K, 4 W, 1.21 ERA, 0.78 WHIP

Manaea came back from the 2018 off-season shoulder surgery to pitch a handful of games in September and he looked great. Given health, he has all the makings of a solid SP3 with the potential to flash SP2 upside. The question will be how many innings will the A's let him throw? He tossed only 66 innings last year between his rehab stints in the minors and the majors, so it's likely he will have a cap this year.

Frankie Montas, age 27, RHP
2019 Stats: 96 IP, 103 K, 9 W, 2.63 ERA, 1.11 WHIP
Montas looked to be a league winner last year… that is until he was handed an 80-game PED suspension. The growth he displayed seemed to be more skill related than anything. He threw a more effective slider that was harder for batters to get good contact on and also induced more strikeouts. Believe in the skills here, they look legit.

Jesus Luzardo, age 22, LHP
2019 Stats: 12 IP, 16 K, 1.50 ERA, 0.67 WHIP
The long awaited arrival of Jesus Luzardo is finally here. The helium on him this year will probably come once spring training arrives and more people see him healthy and striking fools out. In keeper or dynasty, this is your last chance to get him without going crazy. While his innings will be capped this year, he should show why there is so much hype around his arrival.

Chris Bassitt, age 31, RHP
2019 Stats: 144 IP, 141 K, 10 W, 3.81 ERA, 1.19 WHIP
As a late game bench pitcher, you could do worse than Chris Bassitt. His jump in strikeouts last year aren't supported by a particularly high swinging strike rate. So, he might be more of a 7 K/9 guy than a strikeout an inning type.


**Relievers:**
Liam Hendriks, age 31, RHP
2019 Stats: 85 IP, 124 K, 25 SV, 1.80 ERA, 0.96 WHIP
The implosion of Blake Treinen led to the unforeseen rise of Liam Hendricks to lights out closer. The question is, will he pull a Treinen and disappoint this year as well? His BB/9 is a little higher than you might like at 2.22, but his 13.13 K/9 aided by a 17.7% swinging strike rate are incredible. Hendricks has a real shot at 35 saves.

Yusmeiro Petit, age 35, RHP
2019 Stats: 83 IP, 71 K, 2.71 ERA, 0.81 WHIP
You won't get big strikeout numbers from Petit, but he is a more stable reliever than he gets credit for and is a good source of Holds. He would be unlikely to take the closer job should Hendricks falter.

Joakim Soria, age 35, RHP
2019 Stats: 69 IP, 79 K, 4.30 ERA, 1.03 WHIP
Soria is the likeliest candidate to get the occasional save on a rest day for Hendircks or should he get injured. He just isn't the dominant reliever he once was though. He strikes guys out well enough, but his ground ball rate has dropped from 54.8% in 2017 to 37.7% last year. That's a dangerous game to play and makes your margin for error that much smaller in those late inning spots.

Jake Diekman, age 33, LHP
2019 Stats: 62 IP, 84 K, 4.65 ERA, 1.42 WHIP
Well, the strikeout numbers look good… but oh my… you just can't walk guys at a 5.66 BB/9 clip and expect good things to happen. No value here.

Lou Trivino, age 28, RHP
2019 Stats: 60 IP, 57 K, 5.25 ERA, 1.53 WHIP
The thought heading into last year was that if Blake Treinen faltered, Trivino would easily slide into the closer role. Things didn't quite play out that way. Somewhere along the line, his control took a hit and it shows. He's worth keeping an eye on because of the potential, but monitor that WHIP.

J.B. Wendelken, age 27, RHP
2019 Stats: 32.2 IP, 34 K, 3.58 ERA, 0.92 WHIP
Wendelken has all the makings of your standard middle reliever. He doesn't do any one thing so well that his role would be elevated, but he also isn't going to hurt the team either.

T.J. McFarland, age 30, LHP
2019 Stats: 56 IP, 35 K, 4.82 ERA, 1.63 WHIP
I wonder if when McFarland comes into a game in Oakland there is a collective groan. It's the kind of moment where you see his name on the scoreboard and just think to yourself, "Well, they know the game is out of hand and just want to burn through some innings."

Daniel Mengden, age 27, RHP
2019 Stats: 59.2 IP, 42 K, 4.83 ERA, 1.44 WHIP
Mengden tried to stick in the rotation a year ago but he just doesn't have the stuff to hang around a couple of times through the order. A fastball that peaks at 92 mph mixed with a penchant for giving up fly balls doesn't help much either.

By Matt Thompson

### 1. Jesus Luzardo- LHP

The young, advanced lefty made his big league debut in 2019 by making six appearances totaling 12 innings out of the bullpen. He sits in the mid-90s out of the rotation but was sitting 98-99 with no extra effort in short stints for the A's. Luzardo throws three pitches, all of them plus, and he commands them extremely well. The only thing holding him back is his extensive injury history. Originally drafted by the Nationals, Luzardo had Tommy John right after the draft and has never hit the 110 inning mark for a season. Luzardo should start 2020 in the A's rotation, and will likely be their best starter until he's shut down at about 150 innings. **ETA: Arrived.**

### 2. A.J. Puk- LHP

It was a crazy 2019 season for Puk, and after missing the 2018 season due to Tommy John he returned to the mound in June and was pitching in Oakland in August. Like Luzardo, the lefty was limited to the bullpen after getting the call, but it has been recently announced that he will go to camp as a starter to enter 2020. Puk has to be one of the toughest at bats possible, with his tall frame and delivery, it has to look like he's right on top of you with his near 100 MPH heater. His slider is a plus-plus weapon and he also throws a changeup and a slow curveball. The stuff is more explosive than Luzardo but the command makes him much more volatile. Oakland is going to have to get creative to manage the innings of these two phenoms. **ETA: Arrived.**

### 3. Sean Murphy- C

Yet another one of the top fantasy prospects that already made his big league debut. Murphy is a defense first backstop, but he can also hit. He has a simple contact-oriented swing, which mostly produces gap power, and that can turn into homers when he learns how to lift the ball more. Murphy will likely split time with Austin Allen a little more than we love for fantasy, but his high OBP, and developing power give him top 6-8 catcher upside. Perfect target in two catcher formats. I'm slightly gun shy on rookie catchers after what Danny Jansen did to me last year, but in OBP leagues these two should be valued similarly. **ETA: Arrived.**

### 4. Jorge Mateo- SS/2B

Mateo has 80-grade speed. Game changing Billy Hamilton type speed. He's a better hitter than Billy Hamilton ever was, and has the same ability to drastically alter the game. It's a low offensive bar, but Mateo could be an absolute game changer in fantasy. He's a much better fantasy player than real life though. His offensive game is aggressive, and one full of contact issues. He grew into some power in 2019, but some of that comes from the environment in Vegas as well. I've had this take for a while and I'm sticking to it. Mateo absolutely can be a version of Trea Turner for fantasy. Likely outcome? Hell no. But it's there. He's out of options and weill have to be on the big league roster all season. **ETA: 2020.**

### 5. Robert Puason- SS

Puason signed for $5.1 million out of the Dominican Republic, and if it wasn't for Jasson Dominguez, would be getting most of the attention in the J2 ranks. Lean, athletic, and projectable there is plenty of room for him to add strength. The swing is long, and there are some pitch recognition issues here, but the switch-hitter is a future 20/20 type player. If the name sounds familiar this is the international kid the Braves got wrapped up with and caused the loss of their prospects and their GM getting banned. Puason is a potentially special talent. He's got a plus speed and good defensive skills at the six. **ETA: 2024.**

## 6. Daulton Jefferies- RHP
Jefferies missed two full seasons with Tommy John surgery in 2017, so he was invisible on prospect lists entering 2019. His 2019 was magnificent though, as he posted a 93:9 strikeout to walk ratio in 79 innings split between High-A and Double-A. He was limited to mostly three inning appearances, but it's encouraging to see him doing well. The fastball came in around 92-94 and he has plus command on the pitch. He has a plus changeup, and a cutter that's shown progress. He also throws an average breaking ball. Jefferies should return to Double-A next year, you want to keep him out of Vegas, and could make his debut if a window occurs within his likely 120-130 innings limit. **ETA: 2020.**

## 7. James Kaprielian- RHP
The righty was hitting 96 with the fastball while sitting around 94, and this is encouraging news. He missed the better part of the last three seasons with elbow and shoulder injuries, but the upside is still here. He has a curveball, changeup and a slider, with his slider potentially being a plus pitch. He's still likely going to be subject to innings limits next year, but Kaprielian is very much an impact arm, might be more of a multi-inning relief role initially, but his long term role is still a starter in my opinion. **ETA: 2020.**

## 8. Logan Davidson- SS
The switch-hitting shortstop has above average raw power from both sides of the plate, and an average hit tool from both sides. His bat speed is plus and he controls the strike zone very well, but no offensive tool pops here. He's shown some struggles against breaking balls and that could cap his averages around .260, but there's strong OBP skills with enough power and speed. Davidson is good enough defensively to stick at short, but the presence of elite defenders elsewhere makes it more likely he plays second for Oakland. **ETA: 2022.**

## 9. Austin Beck- OF
Beck just flat out hasn't performed like a top ten overall pick, and the plus raw power and speed have been absent from his stat lines thus far. An unstable hit tool has dulled the profile, but he still shows bright enough flashes to stay on this list. His bat speed is elite, and will keep getting him opportunities, as will his plus defensive skills and arm in center. He's one of the best athletes in the minor leagues, he just hasn't been able to show it in games. His batting practice sessions are must see, but as we get to Double-A we need to see in-game production offensively. **ETA: 2022.**

## 10. Lazaro Armenteros- OF
Lazarito is one of the most physically gifted prospects in the minors, and is absolutely chiseled. He's a plus runner with plus raw power and hit 17 homers while stealing 22 bases. Unfortunately he did this while only making contact at a 51% clip. He has posted double digit walk rates, but he's so pull happy that the batting average floor is dangerously low. Armenteros is definitely a fine speculation play, but don't count on anything. High risk, high reward. **ETA: 2022.**

**Next Five:**

Sheldon Neuse- 2B/3B
Greg Deichmann- OF
Nick Allen- SS
Brayan Buelvas- OF
Austin Allen- C

**Top Five in FYPDs:**
Robert Puason- SS
Logan Davidson- SS
Marcus Smith- OF
Tyler Baum- RHP
Jalen Greer- SS

## Seattle Mariners Team Preview
By Tim Lambert

**Projected Lineup:**
1 – J.P. Crawford, SS
2 – Mitch Haniger, RF
3 – Kyle Seager, 3B
4 – Tom Murphy, C
5 – Daniel Vogelbach, DH
6 – Kyle Lewis, LF
7 – Mallex Smith, CF
8 – Evan White, 1B
9 – Dee Gordon, 2B

**Projected Bench:**
Austin Nola, UT
Shed Long Jr., INF/OF
Tim Lopes, INF/ OF
Braden Bishop, OF

**Projected Rotation:**
Marco Gonzales, LHP
Yusei Kikuchi, LHP
Justus Sheffield, LHP
Kendall Graveman, RHP
Justin Dunn, RHP

**Projected Bullpen:**
Matt McGill, RHP
Sam Tuivailala, RHP
Erik Swanson, RHP
Brandon, Brennan, RHP
Dan Altavilla, RHP
Taylor Guilbeau, LHP
Carl Edwards Jr., RHP
Yohan Ramirez, RHP

**Catchers:**
Tom Murphy, age 28, C
2019 stats: 281 PA, 18 HR, 32 Runs, 40 RBI, 2 SB, .273/.324/.535
The trade of Omar Narvaez to the Brewers made Tom Murphy the full-time catcher in Seattle. A better hitter against lefties, Murphy saw a fair amount of righties as well last season and finished with a .273/.324/.535 line and 18 HR and 40 RBI in just 281PAs. According to statcast, he is an above-average framer and by all accounts, the pitching staff loves throwing to him. He should be a great fit as the catcher to mentor all the young pitchers the Mariners are trying to develop. In terms of fantasy upside, however, I'm less optimistic about his fit on my team. There are plenty of red flags in Murphy's profile. He had a high (31%) K rate and a low (6.8%) walk rate.

He hits a lot of fly balls but has also sustained a high BABIP as a major-leaguer. Statcast doesn't have his exit velo numbers, but they do track him having a decent 10.9% barrel percentage. With an xBA of .217, I wouldn't hold out hope for a repeat of 2019 but we know for sure he is getting the playing time so you could do a lot worse than Murphy as a late-rounder in a deep league.


**Infielders:**

Evan White, age 24, 1B
Played in Minor Leagues in 2019
The big news about Evan White this offseason was the major league contract he signed without having ever had a plate appearance in the major leagues and only playing 18 games at the AAA level (in 2018). Regardless of your stance on the contract, it is obvious that the team believes in him and, unless he forgets how to play baseball during spring training, he will be the opening day first baseman. He's got 20+ home run power and his glove should keep him safe at the position(he has gold glove potential), but as a rookie hitting in the bottom of the lineup of a bad team, he should probably stay on your waiver wire to start the season. Keep him on your watchlist. You never know how long it will take for pitchers to figure him out and he could start off hot.

Dan Vogelbach, age 27, eligible at 1B
2019 stats: 558 PA, 23 HR, 73 Runs, 76 RBI, 0 SB, .208/.341/.439
The one they call Vogey started out 2019 very strong with 8 home runs and a .310 average in March and April. He continued his power surge throughout the season finishing with 30 bombs and was able to sustain a high 16.5% walk rate leading to a solid .341 OBP. However, his K% of 26.7% and .208 average could definitely use some work and have led some to speculate on his playing time for the upcoming season. His xstats aren't amazing and he doesn't do anything particularly well besides draw walks and smash homers. There's no reason his job is safe heading into 2020.

Austin Nola, age 30, eligible at 1B
2019 stats: 267 PA, 10 HR, 37 Runs, 31 RBI, 1 SB, .269/.342/.454
Nola is the Isah Kinear-Falefa of 2020 except his name is 20-times less cool and he might actually stick on the roster for the full season. His positional eligibility will be his greatest asset as he doesn't have a particular hitting category where he excels, but don't be surprised if you are contemplating him as a streaming option at some point during the season.

Dee Gordon, age 32, eligible at 2B
2019 stats: 421 PA, 3 HR, 36 Runs, 34 RBI, 22 SB, .275/.304/.359
Here are some alarming numbers for you:

| Year | 2016 | 2017 | 2018 | 2019 |
|---|---|---|---|---|
| Sprint Speed | 98th Percentile | 97th Percentile | 91st Percentile | 84th Percentile |
| Stolen Bases | 30 | 60 | 30 | 22 |
| Games | 79 | 158 | 141 | 117 |

Dee Gordon is getting slower, stealing fewer bases, playing in fewer games, and he sure ain't gettin' any younger.  He's also not a very good hitter and doesn't seem to be making any strides in that department in his advanced age, either.  And with the young position players coming up on this roster his playing time is hardly safe.  If you've gotten yourself in a pickle while drafting and need steals late, Gordon is a good hail mary, but don't be surprised if he goes the way of Billy Hamilton before the season is over.

Shed Long, age 24, eligible at 2B
2019 stats: 168 PA, 5 HR, 21 Runs, 15 RBI, 3 SB, .263/.333/.454
Long will be battling Dee Gordon for playing time at second base, but will also see time in the outfield as he spent 123 innings there in 2019.  He handled his time in the majors pretty well posting a .263/.333/.454 and a 111 wRC+ in 168 plate appearances. He is another young player who isn't incredibly exciting but who's plate skills could make him a contributor to your lineup if the playing time shakes out.

J.P. Crawford, age 25, eligible at SS
2019 stats: 396 PA, 7 HR, 43 Runs, 46 RBI, 5 SB, .226/.313/.371
First and foremost, Crawford is a great defender.  Similar to the situation with Evan White, his defense will keep him in the lineup.  His bat, however, is a different story.  Though he has above average plate discipline, he has little to no power and can't hit lefties.  On top of that, in his three seasons in the major leagues, he can't seem to stay healthy having never played more than the 93 games he played in 2019.  He needs to develop more power to become fantasy relevant and even then, with the injury history, he would be a risky player to roster.

Kyle Seager, 32, eligible at 3B
2019 stats: 443 PA, 23 HR, 55 Runs, 63 RBI, 2 SB, .239/.321/.468
Is this for real?  Is good Kyle Seager back after being utterly worthless in 2018?  I don't see why not. I don't think we will get the 2016 version of Seager that saw him go .278/.359/.499 with 89 runs and 99 RBI again.  That's what I think we will look back on as his career year and it was with the help of a .295 BABIP.  What's more believable is something similar to his numbers from last season.  The x-stats point to a .260-ish batting average (close to his career average) and slugging percentages that aren't too far off either.  His launch angle and exit velocity in 2019 were all close to where they've been over the course of his career.  Really, the only thing that you can point to about his down season in 2018 is that he wasn't barreling the ball - in 2017 he was barreling 8.6% of batted balls, which went down to 5.6% in 2018, then back up to 8.4% in 2019.  He's a great corner infield option late in the draft as his playing time will be unopposed.  There's a chance he gets traded to a contender wherein his counting stat outlook won't be so depressing.

Patrick Wisdom 29 INF
2019 stats: 28 PA, 0 HR, 1 Run, 1 RBI, 0 SB, .154/.185/.192
A DFA cast-off from the Texas Rangers, Wisdom is essentially Evan White insurance. He has some pop in his bat as seen in his most recent season at AAA where he hit 31 homers in only 453 plate appearances.  Unfortunately, that came with a 27% strikeout rate and a 97 wRC+ in a league playing with the juiced ball. Overall, his numbers in the majors haven't been great

(.224/.306/.408 in 86 PAs) but if Evan White struggles out of the gate *and* Kyle Seager gets traded, you can expect to see career-highs across the board for the 29-year-old Wisdom.

## Outfielders:

Mitch Haniger, age 29, eligible at OF
2019 stats: 283 PA, 15 HR, 46 Runs, 32 RBI, 4 SB, .220/.314/.463
The storyline surrounding Mitch Hanigar will be one of the most interesting for the Mariners this season. According to Mariners beat reporter Corey Brock, GM Jerry DiPoto values what Hanigar brings to the team and doesn't want to trade him. On the other hand, if the team is in a full rebuild and Hanigar is one of their most valuable assets (he is) wouldn't you want to trade him while he can still bring back some serious value? If he gets off to a hot start and some team comes knocking with top prospects, don't be surprised if DiPoto pulls the trigger, but for now Mitch is a Mariner.

Anywho! So what will that look like? Well, things got off to a bit of a rocky start for Hanigar in 2019 and it seems to be launch angle-related. An increase in his LA from 12.7 in 2018 to 18.7 helped facilitate an expected batting average of .225 and an actual batting average of .220. It also helped him hit 15 bombs in 63 games which put him on pace for 39 homers. But then he fouled a ball off of his balls and ruptured a testicle, putting him out for the rest of the season. Would he have made the correction and leveled out his swing, or was he just selling out for power to see how many dingers he could hit? I can't imagine DiPoto wants Hanigar on the team to teach the young kids to just go out there and hack so I'm thinking we will get something closer to the 2018 version (.285/.366/.493) than last year's masher. The idea that he will be traded seems unlikely at this point, but with Trader Jerry manning the helm, nobody is safe.

Mallex Smith, age 27, eligible at OF
2019 stats: 566 PA, 6 HR, 70 Runs, 37 RBI, 46 SB, .227/.300/.335
After a fantastic season for the Rays in 2018, Smith was unable to build on his skills in 2019 and was sent down to AAA to work on his swing early in the season. When he came back he was lifting the ball more and hitting the ball harder which worked at first but then that stopped and in the second half he was terrible again. He finished the year with a .227/.300/.335 line, a measly 6 HRs, but still managed to lead the majors with 46 SBs - and therein lies the value. He is going to steal bases. How many is up for debate, unfortunately. When he played for the Rays, his approach was as an aggressive slap hitter and it worked very well. If he can get back to that style, there's no reason he couldn't raise his OBP by 30 points or more and return to pre-2019 batting numbers. If he continues to lift the ball and make easy outs, he could continue to lose playing time and eventually be relegated to 5th outfielder, pinch-runner status.

Kyle Lewis, age 24, eligible at OF
2019 stats: 75 PA, 3 HR, 10 Runs, 13 RBI, 0 SB, .268/.293/.592
Hey look, another 24-year old somewhat underwhelming position player! Unlike some of the other young guys on this team, Lewis has already played in some major league games and already done something interesting - hit homers. In 18 September games, he hit 6 home runs putting him on pace for 54 over a full season. Will that happen? Definitely not, but fangraphs prospect report gives him a 60/65 Raw Power score so the mash potential is there. Also in those 18 games - a nearly 40% strikeout rate and a 4% walk rate. Don't get your hopes up too high, but Lewis is another guy that should at least be added to your watch list at the end of your draft.

Tim Lopes 26 OF, Braden Bishop 26 OF, Jake Fraley 25 OF - It looks like these guys are going to be competing for the 5th outfielder's spot. All of them have minor league options so the ones that don't make it will be sent down but likely called back up at some point. Will any of them be any good? Anything is possible!

**Starting Pitchers:**

Marco Gonzales, age 28
2019 stats: 203 IP, 147 K, 16 Wins, 3.99 ERA, 1.31 WHIP
In a perfect scenario, Marco Gonzales would slot in as a really good #4 starting pitcher but in 2020 on the Mariners, he's the best they've got. He threw 203 innings with a 3.99 ERA and a high-but-not-terrible 1.31 WHIP. With all those innings, he was able to pile up 16 wins so as long as he stays healthy, you can expect Scott Servais to give him the same amount of leash this season.

Yusei Kikuchi, age 29
2019 stats: 161.2 IP, 116 K, 6 Wins, 5.46 ERA, 1.52 WHIP
Kikuchi's first season in the United States wasn't quite what you would call a "disaster", but it was close. A 6-11 record with 5.46 ERA and 1.52 WHIP over 161.2 innings was probably not what the Mariners or Kikuchi were hoping for when he came over from Japan. There is a lot to be said for having gained one year of experience in a different league, not to mention an entirely different country. It's also worth mentioning that his dad died right as the season was getting started and I'm sure that had an effect on him. The main point here is, he needs to improve (by a lot) to be someone you consider outside of the very deepest of leagues.

Justus Sheffield, age 24
2019 stats: 36 IP, 37 K, 0 Wins, 5.45 ERA, 1.72 WHIP
When Jerry DiPoto traded James Paxton to the Yankees last offseason it was for two guys and Justus Sheffield. Well, now we get to see why he wanted him. Sheffield is projected to begin the season in the starting rotation and show the people in Seattle why they said goodbye to "Big Maple". In his 36 big-league innings in 2019, Sheffield was not great sporting a mid-5's ERA and a WHIP of 1.71. It wasn't all bad, however, as he showed a 12.9% swinging strike percentage as well as a 52% groundball rate. If he can limit the walks and homers (something he has had problems with in the past) he could become a very effective pitcher. If not, well at least it won't matter too much this season.

Justin Dunn, age 24
2019 stats: 6.2 IP, 5 K, 0 Wins, 2.70 ERA, 1.65 WHIP
Another DiPoto acquisition from the 2019 off-season, Dunn came over from the Mets in the Robinson Cano/Edwin Diaz deal. Pitching a full season for the Arkansas Travelers, his numbers were solid overall: 9-5, 3.50 ERA, 1.19 WHIP, and 158 K's in 131 IP. When he received the call-up to pitch in September, he promptly walked 5 batters and allowed 2 runs in his ⅔ inning debut. After that, though, he was rock solid striking out 5, walking 4 (3 in his second game), and only allowing two more hits in his final 6IP. He was able to generate a decent 17% swinging-strike rate and a high 57% groundball rate on his slider while his fastball velocity grades out to about average. Based on everything we know about the Seattle rotation, I am very confident in saying he is the one with the highest upside coming into 2020.

Kendall Graveman, age 28

Did not pitch in 2019

Coming off of Tommy John surgery in 2018, Graveman threw a whopping six innings for the Cubs minor league affiliates last season. Prior to that injury, the righty had hardly been the picture of health with his career-high innings pitched being 186 back in 2016. However, in his 466 career Major League innings, he's been a solidly mediocre pitcher with a 1.38 WHIP and a 4.38 ERA. The M's need him to eat innings and not be terrible so as long as he can do one of those things he'll stay up with the big club, but with a minor-league option, he could be riding the bus to Tacoma if he struggles.

**Relief Pitchers:**

Matt Magill, age 30

2019 stats: 22.1 IP, 28 K, 3 Wins, 5 Saves, 3.63 ERA, 1.40 WHIP

Magill is the closer heading into 2020. That's right, I said it: Matt Magill. He was picked up from the Twins in a cash deal and yadda yadda yadda now he's the closer. Who is he? A hard-throwing righty with a solid 28% strikeout rate. But consider this: according to statcast his exit velocities have been some of the highest in the league the last two years, as have his hard-hit percentages. His numbers for Seattle weren't terrible last season and he was able to scratch out 5 saves but how many save opportunities he gets in 2020 and how long he has the job (or if he has it coming out of Spring Training) make him untenable as an asset.

Eric Swanson, age 26

2019 stats: 24.2 IP, 27 K, 0 Wins, 2 Saves, 3.28 ERA, 1.17 WHIP

Swanson got some save opportunities at the end of last season and made the most of it. While the overall numbers don't look great, he could figure in for some saves especially if Magill struggles.

Austin Adams, age 29

2019 stats: 32 IP, 53 K, 2 Wins, 0 Saves, 3.94 ERA, 1.13 WHIP

Unlikely to begin the season on the active roster due to ACL surgery in September.

Carl Edwards Jr., age 28

2019 stats: 17 IP, 19 K, 1 Win, 0 Saves, 8.47 ERA, 1.47 WHIP

Edwards Jr. pitched 17 innings last season and they were not good so he'll be looking for a reset to his pre-2019 self in Seattle. Just the season before his numbers were not bad (52IP, 1.31 WHIP, 2.60 ERA, 3.85 SIERA) but the Cubs cut bait with him anyway, trading him to the Padres at the deadline for Brad Wieck. Walks have been a problem for Edwards Jr. over the last few seasons so if he can cut those down or at least limit big hits around the walks (like he was able to do in 2017) and mitigate the damage, he can be a key piece in the Mariners 'pen and could earn himself a ticket to a contender at the 2020 trade deadline.

Yohan Ramirez, age 24

Pitched in the minor leagues in 2019

The Rule 5 pickup from Houston, Roster Resource has Ramirez starting in the bullpen for the 2020 season. According to Eric Longenhagen at Fangraphs, "His stuff really started to pop in 2018, and then last season he was showing bat-missing, multi-inning stuff — 92-97, up to 99, two plus breaking balls." Sounds good to me! Similar to Carl Edwards Jr., he's got a bit of a BB's problem, but that doesn't seem to scare off this front office.

Nestor Cortez, age 25

2019 stats: 66.2 IP, 69 K, 5 Wins, 0 Saves, 5.67 ERA, 1.55 WHIP

Acquired from the Yankees for international bonus pool money, Nestor Cortez will provide the M's with another lefty option out of the 'pen. Will anyone be pleased with the results? I'm suggesting a "wait and see" approach here as Cortez' numbers in the bigs have not been great (where have I heard that before?). Last season he threw 66.2 innings for the Yanks with a 1.55 WHIP and 5.67 ERA. His SIERA of 4.41 indicates his skills might be better than the numbers show and, like a lot of pitchers in 2019, he was punished by the long ball allowing 16. That number would tie him with Wade LeBlanc for second-most among Mariners "relievers" (LeBlanc was a starter/reliever/follower in 2019) in 20-fewer innings, so I could see his total coming down even if the ball stays the same.

# Seattle Mariners Prospects
## By Matt Thompson

### 1. Jarred Kelenic- OF
Kelenic has been better than advertised since being drafted by the Mets in the first round in 2018. He's bulked up and adjusted his hands in his swing and has taken off. He zoomed through three levels in 2019, starting in the South Atlantic League and ending up in Double-A Arkansas. He even went to the AFL but was removed due to a minor injury. It's a plus hit tool with above-average speed and power tools, but his hit tool is more advanced right now. He's a potential .300 hitter with 30 homer potential that can swipe 20 bags, with strong OBPs. He's a top ten prospect for me. He could see big league time in 2020. **ETA: 2020.**

### 2. Julio Rodriguez- OF
The 19 year-old phenom has all the ingredients to become a future superstar. He saw time at two different levels of A-ball before he ended his season as the league's youngest player in the AFL. Rodriguez has a thick lower half, and will move to right field due to his strong arm. A pair or 70-grade offensive tools in his hit and power give him .315, 30-35 homer upside, but I have him behind Kelenic because of the lack of stolen bases. He could see the big leagues in 2020, but that would be surprising to me. It probably shouldn't be though considering everything else he's done to this point. **ETA: 2021.**

### 3. Noelvi Marte- SS
I'm excited about Marte. The Mariners are going to push Marte aggressively like they did with Julio Rodriguez. He's got plus power, speed and hit tools, but there's a strong chance he loses that plus speed as he fills out and moves to third base. Marte torched the Dominican Summer League, and should start the season in Low-A. He's got a well built frame, six-foot-one, 180 pounds, and I'm betting on him having a strong 2020. His plate skills aren't as advanced as Rodriguez, but Marte is a true five-category guy right now and will be in the top ten this time next year with a strong 2020. **ETA: 2023.**

### 4. Evan White- 1B
I expect Evan White to be the everyday first baseman this season barring a complete meltdown in spring training. White has advanced plate skills and should be a strong source of on-base ability as well as strong defense and gap to gap power at first base. I don't expect the 25 homer power to show through in games right away, but it will come. He will make up for that by chipping in 10-15 steals at peak. Don't get worried about White's lack of power in Double-A, the ballpark in Arkansas was the worst for right-handed power in all of minor league baseball. The contract extension shows how much the Mariners believe in White. You should too. **ETA: 2020.**

### 5. Logan Gilbert- RHP
Gilbert is a pitching prospect I'm looking to aggressively acquire. Gilbert had one of the best statistical seasons in the minor leagues last year and finished his first professional season with 50 innings in Double-A. He's a tall, lean righty with an athletic delivery with long arm action and great extension. His command makes his stuff play up, but all pitches are average or better. His fastball is a plus pitch, and his curveball has flashed that as well, but lacks consistency. He also throws a slider and a change. Gilbert could reach the big leagues in the second half of 2020 if the Mariners want to push him. **ETA: 2021.**

### 6. George Kirby- RHP

Pitchers that typically are gifted with elite command like Kirby are the guys with below average stuff, and that's not the case for the Elon product. Kirby has a low-90s heater with significant wiggle, with an above average change and slider and an average curveball. After signing Kirby tossed 23 innings without issuing a walk. The Mariners hired his pitching coach from Elon to oversee the organization's arms, which is a strong development for Kirby. He's got the frame to add some muscle and velo, and could move quickly. **ETA: 2021.**

### 7. Jake Fraley- OF

The oft-injured Fraley finally eclipsed the 100 game mark last season, but still had his season end prematurely due to a thumb injury. He should be healthy and ready to go this spring, and Fraley is in the mix for a starting outfield job. When he's been healthy he's produced. He gets on-base at an above-average clip, and has 20/20 upside despite the strikeouts that are baked in the profile. The production is real, the tools match. Fraley has plus speed and above-average power, will be an even better real-life player than a fantasy one due to how well he runs the bases and plays defense. Here's hoping Fraley gets an extended look this season. **ETA: Arrived.**

### 8. Kyle Lewis- OF

Injuries suck. I look at Lewis and always wonder what we could've missed out on. The knee injury and everything he dealt with after that have robbed us of some of his explosiveness and game changing speed. It's a high risk profile though. He hits the ball extremely hard, and has elite bat speed. There isn't a park anywhere Lewis can't hit the ball out of. His double digit walk rates he posted in the minors didn't follow him to the bigs, and his 4% walk rate in his brief sample is worrisome. His 38% K rate is terrifying though, and that's a number that can cut the double-plus raw power down at the knees. **ETA: Arrived.**

### 9. Justus Sheffield- LHP

I've never been a Justus Sheffield guy, and the rest of the industry has caught up now, and his stock may be low enough that I'm buying back in. Sheffield has a shallow three pitch arsenal with his fastball, slider and change. His overall command is below average, but his fastball has late movement that makes it difficult to square up. His slider is a plus pitch, but if he can't locate the fastball hitters can just spit on it. With some of the younger arms I listed above quickly approaching the bigs, I'd like the Mariners to put Sheffield in the closer role. He should grab a rotation spot out of spring. **ETA: Arrived.**

### 10. Justin Dunn- RHP

The former collegiate reliever while at Boston College now finds himself trying to lock down a big league rotation spot. It's an athletic delivery, with a little bit of across-body to it. His fastball is above-average and his slider is plus. His changeup lags behind the other two pitches. The difference between him and Sheffield? I think Dunn's command lapse in the majors is only a temporary thing. I think he's a long term number four starter in the bigs. He should grab a rotation spot out of spring training. **ETA: Arrived.**

### Next Five:
Cal Raleigh- C
Brandon Williamson- LHP
Isaiah Campbell- RHP

Juan Then- RHP
Sam Carlson- RHP

**Top Five in FYPDs:**
George Kirby- RHP
Brandon Williamson- LHP
Isaiah Campbell- RHP
George Feliz- OF
Austin Shenton- 3B

**Texas Rangers Team Preview**
By Corey Steiner

**Projected Order:**
1- Shin-Soo Choo
2- Elvis Andrus
3- Joey Gallo
4- Danny Santana
5- Willie Calhoun
6- Nick Solak
7- Rougned Odor
8- Jose Trevino
9- Ronald Guzman

**Projected Bench:**
Jeff Mathis, C
Isaiah Kiner-Falefa, C/3B
Adolis Garcia, OF
Scott Heineman, OF

**Projected Rotation:**
Corey Kluber, RHP
Mike Minor, LHP
Lance Lynn, RHP
Kyle Gibson, RHP
Jordan Lyles, RHP

**Bullpen:**
Jose Leclerc, RHP
Rafael Montero, RHP
Jesse Chavez, RHP
Brett Martin, LHP
Nick Goody, RHP
Joely Rodriguez, LHP
Edinson Volquez, RHP
Yohander Mendez, LHP
Joe Palumbo, LHP
Brock Burke, LHP
Jonathan Hernandez, RHP

**Catchers:**
Jose Trevino, age 27, eligible at C
2019 Stats: 126 PA, 2 HR, 18 Runs, 13 RBI, 0 SB, .258/.272/.383

Trevino's short run in the majors last season isn't necessarily indicative of his abilities. However, he hasn't shown enough power in his minor league career to warrant drafting in two-catcher 15-team leagues. His ability to make contact suggests that he could be worth watching on the waiver wire in the early weeks of 2020 in deeper formats.

Jeff Mathis, age 37, eligible at C
2019 Stats: 244 PA, 2 HR, 17 Runs, 12 RBI, 1 SB, .158/.209/.224
Mathis doesn't need to be rostered in any fantasy leagues heading into 2020 as there is little evidence to suggest that we will see a late-career renaissance.

Isiah Kiner-Falefa, age 25, eligible at C, 3B
2019 Stats: 250 PA, 1 HR, 23 Runs, 21 RBI, 3 SB, .238/.299/.322
After a disappointing 2019 season and entering into a three-way timeshare, Kiner-Falefa doesn't need to be drafted outside of very deep leagues (e.g. 20 teams, 2 catchers). His ability to steal 5-10 bases given enough playing time makes him somewhat unique at the catcher position. Keep an eye on the Rangers' catching situation early as he may be worth adding if he heats up in the early weeks.


**Infielders**:
Elvis Andrus, age 31, eligible at SS
2019 Stats: 648 PA, 12 HR, 81 Runs, 72 RBI, 31 SB, .275/.313/.393
Andrus turned in a surprisingly strong 2019 campaign after underperforming due to injury in the previous season. With stolen bases at a premium in this year's draft, Andrus is one of the few players past pick 100 who can reliably contribute in that category without hurting you anywhere else. A great value play, especially if you choose to target pitching early in your draft.

Danny Santana, age 29, eligible at 1B, OF
2019 Stats: 616 PA, 28 HR, 81 Runs, 81 RBI, 21 SB, .283/.324/.534
Santana is getting drafted early (122 ADP) because of his ability to hit 20 HR and steal 20 bases, even factoring in regression from last year's surprising power production. Still, it should be noted that his low walk rate and high strikeout rate suggest that worse times could be ahead. If he were to lose playing time, this would cut into his SB total. There are more reliable options at this stage in the draft (including his teammate Andrus).

Nick Solak, age 25, eligible at UT
2019 Stats: 135 PA, 5 HR, 19 Runs, 17 RBI, 2 SB, .293/.393/.491
Strong plate discipline, job stability, and the ability to chip in ten stolen bases over the course of a full season make Solak an appealing option with upside at his current ADP (262). While his first appearance in the majors likely included some overperformance in the triple slash line, he is capable of contributing in every category without hurting you anywhere. He should gain eligibility at 3B a few weeks into the season, so don't let his positional-inflexibility prevent you from taking advantage of the value provided by his current price.

Rougned Odor, age 26, eligible at 2B
2019 Stats: 581 PA, 30 HR, 77 Runs, 93 RBI, 11 SB, .205/.283/.439
Odor offers a promising combination of power and speed that could prove valuable if he can put together a decent batting average. Consistently high strikeout rates limit his upside and a poor

SB success rate suggests that this total could come down if the team decides to stop giving him the green light. Still, his rising walk rates over the last few seasons indicates that better plate discipline could be around the corner. If you have constructed a strong BA/OBP base at this point in the draft, he may be worth taking a shot on, but proceed with caution anywhere before pick 250.

Ronald Guzman, age 25, eligible at 1B
2019 Stats: 295 PA, 10 HR, 34 Runs, 36 RBI, 1 SB, .219/.308/.414
Unless you are drafting in a very deep (e.g. AL Only) league, Guzman doesn't need to be on your radar. He can be a serviceable fill-in at CI in case of injury, as he has 20-25 HR upside with competent on-base skills.

**Outfielders**:
Joey Gallo, age 26, eligible at OF
2019 Stats: 297 PA, 22 HR, 54 Runs, 49 RBI, 4 SB, .253/.389/.598
Last year, injury cut short what was looking to be a breakout campaign for Gallo (as much as is possible for someone who had already hit 40 HR twice in his career). Gallo looks primed for another 40 HR campaign and, unlike many power hitters, he can chip in up to 10 SB to go with it. The appeal is obviously much greater in OBP leagues, but if you draft a few high-average players around him, Gallo should return value at his current draft price (76).

Willie Calhoun, age 25, eligible at OF
2019 Stats: 337 PA, 21 HR, 51 Runs, 48 RBI, 0 SB, .269/.323/.524
Calhoun is easily capable of hitting 30 HR in his first full season in the majors and his strong plate discipline (~15% walk rate) indicates that his batting average and runs scored are both likely to remain pluses. The largest questions are his defense and whether he will receive 600 plate appearances given Choo's full-time status at DH. Still, don't be afraid to take him at or even slightly earlier than his current ADP (155) if you decide to wait on drafting power bats.

Shin-Soo Choo, age 37, eligible at OF
2019 Stats: 660 PA, 24 HR, 93 Runs, 61 RBI, 15 SB, .265/.371/.455
Choo has proven to be immensely valuable in the late stages of his career and his hard-hit percentage was 49% in 2019, the highest of his career (per Baseball Savant). There is little to suggest a decline in his profile and he is likely to provide value anywhere after pick 200.

Adolis García, age 27, eligible at OF
2019 Stats: N/A (in minors)
García was acquired from the Cardinals for depth and isn't likely to play enough to provide fantasy value in any format in 2020.

Scott Heineman, age 27, eligible at OF
2019 Stats: 85 PA, 2 HR, 8 Runs, 7 RBI, 1 SB, .213/.306/.373
Barring injury, Heineman won't receive enough playing time to be fantasy relevant. If given the opportunity, he could steal 15 bases over the course of a full season with decent BA, though his power upside is limited.

**Starters**:
Corey Kluber, age 33, RHP

2019 Stats: 35.2 IP, 38 K, 2 W, 5.80 ERA, 1.65 WHIP

Despite a drastically injury-shortened 2019 and declining numbers in three straight seasons, Kluber is getting drafted within the top 100 ADP. His strikeout upside is diminished from his peak years and with Paxton, Berrios, Woodruff, Gray, and Soroka available after him, to name a few, there seems to be little reason to take on this degree of risk at such an important place in the draft.

Mike Minor, age 32, LHP
2019 Stats: 208.1 IP, 200 K, 14 W, 3.59 ERA, 1.24 WHIP

Few could have expected Minor's breakout season at the age of 31. His FIP (4.25) suggests that he was a bit lucky last year. While his strikeout upside is dependent upon the volume of innings he is able to pitch, he is good at limiting baserunners by not issuing many free passes. Home runs, at times, can be an issue. Minor is currently getting drafted at a point where many are targeting relief pitching, which means you may be able to get him later than his ADP (171). It's reasonable to expect regression in both ERA and WHIP, making him a low-upside play, but he also seems to be reliable for 200 solid innings, indicating that he also has a high floor.

Lance Lynn, age 32, RHP
2019 Stats: 208.1 IP, 246 K, 16 W, 3.67 ERA, 1.22 WHIP

Lynn seems to have found a home in Texas, as he struck out more batters in 2019 than at any other point in his major league career. As with Minor, it is fair to expect some regression in the ERA and WHIP categories, however perhaps to a lesser extent. Lynn seems to be a relatively safe option that won't cost too much draft capital; drafting him would pair well with riskier, high-upside plays like Sale and Bauer. Feel comfortable taking him around or even slightly earlier than ADP (133), as he is likely to provide a strong foundation in IP and strikeouts.

Kyle Gibson, age 32, RHP
2019 Stats: 160 IP, 160 K, 13 W, 4.84 ERA, 1.44 WHIP

One problem with rostering Gibson is the erratic nature of his results on a start-to-start basis. While you can probably expect some improvement in ERA, the move to Texas is not likely to help his stats and the WHIP is almost surely going to remain high. I'm looking elsewhere despite his low ADP (363).

Jordan Lyles, age 29, RHP
2019 Stats: 141 IP, 146 K, 12 W, 4.15 ERA, 1.32 WHIP

Lyles showed flashes of brilliance last year, but like Gibson, his results are erratic on a start-to-start basis, making him a frustrating player to roster in fantasy. There are more interesting high-upside players late in the draft.

**Relievers:**

José Leclerc, age 26, RHP
2019 Stats: 68.2 IP, 100 K, 14 SV, 4.33 ERA, 1.33 WHIP

While his rocky 2019 may in part be attributable to bad luck, Leclerc's erratic command – which manifested itself at various points throughout his minor league career – came back to bite him in a significant way. One might argue that this inconsistency is factored into his low price (171

ADP), but with Raisel Iglesias and Hansel Robles available in the same range, it seems like an unnecessary risk to take.

Rafael Montero, age 29, RHP
2019 Stats: 29 IP, 34 K, 0 SV, 2.48 ERA, 0.97 WHIP
Montero is a great gamble to take in the last round of the draft because he demonstrated a new and improved approach in 2019 which is likely to yield strong ratios, even if he does not acquire saves at the beginning of the season. He demonstrates more consistent command than Leclerc and thus seems like a possible candidate to succeed him in the closer role if the opportunity arises.

Jesse Chavez, age 36, RHP
2019 Stats: 78 IP, 72 K, 1 SV, 4.85 ERA, 1.33 WHIP
The veteran doesn't offer enough contribution in terms of ratios or strikeouts to be worth rostering in fantasy leagues.

Brett Martin, age 24, LHP
2019 Stats: 62.1 IP, 62 K, 0 SV, 4.76 ERA, 1.44 WHIP
He may be able to pick up some holds if that is relevant to your league format; however, his ratios likely won't help you enough to warrant rostering him.

Nick Goody, age 28, RHP
2019 Stats: 40.2 IP, 50 K, 0 SV, 3.54 ERA, 1.28 WHIP
Goody's strong 2019 may in part be due to a low BABIP, but if he continues to combine low ratios with a high strikeout rate in the first few weeks of the season, consider adding him to your roster, especially in Holds leagues.

Joely Rodriguez, age 28, LHP
2019 Stats: N/A
After two strong seasons playing for Chunichi in Japan's Nippon League, Rodriguez returns to the MLB in what will likely be a low-leverage role to start the season. Keep an eye on him in April as he may get moved to the later innings if he demonstrates an improved approach.

Edinson Volquez, age 36, RHP
2019 Stats: 16 IP, 10 K, 0 W, 6.75 ERA, 2.00 WHIP
Volquez may be used as a spot starter intermittently throughout the season, in which case he can be used as a streamer, but he should not be drafted in most leagues.

Yohander Mendez, age 25, LHP
2019 Stats: 4.2 IP, 8 K, 1 W, 5.79 ERA, 1.93 WHIP
Mendez is not likely to see high-leverage situations during the 2020 season.

Joe Palumbo, age 25, LHP
2019 Stats: 16.2 IP, 21 K, 0 W, 9.18 ERA, 1.74 WHIP
After receiving Tommy John surgery in 2017, Palumbo returned to the field for his first full season in 2019, performing well in the minor leagues and receiving a brief taste of the majors to end the year. He may not start the year with the major league club, but he is someone to keep

an eye on in spring training, as he has the potential to be a mid-range starter with strikeout upside.

Brock Burke, age 23, LHP
2019 Stats: 26.2 IP, 14 K, 0 W, 7.43 ERA, 1.54 WHIP
In his first full season with the Rangers after being acquired from the Rays, Burke performed well, mostly at the AA level, and briefly played with the major league club at the end of the year. He may be a useful starter in the long term, but he isn't likely to be used in that capacity in 2020.

Jonathan Hernandez, age 23, RHP
2019 Stats: 16.2 IP, 19 K, 2 W, 4.32 ERA, 1.62 WHIP
Hernandez has been working through control issues and, if added to the major league roster, will be used in low-leverage situations as he gets acclimated to the big leagues.

# Texas Rangers Prospects
By Matt Thompson

### 1. Nick Solak- 2B/3B/OF
Solak barely missed graduating from this list, falling just 14 at-bats shy. According to roster resources, Solak is projected to make the big league team but not the starting lineup, and that doesn't make sense to me. Solak doesn't have a true defensive home. If he's not going to play the field everyday he should go to Triple-A to improve defensively. The bat is solidly above average and can help the team win now. It's above-average hit and power tools while walking at a high clip. I have no doubts about Solak's ability to hit, just don't know where he will fit in the lineup. **ETA: Arrived.**

### 2. Josh Jung- 3B
The Rangers stayed local and selected Texas Tech product Josh Jung with the 8th overall pick in the 2019 draft. Jung can hit. The hit tool is above-average and Jung will take what the pitcher gives him. I wish he was more aggressive when he gets his pitch, and would jump on a pitch earlier in the count and use his big powerful frame. His bat-to-ball skills are strong, and he's a plus defender at the hot corner. Jung is one of the safer college bats available. **ETA: 2022.**

### 3. Sherten Apostel- 3B
I'm enamored with Apostel. A guy that constantly hits the ball as hard as he does, while walking at such an elite rate will always be a guy I'm interested in. Big sturdy frame with broad shoulders, Apostel can hit the ball out of any park to all fields. It's a little bit of a three-true-outcomes profile here though, and that 25% strikeout rate is a tad worrisome. Defensively he has a strong arm, but lacks the range and hands to be an asset at third base. His hard hit data and exit velocity numbers are things of beauty though, and I think he hits enough to break into the Rangers lineup. **ETA: 2022.**

### 4. Luisangel Acuña- SS
First things first, yes this is Ronald Acuña's younger brother. The swings look similar mechanically, but their games are very different. Acuna had more walks than strikeouts in his 51 game sample in the DSL, and his game is more based on his advanced feel for the game than loud tools. He also stole 17 bases. He's a prime candidate to develop a power tool to go with his plus hit tool, due to how advanced and selective he is. It will be interesting to see what the Rangers do with Acuña next season. He will make his full season debut, just don't know where yet. **ETA: 2024.**

### 5. Sam Huff- C
Huff finally grew into his 80 game raw power with a breakout 2019 season that resulted in 28 homers. He's a large dude with long levers, and it's not shocking to see that he has strikeout issues. His defense and framing numbers were positive in 2019, and it appears he's made some improvements on that side of the ball. He doesn't move laterally as well as most big league catchers do, and blocking and getting up out of his crouch to make throws are some areas where he can stand to improve a bit. Huff has shown enough that I think he can at least be a part-time catcher in the big leagues, but not the everyday guy. **ETA: 2022.**

### 6. Leody Taveras- OF

Taveras is the best real life prospect in the system, but that doesn't necessarily make him appealing from a fantasy standpoint. He's an elite defender in center, and that's far and away his best tool. He did post the best statistical season of his career in 2019 though, which is a welcome change, but you need to understand that he's consistently been one of the youngest players in every league he's played in. Taveras does have an above-average hit tool, but the lack of power means pitchers will continue to challenge him. His best fantasy asset is the 20+ steals he can get you, and he seems like a perfect bottom of the order bat in the AL. He is likely to start the year in Triple-A as a 21 year-old, and could see the big leagues in the second half as he is the best outfield defender on the 40-man roster. **ETA: 2021.**

## 7. Maximo Acosta- SS
I love Acosta's swing. He's got plus bat speed and hits the ball on the nose frequently. His overall plate approach is mature, and he will take a walk and doesn't try and do too much. He's already grown some since signing, and has added a few inches as well as 10-15 pounds of muscle to his frame. The frame and hometown are the same as Gleyber Torres, and he has some of the same concerns about the frame that came with Torres. He may have to move to second or third, but he should hit enough that it won't matter. **ETA: 2024.**

## 8. Bubba Thompson- OF
Injuries have robbed this premier athlete of the baseball development that he badly needs. Thompson is extremely raw, and the former multi-sport athlete needs to improve the finer things, like his pitch recognition and outfield reads. Thompson is an explosive athlete, and was hitting the ball hard and putting on shows during his BP despite his thin, wiry frame. There's so much power in his wrists and forearms. The swing and miss in his game is a problem, and he just needs more reps to chip away at it. His HRs and SBs can't fully show if he can't make contact and get on base. **ETA: 2022.**

## 9. Joe Palumbo- LHP
The lefties first season back from Tommy John was a success, but he ran into some bumps in the road after his big league debut. He will fill up the strike zone and also miss bats, which is a combination you have to love from a young arm. He gets his plus heater up to the mid-90s and will use the pitch to set up his plus curve and above-average changeup. There's some reliever risk due to how well the fastball and curveball perform in tandem, and also due to his five-foot-ten, 150 pound frame. Palumbo is the next man up in the Rangers rotation, and should start in Triple-A. **ETA: Arrived.**

## 10. Bayron Lora- OF
The top power bat in the 2019 J2 class, the Rangers signed Lora for $3.9 million. He fits the bill. A large human, Lora stands six-foot-five and weighs a muscular 230 pounds despite being only 17. He has some feel for the zone, but will run into some mechanical issues and swing inconsistencies that prevent him from tapping into that enormous raw pop. This is a high risk profile, and bigger guys like this must hit. **ETA: 2025.**

**Next Five:**
Hans Crouse- RHP
Cole Winn- RHP
Heriberto Hernandez- OF
Ricky Vanasco- RHP

Davis Wendzel- 3B

**Top Five in FYPDs:**
Josh Jung- 3B
Maximo Acosta- SS
Bayron Lora- OF
Davis Wendzel- 3B
Ryan Garcia- RHP

# Atlanta Braves Team Preview
By Jim Bay

## Projected Lineup

1- Ronald Acuna Jr. - RF
2- Ozzie Albies - 2B
3- Freddie Freeman - 1B
4- Travis d'Arnaud - C
5- Nick Markakis - LF
6- Dansby Swanson - SS
7- Ender Inciarte - CF
8- Austin Riley - 3B
9- Pitcher

## Projected Bench

Tyler Flowers - C
Johann Camargo - INF/OF
Charlie Culberson - INF/OF
Adam Duvall - OF
Rafael Ortega - OF

## Projected Rotation

Mike Soroka - RHP
Cole Hamels - LHP
Mike Foltynewicz - RHP
Max Fried - LHP
Sean Newcomb - LHP

## Bullpen

Mark Melancon - RHP
Will Smith - LHP
Shane Greene - RHP
Luke Jackson - RHP
Chris Martin - RHP
Darren O'Day - RHP
Grant Dayton - LHP
Jeremy Walker - RHP

## CATCHERS

Travis d'Arnaud, age 31, eligible at C/1B
2019 Stats: (TB,LAD, NYM) 391 PA's, 16 HRs, 52 Runs, 69 RBI, 0 SB, .251/.312/.433

d'Arnaud struggled at the beginning of 2019 before being released by the Mets. He then signed with the Rays and was productive for them for the rest of the season. Signed with the Braves, d'Arnaud will be the primary catcher and should be drafted in the top 15 in fantasy.

Tyler Flowers, age 33, eligible at C
2019 Stats: 310 PAs, 11 HRs, 36 Runs, 34 RBI, 0 SB, .229/.319/.413
Flowers will see enough playing time to warrant consideration in two catcher and deeper leagues.


## INFIELDERS

Ozzie Albies, age 23, eligible at 2B
2019 Stats: 702 PAs, 24 HRs, 102 Runs, 86 RBI, 15 SB, .295/.352/.500
In addition to all the numbers listed here, Albies also led the National League in hits with 189. Also, Albies became the 11th player in history to record at least 40 doubles and 20 home runs in each of his first two seasons. He is a top 3 pick at 2B and in the top 50 overall. A must-have in dynasty and keeper leagues.

Freddy Freeman, age 30, eligible at 1B
2019 Stats: 692 PAs, 38 HRs, 113 Runs, 121 RBI, 6 SB, .295/.389/.549
Fragments in his right elbow dragged down his numbers in the final three weeks of the regular season, which was close to winning him the MVP. Offseason surgery should bring him back healthy and make him one of the top, if not the top fantasy first baseman. Generally considered within the top 15 overall

Dansby Swanson, age 26, eligible at SS
2016 Stats: 545 PAs, 17 HRs, 77 Runs, 65 RBI, 10 SB, .251/.325/.422
At the beginning of 2019, Swanson was hitting the ball hard to all fields. Then he suffered a heel injury in July. Before the injury, he had a hard-hit percentage of 42.6 percent and an opposite-field percentage of 27.1. Those numbers, especially the opposite field percentage dropped after the injury. He has not quite posted numbers as promised, but he could start at SS or Middle Infield in most fantasy formats.

Austin Riley, age 22, eligible at OF with the expectation of being the starting 3B
2019 Stats: 297 PAs, 18 HRs, 41 Runs, 49 RBI, 0 SB, .226/.279/.471
Riley lit the league on fire when he was promoted in May, earning rookie-of-the-month honors. He cooled down afterward and struggled mightily to end the season, hitting .132 with a .454 OPS in 14 September games. He should be given the opportunity to win the starting third base job and if he does, it makes his rosterable in all fantasy formats.

Johan Camargo, age 26, eligible at SS/3B/OF-- 3B (18) SS (25) LF (11) RF (5)
2019 Stats: 248 PAs, 7 HRs, 31 Runs, 32 RBI, 1 SB, .233/.279/.384
Given the opportunity to win the starting 3B job, Fantasy owners could take a flyer and draft him in the later rounds. He started there in 2018 but did not produce much. After a demotion to Triple-A last season, he played well upon his return to the majors in September but saw his season end prematurely by a right-shin fracture.

Charlie Culberson, age 30, eligible at 1B/OF
2019 Stats: 144 PAs, 5 HR, 14 Runs, 20 RBI, 0 SB, .259/.294/.437
Culberson's versatility is his major asset for the Braves, but not so much for fantasy leagues. He'll be coming back from a serious injury sustained with two weeks to go in the 2019 season when he was struck in the face by a pitch while attempting to bunt. He was left with multiple facial fractures but is expected to make a full recovery.

## OUTFIELD

Ronald Acuna Jr., age 22, eligible at OF
2019 Stats: 715 PAs, 41 HRs, 127 Runs, 101 RBI, 37 SB, .280/.365/.518
All you really need to know about the 22-year-old is that he should be taken within the first three picks of most fantasy drafts. If you have the first pick, his stats and age would make him worthy of that pick, especially in dynasty and keeper leagues.

Nick Markakis, age 36, eligible at OF
2019 Stats: 469 PAs, 9 HRs, 61 Runs, 62 RBI, 2 SB
May end up in a platoon, but worthy of being a bench player on fantasy teams.

Ender Inciarte, age 29 eligible at OF
2019 Stats: 230 PAs, 5 HR, 30 Runs, 24 RBI, 7 SB, .246/.343/.397
Inciarte was hurt for most of the second half of the season not allowing him to surge and have the big second half he usually does for Atlanta. However, remember it was only two seasons ago he collected 201-hits and was one of the best hitters on the Braves. That makes him a nice draft pick with some upside that could start at the bottom end of most fantasy teams' outfields.

Adam Duvall, age 31, eligible at OF
2019 Stats: 130 PAs, 10 HRs, 17 Runs, 19 RBI, 0 SB, .267/.315/.567
Duvall, looking at a platoon, which makes him valuable only in deep leagues.

Rafael Ortega, age 28, eligible at OF
2019 Stats: 96 PAs, 2 HR, 7 Runs, 10 RBI, 3 SB, .205/.271/.307
As a depth piece for the Braves, he has no fantasy value.

## PITCHING

### Starting Rotation
Mike Soroka, age 22, RHP
2019 Stats: 174.2 IP, 142 K's, 13 Wins, 2.68 ERA, 1.11 WHIP
Soroka mixes in an above-average four-seamer and changeup that keeps batters off balance and back up his excellent batted ball data. Where Soroka won't contribute is strikeouts as he put up just 7.32 K/9 last year. 13-15 wins and a low-mid 3's ERA is a reasonable expectation for Soroka who will probably be drafted among the top 30 pitchers in fantasy.

Cole Hamels, age 36, LHP
2019 Stats: (CUBS) 141.2 IP, 143 K's, 7 Wins, 3.81 ERA, 1.39 WHIP
The Braves signed Hamels to a one-year deal. What fantasy owners will worry about is how a pitcher in his mid 30's might start to decline. His most troubling number from 2019 is a 9.1 BB%

which tied for his highest walk rate in his career. Over the last two years combined, Hamels has pitched 332.1 innings to the tune of a 3.79 ERA and a 1.32 WHIP. In 2020 he should post about those same numbers, and worthy of at least a reserve spot on fantasy teams.

Mike Foltynewicz, age 28, RHP
2019 Stats: 117 IP, 105 K's, 8 Wins, 4.54 ERA, 1.25 WHIP
Last season was a difficult one, but Foltynewicz's struggles could also be attributed to the right elbow bone spur that sidelined him at the beginning of the season. This supposedly caused a "mental block" according to several Atlanta sources. For somebody who was talked about as a Cy Young candidate in 2018, he makes a nice bounce-back candidate for 2020 as a fantasy owner can expect better numbers for a team that will support him with runs.

Max Fried, age 26, LHP
2019 Stats: 165.2 IP, 173 K's, 17 Wins, 4.02 ERA, 1.33 WHIP
Fried is a take-charge guy on the mound and has an elite two-pitch combination that consists of his fastball and curveball. A fantasy owner should expect similar strikeout numbers to last year and should improve his ERA and WHIP. Will rank just inside the top 40 for starting pitchers in 2020.

Sean Newcomb, age 36, LHP
2019 Stats: 68.1 IP, 65 K's, 6 Wins, 1 Save, 3.16 ERA, 1.32 WHIP
Newcomb is the frontrunner to win the fifth spot in the rotation for the Braves. Newcomb was demoted to Triple-A after walking eight over his first three starts. He returned as a reliever, finding his niche with a 3.04 ERA and 57:19 strikeout-to-walk ratio in 51 appearances. His relief success might've unlocked his potential as a starter. If he wins this spot, playing for a strong team makes him a nice late-round addition to fantasy rosters.

## BULLPEN

Mark Melancon, age 35, RHP
2019 Stats: 67.1 IP, 68 K's, 5 Wins, 12 Saves, 3.61 ERA, 1.32 WHIP
At least, for now, Melancon is expected to open 2020 with the ninth-inning duties in Atlanta. Due to the competition behind him, he is a low-end selection for relief pitchers in fantasy.

Will Smith, age 30, LHP
2019 Stats: (SF) 65.1 IP, 96 K's, 5 Wins, 34 Saves, 2.76 ERA, 1.03 WHIP
Even though the Braves are publically saying that Melancon is the closer, it will be hard to ignore that Smith was one of the better closers in baseball in 2019. Smart money says that he will be the closer at some point in 2020 and fantasy owners should draft him with that in mind.

Shane Greene, age 31, RHP
2019 Stats: (DET, ATL) 62.2 IP, 64 K's, 0 Wins, 23 Saves, 2.30 ERA, 1.01 WHIP
Greene was quickly demoted as the closer after he was acquired from Detroit in mid-season. Will generally only get a chance for holds in 2020.

Grant Dayton, age 32, LHP
2019 Stats: 12 IP, 14 K's, 0 Wins, 0 Saves, 3.00 ERA, 1.33 ERA

A freak injury while playing catch in warmups sidelined him for a big chunk of the season. As a left-hander out of the bullpen, he could garner a bunch of holds.

Luke Jackson, age 28, RHP
2019 Stats: 72.2 IP, 106 K's, 9 Wins, 18 Saves, 3.84 ERA, 1.40
Even as the Braves' leader in saves last season, it is hard to see Jackson not getting anything more than a handful of saves in a crowded Atlanta bullpen.

Chris Martin, age 33, RHP
2019 Stats: 55.2 IP, 65 K's, 1 Win, 4 Saves, 3.40 ERA, 1.02 ERA
Martin has no fantasy value.

Darren O'Day, age 37, RHP
2019 Stats: 5.1 IP, 6 K's, 0 Wins, 0 Saves, 1.69 ERA, 0.75 WHIP
The veteran does not have any fantasy value.

Jeremy Walker, age 24, RHP
2019 Stats: 9.1 IP, 6 K's, 0 Wins, 0 Saves, 1.93 ERA, 1.39 WHIP
No fantasy value

# Atlanta Braves Prospects
By Matt Thompson

## 1. Drew Waters- OF
Waters is a divisive prospect with evaluators I've talked to. I feel like I'm solidly in the middle on Waters, and I think there's significant offensive and defensive skills here. He's a switch-hitter that hits well enough against both sides but has the ability to terrorize right-handers. It's plus bat speed, but a little too linear. He will work gap-to-gap and if he's able to add more loft to his swing, he could pop 25 homers. He's a 15-20 steal candidate as well, and he can play above-average defense at all three spots. Some concerns about his makeup may get in the way, and he needs to hit lefties better, but he's an intriguing hitter. **ETA: 2021.**

## 2. Christian Pache- OF
Pache is a top twenty prospect on real lists due to his incredible defense in center. He's a legit Gold Glove candidate with regular playing time, with the arm to match. His defensive is significantly ahead of his offensive game, but he did improve significantly on that side of the ball. He upped his walk and power frequency without hindering his contact ability. It's going to take two-four years, but he could be a 25 homer bat with some stolen bases as well. He's going to learn on the fly though because his defense is Major League ready. **ETA: 2020.**

## 3. Ian Anderson- RHP
The 2016 first rounder pitched his way to Triple-A in 2019, and should make his big league debut in 2020. Anderson has physically matured since getting drafted and his fastball/curveball combination can miss bats. The stuff has jumped due to improved mechanics, and his changeup is now a big league out-pitch. There are some concerns with Anderson as he's not a high-spin arm, but his fastball has been effective enough as he's climbed through the Braves system. He should go back to Triple-A to start 2020, and he hopefully can find that feeling that eluded him with the new ball. **ETA: 2020.**

## 4. Kyle Wright- RHP
Much like Pache and Waters, if this was a real list Anderson and Wright would be flipped for me. Why? Because Anderson has more upside. Wright has a deep arsenal, but has looked shaky in his big league trials due to an inability to command his fastball. Without his fastball his array of above-average secondaries play down. His slider is tight and misses bats, and he also has an average curveball and changeup. His change is inconsistent but there are times where it looks like his best pitch. He lacks top of the rotation upside, but is a damn near lock to be a long-term number three. **ETA: Arrived.**

## 5. Kyle Muller- LHP
Muller has added some velocity before the 2019 after doing extensive off-season work to do just that. His fastball now sits 92-94 but he can live 95-99 in short bursts. It plays even louder than that due to plus extension. His breaking ball is more of a slider now, and his changeup works well off of his fastball with late drop. Muller needs to improve his command/control, but will fall somewhere between an SP 2 or SP 4, depending on how big of an improvement he makes. Muller is a candidate to hit Atlanta this summer, and could be a high leverage pen arm if the command doesn't improve. **ETA: 2020.**

## 6. Braden Shewmake- SS

Shewmake was an SEC standout while at Texas A&M, and proved how polished he was by making it all the way to Double-A after being drafted. His offensive game is built around making contact and sending liners to all fields. His strong plate skills could make the offensive package play up, but his homer output will be minimal because he lacks strength. Shewmake has a high utility floor, but there's enough here to be a second division starting shortstop if he were to get moved. **ETA: 2021.**

## 7. Bryse Wilson- RHP
Wilson may have the best fastball of any young arm that came through Atlanta last year. The downside here is he lacks a consistent secondary offering. His slider is the best secondary pitch, but it projects as an average pitch at best. Inconsistent shape and control limit the pitch's usefulness. His curveball is a fringe pitch, and changeup is developing though. His fastball can hit the upper 90s with wiggle though, and he does have a future in the bullpen if needed. **ETA: Arrived.**

## 8. Wiliam Contreras- C
On paper it looked like a down year for Contreras, but the strides he made on the defensive side of the ball were very encouraging. Offensively his plus bat speed points to 20-homer upside in the future, but his over aggressiveness will get in the way of that without a change. He expands the zone and in addition to not walking much will struggle to square up pitches consistently. Something like .260 20 is a solid expectation here. Should start 2020 in Triple-A, but could also start in Double-A due to his youth. **ETA: 2021.**

## 9. Michael Harris- OF
Harris was the token Braves pick from the Georgia prep ranks. Just as they do every year they stayed home and plucked a high upside athlete in the third round. Harris has two-way abilities but will just be a hitter in Atlanta. He's raw, and will need significant time to bake, but Harris has exciting offensive skills. He has surprising bat to ball skills despite being as raw as he is, and he should get to 20+ homers easily with his bat speed. He's pull-heavy now as well, and needs to use all fields more. Future corner outfielder. **ETA: 2023.**

## 10. Shea Langeliers- C
If not for Adley he would've gotten more publicity, but he's a catcher with strong defensive skills and plus raw power that was overshadowed despite going inside the top ten of the 2019 draft. His power to his pull side is even double-plus. He will use all fields, but needs to be more selective for his pitch. Has ability to be an all-fields power threat with refinement. Will push Contreras for the catching job, and as soon as 2022 it could be an effective timeshare between the two. **ETA: 2021.**

**Next Five:**
Tucker Davidson- LHP
Bryce Ball- 1B
Jasseel De La Cruz- RHP
Trey Harris- OF
Justin Dean- OF

**Top Five in FYPDs:**
Braden Shewmake- SS

Michael Harris- OF
Shea Langeliers- C
Bryce Ball- 1B
Vaughn Grissom- SS

# Miami Marlins Team Preview
## By Brent Brown

**Projected Order:**
1- Jonathan Villar, 2B
2- Garrett Cooper, RF
3- Harold Ramirez, LF
4- Jorge Alfaro, C
5- Jesus Aguilar, 1B
6- Brian Anderson, 3B
7- Miguel Rojas, SS
8- Lewis Brinson,
CF 9- Pitchers spot

**Projected Bench:**
Chad Wallach, C
Jon Berti, 3B
Isan Diaz, 2B
Austin Dean, OF
Magneuris Sierra, OF
Monte Harrison, OF

**Projected Rotation:**
Sandy Alcantara, RHP
Caleb Smith, LHP
Jordan Yamamoto, RHP
Jose Urena, RHP
Ryne Stanek, RHP

**Bullpen:**
Jarlin Garcia, LHP
Elieser Hernandez, RHP
Austin Brice, RHP
Jeff Brigham, RHP
Drew Steckenrider, RHP
Adam Conley, LHP
Sterling Sharp, RHP

**Catchers:**
Jorge Alfaro, age 27, eligible at C
2019 Stats: 465 PA, 18 HR, 44 Runs, 57 RBI, 4 SB, .262/.312/.736
He's the primary catcher and that keeps him on the field handling this young pitching staff. This also complicates his offensive production as many young catcher struggle with both sides of their game, but I see an improvement on the power numbers with another full year under his belt.

Chad Wallach, age 28, eligible at C
2019 Stats: 231 PAs, 1 HRs, 4 Runs, 3 RBIs, 0 SBs, .250/.333/.708

Less than your classic backup, he's not going to play much and when he does, he's not a fantasy option.

**Infielders**:
Brian Anderson, age 27, eligible at 3B, OF
2019 Stats: 520 PAs, 20 HRs, 57 Runs, 66 RBIs, 5 SBs, .261/.342/.811
Spent half of 2019 in RF, the other half at 3B. He's a solid bat who's not going to kill it or kill your stats. I can see a pick up in RBIs with Villar at the top of the order. A few more steals at the end of a double steal as an improvement into double-digits would be huge.

Miguel Rojas, age 31, eligible at SS
2019 Stats: 526 PAs, 5 HRs, 52 Runs, 46 RBIs, 9 SBs, .284/.331/.710
Just not a lot here with the great overall depth of this position across the league. Maybe he's an injury replacement or a middle infielder in a deep roster style league.

Jonathan Villar, age 29, eligible at 2B, SS
2019 Stats: 714 PAs, 24 HRs, 111 Runs, 78 RBIs, 40 SBs, .274/.339/.792
This guy is gonna run, we'll see what Marlins Park does to his power numbers, but I see this lineup being better so his counting stats should maintain with his 2019 numbers. Change back to the NL after a season and a half with the Orioles.

Jesus Aguilar, age 29, eligible at 1B
2019 Stats: 262 PAs, 12 HRs, 39 Runs, 50 RBIs, 0 SBs, .236/.325/.714
A limited role on two teams in 2019 led to reduced numbers. If he can resume to ¾ of the numbers from 2018 that would lead to a corner infield role for your squad.

Jon Berti, age 30, eligible at 3B, SS, OF 2019 Stats: 287 PAs, 6 HRs, 52 Runs, 24 RBIs, 17 SBs, .273/.348/.755 Light hitting utility player with some decent speed. He's not Ben Zobrist, but with some more playing time, maybe he's a poor man's version.

Isan Diaz, age 24, eligible at 2B
2019 Stats: 201 PAs, 5 HRs, 17 Runs, 23 RBIs, 0 SBs, .173/.259/.566 He's still young, but he has MLB experience and just needs some PT. A younger version of Berti.

**Outfielders**
Harold Ramirez, age 25, eligible at OF
2019 Stats: 446 PAs, 11 HRs, 54 Runs, 50 RBIs, 2 SBs, .276/.312/.728
Making his debut in May of 2019, put up respectable numbers. I would look for an improvement and hopeful of 20 HRs, double-digit steals would lead to his value.

Lewis Brinson, age 26, eligible at OF
2019 Stats: 248 PAs, 0 HRs, 15 Runs, 15 RBIs, 1 SBs, .173/.236/.457
This kid couldn't hit water if he fell out of a boat in 2019. In a season where HRs were up across the league he hit zero and he only stole one base.

Garrett Cooper, age 29, eligible at 1B, OF
2019 Stats:421 PAs, 15 HRs, 52 Runs, 50 RBIs, 0 SBs, .281/.344/.791
Can this guy get to 20 HRs? That would be a slight improvement, but will help and having Villar

at second base a lot will improve his RBIs.

Austin Dean, age 26 , eligible at OF 2019 Stats: 189 PAs, 6 HRs, 17 Runs, 21 RBIs, 0 SBs, .225/.261/.665 A clear backup on this roster and limited fantasy value. Maybe there is a chance for improvement, but it's hard to predict at this point in his career.

Magneuris Sierra, age 24, eligible at OF 2019 Stats: 42 PAs, 0 HRs, 5 Runs, 1RBI, 3 SBs, .350/.381/.806 Not bad numbers on a limited basis. Still hasn't played a full season since his debut in 2017. Could push Brinson for PT in centerfield.

Monte Harrison, age 24, eligible at OF 2019 Stats: DNP, yet to debut in MLB This team is young and this guy could be roaming center very soon. I don't think he opens the season, but could come up if he opens Triple-A off to a hot start. A speedy outfielder with some developing power. There are a handful of prospects that are on the verge, mostly Chisholm, the aforementioned Harrison, and Victor Victor Mesa

**Starters:**
Sandy Alcantara, age 24, RHP
2019 Stats: 197 1/3 IP, 151 K, 6 W, 3.88 ERA, 1.32 WHIP
It's tough for an Ace to be 24, but I think that is what he'll be on this team. An improvement in his K/9 is needed and reduce that WHIP.

Caleb Smith, age 28, LHP
2019 Stats: 153 1/3 IP, 168 K, 10 W, 4.52 ERA, 1.23 WHIP
The deeper your league, the more likely to roster this lefty. A few more solid starts would add to his innings and pick up a few more W's.

Jordan Yamamoto, age 24, RHP
2019 Stats: 78 2/3 IP, 82 K, 4 W, 4.46 ERA, 1.14 WHIP
Making his debut in early June, pitched pretty well. If he can maintain that excellent WHIP of 1.14 while lowering the ERA into the 3's, he would be a useful asset.

Jose Urena, age 28, RHP
2019 Stats: 84 2/3 IP, 62 K, 4 W, 5.21 ERA, 1.48 WHIP
Started 2019 awful, turned it around and had the ERA into the low 4's by early June and his season was derailed by a shoulder injury, which would scare me. Came off IL in September and only pitched out of the bullpen and it wasn't very good.

Ryne Stanek, age 28, RHP
2019 Stats: 77 IP, 89 K, 0 W, 3.97 ERA, 1.30 WHIP
No victories, but was an opener for TB before a mid-season trade and then used out of the bullpen in Miami. If his role returns to an opener, there is something useful as a streamer on those starts.
#1 prospect in the system, Sixto Sanchez could get a promotion.

**Relievers:**
Jarlin Garcia, age 27, LHP 2019 Stats: 50 2/3 IP, 39 K, 4 W, 3.02 ERA, 1.11 WHIP
The best-looking arm in this bullpen, could be tabbed as a low-cost closer in your draft. He won't

get many opportunities, but something is better than nothing.

Elieser Hernandez, age 25, RHP
2019 Stats: 82 1/3 IP, 85 K, 3 W, 5.03 ERA, 1.24 WHIP
Spent most of the 2019 season as a starter with a short stint in the bullpen. The ERA is affected by the small sample size and I believe he can get that down about a run and be a back of the rotation fantasy pitcher if the bullpen thing is unsuccessful again

Austin Brice, age 28, RHP
2019 Stats: 44 2/3 IP, 46 K, 1 W, 3.43 ERA, 1.23 WHIP
Missed parts of the season with forearm injuries, once a starter has shown some success in the bullpen. He could also be the closer showing a solid arm. The injury scare could for certain be an issue.

Jeff Brigham, age 28, RHP
 2019 Stats: 38 1/3 IP, 39 K, 3 W, 4.46 ERA, 1.30 WHIP
He did pick up one save in 2019. Maybe he picks up some holds along the way as the team improves.

Drew Steckenrider, age 29, RHP
2019 Stats: 14 1/3 IP, 14 K, 0 W, 6.28 ERA, 0.98 WHIP
After two pretty good seasons, 2019 was not so good. Battled right elbow and missed most of the season. With no surgery, who knows. I guess we'll wait and see.

Adam Conley, age 30, LHP
2019 Stats: 60 2/3 IP, 53 K, 2 W, 6.53 ERA, 1.73 WHIP
The last season wasn't as productive as 2018. Did have two saves and could be a late inning kind of guy.

Sterling Sharp, age 25, RHP
Yet to make his MLB debut Claimed in the Rule 5 draft from the Washington Nationals, he'll have to remain on the active roster or be returned to Washington. Used as a starter in the minors, his only option at the moment would be a long man in the bullpen.

# Miami Marlins Prospects
By Matt Thompson

## 1. Sixto Sanchez- RHP
You can say I've turned the corner on Sixto. I still don't think he gets the strikeouts you desire in an ace for fantasy, but I do think he offers the Marlins enough to be a constant atop their rotation with the weak contact and plus command. He also appears to be over the health concerns that lingered with the elbow around the time of the move from the Phillies. Sixto re-worked the delivery and now sits 96-98 with the heater which he can manipulate and create different looks. His changeup and slider are also plus pitches, and are designed to get weak contact and ground balls as well as to miss bats. He uses his change mostly against southpaws. He should be an elite ratio and ERA play, and Sixto is somehow still underrated in the fantasy game. **ETA: 2020.**

## 2. JJ Bleday- OF
The centerpiece of the National Championship Vanderbilt Commodore lineup, Bleday had an underwhelming pro debut, but it was a long season for him, and then he was sent to the toughest park in the toughest league for offensive players. The lefty has quick, powerful hands, and easy plus raw power. He's a future fixture in the middle of the Marlins lineup. His strong right field defense is just icing on the cake. It's a high floor bat with the potential for a 55 hit/70 power pairing. He should see Double-A by the Summer. **ETA: 2021.**

## 3. Jazz Chisholm- SS
The Marlins return in a rare prospect-for-prospect challenge trade, Chisholm is the Marlins shortstop of the future and should benefit greatly from the move to Miami. The quick-twitch athletic shortstop has the glove to stick at the six. He's got plus raw power but his over aggressiveness in the box prevents him from fully tapping into it. Jazz has all the ingredients to be an absolute fan favorite in Miami, and the skills to be a star if the Marlins can motivate Jazz to put in the work. **ETA: 2021.**

## 4. Edward Cabrera- RHP
Cabrera simplified his delivery and unlocked more velocity while limiting walks and missing more bats. Yep. That's what you want. His fastball is a plus offering and he backs it up with two above-average secondaries in his curveball and changeup. With Cabrera showing improvements and already being in Double-A and on the 40-man, he's just a phone call away from a call-up. He's likely a number two or three starter long term. **ETA: 2020.**

## 5. Lewin Diaz- 1B
Diaz could always hit, but when you have a 6-foot-4 first baseman with a powerful frame, you're looking for more than just a batting average asset. Diaz unlocked something in the swing when he dropped his hands, and he started hitting the ball harder and farther. Diaz has the unusual combination of power and contact ability, and has a chance to be a strong offensive player due to the hit tool and power combination. Diaz is on the 40-man, but we shouldn't see him in 2020. **ETA: 2021.**

## 6. Jesus Sanchez- OF
Sanchez is a guy I've always been down on compared to the industry. Yes he has plus bat speed, and yes he keeps his bat through the zone for such a long time, and he has plus raw

power. He's so aggressive in the box that I worry about his ability to drive the ball and pitchers with a plan should be able to carve him up. He offers zero to negative defensive value and won't run, so if he doesn't hit it can get ugly here. He's only 22-years-old, so there's time to improve, but he already reached Triple-A last season. **ETA: 2021.**

### 7. Monte Harrison- OF

The ultimate dice roll. If you could give Harrison a 40-hit tool, he would be a star. In a system full of athletes, Harrison may be the best one. He's a double-plus runner who has been successful on the bases at an outstanding 84% clip. He's a plus fielder equipped with a cannon and could win awards for his glove in the future. He's an exciting player, he just strikes out too much. He did cut his 38% K rate down to 30%, but he needs to shave another few points off to have long sustainable success. Harrison is on the 40-man roster. **ETA: 2020.**

### 8. Kameron Misner- OF

The University of Missouri product is yet another plus athlete in a system full of them. Misner is not quite the athlete of Harrison, but the same issues are here. Plus power and speed tools, but the hit tool, specifically the contact part, brings the whole skill set down for me. Misner fell a bit in the draft, down to 35th overall, due to a poor conference season. He's a boom or bust guy, but if he hits you could get something like 25 homers/20 steals out of Misner. **ETA: 2022.**

### 9. Braxton Garrett- LHP

The 2016 first rounder only had 16 pro innings under his belt since entering pro ball, and he took a massive jump in innings by taking the ball every fifth day and throwing 105 innings with strong results in High-A. Garrett sits 94-95 with the fastball and a plus curveball and an above-average change. He will manipulate his fastball and throw multiple versions of the pitch. Garrett should report to Double-A to begin 2020 and projects as a mid-rotation arm with solid ratios. **ETA: 2021.**

### 10. Trevor Rogers- LHP

The big 6-foot-6 lefty with a disappointing fastball, Rogers has added some depth to his arsenal by adding a cutter to go with his curveball and change. There's got to be more velocity in here right? Rogers is the rare tall southpaw that repeats his delivery well, and his frame looks like it can sustain another quality 10-15 pounds. Rogers is an innings eating number four starter unless the stuff pops. **ETA: 2021.**

**Next Five:**
Peyton Burdick- OF
Connor Scott- OF
Jerar Encarnacion- OF
Nick Neidert- RHP
Osiris Johnson- SS

**Top Five in FYPDs:**
JJ Bleday- OF
Kameron Misner- OF
Peyton Burdick- OF
Jose Salas- SS
Nasim Nunez- SS

# New York Mets Team Preview
By Ray Kuhn

**Projected Lineup:**
1 – Brandon Nimmo, CF
2 – Jeff McNeil, 3B
3 – Pete Alonso, 1B
4 – Robinson Cano, 2B
5 – Yoenis Cespedes, LF
6 – Michael Conforto, RF
7 – Wilson Ramos, C
8 – Amed Rosario, SS

**Projected Bench:**
Tomas Nido, C
J.D. Davis, IF/OF
Jed Lowrie, IF
Jake Marisnick, OF
Dominic Smith, IF/OF

**Projected Rotation:**
Jacob deGrom, RHP
Noah Syndergaard, RHP
Marcus Stroman, RHP
Steven Matz, LHP
Rick Porcello, RHP

**Projected Bullpen:**
Edwin Diaz, RHP
Dellin Betances, RHP
Seth Lugo, RHP
Justin Wilson, LHP
Jeurys Familia, RHP
Brad Brach, RHP
Robert Gsellman, RHP
Michael Wacha, RHP

**Catchers:**
Wilson Ramos, age 32, eligible at C
2019 stats: 524 PA, 14 HR, 52 Runs, 73 RBI, 1 SB, .288/.351/.416
Ramos was never a home run hitter, but his power certainly took a step back last season. With a 62% ground ball rate, Ramos' upside is limited despite the fact that he was in the middle of the Mets' lineup for the majority of last season. The batting average is there, especially for a catcher, which makes Ramos a solid option as even with all of the ground balls, he is a solid source of run production.

Tomas Nido, age 25, eligible at C
2019 stats: 144 PA, 4 HR, 9 Runs, 14 RBI, 0 SB, .191/.231/.316

We are dealing with your typical backup catcher here, as the glove and handling of pitchers is Nido's best tool. He doesn't bring any power to the table, puts the ball on the ground too much, and doesn't make enough contact to have an impact. And with the batting average as poor as it is, he hurts you more than helps.

**Infielders:**

Pete Alonso, age 25, eligible 1B
2019 stats: 693 PA, 53 HR, 103 Runs, 120 RBI, 1 SB, .260/.358/.583
Yes, we know everything that Alonso did in his rookie season, and his power tool and skill set is as real as it gets, but expecting 53 home runs once again might not be prudent. With a 69% contact rate last season, the concern for Alonso is that he is closer to his .241 second half batting average, and that isn't exactly what you want out of your second or third round pick. But 45 home runs and 100 RBI are a very reasonable expectation.

Robinson Cano, age 37, eligible at 2B
2019 stats: 423 PA, 13, 46 Runs, 39 RBI, 0 SB, .256/.307/.428
Overall, it was not a good season for the veteran second baseman. He battled both injuries and ineffectiveness, but there were some good flashes in there as well. Before anything, we have to assume there won't be a full season of statistics from Cano as the Mets will also make sure he gets plenty of rest. Cano still makes contact at an above average level, but the plate skills have taken a dip from the prime of his career. Power and hard contact are trending in the wrong direction, and this point, a reverse isn't likely. The Cano we know is still in there, but he's now a late round, middle infield option for deeper leagues at best.

Amed Rosario, age 24, eligible at SS
2019 stats: 655 PA, 15 HR, 75 Runs, 72 RBI, 19 SB, .287/.323/.432
Rosario truly is a tricky player to evaluate. The shortstop is still young and has some time to improve, but we also have a few seasons of track record to go on. Our first variable is the batting order. Batting eighth is never a great thing for fantasy value, but entering the season, that is where Rosario is currently slotted in. Of course, his stat line will get your attention, and those 19 stolen bases have their value, but efficiency (he was caught stealing 10 times) is still an issue. He has gotten his contact up to league average rates and is also improving the quality of his contact, but at 15 we likely have seen the peak of his home run value. Rosario's speed is elite, but don't pay for performance that isn't there yet.

Jeff McNeil, age 27, eligible at OF, 3B, and 2B
2019 stats: 567 PA, 23 HR, 83 Runs, 75 RBI, 5 SB, .318/.384/.531
McNeil's plate skills aren't a surprise, but his second half power surge was to some degree. After posting an 86% contact rate in 2018, he followed that up with an 85% rate last season while also hitting .318 and showing that power we mentioned. After hitting just six home runs in the first half of the season, McNeil followed that up with 23 in the second half as he started attacking first pitches while driving in 75 runs overall. As a whole, McNeil's power metrics are really just slightly above average, but everything here says a repeat is quite possible.

J.D. Davis, age 26, eligible at OF and 3B
2019 stats: 453 PA, 22 HR, 65 Runs, 57 RBI, 3 SB, .307/.369/.527
Finding consistent playing time was key for Davis last season, but the fact that he delivered when in the lineup did lead to more at bats. Where he plays this season, most likely between left

field and third base, will some what impact his value, but if you draft based on skills, there is a solid base to work with at the plate. While he likely won't hit .307 again, Davis' contact and line drive rates do support a solid batting average with power metrics that led to 14 home runs in 240 second half plate appearances being repeatable. More playing time could lead to 30 home runs, but pay for 20.

Jed Lowrie, age 35, eligible at 2B
2019 stats: 8 PA, 0 HR, 0 Runs, 0 RBI, 0 SB, .000/.125/.000
We know the running joke that Lowrie was signed by the Mets and then disappeared with a knee and other injuries, and that is just what happens for New York. Lowrie now enters this season as a super-utility option, and based on what we saw from him in 2017 and 2018, there is something to work with. We are looking at more like 400 plate appearances from Lowrie, and there is nothing wrong with that, in fact, it's probably better for his outlook of making it through a full season. When in the lineup though, he does bring some power and solid plate skills to the table.

**Outfielders:**
Yoenis Cespedes, age 34, eligible at OF
2018 stats: 157 PA, 9 HR, 20 Runs, 29 RBI, 3 SB, .262/.325/.496
Let's go from one Mets' injury problem to another, and Cespedes is even more comical than most. Following an injury at his ranch last season, the outfielder appears poised to return after missing almost two years of action, and he is talking a big game about what he can do at the plate. As he is essentially forgotten, the cost will be free, and let's just assume he will be the starting left fielder. Even if that is the case though, we know his workload will be monitored, and he likely will be removed from games in the late innings for defensive purposes. If all goes well, Cespedes does have a legitimate power tool along with the capability to drive in runs and hit for a solid average. Take the late round flier, because at the very least, you will know who your first drop should be.

Brandon Nimmo, age 26, eligible at OF
2019 stats: 254 PA, 8 HR, 34 Runs, 29 RBI, 2 SB, .221/.375/.407
Even though he struggled to hit for average last season, while also dealing with neck issues, Nimmo does a good job of finding his way on base. Nimmo's other skill is speed, but to this point in his career, that has yet to translate into stolen bases, and he has also struggled to make consistent contact; 65% last season. That is mitigated in OBP leagues, but even despite the fly ball boost last season, we shouldn't be expecting much in the power department from Nimmo either, so he is more like a one trick pony.

Michael Conforto, age 26, eligible at OF
2019 stats: 648 PA, 33 HR, 90 Runs, 92 RBI, 7 SB, .257/.363/.494
Some of Conforto's value stems from him consistently being in the lineup, but we are dealing with a solid hitter here. In fact, based on just visually watching his swing, you would expect to see the batting average be a little higher. And don't think about following him week to week, because there is some streakiness here as well. The 24%-line drive rate is a nice tough and at 73%, Conforto's contact rate is at least trending in the right direction, which ensures we are working with a solid base of plate skills. Perhaps more importantly though, both his power and 20% home run to fly ball rate appear to be both consistent and repeatable, so we can once again count on 30 home runs with upside, and if everything falls right, maybe 100 RBI as well.

Perhaps if Conforto keeps on making slight improvements or finds some more consistency, that batting average gets closer to .270?

Jake Marisnick, age 28, eligible at OF
2019 stats: 318 PA, 10 HR, 46 Runs, 34 RBI, 10 SB, .233/.289/.411
Marisnick will likely be used as some form of fourth outfielder/defensive placement, and what you see is what you get from him. There is some power and speed there, but he likely won't get enough consistent playing time for it truly matter. And if he does, then the batting average will likely be an issue.

Dominic Smith, age, 24, eligible at OF and 1B
2019 stats: 197 PA, 11 HR, 35 Runs, 25 RBI, 1 SB, .282/.355/.525
Playing time is likely going to be the biggest issue for Smith, as the former first round pick finally made some strides last season as he found consistency for the first time. Despite the 11 home runs, Smith's power and home run stroke still seems to be a work in progress (can we trust his 22% home run to fly ball rate), but the contact rate and overall plate skills are moving forward. Unless he finds regular playing time though, he won't do enough to be fantasy relevant other than in the deepest of leagues.

**Starting Pitchers:**
Jacob deGrom, age 31, RHP
2019 stats: 204 IP, 255 K, 11 Wins, 2.43 ERA, 0.97 WHIP
It would be nice if one of the best pitchers in the game could pick up some wins, right? deGrom is the poster child for counting quality starts, and not wins as a category, but it's hard to argue with anything the right-hander does on the mound. Once again, the right-hander's skills remained intact, and if anything, they even slightly improved. Nothing about deGrom suggests that he is going to slow down or that there any chinks in the armor, especially after his 1.51 ERA in the second half of last season. In fact, his average fastball velocity even increased from 96 to 96.9 miles per hour last season.

Noah Syndergaard, age 27, RHP
2019 stats: 197.2 IP, 202 K, 10 Wins, 4.28 ERA, 1.23 WHIP
Based on talent, Syndergaard should be better. At times, there are flashes of such, and in fairness his FIP was 3.60 last season, but he just hasn't completely put it together yet. The first thing to check, is Syndergaard's control, and that has remained unchanged from a year ago, and there is still nothing to worry about there. The five percent increase in fly balls and the right-hander's home run to fly ball rate going from 8% to 13% weren't good signs, but the overall picture is still pretty good. Syndergaard's swinging strike rate was still pretty good, and that, along with his ERA, did take a step forward in the second half of last season. Looking at the right-hander as an SP2 with upside could provide some nice value as he is currently going towards the end of that range.

Marcus Stroman, age 28, RHP
2019 stats: 184.1 IP, 159 K, 10 Wins, 3.22 ERA, 1.31 WHIP
The move to the National League for a full season should benefit the right-hander. He also changed his pitch mix last year as he trended more towards his cutter than sinker, but even with that being said, Stroman's groundball rate was still 54% last season; after consistently running in the low 60's. Stroman is a solid innings eater, but the strikeouts are not going to be there at

the level you need, so keep that in context. Worst case scenario though, his ERA won't be on the wrong side of four.

Steven Matz, age 28, LHP

2019 stats: 160.1 IP, 153 K, 11 Wins, 4.21 ERA, 1.31 WHIP

The first thing the left-hander needs to do is stay healthy through a full season. There is a solid pitcher in there, but Matz just needs to find consistency and put that together. Things did improve for Matz in the second half of the season, and he finally seems to be getting some swinging strikes (10.1%), but he has yet to prove to be the pitcher that can be consistently counted on. Overall, Matz isn't going to stand out from the crowd, but you will get to a point in your draft where he is the best pitcher available, and you could do worse.

Rick Porcello, age 31, RHP

2019 stats: 174.1 IP, 143 K, 14 Wins, 5.52 ERA, 1.39 WHIP

If you want to know why wins aren't necessarily fair, look at Porcello compared to deGrom. It is worth noting, that even for as much as Porcello struggled, he still logged a significant amount of innings, but based on his 4.76 FIP, things should have been a little better. The right-hander has a track record of eating up innings, but you aren't going to get strikeouts from him, and the upside (aside from as a streamer) is limited as he just doesn't get enough swinging strikes. Porcello will be a better pitcher for the Mets than he will be for your fantasy team, but if you are chasing wins, he might find his way onto your team.

**Relief Pitchers:**

Edwin Diaz, age 25, RHP

2019 stats: 58 IP, 99 K, 26 Saves, 5.59 ERA, 1.38 WHIP

For as bad as Diaz was last season, how can you not like those strikeouts? The problem for the right-hander was two-fold; walks and home runs. Of course, there is a little more to the story than that, he did have a 4.51 FIP for whatever that is worth, but Diaz fits perfectly in the age of three true outcomes (strikeout, walk, home run). Diaz's xERA of 3.12 also paints a favorable picture, but he is going to have to keep those fly balls down (35% to 44% last season). The talent is still there, and some form of a bounce back is likely, but do you really want to invest that heavily in a closer?

Dellin Betances, age 31, RHP

2018 stats: 66.2 IP, 115 K, 4 Saves, 2.70 ERA, 1.05 WHIP

Last season, Betances pitched to two batters, and struck both of them out, before injuring his Achilles. The right-hander now appears, once again, to be healthy, and the good news is that his arm woes are behind him. We have to make sure that the velocity is there once we see him in Spring Training, and it should be since he has had a year off, and there is value here even without the saves.

Seth Lugo, age 30, RHP

2019 stats: 80 IP, 104 K, 6 Saves, 2.70 ERA, 0.90 WHIP

Lugo's success out of the bullpen has done him harm in the sense that it has kept from the rotation, as he is too valuable otherwise. He isn't going to be in the running for saves, but the holds will be there, along with everything else. Everything we saw from Lugo last season is repeatable.

Justin Wilson, age 32, LHP

2019 stats: 39 IP, 44 K, 4 Saves, 2.54 ERA, 1.33 WHIP
As the lone southpaw in the Mets' bullpen, Wilson is going to be used often, and that means holds, and about a strikeout per inning. Other than that, there is no upside though.

Jeurys Familia, age 30, RHP
2019 stats: 60 IP, 63 K, 0 Saves, 5.70 ERA, 1.73 WHIP
Familia's return to New York, he didn't leave for long, didn't exactly go according to plan. In fact, far from it. He wasn't really healthy, at least at the beginning of the season, but the only place for it to go for Familia, is up. The right-hander should find some consistency, as long as he is healthy, and his control has to improve after his struggles at finding the plate last season.

Brad Brach, age 33, RHP
2019 stats: 54.1 IP, 60 K, 0 Saves, 5.47 ERA, 1.62 WHIP
Overall, it was a rough season for Brach, but things did pick up for the right-hander once he joined the Mets. From a fantasy perspective though, there really isn't much to see.
Robert Gsellman, age 26, RHP
2019 stats: 63.2 IP, 60 K, 1 Save, 4.66 ERA, 1.37 WHIP
If Gsellman finds his way back into the rotation, he might be worth a closer look, but that's about it. He needs to get back to generating ground balls, but the increased velocity out of the bullpen did help pad his strikeout total.

Michael Wacha, age 28, RHP
2019 stats: 126.2 IP, 104 K, 6 Wins, 4.76 ERA, 1.56 WHIP
If you thought last season was rough for Wacha, it could have actually been worse as his FIP was 5.61. Wacha struggled with his control last season, and the fact that he doesn't over power hitters or generate much in the way of strikeouts does hinder his value. We have seen some flashes of success from Wacha, but he is more of an innings eater than anything else. And for that to happen, he needs to find his way into the rotation before even getting on your radar.

**New York Mets Prospects**
By Matt Thompson

## 1. Ronny Mauricio- SS

The six-foot-three Mauricio is the definition of projectable, as there is room for him to add a solid 20-30 pounds of muscle to his frame. He's a quick twitch athletic shortstop with strong bat-to-ball skills and good feel for the barrel, and he's in the process of developing a solid offensive foundation to build upon. The switch-hitter doesn't have any stats that jump off the page, but his contact ability (79%) was remarkable when you consider the youth and his long limbs. Mauricio has already started to add some mass, as photos from Mets instructs showed. With his frame I'd say it's unlikely he sticks at short but you'll be happy with his .280 30 homer potential from the hot corner. **ETA: 2023.**

## 2. Andres Gimenez- SS

I'm still in on Gimenez, and this is a hill I'm planting my flag on. Gimenez did hit for more power during his second go around in Double-A, but it did come with an uptick in his strikeout rate. His quest for power resulted in mechanical issues with his swing, but the swing looked good as new in the AFL and he led the league in hitting. In talking with several evaluators about Gimenez, I think he can be a 15+ homer threat at peak, and that should come with good batting averages and 20+ steals. Essentially not all that different from Amed Rosario, except Gimenez is a strong defender at the six. Gimenez will start 2020 in Triple-A, and I expect him to spend a full season there. **ETA: 2021.**

## 3. Francisco Alvarez- C

Don't just skip over Alvarez because he's a teenage catching prospect! The 17-year-old Alvarez was aggressively assigned to the GCL, and handled it gracefully. He wasn't there long before they sent him to the Appy League, and he exceeded expectations there also. He showed plate skills advanced beyond his years, with strong contact rates around 75-80% and double digit walk rates. He's got plus raw power but is still learning to fully turn it out in games. His strong arm will slow down the running game and he shows enough on the defensive side to project him there long term. **ETA: 2023.**

## 4. Brett Baty- 3B

Baty compares to 2018 first rounder Nolan Gorman. Both are prep third baseman that are advanced physically. Both are gifted with plus raw power and contact issues that could limit their power. You may not know this, but Baty is actually older than Gorman, despite being a 2019 draftee. Baty was dinged a bit for his advanced age as a prep draft prospect, and will play all of 2020 as a 20-year old. He will make his full season debut next year. There's 30 homer upside, but those come with defensive question marks that may push him to first base. **ETA: 2022.**

## 5. Matt Allan- RHP

Our second highest rated prep arm in the 2019 draft over at Prospects Live, Allan slipped due to the third round of the 2019 draft due to signability concerns over the bonus amount and an alleged strong commitment to the University of Florida. Despite slipping to the third round, the Mets gave him $2.5 million. They shaped their entire draft around Brett Baty, Allan and another prep arm Josh Wolf. Allan has a plus fastball and a plus-to-double-plus curveball, but his changeup lags behind. His command is advanced and he can miss bats at a high clip. He lacks the athleticism of many of the other prep arms, but he trades that for advanced pitchability. He projects as anywhere from a number two to four starter. **ETA: 2023.**

### 6. Mark Vientos- 3B
Vientos is one of the most underrated power bats in the minors, and his average flyball distance data matches his plus-plus raw power. The bat speed is above-average, and there's room to add even more mass to his frame. He's an aggressive hitter with swing and miss concerns, and a lack of footspeed and questionable hands may push him over to first base, which raises the offensive bar. Vientos will only be 20 in 2020, and although it feels like he's been around a bit, now is a good time to scoop him up where available. **ETA: 2022.**

### 7. Robert Dominguez- RHP
When Dominguez signed he was regarded as an interesting arm that sat 90-93, but in the year since an informal agreement was struck Dominguez has grown an inch or two and added some mass to the frame. He now sits 93-96 and can hit 99 with the heater and the curveball projects as an average pitch, and the changeup fringe. He's now six-foot-four, and can probably handle an aggressive stateside assignment to begin 2020. **ETA: 2024.**

### 8. Josh Wolf- RHP
Wolf was a late riser on the Texas prep scene, but impressed the Mets enough to draft him in the second round of the 2019 draft. Wolf sits 94-97 with the heater and a plus curveball. There are some durability concerns here, and he may only be a 160 inning a year arm, but Wolf should be an above average big league starter on a per inning basis. He could also be a dominant pen arm. **ETA: 2023.**

### 9. Thomas Szapucki- LHP
The electric lefty missed roughly a year and a half due to Tommy John, so he was a guy to track in 2019 to see where the stuff ended up. As the season went on, Szapucki got stronger and the stuff looked crisp once again. He still missed bats at a high clip in his 60+ inning sample, and his funky arm angle makes for uncomfortable at bats. An improved changeup would answer a lot of questions about the future role, but as of now he's either a multi-inning reliever or a 4 or 5 starter, depending on who you talk to. He will start 2020 in Double-A. **ETA: 2021.**

### 10. Shervyen Newton- 2B/SS
Newton struggled in 2019, but part of that could be due to a shoulder injury that bothered him all season. The tall, projectable switch-hitter has plus to plus-plus raw power, and will likely fill out and force a move to third base. He's posted two seasons of sub 65% contact rates while in the lower minors, so you can't realistically consider Newton to be much more than a lotto ticket for fantasy. There's a non-zero chance at 30-homer power here, and the athleticism that comes with it makes him even more interesting. **ETA: 2022.**

**Next Five:**
Alexander Ramirez- OF
David Peterson- LHP
Franklyn Kilome- RHP
Freddy Valdez- OF
Junior Tilien- SS

**Top Five in FYPDs:**
Brett Baty- 3B
Matt Allan- RHP
Robert Dominguez- RHP
Josh Wolf- RHP
Alexander Ramirez- OF

# Philadelphia Phillies Team Preview
## By Gabe Zammit

**Projected Order:**
1- Andrew McCutchen, OF
2- J.T. Realmuto, C
3- Bryce Harper, OF
4- Rhys Hoskins, 1B
5- Didi Gregorious, SS
6- Jean Segura, 2B
7- Scott Kingery, 3B
8- Adam Haseley, OF

**Projected Bench:**
Andrew Knapp, C
Josh Harrison, INF
Jay Bruce, OF/1B
Odúbel Herrera, OF
Roman Quinn, OF

**Projected Rotation:**
Aaron Nola, RHP
Zack Wheeler, RHP
Jake Arrieta, RHP
Vince Velasquez, RHP
Zach Eflin, RHP

**Bullpen**:
Héctor Neris, RHP
Seranthony Dominguez, RHP
Adam Morgan, LHP
José Álvarez, LHP
Nick Pivetta, RHP
Ranger Suárez, LHP
Victor Arano, RHP
Cole Irvin, LHP

**Catchers:**
J.T. Realmuto, age 29, eligible at C
2019 Stats: 593 PA, 25 HR, 92 Runs, 83 RBI, 9 SB, .275/.328/.493
Count me among the many who expected Realmuto to greatly surpass his 2018 with his trade from Miami to Philly last offseason. While he didn't bust, he also didn't return the incredible season we had hoped on. All of his advanced stats signal that 2020 will be much the same as 2019. Add to that the potential to get 8+ stolen bases, and he is well worth the draft day price in my mind.

Andrew Knapp, age 28, eligible at C
2019 Stats: 160 PA, 2 HR, 12 Runs, 8 RBI, 0 SB, .213/.318/.324
Knapp owns a poor hit tool and is blocked by one of the best active catchers playing the game. Even with an 11% walk rate, he is not worth your time for the aforementioned reasons.

**Infielders:**
Rhys Hoskins, age 27, eligible at 1B
2019 Stats: 705 PA, 29 HR, 86 Runs, 85 RBI, 2 SB, .226/.364/.454
If you remove Hoskins' last 40 games, after he was hit in the hand by a pitch, his triple slash is a more palatable .243/.381/.488. Still, Hoskins power indicators have slid the wrong way dramatically from his breakout 45 HR 2017. His hard hit rate has fallen from 45.2% down to 38.7% and his barrel percentage has dropped from 13.5% to 9.7%. It's looking like 2017 was the outlier year, but this is still a guy worth grabbing, particularly in OBP leagues.

Jean Segura, age 30, eligible at SS
2019 Stats: 618 PA, 12 HR, 79 Runs, 60 RBI, 10 SB, .280/.323/.420
Every batting metric with Segura from 2019 was just about in line with what he did in 2018. This is remarkable, especially when you consider that Segura fought through a hamstring injury early in the season which may have hindered his production. My projection for the coming season is a guy who can still hit for 8-12 HR and also expect a bounce back to 20 SB. This could be a buying opportunity.

Didi Gregorious, age 30, eligible at SS
2019 Stats: 344 PA, 16 HR, 47 Runs, 61 RBI, 2 SB, .238/.276/.441
Didi returned from TJ surgery last year and actually flashed some of his power again. This could lead you to believe he has 35-40 homer pop, I'm a little skeptical. His launch angle is excellent at 17.2%, but he doesn't barrell the ball up or hit the ball hard enough to warrant big time power. He also adds little to no speed at a deep position. I like him for 20-25 HR with a .250 average, which just isn't as valuable in the game as it once was.

Scott Kingery, age 25, eligible at 3B/OF
2019 Stats: 500 PA, 19 HR, 64 Runs, 55 RBI, 15 SB, .258/.315/.474
This could be the year the Phillies stop moving Kingery all over the field and just let him own a position. His sprint speed is the one metric that stands out, although I'm not crazy about only a 79% success rate on the base paths. Even still, he could break 600 PA this year and be a dual eligible 20/20 player. That's a really nice player for where he's going in drafts... He just needs to hold off stud minor league prospect Alec Bohm.

Josh Harrison, age 32, eligible at 2B
2019 Stats: 147 PA, 1 HR, 10 Runs, 8 RBI, 4 SB, .175/.218/.263
Harrison's plate skills and usefulness have been decaying steadily since 2017. It wouldn't be a surprise to see him off the roster if a more suitable utility player comes along.

**Outfielders:**
Bryce Harper, age 27, eligible at OF
2019 Stats: 682 PA, 35 HR, 98 Runs, 114 RBI, 15 SB, .260/.372/.510

People love to hate this guy, and I don't really understand why. Harper has well exceeded 600 PA in 4 of the last 5 years and is still a threat to get to 50 HR. His opportunity to carry a .300 average seems gone, but everything else is the real deal. I'm happily buying in again.

Andrew McCutchen, age 33, eligible at OF
2019 Stats: 262 PA, 10 HR, 45 Runs, 29 RBI, 2 SB, .256/.378/.457
The big question here is when will Cutch return from injury and how will it affect his play? I'm watching him closely in spring training for any hint as to his health. That being said, you have to love his draft day price and the opportunity here to be in a stacked lineup and get 100 Runs and 70 RBI. Just don't count on more than a few stolen bases.

Adam Haseley, age 23, eligible at OF
2019 Stats: 242 PA, 5 HR, 30 Runs, 26 RBI, 4 SB, .266/.324/.396
Haseley could be the biggest playing time casualty if Bohm is called up. That move would slide Kingery to CF as most likely a platoon partner with Haseley. This is not a skill set to buy right now without a standout skill and a guarantee of playing time anyways.

Jay Bruce, age 32, eligible at OF
2019 Stats: 333 PA, 26 HR, 43 Runs, 59 RBI, 1 SB, .216/.261/.523
Two years now with a variety of injuries sure do make Bruce a tough buy. If you squint hard enough, you can envision a world where he could hit .240 with 30 HR… The likelihood of that seems pretty far away. Barring an injury or a trade, Bruce just won't see the playing time to be useful.

Odúbel Herrera, age 28, eligible at OF
2019 Stats: 139 PA, 1 HR, 12 Runs, 16 RBI, 2 SB, .222/.288/.341
Herrera suffered a hamstring strain early in the year and then got suspended in June for the rest of 2019 for domestic violence. It appears as if the Phillies could be preparing for life without him at this point as the OF picture is looking a little muddy. Although, a setback to Andrew McCutchen's recovery or Haseley laying an egg at the plate could open things up for Herrera again.

Roman Quinn, age 26, eligible at OF
2019 Stats: 122 PA, 4 HR, 18 Runs, 11 RBI, 8 SB, .213/.298/.370
Quinn is the guy I'd actually show some interest in if he can see his way to regular at bats. He might really hurt your average, but the speed here is real and that is a hot commodity in today's game.

**Starters:**
Aaron Nola, age 26, RHP
2019 Stats: 202.1 IP, 229 K, 12 W, 3.87 ERA, 1.27 WHIP
This was a good year from Nola, but was it ace caliber? His BB/9 shot up from 2.46 to 3.56 and his ERA from 2.37 to 3.87. He's starting to look more like a back end SP1 or top tier SP2 than someone who can break into the truly elite at the position. Of course, I would still be very happy with him as my staff anchor. He seems to have established a very safe floor and if he gets those walks back down the upside is a Cy Young contender.

Zack Wheeler, age 29, RHP

2019 Stats: 195.1 IP, 195 K, 11 W, 3.96 ERA, 1.26 WHIP

Philly really went hard after pitching help this off-season and landed Wheeler. He's now given us two healthy years racking up the innings with about a strikeout per inning while improving slightly on his free passes. The move to Philly isn't the best in terms of ball park factors, but there is something to be said about staying in division. I don't see a tone of upside with Wheeler, but I don't see him as a particularly risky arm either.

Jake Arrieta, age 34, RHP
2019 Stats: 135.2 IP, 110 K, 8 W, 4.64 ERA, 1.47 WHIP

Could the bone spurs Arrieta pitched through last season could be to blame for last year's slide, or could it just be that Arrieta has been in a steady decline since his unbelievable 2015? I tend to hedge towards the latter. Arrieta's ceiling this coming season has definitely lowered to a 4.00 ERA with 8 K/9, the floor on the other hand… That could be a ratio killer.

Vince Velasquez, age 27, RHP
2019 Stats: 117.1 IP, 130 K, 7 W, 4.91 ERA, 1.39 WHIP

I'm squinting here and I can still see the upside, but it's getting harder to see. Velasquez teases the fantasy community year after year with strikeout upside, and I know there will be many who buy in again this year. His FIP points to a potentially even higher ERA. As a bench stash only or in a deeper league, he's still worth the risk.

Zach Eflin, age 25, RHP
2019 Stats: 163.1 IP, 129 K, 10 W, 4.13 ERA, 1.35 WHIP

Eflin is like having to settle for a plain bagel with butter because you are out of better breakfast alternatives. It's not bad by any means, but it's nothing to write home about either. He got moved between the bullpen and a starting role last year, and ended the year on a seemingly good note. Still, I'd look for a better alternative.


**Relievers:**

Héctor Neris, age 30, RHP
2019 Stats: 67.2 IP, 89 K, 28 SV, 2.93 ERA, 1.02 WHIP

Neris seems to be one of the less buzzed about closers, but there is some safety that cannot be overlooked with him as compared to the other closers in the same range. Neris Has a good strikeout rate at 11.84 K/9 and also has shown the ability to get that up even higher with his 18% swinging strike rate. He had 6 blown saves last year, so he is not without any risk.

Seranthony Dominguez, age 25, RHP
2019 Stats: 24.2 IP, 29 K, 4.01 ERA, 1.46 WHIP

Last off-season the speculation was that Dominguez could take the closer role. An elbow injury knocked him out of that conversation and needs to be considered before drafting him this year as well. He's a guy to monitor because of the strikeout upside and the potential to close, just keep an eye on the status of his elbow.

Adam Morgan, age 30, LHP
2019 Stats: 29.2 IP, 29 K, 3.94 ERA, 1.01 WHIP

Morgan is a failed starter who looks to have settled into a key late inning role. He's a great get in Holds leagues. The odds of him getting more than the occasional Save are slim.

José Álvarez, age 30, LHP
2019 Stats: 59 IP, 51 K, 3.36 ERA, 1.42 WHIP
Adam Morgan and José Álvarez are essentially the Spiderman pointing at each other meme. Both lefties who couldn't hang onto starting jobs, both fine relievers who have value in Holds leagues and could get a Save here or there.

Nick Pivetta, age 27, RHP
2019 Stats: 93.2 IP, 89 K, 4 W, 5.38 ERA, 1.52 WHIP
One of the more popular "sleepers" last year, Pivetta struggled mightily time and again throughout the course of the season. He elevated the usage of his curveball from 22% to 35%, since that had been his most effective pitch the previous season. Rather than helping him, this seemed to hurt him as he couldn't get the punchouts he'd had before. There's still hope for Pivetta, and he's coming at an extreme discount. He should see starts sooner or later, so I'd speculate on him in deeper leagues.

Ranger Suárez, age 24, LHP
2019 Stats: 48.2 IP, 42 K, 3.14 ERA, 1.32 WHIP
One would think that Suárez would have little to no role in the Phillies bullpen, but because of their right-handed heavy rotation, he will still have opportunities to get some meaningful innings. He has the opportunity to grab 10 or so Holds with the potential for more if either of the more senior lefties get moved to the rotation or get hurt.

Victor Arano, age 25, RHP
2019 Stats: 4.2 IP, 7 K, 3.86 ERA, 0.86 WHIP
An elbow injury knocked Arano out for 2019 after only 4.2 innings. His return this year will put some heat on Dominguez as the backup to Neris for the closer job. Arano has the ability to get strikeouts over a batter an inning if he can regain his form on his slider. He's someone to keep an eye on if the bullpen looks unstable.

Cole Irvin, age 26, LHP
2019 Stats: 41.2 IP, 31 K, 5.83 ERA, 1.39 WHIP
There's not much velocity in Irvin's arm but plenty of control and a decent pitch mix. This unfortunately means he will be relegated to the occasional spot start or some long relief, but that should be about it.

## Philadelphia Phillies Prospects
By Matt Thompson

### 1. Alec Bohm- 3B

On a real life Phillies list I'd slot Bohm number two, but in a fantasy list gimme Bohm and his offensive skills. The third overall pick in the 2018 draft out of Wichita State, Bohm signed for $5.85 million and had a difficult pro debut accompanied by injuries. He flipped the switch in 2019, hitting for power while rarely swinging and missing. It's a strong hit/power tool pairing, and there's enough offensive skills here to be a big league difference maker on offense. There are some concerns over his ultimate defensive home, but he's going to get every opportunity to be a big league third baseman. He may be better suited for first base, but Rhys Hoskins isn't going anywhere soon. Bohm could be up in the second half of 2020. **ETA: 2020.**

### 2. Spencer Howard- RHP

Howard's breakout started in the second half of 2018 and it carried over into 2019, even after the start of his season was delayed due to an early season bout with arm soreness. He dominated the Florida State League in his first seven starts before more of the same in Double-A. Howard's plus changeup is what separates him from the pack, it's a plus pitch and his palm-ball grip allows him to mimic the arm speed of the fastball. It gets double digit separation off of his 93-97 heater. He also mixes in a curveball and a slider. Howard is a future number two and could see the big leagues in 2020. **ETA: 2020.**

### 3. Bryson Stott- SS

For the second year in a row the Phillies grabbed a college bat with their first round pick. Stott lacks a standout tool, and his whole skill set is average which gives him a high floor. He's going to be a big leaguer and should be ready to contribute as a regular in 2022, or a bench bat in 2021. He may be a better fit for second base but he's quick enough and has enough hands to stick up the middle. Stott will likely be around .260 with 15-18 homers and 10-12 steals while providing a solid OBP. Not remarkable, but bankable. **ETA: 2022.**

### 4. Francisco Morales- RHP

The Phillies took it easy with their 6-foot-4 flamethrower, limiting him to only 96 innings spread out over 27 appearances. The lean, projectable Morales sits 94-97 with life, and he's a candidate to pound triple digits with short relief outings. He also has a plus slider in the high-80s. Like many young hurlers he needs to improve his changeup and command, but the ceiling is high. He's either a future number two starter or a two-pitch shutdown reliever, and both carry value. **ETA: 2022.**

### 5. Johan Rojas- OF

Rojas wasn't a high dollar international signing in 2017, but has the production and tools to warrant a spot on this list. Rojas is a strong defender in the outfield and his plus speed and arm are weapons. He's still learning how to fully take advantage of the plus speed on the bases, but he will help out in the steals department. Offensively its an average or slightly above hit tool and average power. He should make the jump to full season ball in 2020. **ETA: 2023.**

### 6. Adonis Medina- RHP

Medina is a three-pitch righty that is more of a floor guy than an upside play. Medina's fastball, changeup, slider trio all project to be above-average offerings, but I don't see any of them improving to the plus level. He's the Bryson Stott of pitchers in the system. The strikeouts have gone the wrong direction over time, and he's relies more on weak contact to get outs. Medina projects as a solid big league number four starter, and that could happen as soon as 2021.**ETA: 2021.**

### 7. Luis Garcia- SS/2B

The Phillies aggressively jumped Garcia over the DSL and brought him to the GCL where he performed well at 17 in 2018. In 2019 they jumped him to full-season ball as an 18-year-old, and it was a flop. Garcia looked overmatched in Lakewood, and his lack of strength enticed pitchers to challenge him. His plate skills still show promise, and he drew positive grades for his defense despite the rawness, and the quality of at bats did improve as the season went on. I'm not bailong on the plus hit tool, and the switch-hitting teenager should give Lakewood another try in 2020. **ETA: 2023.**

### 8. Kendall Simmons- SS/2B

Simmons is a big physical shortstop with some interesting offensive tools. The questions about his hit tool did drive him down draft boards though, and the Phillies were able to snag him in the sixth round in the 2018 draft. I love the athleticism and power here. He has plus power with a plus arm and above-average speed. He did show an ability to take a walk last season, but the hit tool proved to lag behind as he had a near 27% K rate and a 13% SwStr%. He's going to share time in Lakewood up the middle with Garcia to open 2020. **ETA: 2023.**

### 9. Simon Muzziotti- OF

Muzziotti has appealing hit and speed grades, but his complete lack of power throws a big bucket of water on the profile from a fantasy perspective. Plus hit, plus run, and good glove center fielders still have value in today's game, but very few become everyday players with 30 game power. He does have a relatively high floor though, and will likely settle in as a valuable reserve outfielder for the Phillies. Not all that different than Roman Quinn. **ETA: 2022.**

### 10. Mickey Moniak- OF

Moniak isn't all that different from Muzziotti, but he has more power but less of an overall hit tool. Moniak is a polarizing prospect. It appears that there's some Jackie Bradley Jr. in here because I've talked to people that have seen him once or twice and absolutely love him when he's locked in and his JBJ like hot streaks can be quite the thing. On the other side of it, people with more experience around Moniak all essentially believe in him as a fourth outfielder. I like him as a high usage fourth outfielder. **ETA: 2021.**

**Next Five:**
Jamari Baylor- SS
Erik Miller- LHP
Connor Seabold- RHP
Starlyn Castillo- RHP
Rafael Marchan- C

**Top Five in FYPDs:**
Bryston Stott- SS
Jamari Baylor- SS
Erik Miller- LHP
Yhoswar Garcia- OF (Signing in March when eligible)
Gunner Mayer- RHP

## Washington Nationals Team Preview
By Kenny Butrym

**Projected Order:**
1- Adam Eaton, RF
2- Trea Turner, SS
3- Juan Soto, LF
4- Howie Kendrick, 1B
5- Asdrubal Cabrera, 3B
6- Victor Robles, CF
7- Kurt Suzuki, C
8- Starlin Castro, 2B

**Projected Bench:**
Yan Gomes, C
Michael A. Taylor, OF
Wilmer Difo, INF
Adrian Sanchez, INF
Andrew Stevenson, OF

**Projected Rotation:**
Stephen Strasburg, RHP
Max Scherzer, RHP
Patrick Corbin, LHP
Anibal Sanchez, RHP
Joe Ross, RHP

**Bullpen**:
Sean Doolittle, LHP
Will Harris, RHP
Roenis Elias, LHP
Tanner Rainey, RHP
Wander Suero, RHP
Hunter Strickland, RHP
Austin Voth, RHP

**Catchers:**
Kurt Suzuki, age 36, eligible at C
2019 Stats: 309 PA, 17 HR, 37 Runs, 63 RBI, _ SB, .264/.324/.486
Catcher is gross so even projected at about 50% of starts a 36yo backstop can push for C1 status.  Career .260 hitter who can take advantage of the current offensive environment and

give you 12-17 HR without hurting any categories. Not someone I'm bending over backwards to roster but definitely comfortable putting him in my lineup regularly.

Yan Gomes, age 32, eligible at C
2019 Stats:358 PA, 12 HR, 36 Runs, 43 RBI, 2 SB, .000/.000/.000
Does not share the BA floor of his battery mate but can get to double digit home runs even receiving less than half of the PT. He is a low to mid-range C2 and is in the large collection of low average catchers with a little bit of pop. Also worth noting he has a pretty noteworthy platoon splits so matchups w L could be a cheap DFS C play.

**Infielders**:
Trea Turner, age 26, eligible at SS
2019 Stats: 569 PA, 19 HR, 96 Runs, 57 RBI, 35 SB, .298/.353/.497
Turner was a top-10 hitter last season even though he played only 122 games due to a finger injury he incurred while trying to lay down a bunt. He was holding the bat with 9 fingers even after he returned and still managed 19 HR to go with his 35 steals. Turner is a target for me and someone I would consider any time after the top 3 or 4 are off the board. 20+ HR coming from a guy who can threaten 40+ steals is a unique skill set and one that can really give you a leg up on your league mates who have to fill their steals with players who at best offer limited power upside and at worst hurt you in multiple other categories

Howie Kendrick, age 36, eligible at 1B, 2B
2019 Stats: 370 PA, 17 HR, 61 Runs, 62 RBI, 2 SB, .344/.395/.572
Kendrick is currently slated to be the primary 1B for the world champs, though a re-signing of another 1B to ease the burden off the 36 yo world series hero could still be in the offing. Kendrick is not a full time player anymore but he is a hell of a hitter. I certainly would not expect .344 again but he will be an asset to your BA while providing counting stats when he gets the at bats. Definitely a worthy late round draft pick who comes with multi position eligibility as a bonus just keep in mind he won't be a full time player

Starlin Castro, age 30, eligible at 2B, 3B
2019 Stats: 676 PA, 22 HR, 68 Runs, 86 RBI, 2 SB, .270/.300/.436
Castro was a bit of a compiler last year managing to play in all 162 games and amassing 676 plate appearances. However if you just look at the overall numbers you miss a heck of a second half where he hit .302 and 16 of his 22 home runs. He moves out of Miami and gets both a home field boost to at least a neutral field and into a more potent lineup. He will not get the chance to bat in the 3-5 slots in DC and is currently penciled in at 8 but if he can build off of his huge 2nd half he could both move up in the lineup and prove to be a steal in fantasy drafts, though bottom of the order could hamper his counting numbers. OBP leagues take note he does not take walks well so dock him accordingly

Asdrubal Cabrera, age 34, eligible at 2B, 3B
2019 Stats: 592 PA, 23 HR, 68 Runs, 75 RBI, 0 SB, .260/.342/.441
Nats brought back Cabrera on a 1 year 2.5M deal. It is looking like he will be the starting 3B at least to begin the season barring a Donaldson signing or a trade. The Nats also have top prospect Kieboom who up until the Cabrera and Castro signings had been penciled into the starting lineup. All this is to say I wouldn't bank on a full season of starts from Cabrera. When he is getting at bats he can be a productive bat in both real life and fantasy bringing 20 HR

power and an unspectacular career .268 BA.  Last season like with Castro was a tale of two halves. Cabrera's Washington numbers dwarf his numbers in Texas who DFA'd him mid-season. As the starter Cabrera should get the PT he needs to be useful in deeper formats just keep tabs on the Nats depth chart and have a back up plan.

Wilmer Difo, age 27, eligible at SS
2019 Stats: 144 PA, 2 HR, 15 Runs, 8 RBI, 0 SB, .252/.315/.313
Bench piece for the Nats with little power, not on the fantasy radar.

Adrian Sanchez, age 29, eligible at 3B
2019 Stats: 32 PA, 0 HR, 3 Runs, 1 RBI, 0 SB, .226/.250/.226
No Fantasy Value

**Outfielders**:
Adam Eaton, age 31, eligible at OF
2019 Stats: 656 PA, 15 HR,103 Runs, 49 RBI, 15 SB, .279/.365/.428
Eaton enjoyed his first healthy season in DC and responded with a top 30 OF type season.  He is on the wrong side of 30 and as fantasy players are wont to do there is an injury and age tax holding down his value.  Remember in drafts that that injury risk is already baked into his adp. The Nats lineup is still strong even without Rendon and Eaton provides some home run pop as well as some speed with a decent batting average

Juan Soto, age 21, eligible at OF
2019 Stats: 659 PA, 34 HR, 110 Runs, 110 RBI, 12 SB, .282/.401/.548
Youth, power even a little bit of speed (don't discount those 12 steals) Soto has it all.  He is an elite hitter who gives you all of the counting stats and isn't a 0 in the steals department.  His numbers last year included a stay on the IL and he was just 21 yo.  Soto is a first-rounder for fantasy and one that doesn't present a liability in any category.  Low risk, high ceiling, high floor, the fantasy roster trifecta.

Victor Robles, age 22, eligible at OF
2019 Stats: 617 PA, 17 HR, 86 Runs, 65 RBI, 28 SB, .255/.326/.419
It is easy to forget that Robles was once considered the Nats top OF prospect ahead of superstar LF Juan Soto.  If not for an elbow injury in the Minors Robles would have received the call to the majors before Soto and we might still be waiting for Soto's full break out.  Robles is an outstanding defender so playing time is not an issue and offers power and speed not easily found in the fantasy ranks.  There was some disappointment in Robles' real world performance but don't let that cloud your fantasy opinion of him.  He is an excellent source of speed with pop and counting stats to go with it and an opportunity for growth.

Michael A Taylor, age 28, eligible at OF
2019 Stats: 97 PA, 1 HR, 10 Runs, 3 RBI, 6 SB, .250/.305/.364
Taylor shows flashes of a power speed combo but has never hit consistently enough to make it stick.   He hasn't really demonstrated a hit tool at the major league level but if he is playing every day he could have deep league appeal for SBs if nothing else so watch for injuries to the Nats starters

Andrew Stevenson, age 25, eligible at OF
2019 Stats: 37 PA, 0 HR, 4 Runs, 0 RBI, 0 SB, .367/.486/.467
.367 BA as a part time PH is impressive but Stevenson isn't fantasy relevant

**Starters:**
Stephen Strasburg, age 31, RHP
2019 Stats: 209 IP, 251 K, 18 W, 3.32 ERA, 1.04 WHIP
Strasburg turned his second 200+ip season into a career year and a huge payday. He is a fantasy ace but don't pay for last year's numbers. That being said you won't have to. His injury history will keep his ADP down a bit. Another 200 inning season will get you well over 200 strikeouts strong ratios and put him in line for a good number of wins. His arm does make me think twice but all pitchers carry injury risk, don't be afraid to put Strasburg at the top of your fantasy rotation

Max Scherzer, age 35, RHP
2019 Stats: 172.1 IP, 243 K, 11 W, 2.92 ERA, 1.03 WHIP
Scherzer fell victim to a back injury last year around the all-star break that held him back and seemed to linger even into the playoffs where Max needed a cortisone shot in his neck to pick game 7 and he still put up SP1 numbers. Elite strikeouts, elite ratios, elite workload...as long as he can stay on the field. Age-ism and back issues have not really affected his draft value much early on nor should they. If you are comfortable taking the leap that an off-season of rest will get Mad Max back to full health put him at the top of your P board

Patrick Corbin, age 30, LHP
2019 Stats: 202 IP, 238 K, 14 W, 3.25 ERA, 1.18 WHIP
Not many #3 starters double as fantasy #1s that is what you get with Corbin. Another 200 inning work horse with over a strike out an inning, strong ratios and peripheral numbers and backed up by a strong lineup sure to push that win total up. Depending on your draft strategy I would be comfortable starting off with 3 bats and then snagging Corbin as my ace or loading up the top part of my staff with Corbin as my SP2

Anibal Sanchez, age 36, RHP
2019 Stats: 166 IP, 134 K,11 W, 3.85 ERA, 1.27 WHIP
The 36 yo was surprisingly useful both in the real world and fantasy terms last season. Not a high strikeout guy but Sanchez posted a respectable 3.85 ERA. I certainly don't expect a return to the 2.83 ERA he posted in Atlanta in 2018 but also wouldn't regress him as much as early projections which are predicting a 5+ ERA. Sanchez is not going to wow you with his numbers but can serve as a nice mid fantasy rotation piece you can snag in the back half of drafts

Joe Ross, age 26, RHP
2019 Stats: 64 IP, 57 K, 4 W, 5.48 ERA, 1.67 WHIP
5th spot is definitely up for grabs between Joe Ross and Voth and maybe Fedde depending on how spring goes. Barring another edition but I am penciling in the veteran for now though if Voth shows out in spring he may produce a bit more fantasy upside. Ross is a late round flyer for fantasy in deeper leagues for now but the 5th spot in DC is worth keeping an eye on for folks in leagues where such a player is roster-worthy and is probably not more than a streaming options in good 2 start weeks in most leagues.

**Relievers:**

Sean Doolittle, age 33, LHP
2019 Stats: 60 IP, 66 K, 6 W, 29 Sv 4.05 ERA, 1.30 WHIP
A rocky summer topped off with a trip to the IL led to Doolittle not serving as the full-time closer down the stretch for the world champs last year, a role that ended up falling to Daniel Hudson who is not on the roster as of this writing. Doolittle's numbers can be parsed to find periods of the elite performance that made him a top half RP in last years fantasy drafts and gives him the projected lead closer role heading into the season. The Nats do have a couple of relievers who could keep the pressure on Doolittle if he struggles again and reliever performance can disappear quickly so I would feel better with Doolittle as the #2 closer on a fantasy roster than #1and even with a career 3.05 ERA I would probably plan for a number closer to what he put out last season than bank on a return to form. Doolittle does carry some upside as the closer on a top team with elite SPs to create opportunity but carries noteworthy risk as well.

Will Harris, age 35, RHP
2019 Stats: 60 IP, 62 K, 4 W, 1.50 ERA, 0.93 WHIP
Harris joins the Nats bullpen in an effort to turn a weakness into a strength. Harris posted an elite 1.50 ERA last season and should be a good source of holds and would most likely be the first man up for saves if doolittle falters or hits the IL. He isn't an elite K arm out of the pen so that could limit his fantasy value if his ERA and WHIP drift back towards the pack but as long as he is posting those elite ratios probably deserves a spot at the back end of drafts

Roenis Elias, age 31, LHP
2019 Stats: 50 IP, 47 K, 4 W, 14 Sv, 3.96 ERA, 1.28 WHIP
Don't let those saves from last season fool you into thinking he is going to get opportunities this year. His saves all came in Seattle as he suffered an injury shortly after his trade to DC. If things at the back end of the Nats pen get bad the fact that he has closed before could become relevant but until that happens Elias should remain on fantasy waiver wires.

Tanner Rainey, age 27, RHP
2019 Stats: 48.1 IP, 74 K, 2 W, 3.91 ERA, 1.45 WHIP
Rainey has unbelievable stuff as evidenced by his 74 K in 48.1 innings. He also struggles to find the plate as his 7.08 BB/9 number indicates. Rainey would be a very interesting bullpen arm, possibly elite, if he can get command of his pitches so that bears watching during the season but until that happens his blow-ups and WHIP numbers keep him off all but the deepest fantasy rosters where those Ks are enough to look past the walks.

Wander Suero, age 28, RHP
2019 Stats: 71.1 IP, 81 K, 6 W, 4.54 ERA, 1.26 WHIP
Middle reliever, could earn holds if he gets back to the set-up role and in holds leagues could be useful if he can drop his ERA (he did sport a 3.07 FIP last season)

Hunter Strickland, age 31, RHP
2019 Stats: 24.1 IP, 18 K, 2 W, 2 Sv, 5.55 ERA, 1.23 WHIP
Middle reliever fighting for a spot in the bullpen, not fantasy relevant

Austin Voth, age 27, RHP
2019 Stats: 43.2 IP, 44 K, 2 W, 3.30 ERA, 1.05 WHIP
Could make for an interesting flyer if he can wrestle the #5 starter role away from Joe Ross. Voth's 3.30 ERA was mostly supported with a 3.79 FiP in a small sample size and he managed a strikeout an inning.  Not someone I am rushing out to roster but a name I will keep an eye on as the season gets started if he has a rotation spot

# Washington Nationals Prospects
## By Matt Thompson

### 1. Carter Kieboom- SS/3B/2B

Kieboom was amongst the youngest hitters in the PCL in 2019, and although his big league debut didn't go well, it was still a strong season for the 22-year-old infielder. It's an above-average hit tool with plus raw power, but no real defensive home adds some questions and is suppressing his draft cost for 2020. The signings of Asdrubal Cabrera and Starlin Castro should help the lineup by raising the floor after losing Rendon, but Kieboom is the real answer here. Kieboom will get most of the at-bats at an infield position from April on, and his sneaky versatility will be a nice asset. Kieboom was a monster in Triple-A, and he can swat 25+ homers if given the opportunity and he's getting drafted too low. **ETA: Arrived.**

### 2. Jackson Rutledge- RHP

The Nats drafted the JUCO product with the 16th pick in the June draft and gave him a $3.45 million bonus, a record for a Junior College player. Rutledge stuff is loud. Mid-to-high 90s fastball that can touch 98, and it comes with a plus slider that is absolutely death on righties due to his short, ¾ arm slot. His curveball and changeup get future above-average grades as well. He's either a high strikeout number two starter or a dominating reliever due to his fastball/slider combo. He won't be the most efficient guy and will issue walks, but the strikeouts will come in bunches. **ETA: 2022.**

### 3. Luis Garcia- SS/2B

Garcia was the youngest hitter in the upper levels of the minors last season, and I couldn't wrap my head around why people were so quick to write him off last season after underwhelming statistics in tough environments as the youngest hitter. Yes, he's not the flashiest or toolsiest player, but he's a first division regular when it all comes together. His bat-to-ball skills are his offensive bread and butter, and he uses all contact while rarely striking out. He didn't hit the ball very hard as a collective, but the power hasn't shown up yet. It's in there. He's got average power, and should post strong .280-.290 averages with 18-20 homers and 10-12 steals at his peak while playing strong defense up the middle. I'll keep grabbing the shares of Garcia and they'll start paying off in 2021. He should repeat Double-A to start 2020, but it wouldn't surprise me if they pushed him to the Pacific Coast League. **ETA: 2021.**

### 4. Mason Denaburg- RHP

This is a pure upside play here, and Denaburg had a chance at becoming a number two starter when he was drafted. Two injuries have gotten in the way since, but with the rest of this system where it is, why not take the shot on Denaburg in fantasy? When he came out of the draft he had a fastball that could hit 97 with movement, and it came with a plus curveball and the athleticism you want in your arms. Hopefully that's the arsenal when he gets back to it. **ETA: 2023.**

### 5. Andry Lara- RHP

Regarded as the top pitching prospect in the 2019 J2 class, The Nationals signed Lara for $1.25 million out of Venezuela. Lara operates in the low-to-mid-90s with the fastball and his best secondary pitch is a slurvy breaking ball. The delivery is clean and simple, and he gets tremendous downhill plane on his arsenal. Developing a third pitch and maintaining the body are on the to-do list for Lara. **ETA: 2024.**

### 6. Jeremy De La Rosa- OF
The Nats aggressively pushed their $300,000 J2 signing from 2018 to the states quickly, and he's rewarded them by posting good walk rates and showing the foundation of what could be at least plus power in time. He's on this list due to what we think he can do in the future, and in a system that lacks upside De La Rosa offers some. **ETA: 2024.**

### 7. Drew Mendoza- 1B/3B
Mendoza had three solid, but inconsistent years while at Florida State where he primarily played third base. The Nationals played Mendoza primarily at first base, and that's likely a better fit for his massive six-foot-five, 230 pound frame. He is a patient hitter but will also swing through strikes but has plus raw power. Mendoza is worth a flier in OBP formats but in most leagues can be left on the wire unless there are 20+ teams. **ETA: 2023.**

### 8. Tim Cate- LHP
Cate was the Nationals second rounder in the 2018 draft out of UConn. He has one plus pitch and it's his knee-buckling curveball. Everything he does on the mound is to set up that pitch. He knows he won't miss bats with his 90 MPH fastball, so he will try to jam hitters or throw it up or out of the zone to get hitters to chase. His changeup is above-average with some depth, but it needs the fastball to be effective. Cate could play any role on a staff, but most of his value will come from how many innings he can eat as a backend starter. **ETA: 2022.**

### 9. Wil Crowe- RHP
Crowe is Cate with a durable frame essentially. Crowe has a large frame that just looks like he's made to eat innings. It's an awful delivery, a high effort one with nearly every flaw in the book, but those imperfections add deception. His fastball has enough oomph on it to get it by hitters at 95, and he can manipulate it by sinking or cutting it. His best off-speed pitch is a big slider and he also has a fringe loopy curveball. Crowe gets results despite the issues, and is a potential backend starter. **ETA: 2021.**

### 10. Yasel Antuna- SS
Antuna was out until June due to Tommy John surgery he had in late 2018, and he only played three games before he was shut down due to another injury. When healthy there's a chance for above-average power and hit tools, but his aggressive, raw approach causes him to get exposed at times. Antuna is yet another upside play in a system that lacks it. **ETA: 2023.**

**Next Five:**
Seth Romero- LHP

Riosmar Quintana- OF
Israel Pineda- C
Tyler Dyson- RHP
Matt Cronin- LHP

**Top Five in FYPDs:**
Jackson Rutledge- RHP
Andry Lara- RHP
Drew Mendoza- 3B/1B
Riosmar Quintana- OF
Tyler Dyson- RHP

# Chicago Cubs Team Preview
By Jim Bay

## PROJECTED LINEUP

1- Anthony Rizzo, 1B
2- Kris Bryant - 3B
3- Javier Baez - SS
4- Kyle Schwarber - LF
5- Willson Contreras - C
6- Jason Heyward - RF
7- Ian Happ - CF
8- David Bote - 2B
9- Pitcher

## PROJECTED BENCH

Daniel Descalso - INF
Victor Caratini - C
Hernan Perez - INF/OF
Albert Almora Jr. - OF
Tony Kemp - OF/2b

## PROJECTED ROTATION

Yu Darvish - RHP
Jose Quintana - LHP
Kyle Hendricks - RHP
Jon Lester - LHP
Tyler Chatwood - RHP

## PROJECTED BULLPEN

Craig Kimbrel - LHP
Rowan Wick - RHP
Ryan Tepera - RHP
Kyle Ryan - LHP
Brad Wieck - LHP
Duane Underwood Jr. - RHP
Alec Mills - RHP
Trevor Megill - RHP

## CATCHERS

Willson Contreras, age 27, eligible at C
2019 Stats: 409 PAs, 24 HR, 57 Runs, 64 RBI, 1 SB, .272/.355/.533

Following a down second half in 2018, Contreras bounced back in 2019, posting a solid slash line. Despite missing a month, he hit a career-high 24 home runs in 105 games. Contreras is a top-five fantasy catcher.

Victor Caratini, age 26, eligible at C/1B
2019 Stats: 279 PAs, 11 HR, 31 Runs, 34 RBI, 1 SB, .266/.348/.447
He posted a solid slash line in 95 games and provides the fantasy owners with a contact-oriented, professional at-bat. Having first base eligibility gives him some value, mostly in deep leagues.

## INFIELDERS

Anthony Rizzo, age 30, eligible at 1B
2019 Stats: 613 PAs, 27 HRs, 89 Runs, 94 RBI, 5 SB, .293/.405/.520
Nagging injuries limited him to 146 games in 2019, which was a five-year low. In spite of this, Rizzo posted solid numbers and will still be a focal point for the Cubs in 2020. He is still worthy of being a top-five choice at first base for fantasy owners.

Javier Baez, age 27, eligible at SS
2019 Stats: 561 PAs, 29 HRs, 89 Runs, 85 RBI, 11 SB, .281/.316/.531
Last year Baez put up slightly fewer numbers than he did in 2018, when he was the runner-up for the 2018 NL MVP award, posting career highs across the board.: .290/.326/.554, 34 homers, 111 RBI. The ceiling is still high for Baez and drafting him as a top-five shortstop is not unreasonable.

Kris Bryant, age 28, eligible at 3B/OF
2019 Stats: 634 PAs, 31 HRs, 108 Runs, 77 RBI, 4 SB, .282/.382/.521
The 2019 Bryant finally posted numbers similar to this 2016 MVP caliber season. He saw his power stroke return, evidenced by a .521 slugging percentage and the second 30+ homer, 30+ double campaign of his career. Bryant is an elite player when healthy, and having outfield eligibility adds to his value, if not making him somewhat of a bargain, as a top 50 pick in fantasy drafts.

David Bote, age 26, eligible at 2B/3B
2019 Stats: 356 PAs, 11 HRs, 47 Runs, 41 RBI, 5 SB, .257/.362/.422
Potential fantasy owners will have to monitor the Cubs to see where Bote fits into their plans. Obviously, as a starter, he has more value than being a utility player. His numbers suggest that he could provide depth for most fantasy rosters.

Daniel Descalso, age 33, eligible at 2B
2019 Stats: 194 PAs, 2 HR, 20 Runs, 2 HR, 15 RBI, .173/.271/..250
In order for him to have any fantasy value, Descalso would have earned playing time and post numbers like when he slashed .263/.349/.408 in his first 24 games of 2019.

Tony Kemp, age 28, eligible at 2B/OF
2019 Stats: 186 PAs, 8 HR, 31 Runs, 29 RBI, 4 SB, .212/.291/.380

Like Bote and Descalso, potential fantasy owners will have to see what shakes out during the spring to see who emerges with playing time. Kemp posting numbers as he did with Houston in 2018 (.263/.351/.392) would at least make him worthy of deeper fantasy rosters.

Hernan Perez, age 29, eligible at 2B/SS/3B (14 games)
2019 Stats: 246 PAs, 8 HR, 29 Runs, 18 RBI, 5 SB, .228/.262/ .379
Signed as a free agent, the former Brewer's biggest asset has some speed as he stole 34 bases in 2016 and has 69 in his career. Wiggling through the rest of the "average Joes" at 2B may make him a source for some cheap steals. His potential roster versatility, as he can play outfield, could make him useful in deep leagues if he can earn some playing time.

## OUTFIELDERS

Kyle Scwarber, age 27, eligible at OF
2019 Stats: 610 PAs, 38 HRs, 82 Runs, 92 RBI, 2 SB, .250/.339/.531
Schwarber was one of baseball's best overall hitters in the second half of last season. Some mechanical changes, as well as a willingness to hit to all fields, led to a .997 OPS and in the second half of the season. Overall, Schwarber finished as the team leader in home runs this season, raised his batting average, lowered his strikeout rate and raised his contact rate for the second consecutive season. A top 20 OF in fantasy.

Ian Happ, age 25, eligible at OF/2B (13 games)
2019 Stats: 156 PAs, 11 HRs, 25 Runs, 30 RBI, 2 SB, .264/.333/.564
The beginning of the 2019 season was a struggle for Happ. A poor spring and hitting issues led to his demotion to Triple A. His reworked swing was put to the ultimate test when he finally got the call to return to the majors in late July. Happ caught fire down the stretch and went on to hit 11 homers with a .898 OPS. There's no reason to doubt his ability to post decent numbers in 2020. Generally considered a top 100 fantasy outfielder with a lot of upside.

Jason Heyward, age 30, eligible at OF
2019 Stats: 589 PAs, 21 HR, 78 Runs, 62 RBI, 8 SB, .251/.343/.429
Heyward did see some improvement in most offensive stat categories last year. He will begin the season as a starter in the Cubs outfield and is worthy of being on fantasy rosters in all formats as he should post similar numbers to last year.

Albert Almora Jr., age 25, eligible at OF
2019 Stats: 363 PAs, 12 HR, 41 Runs, 32 RBI, 2 SB. .236/.271/.381
The Cubs would love to see Almora start 2020 at center fielder but a poor 2019 will probably not see that happen. Almora spent some time in Triple-A Iowa to figure some things out, which did not help much. Almora does not have much fantasy value.

## PITCHERS

### Starting Rotation

Yu Darvish, age 33, RHP
2019 Stats: 178.2 IP, 229 K's, 6 Wins, 3.98 ERA, 1.10 WHIP

The Veteran right-hander turned things around in 2019, especially in the second half of the season. In 13 post-All-Star break starts, Darvish posted a K/9 of 13, a 2.76 ERA with seven walks through 118 innings. He should be taken in the top 25 of most fantasy drafts.

Kyle Henricks, age 30, RHP
2019 Stats: 177 IP, 150 K's, 11 Wins, 3.46 ERA, 1.13 WHIP
Hendricks as a control artist, a pitcher with elite pitch tunneling that can change speed and location with ease, who maintains a mindset and knowledge of the art of pitching few can truly understand. For example, Hendricks changed his pitching approach in 2019 to exploit the weaknesses of the launch angle revolution. His ability to reinvent himself and remain at the top of his game bodes well for fantasy owners as a truly reliable starting pitching option.

Jose Quintana, age 31, LHP
2019 Stats: 171 IP, 152 K's, 13 Wins, 4.68 ERA, 1.39 ERA
Quintana has not been the pitcher fantasy owners and the Cubs expected when they traded for him. Quintana hasn't been a bust with the Cubs, but he's been up-and-down, showing flashes of brilliance (2.02 ERA in six August starts last season) while also struggling immensely (11.09 ERA in five September starts). Potential fantasy owners will have to deal with the inconsistencies in order to benefit from his upside.

Jon Lester, age 36, LHP
2019 Stats: 171.2 IP, 165 K's, 13 Wins, 4.46 ERA, 1.50 WHIP
Lester struggled a bit last season. His velocity has been down on all of his pitches. This is just what happens on veteran starting pitchers that have a lot of miles on their arms. However, Lester is an intense competitor and there is no reason to not doubt that he will post at least similar numbers to last year.

Tyler Chatwood, age 30, RHP
2019 Stats: 76.2 IP, 74 K's, 5 Wins, 3.76 ERA, 1.33 WHIP
Chatwood is the current front runner to be the fifth starter for the Cubs. Yes, this is the same Chatwood who signed a 38 million dollar deal for 2018 and then imploded. But then, in the second half of 2019, things changed. Over his final 18 games, Chatwood posted a 2.84 ERA in 31 2/3 innings of work and his 3.45 strikeout-to-walk ratio was completely different than what he posted in 2018. Chatwood could be an interesting sleeper in fantasy drafts.

**Bullpen**

Craig Kimbrel, age 31, RHP
2019 Stats: 20.2 IP, 30 K's, 0 Wins, 13 Saves, 6.53 ERA, 1.60 WHIP
Before coming to the Cubs, Kimbrel was a lights-out closer for the Red Sox. He was not exactly lights out for the Cubs after they acquired him in mid-season. However, he still will be the closer for the Cubs and should be drafted with Red Sox numbers in mind, making him at top 10 closer at least.

Rowan Wick, age 27, RHP
2019 Stats: 33.1 IP, 35 K's, 2 Wins, 2 Saves, 2.43 ERA, 1.14 WHIP
Wick is in line to be the set-up man, which gives him some value for holds and the occasional saves.

Alec Mills, age 28, RHP
2019 Stats: 36 IP, 1 Win, 1 Save, 2.75 ERA, 1.17 WHIP
Mills bears watching as he could win the fifth starter spot coming out of spring training. That would give him some fantasy value, especially in deeper leagues.

Ryan Tepera, age 32, RHP
2019 Stats (Toronto): 21.2 IP, 0 Wins, 0 Saves, 4.98 ERA, 1.29 WHIP
Tepera only saw limited action last season due to elbow issues. He was effective for the Blue Jays from 2015-18, and if healthy could work his way into the set-up role.

Kyle Ryan, age 28, LHP
2019 Stats: 61 IP, 58 K's 4 Wins, 0 Saves, 3.54 ERA, 1.38 WHIP
Unless he becomes the set-up man, he has no real fantasy value.

Brad Wieck, age 28, LHP
2019 Stats: 34.2 IP, 49 K's, 2 Wins, 2 Saves, 5.71 ERA, 1.18 WHIP
No fantasy value

Duane Underwood Jr., age 26, RHP
2019 Stats: 11.2 IP, 13 K's, 0 Wins, 0 Saves, 5.40 ERA, 1.37 ERA
No fantasy value

# Chicago Cubs Prospects
By Matt Thompson

### 1. Nico Hoerner- 2B/SS
Injuries hit the Cubs down the stretch, and the Cubs promoted their 2018 first rounder for the stretch run. He had an injury filled year at Double-A, only getting 294 plate appearances before skipping Triple-A to plug the hole at shortstop after the Javy Baez injury. He held his own in his brief big league sample, and he hit as many homers (three) as he did in Double-A. His plate skills aren't mature enough for the big leagues and his 4% walk rate would be in issue with extended run. He's a contact and line-drive oriented player, and he will likely top out around 15-20 homers with a strong average and a sprinkling of stolen bags. He's also a second baseman for my money, and could be up as soon as May. **ETA: Arrived.**

### 2. Brennen Davis- OF
Davis is an elite athlete that has undergone a massive physical transformation since the draft. He reworked his swing and added significant strength while maintaining his plus speed. If you're looking for a potential speed and power threat that's a bit underrated this is your guy. He is the rare power guy that doesn't strike out a ton. He's still raw, but he does also add defensive value to the package. He's an exciting prospect. **ETA: 2023.**

### 3. Brailyn Marquez- LHP
Marquez is rocketing up prospect lists due to his elite velocity and new found control. His command improvements did fall back to 2018 levels after he was promoted to the Carolina League however. It's a low effort delivery that can touch 102 with the heater. He sits 94-96 with a deceptive, cross-body delivery. His secondaries lag behind the fastball right now, and there's signficant reliever risk unless his curveball and/or changeup find another gear. **ETA: 2022.**

### 4. Miguel Amaya- C
One of my personal favorite prospects after seeing him in the AFL this season. He was in the same batting practice group as Jo Adell in the Fall Stars Game, and was matching him homer for homer while consistently hitting them further. He's a strong defender with a plus arm, and his offensive skills are catching up to his defensive skills. He works the count well and should continue to add strength to his sturdy frame. He will have AVG/OBP value in addition to 20-25 homer pop. He will start 2020 as one of the youngest players in Double-A at 21. **ETA: 2021.**

### 5. Cole Roederer- OF
The left-handed hitting outfielder would've been a first round talent coming out in 2018 if it wasn't for a shoulder injury he suffered as an amateur. The power is very real, he just hasn't gotten it to fully translate in games but his exit velocity numbers are amongst the best in the entire organization. He's added strength and mass and while he may not be the stolen base asset he was initially thought of, he can hit .260-.275 with 25 homers at peak. **ETA: 2022.**

### 6. Chase Strumpf- 2B
Strumpf is an offensive-minded second baseman with strong plate skills. He climbed three levels of the organization after getting drafted in the second round this past June. He's going to be an AVG/OBP asset for fantasy, but most of his power will be doubles power as his swing is

set up for more of a line drive approach. He's not an elite athlete and may not stick at second base and have to settle for a utility role. **ETA: 2021.**

## 7. Adbert Alzolay- RHP
The first of the wave of pitching prospects to hit Wrigley Field, Alzolay finally stayed healthy and flashed his impressive skills in 2019. His fastball/curveball combination is strong and he can carve out an important bullpen role off of those two pitches alone. His changeup has flashed plus but lacks consistency at the moment. There's a heavy flyball tendency here, and he's likely a reliever because of that and the lack of a third pitch. Look for him to start the year in Triple-A, and be the first call-up from Iowa early on. **ETA: Arrived.**

## 8. Ryan Jensen- RHP
The Cubs surprise first-rounder out of Fresno State, Jensen has a lively fastball that can hit 99 with movement. His changeup and slider, and overall command, all need to improve, and Jensen is unlikely to move quickly despite the potential reliever tag. Jensen likely hits Double-A at the end of 2020, and can debut in 2021 as either a mid-rotation starter or high octane reliever. **ETA: 2021.**

## 9. Kevin Made- SS
Made was one of the jewels of a busy international class for the Cubs in 2019. He's a million miles away, but projects as a big league shortstop in the future. He lacks a big standout tool but has a well rounded skill set. His instincts and baseball I.Q. are high, and there's an above average shortstop in here, you'll just have to wait. He's on the smaller side but has strong hand-eye coordination and a quick bat.
**ETA: 2024.**

## 10. Ronnier Quintero- C
Quintero is worth a late round flier in your FYPD due to his big raw power and above average speed. Teenage catchers often bust more than not, but Quintero has a strong arm and a chance to be an above-average defender. The power upside alone makes him worth a gamble. **ETA: 2024.**

**Next Five:**
Christopher Morel- 3B
Aramis Ademan- SS
Rafael Morel- SS
Corey Abbott- RHP
Riley Thompson- RHP

**Top Five in FYPDs:**
Chase Strumpf- 2B
Ryan Jensen- RHP
Kevin Made- SS
Ronnier Quintero- C
Ethan Hearn- C

# Cincinnati Reds Team Preview
By Jim Bay and Kenny Butrym

**Projected Order:**
1-Shogo Akiyama, CF
2- Joey Votto, 1B
3- Eugenio Suarez, 3B
4- Mike Moustakas, 2B
5- Nick Castellanos, RF
6- Jesse Winker, LF
7- Freddy Galvis, SS
8- Tucker Barnhart, C


**Projected Bench:**
Josh VanMeter, OF
Phillip Ervin. OF
Nick Senzel, OF
Curt Casali, C
Mark Payton, OF

**Projected Rotation:**
Sonny Gray, RHP
Luis Castillo, RHP
Trevor Bauer, RHP
Wade Miley, RHP
Anthony DeSclafani, RHP

**Bullpen**:
Raisel Iglesias, RHP
Michael Lorenzen, RHP
Amir Garrett, LHP
Robert Stephenson, RHP
Jose De Leon, RHP
Lucas Sims, RHP
Cody Reed, LHP
Sal Romano, RHP

**Catchers:**
Tucker Barnhart, age 29, eligible at C
2019 Stats: 364 PA, 11 HR, 32 Runs, 40 RBI, 1 SB, .231/.328/.380

Back-to-back seasons of subpar offensive performances have many wondering if we have seen the best of Barnhart. The ray of light was when Barnhart came off an IL stint, he came back in a big way. During his time off, Barnhart spent time looking at the techniques of some of the best batters in the league and the research proved to be helpful as he increased all of his stat lines. For Fantasy, Barnhart is a fine selection as a backup or as a starter in a league that employs two catchers.

Curt Casali, age 31, eligible at C
2019 Stats: 236 PA, 4 HR, 15 Runs, 16 RBI, 0 SB, .251/.331/.411
Could produce enough to be a backup in two catcher leagues

**Infielders**:
Joey Votto, age 36, eligible at 1B
2019 Stats: 608 PA, 15 HR, 79 Runs, 47 RBI, 5 SB, .261/.357/.411
Votto will benefit from the new additions to the Reds as much as anybody. The biggest thing for Votto is whether he can sustain or improve upon last season's numbers at 36 years old. He is probably best thought of in around the top 25 basemen in fantasy and should be drafted for at least a bench position with upside potential.

Eugenio Suarez, age 28, eligible at 3B
2019 Stats: 662 PA, 49 HR, 87 Runs, 103 RBI, 3 SB, .271/.358/.572
Suarez is a powerfully built hard-hitting third baseman with tremendous upper-body strength, and at age 28, he is in the prime of his career. Hitting in the newly improved Reds lineup should ensure similar if not increased numbers for 2020. This will easily make him a top 10 third baseman in fantasy, with a high ceiling.

Mike Moustakas, age 31, eligible at 2B, 3B
2019 Stats: 584 PA, 35 HR, 80 Runs, 87 RBI, 3 SB, .254/.329/.516
The former Brewer belted 101 home runs the past three seasons combined, which is 10 more than any other player who has carried second base eligibility in at least one of those years. He also has 267 RBI during that same three-year stretch. In Cincinnati, Moustakas' skills fit his home park even better than they did in Milwaukee. It is not out of the question that he could hit 40 HR in 2020, and can be considered top 15, and almost top 10, at both second and third base for fantasy.

Freddy Galvis, age 30, eligible at 2B, SS
2019 Stats: 589 PA, 23 HR, 67 Runs, 70 RBI, 4 SB, .260/.296/.438
Galvis was claimed from Toronto in August of last year, and while he contributes across the board, he does not do any one thing particularly well. He is a serviceable Fantasy player who should at least have a bench spot in most fantasy rosters.

**Outfielders**:
Shogo Akiyama, age 31, eligible at OF
2019 Stats: Played in Japan
Akiyama has posted particularly impressive numbers over the past five seasons in Japan, hitting for a .320/.398/.497 slash line while averaging 19 home runs and 16 steals. It always remains to

be seen how his tools will translate from overseas, but double-digit home runs and steals alongside a strong, .300-plus average is certainly a reasonable expectation. He is expected to bat lead-off for the Reds.

Aristides Aquino, age 26, eligible at OF
2019 Stats: 225 PA, 19 HR, 31 Runs, 47 RBI, 7 SB, .259/.316/.576
After the Reds brought him to the big league club in August, Aquino hit three home runs in a game against the Cubs. In the first 17 games, Aquino blasted 11 home runs. However, he struggled in September, batting only .167 but did hit five home runs. Which Aquino will fantasy owners see in 2020? He should be considered a top 50 fantasy outfielder with a ton of upside

Jesse Winker, age 26, eligible at OF
2019 Stats: 384 PA, 16 HR, 51 Runs, 38 RBI, 0 SB, .269/.357/.473
In his past two seasons for the Reds, injuries have kept outfielder Jesse Winker from being totally productive. Winker had an encouraging September of 2019 when he batted .364 over his final 17 games. Playing time might be an issue in the crowded Red outfield but he is worthy of taking a look at in the later rounds of drafts.

Nick Senzel, age 24, eligible at OF
2019 Stats: 414 PA, 12 HR, 55 Runs, 42 RBI, 14 SB, .256/.315/.427
In September, Senzel was diagnosed with a torn labrum in his left shoulder and was shut down for the rest of the season. Senzel came into 2019 as one of the top prospects in baseball, but playing time may be an issue. However, he has so much talent that he could be drafted as a bench player to see if he can garner some playing time, as there have been rumblings out of Cincinnati that he might get a look at shortstop.

Josh VanMeter, age 25, eligible at OF
2019 Stats: 260 PA, 8 HR, 33 Runs, 23 RBI, 9 SB, .237/.327/.408
Too many mouths to feed in the Reds outfield to have any significant fantasy value

Phillip Ervin, age 27, eligible at OF
2019 Stats: 260 PA, 7 HR, 30 Runs, 23 RBI, 4 SB, .271/.331/.466
Sure, he had a breakout season in 2019 but where will he fit in the crowded Red's outfield. Maybe worth a bench spot, especially in deeper leagues to see how this plays out.

**Starters:**
Sonny Gray, age 30, RHP
2019 Stats: 175.1 IP, 205 K, 11 W, 2.87 ERA, 1.08 WHIP
After struggling with the Yankees, Gray changed his approach to pitching and he seemed to get more comfortable in his ability by posting a 2.12 ERA and .162 BA in the second half, both top-three numbers in the NL. If the new look Sonny Gray continues, he would make an excellent roster addition as a top 100 player in fantasy.

Luis Castillo, age 27, RHP
2019 Stats: 190.2 IP, 226 K, 15 W, 3.40 ERA, 1.14 WHIP
In 2019 Luis Castillo saw a decline in performance in the second half, with a 4.78 ERA after the all-star break. This could have been due to workload, which has been an issue in the past.

Keeping things in check, as well as having improved run support behind him should make him a top 15 pitcher in fantasy for 2020.

Trevor Bauer, age 29, RHP
2019 Stats: 213 IP, 253 K, 11 W, 4.48 ERA, 1.25 WHIP
Here is what to expect from Bauer: a strikeout artist who makes positive contributions in ERA and doesn't leave the game after five innings. This will make him selected within the top 80 of most fantasy drafts and will make a solid rotation addition to any fantasy roster.

Anthony DeSclafani, age 29, RHP
2019 Stats: 166.2 IP, 167 K, 9 W, 3.89 ERA, 1,20 WHIP
One of the most steady pitchers for the Reds last season was DeSclafani. After an injury-plagued couple of years, he proved that he could remain healthy for a season, and put together a quality one at that. He should be one of the better under the radar selections on draft day and could be a steal in the mid-rounds.

Wade Miley, age 33, LHP
2019 Stats: 167.1 IP, 140 K, 14 W, 3.98 ERA, 1.34 WHIP
Miley got off to a sizzling start in 2019, going 7-4 with a 3.28 ERA over 18 starts. After the break, his ERA ballooned to 5.07 over 15 outings. Which Miley appears in 2020? The durable pitcher has not missed a start since July 12, 2018. Since the start of that season, he has thrown 248 innings with a 3.52 ERA. He is worthy of at least a bench spot in most fantasy formats.

**Relievers:**
Raisel Iglesias, age 30, RHP
2019 Stats: 67 IP, 89 K, 3 W, 34 Sv, 4.16 ERA, 1.22 WHIP
An improved Reds team should give him even more chances to earn saves. This should make him among the top 10 fantasy relievers in 2020.

Michael Lorenzen, age 28, RHP, OF
2019 Stats: 83.1 IP, 85 K, 1 W, 7Sv, 2.92 ERA, 1.15 WHIP
Lorenzen put together a career-year, leading the relievers in ERA (2.92), games played (73), innings pitched (83.1), and was second in strikeouts (85) to Iglesias. Holds and an occasional save makes him valuable in deeper leagues.

Amir Garrett, age 27, LHP
2019 Stats: 56 IP, 78 K, 5 W, 3.21 ERA, 1.41 WHIP
An injury shelved Garrett for a period of time before the All-Star break, and the southpaw never returned to form following his return. Has little fantasy value except for holds.

Robert Stephenson, age 27, RHP
2019 Stats: 64.2 IP, 81 K, 3 W, 3.76 ERA, 1.04 WHIP
Stephenson put together a solid season in 2019 with career-highs in ERA and WHIP but for fantasy, his only value is for holds.

Jose De Leon, age 27, RHP

2019 Stats: 4 IP, 7 K, 1 W, 2.25 ERA, 1.50 WHIP
Once a top prospect, De León has only logged 23 2/3 innings in the majors since debuting in 2016 due to injuries. He is mostly a guy to keep on your radar in case he gets a chance to start in the Reds talented lineup.

Lucas Sims, age 26, RHP
2019 Stats: 43 IP, 57 K, 2 W, 4.60 ERA, 1.16 WHIP
No fantasy value

Cody Reed, age 26, LHP
2019 Stats: 6.1 IP, 7 K, 0 W, 1.42 ERA, 1.11 WHIP
No fantasy value

Sal Romano, age 26, RHP
2019 Stats: 16.1 IP, 16 K, 1 W, 2Sv, 7.71 ERA, 1.84 WHIP
No fantasy value

# Cincinnati Reds Prospects
## By Matt Thompson

**1. Nick Lodolo- LHP**

He was the top arm off the board in the 2019 draft, going seventh overall. Tall, lanky left-hander reminds me of Andrew Miller physically, and also has a similar arm slot, but significantly better command. In fact, after getting drafted Lodolo threw 18 innings for the Reds across two levels of A-ball, and he struck out 30 and didn't walk a hitter. His fastball sits low-90s with arm-side run and can touch 95. His slider has a big sweeping break and is a plus pitch and he also mixes in an average changeup. With the Driveline staff now working closely with the Reds I expect Lodolo to add a tick or two to the heater, and can he be a number two starter. **ETA: 2021.**

**2. Jonathan India- 3B**

A bit of the prospect shine has worn off of India since the Reds selected him with the fifth overall pick in 2018. His best offensive tool is his OBP ability, and the rest of his game falls in the "bucket of fives" category. Every tool is average, but nothing is plus. His raw power is above-average, as is his defensive ability and arm. The hit tool is average and there are some concerns with velocity here. He does a lot of things well, but nothing well enough to push Suarez off of third. He's not going to play short, and potentially settles into a utility role as the Reds are currently constructed. **ETA: 2021.**

**3. Hunter Greene- RHP**

You can make a case for Hunter Greene as the number one fantasy prospect on this list, but I'm slotting him behind India as he's likely to miss most of 2020 while rehabbing from Tommy John surgery. I'm really excited about the prospects of Greene in Cincinnati with the addition of Kyle Boddy and the Driveline philosophy. He already has the potential 80-grade heater, and his secondaries lack consistency. If anyone can maximize his stuff and get his secondaries the ideal shape and spin, it's Boddy. Greene already gets praise for one of the most athletic and smooth deliveries, and we're just waiting for his slider and changeup to return. His slider had shown flashes prior to the elbow injury, but the change was just fringy. Greene has number one starter upside, and if he does pitch this year it will likely be in High-A. **ETA: 2022.**

**4. Jose Garcia- SS**

The Reds gave Garcia $5 million to sign out of Cuba in 2017, and his first professional season in 2018 didn't go well. He put it together in 2019 and his offensive gaines paired with his strong defensive skills make him a future big league starter at shortstop. It's an above-average hit tool with gap-to-gap power. He makes contact at a strong clip, and has a wiry frame that could add a bit of a power element to his game as well. It's an aggressive offensive approach and he will be prone to peaks and valleys. He's a future starting shortstop with a strong average, 15 or so homers and 10-12 steals. He should start 2020 in Double-A. **ETA: 2021.**

**5. Tyler Callihan- 3B/2B**

The Reds selected Callihan in the third round this past June and gave him $1.5 million to sign. He was up there with Riley Greene as one of the best prep bats in the country, and even brings plus raw power to the table. The issue here is he doesn't have a true defensive home. He lacks the lateral quickness to stick long term at second, and that may be the case at third as well. Even if he is a first baseman long term, a lefty that hits the ball in the air as often as he does is a good fit in that park. **ETA: 2023.**

### 6. Tyler Stephenson- C
Two straight healthy seasons have led to two straight seasons with above league average offensive production. Stephenson has battled health issues throughout his professional career, and had a career year in Double-A. He stings the ball with regularity, and his higher than average BABIP numbers are a product of him punishing baseballs. Despite his size his best tool is his hit tool, and he's a hit over power backstop. He's a line drive hitter and should hit 20+ homers with strong averages. His strong walk rates and plate skills provide more value in OBP formats as well. Stephenson's big frame can cause receiving and defensive issues, and his lack of athleticism hurts him defensively. He's an ideal candidate to pair with Tucker Barnhart, or another defensive ace. Should start 2020 in Triple-A. **ETA: 2021.**

### 7. Rece Hinds- 3B
The IMG product is a high risk with a potential chance for a huge payoff. Hinds is an elite athlete with a large frame, built like an NBA two guard. His raw power is 80-grade, but his immature hit tool stands in his way. He missed all but three games and was robbed of all that development time by a quad injury, and Hinds isn't likely to see game action until the summer. He's an above average runner now that likely fills out and is below average at peak. **ETA: 2023.**

### 8. Lyon Richardson- RHP
There was some draft buzz surrounding Richardson with the belief he could be a potential two-way player, but then he hit 97 on the mound and became a day one prospect as a pitcher. The fastball has backed up some since, and sits 90-94 and lacks movement. His slider is an above-average pitch with his curve and change being average offerings. The focus here is just building innings, and Richardson did that in the Midwest League in 2019. He will be sent to the Florida State League in 2020, and will stay there all year putting up above average numbers. He's a future mid-rotation arm for me. **ETA: 2022.**

### 9. Mike Siani- OF
Siani is a defensive artist in center, and his best offensive trait is his game changing speed. That carries value, but there's some upside in the bat. He makes contact at an above-average rate, but his exit velocity numbers are lacking because he doesn't square the ball up as often as you'd like. If Siani can get extended he can drive the ball, but right now there isn't much reason to fear him in the box. Right now you roster for steals with the hope the bat catches up. His elite defense keeps him in the lineup. **ETA: 2022.**

### 10. Stuart Fairchild- OF

The Wake Forest product has above-average raw power and above-average speed, and could be a sneaky power source if he gets regular at bats in Cincinnati. He starts with his hands low at the plate, and hits the ball in the air to his pull-side. He knows his strengths. He's not a very efficient thief on the basepaths, so don't count on speed showing up too much in the future. Nice under the radar sneaky add. **ETA: 2022.**

**Next Five:**
Ivan Johnson- SS/2B
Lyon Richardson- RHP
Braylin Minier- SS
Jacob Heatherly- LHP
Tony Santillan- RHP

**Top Five in FYPDs:**
Nick Lodolo- LHP
Tyler Callihan- 3B/2B
Rece Hinds- 3B
Ivan Johnson- SS/2B
Braylin Minier- SS

## Milwaukee Brewers Team Preview
By Walter McMichael

**Projected Order:**
1- Eric Sogard, 3B
2- Lorenzo Cain, OF
3- Christian Yelich, OF
4- Keston Hiura, 2B
5- Ryan Braun, OF
6- Omar Narváez, C
7- Justin Smoak, 1B
8- Luis Urias, SS


**Projected Bench:**
Manny Piña, C
Ryon Healy, 1B/3B
Orlando Arcia, SS
Ben Gamel, OF
Avisail Garcia,OF


**Projected Rotation:**
Brandon Woodruff, RHP
Adrian Houser, RHP
Brett Anderson, LHP
Josh Lindbloom, RHP
Eric Lauer, LHP


**Bullpen**:
Josh Hader, LHP
Brent Suter, LHP
Corbin Burnes, RHP
Alex Claudio, LHP
Freddy Peralta, RHP
Ray Black, RHP
Deolis Guerra, RHP
Jake Faria, RHP


**Catchers:**
Omar Narváez, age 28, eligible at C
2019 Stats: 482 PA, 22 HR, 63 Runs, 55 RBI, 0 SB, .278/.353/.460
Narváez proved to be one of the true breakouts at the catcher position in 2019. While he was overshadowed by fellow breakouts Mitch Garver and Christian Vazquez, his price is also lower than theirs going into 2020. The move to Milwaukee should be a net positive as the Brewers lineup and park provide upgrades over the Mariners'. His power, plate discipline, and strong lineup make him one of my targets at catcher in 2020.

Manny Piña, age 32, eligible at C

2019 Stats: 179 PA, 7 HR, 10 Runs, 25 RBI, 0 SB, .228/.313/.411

Piña has had fantasy relevance in the past as a fill-in catcher but he will have no fantasy value in 2020 other than a weekly streamer against bad pitching if Narváez gets injured.


**Infielders:**

Justin Smoak, age 33, eligible at 1B

2019 Stats: 500 PA, 22 HR, 54 Runs, 61 RBI, 0 SB, .208/.342/.406

Smoak had a maddening 2019 as he combined elite plate discipline with an inability to hit for power. He looks to fill the Eric Thames role in the Brewers lineup which is a useful streaming option when the Brewers face a right-handed heavy schedule. Outside of those weeks, I do not see enough playing time to make Smoak mixed-league viable.


Keston Hiura age 23, eligible at 2B

2019 Stats: 348 PA, 19 HR, 51 Runs, 49 RBI, 9 SB, .303/.368/.570

Keston Hiura was one of the best rookies in a loaded 2019 rookie class. He has always combined elite hitting ability with above average power. His debut was no different and his sophomore year should be more of the same. The strikeout rate in the majors is a cause for concern so the batting average will regress but Hiura has the makings to provide top 30 value at the thin 2B position.


Eric Sogard, age 33, eligible at 2B

2019 Stats: 442 PA, 13 HR, 59 Runs, 40 RBI, 8 SB, .290/.353/.457

Eric "Prospect Called Up Before Vlad Jr." Sogard actually put together a solid season for the Blue Jays. He projects to slot in as the Brewers starting 3B and leadoff hitter to start the season. I mentioned before the 2B position is very shallow and if it is late in the draft and your team is needing runs, some batting average, and some speed, Sogard can fill the hole until a long-term solution is found off the waiver wire.


Luis Urias, age 22, eligible at 2B/SS

2019 Stats: 249 PA, 4 HR, 27 Runs, 24 RBI, 0 SB, .223/.329/.326

The former Padres prospect was shipped over to the Brewers in the Trent Grisham trade. Urias has always shown an ability to make good contact and due to the contact, has flashed some in-game power. His lack of speed does cap his upside and the current lineup projection of hitting 8th limits his counting stats. I believe he will eventually replace Sogard at the top of the order and be a good source of batting average and runs.


Ryon Healy, age 28, eligible at 3B

2019 Stats: 187 PA, 7 HR, 24 Runs, 26 RBI, 0 SB, .237/.289/.456

Healy appears to be Smoak's platoon partner at 1B. He is an empty power hitter who should remain on the waiver wire outside of the deepest of leagues.


Orlando Arcia, age 25, eligible at SS

2019 Stats: 546 PA, 15 HR, 51 Runs, 59 RBI, 8 SB, .223/.283/.350

At first glance, Arcia appears to have some appeal due to the power and speed combination but I think it is time to admit he just cannot hit at the MLB level. He is not even a streamer if one of the other MIs are injured.

**Outfielders**:
Christian Yelich, age 28, eligible at OF
2019 Stats: 580 PA, 44 HR, 100 Runs, 97 RBI, 30 SB, .329/.429/.671
What more can be said about how great Christian Yelich is? I have him as my #1 overall player coming into 2020 as he has been performing over the past two seasons. His power, speed, and batting average are unmatched by any other player in the pool. Fantasy owners should happily take him within the top three overall.

Lorenzo Cain, age 33, eligible at OF
2019 Stats: 623 PA, 11 HR, 75 Runs, 48 RBI, 18 SB, .260/.325/.372
Cain regressed in 2019 after an awesome 2018 season. The reason for regression is what fantasy owners need to decide when going into the draft. If it was due to injury, he's coming at a major bargain. If it was due to age, he should not be touched at his current price. SInce much of his value is tied into his speed and he does not seem to be aging well, I am personally avoiding him.

Ryan Braun, age 36, eligible at OF
2019 Stats: 508 PA, 22 HR, 70 Runs, 75 RBI, 11 SB, .285/.343/.505
Ryan Braun has continued to churn out solid fantasy seasons even while being one of the most frustrating players to own with the constant DTD tags after lineups lock. There are rumors he could be the 1B platoon partner with Smoak and this would allow him to keep his PAs up even if the likely ceiling is ~500. He is a safe bet for 20 HRs and 10 SBs but there is little upside for more.

Avisail Garcia, age 28, eligible at OF
2019 Stats: 530 PA, 20 HR, 61 Runs, 72 RBI, 10 SB, .282/.332/.464
Garcia has never lived up to the "Little Miggy" hype but he has a very interesting fantasy profile. The issue is he does not have full-time playing time at the moment but the associated cost reflects it. He has similar skills to Braun but the upside to put up a full season of PAs. He is a definite buy at his current cost.

Ben Gamel, age 27, eligible at OF
2019 Stats: 356 PA, 7 HR, 47 Runs, 33 RBI, 2 SB, .248/.337/.373
Gamel is strictly a platoon bat with very little fantasy upside and there is not much power or speed.

**Starters**:
Brandon Woodruff, age 27, RHP
2019 Stats: 121.2 IP, 143 K, 11 W, 3.62 ERA, 1.14 WHIP
Woodruff is not what you would expect of a staff ace of a playoff hopeful but he proved his supporters correct with his breakout 2019. An oblique injury forced him to miss a significant portion of the season but should be a concern coming into 2020. Woodruff is currently being drafted as a low-end SP2 and I think there is actually room for profit at the price since I believe he has the stuff to be an SP1 (below ace tier) for fantasy purposes.

Adrian Houser, age 27, RHP
2019 Stats: 111.1 IP, 117 K, 6 W, 3.72 ERA, 1.24 WHIP

Houser was one of the Brewers' random SP contributors they seem to have every season. His splits as an SP are not very encouraging with a 4.57 ERA, 1.35 WHIP, and 84 Ks in 80.2 IP and Steamer does not believe he will be a good SP in 2019. I think a move to the pen where he dominated is more likely than him being a fantasy option as a SP.

Brett Anderson, age 32, LHP
2019 Stats: 176 IP, 90 K, 13 W, 3.89 ERA, 1.31 WHIP
It seems like Anderson has been around forever (he did debut in 2009) and he continues to be a solid real baseball innings eater. He is irrelevant for fantasy since he lacks strikeout upside and the ratios do not make up for it.

Josh Lindblom, age 32, RHP
2019 Stats: No stats
Lindblom, last seen in the Pirates organization, has dominated the KBO over the past three seasons, including last season where he had a 2.50 ERA and 189 Ks in 194.2 IP. Now a 32-year-old returning to the majors, I have a hard time seeing him producing much at the MLB level since the KBO roughly equates to AA competition. I will not be taking a late-round flier on Lindblom.

Eric Lauer, age 24, LHP
2019 Stats: 149.2 IP, 138 K, 8 W, 4.45 ERA, 1.40 WHIP
Lauer is the other piece who came to Milwaukee in the Urias-Grisham deal. He should be a solid innings-eater type for the Brewers but as a fly-ball pitcher in Milwaukee with moderate strikeout upside, there is little fantasy appeal.

**Relievers:**
Josh Hader, age 25, LHP
2019 Stats: 75.2 IP, 138 K, 3 W, 2.62 ERA, 0.081 WHIP
Hader is the best RP in the game with his ridiculous 47.8 K% (six percentage points better than second place Nick Anderson!!!). He is being drafted as such among relief pitchers but is going much lower than the first RP goes off the board over the past few seasons. This is the year to take the slight bargain and invest in the best closer in baseball and take Josh Hader.

Brent Suter, age 30, LHP
2019 Stats: 18.1 IP, 15 K, 4 W, 0.49 ERA, 0.60 WHIP
Speaking of random Brewers contributors, how about a lefty, former SP who throws an 87 mph fastball 78% of the time dominating over 18 relief innings? I honestly do not know how or why it happened but it will not again. Suter seems poised to be the Brewers' two plus inning middle reliever to come in after starters. There is no fantasy value here.

Corbin Burnes, age 25, RHP
2019 Stats: 49 IP, 70 K, 1 W, 8.82 ERA, 1.84 WHIP
Burnes was a popular wide-awake "sleeper" coming into 2019 and had a disastrous season. They moved him to the bullpen and it did not help his struggled with poor batted ball quality. Since the price is currently free, he is the type of post-hype sleeper I like to take a last round flier on to see if the talent everyone loved last year is there.

Alex Claudio, age 28, LHP

2019 Stats: 62 IP, 44 K, 2 W, 4.06 ERA, 1.31 WHIP

Claudio is a career junk ball middle-reliever who is valuable in real baseball but has no value in fantasy.

Freddy Peralta, age 23, RHP

2019 Stats: 85 IP, 115 K, 7 W, 5.29 ERA, 1.46 WHIP

Peralta, like Burnes, was a popular "sleeper" coming into 2019 who was not quite as bad but still struggled mightily. Peralta is a two-pitch pitcher and it could be what limits his upside but I will be targeting him at his depressed price since I still very much believe in his strikeout upside.

Ray Black, age 29, RHP

2019 Stats: 16 IP, 18 K, 0 W, 5.06 ERA, 1.44 WHIP

Ray Black's fastball velocity, averaged 98 mph, would lead you to believe he has the makings of a dominant closer but it essentially his only pitch and lacks the command to truly harness his natural talent.

Deolis Guerra, age 30, RHP

2019 Stats: 0.2 IP, 0 K, 0 W, 54.00 ERA, 6.00 WHIP

Guerra is a AAAA reliever who will be one of the first off the roster when an upgrade is found.

Jake Faria, age 26, RHP

2019 Stats: 18.2 IP, 19 K, 0 W, 6.75 ERA, 2.14 WHIP

Faria was an interesting prospect but was never able to follow up on his strong debut with Tampa Bay in 2017. He is strictly a long-reliever at this point in his career with no fantasy value.

# Milwaukee Brewers Prospects
## By Matt Thompson

### 1. Brice Turang- SS

For what Turang lacks in ceiling he makes up for in floor. The 2018 first rounder brings a blend of speed, contact ability, strong on-base skills and above-average defense. Turang is going to stick at shortstop due to his hands and range, and is a strong candidate to hit at the top of a big league order. He will use all fields, and understands his skills. He will go the other way more than he pulls the ball, but he needs to pull the ball to hit double digit homers in a season. He's an everyday shortstop that can hit .270 with strong OBPs, 10-12 homers and 20+ steals at peak, while adding even more value with the glove. **ETA: 2021.**

### 2. Hedbert Perez- OF

Hedbert's stock is very much on the up and up, and hopefully you got in when it was free. Now, he's going to cost you a top 40-50 pick. Perez is the son of a big leaguer and has five tool potential. Above-average skills offensively with above-average defense is the hope here. Perez could start his career in the AZL, which would be aggressive for a 2019 J2. **ETA: Arrived.**

### 3. Ethan Small- LHP

The Brewers took Small in the first round in 2019 out of Mississippi State. He's a fiery southpaw with pitchability for days. The arsenal is extremely fastball heavy, and he compliments it with an above-average slider and a changeup. The change was a plus pitch in 2018 but he's had some issues with the consistency of it and hopefully it can get back to that in 2020. Small will challenge anyone and everyone in the box. He's got his quirks but it's hard to argue with the results. **ETA: 2021.**

### 4. Eduardo Garcia- SS

This is an aggressive ranking on Garcia. The 17-year-old shortstop made his debut in the DSL last summer but ended up fracturing his right ankle sliding into a base. I love how projectable the frame is, at a lean 6-foot-2 and hopefully he can add some power to his offensive game. His offensive game is built around contact and speed, but the real headliner to his profile is the advanced defensive skills he's already flashed. We will find out much more about Garcia in a few months, but if you have room for a dart throw this isn't a bad one. **ETA: 2023.**

### 5. Antoine Kelly- LHP

The long-limbed, athletic lefty was the Brewers second round pick out of Wabash Valley Junior College in Illinois. He sits in the mid-90s with the heater and has hit triple digits a few times. That's pretty much where the positive stuff ends (for now), because Kelly lacks any secondary pitches that can get hitters out for a sustained period. The command is also fringe at the moment, and there is tremendous reliever risk here. **ETA: 2023.**

### 6. Mario Feliciano- C

Feliciano reached Double-A as a 20-year-old when he got a brief cup of coffee after a strong season in the Carolina League. He started to tap into his raw power blowing by his previous career high of four homers in a season by hitting 19. The raw power is above-average and there's enough here to swat 20-22 homers when you factor in the playing time subtraction for catchers. The new power came at a price though, and more strikeouts and less overall contact followed him. Defensively he needs some polishing, but there's enough here to believe he can handle the position as he matures. He will start 2020 in Double-A. **ETA: 2021.**

### 7. Tristen Lutz- OF

Lutz spent the year in High-A, and the tough offensive environment took a toll on the slugger as he was limited to just 13 homers in 420 at-bats. Lutz is a traditional masher and the 25-30 homer appeal comes with considerable strikeout and batting average risk. He will take a walk to mitigate the BA hit, and his strong arm makes him a fit for right field. Lutz will start 2020 in Double-A. **ETA: 2021.**

### 8. Aaron Ashby- LHP

The Brewers took Ashby from the junior-college ranks in the fourth round in 2018. Ashby dominated the Midwest League in 2018, while limiting walks and missing bats. He repeated the level to begin 2019, and while the strikeouts were there the walks took a steep jump. Ashby has three above-average offerings in his low-90s heater, curveball and changeup. He's a future bat-missing number three starter. **ETA: 2021.**

### 9. Corey Ray- OF

I liked Ray a lot out of Louisville when the Brewers took him with the fifth pick in the 2016 draft. It became apparent fairly quickly that Ray's swing wasn't made for pro ball and that he was in danger of just not hitting enough. Then he went to Double-A in 2018 and won the MVP of the Southern League with an eye popping, .241/.325/.479 line with 27 homers and 37 stolen bases. I bought back in, and his 2019 was off the rails before it started as he dealt with a myriad of finger and hand injuries that created essentially a lost season for the lefty. Ray is a plus runner, but that hasn't translated to the defensive side either as he takes subpar routes consistently and has a fringy arm. Ray was added to the 40-man this winter, and could be a fourth outfielder at some point in 2020 if he hits. **ETA: 2020.**

### 10. Drew Rasmussen- RHP

Despite having two Tommy John surgeries Rasmussen can still reach back and hit 99 on the gun. The former Oregon State Beaver compliments the fastball with a late breaking slider and changeup. The frame has the looks of an innings eating one, but the elbow has failed him twice, blowing out on two separate occasions. Rasmussen should move quickly due to health concerns. **ETA: 2020.**

**Next Five:**
Thomas Dillard- OF/1B
Luis Medina- OF

Joe Gray Jr.- OF
Max Lazar- RHP
Zack Brown- RHP

**Top Five in FYPDs:**
Hedbert Perez- OF
Ethan Small- LHP
Antoine Kelly- LHP
Thomas Dillard- OF/1B
Luis Medina- OF

## Pittsburgh Pirates Team Preview
### By Andrew Dewhirst

**Projected Order:**
1- Bryan Reynolds - LF
2. Starling Marte - CF
3- Gregory Polanco - RF
4- Josh Bell - 1B
5- Colin Moran - 3B
6- Kevin Newman - SS
7- Adam Frazier - 2B
8- Jacob Stallings - C

**Projected Bench:**
Luke Maile - C
Erik Gonzalez - INF
Kevin Kramer - INF/OF
Jose Osuna - INF/OF
Pablo Reyes - OF/INF

**Projected Rotation:**
Chris Archer, RHP
Joe Musgrove, RHP
Steven Brault, LHP
Trevor Williams, RHP
Mitch Keller, RHP

**Bullpen:**
Keone Kela, RHP
Kyle Crick, RHP
RIchard Rodriguez, RHP
Michael Feliz, RHP
Chris Stratton, RHP
Nick Burdi, RHP
Dovydas Neverauskas, RHP
Clay Holmes, RHP

**Catchers:**
Jacob Stallings, age 30, eligible at C
2019 Stats: 210 PAs, 6 HRs, 26 Runs, 13 RBIs, 0 SBs, .262/.325/.382
Stallings is a defense-first catcher that offers little fantasy value in 2020. I would avoid him in all formats.

Luke Maile, age 28, eligible at C
2019 Stats: 129 PAs, 2 HRs, 9 Runs, 9 RBIs, 1 SBs, .151/.205/.235
There is little reason to consider Maile in your drafts. His production in a more hitter-friendly division last year was abysmal, so the move to Pittsburgh isn't likely to create more production.

**Infielders**:
Josh Bell, age 27, eligible at 1B
2019 Stats: 613 PAs, 37 HRs, 94 Runs, 116 RBIs, 0 SBs, .277/.367/.569
Launch Angle changes(up to 13%), and likely others, lead to a great year for Bell. In 2019 he was near the top of the league in exit velocity, hard hit percentage, xBA, xwOBA, and xSLG. I feel like you should see similar production in 2020, as his gains should be repeatable.

Adam Frazier, age 28, eligible at 2B, OF
2019 Stats: 608 PAs, 10 HR, 80 Runs, 50 RBIs, 5 SB, .278/.336/.417
While Frazier isn't sexy, he can be valuable leagues larger than 15 teams or NL-only, as his average is stable, and he should continue to provide some run production.

Colin Moran, age 27, eligible at 3B
2018 Stats: 503 PAs, 13 HR, 46 Runs, 80 RBIs, 0 SB, .277/.322/.429
Moran continues to be not overly useful in teams with 15 teams or less. His lack of power really hurts his profile. You can consider him in NL only, and really deep leagues as his average is stable, but you will want to offset that average with someone who can provide the power you're going to need.

Kevin Newman, age 25, eligible at 3B/OF
2019 Stats: 531 PAs, 12 HR, 61 Runs, 64 RBI's, 16 SB, .308/.353/.446
Newman is a player that is worth targeting for your MI spot. He has a solid average and is going to provide you with above-average steals numbers. The power isn't great, but if he can find himself in the top half of the lineup, you could see a big jump in his run and RBI totals.

Erik Gonzalez, age 28, eligible at SS
2019 Stats: 156 PAs, 1 HR, 15 Runs, 6 RBI's, 4 SB, .254/.301/.317
The best recommendation I can make to you if you are reading this right now is to keep going down the page. Gonzalez will have no value to you in fantasy this year in any league size or type.

Jose Osuna, age 27, eligible at 1B/OF
2019 Stats: 285 PAs, 10 HR, 41 Runs, 36 RBI's, 0 SB, .264/.310/.456
Without an injury to Josh Bell, it's hard to see where Osuna gets enough playing time to make any sort of impact in 2020. He shouldn't be on your draft radar.

**Outfielders**:
Bryan Reynolds, age 24, eligible at OF
2019 Stats: 546 PAs, 16 HRs, 83 Runs, 68 RBIs, 3 SBs, .314/.377/.503
At the top of the Pirates lineup, Reynolds is going to have a lot of value. His average should be steady, and around 0.300, and he should provide you with enough counting stats to make him viable in all leagues 10 teams or larger.

Starling Marte, age 31, eligible at OF
2019 Stats: 586 PAs, 23 HRs, 97 Runs, 82 RBIs, 25 SBs, .295/.342/.503

Another year, another year where Starling Marte is a top 30 performer. He quietly went about having a 20/20 season while hitting for a good average and helping you in all 5 categories. His profile hasn't changed, and he had his highest hard hit% in years last year.

Gregory Polanco, age 28, eligible at OF
2019 Stats: 167 PAs, 6 HRs, 23 Runs, 17 RBIs, 3 SBs, .242/.301/.425
Health continues to be an issue for Polanco after just 167 PA's last year. When healthy, Polanco could be a 20/10 bat or more, but you also have to consider this he can also be a lost draft pick.

Pablo Reyes, age 26, eligible at OF
2019 Stats: 157 PAs, 2 HR, 18 Runs, 19 RBI's, 1 SB, .203/.274/.322
There isn't a real reason to look at Pablo Reyes in your drafts. He hasn't played much, and when he has, he hasn't been all that good.

**Starters:**

Chris Archer, age 31, RHP
2019 Stats: 119.2 IP, 143 Ks, 3 Wins, 5.19 ERA, 1.41 WHIP
Archer saw his strikeout numbers move up a bit in 2019, however he also saw an uptick in her ERA and his WHIP. The price you will have to pay for Archer is going to be as cheap as it's ever been, and if you can take on the risk with his ratios the strikeout numbers can be helpful.

Trevor Williams, age 27, RHP
2019 Stats: 145.2 IP, 113 Ks, 7 Wins, 5.38 ERA, 1.41 WHIP
Outside of his ERA, and WHIP, Williams did largely what he has done in his successful 2018 campaign. While I noted his success was likely not repeatable this time last year, I think Williams is likely to find himself somewhere in the middle of the two years. This makes him usable in NL only leagues, and that is about it.

Joe Musgrove, age 27, RHP
2019 Stats: 170.1 IP, 157 Ks, 11 Wins, 4.44 ERA, 1.22 WHIP
Musgrove is going to have value in NL only and other formats where innings pitched are useful. With enough volume he could be relevant in 15 team leagues but I wouldn't expect him to be useful in anything smaller.

Steven Brault, age 27, LHP
2019 Stats: 113.1 IP, 100 K's, 4 Wins, 5.16 ERA, 1.50 WHIP
In a larger role in 2019, Brault struggled. I expect his struggles will continue in 2020. He isn't a player you should be looking to draft.

Mitch Keller, age 23, RHP
2019 Stats: 48 IP, 65 Ks, 1 Wins, 7.13 ERA, 1.83 WHIP
Keller is the pitcher on this Pirates squad who has the most upside. He struggled in his 2019 debut, but if he can get his home runs under control he could be useful if he can maintain his strikeout numbers, although I would expect them to regress some this year. He is worth a late round flyer in 2020 in 15 team leagues.

**Relievers:**

Keone Kela, age 26, RHP
29.2 IP, 33 K's, 1 Saves, 2.12 ERA, 1.01 WHIP
The closer job is going to be Kela's to lose. He has experience as a closer, and I expect he should be useful in 12 team leagues and larger this year. He should get you 20+ saves and provide a healthy number of strikeouts.

Richard Rodriguez, age 29,RHP
65.1 IP, 63 K's, 1 Saves, 3.72 ERA, 1.35 WHIP
Rodriguez isn't an arm I would be targeting in any league size in 2020. His strikeout numbers don't warrant the ERA and the WHIP risk.

Kyle Crick, age 27, LHP
49.0 IP, 61 SO, 0 Saves, 4.96 ERA, 1.55 WHIP
Crick needs to get his walk numbers under control if he is going to have any value in 2020. If those numbers can come down from an atrocious 15.5%, then you should see the ERA and WHIP numbers come down to a point where Crick can have value in 15 team leagues, and points leagues.

Chris Stratton, age 29, RHP
76.0 IP, 69 K's, 0 Saves, 5.57 ERA, 1.66 WHIP
I don't expect Stratton to be much more than depth for the Pirates. None of his numbers make me believe that he will produce any value in 2020.

Michael Feliz, age 2, RHP
56.1 IP, 73 K's, 0 Saves, 3.99 ERA, 1.26 WHIP
Feliz has the dynamic duo of things you don't want to see in relievers, giving up walks, and giving up home runs. However, he still managed to produce a decent season for the Pirates in 2019, striking out 30% of his batters while not killing your ERA or WHIP. There is upside here, however it's not a risk you likely need to take on draft day.

Nick Burdi, age 27, RHP
8.2 IP, 17 K's, 0 Saves, 9.35 ERA, 1.62 WHIP
Burdi continues to struggle to stay healthy. He has only pitched 10 innings in the last 2 years. If healthy he could produce some value, but you shouldn't be drafting him.

Dovydas Neverauskas, age 27, RHP
9.1 IP, 10 K's, 0 Saves, 10.61 ERA, 2.36 WHIP
Neverauskas shouldn't be on your fantasy radar in 2020 unless you are required to have a Lithuanian born player.

Clay Holmes, age 26, RHP
50 IP, 56 K's, 0 Saves, 5.58 ERA, 1.62 WHIP
Like much of the Pirates bullpen, walks are a real concern for Holmes. If he gets those under control his numbers should spike, but you shouldn't be looking at him on draft day.

# Pittsburgh Pirates Prospects
## By Matt Thompson

### 1. Oneil Cruz- SS

The 6-foot-7 21-year-old prospect has one of the highest ceilings in the minor leagues, literally and figuratively. Cruz reportedly posts elite exit velocity numbers, and I believe it. His raw power is plus-plus (70 on the 20-80 scale) and he's also a plus runner and is athletic enough defensively to play anywhere behind the pitcher. He even gets positive grades about his ability to play shortstop, but when he fills out it's unlikely he sticks at the position. His hands are good at short, as is the arm so he'd be an ideal fit for third base, but the presence of Hayes likely means right field for Cruz. He's going to swing and miss, but there are enough plate skills and speed to think he still hits for average. The upside here is immense, and the range of realistic outcomes is immensely wide. I'm concerned about the foot injury that robbed Cruz of a chunk of his 2019 season. Bigger guys with foot issues are always concerning. He should start in Triple-A in 2020, with an eye towards the big leagues **ETA: 2021.**

### 2. Mitch Keller- RHP

Just two innings shy of graduating from prospect lists, Keller is the clear, obvious pick for a rebound after a disastrous debut. Watching a Keller start is an interesting exercise. He was prone to one big blow up inning in every start, and it just torpedoed his numbers. He would lose his command after throwing a breaking ball. Go back and watch. Immediately after throwing a breaking ball the next fastball was either a ball or a center-cut heater. The inconsistent arm slot would mess up his timing. Keller has the stuff to be a top-40 starter in 2020. **ETA: Arrived.**

### 3. Ke'Bryan Hayes- 3B

Hayes has moved through the Pirates system one level at a time, and I feel as if there is a bit of prospect fatigue with Hayes. He's a plus runner with elite athleticism and defensive skills. He's one of the best defenders in the minors at any position, and his arm can make all the throws. Offensively he takes a walk, and has a gap-to-gap offensive game. He will hit for a strong average, post elite level OBPs, hit 18-22 homers, hit 30+ doubles and steal 10-12 bases. It's an incredibly useful profile, and while nothing is flashy, he's a plug and play guy. Meaning, you check at the end of the year and are pleased with the production you'll get from him. He is ready for Triple-A in 2020, and hopefully gets a late season taste of the bigs. He's a candidate to break out with the new baseball, if that's still a thing in 2020. **ETA: 2021.**

### 4. Jared Oliva- OF

Oliva was one of the players I came away the most impressed with while I was out at the AFL. He does everything, and has average or better tools across the board. He's an elite base stealing threat that has swiped 69 bases over the last two seasons while only getting caught 18 times. (79%). He's ready for Triple-A in 2020, and the trade of Starling Marte makes him likely the best defensive center fielder in the organization. In addition to his plus speed he has emerging raw power, and is a threat to leave the yard pull-side. He's been hidden in pitcher heavy environments throughout his career, and I'm excited for the University of Arizona product to get to the big leagues. **ETA: 2020.**

### 5. Liover Peguero- SS
Peguero was the latest in the Diamondbacks rich pipeline of shortstops with exciting fantasy tools. He brings a plus hit tool to the table with potential plus raw thump and above-average speed. He should stick at shortstop, but has a stocky build and may fit better at third base. He's already posting exit velo numbers above league average, and that combined with his athleticism makes for an enticing fantasy prospect. **ETA: 2023.**

### 6. Tahnaj Thomas- RHP
The rare-Indians misstep, Tahnaj Thomas is going to breakout in 2020. He knows how to miss bats, and has made huge improvements in his walk rate. His fastball sits in the high-90s, and we have a report I'm working on confirming that said he hit "well over 100" in instructs this fall. His best breaking pitch is his above-average slider, but his curveball has plus potential but lacks consistency now. He's a high waisted, athletic kid that is worth gambling on. He made successful changes to his delivery that allowed him to repeat more consistently, and Thomas has scratched just the tip of what he can become. **ETA: 2023.**

### 7. Quinn Priester- RHP
I tend to traditionally avoid prep arms, but Priester has my attention. I've seen him live, and the arsenal is electric. His fastball can touch 97 and has movement, he will work it up in the zone and as the velo climbs it straightens out. It's particularly lethal at 94-95 due to the movement. He pairs it with a big 12-6 hook and a developing changeup and slider. A two-sport athlete from a cold-weather state, this is the type of athletic arm that intrigues me. He's going to enter a professional organization that's undergone an overhaul this weekend, and a more modern approach to pitching can absolutely do big things for Quinn Priester. **ETA: 2024.**

### 8. Travis Swaggerty- OF
Swaggy-T is a hot button prospect for us over at Prospects Live, if you don't believe me just tag a few of us and ask about him! I'm one of the higher guys on him, and I like his plus power/speed combination to go with his ability to play a strong centerfield. We're split on his defense and some guys on our staff that have seen him love him, others don't defensively. Either way, with the thin depth chart that is the Pirates outfield post Marte trade, Swaggerty is set to seize a spot in as soon as 2021. **ETA: 2022.**

### 9. Brennan Malone- RHP
Malone is a prep arm that we got a lot of collective looks at for Prospects Live, and the consensus here is that he's a potential mid rotation arm. Malone has a mid-90s heater with a 12-6 power curveball, but he's also developing a slider and a change, but those two can't really be relied on right now. It's an athletic delivery that he repeats well, but Malone lacks the ceiling of a front end guy until one of the changeup/slider pops. Nice get for the Pirates in the Marte deal. **ETA: 2023.**

**10. Sammy Siani- OF**

Siani was the Pirates first round pick this past June. He's not considered to be as strong defensively as his brother Mike, but he's still an above-average future big league center fielder. His offensive game right now is gap-to-gap power while drawing walks and steals, but the power is coming. He's going to be 19 for all of 2020, so he's got some time for the power to manifest. He's a future 20/20 candidate with strong OBPs but a potentially weak average around .240. **ETA: 2023.**

**Next Five:**

Alexander Mojica- 3B

Jack Herman- OF

Mason Martin- 1B

Cal Mitchell- OF

Ji-Hwan Bae- 2B

**Top Five in FYPDs:**

Quinn Priester- RHP

Brennan Malone- RHP

Sammy Siani- OF

Jared Triolo- 3B

Matt Gorski- OF

## St. Louis Cardinals Team Preview
By Joe Drake

**Projected Order:**
1- Tommy Edman, LF
2- Kolten Wong, 2B
3- Paul Goldschmidt, 1B
4- Paul DeJong, SS
5- Matt Carpenter, 3B
6- Dexter Fowler, RF
7- Yadier Molina, C
8- Harrison Bader, CF
9- Jose Martinez (DH - In AL Parks)

**Projected Bench:**
Andrew Knizner, C
Rangel Ravelo, 1B
Tyler O'Neill, OF
Yairo Munoz, INF/OF

**Projected Rotation:**
Jack Flaherty, RHP
Carlos Martinez, RHP
Miles Mikolas, RHP
Dakota Hudson, RHP
Adam Wainwright, RHP

**Bullpen:**
Kwang-hyun Kim, LHP
Giovanny Gallegos, RHP
Andrew Miller, LHP
John Brebbia, RHP
John Gant, RHP
Brett Cecil, LHP
Tyler Webb, LHP
Daniel Ponce de Leon, RHP

**Catchers:**
Yadier Molina, age 37, eligible at C
2019 Stats: 452 PA, 10 HR, 45 Runs, 57 RBI, 6 SB, .270/.312/.399
Despite being ancient in catcher years, Yadier Molina continues to be a stalwart at the position. He finished in the top 15 of Runs and RBI and 2nd in steals despite missing 6 weeks on the IL. The batting average was strong, too, ranking 9th among catchers with 250 PAs. Expect similar results from Molina in 2020 and potentially some value here as age will scare others off. Just be aware that his games played trended downward for the 2nd straight year.

Andrew Knizner, age 25, eligible at C

2019 Stats: 58 PA, 2 HR, 7 Runs, 7 RBI, 2 SB, .226/.293/.377

The catcher of the future is still just that unless Yadi misses extended time. Knizner is currently the only other catcher on the roster, so an uptick in PAs is probable, but not enough to move him in roster-able territory.

**Infielders**:

Paul Goldschmidt, age 32, eligible at 1B
2019 Stats: 682 PA, 34 HR, 97 Runs, 97 RBI, 3 SB, .260/.346/.476

2019 was Goldschmidt's worst season since his debut in 2011. It's possible he was pressing to play well for his new team and the second-half surge may indicate that he found his footing in STL. 2020 should look pretty similar but with a return to the norm for the AVG as the plate skills don't appear to have had any major erosion. Draft with confidence this season.

Rangel Ravelo, age 28, eligible at 1B
2019 Stats: 43 PA, 2 HR, 2 Runs, 4 RBI, 0 SB, .205/.256/.410

Ravelo is likely the first guy off the roster should the Cardinals add another hitter in free agency or via trade this winter. Even if he remains on the St. Louis roster, he shouldn't be on yours. Ravelo will see very little playing time behind Goldschmidt and looked lost during the PAs he got in 2019.

Kolten Wong, age 29, eligible at 2B
2019 Stats: 549 PA, 11 HR, 61 Runs, 59 RBI, 24 SB, .285/.361/.423

The 2019 Cardinals ran wild under Mike Shildt's watch and Wong was the biggest beneficiary. In addition to a resurgence at the plate, Wong swiped a career-best 24 bags, too. The AVG probably pulls back near his career levels, but he's a near-lock for 10 HR & 15 SBs with upside for 25-30 SBs with additional PAs from hitting at the top of the lineup.

Paul DeJong, age 26, eligible at SS
2019 Stats: 664 PA, 30 HR, 97 Runs, 78 RBI, 9 SB, .233/.318/.444

DeJong was a solid 4-category contributor at SS in 2019 despite hitting .233. The 9 steals were a pleasant surprise but given his below-average speed, I wouldn't bank on a repeat performance this year. Going forward, Pauly D looks like a 3 category guy who will hit in the middle of a decent lineup. The batting average has fallen off a cliff since 2017 with the BABIP going with it, but Steamer still likes him to rebound to .252. Given that DeJong isn't fast and doesn't hit the ball hard, I'd be more comfortable expecting something around .240.

Yairo Munoz, age 25, eligible at 3B/OF
2019 Stats: 181 PA, 2 HR, 20 Runs, 13 RBI, 8 SB, .267/.298/.355

The best thing about Yairo Munoz is that he could be eligible at 4 different positions by the end of the season. The bad news is, he'll probably never get consistent playing time. Munoz has flashed good contact (.273 AVG) and good speed (13 SB), so he could be a source of stolen bases if DeJong or Wong were to go down for an extended period of time. That said, it's just as likely that Edman moves into the infield and one of the Cardinals' 4000 outfielders gets a shot before Munoz does.

Matt Carpenter, age 34, eligible at 3B
2019 Stats: 492 PA, 15 HR, 59 Runs, 46 RBI, 6 SB, .226/.334/.392

Oh boy, where do we start here? 2019 was a disaster with a capital D. There was a boatload of career-worsts for Carp (K%, HH%, Barrel %, Exit Velo) which led to IL time and inconsistent playing time in the latter half of the season. Despite all that, he still managed a 95 wRC+. What's to like for 2020? The plate skills don't appear to have eroded entirely, he's going to be the starting 3B on Opening Day, and the price is cheap. He should rebound somewhere between 2018 and 19 and if he doesn't, it won't cost you much to find out. There are worse gambles.

Tommy Edman, age 25, eligible at 2B/3B
2019 Stats: 349 PA, 11 HR, 59 Runs, 36 RBI, 15 SB, .304/.350/.500
Cardinals Devil Magic at its finest. Edman was never a heralded prospect (FanGraphs 40 FV) but that didn't stop him from making an impact at the MLB level right away. He played nearly everywhere on the field and racked up double-digit HRs and SBs while hitting .300. Helluva debut. While he doesn't currently qualify there, Edman looks like the Opening Day LF at the moment, and his versatility all but assures him 400+ PAs in 2020 even if the Cardinals happen to bring Ozuna back (or sign another OF). They found creative ways to get him in the lineup in 2019 and I don't see any reason for that to change. Look for another 10/15 season with a 270s AVG from him with room to grow on the steals if the Cardinals get him more PAs.

**Outfielders**:
Dexter Fowler, age 34, eligible at OF
2019 Stats: 574 PA, 19 HR, 69 Runs, 67 RBI, 8 SB, .238/.346/.409
Dex redeemed himself in 2019 after a 2018 season that was so bad that the words to describe it accurately have yet to be invented. That said, there's not much to like here from a fantasy standpoint. The AVG has gone south and likely isn't coming back given the steady increase in K% and SwStr%. The power doesn't stand out (7th percentile Exit Velo) and even on a run-happy team, the SBs didn't come back last year. If he drops from the top of the lineup, which he probably will, the counting stats will fall even further. Steamer likes the track record, but there is no doubt that Dex is on the back half of the aging curve. Watch from a distance.

Tyler O'Neill, age 25, eligible at OF
2019 Stats: 151 PA, 5 HR, 18 Runs, 16 RBI, 1 SB, .262/.311/.411
Tyler O'Neill is a physical specimen with tools out of MLB the Show (70 raw, 10th fastest sprint speed in 2019). He beat AAA to a pulp in 2018. He has also been beaten to a pulp by MLB pitching in his small sample of the big leagues. In his defense, the Cardinals have deployed him sparingly, if not erratically. In 2019, 93 of his 151 PAs came in one month. The remaining 58 were scattered among spot starts and pinch-hitting. During his stint as a starter, he hit .295 with an improved K rate (26.9%) and slugged .466 for a 110 wRC+. O'Neill should be the 4th OF to start the year and the 1st bat off the bench. I wouldn't rule out the chance he wins the LF job out of spring, either. It's worth noting that Jose Martinez is still on the roster and STL still loves him - he's the biggest threat to O'Neill's PT aside from the starters.

Harrison Bader, age 26, eligible at OF
2019 Stats: 406 PA, 12 HR, 54 Runs, 39 RBI, 11 SB, .205/.314/.366
Man, Bader really took a dive in 2019, right? Right?! Well, what if I told you that he hit for slightly more power (ISO .158 -> .161), struck out less (K% 29.3 -> 28.8%), and walked more (7.3% -> 11.3%) than he did in 2018? Not what you expected to hear, I imagine. Yes, the AVG plummeted along with the BABIP and xBA, but his Average Exit Velo and Launch Angle were both better in

2019, as well. Bader's struggles against spin have been well-publicized and will surely be a factor going forward, but the underlying skills are trending in the right direction and his defense is too good not to put him CF. The AVG is risky, but there's an upside for 15 and 25 here if everything clicks. That's nice when you consider he's being drafted outside the top 100 OFs right now.

Jose Martinez, age 31, eligible at OF
2019 Stats: 373 PA, 10 HR, 45 Runs, 42 RBI, 3 SB, .269/.340/.410
I have plenty of fun things to say about Cafecito, but none of them relate to fantasy baseball in 2020. Jose saw his playing time dwindle in 2019 and with a crowded OF and Goldy manning 1st, it is sure to dwindle even more in 2020 as the Cardinals need to see what they're younger guys can do. Unless he's traded, you're hoping for 300 sporadic PAs with a solid AVG and maybe 10 HRs. The outlook would be brighter with regular ABs as a DH for an AL team. Very little upside in STL for him at this point.

Bonus:
Dylan Carlson, age 21, OF
No 2019 Stats
If you're unfamiliar, Dylan Carlson took the minor leagues by storm in 2019 and bulldozed his way to the top of the Cardinals prospect rankings. He was so good that people were clamoring for the 20-year old's inclusion on the playoff roster. While he has yet to crack the 40-man, it's all but a foregone conclusion that Carlson will make his MLB debut at some point in 2020. My best guess is that the Cardinals will let him get a couple months more seasoning at AAA while they sort out their glut of MLB-ready OF talent already on the roster and call up Carlson in late May or Early June. They have zero reason to rush him with so many other options already on the 40-man (O'Neill, Martinez, Arozarena, Thomas). Carlson is currently being drafted as the 81st OF off the board. That makes him one of the first few reserve OFs being taken right now. That's still a little too expensive for someone who might not reach 400 PAs in 2020, in my opinion, but if you are hellbent on rostering him from the jump, there are worse picks you could make.

**Starters:**
Jack Flaherty, age 24, RHP
2019 Stats: 196.1 IP, 231 K, 11 W, 2.75 ERA, 0.97 WHIP
The ultimate tale of two halves. Flaherty was mediocre early on and monstrous to close out the season. What to expect in 2020? Somewhere in between. He took steps forward in K%, BB%, and SwStr% which will help him sustain some of that dominance we saw in the second half and added a full tick of velo on all 5 of his pitches per Statcast. The ERA will probably pull back to the mid-3s based on his FIP (3.46), SIERA (3.68) and Steamer's 2020 projection (3.62). Flaherty looks good for 190 innings and 225+ Ks with very good ratios, but you're going to have to pay for it. He's going in the late second round and will probably rise as we get closer to Opening Day. It may be better to let someone else overpay for his brilliant second half.

Miles Mikolas, age 31, RHP
2019 Stats: 184 IP, 144 K, 9 W, 4.16 ERA, 1.22 WHIP
Magic Mike wasn't quite so magical this time through, but it wasn't due to a major change in his skill set. The K% went up, the SwStr% stayed the same, the BB% only went up a hair... but the HR/FB% skyrocketed from 9.2% to 16.1%. Yowza. The biggest issue appears to be reduced effectiveness from the slider. The wOBA on Mikolas's slider went from .201 in 2018 to .342 in

2019 -- there's your problem. The HR/FB rate should come down a bit in 2020, but I wouldn't bet on a big rebound. Mikolas is a control pitcher with solid stuff -- look for him to eat innings with decent ratios, passable Ks and upside for double-digit wins. At least he won't cost you much.

Dakota Hudson, age 25, RHP
2019 Stats: 174.2 IP, 136 K, 16 W, 3.35 ERA, 1.41 WHIP
Hudson's debut culminated in a beautiful stat line... Don't buy it for a second. Just about every underlying stat and indicator point to Hudson's 2019 success being entirely smoke and mirrors. The sparkling ERA masks a 4.93 FIP and 5.08 SIERA. The K rate was under 20%, the walk rate was over 10%, and his HR/FB was an eye-popping 19.8% -- 1 out of every 5 fly balls went for a home run! A number that high is not just a product of the juiced ball. All that said, Hudson should still be streamable at the least, you're just going to need to temper your expectations and pick your spots. He'll rack up innings and may even tiptoe his way to another good ERA, but the Ks and WHIP are not coming in 2020.

Adam Wainwright, age 38, RHP
2019 Stats: 171.2 IP, 153 K, 14 W, 4.19 ERA, 1.43 WHIP
The Devil Magic seems to work as well for decrepit vets as it does for unknown prospects. That's not to say Waino set the world on fire last year, but he was damn near brilliant in September and October. Nothing against Adam, but I'm certainly not buying that success continuing into 2020. He's just not the man he used to be. You can safely watch from a distance and cherry-pick spot starts when you're in need. No need to spend a draft pick here.

Carlos Martinez, age 28, RHP
2019 Stats: 48.1 IP, 53 K, 4 W, 3.17 ERA, 1.18 WHIP
After moonlighting as closer last year, all signs point to Carlos returning to the rotation for 2020, as long as he is able to. Please note that I'm writing this in December and there may be more recent news confirming this or indicating that he will return to the bullpen. For now, I am assuming that he will start. The last time we saw Carlos as a starter, he was striking out a batter per inning with a low to mid-3s ERA and a WHIP just a tick higher than you'd like. I don't think we can count on that out of the gate in 2020. In all likelihood, Martinez will need a few starts to find his groove before potentially settling into the Carlos we once knew. If he starts the whole year, keep in mind he's thrown just 160 or so innings since the start of 2018. Look for the Cardinals to handle with care -- I doubt he breaks the 150 IP mark by much if at all. What I love about drafting Martinez this year is that you can essentially draft him as a closer right now with the upside of him being a mid-rotation starter for you. Starter or closer, you're going to get value.

**Relievers:**
Kwang-hyun Kim, age 31, LHP
KBO 2019 Stats: 190.1 IP, 180 K, 17 W, 2.51 ERA, 1.24 WHIP
Before we go any further, please note that the stats above are from the KBO. This will be Kim's 1st year in MLB. Though it remains to be seen what his role will be, Kim certainly fills a need for a team without any left-handed starters. The early speculation is that he'll be used as a swingman, starting if/when needed and working out of the pen the remainder of the time. Whether or not Martinez is able to rejoin the rotation could play a large role in how Kim is

deployed. So, what should you expect when he takes the mound? He features a low-90s 4-seamer, a nasty slider, a looping curveball and a forkball. The arsenal is certainly diverse enough to have success as a starter, but the fastball/slider combination appears dominant enough to make him a very effective reliever from the get-go. He's not draft-worthy at the moment, but keep tabs on him if STL decides to see if he can start.

Giovanny Gallegos, age 28, RHP
2019 Stats: 74 IP, 93 K, 3 W, 2.31 ERA, 0.81 WHIP
Gio Gallegos was St. Louis's 2nd most dominant pitcher in 2019, behind Jack Flaherty. He undoubtedly outperformed Carlos Martinez in relief and because of that, he stands a very good chance to break camp as the team's closer in 2020. Jordan Hicks is recovering from Tommy John and I wouldn't expect to see him in the big leagues until the late second half of 2020, if at all. Gallegos was everything you want in a reliever in 2019: K-heavy with low, low ratios. That alone was roster-worthy last year and the potential to be the full time closer on a 90-win club in 2020 should pique your interest even more. He's currently the 81st pitcher off the board, around guys like Sean Doolittle and Marcus Stroman, just ahead of Nick Anderson. If he's announced as the Cardinals' closer for 2020, his ADP will jump even higher.

Andrew Miller, age 35, LHP
2019 Stats: 54.2 IP, 70 K, 6 SV, 4.45 ERA, 1.32 WHIP
Say it with me: Andrew Miller is not the pitcher he used to be. Yes, he looks the same. Yes, his name is the same, but, no, he's not the shutdown reliever he once was. He's 35, after all. Cut him some slack. All that said, if you can stomach the ratios, he will get you Ks and has an outside shot at a handful of saves. Don't forget, the 3-batter minimum rule in 2020 means Miller is either going to face more righties this year or he'll be passed over in situations he would have been summoned in previously.

John Brebbia, age 30, RHP
2019 Stats: 72.2 IP, 87 K, 3 W, 3.59 ERA, 1.18 WHIP
Brebbia is a respectable middle reliever who's good for more than a K per inning and solid ratios. He was one of the regulars out of the pen for the Cardinals in 2019 and should continue to be in 2020.

John Gant, age 27, RHP
2019 Stats: 66.1 IP, 60 K, 11 W, 3.66 ERA, 1.28 WHIP
Yes, the Cardinals like right-handed middle relievers named John. Gant was a step down from his brother-in-name in 2019 across the board except for one category: Wins. Somehow, he squirreled his way into 11 of them. That's more than he had in 2018 when he started 19 games! I would take the under on him getting 11 wins the remainder of his career. Nothing to read into here other than some random win luck.

Tyler Webb, age 29, LHP
2019 Stats: 55 IP, 48 K, 2 W, 3.76 ERA, 1.02 WHIP
Webb was the de facto lefty in relief for STL in 2019 with Miller typically reserved for higher leverage situations. With the new 3-batter minimum and the addition of Kim, I expect Webb to see far less usage in 2020, especially when you consider that he's far less effective against righties than lefties (2019: 3.66 FIP vs L, 5.41 FIP vs R).

Brett Cecil, age 33, LHP
2019 Stats: 0 IP, 0 K, 0 W, 0.00 ERA, 0.00 WHIP
The legend of Brett Cecil lives on in St. Louis. The lefty threw just 32 and ⅔ innings in 2018 and missed all of 2019 recovering from surgery for carpal tunnel. In his last full season of work, in 2017, he struck out 66 in 67.1 innings with a 3.88 ERA and 1.23 WHIP. It's technically possible that nearly 2 years off is exactly what he needed to round into form as a fantasy-relevant reliever... but, you know, maybe not.

Daniel Ponce de Leon, age 28, RHP
2019 Stats: 48.2 IP, 52 K, 1 W, 3.70 ERA, 1.27 WHIP
Unlike the Spanish explorer, it is unlikely that this Ponce de Leon is going to lead an expedition into newfound fantasy success. Ponce will likely serve as a swingman and long reliever again in 2020. His dominance as a starter in AAA gives him a leg up as the likely first guy into the rotation if injury or ineffectiveness strike.

Bonus:
Alex Reyes, age 25, RHP
2019 Stats: 3 IP, 1 K, 0 W, 15.00 ERA, 2.67 WHIP
If you're a glutton for punishment like I am, I know you're going to want to find a reason to roster Alex Reyes in 2020. This is a safe place, friend, we will get through this together. The upside is that for the first time in years, literally, Reyes is supposedly having a completely healthy off-season and is not rehabbing. That might do wonders for his mental state which was not in the best of places when he was punching walls in AAA. Alex still has all the arm talent in the world, but we're getting to the point where you have to wonder if a move to the bullpen will be necessary just to keep him on the mound for a full season. No need to draft, but if you're so inclined, keep him on your watch list and see what he looks like in March. Hey, maybe this is the year, right? ...Right?

## St. Louis Cardinals Prospects
By Matt Thompson

### 1. Dylan Carlson- OF

This is what I mean when I always say that I'm betting on the guy with the advanced plate skills. Breakouts like this happen. Carlson added strength and tweaked his stance and now looks like a future middle of the order bat instead of a fourth outfielder. There's no real weakness to Carlson's game, but there's also nothing here that will blow you away. That being said, he's already spent time in Triple-A and will just be entering his age 21 season. Carlson has a legit chance to break camp with the club out of spring training and is the best all-around outfielder in the organization. **ETA: 2020.**

### 2. Nolan Gorman- 3B

Gorman didn't have a bad year in 2019, but that's the general vibe in the fantasy industry. I'll offer some pushback here though, Gorman put up strong power numbers in two of the most difficult environments for hitters, and did it while being three or four years younger than his peers. Yes the aggressiveness is a problem, and it might stop him from fully tapping into his power. He handles the low pitch well, but pitching him up in the zone gives him fits. He did improve at third and seems likely to stick there now, and I'm excited to see him in an offensive environment in the Texas League. **ETA: 2022.**

### 3. Matthew Liberatore- LHP

The Cardinals acquired Liberatore in an off-season deal sending Jose Martinez and Randy Arozarena to Tampa. Liberatore is a well built lefty, with above-average command and had a successful full season debut only a year after getting drafted in the first round. He has a plus command of his low-90s heater that can hit 97, and he backs it up with a plus curveball, above-average slider and changeup. I actually think his changeup can become his best pitch. The appeal of Liberatore is his high floor. Not too many arms his age have a mid-rotation floor, but that's what we have here in Liberatore. **ETA: 2022.**

### 4. Jhon Torres- OF

The Cardinals challenged Torres with an aggressive full season assignment by sending him to the Midwest League and he faltered, and was sent back to instructional league before getting sent to short season ball. Torres was reworking the swing, and cutting down the big leg kick, and hopefully this is a case of a short term hit for a long term gain. Torres is an elite athlete, with plus raw power and above average speed. He has the makings of a strong future big league right fielder, and middle of the lineup bat. He's always going to swing and miss due to his long limbs and tall frame, but the power is very real. He just needs to get to it more consistently. He should begin the season in the Midwest League. **ETA: 2023.**

### 5. Zack Thompson- LHP

Thompson was the Cardinals first round pick in the 2019 draft out of the University of Kentucky. He would've been off the board prior to the 19th pick, but dropped some due to his history of arm injuries. Despite the injuries he's never gone under the knife. His fastball sits in the low 90s that can touch 97. His slider is his best pitch, but his curveball has made strides since turning pro. He will also mix in a changeup. Despite the injuries Thompson has the makings of a high floor arm. If he stays healthy he's going to start, and he should move quickly because of the previous health concerns. **ETA: 2022.**

### 6. Ivan Herrera- C
The Cardinals aggressively pushed Herrera to High-A and the AFL to end 2019, and he answered the call, positioning himself as the long term successor to Yadier Molina. It's a contact based offensive game now, but based on the exit velocity numbers and the batting practice session I saw in Arizona, its safe to say there's at least average raw power in there to go with an above-average hit tool. Defensively Herrera is still developing, but has shown enough to project as above-average defensively. He should hit for a high average while hitting 15-18 homers at peak, making him a potential top ten fantasy backstop. **ETA: 2022.**

### 7. Tre Fletcher- OF
The tooled-up Fletcher reclassified from the 2020 class to the 2019 class just a few months shy of the draft, and most teams didn't get enough eyes on the tooled up Vanderbilt commit. The Cardinals snagged the cold-weather prep and he immediately became the best athlete in the system. It's potential plus raw and double plus speed, but severe contact issues and raw plate skills need to develop for him to get into the power. Fletcher should play a strong centerfield as well. If you roster Fletcher the only minor league numbers that matter are contact rate and K%, and as long as those numbers are improving you should hold steady. He's so raw that some of the numbers may be ugly as he gets acclimated. Don't panic. **ETA: 2023.**

### 8. Elehuris Montero- 3B
The Cardinals added Montero to the 40-man roster this winter after a disastrous 2019 that saw him completely slowed down due to injuries. Montero can hit, and his first full season run was excellent as he went on to win the Midwest League MVP award. Wrist and hamate injuries as well as a lower body injury took his 2019 season off the rails. I did see him in the AFL and the swing looked better, and more in-sync than previously. His bat-to-ball skills are strong, and the power is above-average. He may or may not stick at third, but his arm is plus and would be wasted if he moved to first base. **ETA: 2021.**

### 9. Justin Williams- OF
Williams has undergone a transformation since his early years as a Diamondbacks prospect. He was a big strong physical kid that showed an ability to hit for average, but it was such a ground ball heavy profile that the power was going to be severely restricted. Fast forward to 2019 and two organizations have attempted to change Williams' swing. The Cardinals may have found something in 2019, as Williams average flyball distance in Triple-A Memphis was an absurd 330

feet. The plate skills are solid and his defense and athleticism have also improved. Williams is on the 40-man, but a big spring could put him in position to seize an outfield job. **ETA: Arrived.**

### 10. Johan Oviedo- RHP

The large-framed Cuban has struggled to consistently throw strikes in the minors, but something changed last season. He was able to command his arsenal more effectively, and he was able to get his off speed pitches over the plate for strikes. He sits 92-95 with the fastball, but has dealt with inconsistent velocity since signing with the Cardinals. His curveball is ahead of his changeup. Oviedo can be a bat missing number three starter at peak. **ETA: 2021.**

**Next Five:**
Andrew Knizner- C
Jose Davila- RHP
Mateo Gil- SS/2B
Malcom Nunez- 3B
Luken Baker- 1B

**Top Five in FYPDs:**
Zack Thompson- LHP
Tre Fletcher- OF
Jose Davila- RHP
Toney Locey- RHP
Jake Burns- C

# Arizona Diamondbacks
## By Gabe Zammit

**Projected Order:**
1- Ketel Marte, OF
2- David Peralta, OF
3- Eduardo Escobar, 2B
4- Christian Walker, 1B
5- Kole Calhoun, OF
6- Nick Ahmed, SS
7- Jake Lamb, 3B
8- Carson Kelly, C

**Projected Bench:**
Stephen Vogt, C
Kevin Cron, 1B
Domingo Leyba, 2B
Ildemaro Vargas, 2B
Tim Locastro, OF

**Projected Rotation:**
Madison Bumgarner, LHP
Mike Leake, RHP
Robbie Ray, LHP
Merrill Kelly, RHP
Luke Weaver, RHP

**Bullpen**:
Archie Bradley, RHP
Junior Guerra, RHP
Andrew Chafin, LHP
Kevin Ginkel, RHP
Yoan López, RHP
Stefan Crichton, RHP
Jimmi Sherfy, RHP
Matt Andriese, RHP

**Catchers:**
Carson Kelly, age 25, eligible at C
2019 Stats: 365 PA, 18 HR, 46 Runs, 47 RBI, 0 SB, .245/.348/.478
The Cardinals might be kicking themselves for trading Kelly to the Diamondbacks last year if he continues on the path he's currently on. Not only is he an above average pitch framer, but he has all the looks of a solid top 10 catcher. There's upside in the bat for 25 HR if he can secure enough at bats.

Stephen Vogt, age 35, eligible at C
2019 Stats: 280 PA, 10 HR, 30 Runs, 40 RBI, 3 SB, .263/.314/.490

Vogt is not much more than an off day fill in for Kelly. He isn't terrible with the bat, but it's simply a playing time issue. Even in a two catcher league, he can be ignored.

**Infielders:**

Christian Walker, age 29, eligible at 1B
2019 Stats: 603 PA, 29 HR, 86 Runs, 73 RBI, 8 SB, .259/.348/.476
Projected to be the cleanup hitter on a decent enough offense, Walker has potential to at least repeat last year's number if not improve on them slightly. While his 25.7% strikeout rate is problematic, he walks at an 11.1% clip which sets his floor nice and high. Walker is going later than he should in drafts and should not be ignored.

Eduardo Escobar, age 31, eligible at 2B/3B
2019 Stats: 699 PA, 35 HR, 94 Runs, 118 RBI, 5 SB, .269/.320/.511
Wow, Escobar blew up last year and increased his HR total from his previous bets of 23 to 35. So he should reach that mark again, right? Not so fast. Digging a little deeper nothing in Escobar's advanced metrics show any real power growth. His launch angle and exit velocity on batted balls is about the same as it's always been, and his hard hit rate is not great as compared to the league average. Escobar is not a bad player by any means, but a regression to 25 HR or so seems more likely than the 35 he had in 2019.

Nick Ahmed, age 30, eligible at SS
2019 Stats: 625 PA, 19 HR, 79 Runs, 82 RBI, 8 SB, .254/.316/.437
Ahmed's calling card has never really been his bat so much as his glove, but last year might have shown that he can at least be serviceable as a late round option. His ground ball and fly ball rate went the wrong direction last year; however, he showed a better eye at the plate and made slightly better contact on the balls he was able to hit in play. There's potential here for a 15/10 season with a pile of Runs and RBI and a so-so AVG.

Jake Lamb, age 29, eligible at 3B
2019 Stats: 226 PA, 6 HR, 26 Runs, 30 RBI, 1 SB, .193/.323/.353
The dream of full time at bats for Jake Lamb is just a memory at this point. After coming back from injury last season, he was relegated to a platoon role, which is likely where he will stay. Without a serious adjustment at the plate, Lamb will become an afterthought.

Kevin Cron, age 27, eligible at 1B
2019 Stats: 78 PA, 6 HR, 12 Runs, 16 RBI, 0 SB, .211/.269/.521
The younger brother of C.J. Cron, Kevin Cron's minor league batting profile would signal that he has massive power in the bat. He hit 38 homers in 82 games at triple-A last year. The problem is, he might not be able to hit major league pitching. The sample size so far is small enough that it's unfair to pass any sort of final judgement. Cron deserves some time to figure things out, just let him do it on waivers first.

Domingo Leyba, age 24, eligible at 2B
2019 Stats: 30 PA, 0 HR, 6 Runs, 5 RBI, 0 SB, .280/.367/.440
Leyba had a really nice year at triple-A in 2019 with a batting line of .300/.351/.519 and 19 homers. The power is unlikely to ever reach 20 HR in the majors and he will probably be a utility infielder, if anything at all.

Ildemaro Vargas, age 28, eligible at 2B
2019 Stats: 211 PA, 6 HR, 25 Runs, 24 RBI, 1 SB, .269/.299/.413
With Josh Rojas waiting in the minors, Vargas will be pushing Leyba for the role of utility infielder this season. Vargas is nothing special with the bat. If he were to get a full season, his upside would be as a 10 homer type with a handful of steals. The odds are that either Vargas or Leyba will be the causality if Rojas gets the call.

**Outfielders**:
Ketel Marte, age 26, eligible at 2B/OF
2019 Stats: 628 PA, 32 HR, 97 Runs, 92 RBI, 10 SB, .329/.389/.592
Raise your hand if you saw Ketel Marte's breakout 2019 coming... If your hand is raised, you are full of it. Even Ketel Marte's own mother didn't think he's bash 32 HR and hit well over .300 on the year. These marks dwarfed his previous bests and although he'd show signs of a breakout, nothing to this extent. The craziest thing about all of this, is that while regression is coming, he could still hit 25 HR and bat .300 and surpass 10 SB. Considering Marte also carries dual eligibility, he is a good buy even at his elevated draft day price.

David Peralta, age 32, eligible at OF
2019 Stats: 423 PA, 12 HR, 48 Runs, 57 RBI, 0 SB, .275/.343/.461
A 30 HR season in 2018 fueled speculation that Peralta would be Arizona's best hitter last year. However, a shoulder injury in the spring and then back surgery in the fall destroyed any chance of returning draft day value. The hope heading into this season is for a full recovery and a return to even 80% of his 2018 numbers.

Kole Calhoun, age 32, eligible at OF
2019 Stats: 632 PA, 33 HR, 92 Runs, 74 RBI, 4 SB, .232/.325/.467
Kole Calhoun is aging like a fine wine as 2019 was one of his better seasons (outside of his BA). The power gains he made last year can be attributed to a new swing path he developed in 2018 and are backed up by an increase in his launch angle and barrell percentage. He's a good source of power later in the draft as long as you can stomach the BA hit.

Tim Locastro, age 27, eligible at OF
2019 Stats: 250 PA, 1 HR, 38 Runs, 17 RBI, 17 SB, .250/.357/.340
Locastro is in an interesting spot as a true utility player on the team. He could see at bats in the OF or as an INF player. The only thing making him worthy of rostering for fantasy is his speed. He has 60 grade speed and could get you 30 steals cheap, but you can't steal first base. Locastro needs to keep his OBP skills up to reach enough playing time to be rosterable.

**Starters:**
Madison Bumgarner, age 30, LHP
2019 Stats: 207.2 IP, 203 K, 9 W, 3.90 ERA, 1.13 WHIP
While he didn't bounce back completely, last year was a really nice rebound for Madison Bumgarner in San Fran. His velocity ticked back up ever so slightly, he surpassed 200 IP, but more importantly, his swinging strike rate jumped to the highest it's been since 2016. Even with a slight park downgrade in Arizona, there's hope for some improvement over last year.

Mike Leake, age 32, RHP
2019 Stats: 197 IP, 127 K, 12 W, 4.29 ERA, 1.29 WHIP

It's really, really hard to sell Mike Leake as an exciting fantasy option outside of deep leagues. He owns a putrid 5.80 K/9, which effectively makes him useless as a strikeout contributor. Leake did reach 6 innings in at least 23 of 32 starts, so there is some streaming appeal in quality start leagues, but that's about it.

Robbie Ray, age 28, LHP
2019 Stats: 174.1 IP, 235 K, 12 W, 4.34 ERA, 1.34 WHIP
Not many starters can boast the type of strikeout rates that Robbie Ray has for three years running. 3 of the last 4 years Ray has had 215 K's without reaching 180 IP. So we know he can get punchouts, but he's also extremely volatile, which is a big reason why his innings haven't reached 200 in a season yet. His problems with walks and his declining velocity could make for a bumpy ride. If you need K's, and you bolster your ERA and WHIP elsewhere, Ray can be a huge asset.

Merrill Kelly, age 31, RHP
2019 Stats: 183.1 IP, 158 K, 13 W, 4.42 ERA, 1.31 WHIP
Many saw Kelly's signing with Arizona after his stint in Korea and drew a parallel to Miles Mikolas doing the same the previous year. Kelly did not have the same initial success and is being dismissed in some fantasy circles due to a pedestrian ERA and strikeout total. Perhaps he needed some time to settle in? His last 10 starts saw a 2.18 ERA and 9.55 ERA. The walks were still an issue, but there could be a 5th starter here.

Luke Weaver, age 26, RHP
2019 Stats: 64.1 IP, 69 K, 4 W, 2.94 ERA, 1.07 WHIP
With a swinging strike rate pushing 12% and velocity back up to 94 MPH, Weaver came out of the chute hot in 2019. We were just ready to forgive his bad performance in 2018 when he went down at the end of May with an elbow injury. Outside of a 2 inning relief appearance in September, we only have the beginning of the season to draw on for this coming year. Weaver has yet to exceed 140 IP in a season between the majors or minors, so logic would dictate that Arizona will be careful with his workload. I'd be more interested in dynasty than redraft for this year.

**Relievers:**
Archie Bradley, age 27, RHP
2019 Stats: 71.2 IP, 87 K, 18 SV, 3.52 ERA, 1.44 WHIP
Finally, Bradley was given the closer and he actually did a fairly good job racking up 18 saves. The WHIP, walks, but most importantly lack of a good 3rd pitch seem to be the things holding him back from breaking into a top option at closer. Bradley needs to continue to develop his changeup and throw it more than 5.8% of the time in order to keep batters off balance. There is hope to be found in his 1st versus 2nd half numbers as his ERA dropped from 4.95 to 1.71.

Junior Guerra, age 35, RHP
2019 Stats: 83.2 IP, 77 K, 3.55 ERA, 1.12 WHIP
Guerra moved from the rotation to the bullpen exclusively last year as a way to extend his career and it certainly worked out. Accompanied by an uptick in velocity and swinging strike rate, Guerra will look to hold down the 8th inning job for Arizona. If Bradley crashes and burns, then there could be more than just Hold opportunities to be had for Guerra.

Andrew Chafin, age 29, LHP
2019 Stats: 52.2 IP, 68 K, 3.76 ERA, 1.33 WHIP
Chafin was thought to have been in live for Saves last year, but the Diamondbacks seem to prefer the lefty in a setup role. He will share Hold opportunities with Guerra and could see a Save here and there.

Kevin Ginkel, age 26, RHP
2019 Stats: 24.1 IP, 28 K, 1.48 ERA, 0.99 WHIP
The dark horse for Saves in this bullpen might be Kevin Ginkel. He has the potential to have a couple of plus pitches and could quietly work his way into the setup role behind Bradley. That means should Bradley falter, Ginkel might be given his shot.

Yoan López, age 27, RHP
2019 Stats: 60.2 IP, 42 K, 3.41 ERA, 1.14 WHIP
López is one of the middle relievers the Diamondbacks deployed for Holds last year. He probably lost that role, or at least will cede much of the opportunities, with the off-season signing of Guerra. Either way, he wouldn't be worth a look for fantasy.

Stefan Crichton, age 28, RHP
2019 Stats: 30.1 IP, 33 K, 3.56 ERA, 1.02 WHIP
Crichton is most effective against righties, which could make his usage this year a little tricky with the new relief minimum rules. He will still find his way to some innings, but nothing useful outside of the real game.

Jimmie Sherfy, age 28, RHP
2019 Stats: 18.1 IP, 22 K, 5.89 ERA, 1.53 WHIP
A middle reliever with limited upside and little to no appeal. Pass on him.

Matt Andriese, age 30, RHP
2019 Stats: 70.2 IP, 79 K, 4.71 ERA, 1.40 WHIP
A former starter, Andriese won't have any value in the bullpen. However, if he can find his way to the rotation, there is some streaming match up appeal.

## Arizona Diamondbacks Prospects
By Matt Thompson

### 1. Kristian Robinson- OF

The Bahamian has one of the highest ceilings of all of the minor leagues. He's built like an NFL wide receiver at six-foot-three, and a chiseled 200 pounds. In addition to double-plus raw power he's also a plus runner, and has the makings of a potential superstar. He has strong pitch recognition, but will always strike out due to his long limbs. He needs to elevate the ball more consistently as he got a little ground ball heavy after his promotion to Kane County. In addition, the walk rate also dipped after the promotion. I expect him to start 2020 back in Kane County and he should hit his way out to Visalia soon after. Robinson is a special talent, and a top fifteen dynasty prospect on any list. **ETA: 2023.**

### 2. Corbin Carroll- OF

Carroll is essentially a more tooled up version of Alek Thomas. Both hit from the left side, have strong defensive skills and profile as top of the order bats. They both also have a stigma attached to them due to their lack of size, but it's not a concern for either player considering their well rounded skill sets. Carroll is the better defender of the two, and has a better feel for contact. His power projects a tick below what Thomas has, but Carroll has also shown flashes like when he led his 18U Team USA squad in homers. He's quieted the swing down since turning pro, but I'm not giving up on the power coming back and sticking around. **ETA: 2023.**

### 3. Alek Thomas- OF

Thomas enjoyed some serious home cooking as the Chicago area native got to play his games less than an hour away from home while he was at Kane County. Thomas won the Midwest League MVP award after hitting .312/.393/.479 with eight homers and 11 stolen bases while showing excellent command of the strike zone. Thomas has registered plus run times for me while also flashing an above-average hit tool. He's growing into power and is very strong for his size. He needs to be more efficient on the basepaths to project as a stolen base threat, but he should hit for average and swat 20 homers at peak. He's a strong defender in center, but the bat may not quite be enough to move to a corner. **ETA: 2022.**

### 4. Daulton Varsho- C

There might not be a more difficult player to evaluate through a fantasy lense than Varsho. His hit tool, power and speed are all above-average tools, and it's a bat that will play anywhere on the diamond. Defensively there are some concerns about his arm and footwork behind the plate, but he's a good enough receiver. When/if robot umpires arrive it might push Varsho out from behind the plate for good because receiving and framing skills will take a back seat to arm strength as a priority for catchers around the league. In a perfect world Varsho is the backup catcher while playing everyday in the outfield, giving him that coveted dual eligibility. He should start 2020 in Triple-A, but should be up in Phoenix this summer. **ETA: 2020.**

### 5. Geraldo Perdomo- SS

The switch-hitting shortstop is a pest in the box, as he works counts and walked more than he struck out across two levels of A-ball in 2019. He's going to be an asset in OBP formats so bump him up a few spots. His glove is enough to stick at the six. He's a much better left-handed hitter than right, but can change into a slap hitter with two strikes. He's a plus runner, and teams pay a high amount of attention to him on the base paths. He needs to be more efficient, but with better body control he can swipe 20 bases annually. The question is how much power he finds. **ETA: 2022.**

### 6. Seth Beer- 1B
Beer can hit, there's nothing you can say to deny that. The question is if he can outhit his deficiencies. Beer's value is entirely tied to his bat. He's a bottom of the scale runner and may not even be a good enough defender to stick at first base. He looks uncomfortable everywhere on the diamond besides the left-handed batters' box. I think he can hit for a strong average with 20-30 homers at peak, but that's dependent on defensive improvements or a DH coming to the National League. He will start out in Triple-A and post monster numbers before possibly getting to Arizona this summer. He's more likely to debut in 2021 though. **ETA: 2021.**

### 7. Blake Walston- LHP
Walston was an under scouted prep arm due to his double duty action as a Division I quarterback recruit in addition to being one of the best prep pitchers in North Carolina. Walston missed many of the showcases due to his football career, and as a result he had inconsistent fastball velocities at his limited viewings. At times he was down as low as 84, but in only a few months of focusing solely on baseball he was hitting 94. At six-foot-five, and only 175 at draft time there's plenty of room for physical projection and velocity. **ETA: 2024.**

### 8. Luis Frias- RHP
Frias is a big, physical righty with a fastball that sits 93-96 and can touch 98. He throws from a high arm slot that makes his 12-6 curveball and splitter tunnel well off the fastball, and also mixes in a slider. At times all four pitches have flashed plus, but it's consistency that's missing from the arsenal. It's a high effort delivery and he can struggle to throw strikes at times, but he's either a big league starter or a late inning reliever, and both carry significant fantasy value. **ETA: 2022.**

### 9. Jon Duplantier- RHP
Duplantier rode the shuttle back and forth from Reno to Phoenix last year, and pitched out of the bullpen for the D-Backs. He's got a checkered health record, but the Diamondbacks are making an effort to rebuild his delivery and cleanup his arm action with hopes he can remain a starter long term. **ETA: Arrived.**

### 10. J.B. Bukauskas- RHP
Bukauskas was the 17th overall pick by the Astros in the 2017 Draft by the Astros, and he was a part of the return for Zack Greinke. The last two seasons have been interrupted by injuries, 2018 was a car accident and 2019 was a bout with elbow soreness. He makes his money with a

mid-90s fastball with wiggle, and a nasty two plane slider that gets plus grades. He needs to add a changeup to give hitters another look, and also needs to be more efficient with the delivery in order to throw more strikes. He should debut in 2020. **ETA: 2020.**

**Next Five:**
Jeferson Espinal- OF
Ronny Polanco- SS
Matt Tabor- RHP
Levi Kelly- RHP
Blaze Alexander- 3B/SS

**Top Five in FYPDs:**
Corbin Carroll- OF
Blake Walston- LHP
Ronny Polanco- SS
Drey Jameson- RHP
Dominic Fletcher- OF

# Colorado Rockies Team Preview
## By Gabe Zammit

**Projected Order:**
1- Charlie Blackmon, OF
2- Trevor Story, SS
3- David Dahl, OF
4- Nolan Arenado, 3B
5- Daniel Murphy, 1B
6- Ryan McMahon, 2B
7- Sam Hilliard, OF
8- Tony Wolters, C

**Projected Bench:**
Drew Butera, C
Josh Fuentes, 1B
Garrett Hampson, 2B/OF
Ian Desmond, OF
Raimel Tapia, OF

**Projected Rotation:**
Jon Gray, RHP
German Márquez, RHP
Kyle Freeland, LHP
Antonio Senzatela, RHP
Jeff Hoffman, RHP

**Bullpen:**
Scott Oberg, RHP
Jairo Diaz, RHP
Carlos Estévez, RHP
Wade Davis, RHP
Jake McGee, LHP
Bryan Shaw, RHP
James Pazos, LHP
Yency Almonte, RHP

**Catchers:**
Tony Wolters, age 27, eligible at C
2019 Stats: 411 PA, 1 HR, 42 Runs, 42 RBI, 0 SB, .262/.337/.329
Is Wolters the worst starting catcher for fantasy on a major league roster? It's gotta be close if not him. Expect zero pop, close to zero speed, and a mediocre batting average. In other words, do not draft Tony Wolters.

Drew Butera, age 36, eligible at C
2019 Stats: 49 PA, 0 HR, 6 Runs, 3 RBI, 0 SB, .163/.229/.233

Butera has a chance to put up better numbers than Wolters, but by how much really? He did show a solid 12.6 walk rate in triple-A last year… but he was also 35 years old. Catcher looks to be a blackhole on the Rockies unless they bring in some help not currently on the major league roster.

**Infielders**:

Daniel Murphy, age 34, eligible at 1B
2019 Stats: 478 PA, 13 HR, 56 Runs, 78 RBI, 1 SB, .279/.328/.452
Two years in a row without reaching 15 HR is not exactly encouraging for Murphy. Anyone hoping for the Coors effect to push him above 25 HR might not want to hold their breath. He still shows a good eye at the plate and should hit for a good average. The Rockies infield is starting to get crowded though and it wouldn't be a surprise to see Murphy cede time as the year wears on.

Ryan McMahon, age 25, eligible at 2B/3B
2019 Stats: 539 PA, 24 HR, 70 Runs, 83 RBI, 5 SB, .250/.329/.450
The big question last year was who would get the 2B job between McMahon and Hampson. After a solid year, it seems that McMahon has full time at bats locked up, if not at 2B then somewhere on this team. He elevated his hard hit rate, barrel rate, and launch angle. These improvements won't see him to be the next 40 homer bat in Colorado, but could he repeat last year's numbers and maybe tack on a few more dingers? Definitely.

Trevor Story, age 27, eligible at SS
2019 Stats: 656 PA, 35 HR, 111 Runs, 85 RBI, 23 SB, .294/.363/.554
Does anyone else remember when Trevor Story was just going to be a placeholder at SS? Even with a thumb injury last year, he showed his batting gains are legitimate. The strikeout rate is still a scary 26.5%, but he walks, has power, and has the green light to steal. Anything less than a 30/20 season would be a disappointment.

Nolan Arenado, age 28, eligible at 3B
2019 Stats: 662 PA, 41 HR, 102 Runs, 118 RBI, 3 SB, .315/.379/.583
Somehow the fantasy community has gotten to the point where Arenado is not an exciting player to draft anymore. Sure, he won't give you more than a couple of steals, but his power and counting number production are one of the most bankable and safe assets in the first round. If you have a backend pick in the draft, just make up the speed somewhere else and enjoy another incredible season from Mr. Arenado.

Garrett Hampson, age 25, eligible at 2B/OF
2019 Stats: 327 PA, 8 HR, 40 Runs, 27 RBI, 15 SB, .247/.302/.385
All of the Garrett Hampson truthers out there lost their minds after watching him struggle to the tune of a .218/.274/.322 line in 232 PA with a 30.2% strikeout rate through the end of August. He looked like the mayor of Bust City. Then September happened, and he hit .318/.368/.534 with 5 HR and 9 SB and the truthers felt vindicated. So what do we expect for 2020? Well, Hampson's unbelievable September will remove any discount he may have had for drafts. The potential is there for 15/30 season or better, but the playing time is still a question as is the validity of his mini-breakout.

Josh Fuentes, age 27, eligible at 1B

2019 Stats: 56 PA, 3 HR, 8 Runs, 7 RBI, 1 SB, .218/.232/.400
A crowded infield and a habit of striking out at an exorbitant rate both combine to make Fuentes nothing more than a bench bat likely to get replaced by the first hot prospect who gets the call.

**Outfielders**:
Charlie Blackmon, age 33, eligible at OF
2019 Stats: 634 PA, 32 HR, 112 Runs, 86 RBI, 2 SB, .314/.364/.576
Blackmon's stolen bases completely evaporated last year, but his contact and power skills remained strong. Is he unable to steal, or was there some other reason? Either way, he is still a solid buy and could be undervalued in drafts as a 4 category stud.

David Dahl, age 25, eligible at OF
2019 Stats: 413 PA, 15 HR, 67 Runs, 61 RBI, 4 SB, .302/.353/.524
Are we really going to spend another year talking about Dahl's potential for 30 HR and 15 SB? Yes, we are. Even though he seems to be looking more like Mr. Glass each year, the skills are real. Drafting Dahl is risky, but can be negated so long as you don't fill your team with other high risk players. The upside is here, and it's legit.

Sam Hilliard, age 26, eligible at OF
2019 Stats: 87 PA, 7 HR, 13 Runs, 13 RBI, 2 SB, .273/.356/.649
Another Rockie, and another question mark of playing time. Hilliard looked great in his callup last year, which fell in line with how he'd been performing in the minors to that point. He could run away with the CF job and return to a great season, but that's only if the Rockies don't sit him for Tapia, Hampson, or someone else. At his current cost, Hilliard is a guy I'm gambling on.

Ian Desmond, age 34, eligible at OF
2019 Stats: 482 PA, 20 HR, 64 Runs, 65 RBI, 3 SB, .255/.310/.479
Could this be the year Ian Desmond finally falls off a cliff (metaphorically of course)? He really can't be counted on for steals anymore, but Desmond is still hitting the ball hard and barreling up. The real question is playing time. Given full-time at bats, he could reach 25 HR and be a real draft-day bargain.

Raimel Tapia, age 26, eligible at OF
2019 Stats: 447 PA, 9 HR, 54 Runs, 44 RBI, 9 SB, .275/.309/.415
A formerly much hyped prospect, Tapia is beginning to show more signs of a replacement level OF than that of a starter. For as crowded as the OF could end up being, Tapia is tough to buy into as more than a deep league stash or a dollar player at the end of an auction.

**Starters:**
Jon Gray, age 28, RHP
2019 Stats: 150 IP, 150 K, 11 W, 3.84 ERA, 1.35 WHIP
Gray's 2019 looked closer to 2017 than his less than memorable 5.12 ERA in 2018. That sounds encouraging, but the simple fact is that Gray will have a hard time ever reaching his potential, so long as he stays in Colorado. The good news is his swinging strike rate has remained steady and his velocity has gone back to where it was in 2017, but the bad news is that he's trending in the wrong direction with free passes. Barring a trade, Gray is a risky buy.

German Márquez, age 25, RHP

2019 Stats: 174 IP, 175 K, 12 W, 4.76 ERA, 1.20 WHIP

I took a lot of grief for not showing caution last year on Máquez when others were ready to declare him as the one who could finally defeat the Coors Field effect. Listen, I think Marquez is an amazing pitcher, and last year was a strong showing by him, but he did not meet the expectations most had when he got drafted.

Kyle Freeland, age 26, LHP
2019 Stats: 104.1 IP, 79 K, 3 W, 6.73 ERA, 1.58 WHIP

Freeland's breakout 17 win and 2.85 ERA in 2018 proved to be a mirage. He crashed back to Earth last year thanks in large part to giving up almost 3 times as many HR/9. His ERA was slightly palatable away from Coors at 4.61, so it's possible as a matchup play he could still be worth a look.

Antonio Senzatela, age 25, RHP
2019 Stats: 124.2 IP, 76 K, 11 W, 6.71 ERA, 1.75 WHIP

We are starting to scrape the bottom of the barrel in Colorado now. Senzatela is nothing more than cannon fodder for the Rockies and should be disregarded in fantasy circles as well. He would end up doing more harm than good to your ratios.

Jeff Hoffman, age 27, RHP
2019 Stats: 70 IP, 68 K, 2 W, 6.56 ERA, 1.59 WHIP

A former first round pick, Hoffman has the capacity to be a startable option, just not any time soon. He is getting closer to striking out a batter an inning, but his control is just not where it needs to be yet, especially given his home park. He's an easy guy to pass on for now.

**Relievers:**

Scott Oberg, age 30, RHP
2019 Stats: 56 IP, 58 K, 5 SV, 2.25 ERA, 1.11 WHIP

Will Oberg be the closer in Colorado this year? He does seem the likeliest candidate, though things could be a little up in the air. He now owns two consecutive years of solid relief production, the one knock on him being his arm injuries. The uncertainty around this bullpen could make him a value, just keep an eye on reports out of spring training.

Jairo Diaz, age 28, RHP
2019 Stats: 57.2 IP, 63 K, 5 SV, 4.53 ERA, 1.30 WHIP

While most owners will be watching Oberg, I'd be keeping an eye on Diaz for save opportunities. He can pump his fastball up to 97 MPH and compliments that with a pretty nasty slider. Diaz was given a handful of save opportunities down the stretch, which may have been an audition for the closer job this year. If he's able to claim the job, he could get you 30+ saves on the cheap.

Carlos Estévez, age 27, RHP
2019 Stats: 72 IP, 81 K, 3.75 ERA, 1.29 WHIP

Well, the Rockies bullpen has no shortage of guys to speculate on for saves, which is probably why some might just avoid it completely. Estévez is another hard throwing rightie who can dial it up to 98 MPH and saw decent success last year out of the bullpen. His numbers don't paint as optimistic a picture as Diaz to usurp the closer role, but the "best" pitcher isn't always the one who ends up with the most saves.

Wade Davis, age 34, RHP
2019 Stats: 42.2 IP, 42 K, 15 SV, 8.65 ERA, 1.88 WHIP
Davis' 2019 was a train wreck you could see coming, but also just couldn't look away from. He lost the closer role in July and did not show any threat to reclaim it. The days of Davis having any shot at closing games out are gone.

Jake McGee, age 33, LHP
2019 Stats: 41.1 IP, 35 K, 4.35 ERA, 1.40 WHIP
McGee has never quite recaptured the form he showed while in Tampa. He has little fantasy relevance now as he won't be seeing opportunities to get Saves or Holds.

Bryan Shaw, age 32, RHP
2019 Stats: 72 IP, 58 K, 5.38 ERA, 1.36 WHIP
Shaw is similar to McGee in the sense that once he came to the thin air of Coors, his baseline re-established itself at an unusable place for fantasy. He's another guy you can easily pass on.

James Pazos, age 28, LHP
2019 Stats: 10.1 IP, 10 K, 1.74 ERA, 1.06 WHIP
Pazos is interesting in the sense that he owns the ability to strike guys out at a decent enough rate. His walk rate and FIP point to just a situational reliever though.

Yency Almonte, age 25, RHP
2019 Stats: 34 IP, 29 K, 5.56 ERA, 1.56 WHIP
Rounding out the bullpen for the Rockies is Yency Almonte. He is equipped with a decent fastball and above average slider. He is unlikely to see any high leverage game action.

# Colorado Rockies Prospects
### By Matt Thompson

### 1. Brendan Rodgers- 2B
Rodgers initial taste of the big leagues didn't go well. He made his debut in May but only played in 25 games due to needing season ending surgery on his right labrum. This is part of who he is though, he's going to look putrid at times due to the subpar plate approach. He's overly aggressive and that with non-everyday playing time is a recipe for disaster. He's the third wheel in what appears to be a two-way battle between Hampson and McMahon for the starting second base gig. Looks like he's slated to start the year in Triple-A. **ETA: Arrived.**

### 2. Sam Hilliard- OF
The Rockies make it tough to get excited about their young players and Hilliard is looking to change that. He got his first taste of the big leagues last summer and faired well, flashing strong power numbers as well as surprising speed. He will always deal with higher than average strikeout totals, but he has the skills to hit 25 bombs and steal 10-12 bags. Did I mention he will get to play his home games in Coors? As of right now he looks to be competing with Raimel Tapia for the fourth outfielder job, but I expect him to seize a starting role soon. **ETA: Arrived.**

### 3. Michael Toglia- 1B
The switch-hitting first baseman was the 23rd overall pick out of UCLA. His best offensive skill is his plus raw power but his exceptional eye and patience aren't far behind. Toglia will always battle with strikeouts which isn't surprising given his six-foot-five frame and the long levers that come with it. He will be a strong source of power and OBP though, and could finally be the long-term answer at first base the team has been seeking since Todd Helton. That is as long as they don't bring in Mark Reynolds to block him. **ETA: 2022.**

### 4. Colton Welker- 3B
Rockies prospects are easily the hardest to evaluate. There is so much noise in all these environments. Every ballpark, except Double-A Hartford, is an absolute launching pad which inflates offensive numbers. Adding another wrinkle, they don't have a team in the AZL, sending all prospects to Grand Junction, which means fewer eyes on them compared to other Arizona clubs. Welker is a bit of a tweener profile. Not quite athletic enough for third base, but not sure if there's enough thump here for a first baseman. He's a guy that makes contact at a better than average clip and consistently hits the ball hard though, which makes him a nice fit in Coors. But where is his defensive home? He's been young for every level, and is ready for Triple-A as a 22 year old. **ETA: 2021.**

### 5. Aaron Schunk- 3B
Schunk was a two-way talent at Georgia and the Rockies liked his work at third base enough to pick him with the 62nd pick. He finally tapped into the raw power his finals season on campus, nearly quadrupling his previous homer total entering the year. He's starting to pull the ball more often and hit the ball in the air, but he needs to continue to do more of the latter to fully maximize his offensive skill set. He's an above-average defender at third, and his arm is plus, but he's blocked by a perennial MVP candidate there. **ETA: 2022.**

### 6. Ryan Vilade- 3B

Vilade looks like a completely different guy from when he was drafted in 2017 to now. He's more physical and has completely re-worked his swing. He's turning that raw power into game power by simplifying the swing, and losing his problematic leg kick that was disrupting his timing. His future defensive home is in question, but he has begun playing the outfield and I have no concerns with him playing in one of the outfield corners in Coors. I think the 24 stolen bases from last year are a bit fluky, and only see him getting around ten or so a year in the big leagues. Vilade brings an average hit tool with above average power to the table and has gotten new life as a prospect. **ETA: 2022.**

### 7. Ryan Rolison- LHP

Rolison was the Rockies first round pick in 2018 out of Ole Miss. He's the rare pitching prospect worth investing in in an organization that is starving for quality arms. Rolison has three above-average offerings, and his fastball is teetering on the edge of plus with his new found command of the pitch. I just need to see it in a longer sample. He can get it up to 96, and it jumps on hitters due to his cross body mechanics. He projects as a mid-rotation arm for me. **ETA: 2021.**

### 8. Terrin Vavra- 2B

The former Golden Gopher was the third round pick in 2018. His calling card is his near elite command of the strike zone. He also added homers to his game, but I fear that could be a product of his environment. 32 doubles and a triple in addition to the ten homers does show skill growth though, so that's something to watch for. He's trending towards a utility role, and his power-OBP combo could be valuable in that spot. **ETA: 2021.**

### 9. Brenton Doyle- OF

Perhaps he should be higher on this list, but Doyle is a bit of an unknown coming out of Division II Shepherd University. He's a physical specimen with plus speed and power tools, but there's some swing and miss here despite strong pitch recognition skills. I've seen D.J. Peters comps put on him, so it's a bit of a hedge, I'll admit, but this feels right. **ETA: 2023.**

### 10. Julio Carreras- SS/3B

The Rockies have a few handfuls of young international kids that play up the middle, and Carreras is the one with the most upside due to his power ceiling. In addition to the power he should also be an above-average runner, even if he fills out and has to slide over to third. Carreras did well against recent college arms, and will report to full-season ball next spring at 20 years-old. **ETA: 2023.**

**Next Five:**
Grant Lavigne- 1B
Tyler Nevin- 1B
Adeal Amador- SS
Vince Fernandez- OF
Eddy Diaz- SS/2B

**Top Five in FYPDs:**
Michael Toglia- 1B
Aaron Schunk- 3B
Brenton Doyle- OF

Adeal Amador- SS
Christian Koss- SS

# Los Angeles Dodgers Team Preview
By Ray Kuhn

**Projected Lineup:**
1 – Joc Pederson, LF
2 – Max Muncy, 2B
3 – Justin Turner, 3B
4 – Cody Bellinger, 1B
5 - Corey Seager, SS
6 - A.J Pollock, CF
7 - Alex Verdugo, RF
8 - Will Smith, C

**Projected Bench:**
Austin Barnes, C
Tyler White, 1B
Matt Beaty, IF/OF
Enrique Hernandez, IF/OF
Chris Taylor, IF/OF

**Projected Rotation:**
Clayton Kershaw, LHP
Walker Buehler, RHP
Kenta Maeda, RHP
Julio Urias, LHP
David Price , LHP

**Projected Bullpen:**
Kenley Jansen, RHP
Blake Treinen, RHP
Pedro Baez, RHP
Joe Kelly, RHP
Adam Kolarek, LHP
Dylan Floro, RHP
Scott Alexander, LHP
Casey Sadler, RHP

**Catchers:**
Will Smith, age 25, eligible at C
2019 stats: 196 PA, 15 HR, 30 Runs, 42 RBI, 2 SB, .253/.337/.571
I, and likely many others, would like to see Smith take the next step in 2020, but I'm not sure how plausible it is. Upon his promotion last season, the hard contact and power metrics were there, but how much of that power do we believe, and Will Smith's contract issues hinder his progress? My guess is that there will be some ups and downs in his performance, but the power numbers will be there despite some streakiness and batting average struggles.

Austin Barnes, age 30, eligible at C
2019 stats: 242 PA, 5 HR, 28 Runs, 25 RBI, 3 SB, .203/.293/.340

After a strong 2017 season, albeit in just 262 plate appearances, the last two years have been pretty rough for Barnes. His contact rate has taken a steep dive, and power isn't his strong suit. We are now three years removed from his 13 stolen bases in 2016, so there really isn't much to see.

**Infielders:**
Cody Bellinger, age 24, eligible at 1B and OF
2019 stats: 661 PA, 47 HR, 121 Runs, 115 RBI, 15 SB, .305/.406/.629
After a down 2018 campaign, Bellinger bounced back in a big way last season, and it makes for an interesting evaluation for 2020. Right now, it looks like we can write off that down campaign of 25 home runs and 76 RBI, but at the same time, I'm not sure we can expect him to go deep 47 times once again. However, the power is real, and perhaps more importantly, Bellinger's contact rate rose from 73% to 81% last season. Factor in 15 stolen bases, and we are talking about a top option, but the concern for Bellinger, is that his .259 batting average in the second half is going to stick around. Even if that's the case, no one would complain based on his elite launch angle.

Max Muncy, age 29, eligible at 1B, 2B, and 3B
2019 stats: 589 PA, 35 HR, 101 Runs, 98 RBI, 4 SB
We just have two years of track record with Muncy, but they have been pretty close to identical, and his profile backs that up. There is the elite power and walk rate, but that comes along with a sub-standard contact rate and a .250 batting. The good thing though, is that you know what you are getting with Muncy, and his dual eligibility at second and third base also helps. It is pretty crazy though, to think that he might be more valuable at first base.

Corey Seager, age 26, eligible at SS
2019 stats: 541 PA, 19 HR, 82 Runs, 87 RBI, 1 SB, .272/.335/.483
Talk about a steep fall from grace. But before we go any further, let's remember that Seager is still just 26 years old and he has dealt with some injury issues over the past two seasons. Last year, it was a hamstring that cost him a month, but he still hit .272 with 19 home runs and 87 RBI in 541 plate appearances. While it doesn't match what our expectations of Seager was, it's not too far away from his 2017 season that saw him hit .295 with 22 home runs and 77 RBI. What we need to do though, is perhaps just adjust our expectations for Seager. There is some power and hard contact there, and perhaps a small adjustment to his swing could bring his 12% home run to fly ball rate back up to his pre-injury levels. We are still working with a solid skill set, and the price is going to be right, and perhaps even a slight bargain.

Justin Turner, age 35, eligible at 3B
2019 stats: 549 PA, 27 HR, 80 Runs, 67 RBI, 2 SB, .290/.372/.509
When it comes to Turner, we just can't factor in health throughout the entire season. But when Turner is in the lineup, the production is there. Health and age are both issues, but it's hard to argue with his hard contact and power metrics. Perhaps age will catch up to Turner at some point from a skills perspective, but that just hasn't happened yet. If you aren't expecting elite production, and look at Turner as a corner infielder while factoring in replacement value, then you shouldn't be disappointed.

Tyler White, age 29, eligible at 1B
2019 stats: 279 PA, 3 HR, 18 Runs, 23 RBI, 0 SB, .208/.308/.304

White has some plate skills, but he has struggled to find consistent footing at the major league level. There isn't anything in his Statcast profile that suggests we will see anything different out of White, but there will likely be one or two flashes of productivity at some point this season. Don't let it fool you unless there is something that changes in his profile.

Matt Beaty, age 27, eligible at 1B and OF
2019 stats: 268 PA, 9 HR, 36 Runs, 46 RBI, 5 SB, .265/.317/.458
Beaty is a platoon option thanks to his struggles against left-handed pitching, but it's hard to argue with his 87% contact rate and above average hard contact rate; granted it does come with marginal power. That lack of true power will keep his value down, but in reality, he is just a slightly better version of White.

Enrique Hernandez, age 28, eligible at 2B and OF
2019 stats: 460 PA, 17 HR, 57 Runs, 64 RBI, 4 SB, .237/.304/.411
At this point in his career, Hernandez is what he is, and that's a solid utility player who will end up seeing around 400 to 450 plate appearances again this season. I'm not sure we will see much of an improvement in him, and you have to live with the batting average, but he will give you put some balls over the fence and provide some solid production when he is in the lineup. Just don't expect anything more.

Chris Taylor, age 29, eligible at OF, 2B, and SS
2019 stats: 414 PA, 12 HR, 52 Runs, 52 RBI, 8 SB, .262/.333/.462
Taylor's contact rate continues to drop, down to 69% last season, so that will hinder his value, but his 27%-line drive rate will keep us interested. While not elite, Taylor does have above average power that gives him 20 home run potential, but it's not something I would bank on. What is more troubling, is the fact that his stolen base metrics have also declined over the past few seasons. If everything falls right, maybe a 15/10 season is possible with a little room for upside, but the last two seasons haven't provided much hope for it.

**Outfielders:**
A.J. Pollock, age 32, eligible at OF
2019 stats: 342 PA, 15 HR, 49 Runs, 47 RBI, 5 SB, .266/.327/.468
If only Pollock could stay healthy. This isn't anything new, but you also can't draft Pollock solely based on his .288 average with 13 home runs and 33 RBI in 227 plate appearances in the second half of last season. We know that is what he is capable of, as the skill set is there, but your ceiling is limited as your investment should be as well.

Mookie Betts, age 27.2, eligible at OF
2019 Stats: 706 PA, 29 HR, 135 Runs, 80 RBI, 16 SB, .295/.391/.524
There isn't much to be said about Mookie that can't be seen by quickly browsing his stat profile. He really does look THAT GOOD in real life and I have no problem with him still being involved in the Top-4 picks. He stole fewer bases last season, but his sprint speed and success rate leaves no reason to believe he can't surpass 20-25 in 2020.

**Starting Pitchers:**
Clayton Kershaw, age 31, LHP
2019 stats: 178.1 IP, 189 K, 16 Wins, 3.03 ERA, 1.04 WHIP

The left-hander isn't the pitcher he once was, but Kershaw is still a pretty good option. Yes, he is good for at least one stint on the Injured List per year, and his velocity is down, but with a 13.7% swinging strike rate, there is still something left in the tank. As long as you adjust your expectations down to allow for the decreased strikeouts, still a batter per inning, Kershaw's control remains an asset, his WHIP will still be elite. Just expect an ERA closer to 3-3.50 and 170 innings, and there shouldn't be a disappointment as we account for the decreased velocity.

Walker Buehler, age 24, RHP
2019 stats: 182.1 IP, 215 K, 14 Wins, 3.26 ERA, 1.04 WHIP
Talk about a complete pitcher. Buehler is now up to four pitches that generate a swinging strike rate of greater than 10%, and the results back it up. Things went the right way for Buehler last season, as the strikeouts went up and the walks went down while he took the next steps towards being a true ace. A touch below the first crop of ace pitchers, Buehler still slides in as an early second round option, but the potential is there for him to take the next step in 2020. While there isn't much more room for him to go, the tools are in place to do so.

David Price, age 34.4, LHP
2019 Stats: 107.1 IP, 128 K, 7 W, 4.28 ERA, 1.31 WHIP
It's been quite some time since we've seen a dominant David Price. 2018 looked like somewhat of a resurgence that is now sandwiched between two highly disappointing years. Being paid like one of the best pitchers in baseball, Price certainly has not lived up to his contract since becoming a member of the Red Sox. The continued decline in velocity and sheer volume of innings on his arm scare me away from taking the risk in 2020.

Julio Urias, age 22, LHP
2019 stats: 79.2 IP, 85 K, 4 Wins, 2.49 ERA, 1.08 WHIP
The former top prospect is certainly talented, and last year he was finally healthy. Los Angeles treaded carefully with the southpaw, he also was suspended for 20 games, as they used him in a variety of roles and he logged just 80 innings. When you look at his ratios, it's hard not to be excited, but the 4.12 xERA does bring us back down to earth. At 95 miles per hour, Urias is just about there as he is working to regain all of his pre-injury velocity, but his 39% fly ball rate last season is still a concern. With a 14.4% swinging strike rate last season, Urias has the stuff to make an impact, and thanks to his lack of production over the past few seasons, the draft price should be affordable.

Ross Stripling, age 27, RHP
2019 stats: 90.2 IP, 93 K, 4 Wins, 3.47 ERA, 1.15 WHIP
The right-hander has been used in a variety of roles, but for now he is primed to start the season in the Dodgers' rotation. It's all about control for Stripling, as he relies on command, and not velocity or many swinging strikes, and for the most part, it has worked for him. The fact that Stripling keeps the ball on the ground, a 50% ground ball rate, does help to mitigate the potential damage.

**Relief Pitchers:**
Kenley Jansen, age 31, RHP
2019 stats: 63 IP, 80 K, 33 Saves, 3.71 ERA, 1.06 WHIP
Jansen was previously as sure of a thing as you could find at the closer's position, and while he is still one of the better options, he has taken a step back. A 16.3% swinging strike rate is

nothing to sneeze at, but it is down from Jansen's previous levels, or really should we say his prime? He has also seen his control take a step back, but I wouldn't fully read into his 4.45 second half ERA. Jansen is no longer completely dominant, but he has a pretty firm grip on the job, and he is still one of the better closers in the league. Just don't overpay.

Blake Treinen, age 31, RHP
2019 stats: 58.2 IP, 59 K, 16 Saves, 4.91 ERA, 1.62 WHIP
Entering last season, Treinen was right there with Jansen as being one of the better closers in the league. Or at least we thought that was the case. I mean, we knew that he wasn't going to repeat his 0.78 ERA, but health issues and poor performance led him to losing the closer's job and posting a 4.91 ERA. Treinen's 5.33 xFIP and 1.62 WHIP do back up those struggles, but how will that translate into next season? The biggest variable in that issue, is the fact that his groundball rate dropped down to 43% last season, a few short years ago it was as high as 66%, and that was a large factor in his struggles as his fly ball rate surged to 33%. Manage your expectations here, and Treinen's value is solely dependent on whether or not he gets some saves at Jansen's expense.

Pedro Baez, age 31, RHP
2019 stats: 69.2 IP, 69 K, 1 Save, 3.10 ERA, 0.95 WHIP
The ERA, strikeouts, and holds will be there for Baez, as his skill set appears to be stable. Baez throws hard and generates swinging strikes, but his propensity for fly balls (48% last season) does give us some cause for concern.

Joe Kelly, age 31, RHP
2019 stats: 51.1 IP, 62 K, 1 Save, 4.56 ERA, 1.38 WHIP
After struggling to the tune of a 5.93 ERA in the first half of the season, bad luck did come into play as he had a 3.83 xERA, Kelly bounced back in the second half. A large part of that was due to the increased usage of his sinker and curveball. Kelly also has the velocity you would expect from a late inning reliever, but he is best left to holds leagues, as his ratios are still more risky than we would like them to be.

Adam Kolarek, age 30, LHP
2019 stats: 55 IP, 45 K, 1 Save, 3.27 ERA, 1.16 WHIP
Acquired from Tampa Bay last season, the left-handed specialist and his 66% groundball rate continued to have success. The strikeouts aren't enough to be considered a true asset, and while his success against left-handed batters leads to holds, there is a new variable to consider. And that, is the three-batter minimum. So, let's stay away here.

Dylan Floro, age 28, RHP
2019 stats: 46.2 IP, 42 K, 0 Save, 4.24 ERA, 1.29 WHIP
Floro is your typical middle reliever who has both good and bad flashes of performance, and there really isn't much fantasy value to be found.

Scott Alexander, age 29, LHP
2019 stats: 17.1 IP, 9 K, 0 Saves, 3.63 ERA, 1.39 WHIP
The southpaw isn't going to blow anyone away, but he keeps the ball on the ground at a high level, and that is about it. From a fantasy perspective, there isn't much to see here.

Casey Sadler, age 29, RHP
2019 stats: 46.1 IP, 31 K, 1 Save, 2.14 ERA, 1.17 WHIP
I'm not sure we can expect a 2.89 ERA again from Sadler, and likely will be on the Triple-A shuttle for the majority of 2020. That also means that Sadler won't get to pitch in any fantasy relevant roles.

# Los Angeles Dodgers Prospects
By Matt Thompson

## 1. Gavin Lux- SS
The strong ending to his 2018 season and whether or not it was sustainable looks like a silly conversation now. Lux obliterated Double-A and Triple-A in 2019, and earned a call-up to the show for the Dodgers and got some meaningful at-bats down the stretch and in the postseason. Lux has the rare combination of ceiling and floor, and is a top five fantasy prospect no matter how you slice it. He's the best second baseman in the organization, and I think he's a better shortstop than Seager. Lux will play a prominent role in the lineup for the Dodgers, but he may start the season in Triple-A due to all the quality depth in the organization. **ETA: Arrived.**

## 2. Dustin May- RHP
May has some of the best stuff in professional baseball, featuring a nasty 94-98 MPH sinking fastball that gets weak contact and misses bats. He compliments it with a 12-6 curve, a cutter and a change. It's a Bronson Arroyo-esque delivery with the versatility to succeed in any role on a staff. My one worry with May is that he doesn't miss bats at an elite rate considering the stuff, and he's more of an 8 K/9 guy but thrives on weak contact and an arsenal that has so much wiggle that it's impossible for hitters to square him up. **ETA: Arrived.**

## 3. Jeter Downs- SS/2B
The first of a pair of former Reds prospects on this list, Jeter Downs is the latest in the long line of Dodgers power breakouts as he went from 13 to 24 homers in his first year in the organization. He had a 24/24 season across High-A and Double-A, showing off his athleticism and above-average speed that plays up due to his plus instincts. The power is real, and Downs can easily clear the 20-homer mark in the bigs, and it will likely come with a high amount of doubles. The lack of arm strength will likely push him to second base long term. He should start 2020 in Double-A. **ETA: 2021.**

## 4. Josiah Gray- RHP
The former Reds prospect was famously dealt to the Dodgers on his birthday, and the young righty pitched at three different levels for the Dodgers in 2019. He started in the Midwest League and ended the season in Double-A. He was a former college shortstop that has elite athleticism for a pitcher. His fastball sits in the low-to-mid 90s with some wiggle and he pairs it with a slider that has shown promise, but he can lose feel for the pitch and will struggle to throw strikes with it. Gray is primarily a two-pitch guy, and needs his changeup to show to stick in the rotation long term. **ETA: 2021.**

## 5. Kody Hoese- 3B
The Dodgers were in the middle of fast-tracking Hoese after drafting him in 2019, but an arm injury slowed him them down and ended his first pro season prematurely. The Tulane product was criticized a bit for facing weaker competition in college, but he drew some rave reviews from scout contacts and I have zero doubts about his ability to hit at the highest level. He's got

the glamour tools in the third baseman's tool belt, the powerful arm and plus raw power, but the overall defense and body may force him to first base. Hoese can hit, and could reach Triple-A by seasons end. **ETA: 2021.**

### 6. Luis Rodriguez- OF

The Dodgers handed the Venezuelan outfielder a $2.7 million bonus. He doesn't have a standout tool here, but he does have a well rounded above-average skill set. The contact skills are strong and he's an interesting flyer in FYPD's who will drop a bit since he didn't play after signing. **ETA: 2024.**

### 7. Michael Busch- 2B/1B

The Dodgers announced Busch as a second baseman on draft day, and he played a little second base during my AFL looks at him. He's not going to be great there, he lacks athleticism and is a bit stiff, but he will blow away the offensive bar there if he sticks at the position. He's value is tied entirely to his bat though, and he's got plus raw pop with enough bat-to-ball skills to make him a prime candidate to take off in 2020. **ETA: 2022.**

### 8. Tony Gonsolin- RHP

On any other club we'd be talking about Gonsolin battling for a rotation spot this spring, but the Dodgers are so deep in the rotation that it's a sure thing that Tony G will either go to Oklahoma City or pitch out of the bullpen for the Dodgers initially. His splitter is one of the best pitches in the minors, a pitch that misses bats and tunnels well off of his fastball, which sits 92-95 as a starter and can touch higher in short stints. He also throws a curveball and a slider. The overall command is above-average, and he will be a successful big league starter. **ETA: Arrived.**

### 9. DJ Peters- OF

You know the story with Peters by now, huge raw power, plus athleticism, near-elite bat speed, but, and here it comes, severe contact issues. Peter's contact rate was sub-65% at both Double-A and Triple-A in 2019 (32% and 29% K%). He's even an above-average runner that can stick in center, but you won't see the speed play on the bases. He will post above-average walk rates, showing that it's not a pitch recognition issue, but a straight up put the bat on the ball issue. If you give Peters a 40-hit tool he can be a star. It's not there, and likely won't ever be. **ETA: 2021.**

### 10. Diego Cartaya- C

I saw Cartaya on the Arizona backfields during my AFL trip, and my dude is a big man. Big but athletic, he should stick behind the plate but the wait time will be a long one. He runs well for a big man, and for a catcher his run times are probably plus. He's strong and doesn't have to square up the ball for it to leave the yard. I'm assuming there are some hustle issues here as the Dodgers staff was riding him hard to get on and off the field quickly and while he was on the base paths during instructs, but I like what I saw. The power is plus, and he covers the plate well. We will see him in five or six years. **ETA: 2024.**

**Next Five:**
Miguel Vargas- 3B
Alex De Jesus- 3B
Jimmy Lewis- RHP
Zach McKinstry- 2B/SS
Ryan Pepiot- RHP

**Top Five in FYPDs:**
Kody Hoese- 3B
Luis Rodriguez- OF
Michael Busch- 2B/1B
Jimmy Lewis- RHP
Ryan Pepiot- RHP

**San Diego Padres Team Preview**
By Gabe Zammit

## Projected Order:
1- Fernando Tatis Jr., SS
2- Tommy Pham, OF
3- Manny Machado, 3B
4- Eric Hosmer, 1B
5- Trent Grisham, OF
6- Francisco Mejia, C
7- Franchy Cordero, OF
8- Jurickson Profar, 2B

## Projected Bench:
Austin Hedges, C
Ty France, INF
Greg Garcia, INF
Manuel Margot, OF
Wil Myers, 1B/OF

## Projected Rotation:
Chris Paddack, RHP
Garrett Richards, RHP
Zach Davies, RHP
Joey Lucchesi, LHP
Dinelson Lamet, RHP

## Bullpen:
Kirby Yates, RHP
Drew Pomeranz, LHP
Andres Munoz, RHP
Craig Stammen, RHP
Matt Strahm, LHP
Pierce Johnson, RHP
José Castillo, LHP
Javy Guerra, RHP

## Catchers:
Francisco Mejia, age 24, eligible at C
2019 Stats: 244 PA, 8 HR, 27 Runs, 22 RBI, 1 SB, .265/.316/.438
The former much hyped Indians prospect got traded to the Padres last year but did not take advantage of the opportunity to grab full time at bats. His xBA of .229 points to a potentially

more grim picture. Sure, there is still upside to be a 15-20 homer guy, but he could also be an anchor to your BA. He's a watchlist guy, but I'm not drafting him.

Austin Hedges, age 27, eligible at C
2019 Stats: 347 PA, 11 HR, 28 Runs, 36 RBI, 1 SB, .176/.252/.311
It's probably too late to expect a breakout from Austin Hedges. His xBA is in the 0th percentile in the majors… No, that's not a typo. That means the leash on Mejia might be longer just because the alternative means more at bats for Hedges.

**Infielders:**
Eric Hosmer, age 30, eligible at 1B
2019 Stats: 667 PA, 22 HR, 72 Runs, 99 RBI, 0 SB, .265/.310/.425
Ho hum…. That pretty much sums up everyone's feelings on Eric Hosmer. The prospect of him being anything special are long, long gone. There is a fine floor here of 18 HR and 150 Runs & RBI combined. That floor is unfortunately not too far from his ceiling either.

Jurickson Profar, age 27, eligible at 2B
2019 Stats: 518 PA, 20 HR, 65 Runs, 67 RBI, 9 SB, .218/.301/.410
Last year was a real let down for Profar backers after his semi-breakout in 2018. Oddly enough, Profar's walk and strikeout rate stayed in line with the previous year. So what happened? His BABIP and xBA both paint an optimistic picture for this year. It's fair to expect a bounce-back to at least his 2018 triple slash of .254/.335/.458.

Fernando Tatis Jr., age 22, eligible at SS
2019 Stats: 372 PA, 22 HR, 61 Runs, 53 RBI, 16 SB, .317/.379/.590
If Tatis hadn't suffered his back injury in August, he might have blown past a 30/20 season. Is there regression coming this year? Well, his 29.6% strikeout rate and .410 BABIP suggest that his BA will drop to maybe the .250 range. Regardless, this is a superstar player blossoming before our eyes.

Manny Machado, age 27, eligible at 3B
2019 Stats: 661 PA, 32 HR, 81 Runs, 85 RBI, 5 SB, .256/.334/.462
Machado signed a huge free agent contract with the Padres last offseason and was a huge disappointment to fantasy owners looking for elite return on their draft day investment. The problem isn't so much that he had a bad year, rather that 30 HR and a handful of steals is not all that special anymore. Don't be too quick to dismiss Machado come draft day. There is still plenty of power in his bat as exit velocity hasn't changed in 5 seasons. A return to 35+ homers is very possible, and with an improved lineup, he could break 100 RBI easily.

Ty France, age 25, eligible at 2B/3B
2019 Stats: 201 PA, 7 HR, 20 Runs, 24 RBI, 0 SB, .234/.294/.402
The acquisition of Profar threw cold water on any hope that Ty France could grab everyday at bats, which means the team either doesn't believe he's an everyday player, or that he would benefit from some more time to develop his bat. He should still get between 150-200 at bats as a fill-in player and could see more time if Profar can't get his act together.

Greg Garcia, age 30, eligible at 2B
2019 Stats: 372 PA, 4 HR, 52 Runs, 31 RBI, 0 SB, .248/.364/.354

The Padres have better options than Greg Garcia should an injury to a starter occur. Outside of his 14.2% walk rate, there is no other real fantasy friendly skill here.

**Outfielders:**
Tommy Pham, age 32, eligible at OF
2019 Stats: 654 PA, 21 HR, 102 Runs, 63 RBI, 15 SB, .273/.369/.450
The move cross-country for Pham shouldn't affect him all that much from the standpoint of playing time or park factors. He is a safe bet for 20 HR and could see upwards of 20-25 SB. He's an underrated draft target and needs to get moved up quite a bit in OBP leagues.

Trent Grisham, age 23, eligible at OF
2019 Stats: 183 PA, 6 HR, 24 Runs, 24 RBI, 1 SB, .231/.328/.410
In an interesting trade, Grisham was moved in the off-season from the Brewers in exchange for Luis Urias. Grisham has an up and down 2019 once he got called up, but his minor league profile shows a capacity to be a plus with his power and OBP. The Padres will give him an opportunity to lock down every day at bats in LF.

Franchy Cordero, age 25, eligible at OF
2019 Stats: 20 PA, 0 HR, 2 Runs, 1 RBI, 1 SB, .333/.450/.400
A myriad of injuries put ended Cordero's season before it could really even start. The tools are there for 20 homers and 10 steals, but it's really going to come down to health and playing time. Cordero is likely to be pushed by Manny Margot, particularly if he can't get his career .240 AVG up.

Manuel Margot, age 25, eligible at OF
2019 Stats: 441 PA, 12 HR, 59 Runs, 37 RBI, 20 SB, .234/.304/.387
Margot continues to tease fantasy owners with his speed potential and would be a real threat for 30+ SB if he had a full season of at bats. Therein lies the problem, his BA has dropped three years in a row which has relegated him to a 4th OF role.

Wil Myers, age 29, eligible at OF
2019 Stats: 490 PA, 18 HR, 58 Runs, 53 RBI, 16 SB, .239/.321/.418
The window for Myers to stay fantasy relevant seems to be closing quickly. Even with a poor BA, he's surprisingly been a good source of power and speed the last few years. The Padres just have a logjam on their major league roster at the corner OF spots and with the bloated contract of Hosmer. Without some sort of injury, or an unbelievable start to the season, Myers will be hard pressed for consistent playing time.

**Starters:**
Chris Paddack, age 24, RHP
2019 Stats: 140.2 IP, 153 K, 9 W, 3.33 ERA, 0.98 WHIP
What a rookie year from Chris Paddack. If it weren't for his inning cap, he may have surpassed 200 K's. His success is especially remarkable when you consider that he primarily throws a fastball and change up with his curveball lagging far behind. He's likely more of a high-end SP2 than an ace if that curveball doesn't take a step forward. If it does… look out.

Garrett Richards, age 31, RHP
2019 Stats: 8.2 IP, 11 K, 8.31 ERA, 1.85 WHIP

Considering his slew of injuries and recovery from TJ surgery, it's hard not to root for Garrett Richards to complete his comeback and find relevance as a fantasy starter again. He made a few starts late last season and the velocity was there but the command hadn't returned yet. Richards is a guy to monitor, although an inning cap is likely.

Zach Davies, age 27, RHP
2019 Stats: 159.2 IP, 102 K, 10 W, 3.55 ERA, 1.29 WHIP
A soft-tosser, Davies can really only be counted on for a cheap win here and there as his ratios won't help much for your fantasy squad. His peak velocity last year was 89 MPH. He's easy to avoid in drafts.

Joey Lucchesi, age 26, LHP
2019 Stats: 163.2 IP, 158 K, 10 W, 4.18 ERA, 1.22 WHIP
There's not a lot of margin for error within Lucchesi's starts, and yet there might be hope for a step forward with him. His K/9 decreased last year from 10.04 to 8.69 even though his swinging strike rate remained virtually the same. The effectiveness of his changeup appears to be the main culprit behind this strikeout decrease. Lucchesi might be a bargain come draft day if he is able to figure out his secondary stuff, but he's best drafted as a bench option.

Dinelson Lamet, age 27, RHP
2019 Stats: 73 IP, 105 K, 3 W, 4.07 ERA, 1.26 WHIP
Lamet seems to be going higher and higher in drafts and for good reason. He returned last year after a successful rehab from TJ surgery and he looked better than ever. He posted an incredible 12.95 K/9 while also recording a 3.91 FIP. He could be a slightly better version of Robbie Ray, the only question is how many innings will he throw? The Padres have been known to limit innings, so Lamet could take a hit in Quality Start leagues.

**Relievers:**
Kirby Yates, age 33, RHP
2019 Stats: 60.2 IP, 101 K, 41 SV, 1.19 ERA, 0.89 WHIP
Could Kirby Yates be the nest reliever this year? All of his metrics show that the insane progress he made last year was not a fluke. His fastball and splitter combo are absolutely deadly and should remain as such this year. The likelihood of another 40 save season has less to do with his skills, and more to do with the fickle nature of saves in general.

Drew Pomeranz, age 31, LHP
2019 Stats: 104 IP, 137 K, 4.85 ERA, 1.43 WHIP
Pomeranz moved full time to a bullpen role in August and saw himself to a 2.53 ERA and 15.61 K/9 over his final 21 innings. It's safe to say, he found his sweet spot. With Yates in the closing role, Pomeranz could take on a late multi-inning relief type role and actually provide quite a bit of value (think 2018 Josh Hader).

Andres Munoz, age 21, RHP
2019 Stats: 23 IP, 30 K, 3.91 ERA, 1.17 WHIP
His strikeout numbers don't reflect it yet, but Andres Munoz has filthy stuff. He can pump his fastball up to 100 MPH on command and make hitters look silly, so long as he places the ball in the strike zone. Because of the depth in the Padres bullpen, Munoz will be able to refine his

command with less pressure. He's a great stash in deep dynasty leagues, but redraft appeal is not there for the time being.

Craig Stammen, age 36, RHP
2019 Stats: 82 IP, 73 K, 8 W, 3.29 ERA, 1.16 WHIP
Attention, those of you who play in holds leagues. You should take note of Craig Stammen and his 31 holds from 2019. Those of you who don't, you can disregard this player.

Matt Strahm, age 28, LHP
2019 Stats: 114.2 IP, 118 K, 4.71 ERA, 1.25 WHIP
Strahm was a very buzzy sleeper a year ago when he was announced as a starter. His curve and slider combo looked like they could have fueled a big breakout. What happened instead was a year worth forgetting. Strahm is better suited in the bullpen or as the occasional spot starter, which essentially makes him worthless for fantasy.

Pierce Johnson, age 28, RHP
2019 Stats: Did Not Play
Johnson spent the 2019 season in Japan and got 40 Holds with a 1.38 ERA across 58 appearances. It's difficult to put a value on him until we see his usage play out. For now, he looks like nothing more than bullpen depth.

José Castillo, age 24, LHP
2019 Stats: 0.2 IP, 2 K, 0.00 ERA, 1.50 WHIP
The innings weren't really there for Castillo in 2019 between the majors or minors as he battled a couple of injuries. When he is healthy, he could end up being a valuable addition to this already crowded bullpen. In the majors in 2018, Castillo struck out 52 batters in 38.1 innings with a 3.29 ERA, so he's worth watching.

Javy Guerra, age 24, RHP
2019 Stats: 8.2 IP, 6 K, 5.19 ERA, 1.15 WHIP
Guerra is a converted hitter and is still finding his way as a pitcher in the major leagues. For now, he is more of a feel good story than someone you'd want to roster.

## San Diego Padres Prospects
By Matt Thompson

### 1. MacKenzie Gore- LHP
Gore has everything you want in a pitching prospect, with advanced command of his four-pitch arsenal, and elite athleticism that just exudes from his delivery. Gore will turn 21 prior to Opening Day, and he's already dominated High-A and made a handful of starts in Double-A. Chris Paddack threw 37 innings in Double-A before breaking camp with the Padres last spring, and that worked out well for the club. Gore has thrown 21 innings in Double-A, and A.J. Preller's seat is getting warm in San Diego. Apples to oranges, but Fernando Tatis got a cup of coffee in Double-A before getting to the big leagues. If anyone is going to do it it will be the Padres. Gore has four potential plus pitches with above-average command. He's a future number one, and he's likely one of the Padres top two or three starters right now. C'mon Preller! Let's do it. **ETA: 2020.**

### 2. CJ Abrams- SS
Abrams has proven to be much more polished than originally thought, and he's proven to be the best prep bat in the class so far. Armed with game-changing true 80-grade speed, Abrams is what we thought Xavier Edwards could've been, but with more thump. His power grade could even be average. The hit tool is plus, and he can pick it at shortstop. If everything goes right he could be a future franchise player, and a rock solid piece up the middle. **ETA: 2023.**

### 3. Luis Patiño- RHP
Patiño gets overshadowed due to the presence of MacKenzie Gore, but he's a top pitching prospect in his own right. The athletic righty has a leg kick similar to Gore and also the elite arm speed. The fastball comes in at 93-95 with late life, and his slider is a swing and miss breaking ball. He also has an above-average curveball and changeup. It's a riskier profile but he still profiles as a number two for me. **ETA: 2021.**

### 4. Taylor Trammell- OF
The former Reds farmhand came over in the three team deal that sent Trevor Bauer to Cincinnati. He's an elite athlete with a strong eye, and 25-30 steal upside. He's flashed an above-average hit tool but has batted ball data shows a pessimistic view on his future power. Trammell doesn't drive or lift the ball consistently. His poor throwing arm may push him to left, but they will try and extract as much value as possible here and keep him in center. **ETA: 2021.**

### 5. Luis Campusano- C
Campusano made significant strides offensively in 2019, and his offensive numbers matched his strong defense. His plate skills were elite, and the early above-average grades on his hit tool may be a bit low. He's got 60 raw, and understands how to work counts and hunt for his pitch. He projects as an above-average defender, and has a chance to be the two-way catcher they hoped Austin Hedges would become. **ETA: 2021.**

### 6. Hudson Head- OF

Despite being drafted in the third round the Padres gave Double-H first round money to get him signed. His $3 million bonus is a record for the third round, and it looks to be a shrewd one so far. Head has plus bat speed and stings the ball with regularity, and is a plus runner with growing power. This was an absolute steal by the Padres. **ETA: 2023.**

### 7. Jake Cronenworth- SS/RHP

The two-way Cronenworth came over to the Padres from the Rays in the Tommy Pham/Hunter Renfroe deal. Cronenworth broke out in Triple-A Durham and was on the cusp of a call-up prior to the trade. When you factor in the approach it's a plus hit tool, and he's an above-average runner that can play a strong defensive shortstop. He can also pitch a bit, and can actually be used as an extra pitcher in the NL parks, which gives him a bit of added value. He can bring it in the low 90s with a usable breaking ball. **ETA: 2020.**

### 8. Edward Olivares- OF

Olivares was originally a Blue Jays prospect and came over to San Diego for Yangervis Solarte. Olivares has shown strong plate skills with above-average speed and growing average power. The power grade is going to jump up as he matures. He can play all three outfield spots, and his plus arm makes him a fit in right, but he's athletic enough and a strong enough fielder to handle center. He might be one of the most underrated prospects in baseball. He can hit, and gets overlooked in this system. He will be in San Diego mid-season if injuries hit. **ETA: 2020.**

### 9. Gabriel Arias- SS

Arias had a reputation as a glove first shortstop, but he had his career best offensive season across the board in 2019, and is looking to grow on that as he heads to Double-A in 2020. Arias can pick it, and may be the strongest defender in the entire organization at any position. It's a plus glove, but with Tatis around, he may be sliding over to second base. It's fun to watch athletes like this go to work, and Arias is certainly that. **ETA: 2022.**

### 10. Reginald Preciado- SS

The Padres signed Preciado for $1.3 million. The teenage switch-hitting shortstop is lean, and lanky with a ton of physical projection. It's hard to say what happens to the body, but he should fill out, and if he continues to barrel the ball as often as he does he could grow into plus power while sticking at shortstop. Exciting profile. **ETA: 2024.**

**Next Five:**
Adrian Morejon- LHP
Junior Perez- OF
Joey Cantillo- LHP
Ryan Weathers- LHP
Ismael Mena- OF

**Top Five in FYPDs:**

CJ Abrams- SS
Hudson Head- OF
Reginald Preciado- SS
Ismael Mena- OF
Joshua Mears- OF

**San Francisco Giants Team Preview**
By Jorge Montanez

## Projected Order
1. Mike Yaztrzemski, RF
2. Buster Posey, C
3. Brandon Belt, 1B
4. Evan Longoria, 3B
5. Alex Dickerson, LF
6. Brandon Crawford, SS
7. Mauricio Dubon, 2B
8. Steven Duggar, CF

## Projected Bench
Aramis Garcia, C
Zack Cozart, INF
Donovan Solano, INF
Jaylin Davis, OF
Austin Slater, OF/INF

## Projected Rotation
Johnny Cueto, RHP
Jeff Samardzija, RHP
Kevin Gausman, RHP
Tyler Beede, RHP
Logan Webb, RHP

## Projected Bullpen
Shaun Anderson, RHP
Tony Watson, LHP
Jandel Gustave, RHP
Tyler Rogers, RHP
Sam Coonrod, RHP
Trevor Gott, RHP
Wandy Peralta, LHP
Dany Jimenez, RHP

## Catchers:
Buster Posey, Age 32
2019 Stats: 445 PA, 7 HR, 43 R, 38 RBI, 0SB, .257/.320/.368
With 1258 games played under his belt, the face of the Giants franchise over the last decade is likely done as a major fantasy contributor. The decline has been in motion for the last three years now with declining slugging, average, and on-base percentage. Many times, eroding plate discipline and contact skills are true signs of age-related decline. Posey had the worst walk-to-strikeout ratio of his career to go with career-low contact rates. Perhaps a year removed from hip surgery can help Posey hit for a decent average, but at this point that's about all we can hope for.

Aramis Garcia, Age 26
2019 Stats: 46 PA, 2 HR, 5 R, 5 RBI, 0 SB, .143/.217/.310
Aramis Garcia has always been an intriguing prospect with power potential. At this point, it doesn't seem like he's going to develop the contact and plate skills necessary to stick in the majors. His last two seasons in Triple-A saw a strikeout rate hovering around 30%. While it's been a small sample size, he's struck out over 45% of the time at the MLB level. With an option remaining, I wouldn't be surprised to see the Giants sign a veteran catcher to back up Buster Posey until Joey Bart is ready for his major league debut.

**Infielders**
Brandon Belt, Age 31, 1B
2019 Stats: 616 PA, 17 HR, 76 R, 57 RBI, 4 SB .234/.339/.403
Well, the Giants are finally going to help out Brandon Belt and move the fences in, albeit just marginally. But moving the bullpen to center field last season would have given Brandon Belt his first 20 home run season with perhaps five or so more home runs. The fact that Belt hasn't had a 20-home run season is astonishing considering his extreme fly ball tendencies. Belt has been at the center of trade rumors for years, but until he's moved, we're operating under the assumption that he'll be a Giant and forever left wondering what could have been of Brandon Belt's career had he played in a different park. Belt still walks at an elite rate, but outside of OBP leagues, he carries little to no value in other categories.

Mauricio Dubon, Age 25, 2B/SS
2019 Stats: 111 PA, 4 HR, 12 R, 9 RBI, 3 SB, .274/.306/.434
Mauricio Dubon was the prize of the trade deadline for Farhan Zaidi after he was acquired in exchange for Drew Pomeranz. Dubon is an interesting mix of power, speed, and hit ability after he totaled 24 home runs and 13 stolen bases between Triple-A and the majors last season. He has a track record of not striking out in the minors, which bodes well for his chances to hit for a decent average at the MLB level. He'll be an interesting late addition in drafts, especially in roto leagues where he can achieve double digit home runs and steals with regular playing time.

Brandon Crawford, Age 32, SS
2019 Stats: 560 PA, 11 HR, 58 R, 59 RBI, 3 SB, .228/.304/.350
Another piece of the Giants' aging core of the 2010's, Brandon Crawford had his worst statistical season with a 74 wRC+. Granted, he's never been the most relevant of fantasy shortstops as he's more renowned for his glovework. Look for the phaseout to begin with the aging core players as Crawford could platoon with guys like Donovan Solano and Mauricio Dubon. Crawford should go undrafted in just about every league.

Evan Longoria, Age 34, 3B
2019 Stats: 508 PA, 20 HR, 59 R, 69 RBI, 3 SB, .254/.325/.437
The numbers might not show it, but Evan Longoria had his best season at the plate since 2016. Had Longoria stayed healthy, he would have been on pace for about 25 home runs. With 129 and 125 games played over the last two seasons, it's fair to question Longoria's durability at this point of his career. But when we did hit, he still hit the ball well with his highest average exit velocity since 2016. He won't be relevant in 12 team leagues, but perhaps a late power source in 15 team leagues at the corner infield position isn't out of the question.

Zack Cozart, Age 34, SS

2019 Stats: 0 HR, 4 R, 7 RBI, 0 SB, .124/.178/.144

In another brilliant move by Farhan Zaidi, the Giants took on Zack Cozart's remaining year on his contract along with one the Angels' top prospects Will Wilson. Wilson was the real prize in the trade. With no open position to play, Cozart will likely be irrelevant this season. Perhaps an injury could open up some playing time and allow Cozart an opportunity to reclaim some value, but I wouldn't count on it. In fact, it wouldn't surprise me to see Cozart cut before the start of the season.

Donovan Solano, Age 32, 2B

2019 Stats: 228 PA, 4 HR, 27 R, 23 RBI, 0 SB, .330/.360/.456

The 32-year-old journeyman played respectably in his role as a utility man for the Giants in 2019. Although his .330 average came with a .409 BABIP in only 228 plate appearances. Solano won't be fantasy relevant as I don't expect an expanded role for him.

**Outfielders**

Mike Yastrzemski, Age 29, OF

2019 Stats: 411 PA, 21 HR, 64 R, 55 RBI, 2 SB, .272/.334/.518

The grandson of a Hall of Famer, Yastrzemski enjoyed a late breakout at 29-years-old. Any time a player has a breakout season this late in their career I find it a little skeptical. Yastrzemski's high strikeout rate and .325 BABIP has me concerned that he won't keep up a .272 average. While the BABIP isn't too crazy, it's well above his career average in the minor leagues. The 11.2%-barrel rate does give some credence to his power output, so perhaps another 20-home run season could come in 2020. Outside of that I don't think Yastrzemski will be relevant in anything other than deeper five outfielder leagues.

Alex Dickerson, Age 29, OF

2019 Stats: 190 PA, 6 HR, 29 R, 28 RBI, 1 SB, .276/.332/.489

Dickerson is tentatively penciled in to start for the Giants after he returned on a one-year contract. He compares similarly to Yastrzemski, although his lower strikeout rate and track record of high BABIPs in the minors lead me to believe he could sustain a decent average. That average is going to come as part of a platoon against right-handed pitchers, as he's struggled against left-handed pitching. I can see a fifth outfielder in a deep league or perhaps relevant in an NL only format if things break right for Dickerson and he can stay healthy.

Steven Duggar, Age 26, OF

2019 Stats: 281 PA, 4 HR, 26 R, 28 RBI, 1 SB, .234/.278/.341

With the departure of Kevin Pillar, Duggar should reclaim his spot in center field. His defense should keep him in the lineup for the most part. Although his strikeout rate and struggles against lefties could lead to him having the strong side of a platoon. Don't expect much in the way of fantasy upside for Duggar. He should be going undrafted everywhere.

Jaylin Davis, Age 25, OF

2019 Stats: 47 PA, 1 HR, 2 R, 3 RBI, 1 SB, .167/.255/.238

The Giants are going to want to see what they have out of the power hitting prospect they acquired from the Minnesota Twins last season. Davis hit 35 home runs between Double-A and Triple-A in 2019. Perhaps we see a platoon situation with Alex Dickerson or Steven Duggar. He should be drafted anywhere at this point but he's an interesting name to keep an eye on for San Francisco.

Austin Slater, Age 27, OF
2019 Stats: 192 PA, 5 HR, 20 R, 21 RBI, 1 SB, .238/.333/.417
Another player in the long list of fantasy irrelevant bodies in the Giants' lineup. Slater hasn't been able to get his strikeouts under control in the majors. The weak side of a platoon, a decent on base percentage, and a hand full of home runs and counting stats, that's it, that's the upside.

**Starters**
Johnny Cueto, Age 33, RHP
2019 Stats: 16 IP, 13 Ks, 1 Win, 5.06 ERA, 1.25 WHIP
Johnny Cueto returned to game action late last season from Tommy John surgery. The small sample size of 16 innings can be mostly dismissed. While he pitched well through 53 innings in 2018, his 4.71 FIP showed he'd been getting lucky with a 3.23 ERA and a mere 6.45 K/9. If a pitcher is going to outpitch his metrics and get away with a low strikeout rate, San Francisco is the place to do it. Cueto might be worth a flier as a home streamer in deep leagues but don't let his name value sway you into taking him in any shallow mixed league format.

Jeff Samardzija, Age 34, RHP
2019 Stats: 181.1 IP, 140 Ks, 11 Wins, 3.52 ERA, 1.11 WHIP
Samardzija bounced back from an injury riddled 2018 season to provide solid volume, contributing in ERA and WHIP. As mentioned previously regarding Cueto, San Francisco is the place to pitch with diminished skills. Samardzija is the perfect example with a 4.59 FIP and 6.95 K/9. If you drafted him last season, you got great value. Can you get lucky two years in a row? Outside of a WHIP stabilizer, I wouldn't expect much else.

Kevin Gausman, Age 28, RHP
2019 Stats: 102.1 IP, 114 Ks, 3 Wins, 5.72 ERA, 1.42 WHIP
The rebuilding Giants team took a chance on Keven Gausman this offseason, signing him to a one-year deal. Gausman spent time with Atlanta and Cincinnati last season. While things didn't work out as a starter, he proved to be much more effective as a reliever. Gausman had a 6.37 ERA with a 1.49 WHIP as a starter and a 3.10 ERA with a 1.13 WHIP as a reliever. Gausman features an excellent splitter, but aside from his fastball, he's just a two pitch pitcher. The plan is for him to start the season in the rotation, but he could ultimately end up in the bullpen. There's an outside chance he could save some games for the Giants. He's worth a gamble late in drafts as it won't cost you much to see how things pan out.

Tyler Beede, Age 26, RHP
2019 Stats: 117 IP, 113 Ks, 5 Wins, 5.08 ERA, 1.48 WHIP
Things didn't go so well for Beede in his first season in the majors. Beede's 5.03 FIP doesn't give much hope for his 5.08 ERA. The former first round pick was hit around hard in 2019, falling in the bottom two percent of the league in average exit velocity allowed and bottom four percent in hard hit percentage allowed. The 1.48 WHIP just exacerbates those problems. Beede has potential, but he needs to correct his control issues and work on suppressing hard contact. He'll go undrafted in most leagues but will remain someone to keep an eye on.

Logan Webb, Age 23, RHP
2019 Stats: 39.2 IP, 37 Ks, 2 Wins, 5.22 ERA, 1.46 WHIP

One of the more interesting young players on the 2020 Giants team will be Logan Webb. Webb will be filling out the rotation as the fifth starter after making eight starts to end the season. A 2.18 ERA and 10.23 K/9 in Double-A earned him a shot with the big club in August. There are some signs that point to positive regression for Webb after putting up a 5.22 ERA in 39.2 major league innings. That ERA came with a 4.12 FIP, 48.8% ground ball rate, 65.4% strand rate, .333 BABIP against him. Across three levels of the minor leagues last season, Webb generated a ground ball rate over 60%. He'll be virtually free in drafts. You'll want to keep him on your watch list.

**Relievers**
Shaun Anderson, Age 25, RHP
2019 Stats: 96 IP, 70 Ks, 2 Saves, 5.44 ERA, 1.55 WHIP
Shaun Anderson made his big-league debut last season and made 16 starts posting a 5.33 ERA before being moved to the bullpen. As a reliever he posted a 6.08 ERA in 13.1 innings. The ERA was a bit inflated by a four-run outing to end the season. Remove his final outing and he has a 3.55 ERA as a reliever. Anderson did fill in for Will Smith to pick up two saves down the stretch and is currently penciled in as the closer for 2020. He's a dart throw for saves in the final rounds of deep leagues.

Tony Watson, Age 34, LHP
2019 Stats: 54 IP, 41 Ks, 4.17 ERA, 1.26 WHIP
Tony Watson exercised his player option to remain with the team after a disappointing season. Watson posted his highest ERA since 2011 at 4.17. He also saw a dip in his strikeout rate at 6.83 K/9, his lowest since 2013. While he's served as a closer before, Watson hasn't recorded a save since 2017. Outside of deep leagues that count holds, Watson holds little to no fantasy value in 2020.

Jandel Gustave, Age 27, RHP
2019 Stats: 24.1 IP, 14 Ks, 1 Save, 2.96 ERA, 1.11 WHIP
Gustave was a bit lucky to have a 2.96 ERA considering he had a .227 BABIP against and a mere 5.18 K/9. There's no reason to draft Gustave even if the San Francisco closing job is up in the air.

Tyler Rogers, Age 29, RHP
2019 Stats: 17.2 IP, 16 Ks, 1.02 ERA, 0.85 WHIP
Tyler Rogers finally earned a shot in the big leagues and took advantage of his opportunity. Rogers posted a 1.02 ERA by limiting base runners and inducing ground balls at a 69.4% rate. He's made his case for a bigger role in 2020 but will remain off the fantasy radar for the time being.

Sam Coonrod, Age 27, RHP
2019 Stats: 27.2 IP, 20 Ks, 3.58 ERA, 1.23 WHIP
Sam Coonrod was another San Francisco Giant to make his MLB debut last season. Coonrod's 3.58 ERA came with a 5.24 FIP and 6.51 K/9. Needless to say he shouldn't be on any fantasy teams in 2020.

Trevor Gott, Age 27, RHP
2019 Stats: 52.2 IP, 57 Ks, 1 Save, 4.44 ERA, 1.10 WHIP

Trevor Gott has a few things to like about his profile including a four-seam fastball that sits in the mid-90's and induces an above average 11.8% swinging strike rate. The disparity between his 4.44 ERA and 3.12 FIP shows he was a better pitcher than what the number indicates. Gott could be a dark horse candidate to save games.

Wandy Peralta, Age 28, LHP
2019 Stats: 39.2 IP, 32 Ks, 5.67 ERA, 1.41 WHIP
Nothing to see here. 5.67 ERA came with a 6.57 FIP. Most of that came in Cincinnati as he made his final eight appearances with the Giants. He faced only one batter in four of those eight appearances for San Francisco. Peralta is irrelevant for 2020 fantasy baseball.

Dany Jimenez, Age 26, RHP
2019 Stats (Double-A): 33.2 IP, 46 Ks, 6 Saves, 1.87 ERA, 1.01 WHIP
Dany Jimenez is an interesting arm acquired by San Francisco in the Rule 5 draft. Considering the other options in the bullpen and the potential Jimenez has, I think there's a good shot he stays with the big-league club. Jimenez dominated Double-A last season with a high-90's fastball to go with a slider and changeup. He's someone to monitor come Spring Training but shouldn't be drafted anywhere until he's established a role with the club.

# San Francisco Giants Prospects
By Matt Thompson

## 1. Marco Luciano- SS
Luciano and Wander Franco are the part of the reason why Jasson Dominguez stock is so high. The track record for top ranked J2 teenagers has been extremely hot, and Luciano has exceeded all expectations for him to this point. The bat speed is plus, if not better and the raw power is 70-grade. He's shown strong walk rates and has the ability to be a five category contributor for fantasy. The only knocks are his proximity and that he may have to move to third base as he fills out. Luciano has the ability to hit .300 with 30-35 bombs and 20-30 stolen bases. **ETA: 2022.**

## 2. Heliot Ramos- OF
Ramos has an exciting power-speed combination, but it comes from a body that is going to require maintenance. Ramos has plus bat speed and will use all fields, and should hit for average while also netting 20-25 homers and 15-20 stolen bases. His above average walk rates add a layer to his floor, and Ramos should be the Giants everyday right fielder soon. The numbers don't pop because he's played in some tough offensive parks, but Ramos has the skills to hit in the middle of the lineup while playing strong outfield defense. **ETA: 2021.**

## 3. Hunter Bishop- OF
The Giants first round pick, Bishop had the best power/speed combination of any collegiate player in the 2019 draft and broke out with a monster junior season at Arizona State. He made some swing adjustments and found that power stroke, hitting .342/.479/.748 with 22 homers. His batting average upside is capped due to some swing and miss concerns, but he can still go 20/20 despite hitting .250. **ETA: 2022.**

## 4. Luis Matos- OF
Matos was another gem from the same 2018 J2 class that unearthed Marco Luciano. Matos began his pro career in the DSL, but did get promoted to the AZL to closeout 2019. He destroyed the DSL by hitting .362/.430/.570 with seven homers and 20 stolen bases over 55 games while also displaying excellent contact skills. The bat speed is plus, and he's also a plus runner that should stick up the middle. He will make his full-season debut at just 18, and is a player worth investing in. **ETA: 2023.**

## 5. Joey Bart- C
This is likely the lowest you'll see Bart on a Giants list, but I'm worried about the two hand injuries and what they can do for his future. There are no questions surrounding the power though. Bart has plus raw power and a better than advertised hit tool. He will take his walks as well, making him a strong four-category offensive player. His defensive skills are plus, and he will stop a running game in its tracks, but the hand injuries have me worried. **ETA: 2021.**

## 6. Will Wilson- SS

The Angels popped Wilson with the 15th overall pick in the 2019 draft out of North Carolina State. Wilson was a steady performer for the Wolfpack, and his biggest weakness is that he has no standout tool. He has more pop than advertised, and it's a 55-power, 50-hit profile for me. He's going to hit, and likely will slide over to second base long-term. It's a high floor and limited ceiling, but Wilson is polished despite being one of the youngest in his draft class. He's a candidate to move quickly. **ETA: 2022.**

### 7. Alexander Canario- OF

Canario is an explosive athlete with top of the scale bat speed. He has massive raw power, but strikes out a ton and has pitch recognition issues with a long swing. Strikeouts were an issue in 2019, and i can see them being a problem for the rest of Canario's career. He should stick in center though, and will steal 10-15 bases as well. He could hit for a strong average and hit 20-25 homers, but he will need to tone down the aggressiveness and free swinging tendencies. The ceiling and floor might be one of the widest gaps in the entire minor leagues. He will make his full season debut in 2020. **ETA: 2023.**

### 8. Mauricio Dubon- 2B

I love players like Dubon, and if he played for most other teams in baseball we'd be wondering when he's coming up or how much of an impact he could have. With the Giants Dubon is likely the best second baseman currently on the 40-man roster and will also play some outfield this spring to add some versatility. Dubon is a plus runner and could steal 25 bags if he gets the playing time. There's also enough of a hit tool to put together a .270 or so average with 8-10 homers. He could be an interesting draft day bargain **ETA: Arrived.**

### 9. Jairo Pomares- OF

Another member of the loaded 2018 J2 class, the Giants signed Pomares for $1 million out of Cuba as an 18-year-old. Pomares showed a plus hit tool by using all fields and only striking out at around a 15% clip, but then he struggled after getting promoted to Salem-Kaiser and put up a 27% K rate while looking lost at the plate. Aggressiveness and over swinging will make it difficult for him to hit unless he makes some changes, but the gap-to-gap power will obviously make him an asset if he hits. He's only an average runner and will likely have to move to a corner defensively so that will put more pressure on the bat. **ETA: 2023.**

### 10. Luis Toribio- 3B

Toribio's offensive calling card is hit ability to take a walk. He's also shown an ability to hit the ball a long way. The hit tool needs some work, especially against lefties, but there's enough here to get excited. He's not very athletic, and could possibly require a platoon partner, but Toribio is worth a late round flier in a dynasty format. He also may have to move to first, which puts more pressure on the bat. **ETA: 2023.**

**Next Five:**
Logan Webb- RHP
Seth Corry- LHP

Jaylin Davis- OF
Sean Hjelle- RHP
Grant McCray- OF

**Top Five in FYPDs:**
Hunter Bishop- OF
Will Wilson- SS
Grant McCray- OF
Logan Wyatt- 1B
Dilan Rosario- SS

# Catcher Ranks

| Rank | Player | Team | Position(s) | Rank | Player | Team | Position(s) |
|------|--------|------|-------------|------|--------|------|-------------|
| 1 | J.T. Realmuto | PHI | C | 21 | Chance Sisco | BAL | C |
| 2 | Gary Sanchez | NYY | C | 22 | Roberto Perez | CLE | C |
| 3 | Yasmani Grandal | CWS | 1B, C | 23 | Tom Murphy | SEA | C |
| 4 | Willson Contreras | CHC | C | 24 | Tucker Barnhart | CIN | C |
| 5 | Mitch Garver | MIN | C | 25 | Mike Zunino | TB | C |
| 6 | Omar Narvaez | MLW | C | 26 | Reese McGuire | TOR | C |
| 7 | Will Smith | LAD | C | 27 | Robinson Chirinos | FA | C |
| 8 | Wilson Ramos | NYM | C | 28 | Willians Astudillo | MIN | C |
| 9 | Carson Kelly | ARZ | C | 29 | Pedro Severino | BAL | C |
| 10 | Sal Perez | KC | C | 30 | Victor Caratini | CHC | C, 1B |
| 11 | Jorge Alfaro | MIA | C | 31 | Joey Bart | SF | C |
| 12 | Yadier Molina | STL | C | 32 | Yan Gomes | WAS | C |
| 13 | Christian Vazquez | BOS | C | 33 | Tyler Flowers | ATL | C |
| 14 | Travis d'Arnaud | ATL | 1B, C | 34 | Welington Castillo | FA | C |
| 15 | Buster Posey | SF | C | 35 | Jacobs Stallings | PIT | C |
| 16 | Sean Murphy | OAK | C | 36 | Tony Wolters | COL | C |
| 17 | Castro, Jason | LAA | C | 37 | Daulton Varsho | ARZ | C |
| 18 | Francisco Mejia | SD | C | 38 | Tyler Stephenson | CIN | C |
| 19 | Danny Jansen | TOR | C | 39 | Austin Hedges | SD | C |
| 20 | Kurt Suzuki | WAS | C | 40 | Austin Allen | OAK | C |

# First Base Ranks

| Rank | Player | Team | Pos | Rank | Player | Team | Pos |
|---|---|---|---|---|---|---|---|
| 1 | Cody Bellinger | LAD | 1B, OF | 26 | Daniel Murphy | COL | 1B |
| 2 | Freddie Freeman | ATL | 1B | 27 | Christian Walker | ARZ | 1B |
| 3 | Pete Alonso | NYM | 1B | 28 | Nate Lowe | TB | 1B |
| 4 | Anthony Rizzo | CHC | 1B | 29 | Rowdy Tellez | TOR | 1B |
| 5 | Paul Goldschmidt | STL | 1B | 30 | C.J. Cron | MIN | 1B |
| 6 | Matt Olson | OAK | 1B | 31 | Miguel Cabrera | DET | 1B |
| 7 | Max Muncy | LAD | 2B, 1B, 3B | 32 | Jesus Aguilar | MIA | 1B |
| 8 | DJ LeMahieu | NYY | 1B, 3B, 2B | 33 | Brandon Belt | SF | 1B |
| 9 | Josh Bell | PIT | 1B | 34 | Evan White | SEA | 1B |
| 10 | Jose Abreu | CWS | 1B | 35 | Jake Bauers | CLE | 1B, OF |
| 11 | Rhys Hoskins | PHI | 1B | 36 | Jake Lamb | ARZ | 1B, 3B |
| 12 | Trey Mancini | BAL | OF, 1B | 37 | Travis d'Arnaud | ATL | 1B, C |
| 13 | Yuli Gurriel | HOU | 1B, 3B | 38 | Howie Kendrick | WAS | 1B, 2B |
| 14 | Yasmani Grandal | CWS | 1B, C | 39 | Marwin Gonzalez | MIN | 1B, 3B, OF |
| 15 | Luke Voit | NYY | 1B | 40 | Jeimer Candelario | DET | 1B, 3B |
| 16 | Carlos Santana | CLE | 1B | 41 | Ji-Man Choi | TB | 1B |
| 17 | Joc Pederson | LAD | 1B, OF | 42 | Dominic Smith | NYM | OF, 1B |
| 18 | Danny Santana | TEX | 1B, OF | 43 | Ryan Mountcastle | BAL | 1B |
| 19 | Joey Votto | CIN | 1B | 44 | Eric Thames | MLW | 1B |
| 20 | Michael Chavis | BOS | 1B, 2B | 45 | Seth Beer | HOU | 1B |
| 21 | Yandy Diaz | TB | 1B, 3B | 46 | Justin Smoak | FA | 1B |
| 22 | Renato Nunez | BAL | 1B | 47 | Ryan O'Hearn | KC | 1B |
| 23 | Edwin Encarnacion | CHW | 1B | 48 | Daniel Vogelbach | SEA | 1B |
| 24 | Eric Hosmer | SD | 1B | 49 | Albert Pujols | LAA | 1B |
| 25 | Garrett Cooper | MIA | 1B, OF | 50 | Ryan Zimmerman | WAS | 1B |

# Second Base Ranks

| Rank | Player | Team | Pos | Rank | Player | Team | Position(s) |
|------|--------|------|-----|------|--------|------|-------------|
| 1 | Gleyber Torres | NYY | 2B, SS | 26 | Tommy La Stella | LAA | 2B, 3B |
| 2 | Jonathan Villar | MIA | SS, 2B | 27 | Robinson Cano | NYM | 2B |
| 3 | Jose Altuve | HOU | 2B | 28 | Mauricio Dubon | SF | 2B |
| 4 | Ketel Marte | ARZ | 2B, OF | 29 | Howie Kendrick | WAS | 1B, 2B |
| 5 | Ozzie Albies | ATL | 2B | 30 | Nick Madrigal | CWS | 2B |
| 6 | Whit Merrifield | KC | 2B, OF | 31 | Jurickson Profar | SD | 2B |
| 7 | Keston Hiura | MLW | 2B | 32 | Adam Frazier | PIT | 2B |
| 8 | Max Muncy | LAD | 2B, 1B, 3B | 33 | Shed Long | SEA | 2B |
| 9 | Mike Moustakas | CIN | 2B, 3B | 34 | Isan Diaz | MIA | 2B |
| 10 | DJ LeMahieu | NYY | 1B, 3B, 2B | 35 | Cesar Hernandez | FA | 2B |
| 11 | Jeff McNeil | NYM | OF, 3B, 2B | 36 | Franklin Barreto | OAK | 2B |
| 12 | Eduardo Escobar | ARZ | 2B, 3B | 37 | Starlin Castro | FA | 3B, 2B |
| 13 | Cavan Biggio | TOR | 2B | 38 | Niko Goodrum | DET | 2B, SS, OF |
| 14 | Gavin Lux | LAD | 2B | 39 | David Fletcher | LAA | SS, OF, 2B, 3B |
| 15 | Kevin Newman | PIT | 2B, SS | 40 | Jose Peraza | BOS | OF, 2B, SS |
| 16 | Garrett Hampson | COL | 2B, OF | 41 | Hanser Alberto | BAL | 2B, 3B |
| 17 | Ryan McMahon | COL | 2B, 3B | 42 | Freddy Galvis | CIN | 2B, SS |
| 18 | Brandon Lowe | TB | 2B | 43 | Wilmer Flores | ARZ | 2B |
| 19 | Rougned Odor | TEX | 2B | 44 | Nicky Lopez | KC | 2B, SS |
| 20 | Tommy Edman | STL | 2B, 3B | 45 | Sheldon Neuse | OAK | 2B |
| 21 | Michael Edman | BOS | 1B, 2B | 46 | Joey Wendle | TB | 2B, 3B |
| 22 | Dee Gordon | SEA | 2B | 47 | Brendan Rodgers | COL | 2B |
| 23 | Kolton Wong | STL | 2B | 48 | Chris Taylor | LAD | 2B, SS, OF |
| 24 | Luis Arraez | MIN | 2B, OF | 49 | Kike Hernandez | LAD | 2B, OF |
| 25 | Luis Urias | MLW | SS, 2B | 50 | Brian Dozier | FA | 2B |

## Shortstop Ranks

| Rank | Player | Team | Pos | Rank | Player | Team | Pos |
|---|---|---|---|---|---|---|---|
| 1 | Francisco Lindor | CLE | SS | 26 | Nico Hoerner | CHC | SS |
| 2 | Trea Turner | WAS | SS | 27 | Jorge Mateo | OAK | SS |
| 3 | Trevor Story | COL | SS | 28 | Carter Kieboom | WAS | SS |
| 4 | Alex Bregman | HOU | 3B, SS | 29 | Dansby Swanson | ATL | SS |
| 5 | Fernando Tatis Jr. | SD | SS | 30 | Andrelton Simmons | LAA | SS |
| 6 | Gleyber Torres | NYY | 2B, SS | 31 | Jon Berti | MIA | 3B, SS, OF |
| 7 | Jonathan Villar | MIA | SS, 2B | 32 | Nick Ahmed | ARZ | SS |
| 8 | Javier Baez | CHC | SS | 33 | Miguel Rojas | MIA | SS |
| 9 | Adalberto Mondesi | KC | SS | 34 | Orlando Arcia | MLW | SS |
| 10 | Xander Bogaerts | BOS | SS | 35 | Niko Goodrum | DET | 2B, SS, OF |
| 11 | Marcus Semien | OAK | SS | 36 | David Fletcher | LAA | SS, OF, 2B, 3B |
| 12 | Carlos Correa | HOU | SS | 37 | Jose Peraza | BOS | OF, 2B, SS |
| 13 | Tim Anderson | CWS | SS | 38 | J.P. Crawford | SEA | SS |
| 14 | Manny Machado | SD | 3B, SS | 39 | Freddy Galvis | CIN | 2B, SS |
| 15 | Bo Bichette | TOR | SS | 40 | Nicky Lopez | KC | 2B, SS |
| 16 | Jorge Polanco | MIN | SS | 41 | Chris Taylor | LAD | 2B, SS, OF |
| 17 | Elvis Andrus | TEX | SS | 42 | Brandon Crawford | SF | SS |
| 18 | Paul DeJong | STL | SS | 43 | Cole Tucker | PIT | SS |
| 19 | Kevin Newman | PIT | 2B, SS | 44 | Royce Lewis | MIN | SS |
| 20 | Amed Rosario | NYM | SS | 45 | Willi Castro | DET | SS |
| 21 | Corey Seager | LAD | SS | 46 | Richie Martin | BAL | SS |
| 22 | Jean Segura | PHI | SS | 47 | Myles Straw | HOU | SS |
| 23 | Didi Gregorius | PHI | SS | 48 | Wander Franco | TB | SS |
| 24 | Willy Adames | TB | SS | 49 | Ehire Adrianza | MIN | 1B, SS, 3B |
| 25 | Luis Uris | MLW | SS, 2B | 50 | Danny Mendick | CWS | SS |

# Third Base Ranks

| Rank | Player | Team | Pos | Rank | Player | Team | Pos |
|---|---|---|---|---|---|---|---|
| 1 | Arenado, Nolan | COL | 3B | 26 | La Stella, Tommy | LAA | 2B, 3B |
| 2 | Rendon, Anthony | LAA | 3B | 27 | Urshela, Gio | NYY | 3B |
| 3 | Bregman, Alex | HOU | 3B, SS | 28 | Berti, Jon | MIA | 3B, SS, OF |
| 4 | Ramirez, Jose | CLE | 3B | 29 | Castro, Starlin | WAS | 3B, 2B |
| 5 | Devers, Rafael | BOS | 3B | 30 | Carpenter, Matt | STL | 3B |
| 6 | Suarez, Eugenio | CIN | 3B | 31 | Diaz, Yandy | TB | 1B, 3B |
| 7 | Guerrero Jr., Vladimir | TOR | 3B | 32 | Seager, Kyle | SEA | 3B |
| 8 | Bryant, Kris | CHC | 3B, OF | 33 | Shaw, Travis | TOR | 3B |
| 9 | Muncy, Max | LAD | 2B, 1B, 3B | 34 | Longoria, Evan | SF | 3B |
| 10 | Moncada, Yoan | CWS | 3B | 35 | Franco, Maikel | KC | 3B |
| 11 | LeMahieu, DJ | NYY | 1B, 3B, 2B | 36 | Frazier, Todd | TEX | 3B |
| 12 | Machado, Manny | SD | 3B, SS | 37 | Fletcher, David | LAA | SS, OF, 2B, 3B |
| 13 | Donaldson, Josh | MIN | 3B | 38 | Alberto, Hanser | BAL | 2B, 3B |
| 14 | Moustakas, Mike | CIN | 2B, 3B | 39 | Cabrera, Asdrubal | WAS | 2B, 3B |
| 15 | Chapman, Matt | OAK | 3B | 40 | Anderson, Brian | MIA | OF, 3B |
| 16 | McNeil, Jeff | NYM | OF, 3B, 2B | 41 | Gonzalez, Marwin | MIN | 1B, 3B, OF |
| 17 | Sano, Miguel | MIN | 3B | 42 | Lamb, Jake | ARZ | 1B, 3B |
| 18 | Escobar, Eduardo | ARZ | 2B, 3B | 43 | Candelario, Jeimer | DET | 1B, 3B |
| 19 | Gurriel, Yuli | HOU | 1B, 3B | 44 | Jones, Nolan | CLE | 3B |
| 20 | McMahon, Ryan | COL | 2B, 3B | 45 | Moran, Colin | PIT | 3B |
| 21 | Turner, Justin | LAD | 3B | 46 | Paredes, Isaac | DET | 3B |
| 22 | Davis, J.D. | NYM | OF, 3B | 47 | Bote, David | CHC | 2B, 3B |
| 23 | Kingery, Scott | PHI | 3B, OF | 48 | Bohm, Alec | PHI | 3B |
| 24 | Edman, Tommy | STL | 2B, 3B | 49 | Hayes, Ke'Bryan | PIT | 3B |
| 25 | Dozier, Hunter | KC | 3B, OF | 50 | Drury, Brandon | TOR | 3B, OF |

# Outfield Ranks

| Rank | Player | Team | Pos | Rank | Player | Team | Pos |
|---|---|---|---|---|---|---|---|
| 1 | Acuna Jr., Ronald | ATL | OF | 26 | Ozuna, Marcell | STL | OF |
| 2 | Yelich, Christian | MLW | OF | 27 | Robert, Luis | CWS | OF |
| 3 | Trout, Mike | LAA | OF | 28 | Mancini, Trey | BAL | OF, 1B |
| 4 | Betts, Mookie | LAD | OF | 29 | Puig, Yasiel | CLE | OF |
| 5 | Bellinger, Cody | LAD | 1B, OF | 30 | Benintendi, Andrew | BOS | OF |
| 6 | Soto, Juan | WAS | OF | 31 | Castellanos, Nicholas | CHC | OF |
| 7 | Martinez, J.D. | BOS | OF | 32 | Mercado, Oscar | CLE | OF |
| 8 | Judge, Aaron | NYY | OF | 33 | Conforto, Michael | NYM | OF |
| 9 | Harper, Bryce | PHI | OF | 34 | Tucker, Kyle | HOU | OF |
| 10 | Marte, Starling | PIT | OF | 35 | Santana, Danny | TEX | 1B, OF |
| 11 | Meadows, Austin | TB | OF | 36 | Brantley, Michael | HOU | OF |
| 12 | Springer, George | HOU | OF | 37 | Aquino, Aristides | CIN | OF |
| 13 | Marte, Ketel | ARZ | 2B, OF | 38 | Kepler, Max | MIN | OF |
| 14 | Blackmon, Charlie | COL | OF | 39 | Reyes, Franmil | CLE | OF |
| 15 | Merrifield, Whit | KC | 2B, OF | 40 | Dahl, David | COL | OF |
| 16 | Stanton, Giancarlo | NYY | OF | 41 | Smith, Mallex | SEA | OF |
| 17 | Jimenez, Eloy | CWS | OF | 42 | Calhoun, Willie | TEX | OF |
| 18 | Robles, Victor | WAS | OF | 43 | Schwarber, Kyle | CHC | OF |
| 19 | Bryant, Kris | CHC | 3B, OF | 44 | Hampson, Garrett | COL | 2B, OF |
| 20 | Pham, Tommy | SD | OF | 45 | Gurriel Jr., Lourdes | TOR | OF |
| 21 | Soler, Jorge | KC | OF | 46 | Buxton, Byron | MIN | OF |
| 22 | Gallo, Joey | TEX | OF | 47 | Kingery, Scott | PHI | 3B, OF |
| 23 | Laureano, Ramon | OAK | OF | 48 | Davis, J.D. | NYM | OF, 3B |
| 24 | McNeil, Jeff | NYM | OF, 3B, 2B | 49 | Dozier, Hunter | KC | 3B, OF |
| 25 | Rosario, Eddie | MIN | OF | 50 | Senzel, Nick | CIN | OF |

| Rank | Player | Team | Pos | Rank | Player | Team | Pos |
|---|---|---|---|---|---|---|---|
| 51 | Haniger, Mitch | SEA | OF | 76 | Canha, Mark | OAK | OF |
| 52 | Cain, Lorenzo | MLW | OF | 77 | Grichuk, Randal | TOR | OF |
| 53 | Adell, Jo | LAA | OF | 78 | Carlson, Dylan | STL | OF |
| 54 | Pederson, Joc | LAD | 1B, OF | 79 | Kiermaier, Kevin | TB | OF |
| 55 | Berti, Jon | MIA | 3B, SS, OF | 80 | Goodrum, Niko | DET | 2B, SS, OF |
| 56 | Reynolds, Bryan | PIT | OF | 81 | Winker, Jesse | CIN | OF |
| 57 | Eaton, Adam | WAS | OF | 82 | Hilliard, Sam | COL | OF |
| 58 | Arraez, Luis | MIN | 2B, OF | 83 | Fletcher, David | LAA | SS, OF, 2B, 3B |
| 59 | McCutchen, Andrew | PHI | OF | 84 | Polanco, Gregory | PIT | OF |
| 60 | Verdugo, Alex | LAD | OF | 85 | Gardner, Brett | NYY | OF |
| 61 | Pollock, A.J. | LAD | OF | 86 | Rojas, Josh | ARZ | OF |
| 62 | Riley, Austin | ATL | OF | 87 | Yastrzemski, Mike | SF | OF |
| 63 | Upton, Justin | LAA | OF | 88 | Cooper, Garrett | MIA | 1B, OF |
| 64 | Braun, Ryan | MLW | OF | 89 | Santander, Anthony | BAL | OF |
| 65 | Pillar, Kevin | SF | OF | 90 | Dickerson, Corey | PHI | OF |
| 66 | Mazara, Nomar | CWS | OF | 91 | Hernandez, Teoscar | TOR | OF |
| 67 | Choo, Shin-Soo | TEX | OF | 92 | Margot, Manuel | SD | OF |
| 68 | Anderson, Brian | MIA | OF, 3B | 93 | Tsutsugo, Yoshitomo | TB | OF |
| 69 | Myers, Wil | SD | OF | 94 | Reyes, Victor | DET | OF |
| 70 | Santana, Domingo | SEA | OF | 95 | Gonzalez, Marwin | MIN | 1B, 3B, OF |
| 71 | Hays, Austin | BAL | OF | 96 | Lewis, Kyle | SEA | OF |
| 72 | Renfroe, Hunter | TB | OF | 97 | Piscotty, Stephen | OAK | OF |
| 73 | Garcia, Avisail | TB | OF | 98 | Inciarte, Ender | ATL | OF |
| 74 | Peralta, David | ARZ | OF | 99 | Nimmo, Brandon | NYM | OF |
| 75 | Grisham, Trent | SD | OF | 100 | Happ, Ian | CHC | OF |

| Rank | Player | Team | Pos | Rank | Player | Team | Pos |
|------|--------|------|-----|------|--------|------|-----|
| 101 | Smith, Dominic | NYM | OF, 1B | 126 | Hernandez, Kike | LAD | 2B, OF |
| 102 | Calhoun, Kole | LAA | OF | 127 | Fowler, Dexter | STL | OF |
| 103 | Bradley Jr., Jackie | BOS | OF | 128 | Goodwin, Brian | LAA | OF |
| 104 | VanMeter, Josh | CIN | OF | 129 | Bruce, Jay | PHI | OF |
| 105 | Tauchman, Mike | NYY | OF | 130 | Pache, Cristian | ATL | OF |
| 106 | Bader, Harrison | STL | OF | 131 | Hicks, Aaron | NYY | OF |
| 107 | Garcia, Leury | CWS | OF | 132 | Dyson, Jarrod | ARZ | OF |
| 108 | DeShields, Delino | CLE | OF | 133 | Luplow, Jordan | CLE | OF |
| 109 | Heyward, Jason | CHC | OF | 134 | Pence, Hunter | TEX | OF |
| 110 | Taylor, Chris | LAD | 2B, SS, OF | 135 | Brown, Seth | OAK | OF |
| 111 | Frazier, Clint | NYY | OF | 136 | Stewart, Christin | DET | OF |
| 112 | Fraley, Jake | SEA | OF | 137 | Gordon, Alex | KC | OF |
| 113 | Tapia, Raimel | COL | OF | 138 | Dixon, Brandon | DET | 1B, OF |
| 114 | O'Neill, Tyler | STL | OF | 139 | Ramirez, Harold | MIA | OF |
| 115 | Akiyama, Shogo | FA | OF | 140 | Reddick, Josh | HOU | OF |
| 116 | Desmond, Ian | COL | OF | 141 | Locastro, Tim | ARZ | OF |
| 117 | Peraza, Jose | BOS | OF, 2B, SS | 142 | Dickerson, Alex | SF | OF |
| 118 | Markakis, Nick | ATL | OF | 143 | Harrison, Monte | MIA | OF |
| 119 | Souza Jr., Steven | ARZ | OF | 144 | Arozarena, Randy | STL | OF |
| 120 | Beaty, Matt | LAD | OF, 1B | 145 | Osuna, Jose | PIT | 1B, OF |
| 121 | Bauers, Jake | CLE | 1B, OF | 146 | Waters, Drew | ATL | OF |
| 122 | Martinez, Jose | STL | OF | 147 | Naylor, Josh | SD | OF |
| 123 | Cordero, Franchy | SD | OF | 148 | Pinder, Chad | OAK | 2B, OF |
| 124 | Jones, JaCoby | DET | OF | 149 | Cespedes, Yoenis | NYM | OF |
| 125 | Kirilloff, Alex | MIN | OF | 150 | Hamilton, Billy | ATL | OF |

# Starting Pitcher Ranks

| Rank | Player | Team | Rank | Player | Team |
|---|---|---|---|---|---|
| 1 | Jacob deGrom | NYM | 26 | José Berríos | MIN |
| 2 | Gerrit Cole | NYY | 27 | Mike Soroka | ATL |
| 3 | Justin Verlander | HOU | 28 | James Paxton | NYY |
| 4 | Max Scherzer | WAS | 29 | Lance Lynn | TEX |
| 5 | Walker Buehler | LAD | 30 | Carlos Carrasco | CLE |
| 6 | Mike Clevinger | CLE | 31 | Zac Gallen | ARZ |
| 7 | Blake Snell | TB | 32 | Frankie Montas | OAK |
| 8 | Chris Sale | BOS | 33 | Sonny Gray | CIN |
| 9 | Shane Bieber | CLE | 34 | Hyun-Jin Ryu | TOR |
| 10 | Jack Flaherty | STL | 35 | Eduardo Rodriguez | BOS |
| 11 | Luis Castillo | CIN | 36 | Jesus Luzardo | OAK |
| 12 | Patrick Corbin | WAS | 37 | Max Fried | ATL |
| 13 | Stephen Strasburg | WAS | 38 | Madison Bumgarner | ARZ |
| 14 | Luis Severino | NYY | 39 | Zack Wheeler | PHI |
| 15 | Aaron Nola | PHI | 40 | Mike Minor | TEX |
| 16 | Lucas Giolito | CWS | 41 | Corey Kluber | TEX |
| 17 | Clayton Kershaw | LAD | 42 | Kyle Hendricks | CHC |
| 18 | Charlie Morton | TB | 43 | Matthew Boyd | DET |
| 19 | Tyler Glasnow | TB | 44 | Andrew Heaney | LAA |
| 20 | Yu Darvish | CHC | 45 | Shohei Ohtani | LAA |
| 21 | Chris Paddack | SD | 46 | Sean Manaea | OAK |
| 22 | Noah Syndergaard | NYM | 47 | Luke Weaver | ARZ |
| 23 | Trevor Bauer | CIN | 48 | Carlos Martinez | STL |
| 24 | Zack Greinke | HOU | 49 | Mike Foltynewicz | ATL |
| 25 | Brandon Woodruff | MIL | 50 | Kenta Maeda | LAD |

| Rank | Player | Team | Rank | Player | Team |
|---|---|---|---|---|---|
| 51 | David Price | BOS | 76 | Johnny Cueto | SF |
| 52 | Robbie Ray | ARZ | 77 | Forrest Whitley | HOU |
| 53 | German Márquez | COL | 78 | Masahiro Tanaka | NYY |
| 54 | Julio Urías | LAD | 79 | Nathan Eovaldi | BOS |
| 55 | Dinelson Lamet | SD | 80 | Joey Lucchesi | SD |
| 56 | Joe Musgrove | PIT | 81 | Anthony DeSclafani | CIN |
| 57 | Mitch Keller | PIT | 82 | Chris Archer | PIT |
| 58 | Jon Gray | COL | 83 | Michael Pineda | MIN |
| 59 | Kyle Gibson | TEX | 84 | Marco Gonzales | SEA |
| 60 | Garrett Richards | SD | 85 | Tyler Beede | SF |
| 61 | Dylan Cease | CWS | 86 | Dallas Keuchel | CWS |
| 62 | MacKenzie Gore | SD | 87 | Reynaldo López | CWS |
| 63 | Lance McCullers Jr. | HOU | 88 | Kevin Gausman | SF |
| 64 | Jeff Samardzija | SF | 89 | Caleb Smith | MIA |
| 65 | Ross Stripling | LAD | 90 | Dustin May | LAD |
| 66 | Sandy Alcantara | MIA | 91 | Aaron Civale | CLE |
| 67 | Marcus Stroman | NYM | 92 | Patrick Sandoval | LAA |
| 68 | Domingo German | NYY | 93 | Brad Peacock | HOU |
| 69 | Chris Bassitt | OAK | 94 | Zach Davies | SD |
| 70 | A.J. Puk | OAK | 95 | Dakota Hudson | STL |
| 71 | Griffin Canning | LAA | 96 | Jose Quintana | CHC |
| 72 | Jake Odorizzi | MIN | 97 | Anibal Sanchez | WAS |
| 73 | Miles Mikolas | STL | 98 | Nate Pearson | TOR |
| 74 | Michael Kopech | CWS | 99 | Steven Matz | NYM |
| 75 | Cole Hamels | ATL | 100 | Sixto Sachez | MIA |

# Top 100 Prospects

| # | | # | | # | | # | |
|---|---|---|---|---|---|---|---|
| 1 | Wander Franco- TB | 26 | Brennen Davis- CHC | 51 | Oneil Cruz- PIT | 76 | Robert Puason- OAK |
| 2 | Luis Robert- CWS | 27 | Alex Kirilloff- MIN | 52 | Nick Madrigal- CWS | 77 | Isaac Paredes- DET |
| 3 | Jo Adell- LAA | 28 | Luis Patiño- SD | 53 | Brandon Marsh- LAA | 78 | Orelvis Martinez- TOR |
| 4 | Gavin Lux- LAD | 29 | Alec Bohm- PHI | 54 | Evan White- SEA | 79 | Triston Casas- BOS |
| 5 | Jarred Kelenic- SEA | 30 | Bobby Witt Jr- KC | 55 | Xavier Edwards- TB | 80 | Nick Lodolo- CIN |
| 6 | Marco Luciano- SF | 31 | Ronny Mauricio- NYM | 56 | Nick Solak- TEX | 81 | Josiah Gray- LAD |
| 7 | Julio Rodriguez- SEA | 32 | Spencer Howard- PHI | 57 | Logan Gilbert- SEA | 82 | Austin Hays- BAL |
| 8 | MacKenzie Gore- SD | 33 | JJ Bleday- MIA | 58 | Shane Baz- TB | 83 | Edward Cabrera- MIA |
| 9 | Jesus Luzardo- OAK | 34 | Corbin Carroll- ARI | 59 | Mitch Keller- PIT | 84 | Josh Lowe- TB |
| 10 | Dylan Carlson- STL | 35 | Jordan Groshans- TOR | 60 | Cristian Pache- ATL | 85 | Jose Garcia- CIN |
| 11 | Andrew Vaughn- CWS | 36 | Trevor Larnach- MIN | 61 | George Valera- CLE | 86 | Sherten Apostel- TEX |
| 12 | Jasson Dominguez- NYY | 37 | Nolan Jones- CLE | 62 | Heliot Ramos- SF | 87 | Aaron Bracho- CLE |
| 13 | Royce Lewis- MIN | 38 | Jazz Chisholm- MIA | 63 | Greg Jones- TB | 88 | Jordyn Adams- LAA |
| 14 | Forrest Whitley- HOU | 39 | Brendan McKay- TB | 64 | Hunter Bishop- SF | 89 | Monte Harrison- MIA |
| 15 | Kristian Robinson- ARI | 40 | Alek Thomas- ARI | 65 | Ethan Hankins- CLE | 90 | Jesus Sanchez- MIA |
| 16 | Carter Kieboom- WSH | 41 | Grayson Rodriguez- BAL | 66 | Daulton Varsho- ARI | 91 | Taylor Trammell- SD |
| 17 | Matt Manning- DET | 42 | Riley Greene- DET | 67 | DL Hall- BAL | 92 | Ian Anderson- ATL |
| 18 | CJ Abrams- SD | 43 | Nolan Gorman- STL | 68 | Lewin Diaz- MIA | 93 | Brayan Rocchio- CLE |
| 19 | Adley Rutschman- BAL | 44 | Nico Hoerner- CHC | 69 | Geraldo Perdomo- ARI | 94 | Brailyn Marquez- CHC |
| 20 | Michael Kopech- CWS | 45 | Jeter Downs- LAD | 70 | George Kirby- SEA | 95 | Ke'Bryan Hayes- PIT |
| 21 | Nate Pearson- TOR | 46 | Sixto Sanchez- MIA | 71 | Joey Bart- SF | 96 | Ryan Mountcastle- BAL |
| 22 | Casey Mize- DET | 47 | Daniel Lynch- KC | 72 | Erick Pena- KC | 97 | Tyler Freeman- CLE |
| 23 | Vidal Brujan- TB | 48 | Dustin May- LAD | 73 | Luis Matos- SF | 98 | Kyle Wright- ATL |
| 24 | Noelvi Marte- SEA | 49 | A.J. Puk- OAK | 74 | Sean Murphy- OAK | 99 | Matthew Liberatore- STL |
| 25 | Drew Waters- ATL | 50 | Brendan Rodgers- COL | 75 | Tarik Skubal- DET | 100 | Jorge Mateo- OAK |

# FYPD Ranks

|    | Player | Team | Position |
|----|--------|------|----------|
| 1  | Andrew Vaughn | Chicago White Sox | 1B |
| 2  | Jasson Dominguez | New York Yankees | OF |
| 3  | CJ Abrams | San Diego Padres | SS |
| 4  | Adley Rutschman | Baltimore Orioles | C |
| 5  | Bobby Witt Jr. | Kansas City Royals | SS |
| 6  | Corbin Carroll | Arizona Diamondbacks | OF |
| 7  | JJ Bleday | Miami Marlins | OF |
| 8  | Greg Jones | Tampa Bay Rays | SS |
| 9  | Riley Greene | Detroit Tigers | OF |
| 10 | Erick Pena | Kansas City Royals | OF |
| 11 | Robert Puason | Oakland Athletics | SS |
| 12 | Hunter Bishop | San Francisco Giants | OF |
| 13 | George Kirby | Seattle Mariners | RHP |
| 14 | Maximo Acosta | Texas Rangers | SS |
| 15 | Josh Jung | Texas Rangers | 3B |
| 16 | Daniel Espino | Cleveland Indians | RHP |
| 17 | Kody Hoese | Los Angeles Dodgers | 3B |
| 18 | Hudson Head | San Diego Padres | OF |
| 19 | Luis Rodriguez | Los Angeles Dodgers | OF |
| 20 | Nick Lodolo | Cincinnati Reds | LHP |
| 21 | Kameron Misner | Miami Marlins | OF |
| 22 | Bryson Stott | Philadelphia Phillies | SS |
| 23 | Brett Baty | New York Mets | 3B |
| 24 | Yoshitomo Tsutsugo | Tampa Bay Rays | OF |
| 25 | Michael Busch | Los Angeles Dodgers | 2B/1B |
| 26 | Brady McConnell | Kansas City Royals | SS |
| 27 | Jackson Rutledge | Washington Nationals | RHP |

| 28 | Michael Toglia | Colorado Rockies | 1B |
|----|----|----|----|
| 29 | Alek Manoah | Toronto Blue Jays | RHP |
| 30 | Keoni Cavaco | Minnesota Twins | SS/3B |
| 31 | Chase Strumpf | Chicago Cubs | 2B |
| 32 | Blake Walston | Arizona Diamondbacks | LHP |
| 33 | Gunnar Henderson | Baltimore Orioles | SS |
| 34 | Trejyn Fletcher | St. Louis Cardinals | OF |
| 35 | Zack Thompson | St. Louis Cardinals | LHP |
| 36 | Reginald Preciado | San Diego Padres | SS |
| 37 | Will Wilson | Los Angeles Angels | SS |
| 38 | Ethan Small | Milwaukee Brewers | LHP |
| 39 | Matt Wallner | Minnesota Twins | OF |
| 40 | Noah Song | Boston Red Sox | RHP |
| 41 | Bayron Lora | Texas Rangers | OF |
| 42 | Braden Shewmake | Atlanta Braves | SS |
| 43 | Ismael Mena | San Diego Padres | OF |
| 44 | Yhoswar Garcia | Philadelphia Phillies | OF |
| 45 | Shogo Akiyama | FREE AGENT | OF |
| 46 | Logan Davidson | Oakland Athletics | SS |
| 47 | Tyler Callihan | Cincinnati Reds | 2B |
| 48 | Seth Johnson | Tampa Bay Rays | RHP |
| 49 | Adael Amador | Colorado Rockies | SS |
| 50 | Quinn Priester | Pittsburgh Pirates | RHP |

# ATC 2020 Hitter Projections

| Player Name | Team | Pos | AB | H | BB | R | RBI | HR | SB | BA | OBP |
|---|---|---|---|---|---|---|---|---|---|---|---|
| Abraham Almonte | ARI | OF | 18 | 4 | 2 | 3 | 2 | 1 | 0 | 0.202 | 0.285 |
| Andy Young | ARI | 2B | 14 | 3 | 1 | 2 | 2 | 1 | 0 | 0.244 | 0.310 |
| Ben DeLuzio | ARI | SS | 8 | 2 | 1 | 1 | 1 | 0 | 0 | 0.239 | 0.299 |
| Caleb Joseph | ARI | C | 43 | 9 | 2 | 4 | 4 | 1 | 0 | 0.207 | 0.247 |
| Carson Kelly | ARI | C | 366 | 91 | 49 | 48 | 53 | 20 | 0 | 0.250 | 0.345 |
| Christian Walker | ARI | 1B | 454 | 113 | 49 | 68 | 69 | 24 | 5 | 0.248 | 0.331 |
| Daulton Varsho | ARI | C | 14 | 4 | 1 | 2 | 2 | 1 | 1 | 0.262 | 0.324 |
| David Peralta | ARI | OF | 524 | 146 | 46 | 69 | 74 | 20 | 2 | 0.279 | 0.343 |
| Domingo Leyba | ARI | 2B | 81 | 20 | 6 | 10 | 10 | 2 | 1 | 0.252 | 0.302 |
| Eduardo Escobar | ARI | 2B/3B | 584 | 152 | 48 | 81 | 90 | 27 | 4 | 0.260 | 0.318 |
| Ildemaro Vargas | ARI | 2B | 208 | 58 | 11 | 24 | 23 | 5 | 3 | 0.278 | 0.317 |
| Jake Lamb | ARI | 1B/3B | 293 | 68 | 43 | 43 | 46 | 12 | 2 | 0.230 | 0.334 |
| Jarrod Dyson | ARI | OF | 266 | 62 | 29 | 36 | 24 | 5 | 18 | 0.232 | 0.312 |
| Josh Rojas | ARI | OF | 266 | 69 | 30 | 37 | 33 | 7 | 10 | 0.259 | 0.339 |
| Ketel Marte | ARI | 2B/OF | 572 | 169 | 56 | 88 | 79 | 23 | 10 | 0.295 | 0.361 |
| Kevin Cron | ARI | 1B | 173 | 43 | 16 | 25 | 32 | 10 | 0 | 0.248 | 0.317 |
| Kole Calhoun | ARI | OF | 513 | 121 | 62 | 78 | 68 | 23 | 4 | 0.236 | 0.323 |
| Nick Ahmed | ARI | SS | 538 | 131 | 46 | 67 | 72 | 17 | 7 | 0.244 | 0.305 |
| Robert Refsnyder | ARI | OF | 15 | 4 | 2 | 2 | 2 | 0 | 0 | 0.252 | 0.325 |
| Stephen Vogt | ARI | C | 253 | 63 | 21 | 29 | 36 | 10 | 2 | 0.248 | 0.307 |
| Steven Souza | ARI | OF | 285 | 68 | 34 | 39 | 42 | 13 | 6 | 0.240 | 0.328 |
| Tim Locastro | ARI | OF | 162 | 40 | 10 | 24 | 16 | 3 | 10 | 0.248 | 0.315 |
| Wilmer Flores | ARI | 2B | 334 | 96 | 21 | 40 | 48 | 15 | 0 | 0.288 | 0.333 |
| Wyatt Mathisen | ARI | 3B | 17 | 4 | 2 | 2 | 2 | 1 | 0 | 0.221 | 0.295 |

| Player Name | Team | Pos | AB | H | BB | R | RBI | HR | SB | BA | OBP |
|---|---|---|---|---|---|---|---|---|---|---|---|
| Adam Duvall | ATL | OF | 160 | 37 | 13 | 21 | 25 | 9 | 1 | 0.231 | 0.295 |
| Adeiny Hechavarria | ATL | 2B/SS | 171 | 44 | 9 | 20 | 21 | 2 | 2 | 0.255 | 0.296 |
| Alex Jackson | ATL | C | 18 | 4 | 1 | 2 | 3 | 1 | 0 | 0.202 | 0.277 |
| Austin Riley | ATL | OF | 402 | 101 | 31 | 57 | 66 | 22 | 1 | 0.250 | 0.311 |
| Billy Hamilton | ATL | OF | 177 | 40 | 16 | 22 | 13 | 1 | 12 | 0.225 | 0.289 |
| Charlie Culberson | ATL | OF | 125 | 31 | 7 | 15 | 15 | 4 | 1 | 0.246 | 0.292 |
| Cristian Pache | ATL | OF | 137 | 35 | 9 | 14 | 15 | 3 | 2 | 0.257 | 0.310 |
| Dansby Swanson | ATL | SS | 508 | 129 | 53 | 70 | 65 | 19 | 10 | 0.255 | 0.328 |
| Drew Waters | ATL | OF | 13 | 3 | 1 | 1 | 1 | 0 | 0 | 0.243 | 0.296 |
| Ender Inciarte | ATL | OF | 416 | 111 | 40 | 57 | 44 | 9 | 14 | 0.266 | 0.334 |
| Freddie Freeman | ATL | 1B | 571 | 169 | 82 | 99 | 106 | 35 | 6 | 0.297 | 0.390 |
| Jace Peterson | ATL | OF | 13 | 3 | 1 | 2 | 1 | 0 | 1 | 0.231 | 0.307 |
| Johan Camargo | ATL | SS | 266 | 71 | 21 | 34 | 37 | 9 | 1 | 0.266 | 0.324 |
| Josh Donaldson | ATL | 3B | 521 | 137 | 91 | 93 | 94 | 34 | 4 | 0.263 | 0.378 |
| Matt Joyce | ATL | OF | 198 | 48 | 31 | 30 | 27 | 8 | 1 | 0.242 | 0.346 |
| Nick Markakis | ATL | OF | 482 | 137 | 53 | 64 | 69 | 11 | 2 | 0.285 | 0.356 |
| Ozzie Albies | ATL | 2B | 613 | 177 | 48 | 96 | 80 | 23 | 17 | 0.288 | 0.342 |
| Rafael Ortega | ATL | OF | 59 | 15 | 6 | 8 | 6 | 2 | 2 | 0.244 | 0.314 |
| Ronald Acuna | ATL | OF | 594 | 168 | 69 | 108 | 92 | 36 | 34 | 0.282 | 0.364 |
| Travis D'Arnaud | ATL | C/1B | 331 | 84 | 27 | 43 | 51 | 14 | 0 | 0.254 | 0.313 |
| Tyler Flowers | ATL | C | 258 | 60 | 29 | 32 | 33 | 9 | 0 | 0.234 | 0.329 |

| Player Name | Team | Pos | AB | H | BB | R | RBI | HR | SB | BA | OBP |
|---|---|---|---|---|---|---|---|---|---|---|---|
| Anthony Santander | BAL | OF | 516 | 131 | 28 | 61 | 71 | 23 | 3 | 0.255 | 0.295 |
| Austin Hays | BAL | OF | 458 | 115 | 25 | 60 | 63 | 20 | 8 | 0.252 | 0.294 |
| Austin Wynns | BAL | C | 61 | 14 | 5 | 7 | 6 | 2 | 0 | 0.238 | 0.300 |
| Cedric Mullins | BAL | OF | 63 | 15 | 5 | 8 | 6 | 2 | 2 | 0.242 | 0.294 |
| Chance Sisco | BAL | C | 254 | 60 | 28 | 35 | 32 | 10 | 1 | 0.235 | 0.331 |
| Chris Davis | BAL | 1B | 295 | 56 | 35 | 32 | 38 | 13 | 0 | 0.191 | 0.282 |
| D.J. Stewart | BAL | OF | 295 | 73 | 34 | 40 | 42 | 11 | 5 | 0.246 | 0.328 |
| Dwight Smith | BAL | OF | 215 | 55 | 19 | 27 | 29 | 7 | 3 | 0.255 | 0.320 |
| Hanser Alberto | BAL | 2B/3B | 513 | 147 | 17 | 60 | 54 | 12 | 4 | 0.287 | 0.314 |
| Jose Iglesias | BAL | SS | 482 | 131 | 21 | 54 | 52 | 8 | 7 | 0.271 | 0.307 |
| Mark Trumbo | BAL | Util | 267 | 59 | 20 | 29 | 40 | 14 | 0 | 0.222 | 0.280 |
| Mason Williams | BAL | OF | 40 | 10 | 3 | 4 | 4 | 1 | 1 | 0.245 | 0.294 |
| Pat Valaika | BAL | 2B | 26 | 6 | 1 | 3 | 3 | 1 | 0 | 0.215 | 0.258 |
| Pedro Severino | BAL | C | 280 | 67 | 23 | 30 | 34 | 10 | 2 | 0.237 | 0.303 |
| Renato Nunez | BAL | 1B | 528 | 130 | 44 | 68 | 80 | 27 | 1 | 0.246 | 0.311 |
| Richard Urena | BAL | SS | 112 | 27 | 6 | 12 | 11 | 2 | 1 | 0.245 | 0.286 |
| Richie Martin | BAL | SS | 207 | 48 | 13 | 23 | 19 | 4 | 7 | 0.233 | 0.281 |
| Rio Ruiz | BAL | 3B | 362 | 87 | 36 | 42 | 46 | 12 | 1 | 0.241 | 0.312 |
| Ryan Mountcastle | BAL | 1B | 113 | 31 | 6 | 14 | 16 | 5 | 1 | 0.272 | 0.310 |
| Rylan Bannon | BAL | 3B | 52 | 13 | 5 | 6 | 6 | 1 | 1 | 0.248 | 0.321 |
| Steve Wilkerson | BAL | OF | 168 | 39 | 12 | 20 | 18 | 4 | 2 | 0.231 | 0.290 |
| Trey Mancini | BAL | 1B/OF | 579 | 158 | 53 | 86 | 86 | 29 | 1 | 0.273 | 0.338 |
| Yusniel Diaz | BAL | OF | 32 | 8 | 4 | 4 | 4 | 1 | 0 | 0.254 | 0.329 |

| Player Name | Team | Pos | AB | H | BB | R | RBI | HR | SB | BA | OBP |
|---|---|---|---|---|---|---|---|---|---|---|---|
| Andrew Benintendi | BOS | OF | 566 | 155 | 65 | 88 | 79 | 17 | 14 | 0.274 | 0.352 |
| Bobby Dalbec | BOS | 3B | 162 | 39 | 17 | 23 | 25 | 8 | 2 | 0.239 | 0.319 |
| Brock Holt | BOS | 2B | 287 | 75 | 33 | 37 | 33 | 5 | 2 | 0.260 | 0.342 |
| Christian Vazquez | BOS | C | 420 | 110 | 27 | 53 | 54 | 14 | 4 | 0.262 | 0.310 |
| Christopher Owings | BOS | 2B | 85 | 21 | 6 | 10 | 10 | 3 | 2 | 0.250 | 0.297 |
| Dustin Pedroia | BOS | 2B | 96 | 25 | 9 | 12 | 11 | 2 | 1 | 0.262 | 0.330 |
| Eduardo Nunez | BOS | 2B | 184 | 50 | 7 | 20 | 23 | 5 | 5 | 0.269 | 0.299 |
| J.D. Martinez | BOS | OF | 548 | 166 | 67 | 95 | 111 | 37 | 2 | 0.304 | 0.380 |
| Jackie Bradley | BOS | OF | 495 | 117 | 52 | 70 | 67 | 18 | 10 | 0.236 | 0.321 |
| Jonathan Arauz | BOS | SS | 46 | 11 | 3 | 6 | 5 | 1 | 1 | 0.237 | 0.295 |
| Jose Peraza | BOS | 2B/SS/OF | 339 | 93 | 16 | 40 | 36 | 6 | 9 | 0.275 | 0.317 |
| Josh Ockimey | BOS | 1B | 63 | 14 | 9 | 9 | 9 | 3 | 1 | 0.228 | 0.329 |
| Juan Centeno | BOS | C | 52 | 12 | 4 | 5 | 6 | 1 | 2 | 0.234 | 0.298 |
| Kevin Plawecki | BOS | C | 186 | 46 | 17 | 24 | 24 | 6 | 0 | 0.246 | 0.320 |
| Marco Hernandez | BOS | 2B | 114 | 29 | 4 | 14 | 10 | 1 | 1 | 0.256 | 0.293 |
| Michael Chavis | BOS | 1B/2B | 417 | 104 | 35 | 59 | 65 | 22 | 3 | 0.250 | 0.316 |
| Mitch Moreland | BOS | 1B | 372 | 91 | 41 | 55 | 63 | 20 | 1 | 0.244 | 0.321 |
| Mookie Betts | BOS | OF | 580 | 174 | 86 | 124 | 88 | 32 | 19 | 0.300 | 0.392 |
| Rafael Devers | BOS | 3B | 598 | 178 | 46 | 109 | 107 | 33 | 7 | 0.298 | 0.352 |
| Rusney Castillo | BOS | OF | 15 | 4 | 1 | 2 | 2 | 0 | 0 | 0.258 | 0.292 |
| Steve Pearce | BOS | 1B | 133 | 28 | 12 | 15 | 16 | 3 | 0 | 0.212 | 0.287 |
| Tzu-Wei Lin | BOS | 2B | 23 | 5 | 2 | 3 | 2 | 0 | 1 | 0.238 | 0.298 |
| Xander Bogaerts | BOS | SS | 577 | 169 | 64 | 94 | 101 | 26 | 6 | 0.293 | 0.366 |

| Player Name | Team | Pos | AB | H | BB | R | RBI | HR | SB | BA | OBP |
|---|---|---|---|---|---|---|---|---|---|---|---|
| Addison Russell | CHC | 2B/SS | 233 | 57 | 22 | 30 | 30 | 8 | 2 | 0.246 | 0.316 |
| Albert Almora | CHC | OF | 322 | 84 | 17 | 40 | 36 | 9 | 2 | 0.260 | 0.299 |
| Anthony Rizzo | CHC | 1B | 544 | 155 | 73 | 92 | 96 | 28 | 5 | 0.285 | 0.385 |
| Ben Zobrist | CHC | 2B | 176 | 45 | 18 | 21 | 18 | 3 | 1 | 0.255 | 0.326 |
| Daniel Descalso | CHC | 2B | 162 | 32 | 23 | 22 | 19 | 7 | 2 | 0.195 | 0.298 |
| David Bote | CHC | 2B/3B | 295 | 73 | 35 | 40 | 40 | 10 | 4 | 0.246 | 0.332 |
| Donnie Dewees | CHC | OF | 6 | 2 | 1 | 1 | 1 | 0 | 0 | 0.238 | 0.305 |
| Ian Happ | CHC | OF | 347 | 83 | 47 | 52 | 52 | 18 | 6 | 0.240 | 0.334 |
| Jason Heyward | CHC | OF | 494 | 128 | 57 | 71 | 63 | 15 | 6 | 0.259 | 0.339 |
| Javier Baez | CHC | SS | 573 | 158 | 32 | 91 | 96 | 30 | 14 | 0.276 | 0.316 |
| Jonathan Lucroy | CHC | C | 187 | 47 | 16 | 20 | 23 | 5 | 0 | 0.251 | 0.317 |
| Kris Bryant | CHC | 3B/OF | 552 | 153 | 76 | 102 | 83 | 29 | 4 | 0.276 | 0.377 |
| Kyle Schwarber | CHC | OF | 487 | 122 | 71 | 79 | 85 | 36 | 3 | 0.251 | 0.351 |
| Mark Zagunis | CHC | OF | 18 | 5 | 2 | 2 | 2 | 0 | 0 | 0.250 | 0.319 |
| Nick Castellanos | CHC | OF | 604 | 170 | 44 | 93 | 88 | 27 | 2 | 0.281 | 0.334 |
| Nico Hoerner | CHC | SS | 330 | 89 | 21 | 42 | 37 | 6 | 4 | 0.270 | 0.318 |
| Robel Garcia | CHC | 2B | 34 | 8 | 3 | 5 | 5 | 2 | 0 | 0.228 | 0.304 |
| Ryan Court | CHC | 1B | 11 | 2 | 1 | 1 | 2 | 0 | 0 | 0.194 | 0.262 |
| Victor Caratini | CHC | C/1B | 231 | 60 | 23 | 29 | 31 | 8 | 1 | 0.260 | 0.335 |
| Willson Contreras | CHC | C | 417 | 108 | 47 | 58 | 65 | 21 | 2 | 0.260 | 0.345 |

| Player Name | Team | Pos | AB | H | BB | R | RBI | HR | SB | BA | OBP |
|---|---|---|---|---|---|---|---|---|---|---|---|
| Adam Engel | CHW | OF | 186 | 42 | 12 | 22 | 19 | 4 | 4 | 0.225 | 0.285 |
| Charlie Tilson | CHW | OF | 22 | 5 | 1 | 2 | 2 | 0 | 1 | 0.234 | 0.290 |
| Daniel Palka | CHW | OF | 16 | 3 | 2 | 2 | 2 | 1 | 0 | 0.209 | 0.298 |
| Danny Mendick | CHW | SS | 111 | 27 | 9 | 14 | 13 | 3 | 2 | 0.240 | 0.307 |
| Edwin Encarnacion | CHW | 1B | 463 | 115 | 63 | 76 | 88 | 32 | 1 | 0.248 | 0.344 |
| Eloy Jimenez | CHW | OF | 562 | 158 | 40 | 84 | 97 | 36 | 0 | 0.282 | 0.333 |
| James McCann | CHW | C | 310 | 76 | 21 | 37 | 40 | 12 | 2 | 0.244 | 0.299 |
| Jon Jay | CHW | OF | 252 | 65 | 16 | 28 | 22 | 2 | 1 | 0.258 | 0.317 |
| Jose Abreu | CHW | 1B | 587 | 163 | 38 | 84 | 103 | 29 | 2 | 0.278 | 0.331 |
| Jose Rondon | CHW | 2B | 11 | 2 | 1 | 1 | 1 | 0 | 0 | 0.175 | 0.242 |
| Leury Garcia | CHW | 2B/OF | 437 | 115 | 19 | 58 | 41 | 8 | 13 | 0.262 | 0.299 |
| Luis Robert | CHW | OF | 507 | 134 | 29 | 73 | 70 | 21 | 18 | 0.265 | 0.311 |
| Matt Skole | CHW | Util | 16 | 3 | 2 | 2 | 2 | 1 | 0 | 0.197 | 0.300 |
| Nick Madrigal | CHW | 2B | 391 | 111 | 28 | 54 | 41 | 4 | 16 | 0.284 | 0.337 |
| Nicky Delmonico | CHW | OF | 9 | 2 | 1 | 1 | 1 | 0 | 0 | 0.244 | 0.307 |
| Nomar Mazara | CHW | OF | 492 | 125 | 38 | 70 | 77 | 22 | 3 | 0.254 | 0.312 |
| Ryan Goins | CHW | 3B | 57 | 14 | 5 | 7 | 7 | 1 | 0 | 0.240 | 0.306 |
| Seby Zavala | CHW | C | 9 | 2 | 1 | 1 | 1 | 0 | 0 | 0.181 | 0.234 |
| Tim Anderson | CHW | SS | 579 | 162 | 22 | 84 | 71 | 20 | 22 | 0.279 | 0.310 |
| Yasmani Grandal | CHW | C/1B | 462 | 111 | 80 | 70 | 72 | 24 | 3 | 0.240 | 0.354 |
| Yoan Moncada | CHW | 3B | 569 | 152 | 58 | 87 | 82 | 25 | 12 | 0.267 | 0.339 |
| Yolmer Sanchez | CHW | 2B | 352 | 88 | 28 | 41 | 36 | 5 | 5 | 0.249 | 0.310 |
| Zack Collins | CHW | Util | 84 | 18 | 14 | 12 | 13 | 4 | 0 | 0.219 | 0.334 |

| Player Name | Team | Pos | AB | H | BB | R | RBI | HR | SB | BA | OBP |
|---|---|---|---|---|---|---|---|---|---|---|---|
| Alex Blandino | CIN | 2B | 51 | 11 | 7 | 6 | 5 | 1 | 0 | 0.223 | 0.312 |
| Aristides Aquino | CIN | OF | 505 | 122 | 38 | 67 | 80 | 31 | 11 | 0.241 | 0.300 |
| Curt Casali | CIN | C | 196 | 47 | 21 | 23 | 26 | 7 | 0 | 0.240 | 0.315 |
| Derek Dietrich | CIN | 1B/2B | 67 | 16 | 6 | 9 | 9 | 3 | 0 | 0.244 | 0.325 |
| Eugenio Suarez | CIN | 3B | 558 | 146 | 71 | 86 | 98 | 38 | 3 | 0.262 | 0.351 |
| Freddy Galvis | CIN | 2B/SS | 551 | 135 | 35 | 63 | 64 | 17 | 5 | 0.246 | 0.292 |
| Jesse Winker | CIN | OF | 411 | 118 | 55 | 63 | 54 | 18 | 1 | 0.286 | 0.378 |
| Joey Votto | CIN | 1B | 513 | 139 | 87 | 80 | 64 | 18 | 4 | 0.272 | 0.381 |
| Josh VanMeter | CIN | OF | 285 | 72 | 32 | 39 | 37 | 11 | 10 | 0.252 | 0.331 |
| Kyle Farmer | CIN | 2B | 86 | 20 | 5 | 9 | 10 | 2 | 2 | 0.231 | 0.285 |
| Mark Payton | CIN | OF | 112 | 27 | 11 | 14 | 14 | 4 | 2 | 0.241 | 0.308 |
| Mike Moustakas | CIN | 2B/3B | 552 | 142 | 50 | 78 | 93 | 34 | 3 | 0.257 | 0.322 |
| Nick Senzel | CIN | OF | 494 | 131 | 44 | 70 | 59 | 16 | 17 | 0.265 | 0.330 |
| Phillip Ervin | CIN | OF | 302 | 75 | 28 | 39 | 37 | 10 | 7 | 0.249 | 0.320 |
| Scooter Gennett | CIN | 2B | 341 | 89 | 19 | 44 | 46 | 11 | 1 | 0.262 | 0.306 |
| Scott Schebler | CIN | OF | 21 | 4 | 2 | 2 | 2 | 1 | 0 | 0.191 | 0.262 |
| Shogo Akiyama | CIN | OF | 464 | 130 | 52 | 69 | 55 | 13 | 9 | 0.280 | 0.358 |
| Travis Jankowski | CIN | OF | 77 | 18 | 8 | 9 | 6 | 1 | 4 | 0.237 | 0.313 |
| Tucker Barnhart | CIN | C | 353 | 85 | 44 | 38 | 41 | 9 | 1 | 0.240 | 0.325 |

| Player Name | Team | Pos | AB | H | BB | R | RBI | HR | SB | BA | OBP |
|---|---|---|---|---|---|---|---|---|---|---|---|
| Andrew Velazquez | CLE | 2B | 30 | 7 | 2 | 4 | 3 | 1 | 1 | 0.234 | 0.282 |
| Bobby Bradley | CLE | Util | 58 | 14 | 6 | 8 | 9 | 3 | 0 | 0.234 | 0.302 |
| Bradley Zimmer | CLE | OF | 50 | 11 | 5 | 7 | 6 | 1 | 1 | 0.223 | 0.299 |
| Carlos Gonzalez | CLE | OF | 105 | 25 | 11 | 13 | 14 | 4 | 0 | 0.237 | 0.308 |
| Carlos Santana | CLE | 1B | 549 | 143 | 99 | 94 | 91 | 28 | 3 | 0.260 | 0.375 |
| Cesar Hernandez | CLE | 2B | 541 | 147 | 58 | 75 | 59 | 12 | 10 | 0.271 | 0.346 |
| Christian Arroyo | CLE | 3B | 63 | 15 | 5 | 8 | 8 | 2 | 0 | 0.247 | 0.307 |
| Daniel Johnson | CLE | OF | 49 | 13 | 4 | 7 | 7 | 2 | 1 | 0.265 | 0.328 |
| Delino DeShields | CLE | OF | 254 | 59 | 28 | 34 | 23 | 4 | 15 | 0.233 | 0.314 |
| Francisco Lindor | CLE | SS | 625 | 178 | 57 | 111 | 88 | 33 | 22 | 0.284 | 0.347 |
| Franmil Reyes | CLE | OF | 497 | 130 | 50 | 74 | 86 | 36 | 0 | 0.262 | 0.330 |
| Greg Allen | CLE | OF | 231 | 57 | 15 | 29 | 24 | 4 | 10 | 0.245 | 0.307 |
| Hanley Ramirez | CLE | Util | 73 | 17 | 8 | 10 | 11 | 4 | 0 | 0.238 | 0.317 |
| Jake Bauers | CLE | 1B/OF | 296 | 70 | 42 | 42 | 41 | 11 | 5 | 0.237 | 0.332 |
| Jason Kipnis | CLE | 2B | 355 | 86 | 34 | 43 | 47 | 12 | 5 | 0.242 | 0.310 |
| Jordan Luplow | CLE | OF | 275 | 70 | 34 | 41 | 39 | 13 | 4 | 0.256 | 0.343 |
| Jose Ramirez | CLE | 3B | 562 | 155 | 70 | 92 | 99 | 30 | 27 | 0.276 | 0.357 |
| Mike Freeman | CLE | 2B | 32 | 8 | 3 | 4 | 3 | 0 | 0 | 0.239 | 0.302 |
| Oscar Mercado | CLE | OF | 540 | 141 | 40 | 81 | 61 | 15 | 21 | 0.261 | 0.318 |
| Roberto Perez | CLE | C | 356 | 78 | 41 | 41 | 50 | 15 | 1 | 0.220 | 0.304 |
| Sandy Leon | CLE | C | 213 | 43 | 15 | 21 | 22 | 5 | 0 | 0.203 | 0.262 |
| Tyler Naquin | CLE | OF | 306 | 83 | 19 | 40 | 42 | 11 | 5 | 0.273 | 0.317 |
| Yasiel Puig | CLE | OF | 513 | 137 | 48 | 72 | 81 | 25 | 16 | 0.267 | 0.332 |
| Yu Chang | CLE | 3B | 38 | 9 | 4 | 5 | 5 | 1 | 0 | 0.230 | 0.297 |

| Player Name | Team | Pos | AB | H | BB | R | RBI | HR | SB | BA | OBP |
|---|---|---|---|---|---|---|---|---|---|---|---|
| Brendan Rodgers | COL | 2B | 161 | 44 | 9 | 21 | 21 | 5 | 1 | 0.272 | 0.313 |
| Charlie Blackmon | COL | OF | 562 | 168 | 47 | 104 | 77 | 28 | 4 | 0.298 | 0.359 |
| Chris Iannetta | COL | C | 65 | 14 | 9 | 9 | 9 | 3 | 0 | 0.215 | 0.316 |
| Daniel Murphy | COL | 1B | 430 | 124 | 33 | 59 | 69 | 16 | 2 | 0.289 | 0.340 |
| David Dahl | COL | OF | 452 | 127 | 34 | 70 | 69 | 22 | 7 | 0.280 | 0.334 |
| Dom Nunez | COL | C | 78 | 18 | 8 | 9 | 10 | 3 | 1 | 0.224 | 0.303 |
| Drew Butera | COL | C | 67 | 16 | 6 | 8 | 8 | 2 | 0 | 0.243 | 0.307 |
| Garrett Hampson | COL | 2B/OF | 354 | 96 | 30 | 47 | 38 | 8 | 20 | 0.271 | 0.332 |
| Ian Desmond | COL | OF | 339 | 87 | 28 | 46 | 49 | 13 | 5 | 0.257 | 0.317 |
| Josh Fuentes | COL | 1B | 81 | 21 | 4 | 10 | 11 | 3 | 1 | 0.261 | 0.302 |
| Mark Reynolds | COL | 1B | 92 | 20 | 12 | 11 | 13 | 4 | 1 | 0.212 | 0.301 |
| Nolan Arenado | COL | 3B | 579 | 172 | 65 | 98 | 114 | 38 | 3 | 0.298 | 0.369 |
| Raimel Tapia | COL | OF | 292 | 80 | 16 | 37 | 33 | 7 | 7 | 0.275 | 0.316 |
| Roberto Ramos | COL | 1B | 8 | 2 | 1 | 1 | 1 | 0 | 0 | 0.273 | 0.346 |
| Ryan McMahon | COL | 2B/3B | 497 | 130 | 52 | 67 | 76 | 21 | 5 | 0.261 | 0.334 |
| Sam Hilliard | COL | OF | 305 | 75 | 27 | 42 | 42 | 13 | 8 | 0.247 | 0.312 |
| Tony Wolters | COL | C | 323 | 79 | 37 | 37 | 37 | 4 | 1 | 0.245 | 0.332 |
| Trevor Story | COL | SS | 572 | 161 | 54 | 97 | 92 | 33 | 20 | 0.281 | 0.348 |
| Yonathan Daza | COL | OF | 47 | 14 | 3 | 5 | 5 | 1 | 1 | 0.298 | 0.335 |
| Yonder Alonso | COL | 1B | 179 | 43 | 22 | 23 | 25 | 8 | 0 | 0.242 | 0.327 |

| Player Name | Team | Pos | AB | H | BB | R | RBI | HR | SB | BA | OBP |
| --- | --- | --- | --- | --- | --- | --- | --- | --- | --- | --- | --- |
| Austin Romine | DET | C | 266 | 68 | 15 | 30 | 35 | 9 | 1 | 0.257 | 0.300 |
| Brandon Dixon | DET | 1B/OF | 198 | 48 | 12 | 23 | 25 | 7 | 3 | 0.244 | 0.293 |
| C.J. Cron | DET | 1B | 491 | 126 | 33 | 61 | 79 | 28 | 1 | 0.258 | 0.317 |
| Christin Stewart | DET | OF | 389 | 95 | 44 | 47 | 54 | 15 | 1 | 0.243 | 0.324 |
| Dawel Lugo | DET | 3B | 313 | 83 | 13 | 35 | 35 | 7 | 2 | 0.266 | 0.299 |
| Daz Cameron | DET | OF | 18 | 4 | 2 | 2 | 2 | 0 | 1 | 0.214 | 0.296 |
| Gordon Beckham | DET | 2B | 65 | 15 | 5 | 7 | 7 | 1 | 1 | 0.233 | 0.295 |
| Grayson Greiner | DET | C | 216 | 48 | 20 | 21 | 23 | 6 | 0 | 0.222 | 0.286 |
| Harold Castro | DET | 2B/OF | 207 | 55 | 7 | 21 | 21 | 4 | 3 | 0.268 | 0.291 |
| Isaac Paredes | DET | 3B | 103 | 28 | 10 | 13 | 13 | 3 | 1 | 0.269 | 0.340 |
| JaCoby Jones | DET | OF | 458 | 107 | 37 | 60 | 49 | 14 | 11 | 0.234 | 0.302 |
| Jake Robson | DET | OF | 17 | 4 | 2 | 2 | 2 | 0 | 1 | 0.242 | 0.310 |
| Jake Rogers | DET | C | 117 | 24 | 12 | 14 | 14 | 4 | 0 | 0.208 | 0.290 |
| Jeimer Candelario | DET | 1B/3B | 413 | 96 | 51 | 54 | 49 | 14 | 3 | 0.233 | 0.326 |
| John Hicks | DET | C/1B | 87 | 19 | 5 | 9 | 10 | 3 | 0 | 0.224 | 0.265 |
| Jonathan Schoop | DET | 2B | 494 | 129 | 24 | 64 | 71 | 25 | 1 | 0.260 | 0.303 |
| Jordy Mercer | DET | SS | 254 | 63 | 19 | 28 | 28 | 7 | 0 | 0.247 | 0.305 |
| Miguel Cabrera | DET | 1B | 455 | 126 | 47 | 51 | 63 | 14 | 0 | 0.276 | 0.346 |
| Niko Goodrum | DET | 2B/SS/OF | 496 | 121 | 47 | 64 | 59 | 17 | 15 | 0.244 | 0.312 |
| Sergio Alcantara | DET | SS | 23 | 6 | 2 | 2 | 2 | 0 | 0 | 0.243 | 0.306 |
| Travis Demeritte | DET | OF | 329 | 77 | 32 | 44 | 41 | 12 | 5 | 0.235 | 0.308 |
| Troy Stokes Jr. | DET | OF | 21 | 5 | 2 | 3 | 2 | 1 | 0 | 0.228 | 0.311 |
| Victor Reyes | DET | OF | 446 | 123 | 21 | 56 | 46 | 7 | 15 | 0.275 | 0.309 |
| Willi Castro | DET | SS | 295 | 76 | 19 | 36 | 32 | 5 | 4 | 0.259 | 0.309 |

| Player Name | Team | Pos | AB | H | BB | R | RBI | HR | SB | BA | OBP |
|---|---|---|---|---|---|---|---|---|---|---|---|
| A.J. Reed | HOU | 1B | 17 | 3 | 2 | 2 | 2 | 1 | 0 | 0.172 | 0.239 |
| Abraham Toro-Hernandez | HOU | 3B | 71 | 18 | 7 | 10 | 10 | 3 | 1 | 0.254 | 0.330 |
| Aledmys Diaz | HOU | 1B/2B | 219 | 57 | 18 | 31 | 33 | 8 | 2 | 0.262 | 0.321 |
| Alex Bregman | HOU | 3B/SS | 557 | 161 | 99 | 110 | 104 | 33 | 6 | 0.289 | 0.401 |
| Carlos Correa | HOU | SS | 488 | 132 | 61 | 76 | 91 | 28 | 3 | 0.271 | 0.352 |
| Dustin Garneau | HOU | C | 92 | 19 | 9 | 11 | 11 | 3 | 0 | 0.207 | 0.291 |
| Garrett Stubbs | HOU | C | 79 | 17 | 7 | 10 | 8 | 2 | 2 | 0.221 | 0.291 |
| George Springer | HOU | OF | 553 | 153 | 70 | 107 | 88 | 34 | 7 | 0.276 | 0.363 |
| Jack Mayfield | HOU | SS | 19 | 4 | 1 | 3 | 3 | 1 | 0 | 0.231 | 0.280 |
| Jose Altuve | HOU | 2B | 568 | 171 | 52 | 97 | 82 | 24 | 10 | 0.302 | 0.365 |
| Josh Reddick | HOU | OF | 390 | 104 | 33 | 51 | 51 | 12 | 4 | 0.268 | 0.322 |
| Kyle Tucker | HOU | OF | 386 | 98 | 35 | 60 | 60 | 19 | 17 | 0.254 | 0.323 |
| Martin Maldonado | HOU | C | 312 | 68 | 22 | 38 | 35 | 10 | 0 | 0.218 | 0.285 |
| Michael Brantley | HOU | OF | 547 | 162 | 48 | 84 | 84 | 19 | 5 | 0.297 | 0.356 |
| Myles Straw | HOU | SS | 208 | 54 | 24 | 31 | 21 | 1 | 16 | 0.258 | 0.338 |
| Taylor Jones | HOU | 1B | 20 | 5 | 2 | 3 | 3 | 1 | 0 | 0.252 | 0.329 |
| Yordan Alvarez | HOU | Util | 535 | 152 | 76 | 91 | 109 | 40 | 2 | 0.283 | 0.375 |
| Yuli Gurriel | HOU | 1B/3B | 560 | 163 | 31 | 78 | 91 | 22 | 5 | 0.291 | 0.331 |

| Player Name | Team | Pos | AB | H | BB | R | RBI | HR | SB | BA | OBP |
| --- | --- | --- | --- | --- | --- | --- | --- | --- | --- | --- | --- |
| Adalberto Mondesi | KC | SS | 501 | 126 | 25 | 70 | 67 | 16 | 48 | 0.252 | 0.289 |
| Alex Gordon | KC | OF | 439 | 111 | 42 | 57 | 55 | 12 | 5 | 0.252 | 0.331 |
| Brett Phillips | KC | OF | 281 | 61 | 35 | 38 | 33 | 9 | 10 | 0.216 | 0.304 |
| Bubba Starling | KC | OF | 252 | 60 | 15 | 30 | 25 | 6 | 4 | 0.237 | 0.285 |
| Cam Gallagher | KC | C | 106 | 26 | 8 | 12 | 12 | 2 | 0 | 0.248 | 0.308 |
| Cheslor Cuthbert | KC | 1B/3B | 170 | 43 | 11 | 16 | 21 | 6 | 0 | 0.250 | 0.296 |
| Dairon Blanco | KC | OF | 6 | 2 | 0 | 1 | 1 | 0 | 0 | 0.242 | 0.281 |
| Erick Mejia | KC | OF | 26 | 6 | 2 | 3 | 3 | 0 | 0 | 0.241 | 0.298 |
| Humberto Arteaga | KC | SS | 19 | 5 | 1 | 2 | 2 | 0 | 0 | 0.260 | 0.292 |
| Hunter Dozier | KC | 3B/OF | 500 | 127 | 52 | 68 | 72 | 21 | 3 | 0.253 | 0.327 |
| Jorge Bonifacio | KC | OF | 92 | 19 | 7 | 11 | 10 | 3 | 0 | 0.208 | 0.269 |
| Jorge Soler | KC | OF | 539 | 139 | 69 | 82 | 94 | 35 | 3 | 0.258 | 0.349 |
| Kelvin Gutierrez | KC | 3B | 34 | 9 | 3 | 4 | 4 | 1 | 1 | 0.254 | 0.305 |
| Lucas Duda | KC | 1B | 98 | 22 | 10 | 13 | 15 | 5 | 0 | 0.223 | 0.301 |
| Maikel Franco | KC | 3B | 419 | 106 | 33 | 52 | 61 | 18 | 0 | 0.253 | 0.308 |
| Meibrys Viloria | KC | C | 65 | 16 | 5 | 6 | 7 | 1 | 0 | 0.242 | 0.301 |
| Nick Dini | KC | C | 15 | 4 | 1 | 2 | 2 | 1 | 0 | 0.244 | 0.318 |
| Nick Heath | KC | OF | 9 | 2 | 1 | 1 | 1 | 0 | 1 | 0.227 | 0.293 |
| Nicky Lopez | KC | 2B/SS | 443 | 119 | 32 | 52 | 41 | 5 | 6 | 0.268 | 0.321 |
| Ryan McBroom | KC | OF | 257 | 68 | 23 | 32 | 32 | 8 | 1 | 0.263 | 0.329 |
| Ryan O'Hearn | KC | 1B | 350 | 80 | 39 | 42 | 49 | 16 | 0 | 0.230 | 0.311 |
| Salvador Perez | KC | C | 466 | 116 | 18 | 54 | 70 | 23 | 1 | 0.250 | 0.287 |
| Whit Merrifield | KC | 2B/OF | 599 | 172 | 43 | 88 | 62 | 14 | 22 | 0.287 | 0.338 |

| Player Name | Team | Pos | AB | H | BB | R | RBI | HR | SB | BA | OBP |
|---|---|---|---|---|---|---|---|---|---|---|---|
| Albert Pujols | LAA | 1B | 445 | 110 | 33 | 54 | 71 | 19 | 2 | 0.248 | 0.302 |
| Andrelton Simmons | LAA | SS | 501 | 138 | 33 | 60 | 61 | 10 | 11 | 0.276 | 0.324 |
| Anthony Bemboom | LAA | C | 30 | 6 | 2 | 3 | 3 | 1 | 0 | 0.207 | 0.262 |
| Anthony Rendon | LAA | 3B | 551 | 161 | 78 | 97 | 104 | 29 | 4 | 0.292 | 0.383 |
| Brandon Marsh | LAA | OF | 10 | 3 | 1 | 1 | 1 | 0 | 0 | 0.262 | 0.349 |
| Brian Goodwin | LAA | OF | 339 | 81 | 32 | 48 | 42 | 13 | 6 | 0.239 | 0.307 |
| David Fletcher | LAA | 2B/3B/SS/OF | 493 | 139 | 38 | 66 | 48 | 6 | 7 | 0.281 | 0.335 |
| Jared Walsh | LAA | 1B | 68 | 16 | 6 | 10 | 10 | 4 | 0 | 0.236 | 0.302 |
| Jason Castro | LAA | C | 306 | 68 | 39 | 41 | 38 | 12 | 0 | 0.221 | 0.315 |
| Jo Adell | LAA | OF | 378 | 93 | 30 | 54 | 48 | 12 | 8 | 0.245 | 0.306 |
| Justin Upton | LAA | OF | 475 | 115 | 58 | 74 | 81 | 26 | 3 | 0.241 | 0.327 |
| Luis Rengifo | LAA | 2B | 120 | 29 | 12 | 15 | 13 | 3 | 2 | 0.241 | 0.320 |
| Matt Thaiss | LAA | 3B | 142 | 34 | 16 | 18 | 19 | 6 | 0 | 0.242 | 0.318 |
| Max Stassi | LAA | C | 189 | 39 | 20 | 21 | 22 | 6 | 0 | 0.205 | 0.286 |
| Michael Hermosillo | LAA | OF | 53 | 11 | 4 | 7 | 6 | 2 | 2 | 0.210 | 0.289 |
| Mike Trout | LAA | OF | 514 | 153 | 121 | 117 | 105 | 43 | 14 | 0.298 | 0.439 |
| Peter Bourjos | LAA | OF | 75 | 17 | 4 | 8 | 8 | 1 | 2 | 0.225 | 0.267 |
| Shohei Ohtani | LAA | Util | 406 | 115 | 40 | 62 | 71 | 22 | 12 | 0.282 | 0.349 |
| Taylor Ward | LAA | OF | 46 | 11 | 5 | 7 | 7 | 1 | 0 | 0.246 | 0.321 |
| Tommy La Stella | LAA | 2B/3B | 352 | 98 | 31 | 52 | 47 | 13 | 1 | 0.277 | 0.340 |

| Player Name | Team | Pos | AB | H | BB | R | RBI | HR | SB | BA | OBP |
|---|---|---|---|---|---|---|---|---|---|---|---|
| A.J. Pollock | LAD | OF | 397 | 102 | 31 | 59 | 58 | 18 | 8 | 0.257 | 0.319 |
| Alex Verdugo | LAD | OF | 418 | 123 | 38 | 54 | 55 | 15 | 5 | 0.295 | 0.356 |
| Austin Barnes | LAD | C | 185 | 41 | 23 | 24 | 22 | 5 | 3 | 0.223 | 0.322 |
| Chris Taylor | LAD | 2B/SS/OF | 348 | 87 | 35 | 50 | 44 | 11 | 7 | 0.251 | 0.324 |
| Cody Bellinger | LAD | 1B/OF | 545 | 157 | 88 | 105 | 110 | 42 | 14 | 0.288 | 0.388 |
| Corey Seager | LAD | SS | 499 | 138 | 49 | 78 | 79 | 21 | 2 | 0.277 | 0.345 |
| Edwin Rios | LAD | 1B | 21 | 5 | 2 | 3 | 3 | 1 | 0 | 0.230 | 0.289 |
| Enrique Hernandez | LAD | 2B/OF | 325 | 79 | 35 | 48 | 47 | 14 | 3 | 0.243 | 0.319 |
| Gavin Lux | LAD | 2B | 425 | 114 | 42 | 62 | 52 | 14 | 10 | 0.269 | 0.337 |
| Joc Pederson | LAD | 1B/OF | 411 | 103 | 48 | 74 | 67 | 28 | 2 | 0.250 | 0.339 |
| Justin Turner | LAD | 3B | 473 | 136 | 53 | 77 | 72 | 23 | 3 | 0.288 | 0.373 |
| Keibert Ruiz | LAD | C | 11 | 3 | 1 | 1 | 1 | 0 | 0 | 0.239 | 0.290 |
| Matt Beaty | LAD | 1B/OF | 160 | 43 | 12 | 21 | 22 | 6 | 2 | 0.267 | 0.327 |
| Max Muncy | LAD | 1B/2B/3B | 477 | 118 | 84 | 88 | 82 | 31 | 4 | 0.247 | 0.365 |
| Rocky Gale | LAD | C | 7 | 2 | 0 | 1 | 1 | 0 | 0 | 0.214 | 0.262 |
| Russell Martin | LAD | C | 96 | 21 | 15 | 13 | 12 | 4 | 1 | 0.223 | 0.341 |
| Tyler White | LAD | 1B | 54 | 13 | 6 | 6 | 7 | 2 | 0 | 0.237 | 0.324 |
| Will Smith | LAD | C | 377 | 87 | 40 | 54 | 62 | 22 | 3 | 0.230 | 0.312 |

| Player Name | Team | Pos | AB | H | BB | R | RBI | HR | SB | BA | OBP |
|---|---|---|---|---|---|---|---|---|---|---|---|
| Brian Anderson | MIA | 3B/OF | 535 | 142 | 53 | 74 | 71 | 22 | 5 | 0.266 | 0.343 |
| Bryan Holaday | MIA | C | 23 | 5 | 2 | 2 | 3 | 0 | 0 | 0.228 | 0.290 |
| Cesar Puello | MIA | OF | 7 | 2 | 1 | 1 | 1 | 0 | 0 | 0.237 | 0.320 |
| Chad Wallach | MIA | C | 13 | 2 | 1 | 1 | 1 | 0 | 0 | 0.189 | 0.259 |
| Corey Dickerson | MIA | OF | 458 | 128 | 26 | 57 | 63 | 17 | 3 | 0.280 | 0.320 |
| Curtis Granderson | MIA | OF | 68 | 15 | 9 | 9 | 9 | 3 | 1 | 0.218 | 0.318 |
| Francisco Cervelli | MIA | C | 227 | 53 | 27 | 25 | 26 | 6 | 1 | 0.234 | 0.330 |
| Garrett Cooper | MIA | 1B/OF | 343 | 92 | 30 | 45 | 48 | 13 | 0 | 0.270 | 0.332 |
| Harold Ramirez | MIA | OF | 333 | 92 | 17 | 40 | 40 | 9 | 3 | 0.277 | 0.320 |
| Isan Diaz | MIA | 2B | 460 | 106 | 51 | 59 | 57 | 15 | 4 | 0.230 | 0.312 |
| J.T. Riddle | MIA | OF | 181 | 41 | 10 | 20 | 22 | 6 | 0 | 0.228 | 0.270 |
| Jesus Aguilar | MIA | 1B | 390 | 96 | 46 | 53 | 66 | 19 | 0 | 0.247 | 0.328 |
| Jesus Sanchez | MIA | OF | 101 | 25 | 6 | 12 | 12 | 3 | 1 | 0.246 | 0.286 |
| Jon Berti | MIA | 3B/SS/OF | 355 | 89 | 34 | 53 | 34 | 8 | 21 | 0.250 | 0.324 |
| Jonathan Villar | MIA | 2B/SS | 552 | 143 | 51 | 77 | 58 | 16 | 33 | 0.258 | 0.325 |
| Jorge Alfaro | MIA | C | 415 | 103 | 22 | 43 | 51 | 16 | 3 | 0.247 | 0.300 |
| Lewin Diaz | MIA | 1B | 18 | 4 | 1 | 2 | 3 | 1 | 0 | 0.249 | 0.308 |
| Lewis Brinson | MIA | OF | 316 | 67 | 22 | 34 | 34 | 8 | 4 | 0.213 | 0.276 |
| Magneuris Sierra | MIA | OF | 148 | 38 | 8 | 16 | 12 | 1 | 8 | 0.253 | 0.293 |
| Miguel Rojas | MIA | SS | 476 | 129 | 31 | 53 | 49 | 8 | 7 | 0.272 | 0.322 |
| Monte Harrison | MIA | OF | 240 | 54 | 18 | 30 | 24 | 8 | 7 | 0.226 | 0.288 |
| Neil Walker | MIA | 1B/3B | 270 | 67 | 32 | 35 | 36 | 9 | 2 | 0.249 | 0.333 |

| Player Name | Team | Pos | AB | H | BB | R | RBI | HR | SB | BA | OBP |
|---|---|---|---|---|---|---|---|---|---|---|---|
| Avisail Garcia | MIL | OF | 461 | 125 | 31 | 61 | 70 | 20 | 7 | 0.271 | 0.324 |
| Ben Gamel | MIL | OF | 230 | 59 | 26 | 32 | 26 | 5 | 2 | 0.257 | 0.336 |
| Christian Yelich | MIL | OF | 555 | 171 | 82 | 109 | 98 | 37 | 25 | 0.309 | 0.402 |
| David Freitas | MIL | C | 14 | 4 | 1 | 2 | 2 | 0 | 0 | 0.278 | 0.340 |
| Eric Sogard | MIL | 2B | 335 | 87 | 36 | 43 | 33 | 7 | 6 | 0.259 | 0.336 |
| Hernan Perez | MIL | 2B/SS | 130 | 32 | 7 | 15 | 16 | 4 | 3 | 0.245 | 0.285 |
| Jacob Nottingham | MIL | C | 14 | 3 | 1 | 2 | 2 | 0 | 0 | 0.189 | 0.254 |
| Jedd Gyorko | MIL | 3B | 196 | 48 | 22 | 25 | 29 | 9 | 3 | 0.245 | 0.322 |
| Justin Smoak | MIL | 1B | 409 | 96 | 69 | 59 | 66 | 22 | 0 | 0.234 | 0.349 |
| Keston Hiura | MIL | 2B | 557 | 155 | 42 | 83 | 85 | 27 | 13 | 0.279 | 0.340 |
| Logan Morrison | MIL | 1B | 50 | 11 | 5 | 7 | 8 | 3 | 0 | 0.210 | 0.286 |
| Lorenzo Cain | MIL | OF | 536 | 149 | 53 | 78 | 52 | 12 | 19 | 0.279 | 0.349 |
| Luis Urias | MIL | 2B/SS | 460 | 115 | 52 | 63 | 54 | 12 | 3 | 0.250 | 0.337 |
| Manuel Pina | MIL | C | 256 | 63 | 21 | 28 | 32 | 9 | 0 | 0.245 | 0.312 |
| Mark Mathias | MIL | 2B | 17 | 4 | 2 | 2 | 2 | 0 | 0 | 0.221 | 0.292 |
| Omar Narvaez | MIL | C | 357 | 95 | 43 | 46 | 46 | 13 | 0 | 0.266 | 0.349 |
| Orlando Arcia | MIL | SS | 293 | 71 | 22 | 32 | 34 | 8 | 5 | 0.243 | 0.297 |
| Ronny Rodriguez | MIL | 2B/SS | 177 | 43 | 9 | 22 | 24 | 7 | 2 | 0.241 | 0.274 |
| Ryan Braun | MIL | OF | 438 | 119 | 35 | 65 | 71 | 21 | 10 | 0.271 | 0.329 |
| Ryon Healy | MIL | 3B | 174 | 44 | 11 | 22 | 26 | 8 | 0 | 0.254 | 0.303 |
| Tyler Austin | MIL | 1B/OF | 65 | 14 | 7 | 9 | 10 | 3 | 1 | 0.222 | 0.295 |
| Tyrone Taylor | MIL | OF | 20 | 5 | 2 | 2 | 2 | 1 | 0 | 0.229 | 0.287 |

| Player Name | Team | Pos | AB | H | BB | R | RBI | HR | SB | BA | OBP |
|---|---|---|---|---|---|---|---|---|---|---|---|
| Alex Avila | MIN | C | 130 | 28 | 23 | 16 | 17 | 5 | 1 | 0.213 | 0.337 |
| Alex Kirilloff | MIN | OF | 30 | 8 | 2 | 4 | 4 | 1 | 0 | 0.276 | 0.328 |
| Brent Rooker | MIN | OF | 11 | 3 | 1 | 2 | 2 | 1 | 0 | 0.242 | 0.305 |
| Byron Buxton | MIN | OF | 430 | 110 | 30 | 63 | 60 | 14 | 21 | 0.255 | 0.309 |
| Eddie Rosario | MIN | OF | 561 | 158 | 29 | 87 | 97 | 31 | 4 | 0.281 | 0.315 |
| Ehire Adrianza | MIN | 1B/3B/SS | 209 | 54 | 18 | 29 | 25 | 5 | 2 | 0.257 | 0.318 |
| Ian Miller | MIN | OF | 6 | 1 | 0 | 1 | 1 | 0 | 0 | 0.223 | 0.282 |
| Jake Cave | MIN | OF | 146 | 38 | 12 | 21 | 20 | 6 | 1 | 0.258 | 0.320 |
| Jorge Polanco | MIN | SS | 586 | 164 | 54 | 91 | 79 | 19 | 6 | 0.280 | 0.343 |
| LaMonte Wade | MIN | OF | 32 | 8 | 5 | 5 | 4 | 1 | 0 | 0.249 | 0.348 |
| Luis Arraez | MIN | 2B/OF | 501 | 156 | 47 | 69 | 54 | 7 | 4 | 0.311 | 0.371 |
| Luke Raley | MIN | OF | 16 | 4 | 1 | 2 | 2 | 1 | 0 | 0.245 | 0.314 |
| Marwin Gonzalez | MIN | 1B/3B/OF | 397 | 106 | 34 | 51 | 57 | 15 | 2 | 0.267 | 0.332 |
| Max Kepler | MIN | OF | 531 | 134 | 62 | 92 | 81 | 28 | 3 | 0.253 | 0.337 |
| Miguel Sano | MIN | 3B | 472 | 115 | 62 | 78 | 88 | 35 | 0 | 0.243 | 0.335 |
| Mitch Garver | MIN | C | 360 | 93 | 43 | 61 | 60 | 21 | 0 | 0.257 | 0.341 |
| Nelson Cruz | MIN | Util | 491 | 139 | 58 | 82 | 102 | 36 | 0 | 0.283 | 0.367 |
| Nick Gordon | MIN | SS | 10 | 2 | 1 | 1 | 1 | 0 | 0 | 0.244 | 0.295 |
| Ronald Torreyes | MIN | SS | 16 | 4 | 1 | 2 | 2 | 0 | 1 | 0.219 | 0.260 |
| Willians Astudillo | MIN | C | 202 | 59 | 7 | 27 | 29 | 6 | 1 | 0.292 | 0.322 |

| Player Name | Team | Pos | AB | H | BB | R | RBI | HR | SB | BA | OBP |
|---|---|---|---|---|---|---|---|---|---|---|---|
| Amed Rosario | NYM | SS | 574 | 158 | 31 | 70 | 64 | 14 | 19 | 0.275 | 0.316 |
| Andres Gimenez | NYM | SS | 12 | 3 | 1 | 1 | 1 | 0 | 1 | 0.237 | 0.302 |
| Brandon Nimmo | NYM | OF | 408 | 97 | 77 | 69 | 50 | 15 | 6 | 0.237 | 0.370 |
| Carlos Gomez | NYM | OF | 46 | 11 | 3 | 6 | 6 | 2 | 2 | 0.228 | 0.301 |
| Dominic Smith | NYM | 1B/OF | 243 | 60 | 20 | 34 | 32 | 11 | 1 | 0.246 | 0.309 |
| J.D. Davis | NYM | 3B/OF | 434 | 119 | 40 | 61 | 64 | 21 | 3 | 0.273 | 0.338 |
| Jacob Marisnick | NYM | OF | 237 | 52 | 16 | 35 | 29 | 9 | 8 | 0.221 | 0.283 |
| Jed Lowrie | NYM | 2B | 284 | 70 | 34 | 36 | 37 | 9 | 0 | 0.246 | 0.330 |
| Jeff McNeil | NYM | 2B/3B/OF | 555 | 164 | 40 | 89 | 72 | 20 | 7 | 0.296 | 0.358 |
| Joe Panik | NYM | 2B | 213 | 56 | 19 | 26 | 22 | 4 | 2 | 0.263 | 0.327 |
| Juan Lagares | NYM | OF | 170 | 41 | 13 | 22 | 18 | 3 | 3 | 0.242 | 0.300 |
| Luis Guillorme | NYM | SS | 65 | 16 | 7 | 7 | 7 | 1 | 1 | 0.249 | 0.333 |
| Matt Kemp | NYM | OF | 21 | 5 | 1 | 2 | 3 | 1 | 0 | 0.236 | 0.270 |
| Michael Conforto | NYM | OF | 540 | 138 | 82 | 88 | 90 | 34 | 6 | 0.255 | 0.359 |
| Pete Alonso | NYM | 1B | 565 | 145 | 69 | 96 | 108 | 43 | 1 | 0.256 | 0.351 |
| Rajai Davis | NYM | OF | 39 | 9 | 2 | 5 | 4 | 1 | 1 | 0.231 | 0.278 |
| Rene Rivera | NYM | C | 29 | 6 | 2 | 3 | 4 | 1 | 0 | 0.218 | 0.278 |
| Robinson Cano | NYM | 2B | 467 | 127 | 37 | 61 | 64 | 17 | 1 | 0.271 | 0.330 |
| Ryan Cordell | NYM | OF | 34 | 7 | 2 | 3 | 4 | 1 | 0 | 0.216 | 0.271 |
| Tomas Nido | NYM | C | 163 | 36 | 9 | 15 | 18 | 4 | 0 | 0.222 | 0.266 |
| Wilson Ramos | NYM | C | 407 | 113 | 35 | 47 | 62 | 15 | 1 | 0.279 | 0.337 |
| Yoenis Cespedes | NYM | OF | 196 | 51 | 18 | 29 | 32 | 11 | 3 | 0.259 | 0.324 |

| Player Name | Team | Pos | AB | H | BB | R | RBI | HR | SB | BA | OBP |
|---|---|---|---|---|---|---|---|---|---|---|---|
| Aaron Hicks | NYY | OF | 97 | 23 | 15 | 16 | 15 | 5 | 1 | 0.238 | 0.335 |
| Aaron Judge | NYY | OF | 519 | 138 | 97 | 103 | 91 | 39 | 5 | 0.265 | 0.384 |
| Brett Gardner | NYY | OF | 449 | 110 | 49 | 72 | 57 | 16 | 11 | 0.246 | 0.325 |
| Cameron Maybin | NYY | OF | 254 | 64 | 31 | 35 | 28 | 7 | 9 | 0.251 | 0.335 |
| Clint Frazier | NYY | OF | 249 | 62 | 21 | 36 | 35 | 12 | 2 | 0.250 | 0.314 |
| D.J. LeMahieu | NYY | 1B/2B/3B | 583 | 172 | 47 | 98 | 76 | 19 | 5 | 0.295 | 0.348 |
| Gary Sanchez | NYY | C | 434 | 103 | 46 | 68 | 81 | 32 | 0 | 0.238 | 0.322 |
| Giancarlo Stanton | NYY | OF | 461 | 123 | 59 | 79 | 92 | 35 | 2 | 0.266 | 0.352 |
| Giovanny Urshela | NYY | 3B | 447 | 123 | 25 | 61 | 62 | 16 | 1 | 0.276 | 0.321 |
| Gleyber Torres | NYY | 2B/SS | 554 | 151 | 53 | 89 | 96 | 33 | 6 | 0.273 | 0.338 |
| Greg Bird | NYY | 1B | 164 | 37 | 20 | 22 | 25 | 8 | 0 | 0.225 | 0.316 |
| Kyle Higashioka | NYY | C | 119 | 26 | 8 | 15 | 18 | 6 | 0 | 0.220 | 0.274 |
| Luke Voit | NYY | 1B | 419 | 108 | 56 | 64 | 63 | 23 | 0 | 0.257 | 0.354 |
| Miguel Andujar | NYY | 3B | 448 | 122 | 24 | 59 | 70 | 19 | 2 | 0.271 | 0.310 |
| Mike Ford | NYY | 1B | 215 | 56 | 29 | 35 | 36 | 13 | 0 | 0.260 | 0.353 |
| Mike Tauchman | NYY | OF | 304 | 77 | 35 | 46 | 42 | 12 | 6 | 0.253 | 0.334 |
| Terrance Gore | NYY | OF | 14 | 2 | 2 | 2 | 0 | 0 | 3 | 0.154 | 0.272 |
| Thairo Estrada | NYY | 2B | 70 | 18 | 4 | 10 | 9 | 2 | 2 | 0.251 | 0.300 |
| Tyler Wade | NYY | 2B/OF | 102 | 25 | 8 | 14 | 11 | 2 | 5 | 0.241 | 0.304 |

| Player Name | Team | Pos | AB | H | BB | R | RBI | HR | SB | BA | OBP |
|---|---|---|---|---|---|---|---|---|---|---|---|
| Austin Allen | OAK | C | 180 | 45 | 12 | 21 | 23 | 7 | 0 | 0.247 | 0.302 |
| Chad Pinder | OAK | 2B/OF | 287 | 71 | 20 | 37 | 38 | 12 | 1 | 0.248 | 0.305 |
| Dustin Fowler | OAK | OF | 38 | 11 | 1 | 5 | 5 | 1 | 0 | 0.280 | 0.303 |
| Franklin Barreto | OAK | 2B | 222 | 53 | 16 | 32 | 29 | 9 | 4 | 0.240 | 0.298 |
| Jonah Heim | OAK | C | 24 | 6 | 2 | 3 | 3 | 1 | 0 | 0.238 | 0.290 |
| Jorge Mateo | OAK | SS | 152 | 37 | 8 | 19 | 16 | 3 | 6 | 0.240 | 0.279 |
| Josh Phegley | OAK | C | 169 | 39 | 10 | 21 | 24 | 5 | 0 | 0.233 | 0.281 |
| Khris Davis | OAK | Util | 527 | 127 | 52 | 78 | 95 | 36 | 0 | 0.241 | 0.314 |
| Marcus Semien | OAK | SS | 591 | 159 | 69 | 100 | 77 | 23 | 10 | 0.270 | 0.346 |
| Mark Canha | OAK | OF | 446 | 113 | 55 | 73 | 66 | 23 | 3 | 0.253 | 0.350 |
| Matt Chapman | OAK | 3B | 573 | 147 | 66 | 97 | 91 | 34 | 1 | 0.256 | 0.341 |
| Matt Olson | OAK | 1B | 549 | 141 | 65 | 84 | 100 | 39 | 0 | 0.256 | 0.345 |
| Nick Hundley | OAK | C | 89 | 20 | 5 | 9 | 11 | 3 | 0 | 0.219 | 0.268 |
| Ramon Laureano | OAK | OF | 508 | 136 | 42 | 82 | 73 | 23 | 16 | 0.269 | 0.330 |
| Robbie Grossman | OAK | OF | 304 | 77 | 45 | 42 | 34 | 6 | 5 | 0.252 | 0.349 |
| Sean Murphy | OAK | C | 318 | 81 | 28 | 47 | 45 | 13 | 1 | 0.253 | 0.321 |
| Seth Brown | OAK | OF | 145 | 34 | 12 | 19 | 20 | 5 | 2 | 0.233 | 0.298 |
| Sheldon Neuse | OAK | 2B | 212 | 53 | 15 | 25 | 26 | 5 | 2 | 0.248 | 0.298 |
| Skye Bolt | OAK | OF | 21 | 4 | 2 | 3 | 3 | 1 | 0 | 0.195 | 0.257 |
| Stephen Piscotty | OAK | OF | 409 | 106 | 36 | 55 | 59 | 17 | 2 | 0.259 | 0.326 |
| Tony Kemp | OAK | 2B/OF | 144 | 36 | 13 | 19 | 16 | 3 | 4 | 0.249 | 0.319 |
| Vimael Machin | OAK | SS | 15 | 3 | 2 | 2 | 2 | 0 | 0 | 0.203 | 0.297 |

| Player Name | Team | Pos | AB | H | BB | R | RBI | HR | SB | BA | OBP |
|---|---|---|---|---|---|---|---|---|---|---|---|
| Austin Allen | OAK | C | 180 | 45 | 12 | 21 | 23 | 7 | 0 | 0.247 | 0.302 |
| Chad Pinder | OAK | 2B/OF | 287 | 71 | 20 | 37 | 38 | 12 | 1 | 0.248 | 0.305 |
| Dustin Fowler | OAK | OF | 38 | 11 | 1 | 5 | 5 | 1 | 0 | 0.280 | 0.303 |
| Franklin Barreto | OAK | 2B | 222 | 53 | 16 | 32 | 29 | 9 | 4 | 0.240 | 0.298 |
| Jonah Heim | OAK | C | 24 | 6 | 2 | 3 | 3 | 1 | 0 | 0.238 | 0.290 |
| Jorge Mateo | OAK | SS | 152 | 37 | 8 | 19 | 16 | 3 | 6 | 0.240 | 0.279 |
| Josh Phegley | OAK | C | 169 | 39 | 10 | 21 | 24 | 5 | 0 | 0.233 | 0.281 |
| Khris Davis | OAK | Util | 527 | 127 | 52 | 78 | 95 | 36 | 0 | 0.241 | 0.314 |
| Marcus Semien | OAK | SS | 591 | 159 | 69 | 100 | 77 | 23 | 10 | 0.270 | 0.346 |
| Mark Canha | OAK | OF | 446 | 113 | 55 | 73 | 66 | 23 | 3 | 0.253 | 0.350 |
| Matt Chapman | OAK | 3B | 573 | 147 | 66 | 97 | 91 | 34 | 1 | 0.256 | 0.341 |
| Matt Olson | OAK | 1B | 549 | 141 | 65 | 84 | 100 | 39 | 0 | 0.256 | 0.345 |
| Nick Hundley | OAK | C | 89 | 20 | 5 | 9 | 11 | 3 | 0 | 0.219 | 0.268 |
| Ramon Laureano | OAK | OF | 508 | 136 | 42 | 82 | 73 | 23 | 16 | 0.269 | 0.330 |
| Robbie Grossman | OAK | OF | 304 | 77 | 45 | 42 | 34 | 6 | 5 | 0.252 | 0.349 |
| Sean Murphy | OAK | C | 318 | 81 | 28 | 47 | 45 | 13 | 1 | 0.253 | 0.321 |
| Seth Brown | OAK | OF | 145 | 34 | 12 | 19 | 20 | 5 | 2 | 0.233 | 0.298 |
| Sheldon Neuse | OAK | 2B | 212 | 53 | 15 | 25 | 26 | 5 | 2 | 0.248 | 0.298 |
| Skye Bolt | OAK | OF | 21 | 4 | 2 | 3 | 3 | 1 | 0 | 0.195 | 0.257 |
| Stephen Piscotty | OAK | OF | 409 | 106 | 36 | 55 | 59 | 17 | 2 | 0.259 | 0.326 |
| Tony Kemp | OAK | 2B/OF | 144 | 36 | 13 | 19 | 16 | 3 | 4 | 0.249 | 0.319 |
| Vimael Machin | OAK | SS | 15 | 3 | 2 | 2 | 2 | 0 | 0 | 0.203 | 0.297 |

| Player Name | Team | Pos | AB | H | BB | R | RBI | HR | SB | BA | OBP |
|---|---|---|---|---|---|---|---|---|---|---|---|
| Adam Frazier | PIT | 2B | 493 | 136 | 40 | 67 | 51 | 10 | 6 | 0.276 | 0.337 |
| Bryan Reynolds | PIT | OF | 572 | 168 | 55 | 88 | 73 | 18 | 5 | 0.294 | 0.359 |
| Christian Kelley | PIT | C | 6 | 1 | 0 | 1 | 1 | 0 | 0 | 0.214 | 0.276 |
| Cole Tucker | PIT | SS | 177 | 44 | 16 | 22 | 18 | 3 | 4 | 0.247 | 0.315 |
| Colin Moran | PIT | 3B | 464 | 125 | 37 | 53 | 68 | 15 | 1 | 0.269 | 0.326 |
| Elias Diaz | PIT | C | 172 | 46 | 13 | 19 | 21 | 4 | 0 | 0.267 | 0.317 |
| Erik Gonzalez | PIT | SS | 223 | 54 | 12 | 23 | 22 | 4 | 5 | 0.241 | 0.283 |
| Gregory Polanco | PIT | OF | 385 | 96 | 40 | 55 | 55 | 16 | 8 | 0.248 | 0.322 |
| Guillermo Heredia | PIT | OF | 146 | 35 | 11 | 16 | 16 | 4 | 2 | 0.238 | 0.304 |
| Jacob Stallings | PIT | C | 302 | 77 | 22 | 34 | 33 | 8 | 1 | 0.256 | 0.312 |
| Jake Elmore | PIT | OF | 15 | 4 | 1 | 1 | 1 | 0 | 0 | 0.245 | 0.300 |
| Jason Martin | PIT | OF | 40 | 10 | 3 | 5 | 5 | 1 | 1 | 0.247 | 0.298 |
| Jose Osuna | PIT | 1B/OF | 239 | 62 | 16 | 33 | 33 | 9 | 1 | 0.259 | 0.309 |
| Josh Bell | PIT | 1B | 538 | 148 | 80 | 85 | 102 | 32 | 1 | 0.274 | 0.369 |
| Jung Ho Kang | PIT | 3B | 109 | 26 | 9 | 14 | 17 | 6 | 0 | 0.236 | 0.297 |
| Ke'Bryan Hayes | PIT | 3B | 41 | 10 | 3 | 4 | 4 | 0 | 0 | 0.243 | 0.300 |
| Kevin Kramer | PIT | OF | 77 | 18 | 7 | 8 | 8 | 2 | 1 | 0.232 | 0.295 |
| Kevin Newman | PIT | 2B/SS | 544 | 155 | 33 | 66 | 57 | 9 | 17 | 0.284 | 0.329 |
| Lonnie Chisenhall | PIT | OF | 57 | 14 | 5 | 6 | 7 | 2 | 1 | 0.245 | 0.310 |
| Luke Maile | PIT | C | 211 | 45 | 15 | 19 | 21 | 3 | 2 | 0.215 | 0.274 |
| Melky Cabrera | PIT | OF | 324 | 89 | 20 | 39 | 42 | 9 | 2 | 0.276 | 0.319 |
| Pablo Reyes | PIT | OF | 144 | 37 | 11 | 17 | 17 | 3 | 2 | 0.259 | 0.312 |
| Starling Marte | PIT | OF | 566 | 163 | 32 | 88 | 77 | 21 | 27 | 0.287 | 0.337 |

| Player Name | Team | Pos | AB | H | BB | R | RBI | HR | SB | BA | OBP |
|---|---|---|---|---|---|---|---|---|---|---|---|
| Austin Hedges | SD | C | 271 | 56 | 21 | 27 | 34 | 11 | 1 | 0.208 | 0.270 |
| Eric Hosmer | SD | 1B | 594 | 155 | 50 | 75 | 86 | 22 | 2 | 0.262 | 0.321 |
| Esteban Quiroz | SD | SS | 13 | 3 | 1 | 2 | 2 | 1 | 0 | 0.226 | 0.298 |
| Fernando Tatis Jr. | SD | SS | 552 | 151 | 54 | 94 | 75 | 29 | 24 | 0.274 | 0.343 |
| Franchy Cordero | SD | OF | 317 | 73 | 28 | 39 | 38 | 13 | 11 | 0.229 | 0.291 |
| Francisco Mejia | SD | C | 369 | 96 | 23 | 45 | 48 | 14 | 2 | 0.260 | 0.311 |
| Greg Garcia | SD | 2B | 211 | 51 | 31 | 28 | 21 | 3 | 1 | 0.239 | 0.343 |
| Jake Cronenworth | SD | SS | 24 | 6 | 2 | 3 | 3 | 1 | 1 | 0.253 | 0.314 |
| Josh Naylor | SD | OF | 268 | 69 | 26 | 36 | 38 | 6 | 1 | 0.257 | 0.323 |
| Jurickson Profar | SD | 2B | 479 | 117 | 52 | 67 | 67 | 18 | 9 | 0.243 | 0.326 |
| Luis Torrens | SD | C | 11 | 3 | 1 | 1 | 1 | 0 | 0 | 0.256 | 0.317 |
| Manny Machado | SD | 3B/SS | 590 | 160 | 62 | 85 | 96 | 33 | 6 | 0.271 | 0.342 |
| Manuel Margot | SD | OF | 372 | 93 | 31 | 48 | 42 | 10 | 16 | 0.249 | 0.309 |
| Taylor Trammell | SD | OF | 10 | 2 | 1 | 1 | 1 | 0 | 0 | 0.214 | 0.299 |
| Thomas Pham | SD | OF | 545 | 150 | 75 | 88 | 71 | 22 | 23 | 0.276 | 0.369 |
| Trent Grisham | SD | OF | 393 | 97 | 56 | 57 | 50 | 14 | 6 | 0.246 | 0.342 |
| Ty France | SD | 2B/3B | 229 | 59 | 15 | 30 | 32 | 9 | 1 | 0.257 | 0.319 |
| Wil Myers | SD | OF | 374 | 88 | 42 | 49 | 49 | 16 | 13 | 0.235 | 0.314 |

| Player Name | Team | Pos | AB | H | BB | R | RBI | HR | SB | BA | OBP |
|---|---|---|---|---|---|---|---|---|---|---|---|
| Austin Nola | SEA | 1B | 311 | 77 | 32 | 39 | 38 | 9 | 2 | 0.248 | 0.324 |
| Braden Bishop | SEA | OF | 89 | 20 | 7 | 10 | 9 | 2 | 0 | 0.224 | 0.285 |
| Cal Raleigh | SEA | C | 17 | 4 | 1 | 2 | 2 | 1 | 0 | 0.225 | 0.289 |
| Dan Vogelbach | SEA | 1B | 412 | 95 | 75 | 59 | 63 | 23 | 0 | 0.232 | 0.353 |
| Dee Gordon | SEA | 2B | 461 | 126 | 19 | 49 | 38 | 3 | 25 | 0.274 | 0.306 |
| Domingo Santana | SEA | OF | 423 | 107 | 54 | 59 | 62 | 23 | 7 | 0.252 | 0.339 |
| Donnie Walton | SEA | SS | 30 | 8 | 3 | 4 | 3 | 0 | 0 | 0.250 | 0.324 |
| Dylan Moore | SEA | SS/OF | 109 | 24 | 9 | 13 | 12 | 4 | 4 | 0.221 | 0.295 |
| Evan White | SEA | 1B | 335 | 88 | 28 | 45 | 44 | 13 | 2 | 0.264 | 0.326 |
| J.P. Crawford | SEA | SS | 467 | 108 | 59 | 63 | 55 | 11 | 7 | 0.230 | 0.321 |
| Jake Fraley | SEA | OF | 231 | 58 | 15 | 29 | 29 | 8 | 5 | 0.251 | 0.304 |
| Jarred Kelenic | SEA | OF | 42 | 10 | 4 | 5 | 7 | 2 | 1 | 0.243 | 0.299 |
| Keon Broxton | SEA | OF | 40 | 7 | 5 | 5 | 5 | 1 | 1 | 0.182 | 0.274 |
| Kyle Lewis | SEA | OF | 327 | 77 | 27 | 39 | 41 | 13 | 2 | 0.237 | 0.297 |
| Kyle Seager | SEA | 3B | 518 | 125 | 48 | 67 | 77 | 25 | 2 | 0.241 | 0.309 |
| Mallex Smith | SEA | OF | 474 | 119 | 42 | 60 | 39 | 5 | 41 | 0.251 | 0.320 |
| Mitch Haniger | SEA | OF | 531 | 135 | 60 | 83 | 74 | 25 | 7 | 0.254 | 0.339 |
| Patrick Wisdom | SEA | 1B | 35 | 7 | 3 | 4 | 4 | 2 | 0 | 0.203 | 0.271 |
| Sam Haggerty | SEA | 2B | 13 | 3 | 1 | 2 | 1 | 0 | 0 | 0.243 | 0.299 |
| Shed Long | SEA | 2B | 341 | 85 | 33 | 44 | 40 | 11 | 6 | 0.250 | 0.320 |
| Tim Beckham | SEA | SS | 224 | 54 | 17 | 27 | 29 | 9 | 1 | 0.241 | 0.300 |
| Tim Lopes | SEA | OF | 41 | 10 | 4 | 5 | 4 | 1 | 2 | 0.244 | 0.303 |
| Tom Murphy | SEA | C | 333 | 76 | 23 | 37 | 43 | 16 | 2 | 0.228 | 0.285 |

| Player Name | Team | Pos | AB | H | BB | R | RBI | HR | SB | BA | OBP |
|---|---|---|---|---|---|---|---|---|---|---|---|
| Abiatal Avelino | SF | SS | 7 | 2 | 0 | 1 | 1 | 0 | 0 | 0.245 | 0.282 |
| Alex Dickerson | SF | OF | 308 | 84 | 26 | 43 | 44 | 11 | 2 | 0.273 | 0.337 |
| Aramis Garcia | SF | C | 185 | 39 | 13 | 20 | 21 | 6 | 0 | 0.213 | 0.271 |
| Austin Jackson | SF | OF | 28 | 7 | 2 | 3 | 3 | 0 | 0 | 0.242 | 0.309 |
| Austin Slater | SF | OF | 249 | 62 | 28 | 30 | 29 | 7 | 3 | 0.250 | 0.334 |
| Brandon Belt | SF | 1B | 466 | 115 | 70 | 65 | 58 | 17 | 4 | 0.247 | 0.349 |
| Brandon Crawford | SF | SS | 502 | 122 | 50 | 57 | 60 | 13 | 3 | 0.244 | 0.315 |
| Buster Posey | SF | C | 437 | 119 | 43 | 50 | 49 | 9 | 1 | 0.272 | 0.343 |
| Chris Shaw | SF | 1B | 76 | 18 | 6 | 9 | 10 | 3 | 0 | 0.235 | 0.293 |
| Donovan Solano | SF | 2B | 232 | 63 | 14 | 25 | 24 | 3 | 1 | 0.271 | 0.316 |
| Drew Robinson | SF | OF | 8 | 2 | 1 | 1 | 1 | 0 | 0 | 0.201 | 0.285 |
| Erik Kratz | SF | C | 9 | 2 | 1 | 1 | 1 | 0 | 0 | 0.252 | 0.305 |
| Evan Longoria | SF | 3B | 498 | 126 | 38 | 60 | 70 | 20 | 3 | 0.253 | 0.310 |
| Heliot Ramos | SF | OF | 11 | 3 | 1 | 1 | 2 | 0 | 0 | 0.239 | 0.323 |
| Jaylin Davis | SF | OF | 238 | 58 | 23 | 30 | 31 | 10 | 4 | 0.244 | 0.318 |
| Joe McCarthy | SF | OF | 38 | 8 | 5 | 4 | 4 | 1 | 1 | 0.214 | 0.310 |
| Joey Bart | SF | C | 36 | 10 | 3 | 4 | 4 | 1 | 0 | 0.277 | 0.330 |
| Kean Wong | SF | 2B | 71 | 18 | 5 | 8 | 7 | 1 | 1 | 0.253 | 0.308 |
| Kevin Pillar | SF | OF | 514 | 134 | 20 | 64 | 66 | 16 | 12 | 0.261 | 0.295 |
| Mauricio Dubon | SF | 2B | 491 | 131 | 25 | 57 | 52 | 14 | 13 | 0.268 | 0.308 |
| Mike Yastrzemski | SF | OF | 512 | 127 | 51 | 74 | 63 | 22 | 4 | 0.249 | 0.322 |
| Pablo Sandoval | SF | 1B/3B | 66 | 16 | 5 | 8 | 9 | 3 | 0 | 0.246 | 0.300 |
| Steven Duggar | SF | OF | 356 | 85 | 33 | 42 | 35 | 6 | 5 | 0.239 | 0.305 |
| Zach Green | SF | 3B | 43 | 10 | 5 | 5 | 7 | 2 | 0 | 0.223 | 0.309 |

| Player Name | Team | Pos | AB | H | BB | R | RBI | HR | SB | BA | OBP |
|---|---|---|---|---|---|---|---|---|---|---|---|
| Andrew Knizner | STL | C | 139 | 36 | 10 | 16 | 17 | 5 | 2 | 0.256 | 0.315 |
| Austin Dean | STL | OF | 175 | 47 | 12 | 23 | 24 | 6 | 0 | 0.268 | 0.315 |
| Dexter Fowler | STL | OF | 441 | 103 | 63 | 62 | 56 | 16 | 7 | 0.233 | 0.334 |
| Dylan Carlson | STL | OF | 134 | 34 | 13 | 19 | 16 | 5 | 3 | 0.256 | 0.331 |
| Edmundo Sosa | STL | 2B | 17 | 4 | 1 | 2 | 2 | 1 | 1 | 0.249 | 0.299 |
| Harrison Bader | STL | OF | 391 | 92 | 40 | 58 | 47 | 16 | 14 | 0.235 | 0.318 |
| Kolten Wong | STL | 2B | 474 | 125 | 45 | 60 | 56 | 10 | 16 | 0.264 | 0.342 |
| Lane Thomas | STL | OF | 165 | 40 | 15 | 21 | 23 | 6 | 4 | 0.242 | 0.313 |
| Marcell Ozuna | STL | OF | 544 | 148 | 56 | 80 | 96 | 30 | 9 | 0.271 | 0.341 |
| Matt Carpenter | STL | 3B | 424 | 101 | 70 | 67 | 56 | 20 | 5 | 0.238 | 0.351 |
| Matt Wieters | STL | C | 197 | 46 | 18 | 22 | 27 | 9 | 1 | 0.231 | 0.298 |
| Paul DeJong | STL | SS | 571 | 142 | 51 | 85 | 86 | 29 | 7 | 0.249 | 0.321 |
| Paul Goldschmidt | STL | 1B | 573 | 157 | 81 | 93 | 95 | 32 | 4 | 0.274 | 0.368 |
| Ramon Urias | STL | 2B | 9 | 2 | 1 | 1 | 1 | 0 | 0 | 0.240 | 0.300 |
| Rangel Ravelo | STL | 1B | 34 | 9 | 3 | 4 | 4 | 1 | 0 | 0.258 | 0.322 |
| Tommy Edman | STL | 2B/3B | 499 | 139 | 31 | 70 | 54 | 14 | 20 | 0.278 | 0.328 |
| Tyler O'Neill | STL | OF | 361 | 88 | 30 | 51 | 55 | 19 | 3 | 0.243 | 0.304 |
| Yadier Molina | STL | C | 419 | 111 | 25 | 47 | 56 | 13 | 5 | 0.265 | 0.309 |
| Yairo Munoz | STL | 3B/OF | 185 | 47 | 12 | 22 | 21 | 4 | 7 | 0.255 | 0.304 |

| Player Name | Team | Pos | AB | H | BB | R | RBI | HR | SB | BA | OBP |
|---|---|---|---|---|---|---|---|---|---|---|---|
| Austin Meadows | TB | OF | 544 | 153 | 50 | 86 | 83 | 31 | 14 | 0.281 | 0.346 |
| Brandon Lowe | TB | 2B | 490 | 123 | 48 | 71 | 73 | 25 | 7 | 0.250 | 0.323 |
| Brendan McKay | TB | Util | 22 | 5 | 2 | 3 | 3 | 1 | 0 | 0.204 | 0.265 |
| Brian O'Grady | TB | OF | 37 | 8 | 3 | 5 | 5 | 2 | 1 | 0.229 | 0.297 |
| Chris Herrmann | TB | C | 66 | 14 | 8 | 8 | 8 | 2 | 0 | 0.208 | 0.291 |
| Dan Robertson | TB | 2B/3B | 166 | 38 | 21 | 20 | 17 | 3 | 1 | 0.232 | 0.332 |
| Hunter Renfroe | TB | OF | 501 | 117 | 43 | 70 | 77 | 34 | 4 | 0.233 | 0.296 |
| Ji-Man Choi | TB | 1B | 428 | 109 | 63 | 58 | 67 | 21 | 2 | 0.256 | 0.352 |
| Joey Wendle | TB | 2B/3B | 345 | 89 | 21 | 44 | 37 | 6 | 12 | 0.259 | 0.311 |
| Jose Martinez | TB | OF | 374 | 103 | 37 | 51 | 52 | 14 | 3 | 0.275 | 0.342 |
| Kevan Smith | TB | C | 183 | 49 | 13 | 20 | 22 | 5 | 1 | 0.269 | 0.325 |
| Kevin Kiermaier | TB | OF | 481 | 115 | 35 | 64 | 57 | 15 | 18 | 0.239 | 0.298 |
| Matt Duffy | TB | 3B | 257 | 70 | 24 | 31 | 27 | 5 | 2 | 0.274 | 0.342 |
| Michael Perez | TB | C | 164 | 37 | 17 | 19 | 20 | 6 | 0 | 0.223 | 0.297 |
| Mike Brosseau | TB | 2B | 230 | 59 | 16 | 31 | 30 | 9 | 3 | 0.256 | 0.316 |
| Mike Zunino | TB | C | 348 | 70 | 28 | 40 | 45 | 17 | 0 | 0.201 | 0.270 |
| Nathaniel Lowe | TB | 1B | 294 | 78 | 37 | 44 | 45 | 13 | 1 | 0.264 | 0.348 |
| Randy Arozarena | TB | OF | 102 | 26 | 9 | 14 | 12 | 3 | 6 | 0.258 | 0.331 |
| Ryan Lamarre | TB | OF | 7 | 2 | 1 | 1 | 1 | 0 | 0 | 0.230 | 0.303 |
| Willy Adames | TB | SS | 543 | 140 | 54 | 72 | 65 | 19 | 6 | 0.258 | 0.327 |
| Yandy Diaz | TB | 1B/3B | 450 | 122 | 55 | 69 | 57 | 16 | 2 | 0.271 | 0.353 |
| Yoshitomo Tsutsugo | TB | OF | 397 | 102 | 54 | 58 | 62 | 19 | 2 | 0.257 | 0.351 |

| Player Name | Team | Pos | AB | H | BB | R | RBI | HR | SB | BA | OBP |
|---|---|---|---|---|---|---|---|---|---|---|---|
| Adolis Garcia | TEX | OF | 69 | 16 | 3 | 9 | 9 | 3 | 2 | 0.226 | 0.262 |
| Blake Swihart | TEX | OF | 15 | 3 | 1 | 2 | 1 | 0 | 0 | 0.212 | 0.275 |
| Daniel Santana | TEX | 1B/OF | 482 | 121 | 26 | 68 | 66 | 19 | 19 | 0.251 | 0.297 |
| Eli White | TEX | SS | 35 | 8 | 3 | 4 | 3 | 1 | 1 | 0.231 | 0.298 |
| Elvis Andrus | TEX | SS | 598 | 161 | 38 | 80 | 70 | 14 | 24 | 0.268 | 0.315 |
| Hunter Pence | TEX | OF | 231 | 61 | 18 | 29 | 34 | 9 | 4 | 0.262 | 0.317 |
| Isiah Kiner-Falefa | TEX | C/3B | 123 | 31 | 9 | 13 | 12 | 1 | 3 | 0.252 | 0.305 |
| Jeff Mathis | TEX | C | 203 | 41 | 16 | 20 | 18 | 3 | 1 | 0.199 | 0.261 |
| Jett Bandy | TEX | C | 10 | 2 | 1 | 1 | 1 | 0 | 0 | 0.225 | 0.271 |
| Joey Gallo | TEX | OF | 481 | 114 | 86 | 86 | 91 | 41 | 6 | 0.236 | 0.357 |
| Jose Trevino | TEX | C | 118 | 28 | 5 | 13 | 12 | 2 | 0 | 0.237 | 0.265 |
| Logan Forsythe | TEX | 1B/3B | 235 | 54 | 30 | 27 | 25 | 5 | 2 | 0.230 | 0.322 |
| Nick Solak | TEX | Util | 419 | 113 | 46 | 58 | 57 | 17 | 7 | 0.270 | 0.351 |
| Robinson Chirinos | TEX | C | 339 | 78 | 43 | 48 | 51 | 15 | 1 | 0.229 | 0.334 |
| Ronald Guzman | TEX | 1B | 376 | 91 | 38 | 49 | 52 | 15 | 2 | 0.243 | 0.319 |
| Rougned Odor | TEX | 2B | 513 | 117 | 44 | 72 | 77 | 29 | 11 | 0.228 | 0.297 |
| Sam Travis | TEX | 1B | 154 | 39 | 13 | 19 | 19 | 4 | 2 | 0.251 | 0.316 |
| Scott Heineman | TEX | OF | 162 | 42 | 14 | 21 | 19 | 5 | 3 | 0.258 | 0.326 |
| Shin-Soo Choo | TEX | OF | 504 | 129 | 71 | 80 | 59 | 20 | 10 | 0.255 | 0.358 |
| Tim Federowicz | TEX | C | 21 | 4 | 1 | 1 | 2 | 0 | 0 | 0.166 | 0.217 |
| Todd Frazier | TEX | 3B | 372 | 88 | 42 | 54 | 58 | 18 | 2 | 0.237 | 0.325 |
| Welington Castillo | TEX | C | 211 | 48 | 9 | 19 | 32 | 10 | 0 | 0.227 | 0.265 |
| Willie Calhoun | TEX | OF | 521 | 140 | 43 | 75 | 78 | 27 | 1 | 0.270 | 0.329 |
| Yadiel Rivera | TEX | 3B/SS | 21 | 5 | 1 | 2 | 3 | 1 | 1 | 0.228 | 0.258 |

| Player Name | Team | Pos | AB | H | BB | R | RBI | HR | SB | BA | OBP |
|---|---|---|---|---|---|---|---|---|---|---|---|
| Anthony Alford | TOR | OF | 112 | 25 | 9 | 14 | 12 | 2 | 6 | 0.223 | 0.292 |
| Billy McKinney | TOR | OF | 162 | 38 | 15 | 22 | 21 | 7 | 1 | 0.236 | 0.301 |
| Bo Bichette | TOR | SS | 590 | 164 | 46 | 91 | 71 | 22 | 18 | 0.277 | 0.332 |
| Brandon Drury | TOR | 3B/OF | 350 | 82 | 25 | 40 | 42 | 12 | 1 | 0.235 | 0.291 |
| Breyvic Valera | TOR | 2B | 59 | 15 | 5 | 7 | 7 | 2 | 1 | 0.258 | 0.325 |
| Cavan Biggio | TOR | 2B | 492 | 117 | 92 | 79 | 68 | 20 | 17 | 0.237 | 0.360 |
| Danny Jansen | TOR | C | 337 | 83 | 34 | 44 | 46 | 15 | 1 | 0.245 | 0.323 |
| Derek Fisher | TOR | OF | 374 | 84 | 44 | 51 | 48 | 15 | 10 | 0.225 | 0.310 |
| Devon Travis | TOR | 2B | 128 | 33 | 6 | 15 | 16 | 4 | 2 | 0.259 | 0.302 |
| Jonathan Davis | TOR | OF | 88 | 20 | 8 | 12 | 9 | 2 | 3 | 0.225 | 0.305 |
| Kendrys Morales | TOR | 1B | 195 | 49 | 21 | 25 | 29 | 9 | 0 | 0.251 | 0.331 |
| Lourdes Gurriel | TOR | OF | 512 | 136 | 27 | 72 | 79 | 25 | 8 | 0.265 | 0.308 |
| Randal Grichuk | TOR | OF | 522 | 127 | 34 | 71 | 80 | 29 | 3 | 0.243 | 0.295 |
| Reese McGuire | TOR | C | 279 | 68 | 24 | 34 | 33 | 9 | 2 | 0.243 | 0.309 |
| Rowdy Tellez | TOR | 1B | 367 | 92 | 33 | 49 | 55 | 18 | 2 | 0.250 | 0.316 |
| Santiago Espinal | TOR | SS | 8 | 2 | 1 | 1 | 1 | 0 | 0 | 0.251 | 0.293 |
| Teoscar Hernandez | TOR | OF | 445 | 104 | 44 | 62 | 65 | 24 | 6 | 0.233 | 0.303 |
| Travis Shaw | TOR | 3B | 381 | 87 | 53 | 52 | 57 | 20 | 2 | 0.228 | 0.327 |
| Vladimir Guerrero Jr. | TOR | 3B | 565 | 166 | 58 | 78 | 89 | 24 | 1 | 0.294 | 0.364 |

| Player Name | Team | Pos | AB | H | BB | R | RBI | HR | SB | BA | OBP |
|---|---|---|---|---|---|---|---|---|---|---|---|
| Adam Eaton | WAS | OF | 503 | 143 | 57 | 86 | 54 | 13 | 13 | 0.283 | 0.367 |
| Adrian Sanchez | WAS | 3B | 32 | 8 | 2 | 3 | 3 | 0 | 0 | 0.246 | 0.295 |
| Andrew Stevenson | WAS | OF | 77 | 20 | 6 | 10 | 8 | 1 | 1 | 0.253 | 0.313 |
| Asdrubal Cabrera | WAS | 2B/3B | 429 | 113 | 44 | 58 | 60 | 16 | 3 | 0.264 | 0.334 |
| Brian Dozier | WAS | 2B | 379 | 89 | 51 | 55 | 52 | 18 | 5 | 0.235 | 0.330 |
| Carter Kieboom | WAS | SS | 273 | 71 | 28 | 36 | 34 | 10 | 2 | 0.258 | 0.332 |
| Eric Thames | WAS | 1B | 370 | 88 | 48 | 58 | 55 | 21 | 4 | 0.238 | 0.335 |
| Howie Kendrick | WAS | 1B/2B | 315 | 97 | 22 | 46 | 47 | 12 | 2 | 0.308 | 0.358 |
| Jake Noll | WAS | 1B | 24 | 6 | 2 | 3 | 2 | 0 | 0 | 0.248 | 0.297 |
| Juan Soto | WAS | OF | 548 | 160 | 106 | 105 | 109 | 36 | 9 | 0.291 | 0.407 |
| Kurt Suzuki | WAS | C | 301 | 80 | 20 | 40 | 51 | 14 | 0 | 0.266 | 0.325 |
| Matt Adams | WAS | 1B | 287 | 68 | 21 | 38 | 49 | 18 | 0 | 0.235 | 0.293 |
| Matt Reynolds | WAS | 3B | 34 | 8 | 4 | 4 | 4 | 1 | 0 | 0.241 | 0.321 |
| Michael Taylor | WAS | OF | 167 | 39 | 14 | 21 | 20 | 5 | 9 | 0.231 | 0.295 |
| Raudy Read | WAS | C | 19 | 4 | 1 | 2 | 2 | 1 | 0 | 0.230 | 0.270 |
| Ryan Zimmerman | WAS | 1B | 244 | 64 | 23 | 32 | 40 | 12 | 0 | 0.263 | 0.329 |
| Starlin Castro | WAS | 2B/3B | 540 | 152 | 32 | 68 | 74 | 18 | 3 | 0.281 | 0.322 |
| Trea Turner | WAS | SS | 596 | 171 | 52 | 100 | 68 | 20 | 39 | 0.288 | 0.349 |
| Tres Barrera | WAS | C | 10 | 2 | 1 | 1 | 1 | 0 | 0 | 0.250 | 0.305 |
| Victor Robles | WAS | OF | 546 | 144 | 39 | 80 | 67 | 17 | 32 | 0.264 | 0.330 |
| Wilmer Difo | WAS | SS | 216 | 53 | 18 | 28 | 21 | 2 | 4 | 0.245 | 0.305 |
| Yadiel Hernandez | WAS | OF | 8 | 2 | 1 | 1 | 1 | 0 | 0 | 0.294 | 0.371 |
| Yan Gomes | WAS | C | 303 | 72 | 27 | 36 | 42 | 12 | 1 | 0.237 | 0.308 |

# ATC Pitching Projections

| Player Name | Team | IP | ER | W | S | K | ERA | WHIP | QS | HLD |
|---|---|---|---|---|---|---|---|---|---|---|
| Madison Bumgarner | ARI | 185 | 86 | 11 | 0 | 177 | 4.18 | 1.24 | 17 | 0 |
| Robbie Ray | ARI | 163 | 74 | 11 | 0 | 207 | 4.11 | 1.33 | 13 | 0 |
| Zac Gallen | ARI | 148 | 63 | 9 | 0 | 160 | 3.82 | 1.28 | 12 | 0 |
| Mike Leake | ARI | 144 | 73 | 8 | 0 | 96 | 4.58 | 1.32 | 14 | 0 |
| Merrill Kelly | ARI | 143 | 71 | 9 | 0 | 130 | 4.47 | 1.34 | 11 | 0 |
| Luke Weaver | ARI | 133 | 62 | 9 | 0 | 136 | 4.18 | 1.28 | 12 | 0 |
| Taijuan Walker | ARI | 77 | 40 | 5 | 0 | 69 | 4.67 | 1.39 | 3 | 2 |
| Archie Bradley | ARI | 65 | 27 | 3 | 30 | 73 | 3.68 | 1.29 | 0 | 2 |
| Alex Young | ARI | 63 | 29 | 4 | 0 | 55 | 4.19 | 1.38 | 4 | 1 |
| Hector Rondon | ARI | 57 | 25 | 3 | 1 | 55 | 3.96 | 1.31 | 0 | 14 |
| Junior Guerra | ARI | 55 | 27 | 3 | 1 | 53 | 4.32 | 1.38 | 0 | 11 |
| Andrew Chafin | ARI | 52 | 21 | 2 | 1 | 62 | 3.57 | 1.31 | 0 | 18 |
| Kevin Ginkel | ARI | 52 | 19 | 4 | 2 | 62 | 3.35 | 1.22 | 0 | 10 |
| Jon Duplantier | ARI | 48 | 22 | 2 | 0 | 48 | 4.08 | 1.40 | 1 | 1 |
| Stefan Crichton | ARI | 45 | 20 | 2 | 0 | 44 | 4.06 | 1.34 | 0 | 6 |
| Yoan Lopez | ARI | 44 | 20 | 1 | 0 | 38 | 4.01 | 1.28 | 0 | 12 |
| Taylor Clarke | ARI | 38 | 21 | 2 | 0 | 31 | 5.08 | 1.39 | 2 | 0 |
| Yoshihisa Hirano | ARI | 26 | 13 | 2 | 0 | 26 | 4.53 | 1.36 | 0 | 4 |
| Greg Holland | ARI | 24 | 13 | 1 | 2 | 24 | 4.96 | 1.51 | 0 | 0 |
| Jimmie Sherfy | ARI | 17 | 8 | 1 | 0 | 20 | 4.02 | 1.36 | 0 | 1 |

| Player Name | Team | IP | ER | W | S | K | ERA | WHIP | QS | HLD |
|---|---|---|---|---|---|---|---|---|---|---|
| Mike Soroka | ATL | 178 | 73 | 13 | 0 | 154 | 3.68 | 1.26 | 18 | 0 |
| Mike Foltynewicz | ATL | 169 | 82 | 11 | 0 | 160 | 4.35 | 1.33 | 13 | 0 |
| Max Fried | ATL | 167 | 67 | 13 | 0 | 175 | 3.63 | 1.32 | 16 | 0 |
| Cole Hamels | ATL | 158 | 72 | 9 | 0 | 155 | 4.10 | 1.35 | 14 | 0 |
| Sean Newcomb | ATL | 79 | 37 | 5 | 0 | 78 | 4.22 | 1.41 | 3 | 8 |
| Kyle Wright | ATL | 70 | 35 | 4 | 0 | 65 | 4.44 | 1.40 | 5 | 0 |
| Shane Greene | ATL | 64 | 27 | 3 | 5 | 65 | 3.79 | 1.27 | 0 | 10 |
| Bryse Wilson | ATL | 62 | 31 | 5 | 0 | 58 | 4.48 | 1.33 | 4 | 0 |
| Luke Jackson | ATL | 62 | 26 | 4 | 1 | 78 | 3.75 | 1.29 | 0 | 10 |
| Will Smith | ATL | 62 | 22 | 4 | 14 | 83 | 3.20 | 1.14 | 0 | 8 |
| Mark Melancon | ATL | 61 | 26 | 3 | 21 | 58 | 3.81 | 1.30 | 0 | 7 |
| Chris Martin | ATL | 56 | 22 | 2 | 1 | 63 | 3.47 | 1.08 | 0 | 15 |
| Josh Tomlin | ATL | 50 | 29 | 2 | 0 | 34 | 5.24 | 1.35 | 0 | 5 |
| Touki Toussaint | ATL | 50 | 25 | 3 | 0 | 52 | 4.62 | 1.46 | 1 | 2 |
| Darren O'Day | ATL | 40 | 17 | 1 | 0 | 47 | 3.87 | 1.25 | 0 | 2 |
| Grant Dayton | ATL | 33 | 15 | 1 | 0 | 37 | 4.01 | 1.21 | 0 | 2 |
| Anthony Swarzak | ATL | 31 | 16 | 2 | 0 | 30 | 4.73 | 1.42 | 0 | 6 |
| Jacob Webb | ATL | 29 | 13 | 2 | 0 | 28 | 3.93 | 1.36 | 0 | 4 |
| Chad Sobotka | ATL | 23 | 11 | 1 | 0 | 28 | 4.40 | 1.31 | 0 | 3 |
| A.J. Minter | ATL | 22 | 10 | 1 | 0 | 26 | 4.30 | 1.32 | 0 | 1 |
| Ian Anderson | ATL | 21 | 9 | 1 | 0 | 22 | 4.04 | 1.45 | 2 | 0 |
| Jerry Blevins | ATL | 18 | 10 | 1 | 0 | 20 | 4.91 | 1.44 | 0 | 5 |
| Jeremy Walker | ATL | 14 | 6 | 1 | 0 | 11 | 4.05 | 1.30 | 0 | 1 |
| Huascar Ynoa | ATL | 10 | 5 | 0 | 0 | 11 | 4.37 | 1.50 | 0 | 0 |

| Player Name | Team | IP | ER | W | S | K | ERA | WHIP | QS | HLD |
|---|---|---|---|---|---|---|---|---|---|---|
| John Means | BAL | 167 | 90 | 10 | 0 | 130 | 4.83 | 1.34 | 12 | 0 |
| Alex Cobb | BAL | 145 | 82 | 7 | 0 | 102 | 5.09 | 1.42 | 11 | 0 |
| Asher Wojciechowski | BAL | 136 | 81 | 7 | 0 | 122 | 5.34 | 1.40 | 8 | 0 |
| Kohl Stewart | BAL | 91 | 55 | 5 | 0 | 60 | 5.48 | 1.61 | 5 | 0 |
| Dean Kremer | BAL | 82 | 48 | 5 | 0 | 72 | 5.30 | 1.48 | 5 | 0 |
| David Hess | BAL | 70 | 43 | 4 | 0 | 60 | 5.52 | 1.46 | 3 | 0 |
| Miguel Castro | BAL | 70 | 36 | 2 | 1 | 62 | 4.60 | 1.48 | 0 | 11 |
| Mychal Givens | BAL | 68 | 31 | 3 | 16 | 82 | 4.10 | 1.24 | 0 | 4 |
| Richard Bleier | BAL | 65 | 32 | 3 | 1 | 38 | 4.43 | 1.38 | 0 | 9 |
| Hunter Harvey | BAL | 58 | 28 | 3 | 4 | 66 | 4.36 | 1.37 | 0 | 5 |
| Shawn Armstrong | BAL | 57 | 30 | 2 | 3 | 60 | 4.75 | 1.42 | 0 | 11 |
| Brandon Bailey | BAL | 55 | 34 | 2 | 0 | 48 | 5.58 | 1.57 | 3 | 0 |
| Keegan Akin | BAL | 47 | 29 | 2 | 0 | 44 | 5.46 | 1.58 | 3 | 0 |
| Tanner Scott | BAL | 38 | 17 | 2 | 0 | 47 | 4.12 | 1.34 | 0 | 3 |
| Dillon Tate | BAL | 35 | 19 | 1 | 0 | 28 | 4.93 | 1.41 | 0 | 1 |
| Zac Lowther | BAL | 33 | 21 | 2 | 0 | 27 | 5.60 | 1.54 | 2 | 0 |
| Aaron Brooks | BAL | 28 | 16 | 2 | 0 | 19 | 5.02 | 1.46 | 0 | 0 |
| Michael Rucker | BAL | 28 | 15 | 1 | 0 | 25 | 4.99 | 1.40 | 0 | 0 |
| Evan Phillips | BAL | 25 | 14 | 1 | 0 | 26 | 5.23 | 1.46 | 0 | 2 |
| Michael Baumann | BAL | 24 | 16 | 1 | 0 | 19 | 5.92 | 1.64 | 1 | 0 |
| Branden Kline | BAL | 19 | 11 | 1 | 0 | 17 | 5.32 | 1.61 | 0 | 2 |
| Tayler Scott | BAL | 17 | 16 | 1 | 0 | 16 | 8.82 | 1.65 | 0 | 0 |
| Gabriel Ynoa | BAL | 15 | 9 | 0 | 0 | 9 | 5.35 | 1.53 | 1 | 0 |

| Player Name | Team | IP | ER | W | S | K | ERA | WHIP | QS | HLD |
|---|---|---|---|---|---|---|---|---|---|---|
| Eduardo Rodriguez | BOS | 180 | 80 | 14 | 0 | 190 | 3.98 | 1.30 | 15 | 0 |
| Chris Sale | BOS | 167 | 62 | 12 | 0 | 231 | 3.34 | 1.03 | 17 | 0 |
| Martin Perez | BOS | 150 | 77 | 8 | 0 | 119 | 4.65 | 1.46 | 9 | 0 |
| David Price | BOS | 148 | 67 | 11 | 0 | 158 | 4.10 | 1.25 | 14 | 0 |
| Nathan Eovaldi | BOS | 129 | 65 | 8 | 0 | 124 | 4.51 | 1.34 | 10 | 0 |
| Jhoulys Chacin | BOS | 97 | 53 | 5 | 0 | 83 | 4.95 | 1.43 | 6 | 0 |
| Andrew Cashner | BOS | 84 | 44 | 4 | 1 | 64 | 4.75 | 1.43 | 3 | 3 |
| Brandon Workman | BOS | 67 | 24 | 5 | 28 | 85 | 3.19 | 1.26 | 0 | 6 |
| Marcus Walden | BOS | 67 | 30 | 4 | 1 | 62 | 4.06 | 1.35 | 0 | 9 |
| Matt Barnes | BOS | 63 | 24 | 4 | 4 | 93 | 3.48 | 1.28 | 0 | 23 |
| Josh Taylor | BOS | 53 | 22 | 3 | 1 | 62 | 3.73 | 1.31 | 0 | 10 |
| Darwinzon Hernandez | BOS | 50 | 22 | 2 | 0 | 72 | 3.96 | 1.50 | 0 | 4 |
| Ryan Brasier | BOS | 48 | 23 | 2 | 0 | 50 | 4.25 | 1.24 | 1 | 6 |
| Heath Hembree | BOS | 48 | 24 | 2 | 0 | 53 | 4.43 | 1.34 | 0 | 9 |
| Hector Velazquez | BOS | 41 | 23 | 2 | 0 | 30 | 5.03 | 1.58 | 1 | 1 |
| Brian Johnson | BOS | 36 | 21 | 2 | 0 | 29 | 5.35 | 1.65 | 1 | 0 |
| Colten Brewer | BOS | 33 | 19 | 1 | 0 | 35 | 5.23 | 1.48 | 0 | 4 |
| Ryan Weber | BOS | 32 | 16 | 2 | 0 | 22 | 4.61 | 1.43 | 0 | 1 |
| Josh Osich | BOS | 21 | 11 | 1 | 0 | 19 | 4.86 | 1.36 | 0 | 2 |
| Travis Lakins | BOS | 18 | 10 | 1 | 0 | 15 | 4.70 | 1.54 | 0 | 0 |
| Trevor Hildenberger | BOS | 18 | 10 | 1 | 0 | 14 | 5.09 | 1.45 | 0 | 2 |
| Austin Brice | BOS | 15 | 8 | 1 | 0 | 14 | 4.68 | 1.37 | 0 | 0 |

| Player Name | Team | IP | ER | W | S | K | ERA | WHIP | QS | HLD |
|---|---|---|---|---|---|---|---|---|---|---|
| Lucas Giolito | CHA | 180 | 83 | 12 | 0 | 208 | 4.15 | 1.22 | 18 | 0 |
| Dallas Keuchel | CHA | 179 | 83 | 11 | 0 | 141 | 4.18 | 1.38 | 16 | 0 |
| Reynaldo Lopez | CHA | 171 | 88 | 9 | 0 | 156 | 4.65 | 1.34 | 14 | 0 |
| Gio Gonzalez | CHA | 139 | 76 | 8 | 0 | 120 | 4.88 | 1.45 | 8 | 0 |
| Dylan Cease | CHA | 110 | 56 | 7 | 0 | 118 | 4.60 | 1.41 | 9 | 0 |
| Michael Kopech | CHA | 97 | 49 | 6 | 0 | 108 | 4.50 | 1.38 | 8 | 0 |
| Alex Colome | CHA | 63 | 27 | 4 | 28 | 63 | 3.88 | 1.29 | 0 | 3 |
| Steven Cishek | CHA | 62 | 27 | 4 | 2 | 60 | 3.89 | 1.34 | 0 | 9 |
| Aaron Bummer | CHA | 62 | 22 | 2 | 2 | 61 | 3.18 | 1.27 | 0 | 16 |
| Dylan Covey | CHA | 62 | 35 | 2 | 0 | 47 | 5.17 | 1.47 | 2 | 0 |
| Jace Fry | CHA | 53 | 25 | 2 | 1 | 64 | 4.19 | 1.40 | 0 | 10 |
| Evan Marshall | CHA | 52 | 24 | 3 | 0 | 47 | 4.08 | 1.40 | 0 | 16 |
| Kelvin Herrera | CHA | 47 | 24 | 2 | 2 | 47 | 4.63 | 1.36 | 0 | 7 |
| Jimmy Cordero | CHA | 38 | 18 | 3 | 0 | 33 | 4.20 | 1.46 | 0 | 3 |
| Hector Santiago | CHA | 35 | 19 | 2 | 0 | 34 | 4.80 | 1.41 | 0 | 0 |
| Carlos Rodon | CHA | 35 | 18 | 2 | 0 | 35 | 4.54 | 1.38 | 3 | 0 |
| Ross Detwiler | CHA | 29 | 18 | 1 | 0 | 18 | 5.64 | 1.55 | 1 | 0 |
| Ervin Santana | CHA | 27 | 17 | 1 | 0 | 18 | 5.71 | 1.51 | 2 | 0 |
| Carson Fulmer | CHA | 27 | 16 | 1 | 0 | 28 | 5.33 | 1.57 | 0 | 0 |
| Tayron Guerrero | CHA | 24 | 13 | 0 | 6 | 25 | 4.92 | 1.58 | 0 | 2 |
| Jose Ruiz | CHA | 18 | 10 | 1 | 0 | 17 | 4.99 | 1.49 | 0 | 0 |
| Ian Hamilton | CHA | 16 | 8 | 1 | 0 | 16 | 4.47 | 1.36 | 0 | 0 |
| Ryan Burr | CHA | 9 | 6 | 0 | 0 | 9 | 5.41 | 1.39 | 0 | 0 |

| Player Name | Team | IP | ER | W | S | K | ERA | WHIP | QS | HLD |
|---|---|---|---|---|---|---|---|---|---|---|
| Yu Darvish | CHN | 181 | 75 | 12 | 0 | 220 | 3.72 | 1.15 | 16 | 0 |
| Kyle Hendricks | CHN | 176 | 79 | 11 | 0 | 151 | 4.01 | 1.24 | 16 | 0 |
| Jose Quintana | CHN | 172 | 81 | 12 | 0 | 158 | 4.24 | 1.33 | 14 | 0 |
| Jon Lester | CHN | 170 | 88 | 12 | 0 | 155 | 4.65 | 1.43 | 13 | 0 |
| Alec Mills | CHN | 92 | 46 | 5 | 0 | 83 | 4.52 | 1.40 | 5 | 0 |
| Tyler Chatwood | CHN | 90 | 45 | 5 | 0 | 85 | 4.45 | 1.51 | 3 | 2 |
| Derek Holland | CHN | 82 | 44 | 4 | 0 | 78 | 4.84 | 1.43 | 2 | 4 |
| Rowan Wick | CHN | 61 | 26 | 3 | 1 | 64 | 3.76 | 1.33 | 0 | 18 |
| Kyle Ryan | CHN | 58 | 26 | 3 | 1 | 52 | 3.99 | 1.42 | 0 | 13 |
| Brandon Kintzler | CHN | 56 | 25 | 3 | 2 | 45 | 3.97 | 1.31 | 0 | 15 |
| Craig Kimbrel | CHN | 54 | 23 | 3 | 25 | 75 | 3.89 | 1.20 | 0 | 0 |
| Ryan Tepera | CHN | 53 | 26 | 3 | 0 | 49 | 4.43 | 1.37 | 0 | 12 |
| Pedro Strop | CHN | 52 | 24 | 3 | 2 | 55 | 4.09 | 1.33 | 0 | 6 |
| Brad Wieck | CHN | 47 | 22 | 2 | 0 | 63 | 4.08 | 1.24 | 0 | 10 |
| Jharel Cotton | CHN | 45 | 21 | 2 | 0 | 45 | 4.11 | 1.55 | 3 | 0 |
| Adbert Alzolay | CHN | 45 | 25 | 2 | 0 | 46 | 4.88 | 1.44 | 3 | 0 |
| David Phelps | CHN | 32 | 15 | 2 | 0 | 33 | 4.20 | 1.39 | 0 | 4 |
| Daniel Winkler | CHN | 31 | 16 | 2 | 0 | 32 | 4.73 | 1.44 | 0 | 7 |
| Duane Underwood | CHN | 20 | 10 | 1 | 0 | 20 | 4.41 | 1.43 | 0 | 0 |
| Trevor Megill | CHN | 19 | 10 | 1 | 0 | 22 | 4.44 | 1.33 | 0 | 2 |
| Dillon Maples | CHN | 16 | 8 | 1 | 0 | 23 | 4.48 | 1.54 | 0 | 1 |
| Brandon Morrow | CHN | 15 | 6 | 1 | 0 | 16 | 3.60 | 1.25 | 0 | 2 |
| Colin Rea | CHN | 15 | 8 | 0 | 0 | 13 | 5.21 | 1.50 | 0 | 1 |

| Player Name | Team | IP | ER | W | S | K | ERA | WHIP | QS | HLD |
|---|---|---|---|---|---|---|---|---|---|---|
| Trevor Bauer | CIN | 191 | 83 | 12 | 0 | 225 | 3.90 | 1.24 | 18 | 0 |
| Luis Castillo | CIN | 188 | 74 | 13 | 0 | 219 | 3.53 | 1.20 | 19 | 0 |
| Sonny Gray | CIN | 172 | 72 | 12 | 0 | 185 | 3.79 | 1.28 | 17 | 0 |
| Anthony DeSclafani | CIN | 154 | 74 | 9 | 0 | 151 | 4.35 | 1.27 | 12 | 0 |
| Wade Miley | CIN | 140 | 67 | 9 | 0 | 118 | 4.30 | 1.44 | 11 | 0 |
| Tyler Mahle | CIN | 101 | 48 | 6 | 0 | 99 | 4.32 | 1.31 | 8 | 0 |
| Michael Lorenzen | CIN | 76 | 32 | 3 | 8 | 74 | 3.81 | 1.32 | 0 | 19 |
| Raisel Iglesias | CIN | 68 | 28 | 3 | 30 | 83 | 3.77 | 1.20 | 0 | 2 |
| Robert Stephenson | CIN | 65 | 28 | 3 | 4 | 79 | 3.94 | 1.22 | 0 | 10 |
| Amir Garrett | CIN | 62 | 26 | 3 | 1 | 78 | 3.77 | 1.37 | 0 | 21 |
| Lucas Sims | CIN | 61 | 29 | 3 | 0 | 75 | 4.27 | 1.28 | 0 | 4 |
| Cody Reed | CIN | 36 | 15 | 1 | 0 | 37 | 3.82 | 1.31 | 0 | 0 |
| Joel Kuhnel | CIN | 34 | 17 | 2 | 0 | 30 | 4.58 | 1.37 | 0 | 2 |
| Sal Romano | CIN | 32 | 16 | 2 | 0 | 29 | 4.58 | 1.40 | 0 | 1 |
| Jose De Leon | CIN | 29 | 13 | 2 | 0 | 36 | 4.21 | 1.43 | 0 | 0 |
| Matt Bowman | CIN | 23 | 11 | 1 | 0 | 20 | 4.33 | 1.46 | 0 | 0 |
| Josh Smith | CIN | 22 | 16 | 1 | 0 | 20 | 6.37 | 1.58 | 0 | 1 |
| Justin Shafer | CIN | 18 | 9 | 1 | 0 | 17 | 4.86 | 1.48 | 0 | 1 |
| Zach Duke | CIN | 14 | 7 | 1 | 0 | 11 | 4.36 | 1.49 | 0 | 3 |
| Ruben Alaniz | CIN | 11 | 8 | 1 | 0 | 10 | 6.70 | 1.40 | 0 | 1 |
| David Hernandez | CIN | 6 | 2 | 0 | 0 | 6 | 3.74 | 1.40 | 0 | 1 |

| Player Name | Team | IP | ER | W | S | K | ERA | WHIP | QS | HLD |
| --- | --- | --- | --- | --- | --- | --- | --- | --- | --- | --- |
| Shane Bieber | CLE | 198 | 79 | 14 | 0 | 221 | 3.59 | 1.12 | 20 | 0 |
| Mike Clevinger | CLE | 186 | 69 | 15 | 0 | 226 | 3.33 | 1.16 | 19 | 0 |
| Carlos Carrasco | CLE | 160 | 68 | 12 | 0 | 181 | 3.84 | 1.18 | 12 | 0 |
| Aaron Civale | CLE | 141 | 67 | 8 | 0 | 114 | 4.25 | 1.30 | 12 | 0 |
| Zach Plesac | CLE | 127 | 64 | 8 | 0 | 105 | 4.53 | 1.34 | 10 | 0 |
| Adam Plutko | CLE | 77 | 43 | 4 | 0 | 61 | 5.09 | 1.34 | 2 | 1 |
| Logan Allen | CLE | 67 | 36 | 4 | 0 | 55 | 4.88 | 1.45 | 3 | 0 |
| Brad Hand | CLE | 64 | 25 | 4 | 32 | 86 | 3.46 | 1.17 | 0 | 0 |
| Danny Salazar | CLE | 63 | 37 | 3 | 0 | 53 | 5.22 | 1.53 | 4 | 0 |
| Emmanuel Clase | CLE | 60 | 23 | 3 | 6 | 60 | 3.37 | 1.25 | 0 | 14 |
| Nick Wittgren | CLE | 59 | 26 | 3 | 1 | 59 | 3.89 | 1.26 | 0 | 15 |
| Adam Cimber | CLE | 58 | 27 | 4 | 1 | 44 | 4.22 | 1.33 | 0 | 13 |
| Oliver Perez | CLE | 46 | 21 | 2 | 1 | 53 | 4.08 | 1.24 | 0 | 18 |
| James Karinchak | CLE | 41 | 15 | 1 | 1 | 61 | 3.38 | 1.30 | 0 | 5 |
| Jefry Rodriguez | CLE | 39 | 22 | 2 | 0 | 30 | 5.14 | 1.52 | 2 | 0 |
| Hunter Wood | CLE | 39 | 18 | 2 | 0 | 37 | 4.12 | 1.29 | 0 | 4 |
| Phil Maton | CLE | 28 | 14 | 1 | 0 | 29 | 4.57 | 1.35 | 0 | 2 |
| A.J. Cole | CLE | 25 | 13 | 1 | 0 | 26 | 4.69 | 1.38 | 0 | 0 |
| Tyler Olson | CLE | 23 | 12 | 1 | 0 | 24 | 4.51 | 1.38 | 0 | 1 |
| Danny Otero | CLE | 21 | 11 | 1 | 0 | 13 | 4.56 | 1.35 | 0 | 0 |
| James Hoyt | CLE | 20 | 10 | 1 | 0 | 22 | 4.25 | 1.37 | 0 | 1 |
| Cody Anderson | CLE | 10 | 6 | 1 | 0 | 9 | 5.02 | 1.41 | 1 | 0 |
| Jon Edwards | CLE | 7 | 4 | 1 | 0 | 6 | 4.84 | 1.77 | 0 | 0 |

| Player Name | Team | IP | ER | W | S | K | ERA | WHIP | QS | HLD |
|---|---|---|---|---|---|---|---|---|---|---|
| German Marquez | COL | 185 | 87 | 12 | 0 | 193 | 4.25 | 1.25 | 15 | 0 |
| Jon Gray | COL | 178 | 86 | 12 | 0 | 182 | 4.35 | 1.33 | 15 | 0 |
| Kyle Freeland | COL | 151 | 82 | 8 | 0 | 121 | 4.87 | 1.48 | 11 | 0 |
| Antonio Senzatela | COL | 140 | 83 | 8 | 0 | 94 | 5.32 | 1.56 | 8 | 0 |
| Peter Lambert | COL | 91 | 57 | 4 | 0 | 61 | 5.67 | 1.51 | 5 | 0 |
| Jeff Hoffman | COL | 82 | 51 | 4 | 0 | 75 | 5.54 | 1.50 | 3 | 0 |
| Chi Chi Gonzalez | COL | 70 | 41 | 3 | 0 | 54 | 5.29 | 1.55 | 4 | 0 |
| Carlos Estevez | COL | 66 | 31 | 3 | 7 | 72 | 4.26 | 1.33 | 0 | 12 |
| Jairo Diaz | COL | 63 | 30 | 4 | 6 | 65 | 4.32 | 1.36 | 0 | 10 |
| Scott Oberg | COL | 62 | 26 | 4 | 20 | 62 | 3.77 | 1.32 | 0 | 9 |
| Bryan Shaw | COL | 55 | 30 | 3 | 0 | 48 | 5.00 | 1.50 | 0 | 11 |
| Wade Davis | COL | 50 | 29 | 2 | 5 | 52 | 5.28 | 1.50 | 0 | 4 |
| Jake McGee | COL | 49 | 28 | 2 | 1 | 44 | 5.20 | 1.44 | 0 | 9 |
| James Pazos | COL | 37 | 19 | 2 | 0 | 35 | 4.48 | 1.50 | 0 | 9 |
| Yency Almonte | COL | 33 | 19 | 2 | 0 | 30 | 5.28 | 1.67 | 0 | 4 |
| Chad Bettis | COL | 33 | 18 | 1 | 0 | 23 | 4.90 | 1.46 | 1 | 2 |
| Tyler Kinley | COL | 32 | 18 | 1 | 0 | 31 | 5.05 | 1.58 | 0 | 2 |
| Jesus Tinoco | COL | 27 | 16 | 1 | 0 | 21 | 5.27 | 1.57 | 0 | 1 |
| Wes Parsons | COL | 19 | 11 | 0 | 0 | 13 | 5.16 | 1.58 | 0 | 0 |
| Tim Melville | COL | 16 | 8 | 1 | 0 | 13 | 4.83 | 1.55 | 1 | 0 |
| Mike Dunn | COL | 13 | 7 | 1 | 0 | 12 | 5.17 | 1.49 | 0 | 3 |
| Joe Harvey | COL | 12 | 7 | 0 | 0 | 12 | 5.15 | 1.48 | 0 | 0 |
| Phillip Diehl | COL | 12 | 7 | 0 | 0 | 13 | 5.10 | 1.45 | 0 | 0 |

| Player Name | Team | IP | ER | W | S | K | ERA | WHIP | QS | HLD |
|---|---|---|---|---|---|---|---|---|---|---|
| Matt Boyd | DET | 185 | 90 | 10 | 0 | 209 | 4.36 | 1.21 | 15 | 0 |
| Spencer Turnbull | DET | 155 | 80 | 6 | 0 | 146 | 4.66 | 1.38 | 12 | 0 |
| Daniel Norris | DET | 134 | 73 | 5 | 0 | 120 | 4.88 | 1.40 | 7 | 0 |
| Ivan Nova | DET | 127 | 75 | 7 | 0 | 84 | 5.31 | 1.43 | 5 | 0 |
| Jordan Zimmermann | DET | 123 | 74 | 5 | 0 | 90 | 5.43 | 1.41 | 6 | 0 |
| Tyson Ross | DET | 78 | 39 | 4 | 0 | 61 | 4.52 | 1.50 | 6 | 0 |
| Tyler Alexander | DET | 77 | 41 | 3 | 0 | 65 | 4.82 | 1.35 | 4 | 0 |
| Drew VerHagen | DET | 73 | 42 | 5 | 0 | 62 | 5.16 | 1.44 | 4 | 0 |
| Buck Farmer | DET | 67 | 31 | 4 | 1 | 69 | 4.17 | 1.35 | 0 | 15 |
| Joe Jimenez | DET | 63 | 28 | 3 | 25 | 80 | 4.06 | 1.24 | 0 | 1 |
| Michael Fulmer | DET | 55 | 28 | 3 | 0 | 46 | 4.58 | 1.33 | 5 | 0 |
| Gregory Soto | DET | 53 | 29 | 1 | 0 | 47 | 4.93 | 1.51 | 1 | 3 |
| Casey Mize | DET | 50 | 20 | 2 | 0 | 43 | 3.58 | 1.27 | 2 | 0 |
| John Schreiber | DET | 50 | 27 | 4 | 0 | 52 | 4.86 | 1.37 | 0 | 8 |
| Matt Moore | DET | 50 | 29 | 2 | 0 | 44 | 5.19 | 1.26 | 3 | 0 |
| Bryan Garcia | DET | 47 | 28 | 2 | 0 | 44 | 5.30 | 1.44 | 0 | 4 |
| Matt Manning | DET | 46 | 21 | 3 | 0 | 44 | 4.18 | 1.27 | 2 | 0 |
| David McKay | DET | 36 | 20 | 1 | 0 | 42 | 4.92 | 1.48 | 0 | 1 |
| Rony Garcia | DET | 31 | 18 | 1 | 0 | 28 | 5.25 | 1.42 | 0 | 2 |
| Tarik Skubal | DET | 31 | 17 | 1 | 0 | 35 | 4.88 | 1.39 | 2 | 0 |
| Matt Hall | DET | 31 | 17 | 1 | 0 | 31 | 4.86 | 1.48 | 0 | 0 |
| Dario Agrazal | DET | 30 | 18 | 1 | 0 | 21 | 5.19 | 1.37 | 1 | 1 |
| Joey Wentz | DET | 29 | 19 | 1 | 0 | 24 | 5.79 | 1.51 | 2 | 0 |

| Player Name | Team | IP | ER | W | S | K | ERA | WHIP | QS | HLD |
|---|---|---|---|---|---|---|---|---|---|---|
| Justin Verlander | HOU | 202 | 74 | 17 | 0 | 262 | 3.29 | 1.01 | 22 | 0 |
| Zack Greinke | HOU | 195 | 82 | 15 | 0 | 183 | 3.78 | 1.17 | 19 | 0 |
| Jose Urquidy | HOU | 137 | 62 | 9 | 0 | 137 | 4.07 | 1.19 | 11 | 0 |
| Lance McCullers | HOU | 124 | 54 | 9 | 0 | 134 | 3.91 | 1.32 | 11 | 0 |
| Framber Valdez | HOU | 88 | 35 | 6 | 0 | 95 | 3.54 | 1.35 | 3 | 0 |
| Bradley Peacock | HOU | 83 | 39 | 6 | 0 | 92 | 4.29 | 1.29 | 6 | 1 |
| Josh James | HOU | 65 | 27 | 5 | 0 | 92 | 3.73 | 1.19 | 1 | 6 |
| Roberto Osuna | HOU | 62 | 22 | 3 | 37 | 70 | 3.15 | 1.03 | 0 | 0 |
| Collin McHugh | HOU | 62 | 28 | 4 | 0 | 68 | 4.02 | 1.26 | 3 | 3 |
| Ryan Pressly | HOU | 60 | 21 | 3 | 7 | 77 | 3.12 | 1.08 | 0 | 14 |
| Chris Devenski | HOU | 57 | 28 | 3 | 0 | 61 | 4.41 | 1.24 | 0 | 11 |
| Rogelio Armenteros | HOU | 53 | 29 | 3 | 0 | 49 | 4.85 | 1.39 | 3 | 0 |
| Joe Smith | HOU | 50 | 22 | 3 | 0 | 48 | 4.02 | 1.24 | 0 | 10 |
| Forrest Whitley | HOU | 43 | 22 | 3 | 0 | 49 | 4.54 | 1.37 | 2 | 0 |
| Bryan Abreu | HOU | 40 | 19 | 2 | 0 | 49 | 4.17 | 1.43 | 0 | 1 |
| Joe Biagini | HOU | 39 | 21 | 2 | 0 | 34 | 4.73 | 1.44 | 0 | 6 |
| Aaron Sanchez | HOU | 38 | 21 | 2 | 0 | 33 | 4.85 | 1.48 | 2 | 0 |
| Cy Sneed | HOU | 25 | 13 | 2 | 0 | 23 | 4.70 | 1.33 | 0 | 0 |
| Cristian Javier | HOU | 23 | 14 | 2 | 0 | 27 | 5.21 | 1.44 | 2 | 0 |
| Cionel Perez | HOU | 15 | 8 | 1 | 0 | 14 | 4.95 | 1.40 | 0 | 0 |
| Brandon Bielak | HOU | 9 | 5 | 0 | 0 | 8 | 4.99 | 1.50 | 1 | 0 |

| Player Name | Team | IP | ER | W | S | K | ERA | WHIP | QS | HLD |
|---|---|---|---|---|---|---|---|---|---|---|
| Jake Junis | KCA | 177 | 93 | 10 | 0 | 158 | 4.72 | 1.31 | 13 | 0 |
| Brad Keller | KCA | 169 | 83 | 9 | 0 | 127 | 4.43 | 1.44 | 13 | 0 |
| Danny Duffy | KCA | 150 | 77 | 8 | 0 | 132 | 4.64 | 1.38 | 13 | 0 |
| Mike Montgomery | KCA | 126 | 67 | 6 | 0 | 92 | 4.75 | 1.48 | 8 | 0 |
| Jorge Lopez | KCA | 99 | 54 | 5 | 0 | 83 | 4.89 | 1.43 | 4 | 2 |
| Glenn Sparkman | KCA | 94 | 60 | 4 | 0 | 57 | 5.73 | 1.49 | 5 | 0 |
| Scott Barlow | KCA | 73 | 33 | 3 | 1 | 84 | 4.04 | 1.34 | 0 | 15 |
| Ian Kennedy | KCA | 66 | 29 | 3 | 27 | 69 | 3.94 | 1.26 | 0 | 3 |
| Kevin McCarthy | KCA | 62 | 30 | 3 | 1 | 40 | 4.38 | 1.44 | 0 | 12 |
| Tim Hill | KCA | 52 | 23 | 2 | 2 | 47 | 4.05 | 1.32 | 0 | 14 |
| Eric Skoglund | KCA | 45 | 29 | 2 | 0 | 24 | 5.70 | 1.52 | 2 | 0 |
| Jesse Hahn | KCA | 43 | 23 | 2 | 0 | 38 | 4.93 | 1.46 | 3 | 0 |
| Josh Staumont | KCA | 43 | 21 | 1 | 0 | 44 | 4.51 | 1.54 | 0 | 1 |
| Kyle Zimmer | KCA | 41 | 26 | 1 | 0 | 37 | 5.84 | 1.61 | 0 | 1 |
| Heath Fillmyer | KCA | 39 | 21 | 1 | 0 | 30 | 4.80 | 1.50 | 0 | 1 |
| Jake Newberry | KCA | 32 | 18 | 2 | 0 | 28 | 5.07 | 1.51 | 0 | 2 |
| Randy Rosario | KCA | 23 | 12 | 1 | 0 | 18 | 4.69 | 1.51 | 0 | 1 |
| Jacob Barnes | KCA | 23 | 14 | 1 | 0 | 23 | 5.42 | 1.57 | 0 | 2 |
| Brad Boxberger | KCA | 22 | 13 | 1 | 0 | 23 | 5.04 | 1.56 | 0 | 0 |
| Richard Lovelady | KCA | 21 | 11 | 0 | 0 | 19 | 4.49 | 1.37 | 0 | 0 |
| Wily Peralta | KCA | 20 | 11 | 1 | 0 | 17 | 4.94 | 1.53 | 0 | 3 |
| Chance Adams | KCA | 16 | 10 | 0 | 0 | 14 | 5.64 | 1.54 | 0 | 0 |
| Trevor Rosenthal | KCA | 7 | 4 | 0 | 0 | 8 | 4.41 | 1.50 | 0 | 0 |

| Player Name | Team | IP | ER | W | S | K | ERA | WHIP | QS | HLD |
|---|---|---|---|---|---|---|---|---|---|---|
| Dylan Bundy | LAA | 163 | 82 | 10 | 0 | 165 | 4.53 | 1.29 | 12 | 0 |
| Julio Teheran | LAA | 158 | 83 | 9 | 0 | 142 | 4.76 | 1.42 | 13 | 0 |
| Andrew Heaney | LAA | 144 | 67 | 8 | 0 | 160 | 4.21 | 1.22 | 13 | 0 |
| Griffin Canning | LAA | 127 | 61 | 8 | 0 | 132 | 4.32 | 1.28 | 12 | 0 |
| Shohei Ohtani | LAA | 103 | 42 | 7 | 0 | 122 | 3.64 | 1.24 | 9 | 0 |
| Patrick Sandoval | LAA | 80 | 41 | 4 | 0 | 80 | 4.59 | 1.43 | 5 | 0 |
| Hansel Robles | LAA | 69 | 28 | 4 | 26 | 74 | 3.68 | 1.24 | 0 | 4 |
| Jaime Barria | LAA | 68 | 36 | 4 | 0 | 60 | 4.79 | 1.35 | 3 | 0 |
| Ty Buttrey | LAA | 65 | 27 | 4 | 4 | 76 | 3.74 | 1.24 | 0 | 21 |
| Felix Pena | LAA | 62 | 31 | 4 | 0 | 62 | 4.47 | 1.23 | 1 | 0 |
| Trevor Cahill | LAA | 62 | 30 | 3 | 0 | 57 | 4.36 | 1.36 | 0 | 1 |
| Noe Ramirez | LAA | 60 | 28 | 4 | 0 | 66 | 4.26 | 1.26 | 0 | 7 |
| Cam Bedrosian | LAA | 59 | 25 | 3 | 1 | 60 | 3.81 | 1.29 | 0 | 12 |
| Matt Andriese | LAA | 56 | 28 | 3 | 0 | 56 | 4.40 | 1.33 | 1 | 5 |
| Jose Suarez | LAA | 51 | 29 | 2 | 0 | 47 | 5.16 | 1.43 | 2 | 0 |
| Keynan Middleton | LAA | 46 | 19 | 3 | 6 | 46 | 3.69 | 1.36 | 0 | 6 |
| Taylor Cole | LAA | 41 | 20 | 3 | 0 | 40 | 4.49 | 1.39 | 0 | 4 |
| Justin Anderson | LAA | 40 | 20 | 2 | 0 | 45 | 4.44 | 1.49 | 0 | 8 |
| Dillon Peters | LAA | 37 | 20 | 2 | 0 | 28 | 4.84 | 1.46 | 2 | 0 |
| Luke Bard | LAA | 33 | 18 | 2 | 0 | 33 | 4.77 | 1.46 | 0 | 1 |
| Adalberto Mejia | LAA | 31 | 15 | 1 | 0 | 29 | 4.30 | 1.44 | 0 | 3 |
| Matt Harvey | LAA | 26 | 15 | 1 | 0 | 20 | 5.29 | 1.47 | 2 | 0 |
| Mike Mayers | LAA | 22 | 12 | 1 | 0 | 21 | 4.78 | 1.36 | 0 | 1 |

| Player Name | Team | IP | ER | W | S | K | ERA | WHIP | QS | HLD |
|---|---|---|---|---|---|---|---|---|---|---|
| Walker Buehler | LAN | 189 | 68 | 15 | 0 | 217 | 3.26 | 1.07 | 20 | 0 |
| Clayton Kershaw | LAN | 174 | 66 | 13 | 0 | 180 | 3.43 | 1.15 | 17 | 0 |
| Julio Urias | LAN | 123 | 49 | 8 | 0 | 130 | 3.60 | 1.28 | 8 | 5 |
| Kenta Maeda | LAN | 123 | 55 | 9 | 1 | 137 | 4.06 | 1.21 | 10 | 3 |
| Dustin May | LAN | 111 | 48 | 7 | 0 | 98 | 3.87 | 1.23 | 7 | 1 |
| Alex Wood | LAN | 109 | 48 | 7 | 0 | 97 | 3.97 | 1.27 | 10 | 0 |
| Ross Stripling | LAN | 92 | 38 | 6 | 0 | 94 | 3.65 | 1.19 | 5 | 2 |
| Blake Treinen | LAN | 65 | 26 | 4 | 9 | 70 | 3.56 | 1.32 | 0 | 6 |
| Kenley Jansen | LAN | 63 | 26 | 3 | 35 | 76 | 3.77 | 1.11 | 0 | 0 |
| Pedro Baez | LAN | 60 | 25 | 4 | 1 | 62 | 3.80 | 1.25 | 0 | 16 |
| Joe Kelly | LAN | 59 | 26 | 4 | 6 | 67 | 4.02 | 1.30 | 0 | 12 |
| Tony Gonsolin | LAN | 58 | 26 | 4 | 0 | 55 | 4.09 | 1.32 | 4 | 0 |
| Jimmy Nelson | LAN | 53 | 27 | 3 | 0 | 55 | 4.57 | 1.38 | 4 | 0 |
| Adam Kolarek | LAN | 45 | 17 | 3 | 0 | 38 | 3.49 | 1.27 | 0 | 10 |
| Scott Alexander | LAN | 36 | 14 | 2 | 0 | 30 | 3.47 | 1.38 | 0 | 8 |
| Caleb Ferguson | LAN | 35 | 15 | 2 | 0 | 43 | 3.83 | 1.28 | 0 | 2 |
| Casey Sadler | LAN | 30 | 13 | 2 | 0 | 26 | 3.79 | 1.30 | 0 | 3 |
| Dylan Floro | LAN | 28 | 12 | 2 | 0 | 25 | 3.99 | 1.32 | 0 | 4 |
| Dennis Santana | LAN | 5 | 3 | 1 | 0 | 5 | 5.68 | 1.68 | 0 | 0 |

| Player Name | Team | IP | ER | W | S | K | ERA | WHIP | QS | HLD |
|---|---|---|---|---|---|---|---|---|---|---|
| Sandy Alcantara | MIA | 175 | 85 | 8 | 0 | 143 | 4.39 | 1.41 | 13 | 0 |
| Caleb Smith | MIA | 161 | 81 | 10 | 0 | 171 | 4.54 | 1.30 | 11 | 0 |
| Pablo Lopez | MIA | 144 | 68 | 7 | 0 | 124 | 4.24 | 1.28 | 12 | 0 |
| Jordan Yamamoto | MIA | 136 | 68 | 7 | 0 | 131 | 4.49 | 1.37 | 8 | 0 |
| Elieser Hernandez | MIA | 105 | 54 | 5 | 0 | 102 | 4.62 | 1.30 | 6 | 0 |
| Jose Urena | MIA | 92 | 44 | 4 | 8 | 74 | 4.30 | 1.32 | 2 | 2 |
| Robert Dugger | MIA | 73 | 41 | 3 | 0 | 59 | 4.97 | 1.42 | 6 | 0 |
| Ryne Stanek | MIA | 67 | 27 | 2 | 11 | 82 | 3.59 | 1.26 | 0 | 10 |
| Wei-Yin Chen | MIA | 63 | 36 | 3 | 0 | 53 | 5.19 | 1.40 | 4 | 2 |
| Jarlin Garcia | MIA | 61 | 29 | 3 | 1 | 48 | 4.27 | 1.35 | 0 | 8 |
| Jeff Brigham | MIA | 58 | 29 | 2 | 0 | 59 | 4.44 | 1.29 | 0 | 7 |
| Yimi Garcia | MIA | 53 | 26 | 1 | 2 | 53 | 4.43 | 1.24 | 0 | 7 |
| Adam Conley | MIA | 51 | 26 | 2 | 2 | 47 | 4.56 | 1.43 | 0 | 9 |
| Sterling Sharp | MIA | 46 | 21 | 2 | 0 | 39 | 4.03 | 1.37 | 0 | 2 |
| Sixto Sanchez | MIA | 45 | 22 | 3 | 0 | 37 | 4.33 | 1.32 | 3 | 0 |
| Jose Quijada | MIA | 32 | 16 | 1 | 0 | 38 | 4.36 | 1.41 | 0 | 5 |
| Brian Moran | MIA | 28 | 13 | 2 | 0 | 31 | 4.11 | 1.40 | 0 | 4 |
| Stephen Tarpley | MIA | 27 | 14 | 2 | 0 | 29 | 4.76 | 1.40 | 0 | 3 |
| Drew Steckenrider | MIA | 27 | 13 | 1 | 0 | 30 | 4.29 | 1.29 | 0 | 5 |
| Nick Neidert | MIA | 23 | 12 | 1 | 0 | 19 | 4.73 | 1.40 | 2 | 0 |
| Josh D. Smith | MIA | 15 | 6 | 1 | 0 | 17 | 3.77 | 1.30 | 0 | 1 |
| Alex Vesia | MIA | 9 | 4 | 0 | 0 | 10 | 4.04 | 1.31 | 0 | 0 |

| Player Name | Team | IP | ER | W | S | K | ERA | WHIP | QS | HLD |
|---|---|---|---|---|---|---|---|---|---|---|
| Brandon Woodruff | MIL | 162 | 68 | 12 | 0 | 178 | 3.78 | 1.20 | 14 | 0 |
| Eric Lauer | MIL | 148 | 75 | 9 | 0 | 137 | 4.58 | 1.39 | 11 | 0 |
| Josh Lindblom | MIL | 147 | 72 | 9 | 0 | 142 | 4.37 | 1.31 | 11 | 0 |
| Adrian Houser | MIL | 141 | 65 | 8 | 0 | 133 | 4.14 | 1.35 | 9 | 0 |
| Brett Anderson | MIL | 133 | 66 | 8 | 0 | 85 | 4.43 | 1.40 | 12 | 0 |
| Freddy Peralta | MIL | 93 | 43 | 6 | 0 | 125 | 4.15 | 1.31 | 4 | 12 |
| Brent Suter | MIL | 83 | 37 | 5 | 0 | 73 | 4.04 | 1.22 | 3 | 4 |
| Corbin Burnes | MIL | 79 | 41 | 4 | 0 | 88 | 4.71 | 1.33 | 3 | 4 |
| Josh Hader | MIL | 76 | 24 | 4 | 34 | 132 | 2.84 | 0.99 | 0 | 2 |
| Alex Claudio | MIL | 60 | 28 | 3 | 1 | 42 | 4.18 | 1.41 | 0 | 16 |
| Corey Knebel | MIL | 48 | 18 | 2 | 3 | 69 | 3.49 | 1.24 | 0 | 9 |
| Ray Black | MIL | 48 | 23 | 2 | 0 | 61 | 4.32 | 1.32 | 0 | 4 |
| Jay Jackson | MIL | 45 | 22 | 3 | 1 | 67 | 4.36 | 1.30 | 0 | 4 |
| Matt Albers | MIL | 34 | 18 | 2 | 0 | 31 | 4.89 | 1.43 | 0 | 5 |
| Jeremy Jeffress | MIL | 30 | 14 | 2 | 0 | 27 | 4.27 | 1.37 | 0 | 4 |
| Devin Williams | MIL | 25 | 13 | 2 | 0 | 27 | 4.57 | 1.48 | 0 | 1 |
| Jacob Faria | MIL | 25 | 13 | 1 | 0 | 26 | 4.85 | 1.36 | 0 | 2 |
| Taylor Williams | MIL | 23 | 12 | 1 | 0 | 23 | 4.66 | 1.45 | 0 | 0 |
| Trey Supak | MIL | 21 | 13 | 1 | 0 | 16 | 5.48 | 1.47 | 1 | 0 |
| Alex Wilson | MIL | 16 | 9 | 1 | 0 | 12 | 5.03 | 1.41 | 0 | 0 |
| Bobby Wahl | MIL | 15 | 8 | 1 | 0 | 20 | 4.66 | 1.33 | 0 | 1 |
| Deolis Guerra | MIL | 14 | 10 | 1 | 0 | 11 | 6.00 | 1.47 | 0 | 2 |
| Eric Yardley | MIL | 14 | 7 | 0 | 0 | 9 | 4.31 | 1.36 | 0 | 0 |

| Player Name | Team | IP | ER | W | S | K | ERA | WHIP | QS | HLD |
| --- | --- | --- | --- | --- | --- | --- | --- | --- | --- | --- |
| Jose Berrios | MIN | 196 | 89 | 14 | 0 | 192 | 4.11 | 1.25 | 18 | 0 |
| Jake Odorizzi | MIN | 166 | 80 | 12 | 0 | 173 | 4.33 | 1.29 | 11 | 0 |
| Homer Bailey | MIN | 144 | 78 | 9 | 0 | 121 | 4.88 | 1.41 | 10 | 0 |
| Michael Pineda | MIN | 124 | 61 | 9 | 0 | 118 | 4.46 | 1.26 | 10 | 0 |
| Randy Dobnak | MIN | 100 | 49 | 7 | 0 | 72 | 4.36 | 1.35 | 6 | 0 |
| Devin Smeltzer | MIN | 78 | 41 | 4 | 0 | 63 | 4.73 | 1.34 | 5 | 0 |
| Rich Hill | MIN | 74 | 35 | 5 | 0 | 79 | 4.23 | 1.27 | 6 | 0 |
| Taylor Rogers | MIN | 69 | 24 | 3 | 30 | 83 | 3.17 | 1.09 | 0 | 4 |
| Tyler Duffey | MIN | 61 | 25 | 4 | 1 | 73 | 3.66 | 1.14 | 0 | 12 |
| Trevor May | MIN | 59 | 24 | 4 | 1 | 71 | 3.73 | 1.22 | 0 | 14 |
| Sergio Romo | MIN | 57 | 29 | 2 | 8 | 57 | 4.52 | 1.30 | 0 | 15 |
| Lewis Thorpe | MIN | 55 | 29 | 4 | 0 | 57 | 4.69 | 1.32 | 3 | 1 |
| Tyler Clippard | MIN | 53 | 27 | 2 | 2 | 56 | 4.62 | 1.29 | 0 | 9 |
| Matt Wisler | MIN | 44 | 23 | 2 | 0 | 43 | 4.81 | 1.30 | 0 | 3 |
| Brusdar Graterol | MIN | 38 | 17 | 3 | 0 | 38 | 4.06 | 1.31 | 1 | 0 |
| Ryne Harper | MIN | 38 | 17 | 2 | 0 | 35 | 4.01 | 1.26 | 0 | 8 |
| Zack Littell | MIN | 33 | 16 | 2 | 0 | 31 | 4.32 | 1.29 | 0 | 2 |
| Sam Dyson | MIN | 30 | 14 | 2 | 0 | 25 | 4.15 | 1.34 | 0 | 3 |
| Cody Stashak | MIN | 29 | 15 | 2 | 0 | 29 | 4.54 | 1.22 | 0 | 4 |
| Fernando Romero | MIN | 24 | 13 | 1 | 0 | 22 | 4.76 | 1.46 | 0 | 1 |
| Cody Allen | MIN | 21 | 11 | 1 | 1 | 23 | 4.89 | 1.41 | 0 | 0 |
| Addison Reed | MIN | 14 | 7 | 1 | 0 | 11 | 4.90 | 1.34 | 0 | 0 |
| Sean Poppen | MIN | 8 | 5 | 0 | 0 | 7 | 5.17 | 1.54 | 0 | 0 |

| Player Name | Team | IP | ER | W | S | K | ERA | WHIP | QS | HLD |
|---|---|---|---|---|---|---|---|---|---|---|
| Gerrit Cole | NYA | 204 | 72 | 16 | 0 | 279 | 3.16 | 1.03 | 23 | 0 |
| Masahiro Tanaka | NYA | 169 | 84 | 11 | 0 | 150 | 4.47 | 1.28 | 14 | 0 |
| James Paxton | NYA | 167 | 70 | 14 | 0 | 199 | 3.81 | 1.18 | 15 | 0 |
| Luis Severino | NYA | 166 | 68 | 13 | 0 | 186 | 3.71 | 1.19 | 14 | 0 |
| J.A. Happ | NYA | 124 | 63 | 9 | 0 | 118 | 4.54 | 1.30 | 9 | 0 |
| Chad Green | NYA | 66 | 26 | 4 | 1 | 88 | 3.56 | 1.08 | 0 | 9 |
| Domingo German | NYA | 65 | 33 | 5 | 0 | 69 | 4.52 | 1.27 | 5 | 0 |
| Adam Ottavino | NYA | 62 | 25 | 4 | 2 | 79 | 3.60 | 1.32 | 0 | 21 |
| Zack Britton | NYA | 58 | 19 | 3 | 3 | 53 | 2.96 | 1.33 | 0 | 20 |
| Aroldis Chapman | NYA | 58 | 18 | 4 | 35 | 87 | 2.80 | 1.15 | 0 | 0 |
| Thomas Kahnle | NYA | 57 | 23 | 3 | 0 | 77 | 3.63 | 1.17 | 0 | 16 |
| Jordan Montgomery | NYA | 55 | 28 | 3 | 0 | 54 | 4.52 | 1.32 | 3 | 0 |
| Jonathan Loaisiga | NYA | 53 | 25 | 3 | 0 | 60 | 4.25 | 1.27 | 1 | 1 |
| Luis Cessa | NYA | 45 | 23 | 2 | 0 | 42 | 4.60 | 1.34 | 0 | 3 |
| Ben Heller | NYA | 36 | 17 | 3 | 0 | 39 | 4.23 | 1.37 | 0 | 1 |
| Jonathan Holder | NYA | 28 | 15 | 1 | 0 | 29 | 4.85 | 1.29 | 0 | 3 |
| Cory Gearrin | NYA | 26 | 13 | 1 | 0 | 23 | 4.47 | 1.45 | 0 | 4 |
| Tyler Lyons | NYA | 15 | 9 | 1 | 0 | 18 | 5.35 | 1.36 | 0 | 2 |
| Deivi Garcia | NYA | 8 | 4 | 0 | 0 | 9 | 4.87 | 1.44 | 0 | 0 |

| Player Name | Team | IP | ER | W | S | K | ERA | WHIP | QS | HLD |
|---|---|---|---|---|---|---|---|---|---|---|
| Jacob deGrom | NYN | 200 | 62 | 14 | 0 | 248 | 2.80 | 1.04 | 22 | 0 |
| Noah Syndergaard | NYN | 186 | 78 | 12 | 0 | 191 | 3.80 | 1.20 | 16 | 0 |
| Marcus Stroman | NYN | 173 | 75 | 11 | 0 | 152 | 3.87 | 1.35 | 15 | 0 |
| Rick Porcello | NYN | 167 | 86 | 12 | 0 | 150 | 4.61 | 1.29 | 13 | 0 |
| Steven Matz | NYN | 153 | 71 | 9 | 0 | 147 | 4.19 | 1.33 | 13 | 0 |
| Michael Wacha | NYN | 76 | 37 | 4 | 0 | 68 | 4.41 | 1.39 | 4 | 0 |
| Seth Lugo | NYN | 73 | 26 | 4 | 6 | 85 | 3.19 | 1.07 | 0 | 19 |
| Edwin Diaz | NYN | 63 | 23 | 3 | 29 | 100 | 3.24 | 1.07 | 0 | 3 |
| Dellin Betances | NYN | 54 | 18 | 3 | 3 | 86 | 3.02 | 1.18 | 0 | 11 |
| Justin Wilson | NYN | 54 | 20 | 4 | 1 | 65 | 3.38 | 1.27 | 0 | 13 |
| Jeurys Familia | NYN | 54 | 25 | 3 | 1 | 58 | 4.17 | 1.42 | 0 | 10 |
| Robert Gsellman | NYN | 46 | 22 | 2 | 0 | 42 | 4.25 | 1.33 | 0 | 4 |
| Brad Brach | NYN | 44 | 21 | 2 | 1 | 47 | 4.26 | 1.37 | 0 | 8 |
| Luis Avilan | NYN | 38 | 19 | 2 | 0 | 38 | 4.49 | 1.43 | 0 | 7 |
| Paul Sewald | NYN | 24 | 13 | 1 | 0 | 23 | 4.76 | 1.36 | 0 | 1 |
| Drew Gagnon | NYN | 23 | 16 | 2 | 0 | 16 | 6.41 | 1.37 | 0 | 1 |
| Walker Lockett | NYN | 18 | 10 | 1 | 0 | 14 | 5.00 | 1.36 | 0 | 1 |
| A.J. Ramos | NYN | 13 | 7 | 1 | 0 | 13 | 4.97 | 1.50 | 0 | 0 |
| Tyler Bashlor | NYN | 12 | 7 | 0 | 0 | 11 | 5.15 | 1.42 | 0 | 1 |
| Daniel Zamora | NYN | 11 | 5 | 1 | 0 | 12 | 4.46 | 1.29 | 0 | 1 |
| Donnie Hart | NYN | 9 | 4 | 0 | 0 | 6 | 4.49 | 1.52 | 0 | 0 |
| Corey Oswalt | NYN | 8 | 4 | 1 | 0 | 7 | 3.87 | 1.26 | 0 | 0 |

| Player Name | Team | IP | ER | W | S | K | ERA | WHIP | QS | HLD |
|---|---|---|---|---|---|---|---|---|---|---|
| Michael Fiers | OAK | 170 | 87 | 11 | 0 | 130 | 4.61 | 1.35 | 15 | 0 |
| Frankie Montas | OAK | 160 | 69 | 11 | 0 | 156 | 3.88 | 1.28 | 15 | 0 |
| Sean Manaea | OAK | 160 | 74 | 13 | 0 | 137 | 4.15 | 1.27 | 13 | 0 |
| Jesus Luzardo | OAK | 122 | 51 | 7 | 1 | 126 | 3.75 | 1.23 | 9 | 0 |
| Chris Bassitt | OAK | 122 | 57 | 8 | 0 | 113 | 4.22 | 1.30 | 10 | 0 |
| A.J. Puk | OAK | 98 | 45 | 8 | 0 | 106 | 4.13 | 1.31 | 7 | 1 |
| Yusmeiro Petit | OAK | 75 | 34 | 4 | 1 | 66 | 4.05 | 1.15 | 0 | 20 |
| Liam Hendriks | OAK | 67 | 22 | 4 | 30 | 90 | 2.95 | 1.10 | 0 | 1 |
| Marco Estrada | OAK | 65 | 42 | 3 | 0 | 48 | 5.83 | 1.47 | 4 | 0 |
| Lou Trivino | OAK | 59 | 28 | 4 | 0 | 60 | 4.29 | 1.36 | 0 | 14 |
| Joakim Soria | OAK | 59 | 26 | 3 | 2 | 67 | 4.00 | 1.22 | 0 | 15 |
| Daniel Mengden | OAK | 56 | 31 | 3 | 0 | 41 | 4.95 | 1.37 | 2 | 0 |
| Jacob Diekman | OAK | 55 | 24 | 2 | 1 | 69 | 3.92 | 1.33 | 0 | 22 |
| J.B. Wendelken | OAK | 38 | 18 | 3 | 0 | 38 | 4.13 | 1.41 | 0 | 1 |
| T.J. McFarland | OAK | 35 | 18 | 1 | 0 | 21 | 4.54 | 1.50 | 0 | 4 |
| Paul Blackburn | OAK | 22 | 12 | 1 | 0 | 15 | 4.83 | 1.36 | 0 | 1 |
| Ryan Buchter | OAK | 17 | 6 | 1 | 0 | 19 | 3.15 | 1.36 | 0 | 5 |
| Grant Holmes | OAK | 10 | 5 | 1 | 0 | 9 | 4.43 | 1.30 | 0 | 0 |
| James Kaprielian | OAK | 6 | 4 | 0 | 0 | 6 | 5.30 | 1.41 | 1 | 0 |

| Player Name | Team | IP | ER | W | S | K | ERA | WHIP | QS | HLD |
|---|---|---|---|---|---|---|---|---|---|---|
| Aaron Nola | PHI | 191 | 79 | 13 | 0 | 212 | 3.72 | 1.24 | 18 | 0 |
| Zack Wheeler | PHI | 189 | 83 | 12 | 0 | 191 | 3.98 | 1.26 | 17 | 0 |
| Jake Arrieta | PHI | 152 | 77 | 9 | 0 | 128 | 4.56 | 1.39 | 11 | 0 |
| Zach Eflin | PHI | 146 | 75 | 9 | 0 | 120 | 4.60 | 1.36 | 12 | 0 |
| Vincent Velasquez | PHI | 116 | 62 | 7 | 0 | 123 | 4.79 | 1.36 | 8 | 0 |
| Drew Smyly | PHI | 93 | 53 | 4 | 0 | 94 | 5.10 | 1.37 | 6 | 0 |
| Jason Vargas | PHI | 89 | 51 | 5 | 0 | 71 | 5.17 | 1.46 | 6 | 0 |
| Nick Pivetta | PHI | 81 | 40 | 5 | 0 | 87 | 4.40 | 1.33 | 2 | 4 |
| Hector Neris | PHI | 67 | 26 | 3 | 32 | 88 | 3.47 | 1.15 | 0 | 2 |
| Ranger Suarez | PHI | 59 | 25 | 4 | 0 | 51 | 3.91 | 1.32 | 0 | 9 |
| Jose Alvarez | PHI | 57 | 24 | 3 | 1 | 53 | 3.71 | 1.32 | 0 | 15 |
| Jared Hughes | PHI | 55 | 25 | 3 | 0 | 42 | 4.18 | 1.41 | 0 | 7 |
| Seranthony Dominguez | PHI | 50 | 20 | 3 | 2 | 61 | 3.60 | 1.26 | 0 | 9 |
| Juan Nicasio | PHI | 48 | 24 | 2 | 1 | 47 | 4.48 | 1.36 | 0 | 9 |
| Jerad Eickhoff | PHI | 45 | 25 | 2 | 0 | 38 | 5.07 | 1.40 | 2 | 0 |
| Edgar Garcia | PHI | 42 | 24 | 2 | 0 | 48 | 5.03 | 1.26 | 0 | 5 |
| Cole Irvin | PHI | 41 | 22 | 2 | 0 | 31 | 4.78 | 1.33 | 2 | 1 |
| Adam Morgan | PHI | 39 | 18 | 2 | 0 | 39 | 4.14 | 1.30 | 0 | 17 |
| Blake Parker | PHI | 38 | 19 | 2 | 1 | 39 | 4.46 | 1.32 | 0 | 8 |
| Austin Davis | PHI | 34 | 17 | 2 | 0 | 37 | 4.64 | 1.39 | 0 | 3 |
| Victor Arano | PHI | 30 | 14 | 1 | 0 | 35 | 4.15 | 1.29 | 0 | 2 |
| Nick Vincent | PHI | 27 | 14 | 1 | 0 | 26 | 4.70 | 1.26 | 0 | 1 |

| Player Name | Team | IP | ER | W | S | K | ERA | WHIP | QS | HLD |
|---|---|---|---|---|---|---|---|---|---|---|
| Joe Musgrove | PIT | 172 | 80 | 11 | 0 | 157 | 4.18 | 1.25 | 16 | 0 |
| Trevor Williams | PIT | 161 | 86 | 9 | 0 | 127 | 4.80 | 1.39 | 13 | 0 |
| Chris Archer | PIT | 160 | 78 | 8 | 0 | 181 | 4.36 | 1.33 | 12 | 0 |
| Mitch Keller | PIT | 134 | 63 | 7 | 0 | 146 | 4.20 | 1.33 | 10 | 0 |
| Steven Brault | PIT | 130 | 67 | 6 | 0 | 112 | 4.67 | 1.51 | 7 | 0 |
| Francisco Liriano | PIT | 71 | 34 | 4 | 0 | 68 | 4.27 | 1.39 | 0 | 10 |
| Richard Rodriguez | PIT | 65 | 28 | 3 | 2 | 69 | 3.92 | 1.28 | 0 | 15 |
| Kyle Crick | PIT | 61 | 28 | 3 | 8 | 70 | 4.07 | 1.40 | 0 | 11 |
| Michael Feliz | PIT | 60 | 27 | 3 | 5 | 74 | 4.07 | 1.29 | 0 | 11 |
| Keone Kela | PIT | 60 | 21 | 4 | 19 | 72 | 3.14 | 1.15 | 0 | 10 |
| Clay Holmes | PIT | 54 | 28 | 4 | 0 | 51 | 4.62 | 1.65 | 0 | 1 |
| Chad Kuhl | PIT | 54 | 27 | 3 | 0 | 51 | 4.60 | 1.39 | 5 | 0 |
| Chris Stratton | PIT | 52 | 26 | 2 | 1 | 48 | 4.51 | 1.38 | 1 | 3 |
| Geoff Hartlieb | PIT | 28 | 15 | 2 | 0 | 28 | 4.83 | 1.41 | 0 | 2 |
| James Marvel | PIT | 27 | 16 | 2 | 0 | 19 | 5.12 | 1.45 | 2 | 0 |
| Yacksel Rios | PIT | 26 | 15 | 1 | 0 | 24 | 5.13 | 1.55 | 0 | 0 |
| Nick Burdi | PIT | 24 | 12 | 2 | 0 | 32 | 4.61 | 1.31 | 0 | 1 |
| Yefry Ramirez | PIT | 19 | 14 | 1 | 0 | 20 | 6.48 | 1.68 | 0 | 1 |
| J.T. Brubaker | PIT | 18 | 9 | 1 | 0 | 16 | 4.58 | 1.40 | 1 | 0 |
| Dovydas Neverauskas | PIT | 18 | 9 | 1 | 0 | 19 | 4.48 | 1.45 | 0 | 1 |
| Alex McRae | PIT | 14 | 10 | 1 | 0 | 10 | 6.77 | 1.74 | 0 | 0 |
| Wei-Chung Wang | PIT | 13 | 7 | 1 | 0 | 8 | 4.70 | 1.59 | 0 | 0 |

| Player Name | Team | IP | ER | W | S | K | ERA | WHIP | QS | HLD |
|---|---|---|---|---|---|---|---|---|---|---|
| Chris Paddack | SDN | 168 | 66 | 11 | 0 | 183 | 3.52 | 1.11 | 15 | 0 |
| Joey Lucchesi | SDN | 164 | 78 | 10 | 0 | 159 | 4.25 | 1.32 | 12 | 0 |
| Dinelson Lamet | SDN | 151 | 64 | 9 | 0 | 190 | 3.78 | 1.22 | 13 | 0 |
| Zach Davies | SDN | 144 | 73 | 8 | 0 | 101 | 4.53 | 1.42 | 10 | 0 |
| Garrett Richards | SDN | 108 | 50 | 6 | 0 | 113 | 4.14 | 1.35 | 8 | 2 |
| Cal Quantrill | SDN | 85 | 44 | 5 | 0 | 73 | 4.70 | 1.36 | 5 | 0 |
| Craig Stammen | SDN | 71 | 29 | 5 | 1 | 68 | 3.65 | 1.22 | 0 | 21 |
| Matt Strahm | SDN | 69 | 30 | 4 | 0 | 74 | 3.91 | 1.17 | 2 | 8 |
| Drew Pomeranz | SDN | 66 | 25 | 2 | 6 | 81 | 3.45 | 1.18 | 0 | 12 |
| Kirby Yates | SDN | 62 | 18 | 3 | 34 | 91 | 2.61 | 1.03 | 0 | 0 |
| Andres Munoz | SDN | 58 | 22 | 3 | 5 | 76 | 3.38 | 1.23 | 0 | 14 |
| Luis Perdomo | SDN | 44 | 20 | 2 | 0 | 37 | 4.08 | 1.32 | 0 | 6 |
| MacKenzie Gore | SDN | 41 | 19 | 3 | 0 | 43 | 4.14 | 1.32 | 3 | 0 |
| Nick Margevicius | SDN | 38 | 24 | 2 | 0 | 27 | 5.79 | 1.50 | 2 | 0 |
| Robert Erlin | SDN | 36 | 18 | 1 | 0 | 30 | 4.52 | 1.34 | 1 | 2 |
| Pierce Johnson | SDN | 36 | 18 | 2 | 0 | 36 | 4.67 | 1.38 | 0 | 2 |
| Trey Wingenter | SDN | 35 | 17 | 1 | 0 | 46 | 4.31 | 1.28 | 0 | 7 |
| Luis Patino | SDN | 33 | 12 | 2 | 0 | 32 | 3.16 | 1.43 | 2 | 0 |
| Jose Castillo | SDN | 29 | 12 | 1 | 0 | 43 | 3.61 | 1.27 | 0 | 3 |
| Ronald Bolanos | SDN | 24 | 13 | 1 | 0 | 22 | 4.97 | 1.47 | 2 | 0 |
| Michel Baez | SDN | 22 | 10 | 1 | 0 | 24 | 3.93 | 1.32 | 0 | 1 |
| Adrian Morejon | SDN | 16 | 8 | 0 | 0 | 19 | 4.18 | 1.28 | 0 | 1 |
| Gerardo Reyes | SDN | 16 | 8 | 1 | 0 | 20 | 4.65 | 1.34 | 0 | 0 |

| Player Name | Team | IP | ER | W | S | K | ERA | WHIP | QS | HLD |
|---|---|---|---|---|---|---|---|---|---|---|
| Marco Gonzales | SEA | 189 | 94 | 12 | 0 | 145 | 4.47 | 1.34 | 15 | 0 |
| Yusei Kikuchi | SEA | 163 | 87 | 8 | 0 | 127 | 4.81 | 1.38 | 13 | 0 |
| Justus Sheffield | SEA | 137 | 70 | 6 | 0 | 124 | 4.61 | 1.46 | 9 | 0 |
| Kendall Graveman | SEA | 123 | 66 | 6 | 0 | 96 | 4.82 | 1.41 | 9 | 0 |
| Justin Dunn | SEA | 88 | 47 | 4 | 0 | 80 | 4.81 | 1.44 | 3 | 0 |
| Felix Hernandez | SEA | 81 | 47 | 3 | 0 | 65 | 5.23 | 1.48 | 5 | 0 |
| Erik Swanson | SEA | 77 | 40 | 3 | 2 | 73 | 4.66 | 1.24 | 4 | 2 |
| Wade LeBlanc | SEA | 76 | 44 | 5 | 0 | 57 | 5.22 | 1.42 | 3 | 1 |
| Tommy Milone | SEA | 69 | 39 | 3 | 0 | 56 | 5.09 | 1.36 | 4 | 0 |
| Brandon Brennan | SEA | 61 | 28 | 3 | 4 | 59 | 4.17 | 1.36 | 0 | 9 |
| Samuel Tuivailala | SEA | 60 | 26 | 3 | 3 | 58 | 3.95 | 1.37 | 0 | 12 |
| Matt Magill | SEA | 58 | 27 | 3 | 16 | 64 | 4.14 | 1.31 | 0 | 6 |
| Arodys Vizcaino | SEA | 45 | 20 | 3 | 1 | 51 | 4.00 | 1.37 | 0 | 4 |
| Carl Edwards | SEA | 42 | 22 | 3 | 1 | 46 | 4.58 | 1.37 | 0 | 7 |
| Dan Altavilla | SEA | 38 | 18 | 4 | 0 | 46 | 4.28 | 1.35 | 0 | 4 |
| Zac Grotz | SEA | 30 | 13 | 1 | 0 | 30 | 3.78 | 1.31 | 0 | 4 |
| Taylor Guilbeau | SEA | 29 | 13 | 1 | 0 | 23 | 4.15 | 1.38 | 0 | 5 |
| Nestor Cortes | SEA | 28 | 14 | 1 | 0 | 27 | 4.72 | 1.35 | 0 | 0 |
| Ljay Newsome | SEA | 27 | 16 | 1 | 0 | 21 | 5.28 | 1.29 | 2 | 0 |
| Austin Adams | SEA | 26 | 11 | 1 | 0 | 42 | 3.84 | 1.26 | 0 | 8 |
| Reggie McClain | SEA | 21 | 11 | 1 | 0 | 15 | 4.84 | 1.39 | 0 | 0 |
| Phillips Valdez | SEA | 19 | 11 | 1 | 0 | 16 | 5.00 | 1.58 | 1 | 0 |
| Gerson Bautista | SEA | 19 | 11 | 0 | 0 | 19 | 5.15 | 1.56 | 0 | 0 |

| Player Name | Team | IP | ER | W | S | K | ERA | WHIP | QS | HLD |
|---|---|---|---|---|---|---|---|---|---|---|
| Jeff Samardzija | SFN | 175 | 87 | 8 | 0 | 141 | 4.46 | 1.32 | 12 | 0 |
| Kevin Gausman | SFN | 145 | 67 | 7 | 0 | 140 | 4.17 | 1.30 | 13 | 2 |
| Johnny Cueto | SFN | 142 | 67 | 8 | 0 | 120 | 4.23 | 1.34 | 10 | 0 |
| Tyler Beede | SFN | 113 | 58 | 5 | 0 | 109 | 4.63 | 1.43 | 7 | 0 |
| Logan Webb | SFN | 102 | 49 | 5 | 0 | 90 | 4.33 | 1.39 | 8 | 0 |
| Tyler Anderson | SFN | 91 | 44 | 5 | 0 | 89 | 4.40 | 1.30 | 8 | 0 |
| Dereck Rodriguez | SFN | 75 | 37 | 3 | 0 | 61 | 4.45 | 1.33 | 3 | 2 |
| Shaun Anderson | SFN | 66 | 31 | 2 | 10 | 55 | 4.31 | 1.33 | 0 | 2 |
| Tony Watson | SFN | 62 | 26 | 3 | 9 | 56 | 3.80 | 1.26 | 0 | 15 |
| Jandel Gustave | SFN | 52 | 24 | 2 | 1 | 41 | 4.13 | 1.46 | 0 | 7 |
| Tyler Rogers | SFN | 51 | 20 | 3 | 3 | 41 | 3.44 | 1.44 | 0 | 8 |
| Trevor Gott | SFN | 49 | 23 | 3 | 0 | 50 | 4.15 | 1.30 | 0 | 4 |
| Sam Coonrod | SFN | 47 | 22 | 3 | 1 | 44 | 4.14 | 1.50 | 0 | 2 |
| Conner Menez | SFN | 36 | 18 | 1 | 0 | 40 | 4.36 | 1.37 | 2 | 1 |
| Andrew Suarez | SFN | 35 | 17 | 2 | 0 | 27 | 4.38 | 1.43 | 0 | 1 |
| Burch Smith | SFN | 35 | 18 | 2 | 0 | 35 | 4.60 | 1.45 | 0 | 2 |
| Sam Selman | SFN | 30 | 13 | 0 | 0 | 34 | 3.85 | 1.31 | 0 | 4 |
| Trevor Oaks | SFN | 30 | 15 | 2 | 0 | 24 | 4.39 | 1.42 | 1 | 0 |
| Wandy Peralta | SFN | 28 | 14 | 1 | 0 | 24 | 4.42 | 1.42 | 0 | 5 |
| Fernando Abad | SFN | 27 | 13 | 2 | 0 | 24 | 4.21 | 1.31 | 0 | 3 |
| Kyle Barraclough | SFN | 26 | 14 | 1 | 1 | 28 | 4.76 | 1.53 | 0 | 3 |
| Rico Garcia | SFN | 25 | 15 | 1 | 0 | 18 | 5.43 | 1.51 | 2 | 0 |
| Pat Venditte | SFN | 19 | 13 | 1 | 0 | 15 | 5.95 | 1.29 | 0 | 1 |

| Player Name | Team | IP | ER | W | S | K | ERA | WHIP | QS | HLD |
|---|---|---|---|---|---|---|---|---|---|---|
| Jack Flaherty | STL | 189 | 69 | 13 | 0 | 220 | 3.31 | 1.11 | 20 | 0 |
| Miles Mikolas | STL | 182 | 82 | 12 | 0 | 144 | 4.04 | 1.23 | 16 | 0 |
| Dakota Hudson | STL | 158 | 74 | 11 | 0 | 121 | 4.25 | 1.47 | 14 | 0 |
| Adam Wainwright | STL | 136 | 67 | 10 | 0 | 119 | 4.41 | 1.41 | 11 | 0 |
| Daniel Poncedeleon | STL | 87 | 43 | 4 | 0 | 84 | 4.39 | 1.38 | 6 | 1 |
| Kwang-Hyun Kim | STL | 81 | 34 | 5 | 0 | 71 | 3.77 | 1.30 | 0 | 2 |
| Giovanny Gallegos | STL | 70 | 25 | 3 | 10 | 85 | 3.27 | 1.07 | 0 | 14 |
| Carlos Martinez | STL | 66 | 27 | 4 | 35 | 68 | 3.70 | 1.31 | 1 | 2 |
| John Brebbia | STL | 62 | 26 | 3 | 1 | 70 | 3.80 | 1.21 | 0 | 11 |
| John Gant | STL | 60 | 26 | 5 | 1 | 56 | 3.91 | 1.38 | 0 | 12 |
| Andrew Miller | STL | 59 | 26 | 4 | 5 | 73 | 4.00 | 1.29 | 0 | 20 |
| Alex Reyes | STL | 45 | 23 | 3 | 0 | 45 | 4.70 | 1.48 | 2 | 3 |
| Tyler Webb | STL | 43 | 21 | 2 | 0 | 39 | 4.28 | 1.34 | 0 | 5 |
| Ryan Helsley | STL | 40 | 17 | 2 | 0 | 40 | 3.83 | 1.32 | 0 | 4 |
| Junior Fernandez | STL | 34 | 17 | 1 | 0 | 38 | 4.46 | 1.37 | 0 | 2 |
| Austin Gomber | STL | 32 | 15 | 2 | 0 | 29 | 4.35 | 1.37 | 2 | 0 |
| Genesis Cabrera | STL | 29 | 14 | 1 | 0 | 29 | 4.41 | 1.40 | 1 | 1 |
| Dominic Leone | STL | 25 | 13 | 1 | 0 | 28 | 4.88 | 1.38 | 0 | 1 |
| Luke Gregerson | STL | 20 | 10 | 1 | 0 | 16 | 4.60 | 1.41 | 0 | 0 |
| Tony Cingrani | STL | 17 | 10 | 1 | 0 | 24 | 5.13 | 1.40 | 0 | 4 |
| Brett Cecil | STL | 16 | 10 | 1 | 0 | 13 | 5.27 | 1.46 | 0 | 1 |
| Jordan Hicks | STL | 15 | 6 | 1 | 1 | 17 | 3.66 | 1.29 | 0 | 2 |
| Zach Rosscup | STL | 7 | 4 | 0 | 0 | 8 | 5.45 | 2.09 | 0 | 1 |

| Player Name | Team | IP | ER | W | S | K | ERA | WHIP | QS | HLD |
|---|---|---|---|---|---|---|---|---|---|---|
| Charlie Morton | TBA | 179 | 68 | 14 | 0 | 209 | 3.44 | 1.17 | 17 | 0 |
| Blake Snell | TBA | 162 | 59 | 12 | 0 | 205 | 3.30 | 1.18 | 16 | 0 |
| Tyler Glasnow | TBA | 141 | 55 | 10 | 0 | 169 | 3.49 | 1.11 | 11 | 0 |
| Ryan Yarbrough | TBA | 133 | 61 | 10 | 0 | 113 | 4.11 | 1.24 | 10 | 0 |
| Yonny Chirinos | TBA | 125 | 56 | 8 | 0 | 107 | 4.04 | 1.23 | 9 | 0 |
| Brendan McKay | TBA | 102 | 43 | 6 | 0 | 113 | 3.84 | 1.21 | 6 | 0 |
| Diego Castillo | TBA | 65 | 24 | 4 | 8 | 77 | 3.30 | 1.17 | 0 | 17 |
| Nick Anderson | TBA | 64 | 23 | 5 | 10 | 95 | 3.17 | 1.06 | 0 | 19 |
| Emilio Pagan | TBA | 64 | 24 | 3 | 29 | 80 | 3.45 | 1.04 | 0 | 5 |
| Trevor Richards | TBA | 57 | 26 | 3 | 0 | 59 | 4.05 | 1.28 | 2 | 0 |
| Jalen Beeks | TBA | 57 | 25 | 4 | 0 | 53 | 3.92 | 1.36 | 2 | 0 |
| Austin Pruitt | TBA | 55 | 29 | 3 | 0 | 44 | 4.66 | 1.34 | 3 | 0 |
| Colin Poche | TBA | 52 | 22 | 4 | 1 | 72 | 3.84 | 1.15 | 0 | 14 |
| Chaz Roe | TBA | 46 | 22 | 2 | 1 | 52 | 4.21 | 1.34 | 0 | 17 |
| Oliver Drake | TBA | 46 | 18 | 2 | 0 | 54 | 3.60 | 1.22 | 0 | 4 |
| Jose Alvarado | TBA | 39 | 15 | 1 | 2 | 50 | 3.52 | 1.32 | 0 | 7 |
| Andrew Kittredge | TBA | 34 | 15 | 2 | 4 | 38 | 3.96 | 1.17 | 0 | 3 |
| Brent Honeywell | TBA | 33 | 15 | 2 | 0 | 34 | 4.16 | 1.28 | 3 | 0 |
| Peter Fairbanks | TBA | 28 | 13 | 2 | 0 | 36 | 4.26 | 1.24 | 0 | 2 |
| Anthony Banda | TBA | 25 | 12 | 2 | 0 | 23 | 4.42 | 1.38 | 1 | 0 |

| Player Name | Team | IP | ER | W | S | K | ERA | WHIP | QS | HLD |
|---|---|---|---|---|---|---|---|---|---|---|
| Mike Minor | TEX | 185 | 89 | 12 | 0 | 173 | 4.35 | 1.29 | 15 | 0 |
| Lance Lynn | TEX | 183 | 84 | 12 | 0 | 198 | 4.12 | 1.27 | 17 | 0 |
| Corey Kluber | TEX | 178 | 82 | 12 | 0 | 185 | 4.12 | 1.22 | 16 | 0 |
| Kyle Gibson | TEX | 172 | 88 | 10 | 0 | 159 | 4.57 | 1.39 | 13 | 0 |
| Jordan Lyles | TEX | 129 | 71 | 7 | 0 | 117 | 4.96 | 1.43 | 9 | 0 |
| Jesse Chavez | TEX | 73 | 37 | 3 | 2 | 67 | 4.58 | 1.35 | 0 | 10 |
| Rafael Montero | TEX | 66 | 27 | 3 | 5 | 72 | 3.66 | 1.23 | 0 | 12 |
| Jose Leclerc | TEX | 64 | 26 | 3 | 24 | 90 | 3.61 | 1.29 | 0 | 2 |
| Brett Martin | TEX | 59 | 28 | 2 | 1 | 58 | 4.25 | 1.34 | 0 | 9 |
| Kolby Allard | TEX | 51 | 28 | 3 | 0 | 40 | 5.00 | 1.47 | 3 | 0 |
| Joely Rodriguez | TEX | 49 | 25 | 2 | 1 | 44 | 4.56 | 1.48 | 0 | 4 |
| Shawn Kelley | TEX | 47 | 24 | 3 | 2 | 46 | 4.67 | 1.27 | 0 | 4 |
| Luke Farrell | TEX | 42 | 24 | 2 | 0 | 43 | 5.12 | 1.45 | 0 | 1 |
| Ariel Jurado | TEX | 41 | 23 | 2 | 0 | 26 | 5.11 | 1.49 | 3 | 0 |
| Nick Goody | TEX | 38 | 20 | 2 | 0 | 43 | 4.67 | 1.41 | 0 | 4 |
| Shelby Miller | TEX | 34 | 21 | 1 | 0 | 27 | 5.54 | 1.55 | 2 | 0 |
| Brock Burke | TEX | 30 | 18 | 2 | 0 | 24 | 5.36 | 1.42 | 2 | 0 |
| Taylor Hearn | TEX | 30 | 25 | 1 | 0 | 26 | 7.73 | 2.02 | 0 | 1 |
| Taylor Guerrieri | TEX | 26 | 15 | 0 | 0 | 25 | 5.16 | 1.43 | 0 | 0 |
| Ian Gibaut | TEX | 26 | 14 | 1 | 0 | 28 | 5.08 | 1.90 | 0 | 1 |
| Luis Garcia | TEX | 24 | 13 | 1 | 3 | 23 | 4.89 | 1.44 | 0 | 4 |
| Yohander Mendez | TEX | 22 | 12 | 1 | 0 | 22 | 4.77 | 1.50 | 0 | 0 |
| Joe Palumbo | TEX | 21 | 13 | 1 | 0 | 24 | 5.70 | 1.36 | 1 | 0 |

| Player Name | Team | IP | ER | W | S | K | ERA | WHIP | QS | HLD |
|---|---|---|---|---|---|---|---|---|---|---|
| Hyun-Jin Ryu | TOR | 165 | 71 | 11 | 0 | 147 | 3.88 | 1.22 | 16 | 0 |
| Tanner Roark | TOR | 159 | 88 | 8 | 0 | 138 | 4.96 | 1.39 | 11 | 0 |
| Chase Anderson | TOR | 134 | 72 | 7 | 0 | 115 | 4.84 | 1.36 | 9 | 0 |
| Trent Thornton | TOR | 121 | 64 | 6 | 0 | 112 | 4.75 | 1.33 | 8 | 1 |
| Matt Shoemaker | TOR | 119 | 60 | 8 | 0 | 106 | 4.55 | 1.33 | 9 | 0 |
| Shun Yamaguchi | TOR | 95 | 45 | 5 | 0 | 87 | 4.24 | 1.39 | 7 | 2 |
| Ryan Borucki | TOR | 77 | 42 | 4 | 0 | 61 | 4.95 | 1.45 | 7 | 2 |
| Sam Gaviglio | TOR | 76 | 39 | 3 | 0 | 67 | 4.59 | 1.29 | 0 | 8 |
| Wilmer Font | TOR | 65 | 31 | 3 | 0 | 71 | 4.33 | 1.25 | 0 | 6 |
| Jacob Waguespack | TOR | 65 | 33 | 4 | 0 | 55 | 4.64 | 1.42 | 3 | 1 |
| Ken Giles | TOR | 61 | 22 | 2 | 30 | 82 | 3.20 | 1.13 | 0 | 1 |
| Nate Pearson | TOR | 59 | 25 | 4 | 0 | 58 | 3.88 | 1.18 | 4 | 0 |
| Clay Buchholz | TOR | 59 | 33 | 3 | 0 | 43 | 4.99 | 1.41 | 5 | 0 |
| Anthony Bass | TOR | 58 | 26 | 2 | 2 | 53 | 4.02 | 1.30 | 0 | 9 |
| Thomas Pannone | TOR | 57 | 31 | 3 | 0 | 54 | 4.87 | 1.32 | 0 | 2 |
| Derek Law | TOR | 51 | 26 | 2 | 1 | 52 | 4.55 | 1.47 | 0 | 8 |
| Jordan Romano | TOR | 46 | 27 | 2 | 0 | 51 | 5.24 | 1.37 | 0 | 10 |
| Sean Reid-Foley | TOR | 39 | 19 | 2 | 0 | 41 | 4.49 | 1.47 | 0 | 0 |
| Anthony Kay | TOR | 38 | 22 | 2 | 0 | 34 | 5.16 | 1.49 | 3 | 0 |
| Clayton Richard | TOR | 38 | 20 | 2 | 0 | 25 | 4.69 | 1.48 | 3 | 0 |
| T.J. Zeuch | TOR | 27 | 16 | 1 | 0 | 18 | 5.24 | 1.56 | 1 | 1 |
| Buddy Boshers | TOR | 26 | 12 | 1 | 1 | 32 | 4.24 | 1.44 | 0 | 5 |
| Brock Stewart | TOR | 26 | 23 | 2 | 0 | 19 | 7.98 | 2.16 | 0 | 1 |

| Player Name | Team | IP | ER | W | S | K | ERA | WHIP | QS | HLD |
|-------------|------|-----|-----|-----|-----|-----|------|------|-----|-----|
| Max Scherzer | WAS | 197 | 69 | 14 | 0 | 263 | 3.13 | 1.02 | 20 | 0 |
| Stephen Strasburg | WAS | 193 | 74 | 15 | 0 | 225 | 3.44 | 1.15 | 20 | 0 |
| Patrick Corbin | WAS | 192 | 75 | 13 | 0 | 220 | 3.52 | 1.23 | 19 | 0 |
| Anibal Sanchez | WAS | 154 | 76 | 9 | 0 | 135 | 4.47 | 1.38 | 13 | 0 |
| Joe Ross | WAS | 95 | 50 | 5 | 0 | 78 | 4.75 | 1.43 | 6 | 0 |
| Austin Voth | WAS | 63 | 30 | 4 | 0 | 60 | 4.25 | 1.32 | 4 | 0 |
| Jeremy Hellickson | WAS | 63 | 38 | 3 | 0 | 44 | 5.41 | 1.45 | 3 | 0 |
| Dan Hudson | WAS | 62 | 27 | 4 | 9 | 63 | 3.85 | 1.31 | 0 | 10 |
| Will Harris | WAS | 58 | 20 | 3 | 3 | 62 | 3.15 | 1.16 | 0 | 20 |
| Sean Doolittle | WAS | 58 | 25 | 3 | 26 | 65 | 3.86 | 1.13 | 0 | 3 |
| Tanner Rainey | WAS | 57 | 27 | 3 | 1 | 78 | 4.22 | 1.44 | 0 | 11 |
| Roenis Elias | WAS | 53 | 24 | 3 | 1 | 48 | 4.00 | 1.31 | 0 | 7 |
| Wander Suero | WAS | 52 | 24 | 3 | 0 | 55 | 4.16 | 1.29 | 0 | 9 |
| Erick Fedde | WAS | 42 | 22 | 2 | 0 | 30 | 4.80 | 1.50 | 1 | 1 |
| Hunter Strickland | WAS | 38 | 20 | 2 | 0 | 33 | 4.79 | 1.40 | 0 | 6 |
| Fernando Rodney | WAS | 30 | 15 | 1 | 1 | 31 | 4.47 | 1.46 | 0 | 5 |
| Kyle McGowin | WAS | 23 | 13 | 1 | 0 | 22 | 4.89 | 1.35 | 1 | 1 |
| Aaron Barrett | WAS | 22 | 12 | 1 | 0 | 20 | 4.98 | 1.47 | 0 | 1 |
| Tony Sipp | WAS | 18 | 9 | 1 | 0 | 18 | 4.58 | 1.39 | 0 | 3 |
| Javy Guerra | WAS | 15 | 9 | 0 | 0 | 12 | 5.28 | 1.37 | 0 | 1 |
| Jonny Venters | WAS | 11 | 5 | 1 | 0 | 10 | 4.39 | 1.54 | 0 | 3 |
| Kyle Finnegan | WAS | 7 | 4 | 0 | 0 | 8 | 4.42 | 1.40 | 0 | 0 |
| James Bourque | WAS | 6 | 3 | 0 | 0 | 6 | 4.58 | 1.56 | 0 | 0 |

## ATC 10-Team 1 Catcher League Auction Values
## (Hitters)

| Player Name | Team | Pos | $ | Player Name | Team | Pos | $ | Player Name | Team | Pos | $ |
|---|---|---|---|---|---|---|---|---|---|---|---|
| Christian Yelich | MIL | OF | 39 | Starling Marte | PIT | OF | 21 | Tim Anderson | CHW | SS | 15 |
| Mike Trout | LAA | OF | 39 | Ozzie Albies | ATL | 2B | 21 | Marcus Semien | OAK | SS | 15 |
| Ronald Acuna | ATL | OF | 36 | Charlie Blackmon | COL | OF | 21 | Adalberto Mondesi | KC | SS | 15 |
| Mookie Betts | BOS | OF | 36 | Anthony Rizzo | CHC | 1B | 20 | Michael Conforto | NYM | OF | 14 |
| Cody Bellinger | LAD | 1B/OF | 35 | Nelson Cruz | MIN | Util | 19 | Joey Gallo | TEX | OF | 14 |
| Rafael Devers | BOS | 3B | 31 | Austin Meadows | TB | OF | 19 | Yuli Gurriel | HOU | 1B/3B | 14 |
| Francisco Lindor | CLE | SS | 31 | Gleyber Torres | NYY | 2B/SS | 19 | Carlos Santana | CLE | 1B | 14 |
| Juan Soto | WAS | OF | 31 | Paul Goldschmidt | STL | 1B | 19 | Yoan Moncada | CHW | 3B | 14 |
| Nolan Arenado | COL | 3B | 31 | Eddie Rosario | MIN | OF | 19 | Vladimir Guerrero Jr. | TOR | 3B | 14 |
| J.D. Martinez | BOS | OF | 29 | Eloy Jimenez | CHW | OF | 18 | Giancarlo Stanton | NYY | OF | 14 |
| Freddie Freeman | ATL | 1B | 29 | Manny Machado | SD | 3B/SS | 18 | Jorge Soler | KC | OF | 14 |
| Alex Bregman | HOU | 3B/SS | 28 | Kris Bryant | CHC | 3B/OF | 18 | Jeff McNeil | NYM | 2B/3B/OF | 13 |
| Jose Ramirez | CLE | 3B | 28 | Josh Donaldson | ATL | 3B | 18 | Victor Robles | WAS | OF | 13 |
| Trevor Story | COL | SS | 27 | Eugenio Suarez | CIN | 3B | 18 | Michael Brantley | HOU | OF | 13 |
| Trea Turner | WAS | SS | 27 | Jose Abreu | CHW | 1B | 17 | Whit Merrifield | KC | 2B/OF | 13 |
| Yordan Alvarez | HOU | Util | 25 | Josh Bell | PIT | 1B | 17 | Rhys Hoskins | PHI | 1B | 13 |
| Anthony Rendon | LAA | 3B | 24 | Ketel Marte | ARI | 2B/OF | 17 | Jacob Realmuto | PHI | C | 13 |
| Bryce Harper | PHI | OF | 24 | Keston Hiura | MIL | 2B | 17 | Trey Mancini | BAL | 1B/OF | 13 |
| George Springer | HOU | OF | 23 | Thomas Pham | SD | OF | 17 | Andrew Benintendi | BOS | OF | 12 |
| Pete Alonso | NYM | 1B | 22 | Marcell Ozuna | STL | OF | 16 | Ramon Laureano | OAK | OF | 12 |
| Xander Bogaerts | BOS | SS | 22 | Nick Castellanos | CHC | OF | 16 | Bryan Reynolds | PIT | OF | 12 |
| Javier Baez | CHC | SS | 22 | Matt Olson | OAK | 1B | 16 | Mike Moustakas | CIN | 2B/3B | 12 |
| Aaron Judge | NYY | OF | 22 | Matt Chapman | OAK | 3B | 16 | Jorge Polanco | MIN | SS | 12 |
| Fernando Tatis Jr. | SD | SS | 22 | Bo Bichette | TOR | SS | 15 | Yasiel Puig | CLE | OF | 12 |
| Jose Altuve | HOU | 2B | 21 | D.J. LeMahieu | NYY | 1B/2B/3B | 15 | Carlos Correa | HOU | SS | 11 |

## ATC 10-Team 1 Catcher League Auction Values
### (Hitters)

| Player Name | Team | Pos | $ | Player Name | Team | Pos | $ | Player Name | Team | Pos | $ |
|---|---|---|---|---|---|---|---|---|---|---|---|
| Kyle Schwarber | CHC | OF | 10 | Aristides Aquino | CIN | OF | 6 | Nomar Mazara | CHW | OF | 2 |
| Franmil Reyes | CLE | OF | 10 | Eric Hosmer | SD | 1B | 6 | Renato Nunez | BAL | 1B | 2 |
| Paul DeJong | STL | SS | 10 | Lorenzo Cain | MIL | OF | 5 | Avisail Garcia | MIL | OF | 2 |
| Eduardo Escobar | ARI | 2B/3B | 10 | Tommy Edman | STL | 2B/3B | 5 | Willson Contreras | CHC | C | 1 |
| Elvis Andrus | TEX | SS | 10 | Brian Anderson | MIA | 3B/OF | 5 | Cesar Hernandez | CLE | 2B | 1 |
| Max Muncy | LAD | 1B/2B/3B | 10 | Ryan Braun | MIL | OF | 5 | Byron Buxton | MIN | OF | 1 |
| Max Kepler | MIN | OF | 10 | Cavan Biggio | TOR | 2B | 5 | Kyle Tucker | HOU | OF | 1 |
| Jonathan Villar | MIA | 2B/SS | 10 | Yasmani Grandal | CHW | C/1B | 4 | Luis Arraez | MIN | 2B/OF | 1 |
| Khris Davis | OAK | Util | 9 | Daniel Santana | TEX | 1B/OF | 4 | Christian Walker | ARI | 1B | 1 |
| Miguel Sano | MIN | 3B | 9 | David Peralta | ARI | OF | 4 | Mark Canha | OAK | OF | 1 |
| Justin Turner | LAD | 3B | 9 | Joey Votto | CIN | 1B | 4 | Dansby Swanson | ATL | SS | 1 |
| Luis Robert | CHW | OF | 8 | Starlin Castro | WAS | 2B/3B | 4 | Kevin Pillar | SF | OF | 1 |
| Edwin Encarnacion | CHW | 1B | 8 | Rougned Odor | TEX | 2B | 4 | Willy Adames | TB | SS | 1 |
| Lourdes Gurriel | TOR | OF | 8 | Andrew McCutchen | PHI | OF | 4 | Jonathan Schoop | DET | 2B | 1 |
| Jean Segura | PHI | SS | 8 | Brandon Lowe | TB | 2B | 4 | Mitch Garver | MIN | C | 0 |
| Gary Sanchez | NYY | C | 8 | Justin Upton | LAA | OF | 4 | Daniel Murphy | COL | 1B | 0 |
| Mitch Haniger | SEA | OF | 7 | Randal Grichuk | TOR | OF | 3 | J.D. Davis | NYM | 3B/OF | 0 |
| Corey Seager | LAD | SS | 7 | Nick Senzel | CIN | OF | 3 | Shogo Akiyama | CIN | OF | 0 |
| Didi Gregorius | PHI | SS | 7 | Hunter Renfroe | TB | OF | 3 | Kyle Seager | SEA | 3B | 0 |
| Willie Calhoun | TEX | OF | 7 | Ryan McMahon | COL | 2B/3B | 3 | Mallex Smith | SEA | OF | 0 |
| Oscar Mercado | CLE | OF | 7 | Scott Kingery | PHI | 3B/OF | 3 | Hunter Dozier | KC | 3B/OF | 0 |
| Shohei Ohtani | LAA | Util | 7 | Shin-Soo Choo | TEX | OF | 3 | Kole Calhoun | ARI | OF | 0 |
| Adam Eaton | WAS | OF | 6 | Kevin Newman | PIT | 2B/SS | 3 | Salvador Perez | KC | C | 0 |
| Amed Rosario | NYM | SS | 6 | C.J. Cron | DET | 1B | 3 | Mike Yastrzemski | SF | OF | 0 |
| David Dahl | COL | OF | 6 | Joc Pederson | LAD | 1B/OF | 2 | Nick Markakis | ATL | OF | -1 |

## ATC 10-Team 1 Catcher League Auction Values
### (Hitters)

| Player Name | Team | Pos | $ | Player Name | Team | Pos | $ |
|---|---|---|---|---|---|---|---|
| Miguel Andujar | NYY | 3B | -1 | Will Smith | LAD | C | -3 |
| Anthony Santander | BAL | OF | -1 | Mauricio Dubon | SF | 2B | -3 |
| Jason Heyward | CHC | OF | -1 | Teoscar Hernandez | TOR | OF | -3 |
| Andrelton Simmons | LAA | SS | -1 | A.J. Pollock | LAD | OF | -3 |
| Corey Dickerson | MIA | OF | -2 | Hanser Alberto | BAL | 2B/3B | -3 |
| Jackie Bradley | BOS | OF | -2 | Christian Vazquez | BOS | C | -4 |
| Jurickson Profar | SD | 2B | -2 | Michael Chavis | BOS | 1B/2B | -4 |
| Yandy Diaz | TB | 1B/3B | -2 | Adam Frazier | PIT | 2B | -4 |
| Luke Voit | NYY | 1B | -2 | Austin Riley | ATL | OF | -4 |
| Domingo Santana | SEA | OF | -2 | Yadier Molina | STL | C | -4 |
| Brett Gardner | NYY | OF | -2 | Colin Moran | PIT | 3B | -5 |
| Niko Goodrum | DET | 2B/SS/OF | -2 | Albert Pujols | LAA | 1B | -5 |
| Austin Hays | BAL | OF | -2 | Yoshitomo Tsutsugo | TB | OF | -5 |
| Jesse Winker | CIN | OF | -2 | Matt Carpenter | STL | 3B | -5 |
| Wilson Ramos | NYM | C | -2 | Asdrubal Cabrera | WAS | 2B/3B | -5 |
| Nick Ahmed | ARI | SS | -2 | Brandon Belt | SF | 1B | -5 |
| Alex Verdugo | LAD | OF | -2 | Freddy Galvis | CIN | 2B/SS | -5 |
| Kolten Wong | STL | 2B | -2 | David Fletcher | LAA | 2B/3B/SS/OF | -5 |
| Ji-Man Choi | TB | 1B | -3 | Victor Reyes | DET | OF | -5 |
| Evan Longoria | SF | 3B | -3 | Carson Kelly | ARI | C | -5 |
| Kevin Kiermaier | TB | OF | -3 | Justin Smoak | MIL | 1B | -6 |
| Giovanny Urshela | NYY | 3B | -3 | Miguel Cabrera | DET | 1B | -6 |
| Gavin Lux | LAD | 2B | -3 | | | | |
| Nick Solak | TEX | Util | -3 | | | | |
| Robinson Cano | NYM | 2B | -3 | | | | |

# ATC 10-Team 1 Catcher League Auction Values
## (Pitchers)

| Player Name | Team | $ | Player Name | Team | $ | Player Name | Team | $ | Player Name | Team | $ |
|---|---|---|---|---|---|---|---|---|---|---|---|
| Jacob deGrom | NYN | 34 | Taylor Rogers | MIN | 12 | Archie Bradley | ARI | 5 | Jesus Luzardo | OAK | 2 |
| Gerrit Cole | NYA | 33 | James Paxton | NYA | 11 | Max Fried | ATL | 5 | Frankie Montas | OAK | 2 |
| Justin Verlander | HOU | 32 | Luis Severino | NYA | 11 | Lucas Giolito | CHA | 5 | Zac Gallen | ARI | 2 |
| Max Scherzer | WAS | 31 | Emilio Pagan | TBA | 11 | Sonny Gray | CIN | 5 | Julio Urias | LAN | 2 |
| Walker Buehler | LAN | 25 | Brad Hand | CLE | 10 | Hyun-Jin Ryu | TOR | 5 | Scott Oberg | COL | 2 |
| Chris Sale | BOS | 24 | Ken Giles | TOR | 10 | Craig Kimbrel | CHN | 5 | Will Harris | WAS | 2 |
| Jack Flaherty | STL | 21 | Hector Neris | PHI | 10 | Ryan Pressly | HOU | 5 | Ross Stripling | LAN | 2 |
| Josh Hader | MIL | 20 | Kenley Jansen | LAN | 10 | Jose Leclerc | TEX | 4 | Matt Boyd | DET | 1 |
| Mike Clevinger | CLE | 20 | Aaron Nola | PHI | 10 | Corey Kluber | TEX | 4 | German Marquez | COL | 1 |
| Stephen Strasburg | WAS | 20 | Carlos Carrasco | CLE | 9 | Zack Wheeler | PHI | 4 | Brendan McKay | TBA | 1 |
| Shane Bieber | CLE | 18 | Brandon Workman | BOS | 9 | Alex Colome | CHA | 4 | Drew Pomeranz | SDN | 1 |
| Charlie Morton | TBA | 16 | Noah Syndergaard | NYN | 9 | Diego Castillo | TBA | 4 | Matt Barnes | BOS | 1 |
| Blake Snell | TBA | 16 | Brandon Woodruff | MIL | 9 | Joe Jimenez | DET | 4 | Andrew Heaney | LAA | 1 |
| Kirby Yates | SDN | 16 | Nick Anderson | TBA | 8 | Ian Kennedy | KCA | 3 | Madison Bumgarner | ARI | 1 |
| Clayton Kershaw | LAN | 16 | Trevor Bauer | CIN | 7 | Jose Berrios | MIN | 3 | Mark Melancon | ATL | 1 |
| Chris Paddack | SDN | 15 | Keone Kela | PIT | 7 | Eduardo Rodriguez | BOS | 3 | Andres Munoz | SDN | 1 |
| Luis Castillo | CIN | 14 | Raisel Iglesias | CIN | 7 | Chad Green | NYA | 3 | Mychal Givens | BAL | 1 |
| Roberto Osuna | HOU | 14 | Dinelson Lamet | SDN | 7 | Shohei Ohtani | LAA | 3 | Josh James | HOU | 1 |
| Yu Darvish | CHN | 14 | Will Smith | ATL | 7 | Kenta Maeda | LAN | 3 | Ryne Stanek | MIA | 0 |
| Aroldis Chapman | NYA | 13 | Carlos Martinez | STL | 6 | Jose Urquidy | HOU | 3 | Sean Manaea | OAK | 0 |
| Tyler Glasnow | TBA | 13 | Giovanny Gallegos | STL | 6 | David Price | BOS | 2 | Chris Martin | ATL | 0 |
| Liam Hendriks | OAK | 13 | Seth Lugo | NYN | 6 | Dellin Betances | NYN | 2 | Tyler Duffey | MIN | 0 |
| Patrick Corbin | WAS | 12 | Mike Soroka | ATL | 6 | Lance Lynn | TEX | 2 | Dustin May | LAN | 0 |
| Zack Greinke | HOU | 12 | Sean Doolittle | WAS | 6 | Kyle Hendricks | CHN | 2 | Shun Yamaguchi | TOR | 0 |
| Edwin Diaz | NYN | 12 | Hansel Robles | LAA | 5 | Miles Mikolas | STL | 2 | Kwang-Hyun Kim | STL | 0 |

## ATC 10-Team 1 Catcher League Auction Values
### (Pitchers)

| Player Name | Team | $ | Player Name | Team | $ | Player Name | Team | $ | Player Name | Team | $ |
|---|---|---|---|---|---|---|---|---|---|---|---|
| Nate Pearson | TOR | 0 | Kevin Ginkel | ARI | 0 | Marcus Stroman | NYN | -2 | Nick Wittgren | CLE | -3 |
| Brandon Bailey | BAL | 0 | Emmanuel Clase | CLE | 0 | Alex Wood | LAN | -2 | Chris Bassitt | OAK | -4 |
| Casey Mize | DET | 0 | Ryan Yarbrough | TBA | 0 | Luke Jackson | ATL | -2 | James Karinchak | CLE | -4 |
| Matt Manning | DET | 0 | Lance McCullers | HOU | 0 | John Brebbia | STL | -2 | Michael Pineda | MIN | -4 |
| Sterling Sharp | MIA | 0 | Yonny Chirinos | TBA | 0 | Adam Ottavino | NYA | -2 | Collin McHugh | HOU | -4 |
| Sixto Sanchez | MIA | 0 | Joe Musgrove | PIT | 0 | Seranthony Dominguez | PHI | -2 | Andrew Chafin | ARI | -4 |
| MacKenzie Gore | SDN | 0 | Thomas Kahnle | NYA | 0 | Joe Kelly | LAN | -2 | Bradley Peacock | HOU | -4 |
| Luis Patino | SDN | 0 | Colin Poche | TBA | 0 | A.J. Puk | OAK | -2 | Josh Taylor | BOS | -4 |
| Rony Garcia | DET | 0 | Craig Stammen | SDN | -1 | Brent Suter | MIL | -2 | Joey Lucchesi | SDN | -4 |
| Michael Rucker | BAL | 0 | Rafael Montero | TEX | -1 | Andrew Miller | STL | -2 | Cole Hamels | ATL | -4 |
| Austin Adams | SEA | 0 | Matt Magill | SEA | -1 | Freddy Peralta | MIL | -2 | Joe Smith | HOU | -4 |
| Trevor Megill | CHN | 0 | Ty Buttrey | LAA | -1 | Michael Lorenzen | CIN | -2 | Steven Matz | NYN | -4 |
| Yohan Ramirez | SEA | 0 | Zack Britton | NYA | -1 | Pedro Baez | LAN | -3 | Cam Bedrosian | LAA | -4 |
| Stephen Woods | KCA | 0 | Justin Wilson | NYN | -1 | Shane Greene | ATL | -3 | Kevin Gausman | SFN | -4 |
| Dany Jimenez | SFN | 0 | Jake Odorizzi | MIN | -1 | Oliver Drake | TBA | -3 | Jose Alvarado | TBA | -4 |
| J.P. Feyereisen | MIL | 0 | Corey Knebel | MIL | -1 | Michael Feliz | PIT | -3 | Mitch Keller | PIT | -4 |
| Bruce Zimmermann | BAL | 0 | Trevor May | MIN | -1 | Joakim Soria | OAK | -3 | Brad Wieck | CHN | -4 |
| Spencer Howard | PHI | 0 | Robert Stephenson | CIN | -1 | Anthony DeSclafani | CIN | -3 | Jose Quintana | CHN | -4 |
| Garrett Cleavinger | PHI | 0 | Luke Weaver | ARI | -1 | Mike Minor | TEX | -3 | Jon Gray | COL | -4 |
| Deivi Garcia | NYA | 0 | Matt Strahm | SDN | -1 | Adam Kolarek | LAN | -3 | Rowan Wick | CHN | -4 |
| Ashton Goudeau | COL | 0 | Yusmeiro Petit | OAK | -1 | Andrew Kittredge | TBA | -3 | David Hale | NYA | -4 |
| Kyle Finnegan | WAS | 0 | Framber Valdez | HOU | -2 | Rich Hill | MIN | -3 | Masahiro Tanaka | NYA | -4 |
| Logan Gilbert | SEA | 0 | Tony Watson | SFN | -2 | Richard Rodriguez | PIT | -3 | Pablo Lopez | MIA | -4 |
| Robbie Ray | ARI | 0 | Aaron Bummer | CHA | -2 | Griffin Canning | LAA | -3 | Amir Garrett | CIN | -4 |
| Blake Treinen | LAN | 0 | Dan Hudson | WAS | -2 | Keynan Middleton | LAA | -3 | Jose Castillo | SDN | |

455

# ATC 12-Team 1 Catcher League Auction Values
## (Hitters)

| Player Name | Team | Pos | $ | Player Name | Team | Pos | $ | Player Name | Team | Pos | $ |
|---|---|---|---|---|---|---|---|---|---|---|---|
| Christian Yelich | MIL | OF | 40 | Aaron Judge | NYY | OF | 23 | Matt Chapman | OAK | 3B | 17 |
| Mike Trout | LAA | OF | 39 | Ozzie Albies | ATL | 2B | 22 | D.J. LeMahieu | NYY | 1B/2B/3B | 17 |
| Ronald Acuna | ATL | OF | 37 | Charlie Blackmon | COL | OF | 22 | Marcus Semien | OAK | SS | 16 |
| Mookie Betts | BOS | OF | 36 | Anthony Rizzo | CHC | 1B | 21 | Michael Conforto | NYM | OF | 16 |
| Cody Bellinger | LAD | 1B/OF | 35 | Austin Meadows | TB | OF | 21 | Joey Gallo | TEX | OF | 16 |
| Francisco Lindor | CLE | SS | 32 | Gleyber Torres | NYY | 2B/SS | 20 | Victor Robles | WAS | OF | 16 |
| Rafael Devers | BOS | 3B | 32 | Nelson Cruz | MIN | Util | 20 | Yuli Gurriel | HOU | 1B/3B | 16 |
| Juan Soto | WAS | OF | 31 | Eddie Rosario | MIN | OF | 20 | Yoan Moncada | CHW | 3B | 16 |
| Nolan Arenado | COL | 3B | 31 | Paul Goldschmidt | STL | 1B | 20 | Giancarlo Stanton | NYY | OF | 16 |
| J.D. Martinez | BOS | OF | 29 | Eloy Jimenez | CHW | OF | 20 | Vladimir Guerrero Jr. | TOR | 3B | 16 |
| Freddie Freeman | ATL | 1B | 29 | Manny Machado | SD | 3B/SS | 19 | Carlos Santana | CLE | 1B | 15 |
| Jose Ramirez | CLE | 3B | 29 | Kris Bryant | CHC | 3B/OF | 19 | Whit Merrifield | KC | 2B/OF | 15 |
| Alex Bregman | HOU | 3B/SS | 29 | Josh Donaldson | ATL | 3B | 19 | Jorge Soler | KC | OF | 15 |
| Trea Turner | WAS | SS | 28 | Eugenio Suarez | CIN | 3B | 19 | Jeff McNeil | NYM | 2B/3B/OF | 15 |
| Trevor Story | COL | SS | 28 | Jose Abreu | CHW | 1B | 19 | Michael Brantley | HOU | OF | 15 |
| Yordan Alvarez | HOU | Util | 26 | Ketel Marte | ARI | 2B/OF | 19 | Rhys Hoskins | PHI | 1B | 14 |
| Bryce Harper | PHI | OF | 25 | Josh Bell | PIT | 1B | 19 | Trey Mancini | BAL | 1B/OF | 14 |
| Anthony Rendon | LAA | 3B | 25 | Thomas Pham | SD | OF | 19 | Andrew Benintendi | BOS | OF | 14 |
| George Springer | HOU | OF | 24 | Keston Hiura | MIL | 2B | 18 | Ramon Laureano | OAK | OF | 14 |
| Javier Baez | CHC | SS | 23 | Marcell Ozuna | STL | OF | 18 | Yasiel Puig | CLE | OF | 14 |
| Fernando Tatis Jr. | SD | SS | 23 | Adalberto Mondesi | KC | SS | 18 | Bryan Reynolds | PIT | OF | 14 |
| Xander Bogaerts | BOS | SS | 23 | Nick Castellanos | CHC | OF | 17 | Mike Moustakas | CIN | 2B/3B | 14 |
| Starling Marte | PIT | OF | 23 | Matt Olson | OAK | 1B | 17 | Jorge Polanco | MIN | SS | 13 |
| Pete Alonso | NYM | 1B | 23 | Tim Anderson | CHW | SS | 17 | Carlos Correa | HOU | SS | 13 |
| Jose Altuve | HOU | 2B | 23 | Bo Bichette | TOR | SS | 17 | Jacob Realmuto | PHI | C | 13 |

## ATC 12-Team 1 Catcher League Auction Values
### (Hitters)

| Player Name | Team | Pos | $ | Player Name | Team | Pos | $ | Player Name | Team | Pos | $ |
|---|---|---|---|---|---|---|---|---|---|---|---|
| Elvis Andrus | TEX | SS | 13 | Gary Sanchez | NYY | C | 8 | Nomar Mazara | CHW | OF | 5 |
| Jonathan Villar | MIA | 2B/SS | 12 | Lorenzo Cain | MIL | OF | 8 | Avisail Garcia | MIL | OF | 5 |
| Kyle Schwarber | CHC | OF | 12 | Eric Hosmer | SD | 1B | 8 | Renato Nunez | BAL | 1B | 4 |
| Franmil Reyes | CLE | OF | 12 | Tommy Edman | STL | 2B/3B | 8 | Byron Buxton | MIN | OF | 4 |
| Paul DeJong | STL | SS | 12 | Ryan Braun | MIL | OF | 7 | Kyle Tucker | HOU | OF | 4 |
| Eduardo Escobar | ARI | 2B/3B | 12 | Cavan Biggio | TOR | 2B | 7 | Cesar Hernandez | CLE | 2B | 4 |
| Max Muncy | LAD | 1B/2B/3B | 12 | Brian Anderson | MIA | 3B/OF | 7 | Luis Arraez | MIN | 2B/OF | 4 |
| Max Kepler | MIN | OF | 12 | Daniel Santana | TEX | 1B/OF | 7 | Kevin Pillar | SF | OF | 4 |
| Khris Davis | OAK | Util | 11 | David Peralta | ARI | OF | 7 | Dansby Swanson | ATL | SS | 4 |
| Luis Robert | CHW | OF | 11 | Rougned Odor | TEX | 2B | 6 | Mallex Smith | SEA | OF | 4 |
| Miguel Sano | MIN | 3B | 11 | Starlin Castro | WAS | 2B/3B | 6 | Christian Walker | ARI | 1B | 4 |
| Justin Turner | LAD | 3B | 11 | Joey Votto | CIN | 1B | 6 | Mark Canha | OAK | OF | 3 |
| Edwin Encarnacion | CHW | 1B | 10 | Brandon Lowe | TB | 2B | 6 | Willy Adames | TB | SS | 3 |
| Jean Segura | PHI | SS | 10 | Andrew McCutchen | PHI | OF | 6 | Jonathan Schoop | DET | 2B | 3 |
| Lourdes Gurriel | TOR | OF | 10 | Nick Senzel | CIN | OF | 6 | Shogo Akiyama | CIN | OF | 3 |
| Mitch Haniger | SEA | OF | 9 | Justin Upton | LAA | OF | 6 | J.D. Davis | NYM | 3B/OF | 3 |
| Oscar Mercado | CLE | OF | 9 | Randal Grichuk | TOR | OF | 6 | Daniel Murphy | COL | 1B | 3 |
| Didi Gregorius | PHI | SS | 9 | Hunter Renfroe | TB | OF | 6 | Willson Contreras | CHC | C | 3 |
| Corey Seager | LAD | SS | 9 | Kevin Newman | PIT | 2B/SS | 6 | Kyle Seager | SEA | 3B | 2 |
| Willie Calhoun | TEX | OF | 9 | Scott Kingery | PHI | 3B/OF | 6 | Hunter Dozier | KC | 3B/OF | 2 |
| Shohei Ohtani | LAA | Util | 9 | Ryan McMahon | COL | 2B/3B | 5 | Kole Calhoun | ARI | OF | 2 |
| Amed Rosario | NYM | SS | 9 | Shin-Soo Choo | TEX | OF | 5 | Mike Yastrzemski | SF | OF | 2 |
| Adam Eaton | WAS | OF | 9 | Yasmani Grandal | CHW | C/1B | 5 | Nick Markakis | ATL | OF | 2 |
| Aristides Aquino | CIN | OF | 9 | C.J. Cron | DET | 1B | 5 | Anthony Santander | BAL | OF | 2 |
| David Dahl | COL | OF | 9 | Joc Pederson | LAD | 1B/OF | 5 | Miguel Andujar | NYY | 3B | 2 |

## ATC 12-Team 1 Catcher League Auction Values
### (Hitters)

| Player Name | Team | Pos | $ | Player Name | Team | Pos | $ | Player Name | Team | Pos | $ |
|---|---|---|---|---|---|---|---|---|---|---|---|
| Andrelton Simmons | LAA | SS | 2 | Teoscar Hernandez | TOR | OF | 0 | Stephen Piscotty | OAK | OF | -3 |
| Jason Heyward | CHC | OF | 2 | A.J. Pollock | LAD | OF | 0 | Mitch Moreland | BOS | 1B | -3 |
| Mitch Garver | MIN | C | 1 | Hanser Alberto | BAL | 2B/3B | 0 | Eric Thames | WAS | 1B | -3 |
| Corey Dickerson | MIA | OF | 1 | Michael Chavis | BOS | 1B/2B | -1 | Jesus Aguilar | MIA | 1B | -3 |
| Jackie Bradley | BOS | OF | 1 | Wilson Ramos | NYM | C | -1 | Harrison Bader | STL | OF | -3 |
| Jurickson Profar | SD | 2B | 1 | Adam Frazier | PIT | 2B | -1 | Dan Vogelbach | SEA | 1B | -3 |
| Niko Goodrum | DET | 2B/SS/OF | 1 | Austin Riley | ATL | OF | -1 | Garrett Hampson | COL | 2B/OF | -4 |
| Domingo Santana | SEA | OF | 1 | Colin Moran | PIT | 3B | -2 | Brandon Nimmo | NYM | OF | -4 |
| Austin Hays | BAL | OF | 1 | Yoshitomo Tsutsugo | TB | OF | -2 | Carson Kelly | ARI | C | -4 |
| Yandy Diaz | TB | 1B/3B | 1 | Albert Pujols | LAA | 1B | -2 | Maikel Franco | KC | 3B | -4 |
| Brett Gardner | NYY | OF | 1 | Matt Carpenter | STL | 3B | -2 | Howie Kendrick | WAS | 1B/2B | -4 |
| Salvador Perez | KC | C | 1 | Victor Reyes | DET | OF | -2 | Marwin Gonzalez | MIN | 1B/3B/OF | -4 |
| Luke Voit | NYY | 1B | 1 | Asdrubal Cabrera | WAS | 2B/3B | -2 | Jose Iglesias | BAL | SS | -4 |
| Alex Verdugo | LAD | OF | 1 | Will Smith | LAD | C | -2 | Dexter Fowler | STL | OF | -5 |
| Nick Ahmed | ARI | SS | 1 | Freddy Galvis | CIN | 2B/SS | -2 | Leury Garcia | CHW | 2B/OF | -5 |
| Jesse Winker | CIN | OF | 1 | Christian Vazquez | BOS | C | -2 | Jose Martinez | TB | OF | -5 |
| Kolten Wong | STL | 2B | 1 | David Fletcher | LAA | 2B/3B/SS/OF | -2 | Ian Happ | CHC | OF | -5 |
| Kevin Kiermaier | TB | OF | 1 | Brandon Belt | SF | 1B | -2 | Miguel Rojas | MIA | SS | -5 |
| Mauricio Dubon | SF | 2B | 0 | Dee Gordon | SEA | 2B | -2 | Wil Myers | SD | OF | -5 |
| Ji-Man Choi | TB | 1B | 0 | Miguel Cabrera | DET | 1B | -3 | Tyler O'Neill | STL | OF | -5 |
| Evan Longoria | SF | 3B | 0 | Justin Smoak | MIL | 1B | -3 | Alex Gordon | KC | OF | -5 |
| Gavin Lux | LAD | 2B | 0 | Yadier Molina | STL | C | -3 | Jon Berti | MIA | 3B/SS/OF | -5 |
| Nick Solak | TEX | Util | 0 | Nick Madrigal | CHW | 2B | -3 | Buster Posey | SF | C | -5 |
| Giovanny Urshela | NYY | 3B | 0 | Gregory Polanco | PIT | OF | -3 | Trent Grisham | SD | OF | -5 |
| Robinson Cano | NYM | 2B | 0 | Ender Inciarte | ATL | OF | -3 | Luis Urias | MIL | 2B/SS | -5 |

## ATC 12-Team 1 Catcher League Auction Values
## (Pitchers)

| Player Name | Team | $ | Player Name | Team | $ | Player Name | Team | $ | Player Name | Team | $ |
|---|---|---|---|---|---|---|---|---|---|---|---|
| Jacob deGrom | NYN | 37 | Liam Hendriks | OAK | 14 | Zack Wheeler | PHI | 7 | Ian Kennedy | KCA | 4 |
| Gerrit Cole | NYA | 36 | Aaron Nola | PHI | 13 | Will Smith | ATL | 7 | Joe Jimenez | DET | 4 |
| Justin Verlander | HOU | 35 | Carlos Carrasco | CLE | 13 | Jose Berrios | MIN | 7 | Andrew Heaney | LAA | 4 |
| Max Scherzer | WAS | 34 | Edwin Diaz | NYN | 12 | Eduardo Rodriguez | BOS | 7 | Brendan McKay | TBA | 4 |
| Walker Buehler | LAN | 28 | Taylor Rogers | MIN | 12 | Giovanny Gallegos | STL | 7 | Diego Castillo | TBA | 4 |
| Chris Sale | BOS | 27 | Noah Syndergaard | NYN | 12 | Seth Lugo | NYN | 7 | Sean Manaea | OAK | 4 |
| Jack Flaherty | STL | 24 | Brandon Woodruff | MIL | 12 | Sean Doolittle | WAS | 7 | Robbie Ray | ARI | 4 |
| Mike Clevinger | CLE | 23 | Emilio Pagan | TBA | 11 | Hansel Robles | LAA | 6 | Chad Green | NYA | 3 |
| Stephen Strasburg | WAS | 23 | Trevor Bauer | CIN | 11 | Archie Bradley | ARI | 6 | Joe Musgrove | PIT | 3 |
| Shane Bieber | CLE | 21 | Brad Hand | CLE | 11 | Lance Lynn | TEX | 6 | Jesus Luzardo | OAK | 3 |
| Josh Hader | MIL | 20 | Hector Neris | PHI | 11 | Miles Mikolas | STL | 6 | Lance McCullers | HOU | 3 |
| Charlie Morton | TBA | 19 | Kenley Jansen | LAN | 11 | David Price | BOS | 6 | Julio Urias | LAN | 3 |
| Blake Snell | TBA | 19 | Ken Giles | TOR | 11 | Kenta Maeda | LAN | 6 | Yonny Chirinos | TBA | 3 |
| Clayton Kershaw | LAN | 19 | Brandon Workman | BOS | 10 | Kyle Hendricks | CHN | 6 | Dellin Betances | NYN | 3 |
| Chris Paddack | SDN | 18 | Dinelson Lamet | SDN | 10 | Jose Urquidy | HOU | 6 | Scott Oberg | COL | 3 |
| Luis Castillo | CIN | 17 | Mike Soroka | ATL | 9 | Shohei Ohtani | LAA | 6 | Jake Odorizzi | MIN | 3 |
| Yu Darvish | CHN | 17 | Max Fried | ATL | 9 | Frankie Montas | OAK | 6 | Ross Stripling | LAN | 2 |
| Kirby Yates | SDN | 16 | Lucas Giolito | CHA | 8 | Zac Gallen | ARI | 5 | Will Harris | WAS | 2 |
| Patrick Corbin | WAS | 16 | Sonny Gray | CIN | 8 | Craig Kimbrel | CHN | 5 | Luke Weaver | ARI | 2 |
| Tyler Glasnow | TBA | 16 | Nick Anderson | TBA | 8 | Jose Leclerc | TEX | 5 | Marcus Stroman | NYN | 2 |
| Zack Greinke | HOU | 15 | Hyun-Jin Ryu | TOR | 8 | Ryan Pressly | HOU | 5 | Mark Melancon | ATL | 2 |
| Roberto Osuna | HOU | 14 | Corey Kluber | TEX | 8 | Matt Boyd | DET | 5 | Drew Pomeranz | SDN | 2 |
| James Paxton | NYA | 14 | Keone Kela | PIT | 8 | German Marquez | COL | 5 | Matt Barnes | BOS | 2 |
| Luis Severino | NYA | 14 | Raisel Iglesias | CIN | 8 | Madison Bumgarner | ARI | 5 | Mychal Givens | BAL | 2 |
| Aroldis Chapman | NYA | 14 | Carlos Martinez | STL | 7 | Alex Colome | CHA | 5 | Andres Munoz | SDN | 1 |

# ATC 12-Team 1 Catcher League Auction Values
## (Pitchers)

| Player Name | Team | $ | Player Name | Team | $ | Player Name | Team | $ | Player Name | Team | $ |
|---|---|---|---|---|---|---|---|---|---|---|---|
| Josh James | HOU | 1 | Sterling Sharp | MIA | 0 | Rich Hill | MIN | 0 | Joe Kelly | LAN | -1 |
| Ryne Stanek | MIA | 1 | Sixto Sanchez | MIA | 0 | Steven Matz | NYN | 0 | Mike Foltynewicz | ATL | -1 |
| Alex Wood | LAN | 1 | MacKenzie Gore | SDN | 0 | Zack Britton | NYA | 0 | Freddy Peralta | MIL | -1 |
| Dustin May | LAN | 1 | Luis Patino | SDN | 0 | Masahiro Tanaka | NYA | 0 | Caleb Smith | MIA | -1 |
| Ryan Yarbrough | TBA | 1 | Rony Garcia | DET | 0 | Kevin Gausman | SFN | 0 | Seranthony Dominguez | PHI | -1 |
| Tyler Duffey | MIN | 1 | Michael Rucker | BAL | 0 | Justin Wilson | NYN | 0 | Brent Suter | MIL | -1 |
| Chris Martin | ATL | 1 | Austin Adams | SEA | 0 | Robert Stephenson | CIN | 0 | Michael Lorenzen | CIN | -1 |
| Blake Treinen | LAN | 1 | Trevor Megill | CHN | 0 | Framber Valdez | HOU | 0 | Adrian Houser | MIL | -1 |
| Mike Minor | TEX | 1 | Yohan Ramirez | SEA | 0 | Mitch Keller | PIT | -1 | Tyler Mahle | CIN | -1 |
| Emmanuel Clase | CLE | 1 | Stephen Woods | KCA | 0 | Trevor May | MIN | -1 | Shaun Anderson | SFN | -1 |
| Anthony DeSclafani | CIN | 1 | Dany Jimenez | SFN | 0 | Corey Knebel | MIL | -1 | Andrew Miller | STL | -2 |
| Kevin Ginkel | ARI | 1 | J.P. Feyereisen | MIL | 0 | Pablo Lopez | MIA | -1 | Chris Archer | PIT | -2 |
| Thomas Kahnle | NYA | 0 | Bruce Zimmermann | BAL | 0 | Matt Strahm | SDN | -1 | Jose Urena | MIA | -2 |
| Matt Magill | SEA | 0 | Spencer Howard | PHI | 0 | Bradley Peacock | HOU | -1 | Tony Gonsolin | LAN | -2 |
| Craig Stammen | SDN | 0 | Garrett Cleavinger | PHI | 0 | Yusmeiro Petit | OAK | -1 | Shane Greene | ATL | -2 |
| Rafael Montero | TEX | 0 | Deivi Garcia | NYA | 0 | Tony Watson | SFN | -1 | Trevor Richards | TBA | -2 |
| Colin Poche | TBA | 0 | Ashton Goudeau | COL | 0 | Aaron Bummer | CHA | -1 | Pedro Baez | LAN | -2 |
| Griffin Canning | LAA | 0 | Kyle Finnegan | WAS | 0 | Dan Hudson | WAS | -1 | Domingo German | NYA | -2 |
| Ty Buttrey | LAA | 0 | Logan Gilbert | SEA | 0 | A.J. Puk | OAK | -1 | Michael Feliz | PIT | -2 |
| Shun Yamaguchi | TOR | 0 | Joey Lucchesi | SDN | 0 | Luke Jackson | ATL | -1 | Rick Porcello | NYN | -2 |
| Kwang-Hyun Kim | STL | 0 | Chris Bassitt | OAK | 0 | Garrett Richards | SDN | -1 | Oliver Drake | TBA | -2 |
| Nate Pearson | TOR | 0 | Michael Pineda | MIN | 0 | Adam Ottavino | NYA | -1 | J.A. Happ | NYA | -2 |
| Brandon Bailey | BAL | 0 | Jon Gray | COL | 0 | Aaron Civale | CLE | -1 | Joakim Soria | OAK | -2 |
| Casey Mize | DET | 0 | Cole Hamels | ATL | 0 | John Brebbia | STL | -1 | Richard Rodriguez | PIT | -2 |
| Matt Manning | DET | 0 | Jose Quintana | CHN | 0 | Dylan Bundy | LAA | -1 | Adam Kolarek | LAN | -2 |

## ATC 15-Team 2 Catcher League Auction Values
## (Hitters)

| Player Name | Team | Pos | $ | Player Name | Team | Pos | $ | Player Name | Team | Pos | $ |
|---|---|---|---|---|---|---|---|---|---|---|---|
| Christian Yelich | MIL | OF | 42 | Ozzie Albies | ATL | 2B | 24 | Bo Bichette | TOR | SS | 19 |
| Mike Trout | LAA | OF | 40 | Anthony Rizzo | CHC | 1B | 24 | Matt Chapman | OAK | 3B | 19 |
| Ronald Acuna | ATL | OF | 39 | Aaron Judge | NYY | OF | 24 | Nick Castellanos | CHC | OF | 19 |
| Mookie Betts | BOS | OF | 38 | Charlie Blackmon | COL | OF | 23 | Vladimir Guerrero Jr. | TOR | 3B | 19 |
| Cody Bellinger | LAD | 1B/OF | 36 | Austin Meadows | TB | OF | 23 | Yoan Moncada | CHW | 3B | 19 |
| Rafael Devers | BOS | 3B | 34 | Paul Goldschmidt | STL | 1B | 23 | Victor Robles | WAS | OF | 19 |
| Nolan Arenado | COL | 3B | 34 | Jacob Realmuto | PHI | C | 22 | D.J. LeMahieu | NYY | 1B/2B/3B | 18 |
| Francisco Lindor | CLE | SS | 34 | Eddie Rosario | MIN | OF | 22 | Carlos Santana | CLE | 1B | 18 |
| Juan Soto | WAS | OF | 33 | Nelson Cruz | MIN | Util | 22 | Marcus Semien | OAK | SS | 18 |
| Jose Ramirez | CLE | 3B | 33 | Gleyber Torres | NYY | 2B/SS | 22 | Whit Merrifield | KC | 2B/OF | 18 |
| Freddie Freeman | ATL | 1B | 32 | Jose Abreu | CHW | 1B | 22 | Michael Conforto | NYM | OF | 17 |
| J.D. Martinez | BOS | OF | 31 | Kris Bryant | CHC | 3B/OF | 22 | Michael Brantley | HOU | OF | 17 |
| Trea Turner | WAS | SS | 31 | Eugenio Suarez | CIN | 3B | 21 | Giancarlo Stanton | NYY | OF | 17 |
| Trevor Story | COL | SS | 30 | Josh Donaldson | ATL | 3B | 21 | Joey Gallo | TEX | OF | 17 |
| Alex Bregman | HOU | 3B/SS | 30 | Josh Bell | PIT | 1B | 21 | Jeff McNeil | NYM | 2B/3B/OF | 17 |
| Anthony Rendon | LAA | 3B | 28 | Eloy Jimenez | CHW | OF | 21 | Gary Sanchez | NYY | C | 17 |
| Yordan Alvarez | HOU | Util | 27 | Thomas Pham | SD | OF | 21 | Rhys Hoskins | PHI | 1B | 17 |
| Bryce Harper | PHI | OF | 26 | Adalberto Mondesi | KC | SS | 21 | Jorge Soler | KC | OF | 17 |
| Starling Marte | PIT | OF | 26 | Manny Machado | SD | 3B/SS | 21 | Andrew Benintendi | BOS | OF | 16 |
| George Springer | HOU | OF | 25 | Ketel Marte | ARI | 2B/OF | 21 | Ramon Laureano | OAK | OF | 16 |
| Fernando Tatis Jr. | SD | SS | 25 | Keston Hiura | MIL | 2B | 20 | Trey Mancini | BAL | 1B/OF | 16 |
| Pete Alonso | NYM | 1B | 25 | Marcell Ozuna | STL | OF | 20 | Yasiel Puig | CLE | OF | 16 |
| Javier Baez | CHC | SS | 25 | Matt Olson | OAK | 1B | 20 | Bryan Reynolds | PIT | OF | 16 |
| Xander Bogaerts | BOS | SS | 24 | Tim Anderson | CHW | SS | 19 | Jonathan Villar | MIA | 2B/SS | 15 |
| Jose Altuve | HOU | 2B | 24 | Yuli Gurriel | HOU | 1B/3B | 19 | Jorge Polanco | MIN | SS | 15 |

# ATC 15-Team 2 Catcher League Auction Values
## (Hitters)

| Player Name | Team | Pos | $ | Player Name | Team | Pos | $ | Player Name | Team | Pos | $ |
|---|---|---|---|---|---|---|---|---|---|---|---|
| Elvis Andrus | TEX | SS | 15 | David Dahl | COL | OF | 11 | Justin Upton | LAA | OF | 7 |
| Mike Moustakas | CIN | 2B/3B | 15 | Lorenzo Cain | MIL | OF | 11 | Renato Nunez | BAL | 1B | 7 |
| Carlos Correa | HOU | SS | 15 | Corey Seager | LAD | SS | 11 | Randal Grichuk | TOR | OF | 7 |
| Justin Turner | LAD | 3B | 14 | Didi Gregorius | PHI | SS | 11 | Shin-Soo Choo | TEX | OF | 7 |
| Yasmani Grandal | CHW | C/1B | 14 | Mitch Garver | MIN | C | 11 | Hunter Renfroe | TB | OF | 7 |
| Kyle Schwarber | CHC | OF | 14 | Aristides Aquino | CIN | OF | 10 | Mallex Smith | SEA | OF | 7 |
| Franmil Reyes | CLE | OF | 14 | Brian Anderson | MIA | 3B/OF | 10 | Ryan McMahon | COL | 2B/3B | 7 |
| Luis Robert | CHW | OF | 13 | Tommy Edman | STL | 2B/3B | 10 | Avisail Garcia | MIL | OF | 7 |
| Miguel Sano | MIN | 3B | 13 | Salvador Perez | KC | C | 10 | Yadier Molina | STL | C | 7 |
| Eduardo Escobar | ARI | 2B/3B | 13 | Ryan Braun | MIL | OF | 10 | Byron Buxton | MIN | OF | 7 |
| Paul DeJong | STL | SS | 13 | Daniel Santana | TEX | 1B/OF | 9 | Christian Walker | ARI | 1B | 7 |
| Max Kepler | MIN | OF | 13 | Joey Votto | CIN | 1B | 9 | Daniel Murphy | COL | 1B | 7 |
| Max Muncy | LAD | 1B/2B/3B | 13 | Scott Kingery | PHI | 3B/OF | 9 | Kyle Tucker | HOU | OF | 7 |
| Edwin Encarnacion | CHW | 1B | 13 | Wilson Ramos | NYM | C | 9 | J.D. Davis | NYM | 3B/OF | 6 |
| Jean Segura | PHI | SS | 12 | David Peralta | ARI | OF | 9 | Nomar Mazara | CHW | OF | 6 |
| Khris Davis | OAK | Util | 12 | Cavan Biggio | TOR | 2B | 9 | Joc Pederson | LAD | 1B/OF | 6 |
| Lourdes Gurriel | TOR | OF | 12 | Nick Senzel | CIN | OF | 9 | Luis Arraez | MIN | 2B/OF | 6 |
| Willson Contreras | CHC | C | 12 | Kevin Newman | PIT | 2B/SS | 8 | Kevin Pillar | SF | OF | 6 |
| Oscar Mercado | CLE | OF | 12 | C.J. Cron | DET | 1B | 8 | Cesar Hernandez | CLE | 2B | 6 |
| Shohei Ohtani | LAA | Util | 11 | Starlin Castro | WAS | 2B/3B | 8 | Carson Kelly | ARI | C | 5 |
| Amed Rosario | NYM | SS | 11 | Andrew McCutchen | PHI | OF | 8 | Miguel Andujar | NYY | 3B | 5 |
| Adam Eaton | WAS | OF | 11 | Brandon Lowe | TB | 2B | 8 | Hunter Dozier | KC | 3B/OF | 5 |
| Willie Calhoun | TEX | OF | 11 | Will Smith | LAD | C | 8 | Shogo Akiyama | CIN | OF | 5 |
| Mitch Haniger | SEA | OF | 11 | Rougned Odor | TEX | 2B | 8 | Dansby Swanson | ATL | SS | 5 |
| Eric Hosmer | SD | 1B | 11 | Christian Vazquez | BOS | C | 8 | Kyle Seager | SEA | 3B | 5 |

## ATC 15-Team 2 Catcher League Auction Values
### (Hitters)

| Player Name | Team | Pos | $ | Player Name | Team | Pos | $ | Player Name | Team | Pos | $ |
|---|---|---|---|---|---|---|---|---|---|---|---|
| Mark Canha | OAK | OF | 5 | Kolten Wong | STL | 2B | 3 | Dee Gordon | SEA | 2B | 1 |
| Willy Adames | TB | SS | 5 | Jackie Bradley | BOS | OF | 3 | Austin Riley | ATL | OF | 1 |
| Jonathan Schoop | DET | 2B | 5 | Brett Gardner | NYY | OF | 3 | Yoshitomo Tsutsugo | TB | OF | 0 |
| Nick Markakis | ATL | OF | 4 | Kevin Kiermaier | TB | OF | 3 | Justin Smoak | MIL | 1B | 0 |
| Buster Posey | SF | C | 4 | Travis D'Arnaud | ATL | C/1B | 3 | Mitch Moreland | BOS | 1B | 0 |
| Yandy Diaz | TB | 1B/3B | 4 | Jurickson Profar | SD | 2B | 3 | David Fletcher | LAA | 2B/3B/SS/OF | 0 |
| Luke Voit | NYY | 1B | 4 | Mauricio Dubon | SF | 2B | 3 | Eric Thames | WAS | 1B | 0 |
| Andrelton Simmons | LAA | SS | 4 | Gavin Lux | LAD | 2B | 2 | Nick Madrigal | CHW | 2B | 0 |
| Anthony Santander | BAL | OF | 4 | Nick Solak | TEX | Util | 2 | Asdrubal Cabrera | WAS | 2B/3B | 0 |
| Mike Yastrzemski | SF | OF | 4 | Nick Ahmed | ARI | SS | 2 | Jesus Aguilar | MIA | 1B | 0 |
| Kole Calhoun | ARI | OF | 4 | A.J. Pollock | LAD | OF | 2 | Ender Inciarte | ATL | OF | 0 |
| Corey Dickerson | MIA | OF | 4 | Sean Murphy | OAK | C | 2 | Freddy Galvis | CIN | 2B/SS | 0 |
| Alex Verdugo | LAD | OF | 4 | Hanser Alberto | BAL | 2B/3B | 2 | Dan Vogelbach | SEA | 1B | 0 |
| Kurt Suzuki | WAS | C | 4 | Colin Moran | PIT | 3B | 2 | Gregory Polanco | PIT | OF | -1 |
| Jason Heyward | CHC | OF | 4 | Robinson Cano | NYM | 2B | 2 | Garrett Hampson | COL | 2B/OF | -1 |
| Francisco Mejia | SD | C | 4 | Teoscar Hernandez | TOR | OF | 2 | Maikel Franco | KC | 3B | -1 |
| Ji-Man Choi | TB | 1B | 4 | Robinson Chirinos | TEX | C | 2 | Stephen Piscotty | OAK | OF | -1 |
| Giovanny Urshela | NYY | 3B | 3 | Albert Pujols | LAA | 1B | 2 | Harrison Bader | STL | OF | -1 |
| Evan Longoria | SF | 3B | 3 | Danny Jansen | TOR | C | 1 | Tom Murphy | SEA | C | -1 |
| Omar Narvaez | MIL | C | 3 | Matt Carpenter | STL | 3B | 1 | James McCann | CHW | C | -1 |
| Jorge Alfaro | MIA | C | 3 | Miguel Cabrera | DET | 1B | 1 | Roberto Perez | CLE | C | -1 |
| Domingo Santana | SEA | OF | 3 | Adam Frazier | PIT | 2B | 1 | Howie Kendrick | WAS | 1B/2B | -2 |
| Austin Hays | BAL | OF | 3 | Brandon Belt | SF | 1B | 1 | Rowdy Tellez | TOR | 1B | -2 |
| Jesse Winker | CIN | OF | 3 | Victor Reyes | DET | OF | 1 | Brandon Nimmo | NYM | OF | -2 |
| Niko Goodrum | DET | 2B/SS/OF | 3 | Michael Chavis | BOS | 1B/2B | 1 | Jose Martinez | TB | OF | -2 |

## ATC 15-Team 2 Catcher League Auction Values
### (Pitchers)

| Player Name | Team | $ | Player Name | Team | $ | Player Name | Team | $ | Player Name | Team | $ |
|---|---|---|---|---|---|---|---|---|---|---|---|
| Jacob deGrom | NYN | 40 | Liam Hendriks | OAK | 16 | Jose Berrios | MIN | 10 | Joe Jimenez | DET | 7 |
| Gerrit Cole | NYA | 39 | Aaron Nola | PHI | 16 | Eduardo Rodriguez | BOS | 10 | Ryan Pressly | HOU | 7 |
| Justin Verlander | HOU | 38 | Carlos Carrasco | CLE | 15 | Keone Kela | PIT | 10 | Andrew Heaney | LAA | 6 |
| Max Scherzer | WAS | 37 | Edwin Diaz | NYN | 15 | Will Smith | ATL | 9 | Sean Manaea | OAK | 6 |
| Walker Buehler | LAN | 31 | Taylor Rogers | MIN | 15 | Sean Doolittle | WAS | 9 | Robbie Ray | ARI | 6 |
| Chris Sale | BOS | 29 | Noah Syndergaard | NYN | 15 | Giovanny Gallegos | STL | 9 | Diego Castillo | TBA | 6 |
| Jack Flaherty | STL | 26 | Brandon Woodruff | MIL | 14 | Lance Lynn | TEX | 9 | Joe Musgrove | PIT | 6 |
| Stephen Strasburg | WAS | 26 | Emilio Pagan | TBA | 14 | Seth Lugo | NYN | 9 | Jesus Luzardo | OAK | 6 |
| Mike Clevinger | CLE | 26 | Trevor Bauer | CIN | 14 | Hansel Robles | LAA | 9 | Julio Urias | LAN | 5 |
| Shane Bieber | CLE | 24 | Kenley Jansen | LAN | 13 | Archie Bradley | ARI | 8 | Brendan McKay | TBA | 5 |
| Josh Hader | MIL | 23 | Brad Hand | CLE | 13 | Miles Mikolas | STL | 8 | Jake Odorizzi | MIN | 5 |
| Charlie Morton | TBA | 22 | Hector Neris | PHI | 13 | Kyle Hendricks | CHN | 8 | Chad Green | NYA | 5 |
| Blake Snell | TBA | 21 | Ken Giles | TOR | 13 | David Price | BOS | 8 | Lance McCullers | HOU | 5 |
| Clayton Kershaw | LAN | 21 | Brandon Workman | BOS | 13 | German Marquez | COL | 8 | Scott Oberg | COL | 5 |
| Chris Paddack | SDN | 21 | Dinelson Lamet | SDN | 12 | Matt Boyd | DET | 8 | Yonny Chirinos | TBA | 4 |
| Luis Castillo | CIN | 20 | Mike Soroka | ATL | 12 | Frankie Montas | OAK | 8 | Dellin Betances | NYN | 4 |
| Yu Darvish | CHN | 20 | Lucas Giolito | CHA | 11 | Jose Urquidy | HOU | 8 | Ross Stripling | LAN | 4 |
| Kirby Yates | SDN | 19 | Max Fried | ATL | 11 | Kenta Maeda | LAN | 7 | Marcus Stroman | NYN | 4 |
| Patrick Corbin | WAS | 19 | Sonny Gray | CIN | 11 | Craig Kimbrel | CHN | 7 | Mark Melancon | ATL | 4 |
| Zack Greinke | HOU | 18 | Nick Anderson | TBA | 10 | Jose Leclerc | TEX | 7 | Ryan Yarbrough | TBA | 4 |
| Tyler Glasnow | TBA | 18 | Corey Kluber | TEX | 10 | Zac Gallen | ARI | 7 | Luke Weaver | ARI | 4 |
| Roberto Osuna | HOU | 17 | Hyun-Jin Ryu | TOR | 10 | Madison Bumgarner | ARI | 7 | Mychal Givens | BAL | 3 |
| James Paxton | NYA | 17 | Raisel Iglesias | CIN | 10 | Shohei Ohtani | LAA | 7 | Will Harris | WAS | 3 |
| Luis Severino | NYA | 17 | Zack Wheeler | PHI | 10 | Alex Colome | CHA | 7 | Matt Barnes | BOS | 3 |
| Aroldis Chapman | NYA | 17 | Carlos Martinez | STL | 10 | Ian Kennedy | KCA | 7 | Mike Minor | TEX | 3 |

## ATC 15-Team 2 Catcher League Auction Values
### (Pitchers)

| Player Name | Team | $ | Player Name | Team | $ | Player Name | Team | $ | Player Name | Team | $ |
|---|---|---|---|---|---|---|---|---|---|---|---|
| Drew Pomeranz | SDN | 3 | Michael Pineda | MIN | 1 | Brent Suter | MIL | 0 | J.P. Feyereisen | MIL | 0 |
| Dustin May | LAN | 3 | Chris Bassitt | OAK | 1 | Luke Jackson | ATL | 0 | Bruce Zimmermann | BAL | 0 |
| Ryne Stanek | MIA | 3 | Kevin Gausman | SFN | 1 | Michael Lorenzen | CIN | 0 | Spencer Howard | PHI | 0 |
| Josh James | HOU | 3 | Framber Valdez | HOU | 1 | Joe Kelly | LAN | 0 | Garrett Cleavinger | PHI | 0 |
| Andres Munoz | SDN | 3 | A.J. Puk | OAK | 1 | Adam Ottavino | NYA | 0 | Deivi Garcia | NYA | 0 |
| Anthony DeSclafani | CIN | 3 | Mitch Keller | PIT | 1 | Adrian Houser | MIL | 0 | Ashton Goudeau | COL | 0 |
| Blake Treinen | LAN | 2 | Dylan Bundy | LAA | 1 | Bradley Peacock | HOU | 0 | Kyle Finnegan | WAS | 0 |
| Alex Wood | LAN | 2 | Pablo Lopez | MIA | 1 | John Brebbia | STL | 0 | Logan Gilbert | SEA | 0 |
| Tyler Duffey | MIN | 2 | Robert Stephenson | CIN | 1 | Shun Yamaguchi | TOR | 0 | Garrett Richards | SDN | 0 |
| Jon Gray | COL | 2 | Mike Foltynewicz | ATL | 1 | Kwang-Hyun Kim | STL | 0 | Andrew Miller | STL | 0 |
| Chris Martin | ATL | 2 | Yusmeiro Petit | OAK | 1 | Nate Pearson | TOR | 0 | Seranthony Dominguez | PHI | 0 |
| Emmanuel Clase | CLE | 2 | Caleb Smith | MIA | 1 | Brandon Bailey | BAL | 0 | Shane Greene | ATL | 0 |
| Joey Lucchesi | SDN | 2 | Zack Britton | NYA | 1 | Casey Mize | DET | 0 | Pedro Baez | LAN | 0 |
| Jose Quintana | CHN | 2 | Matt Strahm | SDN | 1 | Matt Manning | DET | 0 | Michael Feliz | PIT | 0 |
| Matt Magill | SEA | 2 | Justin Wilson | NYN | 1 | Sterling Sharp | MIA | 0 | Tyler Mahle | CIN | 0 |
| Masahiro Tanaka | NYA | 2 | Tony Watson | SFN | 1 | Sixto Sanchez | MIA | 0 | J.A. Happ | NYA | -1 |
| Kevin Ginkel | ARI | 2 | Trevor May | MIN | 1 | MacKenzie Gore | SDN | 0 | Jose Urena | MIA | -1 |
| Cole Hamels | ATL | 2 | Freddy Peralta | MIL | 1 | Luis Patino | SDN | 0 | Josh Lindblom | MIL | -1 |
| Craig Stammen | SDN | 2 | Dan Hudson | WAS | 1 | Rony Garcia | DET | 0 | Joakim Soria | OAK | -1 |
| Rafael Montero | TEX | 2 | Corey Knebel | MIL | 1 | Michael Rucker | BAL | 0 | Shaun Anderson | SFN | -1 |
| Griffin Canning | LAA | 2 | Chris Archer | PIT | 1 | Austin Adams | SEA | 0 | Richard Rodriguez | PIT | -1 |
| Steven Matz | NYN | 2 | Aaron Civale | CLE | 0 | Trevor Megill | CHN | 0 | Oliver Drake | TBA | -1 |
| Ty Buttrey | LAA | 2 | Rich Hill | MIN | 0 | Yohan Ramirez | SEA | 0 | Domingo German | NYA | -1 |
| Thomas Kahnle | NYA | 2 | Rick Porcello | NYN | 0 | Stephen Woods | KCA | 0 | Merrill Kelly | ARI | -1 |
| Colin Poche | TBA | 1 | Aaron Bummer | CHA | 0 | Dany Jimenez | SFN | 0 | Johnny Cueto | SFN | -1 |

# ATC 15-Team 2 Catcher League Auction Values
## (Pitchers)

| Player Name | Team | $ | Player Name | Team | $ | Player Name | Team | $ | Player Name | Team | $ |
|---|---|---|---|---|---|---|---|---|---|---|---|
| Keynan Middleton | LAA | -1 | Jose Alvarado | TBA | -2 | Roenis Elias | WAS | -3 | Reynaldo Lopez | CHA | -4 |
| Dallas Keuchel | CHA | -1 | Wilmer Font | TOR | -3 | Darren O'Day | ATL | -3 | Ryne Harper | MIN | -4 |
| Nick Wittgren | CLE | -1 | Jairo Diaz | COL | -3 | Jay Jackson | MIL | -3 | Daniel Poncedeleon | STL | -4 |
| Tony Gonsolin | LAN | -1 | Jose Alvarez | PHI | -3 | David Hale | NYA | -3 | Anibal Sanchez | WAS | -4 |
| Adam Kolarek | LAN | -1 | Samuel Tuivailala | SEA | -3 | Trevor Gott | SFN | -3 | Shawn Kelley | TEX | -4 |
| Collin McHugh | HOU | -1 | Bryse Wilson | ATL | -3 | Brandon Kintzler | CHN | -3 | Forrest Whitley | HOU | -4 |
| Trevor Richards | TBA | -1 | Jacob Diekman | OAK | -3 | Jalen Beeks | TBA | -3 | Grant Dayton | ATL | -4 |
| Andrew Kittredge | TBA | -2 | Felix Pena | LAA | -3 | Hunter Harvey | BAL | -3 | Tim Hill | KCA | -4 |
| Tyler Anderson | SFN | -2 | Oliver Perez | CLE | -3 | Zach Plesac | CLE | -3 | Lou Trivino | OAK | -4 |
| Andrew Chafin | ARI | -2 | Brent Honeywell | TBA | -3 | Elieser Hernandez | MIA | -3 | Scott Alexander | LAN | -4 |
| Josh Taylor | BOS | -2 | John Gant | STL | -3 | Anthony Bass | TOR | -3 | Yimi Garcia | MIA | -4 |
| James Karinchak | CLE | -2 | Tyler Rogers | SFN | -3 | Michael Kopech | CHA | -3 | Julian Merryweather | TOR | -4 |
| Cam Bedrosian | LAA | -2 | Lucas Sims | CIN | -3 | Chris Devenski | HOU | -3 | Peter Fairbanks | TBA | -4 |
| Amir Garrett | CIN | -2 | Wander Suero | WAS | -3 | Ryan Brasier | BOS | -3 | Michael Fiers | OAK | -4 |
| Carlos Estevez | COL | -2 | Caleb Ferguson | LAN | -3 | Alex Young | ARI | -3 | Jordan Yamamoto | MIA | -4 |
| Kyle Crick | PIT | -2 | Scott Barlow | KCA | -3 | Jordan Montgomery | NYA | -3 | Jameson Taillon | PIT | -4 |
| Rowan Wick | CHN | -2 | Ranger Suarez | PHI | -3 | Brusdar Graterol | MIN | -3 | Cody Reed | CIN | -4 |
| Marco Gonzales | SEA | -2 | Sergio Romo | MIN | -3 | Buck Farmer | DET | -3 | Dereck Rodriguez | SFN | -4 |
| Nathan Eovaldi | BOS | -2 | Pedro Strop | CHN | -3 | Jake Junis | KCA | -3 | Erik Swanson | SEA | -4 |
| Joe Smith | HOU | -2 | Jeff Samardzija | SFN | -3 | Arodys Vizcaino | SEA | -3 | Ray Black | MIL | -4 |
| Austin Voth | WAS | -2 | Jose Castillo | SDN | -3 | Nick Pivetta | PHI | -3 | Ian Anderson | ATL | -4 |
| Steven Cishek | CHA | -2 | Jonathan Loaisiga | NYA | -3 | Adam Wainwright | STL | -4 | Casey Sadler | LAN | -4 |
| Brad Wieck | CHN | -2 | Hector Rondon | ARI | -3 | Dan Altavilla | SEA | -4 | Alex Vesia | MIA | -4 |
| Noe Ramirez | LAA | -2 | Marcus Walden | BOS | -3 | Brandon Brennan | SEA | -4 | Carlos Rodon | CHA | -4 |
| Matt Shoemaker | TOR | -2 | Randy Dobnak | MIN | -3 | Ryan Helsley | STL | -4 | Jacob Webb | ATL | -4 |

# ATC 12-Team 2 Catcher AL Only League Auction Values
## (Hitters)

| Player Name | Team | Pos | $ | Player Name | Team | Pos | $ | Player Name | Team | Pos | $ |
|---|---|---|---|---|---|---|---|---|---|---|---|
| Mike Trout | LAA | OF | 38 | Yoan Moncada | CHW | 3B | 22 | Yasmani Grandal | CHW | C/1B | 17 |
| Mookie Betts | BOS | OF | 37 | Yuli Gurriel | HOU | 1B/3B | 22 | Khris Davis | OAK | Util | 17 |
| Francisco Lindor | CLE | SS | 34 | Elvis Andrus | TEX | SS | 21 | Daniel Santana | TEX | 1B/OF | 17 |
| Jose Ramirez | CLE | 3B | 33 | Michael Brantley | HOU | OF | 21 | Mitch Haniger | SEA | OF | 17 |
| Rafael Devers | BOS | 3B | 32 | Vladimir Guerrero Jr. | TOR | 3B | 21 | Willie Calhoun | TEX | OF | 16 |
| J.D. Martinez | BOS | OF | 31 | Ramon Laureano | OAK | OF | 21 | Miguel Sano | MIN | 3B | 16 |
| Alex Bregman | HOU | 3B/SS | 30 | Andrew Benintendi | BOS | OF | 21 | Edwin Encarnacion | CHW | 1B | 16 |
| Yordan Alvarez | HOU | Util | 28 | Yasiel Puig | CLE | OF | 21 | Cavan Biggio | TOR | 2B | 16 |
| Adalberto Mondesi | KC | SS | 28 | Matt Olson | OAK | 1B | 21 | Byron Buxton | MIN | OF | 15 |
| Anthony Rendon | LAA | 3B | 27 | Giancarlo Stanton | NYY | OF | 21 | Mitch Garver | MIN | C | 15 |
| Jose Altuve | HOU | 2B | 27 | Matt Chapman | OAK | 3B | 20 | Salvador Perez | KC | C | 15 |
| George Springer | HOU | OF | 27 | Joey Gallo | TEX | OF | 20 | Kyle Tucker | HOU | OF | 15 |
| Xander Bogaerts | BOS | SS | 27 | Jorge Soler | KC | OF | 20 | Brandon Lowe | TB | 2B | 15 |
| Austin Meadows | TB | OF | 26 | Trey Mancini | BAL | 1B/OF | 20 | Rougned Odor | TEX | 2B | 15 |
| Aaron Judge | NYY | OF | 25 | Carlos Santana | CLE | 1B | 20 | Shin-Soo Choo | TEX | OF | 14 |
| Tim Anderson | CHW | SS | 25 | Jorge Polanco | MIN | SS | 20 | Luis Arraez | MIN | 2B/OF | 14 |
| Gleyber Torres | NYY | 2B/SS | 24 | Luis Robert | CHW | OF | 20 | Cesar Hernandez | CLE | 2B | 14 |
| Eddie Rosario | MIN | OF | 24 | Carlos Correa | HOU | SS | 19 | Justin Upton | LAA | OF | 14 |
| Nelson Cruz | MIN | Util | 24 | Gary Sanchez | NYY | C | 19 | Randal Grichuk | TOR | OF | 14 |
| Bo Bichette | TOR | SS | 24 | Oscar Mercado | CLE | OF | 19 | Hunter Renfroe | TB | OF | 13 |
| Whit Merrifield | KC | 2B/OF | 24 | Franmil Reyes | CLE | OF | 18 | Christian Vazquez | BOS | C | 13 |
| Eloy Jimenez | CHW | OF | 24 | Shohei Ohtani | LAA | Util | 18 | C.J. Cron | DET | 1B | 13 |
| Jose Abreu | CHW | 1B | 23 | Lourdes Gurriel | TOR | OF | 18 | Nomar Mazara | CHW | OF | 13 |
| D.J. LeMahieu | NYY | 1B/2B/3B | 22 | Mallex Smith | SEA | OF | 17 | Andrelton Simmons | LAA | SS | 13 |
| Marcus Semien | OAK | SS | 22 | Max Kepler | MIN | OF | 17 | Willy Adames | TB | SS | 13 |

# ATC 12-Team 2 Catcher AL Only League Auction Values
## (Hitters)

| Player Name | Team | Pos | $ | Player Name | Team | Pos | $ | Player Name | Team | Pos | $ |
|---|---|---|---|---|---|---|---|---|---|---|---|
| Renato Nunez | BAL | 1B | 13 | Sean Murphy | OAK | C | 9 | Austin Romine | DET | C | 6 |
| Dee Gordon | SEA | 2B | 12 | Yoshitomo Tsutsugo | TB | OF | 9 | Willians Astudillo | MIN | C | 6 |
| Jonathan Schoop | DET | 2B | 12 | Miguel Cabrera | DET | 1B | 9 | Jose Peraza | BOS | 2B/SS/OF | 5 |
| Niko Goodrum | DET | 2B/SS/OF | 12 | Leury Garcia | CHW | 2B/OF | 9 | J.P. Crawford | SEA | SS | 5 |
| Mark Canha | OAK | OF | 12 | Danny Jansen | TOR | C | 9 | Nicky Lopez | KC | 2B/SS | 5 |
| Kevin Kiermaier | TB | OF | 12 | Albert Pujols | LAA | 1B | 9 | Joey Wendle | TB | 2B/3B | 5 |
| Anthony Santander | BAL | OF | 12 | Robinson Chirinos | TEX | C | 9 | Reese McGuire | TOR | C | 5 |
| Miguel Andujar | NYY | 3B | 12 | Jose Iglesias | BAL | SS | 8 | Mike Tauchman | NYY | OF | 5 |
| Austin Hays | BAL | OF | 12 | Stephen Piscotty | OAK | OF | 8 | Travis Shaw | TOR | 3B | 5 |
| Domingo Santana | SEA | OF | 12 | Jose Martinez | TB | OF | 8 | Tyler Naquin | CLE | OF | 5 |
| Hunter Dozier | KC | 3B/OF | 11 | Mitch Moreland | BOS | 1B | 8 | Evan White | SEA | 1B | 5 |
| Brett Gardner | NYY | OF | 11 | Marwin Gonzalez | MIN | 1B/3B/OF | 8 | Jason Castro | LAA | C | 5 |
| Hanser Alberto | BAL | 2B/3B | 11 | Maikel Franco | KC | 3B | 7 | Pedro Severino | BAL | C | 4 |
| Nick Solak | TEX | Util | 11 | James McCann | CHW | C | 7 | Chance Sisco | BAL | C | 4 |
| Jackie Bradley | BOS | OF | 11 | JaCoby Jones | DET | OF | 7 | Mike Zunino | TB | C | 4 |
| Kyle Seager | SEA | 3B | 11 | Josh Reddick | HOU | OF | 7 | Ronald Guzman | TEX | 1B | 4 |
| Victor Reyes | DET | OF | 11 | Alex Gordon | KC | OF | 7 | Nathaniel Lowe | TB | 1B | 4 |
| Yandy Diaz | TB | 1B/3B | 11 | Dan Vogelbach | SEA | 1B | 7 | Shed Long | SEA | 2B | 4 |
| Nick Madrigal | CHW | 2B | 11 | Tom Murphy | SEA | C | 7 | Brian Goodwin | LAA | OF | 4 |
| Luke Voit | NYY | 1B | 10 | Tommy La Stella | LAA | 2B/3B | 7 | Christin Stewart | DET | OF | 4 |
| Giovanny Urshela | NYY | 3B | 10 | Rowdy Tellez | TOR | 1B | 7 | Jordan Luplow | CLE | OF | 4 |
| Ji-Man Choi | TB | 1B | 10 | Roberto Perez | CLE | C | 7 | Jeimer Candelario | DET | 1B/3B | 4 |
| David Fletcher | LAA | 2B/3B/SS/OF | 10 | Jo Adell | LAA | OF | 6 | Jason Kipnis | CLE | 2B | 4 |
| Teoscar Hernandez | TOR | OF | 10 | Todd Frazier | TEX | 3B | 6 | Martin Maldonado | HOU | C | 3 |
| Michael Chavis | BOS | 1B/2B | 10 | Derek Fisher | TOR | OF | 6 | D.J. Stewart | BAL | OF | 3 |

# ATC 12-Team 2 Catcher AL Only League Auction Values
## (Hitters)

| Player Name | Team | Pos | $ | Player Name | Team | Pos | $ | Player Name | Team | Pos | $ |
|---|---|---|---|---|---|---|---|---|---|---|---|
| Kevan Smith | TB | C | 3 | Mike Brosseau | TB | 2B | 0 | Dustin Garneau | HOU | C | -2 |
| Travis Demeritte | DET | OF | 2 | Michael Perez | TB | C | 0 | Ehire Adrianza | MIN | 1B/3B/SS | -2 |
| Jake Bauers | CLE | 1B/OF | 2 | Brock Holt | BOS | 2B | 0 | John Hicks | DET | C/1B | -2 |
| Welington Castillo | TEX | C | 2 | Jake Fraley | SEA | OF | 0 | Bubba Starling | KC | OF | -3 |
| Myles Straw | HOU | SS | 2 | Grayson Greiner | DET | C | 0 | Harold Castro | DET | 2B/OF | -3 |
| Cameron Maybin | NYY | OF | 2 | Greg Allen | CLE | OF | 0 | Brandon Dixon | DET | 1B/OF | -3 |
| Austin Allen | OAK | C | 2 | Kyle Higashioka | NYY | C | 0 | Jordy Mercer | DET | SS | -3 |
| Kevin Plawecki | BOS | C | 2 | Ryan McBroom | KC | OF | 0 | Juan Centeno | BOS | C | -3 |
| Ryan O'Hearn | KC | 1B | 2 | Franklin Barreto | OAK | 2B | 0 | Sheldon Neuse | OAK | 2B | -3 |
| Rio Ruiz | BAL | 3B | 2 | Matt Duffy | TB | 3B | 0 | Richie Martin | BAL | SS | -3 |
| Delino DeShields | CLE | OF | 1 | Isiah Kiner-Falefa | TEX | C/3B | -1 | Meibrys Viloria | KC | C | -3 |
| Mike Ford | NYY | 1B | 1 | Max Stassi | LAA | C | -1 | Austin Wynns | BAL | C | -3 |
| Clint Frazier | NYY | OF | 1 | Alex Avila | MIN | C | -1 | Bobby Dalbec | BOS | 3B | -3 |
| Robbie Grossman | OAK | OF | 1 | Dwight Smith | BAL | OF | -1 | Chris Herrmann | TB | C | -3 |
| Kyle Lewis | SEA | OF | 1 | Mark Trumbo | BAL | Util | -1 | Scott Heineman | TEX | OF | -3 |
| Hunter Pence | TEX | OF | 1 | Cam Gallagher | KC | C | -1 | Jon Jay | CHW | OF | -3 |
| Chad Pinder | OAK | 2B/OF | 1 | Sandy Leon | CLE | C | -1 | Jake Cave | MIN | OF | -4 |
| Josh Phegley | OAK | C | 1 | Jose Trevino | TEX | C | -2 | Nick Dini | KC | C | -4 |
| Brett Phillips | KC | OF | 1 | Jake Rogers | DET | C | -2 | Jonah Heim | OAK | C | -4 |
| Dawel Lugo | DET | 3B | 1 | Eduardo Nunez | BOS | 2B | -2 | Jorge Mateo | OAK | SS | -4 |
| Yolmer Sanchez | CHW | 2B | 1 | Kendrys Morales | TOR | 1B | -2 | Anthony Bemboom | LAA | C | -4 |
| Austin Nola | SEA | 1B | 1 | Tim Beckham | SEA | SS | -2 | Eric Haase | DET | C | -4 |
| Willi Castro | DET | SS | 1 | Garrett Stubbs | HOU | C | -2 | Chris Davis | BAL | 1B | -4 |
| Brandon Drury | TOR | 3B/OF | 0 | Jeff Mathis | TEX | C | -2 | Cal Raleigh | SEA | C | -4 |
| Aledmys Diaz | HOU | 1B/2B | 0 | Nick Hundley | OAK | C | -2 | Randy Arozarena | TB | OF | -4 |

# ATC 12-Team 2 Catcher AL Only League Auction Values
## (Pitchers)

| Player Name | Team | $ | Player Name | Team | $ | Player Name | Team | $ | Player Name | Team | $ |
|---|---|---|---|---|---|---|---|---|---|---|---|
| Gerrit Cole | NYA | 39 | Lance Lynn | TEX | 13 | Mychal Givens | BAL | 7 | Nathan Eovaldi | BOS | 3 |
| Justin Verlander | HOU | 38 | Matt Boyd | DET | 13 | Dylan Bundy | LAA | 7 | Jake Junis | KCA | 3 |
| Chris Sale | BOS | 30 | David Price | BOS | 12 | Griffin Canning | LAA | 6 | Aaron Bummer | CHA | 3 |
| Mike Clevinger | CLE | 27 | Frankie Montas | OAK | 12 | Michael Pineda | MIN | 6 | Adam Ottavino | NYA | 3 |
| Shane Bieber | CLE | 26 | Nick Anderson | TBA | 12 | Chris Bassitt | OAK | 6 | Domingo German | NYA | 3 |
| Charlie Morton | TBA | 24 | Jose Urquidy | HOU | 12 | Matt Barnes | BOS | 6 | Matt Shoemaker | TOR | 3 |
| Blake Snell | TBA | 23 | Hansel Robles | LAA | 11 | Aaron Civale | CLE | 6 | Reynaldo Lopez | CHA | 3 |
| Zack Greinke | HOU | 21 | Sean Manaea | OAK | 11 | Josh James | HOU | 5 | Trevor Richards | TBA | 3 |
| Tyler Glasnow | TBA | 20 | Andrew Heaney | LAA | 11 | Matt Magill | SEA | 5 | Michael Fiers | OAK | 2 |
| James Paxton | NYA | 20 | Shohei Ohtani | LAA | 10 | Tyler Duffey | MIN | 5 | Zach Plesac | CLE | 2 |
| Luis Severino | NYA | 20 | Jose Leclerc | TEX | 10 | Emmanuel Clase | CLE | 5 | Joakim Soria | OAK | 2 |
| Roberto Osuna | HOU | 19 | Jake Odorizzi | MIN | 10 | Dallas Keuchel | CHA | 5 | Randy Dobnak | MIN | 2 |
| Carlos Carrasco | CLE | 18 | Alex Colome | CHA | 10 | J.A. Happ | NYA | 5 | Michael Kopech | CHA | 2 |
| Aroldis Chapman | NYA | 18 | Ian Kennedy | KCA | 10 | Rafael Montero | TEX | 5 | Oliver Drake | TBA | 2 |
| Liam Hendriks | OAK | 18 | Joe Jimenez | DET | 10 | Rich Hill | MIN | 5 | Nick Wittgren | CLE | 2 |
| Taylor Rogers | MIN | 17 | Brendan McKay | TBA | 9 | Ty Buttrey | LAA | 5 | Keynan Middleton | LAA | 2 |
| Emilio Pagan | TBA | 16 | Mike Minor | TEX | 9 | Bradley Peacock | HOU | 4 | Kyle Gibson | TEX | 2 |
| Lucas Giolito | CHA | 15 | Lance McCullers | HOU | 9 | A.J. Puk | OAK | 4 | Collin McHugh | HOU | 2 |
| Brad Hand | CLE | 15 | Ryan Pressly | HOU | 9 | Marco Gonzales | SEA | 4 | Josh Taylor | BOS | 1 |
| Ken Giles | TOR | 15 | Yonny Chirinos | TBA | 9 | Framber Valdez | HOU | 4 | Cam Bedrosian | LAA | 1 |
| Brandon Workman | BOS | 15 | Jesus Luzardo | OAK | 9 | Thomas Kahnle | NYA | 4 | Andrew Kittredge | TBA | 1 |
| Jose Berrios | MIN | 15 | Diego Castillo | TBA | 8 | Colin Poche | TBA | 4 | Steven Cishek | CHA | 1 |
| Corey Kluber | TEX | 14 | Masahiro Tanaka | NYA | 7 | Yusmeiro Petit | OAK | 4 | Brent Honeywell | TBA | 1 |
| Hyun-Jin Ryu | TOR | 14 | Ryan Yarbrough | TBA | 7 | Zack Britton | NYA | 4 | Trent Thornton | TOR | 1 |
| Eduardo Rodriguez | BOS | 14 | Chad Green | NYA | 7 | Trevor May | MIN | 4 | Jordan Montgomery | NYA | 1 |

# ATC 12-Team 2 Catcher AL Only League Auction Values
## (Pitchers)

| Player Name | Team | $ | Player Name | Team | $ | Player Name | Team | $ | Player Name | Team | $ |
|---|---|---|---|---|---|---|---|---|---|---|---|
| Noe Ramirez | LAA | 1 | Kwang-Hyun Kim | STL | 0 | Carlos Rodon | CHA | 0 | Chaz Roe | TBA | -1 |
| James Karinchak | CLE | 1 | Nate Pearson | TOR | 0 | Julian Merryweather | TOR | 0 | Jacob Waguespack | TOR | -1 |
| Dylan Cease | CHA | 1 | Brandon Bailey | BAL | 0 | Jaime Barria | LAA | 0 | Julio Teheran | LAA | -1 |
| Joe Smith | HOU | 1 | Casey Mize | DET | 0 | Arodys Vizcaino | SEA | 0 | Matt Moore | DET | -1 |
| Wilmer Font | TOR | 1 | Matt Manning | DET | 0 | Erik Swanson | SEA | 0 | Lewis Thorpe | MIN | -1 |
| Samuel Tuivailala | SEA | 1 | Sterling Sharp | MIA | 0 | Brusdar Graterol | MIN | 0 | Thomas Hatch | TOR | -1 |
| Sergio Romo | MIN | 1 | Sixto Sanchez | MIA | 0 | Spencer Turnbull | DET | 0 | Tanner Scott | BAL | -1 |
| Scott Barlow | KCA | 1 | MacKenzie Gore | SDN | 0 | Devin Smeltzer | MIN | 0 | Hunter Wood | CLE | -1 |
| Danny Duffy | KCA | 1 | Luis Patino | SDN | 0 | Lou Trivino | OAK | 0 | Tyler Clippard | MIN | -1 |
| Felix Pena | LAA | 1 | Rony Garcia | DET | 0 | Dan Altavilla | SEA | 0 | J.B. Wendelken | OAK | -1 |
| Jose Alvarado | TBA | 1 | Michael Rucker | BAL | 0 | Shawn Kelley | TEX | 0 | Tyler Alexander | DET | -1 |
| Marcus Walden | BOS | 1 | Austin Adams | SEA | 0 | David Hale | NYA | 0 | Brady Singer | KCA | -1 |
| Jacob Diekman | OAK | 1 | Trevor Megill | CHN | 0 | Tim Hill | KCA | 0 | Cody Stashak | MIN | -1 |
| Forrest Whitley | HOU | 0 | Yohan Ramirez | SEA | 0 | Ryne Harper | MIN | -1 | Zac Grotz | SEA | -1 |
| John Means | BAL | 0 | Stephen Woods | KCA | 0 | Grant Holmes | OAK | -1 | Cristian Javier | HOU | -1 |
| Oliver Perez | CLE | 0 | Dany Jimenez | SFN | 0 | Chase Anderson | TOR | -1 | Matt Andriese | LAA | -1 |
| Hunter Harvey | BAL | 0 | J.P. Feyereisen | MIL | 0 | Sean Reid-Foley | TOR | -1 | Brandon Bielak | HOU | -1 |
| Jonathan Loaisiga | NYA | 0 | Bruce Zimmermann | BAL | 0 | Adam Cimber | CLE | -1 | James Kaprielian | OAK | -1 |
| Buck Farmer | DET | 0 | Spencer Howard | PHI | 0 | Patrick Sandoval | LAA | -1 | Ben Heller | NYA | -1 |
| Michael Fulmer | DET | 0 | Garrett Cleavinger | PHI | 0 | Tarik Skubal | DET | -1 | Ljay Newsome | SEA | -1 |
| Anthony Bass | TOR | 0 | Deivi Garcia | NYA | 0 | Bernardo Flores | CHA | -1 | Darwinzon Hernandez | BOS | -1 |
| Jalen Beeks | TBA | 0 | Ashton Goudeau | COL | 0 | Peter Fairbanks | TBA | -1 | Trevor Cahill | LAA | -1 |
| Chris Devenski | HOU | 0 | Kyle Finnegan | WAS | 0 | Brad Keller | KCA | -1 | Sam Gaviglio | TOR | -1 |
| Brandon Brennan | SEA | 0 | Logan Gilbert | SEA | 0 | Brett Martin | TEX | -1 | Zack Littell | MIN | -1 |
| Shun Yamaguchi | TOR | 0 | Ryan Brasier | BOS | 0 | Jace Fry | CHA | -1 | Daniel Mengden | OAK | -1 |

## ATC 12-Team 2 Catcher NL Only League Auction Values
### (Hitters)

| Player Name | Team | Pos | $ | Player Name | Team | Pos | $ | Player Name | Team | Pos | $ |
|---|---|---|---|---|---|---|---|---|---|---|---|
| Christian Yelich | MIL | OF | 41 | Manny Machado | SD | 3B/SS | 23 | David Dahl | COL | OF | 17 |
| Ronald Acuna | ATL | OF | 39 | Jacob Realmuto | PHI | C | 23 | Christian Walker | ARI | 1B | 17 |
| Nolan Arenado | COL | 3B | 37 | Rhys Hoskins | PHI | 1B | 23 | Max Muncy | LAD | 1B/2B/3B | 17 |
| Freddie Freeman | ATL | 1B | 36 | Marcell Ozuna | STL | OF | 23 | Kevin Newman | PIT | 2B/SS | 16 |
| Cody Bellinger | LAD | 1B/OF | 35 | Justin Turner | LAD | 3B | 23 | Corey Seager | LAD | SS | 16 |
| Trea Turner | WAS | SS | 34 | Nick Castellanos | CHC | OF | 22 | Ryan Braun | MIL | OF | 16 |
| Juan Soto | WAS | OF | 32 | Jeff McNeil | NYM | 2B/3B/OF | 22 | Didi Gregorius | PHI | SS | 16 |
| Trevor Story | COL | SS | 31 | Jonathan Villar | MIA | 2B/SS | 22 | Aristides Aquino | CIN | OF | 16 |
| Anthony Rizzo | CHC | 1B | 29 | Bryan Reynolds | PIT | OF | 20 | Nick Senzel | CIN | OF | 16 |
| Starling Marte | PIT | OF | 29 | Michael Conforto | NYM | OF | 20 | Willson Contreras | CHC | C | 16 |
| Pete Alonso | NYM | 1B | 29 | Brian Anderson | MIA | 3B/OF | 20 | David Peralta | ARI | OF | 15 |
| Fernando Tatis Jr. | SD | SS | 28 | Scott Kingery | PHI | 3B/OF | 20 | Starlin Castro | WAS | 2B/3B | 15 |
| Paul Goldschmidt | STL | 1B | 28 | Eric Hosmer | SD | 1B | 19 | Evan Longoria | SF | 3B | 14 |
| Ozzie Albies | ATL | 2B | 27 | Joey Votto | CIN | 1B | 19 | Wilson Ramos | NYM | C | 14 |
| Kris Bryant | CHC | 3B/OF | 27 | Jean Segura | PHI | SS | 19 | Avisail Garcia | MIL | OF | 14 |
| Bryce Harper | PHI | OF | 27 | Mike Moustakas | CIN | 2B/3B | 18 | Andrew McCutchen | PHI | OF | 14 |
| Josh Bell | PIT | 1B | 27 | Amed Rosario | NYM | SS | 18 | Colin Moran | PIT | 3B | 14 |
| Eugenio Suarez | CIN | 3B | 27 | Lorenzo Cain | MIL | OF | 18 | Ryan McMahon | COL | 2B/3B | 14 |
| Josh Donaldson | ATL | 3B | 27 | Tommy Edman | STL | 2B/3B | 18 | Kevin Pillar | SF | OF | 13 |
| Javier Baez | CHC | SS | 27 | Kyle Schwarber | CHC | OF | 17 | Shogo Akiyama | CIN | OF | 13 |
| Charlie Blackmon | COL | OF | 26 | Eduardo Escobar | ARI | 2B/3B | 17 | Will Smith | LAD | C | 13 |
| Thomas Pham | SD | OF | 25 | Daniel Murphy | COL | 1B | 17 | Yadier Molina | STL | C | 13 |
| Ketel Marte | ARI | 2B/OF | 24 | Paul DeJong | STL | SS | 17 | Matt Carpenter | STL | 3B | 13 |
| Keston Hiura | MIL | 2B | 24 | Adam Eaton | WAS | OF | 17 | Brandon Belt | SF | 1B | 13 |
| Victor Robles | WAS | OF | 24 | J.D. Davis | NYM | 3B/OF | 17 | Dansby Swanson | ATL | SS | 13 |

# ATC 12-Team 2 Catcher NL Only League Auction Values
## (Hitters)

| Player Name | Team | Pos | $ | Player Name | Team | Pos | $ | Player Name | Team | Pos | $ |
|---|---|---|---|---|---|---|---|---|---|---|---|
| Joc Pederson | LAD | 1B/OF | 12 | Nick Ahmed | ARI | SS | 10 | Brian Dozier | WAS | 2B | 5 |
| Alex Verdugo | LAD | OF | 12 | Ender Inciarte | ATL | OF | 9 | Stephen Vogt | ARI | C | 5 |
| Eric Thames | WAS | 1B | 12 | Travis D'Arnaud | ATL | C/1B | 9 | Chris Taylor | LAD | 2B/SS/OF | 5 |
| Kolten Wong | STL | 2B | 12 | Howie Kendrick | WAS | 1B/2B | 9 | Tucker Barnhart | CIN | C | 5 |
| Nick Markakis | ATL | OF | 12 | Asdrubal Cabrera | WAS | 2B/3B | 9 | Brandon Crawford | SF | SS | 5 |
| Mauricio Dubon | SF | 2B | 12 | Austin Riley | ATL | OF | 9 | Jacob Stallings | PIT | C | 5 |
| Jesus Aguilar | MIA | 1B | 12 | Jon Berti | MIA | 3B/SS/OF | 8 | Neil Walker | MIA | 1B/3B | 5 |
| Justin Smoak | MIL | 1B | 12 | Gregory Polanco | PIT | OF | 8 | Garrett Cooper | MIA | 1B/OF | 4 |
| Corey Dickerson | MIA | OF | 12 | Harrison Bader | STL | OF | 8 | Victor Caratini | CHC | C/1B | 4 |
| Gavin Lux | LAD | 2B | 11 | Freddy Galvis | CIN | 2B/SS | 8 | Alex Dickerson | SF | OF | 4 |
| Jesse Winker | CIN | OF | 11 | Miguel Rojas | MIA | SS | 7 | Sam Hilliard | COL | OF | 4 |
| Carson Kelly | ARI | C | 11 | Manuel Margot | SD | OF | 7 | Josh VanMeter | CIN | OF | 4 |
| Jason Heyward | CHC | OF | 11 | Matt Adams | WAS | 1B | 7 | Isan Diaz | MIA | 2B | 4 |
| Buster Posey | SF | C | 11 | Wil Myers | SD | OF | 7 | Adam Haseley | PHI | OF | 4 |
| Mike Yastrzemski | SF | OF | 11 | Brandon Nimmo | NYM | OF | 7 | Harold Ramirez | MIA | OF | 4 |
| Jurickson Profar | SD | 2B | 10 | Ian Happ | CHC | OF | 6 | Enrique Hernandez | LAD | 2B/OF | 3 |
| A.J. Pollock | LAD | OF | 10 | Wilmer Flores | ARI | 2B | 6 | Manuel Pina | MIL | C | 3 |
| Garrett Hampson | COL | 2B/OF | 10 | Ryan Zimmerman | WAS | 1B | 6 | Raimel Tapia | COL | OF | 3 |
| Kurt Suzuki | WAS | C | 10 | Trent Grisham | SD | OF | 6 | Tony Wolters | COL | C | 3 |
| Kole Calhoun | ARI | OF | 10 | Tyler O'Neill | STL | OF | 6 | Kevin Cron | ARI | 1B | 3 |
| Francisco Mejia | SD | C | 10 | Dexter Fowler | STL | OF | 6 | Scooter Gennett | CIN | 2B | 3 |
| Omar Narvaez | MIL | C | 10 | Jake Lamb | ARI | 1B/3B | 6 | Tyler Flowers | ATL | C | 3 |
| Adam Frazier | PIT | 2B | 10 | Luis Urias | MIL | 2B/SS | 6 | Melky Cabrera | PIT | OF | 3 |
| Robinson Cano | NYM | 2B | 10 | Yan Gomes | WAS | C | 5 | Jedd Gyorko | MIL | 3B | 3 |
| Jorge Alfaro | MIA | C | 10 | Ian Desmond | COL | OF | 5 | Josh Rojas | ARI | OF | 3 |

473

# ATC 12-Team 2 Catcher NL Only League Auction Values
## (Hitters)

| Player Name | Team | Pos | $ | Player Name | Team | Pos | $ | Player Name | Team | Pos | $ |
|---|---|---|---|---|---|---|---|---|---|---|---|
| Franchy Cordero | SD | OF | 3 | Jaylin Davis | SF | OF | 0 | Drew Butera | COL | C | -3 |
| Alec Bohm | PHI | 3B | 3 | Josh Naylor | SD | OF | 0 | Mark Reynolds | COL | 1B | -3 |
| Steven Souza | ARI | OF | 3 | Orlando Arcia | MIL | SS | 0 | Matt Joyce | ATL | OF | -3 |
| Yairo Munoz | STL | 3B/OF | 3 | Jose Osuna | PIT | 1B/OF | -1 | Chris Iannetta | COL | C | -3 |
| Nico Hoerner | CHC | SS | 2 | Jacob Marisnick | NYM | OF | -1 | Matt Beaty | LAD | 1B/OF | -3 |
| Phillip Ervin | CIN | OF | 2 | Dominic Smith | NYM | 1B/OF | -1 | Pablo Sandoval | SF | 1B/3B | -3 |
| Jarrod Dyson | ARI | OF | 2 | Steven Duggar | SF | OF | -1 | Andrew Knapp | PHI | C | -3 |
| Eric Sogard | MIL | 2B | 2 | Ty France | SD | 2B/3B | -1 | Chris Shaw | SF | 1B | -3 |
| Ryon Healy | MIL | 3B | 2 | Roman Quinn | PHI | OF | -1 | Donovan Solano | SF | 2B | -3 |
| Matt Wieters | STL | C | 2 | Jung Ho Kang | PIT | 3B | -1 | Austin Dean | STL | OF | -3 |
| Curt Casali | CIN | C | 1 | Jed Lowrie | NYM | 2B | -1 | Joe Panik | NYM | 2B | -3 |
| David Bote | CHC | 2B/3B | 1 | Aramis Garcia | SF | C | -1 | Zack Cozart | SF | 3B | -3 |
| Francisco Cervelli | MIA | C | 1 | Luke Maile | PIT | C | -2 | Lane Thomas | STL | OF | -3 |
| Austin Hedges | SD | C | 1 | Austin Slater | SF | OF | -2 | Joey Bart | SF | C | -3 |
| Jay Bruce | PHI | OF | 1 | Tomas Nido | NYM | C | -2 | Brendan Rodgers | COL | 2B | -3 |
| Yonder Alonso | COL | 1B | 1 | Addison Russell | CHC | 2B/SS | -2 | Billy Hamilton | ATL | OF | -4 |
| Albert Almora | CHC | OF | 1 | Tim Locastro | ARI | OF | -2 | Ronny Rodriguez | MIL | 2B/SS | -4 |
| Elias Diaz | PIT | C | 1 | Russell Martin | LAD | C | -2 | Tyler White | LAD | 1B | -4 |
| Brad Miller | PHI | 3B | 1 | Ildemaro Vargas | ARI | 2B | -2 | Lewis Brinson | MIA | OF | -4 |
| Jonathan Lucroy | CHC | C | 1 | Josh Fuentes | COL | 1B | -2 | Logan Morrison | MIL | 1B | -4 |
| Johan Camargo | ATL | SS | 1 | Ben Gamel | MIL | OF | -2 | Erik Gonzalez | PIT | SS | -4 |
| Andrew Knizner | STL | C | 1 | Monte Harrison | MIA | OF | -2 | Rene Rivera | NYM | C | -4 |
| Carter Kieboom | WAS | SS | 1 | Dom Nunez | COL | C | -2 | Daulton Varsho | ARI | C | -4 |
| Austin Barnes | LAD | C | 1 | Sean Rodriguez | PHI | 3B | -3 | Adam Duvall | ATL | OF | -4 |
| Yoenis Cespedes | NYM | OF | 0 | Michael Taylor | WAS | OF | -3 | Zach Green | SF | 3B | -4 |

# ATC 12-Team 2 Catcher NL Only League Auction Values
## (Pitchers)

| Player Name | Team | $ | Player Name | Team | $ | Player Name | Team | $ | Player Name | Team | $ |
|---|---|---|---|---|---|---|---|---|---|---|---|
| Jacob deGrom | NYN | 38 | Raisel Iglesias | CIN | 12 | Ross Stripling | LAN | 6 | Tyler Mahle | CIN | 3 |
| Max Scherzer | WAS | 36 | Miles Mikolas | STL | 12 | Cole Hamels | ATL | 6 | Freddy Peralta | MIL | 3 |
| Walker Buehler | LAN | 31 | Kyle Hendricks | CHN | 12 | Steven Matz | NYN | 6 | Johnny Cueto | SFN | 3 |
| Jack Flaherty | STL | 27 | German Marquez | COL | 12 | Alex Wood | LAN | 6 | Robert Stephenson | CIN | 3 |
| Stephen Strasburg | WAS | 27 | Madison Bumgarner | ARI | 11 | Mike Foltynewicz | ATL | 6 | Tony Watson | SFN | 3 |
| Josh Hader | MIL | 23 | Keone Kela | PIT | 11 | Dustin May | LAN | 6 | Dan Hudson | WAS | 3 |
| Clayton Kershaw | LAN | 22 | Sean Doolittle | WAS | 11 | Dellin Betances | NYN | 6 | Josh Lindblom | MIL | 3 |
| Luis Castillo | CIN | 22 | Archie Bradley | ARI | 11 | Caleb Smith | MIA | 6 | Matt Strahm | SDN | 3 |
| Chris Paddack | SDN | 22 | Zac Gallen | ARI | 10 | Kevin Gausman | SFN | 5 | Michael Lorenzen | CIN | 3 |
| Yu Darvish | CHN | 21 | Will Smith | ATL | 10 | Rick Porcello | NYN | 5 | Shaun Anderson | SFN | 3 |
| Patrick Corbin | WAS | 21 | Kenta Maeda | LAN | 10 | Drew Pomeranz | SDN | 5 | Brent Suter | MIL | 3 |
| Kirby Yates | SDN | 19 | Giovanny Gallegos | STL | 10 | Pablo Lopez | MIA | 5 | Justin Wilson | NYN | 3 |
| Aaron Nola | PHI | 18 | Robbie Ray | ARI | 10 | Ryne Stanek | MIA | 5 | Joe Kelly | LAN | 3 |
| Noah Syndergaard | NYN | 17 | Seth Lugo | NYN | 10 | Mitch Keller | PIT | 5 | Corey Knebel | MIL | 3 |
| Brandon Woodruff | MIL | 17 | Joe Musgrove | PIT | 10 | Chris Archer | PIT | 5 | Luke Jackson | ATL | 3 |
| Trevor Bauer | CIN | 16 | Craig Kimbrel | CHN | 10 | Will Harris | WAS | 5 | Jeff Samardzija | SFN | 2 |
| Edwin Diaz | NYN | 16 | Marcus Stroman | NYN | 8 | Blake Treinen | LAN | 5 | Andrew Miller | STL | 2 |
| Kenley Jansen | LAN | 15 | Julio Urias | LAN | 8 | Andres Munoz | SDN | 5 | John Brebbia | STL | 2 |
| Hector Neris | PHI | 15 | Luke Weaver | ARI | 7 | Adrian Houser | MIL | 5 | Shane Greene | ATL | 2 |
| Mike Soroka | ATL | 15 | Jon Gray | COL | 7 | Chris Martin | ATL | 4 | Tyler Anderson | SFN | 2 |
| Dinelson Lamet | SDN | 15 | Scott Oberg | COL | 7 | Garrett Richards | SDN | 4 | Michael Feliz | PIT | 2 |
| Sonny Gray | CIN | 14 | Anthony DeSclafani | CIN | 7 | Craig Stammen | SDN | 4 | Seranthony Dominguez | PHI | 2 |
| Max Fried | ATL | 14 | Jose Quintana | CHN | 7 | Kevin Ginkel | ARI | 4 | Tony Gonsolin | LAN | 2 |
| Zack Wheeler | PHI | 14 | Joey Lucchesi | SDN | 7 | Jose Urena | MIA | 4 | Pedro Baez | LAN | 2 |
| Carlos Martinez | STL | 12 | Mark Melancon | ATL | 6 | Merrill Kelly | ARI | 3 | Richard Rodriguez | PIT | 2 |

# ATC 12-Team 2 Catcher NL Only League Auction Values
## (Pitchers)

| Player Name | Team | $ | Player Name | Team | $ | Player Name | Team | $ | Player Name | Team | $ |
|---|---|---|---|---|---|---|---|---|---|---|---|
| Adam Wainwright | STL | 2 | Sterling Sharp | MIA | 0 | Michael Wacha | NYN | 0 | Yoan Lopez | ARI | -2 |
| Anibal Sanchez | WAS | 1 | Sixto Sanchez | MIA | 0 | Kyle Wright | ATL | 0 | Jeurys Familia | NYN | -2 |
| Austin Voth | WAS | 1 | MacKenzie Gore | SDN | 0 | Roenis Elias | WAS | 0 | J.T. Brubaker | PIT | -2 |
| Elieser Hernandez | MIA | 1 | Luis Patino | SDN | 0 | Brandon Kintzler | CHN | 0 | Damon Jones | PHI | -2 |
| Carlos Estevez | COL | 1 | Trevor Megill | CHN | 0 | Jay Jackson | MIL | -1 | Adam Morgan | PHI | -2 |
| Bryse Wilson | ATL | 1 | Dany Jimenez | SFN | 0 | Caleb Ferguson | LAN | -1 | Stefan Crichton | ARI | -2 |
| Jordan Yamamoto | MIA | 1 | J.P. Feyereisen | MIL | 0 | Trevor Gott | SFN | -1 | Nick Neidert | MIA | -2 |
| Kyle Crick | PIT | 1 | Spencer Howard | PHI | 0 | Sandy Alcantara | MIA | -1 | Jarlin Garcia | MIA | -2 |
| Mike Leake | ARI | 1 | Garrett Cleavinger | PHI | 0 | Darren O'Day | ATL | -1 | Casey Sadler | LAN | -2 |
| Eric Lauer | MIL | 1 | Ashton Goudeau | COL | 0 | Jose Castillo | SDN | -1 | Jacob Webb | ATL | -2 |
| Zach Eflin | PHI | 1 | Kyle Finnegan | WAS | 0 | Taijuan Walker | ARI | -1 | Zach Davies | SDN | -2 |
| Adam Kolarek | LAN | 1 | John Gant | STL | 0 | Chad Kuhl | PIT | -1 | Tyler Beede | SFN | -2 |
| Amir Garrett | CIN | 1 | Jose Alvarez | PHI | 0 | Ian Anderson | ATL | -1 | Brad Brach | NYN | -2 |
| Wade Miley | CIN | 1 | Dereck Rodriguez | SFN | 0 | Jameson Taillon | PIT | -1 | Francisco Liriano | PIT | -2 |
| Rowan Wick | CHN | 1 | Lucas Sims | CIN | 0 | Ryan Helsley | STL | -1 | Junior Guerra | ARI | -2 |
| Andrew Chafin | ARI | 1 | Tyler Rogers | SFN | 0 | Yimi Garcia | MIA | -1 | Jeff Brigham | MIA | -2 |
| Jairo Diaz | COL | 0 | Jon Lester | CHN | 0 | Sean Newcomb | ATL | -1 | Trey Wingenter | SDN | -2 |
| Alex Young | ARI | 0 | Ranger Suarez | PHI | 0 | Alex Vesia | MIA | -1 | Kyle Ryan | CHN | -2 |
| Daniel Poncedeleon | STL | 0 | Wander Suero | WAS | 0 | Trevor Oaks | SFN | -1 | Robert Gsellman | NYN | -2 |
| Vincent Velasquez | PHI | 0 | Pedro Strop | CHN | 0 | Tanner Rainey | WAS | -1 | Victor Arano | PHI | -2 |
| Brad Wieck | CHN | 0 | Jake Arrieta | PHI | 0 | Scott Alexander | LAN | -1 | Matt Carasiti | SFN | -2 |
| Dakota Hudson | STL | 0 | Brett Anderson | MIL | 0 | Grant Dayton | ATL | -1 | Dan Straily | PHI | -2 |
| Logan Webb | SFN | 0 | Nick Pivetta | PHI | 0 | Ray Black | MIL | -1 | Dylan Floro | LAN | -2 |
| Shun Yamaguchi | TOR | 0 | Hector Rondon | ARI | 0 | Cody Reed | CIN | -2 | Jharel Cotton | CHN | -2 |
| Kwang-Hyun Kim | STL | 0 | Cal Quantrill | SDN | 0 | Corbin Burnes | MIL | -2 | Taylor Clarke | ARI | -2 |

Made in the USA
Coppell, TX
20 February 2020